Purpose

AND

Process

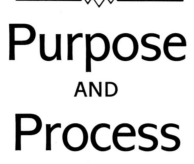

Purpose
AND
Process

Jeffrey D. Hoeper
Arkansas State University

James H. Pickering
University of Houston

Macmillan Publishing Company
New York

Macmillan Publishing Company
866 Third Avenue, New York, New York 10022

Library of Congress Cataloging-in-Publication Data

Hoeper, Jeffrey D.
  Purpose and process / Jeffrey D. Hoeper, James H. Pickering.
    p. cm.
  ISBN 0-02-395470-1
  1. Authorship. I. Pickering, James H. II. Title.
PN145.H53 1989
808'.0427—dc19   88-11079
                      CIP

Printing: 1 2 3 4 5 6 7   Year: 9 0 1 2 3 4 5

ACKNOWLEDGMENTS

Abbey, Edward. "The Damnation of a
Canyon." From *Beyond the Wall* by Edward
Abbey. Copyright © 1984 by Edward
Abbey. Reprinted by permission of Henry
Holt and Company, Inc.

Angell, Roger. "Reggie Rex." *Late
Innings.* Copyright © 1982 by Roger An-
gell. Reprinted by permission of Simon &
Schuster, Inc.

Azimov, Isaac. "Colonizing the
Heavens," *Saturday Review* (28 June
1975). Reprinted by permission.

Baumrind, Diana. "Some Thoughts
on the Ethics of Research," *American Psychologist* 19 (1964): 421–23. Copyright
1964 by the American Psychological Association. Reprinted by permission of the publisher and author.

Bethe, Hans, Richard Garwin, Kurt
Gottfried, Henry Kendall, Carl Sagan, and
Victor Weisskopf. "Response to Robert Jas-
trow," *Commentary* (March 1985): 6–11.
Reprinted by permission.

Boyle, Kay. "Astronomer's Wife,"
from *The White Horses of Vienna and
Other Stories.* Copyright © 1936. Reprinted

by permission of Watkins/Loomis Agency
for the author.

Britt, Susan. "That Lean and Hungry
Look." Reprinted by permission of the
author.

Brush, Katharine. "Birthday Party."
Copyright © 1946 by Katharine Brush.
Originally published in *The New Yorker*,
March 16, 1946. Reprinted by permission of
Thomas S. Brush.

Calandra, Alexander. "Angels on a
Pin," *Saturday Review* (December 1968).
Reprinted by permission.

Crichton, Michael. "Mousetrap." Reprinted by permission of International Creative Management, Inc. First published in
Life magazine. Copyright © 1984 by
Michael Crichton. Also reprinted from *Creative Computing* June 1984. Copyright ©
1984 Ziff Communications Company.

Crist, Judith. "Against the Latest Howl
for Censorship." From *Censorship: For and
Against* ed. Harold Hart. New York: Hart
Publishing Company, 1971. Reprinted by
permission of the author.

Dillard, Annie. "Sight into Insight."

1950 by Sonia Brownell Orwell; renewed 1978 by Sonia Pitt-Rivers. Reprinted by permission of Harcourt Brace Jovanovich, Inc.

Ouchi, William. "Japanese and American Workers: Two Casts of Mind," *Theory Z: How American Business Can Meet the Japanese Challenge* © 1981, Addison-Wesley Publishing Co., Reading, Massachusetts. Pages 47–51 and 64–66. Reprinted with permission.

Perrin, Noel. "The Androgynous Man," *New York Times Magazine* (5 February 1984). Copyright © 1984 by The New York Times Company. Reprinted by permission.

Peter, Lawrence J., and Raymond Hull. From pp. 119–23 in *The Peter Principle* by Lawrence J. Peter and Raymond Hull. Copyright © 1969 by William Morrow & Company, Inc. By permission of William Morrow & Company, Inc.

Porter, Katherine Anne. "The Grave." From *The Leaning Tower and Other Stories*, copyright 1944, 1972 by Katherine Anne Porter. Reprinted by permission of Harcourt Brace Jovanovich, Inc.

Riley, Noel, S.M. "Getting a Big Bang Out of Creation Theories," *Los Angeles Times* (10 March 1981).

Roberts, Paul. "How to Say Nothing in 500 Words" from *Understanding English* by Paul Roberts. Copyright © 1958 by Paul Roberts. Reprinted by permission of Harper & Row, Publishers, Inc.

Rosenblatt, Roger. "Oops! How's That Again?" Copyright 1987 Time Inc. All rights reserved. Reprinted by permission from *Time*.

Royko, Mike. "Maybe He's a Nerd." Reprinted with permission of the author.

Russell, Bertrand. "On Comets," *In Praise of Idleness*. London: George Allen & Unwin (Publishers) Ltd., 1935. Reprinted by permission of the publishers.

Shōnagon, Sei. "Hateful Things and Rare Things", *The Pillow Book of Sei Shōnagon*, trans. and ed. Ivan Morris. Oxford: Oxford University Press, 1967. Reprinted by permission of the publisher.

Shulman, Max. "Love Is a Fallacy," *The Many Lives of Dobie Gillis*. Copyright 1951, © renewed 1978 by Max Shulman.

Reprinted by permission of Harold Matson Company, Inc.

Singer, Isaac Bashevis. "Gimpel the Fool," by Isaac Bashevis Singer from *A Treasury of Yiddish Stories*, edited by Irving Howe and Eliezer Greenberg. Copyright © 1953, 1954 by The Viking Press, Inc. Copyright © renewed 1981 by Isaac Bashevis Singer. All rights reserved. Reprinted by permission of Viking Penguin Inc.

Smith, Ronald E., Irwin G. Sarason, and Barbara R. Sarason. "The Milgram Experiment." Pages 19–22 from *Psychology: The Frontiers of Behavior* by Ronald E. Smith, Irwin G. Sarason, and Barbara R. Sarason. Copyright © 1978 by Ronald Smith. Reprinted by permission of Harper & Row, Publishers, Inc.

Sowell, Thomas. "We're Not Really 'Equal'." Reprinted by permission of the author.

Starkey, Marion L. "The Arraignment of Martha Cory," *The Devil in Massachusetts*. New York: Curtis Brown, 1969.

Steinem, Gloria. "The Politics of Food," *Outrageous Acts and Everyday Rebellions*. New York: Holt, Rinehart and Winston, 1983.

Stone, M. David, and Linda Koebner. "Do Chimps Share Human Rights?" Reprinted by permission from the July/August issue of *Science '82*. Copyright © 1982 by the American Association for the Advancement of Science.

Thomson, Judith Jarvis. "A Defense of Abortion," *Philosophy and Public Affairs* 1, no. 1 (Fall 1971). Copyright © 1971 by Princeton University Press. Reprinted by permission of Princeton University Press.

Updike, John. "A & P." Copyright © 1962 by John Updike. Reprinted from *Pigeon Feathers and Other Stories* by John Updike, by permission of Alfred A. Knopf, Inc. Originally appeared in *The New Yorker*.

Vonnegut, Kurt, Jr., "Harrison Bergeron." From *Welcome to the Monkey House* by Kurt Vonnegut, Jr. Copyright © 1950 to 1968 by Kurt Vonnegut, Jr. Reprinted by arrangement with Delacorte Press/Seymour Lawrence. All rights reserved.

Wilson, L. I. "Glen Canyon's Azure Jewel." Reprinted from *The Saturday Evening Post* © 1980 The Curtis Publishing Co.

Winn, Marie. "Childhood and the Garden of Eden," from *Children without Childhood* by Marie Winn. Copyright © 1981, 1983, by Marie Winn. Reprinted by permission of Pantheon Books, a division of Random House, Inc.

Wolfe, Tom. "Las Vegas (What?) Las Vegas (Can't Hear You! Too Noisy) Las Vegas!!" from *The Kandy-Kolored Tangerine-Flake Streamline Baby* by Tom Wolfe. Copyright © 1963, 1964, 1965 by Thomas K. Wolfe, Jr., and New York Herald Tribune, Inc. Reprinted by permission of Farrar, Straus and Giroux, Inc.

————. "The Sexed-up, Doped-up Hedonistic Heaven of the Boom-Boom '70s." Reprinted by permission of International Creative Management, Inc. (First published in *Esquire*.) Copyright © 1979 by Tom Wolfe.

PREFACE
TO THE INSTRUCTOR

Abraham Lincoln once observed, "Books serve to show a man that those original thoughts of his really aren't very new after all." Our experience in writing *Purpose and Process* is certainly no exception to Lincoln's dictum. Not only are we indebted to composition theorists ranging from Aristotle to Emig, we are also indebted to the scores of textbook authors and editors who have contributed incrementally to current thinking about the composing process.

Purpose and Process quite consciously attempts to situate itself within the mainstream of current composition pedagogy. Like many other readers, it is rhetorically arranged. Like many other readers, it emphasizes the importance of a strong thesis and a clear structure in a solid essay. And like several others, it provides a detailed introduction to the process of writing and revising an essay.

However, *Purpose and Process* is not just another clone of existing texts. One key premise sets our text apart and influences every decision we have made in composing it. We believe that writing should be *purposeful*, and hence that a good writer must at all times keep in mind the reader's desire to be informed, persuaded, and entertained. A crucial point here is our belief that *writing becomes stronger when these purposes are combined*. A single piece of twine is easily snapped, but several pieces woven together can form a rope capable of carrying the load of a weighty argument. Truly memorable writing almost invariably interweaves persuasion, information, and entertainment in some combination. George Orwell's "Shooting an Elephant" is a classic essay in part because it informs us about the racial tensions resulting from the British colonization of India, it persuades us that colonial imperilism is inherently harmful, and it entertains us with a dramatic account of Orwell's

ix

actions. Similarly, Jessica Mitford's "The Embalmer's Art" is a classic piece of journalism because it entertains us with its gruesome wit, it informs us about the details of embalming, and it persuades us that this attempt to make the dead look healthily alive is both wasteful and, ultimately, disrespectful. Indeed, we contend that virtually all forms of writing for general audiences can be made more effective if the writer consciously attempts to combine entertainment, information, and persuasion in some measure.

Thus, we come to a second unusual feature of this text: the inclusion in every chapter of representative pieces drawn from each of the three major forms of modern prose—journalism, fiction, and advertising. This combination of essays, stories, and advertisements is intended to facilitate the classroom analysis of the ways in which different forms of writing achieve their purposes. As a working postulate, one might hypothesize that journalism will emphasize information, fiction will emphasize entertainment, and advertisements will emphasize persuasion. The writing in this text does on the whole support that postulate, but what particularly interests us is the extent to which the *best* modern writing in journalism, fiction, and advertising is that which most successfully combines informing, persuading, and entertaining.

There are still other reasons for the inclusion of stories and advertisements in a text that is primarily designed to help students improve their skills as essayists. We wish to demonstrate that the use of the standard rhetorical patterns is not exclusively confined to essays. In addition, we wish to represent the wide range of modern prose intended for general audiences. We wish to provide students and teachers alike with a stimulating variety of pieces to discuss. And we wish to increase the number of potential writing assignments by including topics that invite the analysis of the ways in which the various patterns and purposes are combined within different forms of prose. This, by the way, is also the reason for the artwork preceding some of the chapters in the text. Each piece of art either illustrates a particular rhetorical pattern or lends itself to analysis through that pattern.

A third key feature of this text is the emphasis we give to the writing process itself. Acknowledgment that writing is a complex and recursive process is by no means new. In this text, however, we have gone far beyond the typical passing nod to the process approach. We try to emphasize that writing is a process in four complementary ways:

1. Chapter 3, "The Writing Process," provides a brief, but thorough introduction to prewriting, writing, and revision.
2. The organization of the chapters in the text is designed to complement the process approach. We devote two chapters to self-expressive writing in Part II, "Writing for Oneself," to introduce

students to the prewriting techniques that they will continue to use in the nine chapters on "Writing for Others."
3. Within each of the introductions to the rhetorical patterns, we reemphasize the writing process by explicitly considering prewriting, planning, drafting, combining purposes, and revising.
4. Each of these chapter introductions concludes with at least two drafts of a student's essay in order to illustrate both the pattern itself and the process of revision.

A final innovative feature in *Purpose and Process* is found in Part IV, entitled "Further Reading: Paired Essays on Controversial Issues." The thirteen essays in that section use the various rhetorical patterns in flexible combinations and form a natural sequel to the nine chapters introducing those patterns. We presume that these essays will also suggest a number of topics that students will wish to explore in their own writing. In our view, however, the most important function of these essays is to underscore an important point about the previous chapters in the text. That point is that the rhetorical patterns provide structures that writers often find helpful in developing an argument, but using them is not a goal in itself. By mastering causal analysis, classification, or comparison, students increase their ability to use combinations of these patterns in supporting a thesis.

Ultimately, writing requires the mastery of *combinations*. Yet learning to write well is not like learning to open a combination lock. There is no simple sequence of steps that will unfailingly unlock the precious secrets of prose style. Indeed, the rules of writing are closer to the combinations of probability theory and quantum physics than to the combination of a padlock. Writing improves when one understands purposes and combines them effectively, when one understands rhetorical structures and chooses them appropriately, and when one moves flexibly and fluidly through the recursive stages of the writing process itself. Ours is the Age of Uncertainty, and it is only fitting that in composition pedagogy, as in everything else, the fixed rules are failing us and we achieve understanding through approximation.

This book has had a lengthy genesis, and we would here like to express our thanks to the many individuals who have assisted us in the process of writing and revision. In addition to our general indebtedness to the published work of many experts in composition pedagogy and theory, we are specifically indebted to the following individuals for their many helpful suggestions about the early drafts of this text: Kirk H. Beetz, National University; Hallman B. Bryant, Clemson University; George Gleason, Southwest Missouri State University; George D. Haich, University of Georgia; Michael Hennessy, Southwest Texas State University; Francis A. Hubbard, Marquette University; Wayne Losano, University of Florida; Steven Lynn, University of South Carolina, Barry M. Maid, University of Arkansas at Little Rock; Mary E. McGann, Rhode Island College; Elizabeth Metzger, University of South Florida; Donavan Ochs, University of Iowa; Carl Singleton, Fort Hays State University; Norman Stafford, Arkansas State University; Judith Stanford, River College; Bonnie K. Stevens, The College of Wooster; James Thompson, University of North Carolina; and Robert Wrigley, Lewis–Clark State College. We are also grateful to our editors at Macmillan: Jennifer Crewe, Susan Didriksen, Tony English, and Katherine Evancie. Our greatest debt, however, is to the many composition students at Michigan State University, University of Houston, and Arkansas State University from whom we have learned most of what we know about the composing process. Our very warmest thanks go to the nine students from Arkansas State University who have allowed us to reprint the early drafts of their essays. From these drafts we hope that the students using this text will learn how varied the writing process can be and yet how much is to be gained by careful and methodical revision.

J.D.H.
J.H.P.

CONTENTS

Part I
PRINCIPLES OF WRITING AND READING

Part II
WRITING FOR ONESELF

◇◇◇

Part III
WRITING FOR OTHERS

Chapter 11
Comparison and Contrast   **374**

Part IV
FURTHER READING
Paired Essays
on Controversial Issues

PART I

PRINCIPLES OF WRITING AND READING

Chapter 1

PURPOSE IN WRITING

Most of the writing we do begins as an assignment, and the immediate purpose is simply to fulfill the assignment. Thus, reporters cover stories, marketing specialists write advertisements, authors fulfill contracts with their publishers, and college students write assigned essays. Indeed, most writers need the pressure of an assignment and a deadline; without that pressure they have great difficulty settling down before an intimidating stack of blank paper.

Writing *just* to complete an assignment can, however, be a serious mistake because that purpose alone often seems unrewarding. Essays written just to fulfill an assignment are frequently boring — in part because the writing is seen as a chore or even a punishment. Hence, some students speak of "chaining themselves to their desks" or regard an approaching deadline as a "date of execution." To escape from the convict mentality into the joy of creativity, all writers must discover for themselves a purpose that reaches beyond fulfilling a mere assignment.

What other purposes are there? To answer that question, let us look at a number of paragraphs written by college students.

SELF-EXPRESSION

This first extract is from a journal in which the student was asked to reflect on past or present experiences. It demonstrates that writing to express one's feelings can often lend to prose the force of heartfelt conviction. Such writing is also a useful vent for the emotions, allowing the writer to examine his or her feelings closely and thereby understand them more clearly.

"THE REST HOME"

Mama and I went to see Great Grandma this evening. I hate the rest home. The air inside is stale and filled with unhappy sounds. Loneliness virtually blankets the place. I'm frightened by rest homes. I'd rather be dead than "live" as some of its residents—which isn't living but existing. I knew Grandma wasn't doing so well, but I never expected what I saw. It made tears well up in my eyes, and a sick feeling came over me. I didn't even recognize her. Grandma was little more than skin stretched over a skeleton.

"Mouth dry," she squeaked, so I put the cup of water in her hand and the straw to her mouth. She was barely able to draw the water through the straw—what little she did manage to get to her mouth she choked on. I watched Mama rub her dry old skin with lotion and gently brush her balding head. I watched her trim Grandma's nails and massage her feet. Grandma was worried about losing her rings. A very special man gave them to her some 70 odd years ago. It's been 11 years since Grandpa died. I think Grandma's ready to join him. She feels betrayed, angry, lonely, and bitter—with good reason. We—her family—put her there—in that place. It doesn't matter that Aunt Jane made the decision; the point is that the family has allowed her to stay there. No one's done anything for her. Very few people go to see her. I felt so guilty for having to leave her there. I have a horrible feeling that it was the last time I'd ever see her alive—or rather existing.

I went to Carol's house later that evening. We talked for a long while and looked at the proofs from her wedding.

These paragraphs are moving, powerful, and effective for a number of reasons. The author describes the atmosphere in the rest home clearly with its "unhappy sounds" and the feeling of loneliness that "virtually blankets the place." She also describes what happens simply and vividly —particularly when her great grandmother struggles to suck a little water up through a straw. The passage also ends effectively when the author, unable to improve her great grandmother's lot, turns away from somber thoughts about death to the happy memories recorded in the proofs from Carol's wedding.

Effective as the passage is, it is clearly not intended to be an essay in any conventional sense. The author wrote what she did to express and record her own feelings and probably had no intention of sharing her writing with others. The fact that she wrote so very well, however, is not entirely accidental. She wrote powerfully in part because she felt strongly. In other words, her desire for self-expression gave her a purpose, and her purpose of expressing revulsion and shame about the plight of her great grandmother helped her to recognize just which details to use in describing the rest home and its occupants. She did not need to plan or struggle in writing these paragraphs; she had feelings and images on her mind and her main task was to put down on paper just what had affected her most strongly. By doing so, she was able to discover more clearly how she felt about committing a relative to the rest home. In expressing her feelings, she recorded incidents that could become the basis of a persuasive essay about a tragic situation facing many Americans with aging parents.

Thus, writing for the purpose of self-expression can be a means of growth and discovery as well as a way to find subjects worth writing about. By writing, we not only learn what we think, but also reassert who we are. We discover ourselves and give our daily lives and fleeting thoughts a degree of solidity and permanence. Such an opportunity for self-expression motivates many people to keep diaries and journals or to write their autobiographies. Benjamin Franklin states that motive clearly: "The next thing most like living one's life over again seems to be a recollection of that life, and to make that recollection as durable as possible by putting it down in writing" (*Autobiography*, 1790).

Writing intended as self-expression can be practical as well as enjoyable. Indeed, many of the methods of self-expression that we will examine in subsequent chapters are also techniques of invention that can be used to generate ideas before beginning an assigned essay. Journals and diaries record thoughts that writers may use later in formal essays; similarly, such techniques of invention as free writing, free association, and listing are powerful methods of discovering what one wishes to communicate to others and of recording those discoveries in a format that is meaningful, at least to oneself.

By definition, however, when we write for self-expression, we need not concern ourselves with communicating ideas to others. Despite the continuing popularity of such works as Benjamin Franklin's *Autobiography*, self-expressive writing normally appeals to an audience of just one, its author. Although popular fascination with the lives of famous men and women may lend temporary interest to their diaries, lists, and doodles, the nation's readers would most likely greet similar books by nonentities — say, Herbert Tiptoe's *Memoir of My Years in Goobertown, Arkansas* — with a yawn.

This is hardly surprising. The self-expressive writing of the famous is of interest precisely because we are interested in their "selves" — in discovering who they are, what their lives are like, and what makes them different from the rest of us. Most writing, however, is a form of interpersonal communication. If we are not famous, our audience is unlikely to be immediately interested in us and we need to find a purpose in writing that also gives our audience a reason for reading. In doing so, we will not entirely abandon self-expression—for to express ourselves to others, we must first discover precisely what we wish to express.

Exercise 1-1

As you read these words, you are inevitably experiencing sensations and feelings. There may be a dryness in your mouth, a consequence of having eaten nothing but a peanut butter sandwich for lunch. Your muscles may be aching from a hard workout with weights before lunch. You may be feeling harried and intimidated by the stacks of books you must study before tomorrow's classes. Whatever you are feeling *right now* should be the subject of a paragraph or two of self-expressive writing. Your goal is to put into words your physical and emotional sensations and your speculations about their causes.

Exercise 1-2

Write a paragraph or two about some relatively minor event in your life that nevertheless affected you powerfully. Try to write down what actually happened and how you felt about what happened. Your goal is to look into yourself and reveal your true feelings *to yourself.*

Exercise 1-3

Review what you have written in exercises 1-1 and 1-2. What parts of this self-expressive writing would you choose not to share with an audience? Why not? What parts would you be willing to share? Would they need to be revised or developed before an audience of strangers could truly understand your experiences?

WRITING FOR READERS

Truly worthwhile writing is always self-expressive to some extent, but the prevailing purpose of an essay must be directed toward serving the needs of readers. Ernest Hemingway stated the writer's basic task with exceptional clarity:

> A writer's problem does not change. He himself changes and the world he lives in changes but his problem remains the same. It is always how to write truly and having found what is true, to project it in such a way that it becomes part of the experience of the person who reads it.

In the end, then, the writer's purpose must mesh with the purposes of the reader. What are those purposes? Let us begin to find the answers by turning to three more passages of student writing.

Passage 1 from "The Grass Is Always Greener on the Football Field" by Keith Martin:

A couple of years ago, a memo entered the office of Barry Casewell, head football coach here at A-State. The memo informed him that the playoff game against Northeast Louisiana would be televised nationally on a cable channel. A few days later at practice, Casewell discovered something that bothered him. It was mid-winter, and we all know what happens to the grass as sub-zero temperatures approach. The turf was a nice shade of tan, leaning toward brown. Casewell began thinking, "What if someone important is watching the game? Why, they'll think we ain't nothin' more than a hick school." He immediately made out an order for dozens of cases of green spray paint and had twelve university employees spray the football field with it. The total cost was about $35,000, give or take a few thousand. What did it matter anyway? The athletic program had a budget of a million dollars. Who would notice?

Passage 2 from "So You Want to Read a Romance?" by Deborah Chappel:

Several years ago, after reading a quotation from a popular romance depicting a heroine feeling quivers of excitement, chills, and palpitations when the hero kissed her hand, Germaine Greer stated, "Indeed, if hand kissing can produce orgasm, actual intercourse might well bring on epilepsy." That kind of attitude toward romances continues today, partly because it is fun and easy to write disdainful commentary on these works, and partly because some of this disdainful commentary is so richly deserved. Few would dispute the fact that the majority of romances on the shelves at the local grocery store cannot be classified as literature. However, these books do serve valuable and constructive purposes, offering vicarious fulfillment of the need for romance and semi-challenging reading material for the semi-literate.

Passage 3 from "A Taste of Blood" by Kenneth Neely:

I glanced at the picture of George Washington as Terry and I walked toward the principal's office. My first fight, I thought to myself, my first trip to the principal's office. I suppose I could ask Terry about what it is like. Everybody knows that he has been in trouble at least eight times this semester, I continued to think.

Just then Terry seemed as if he read my thoughts. He said that I probably wouldn't get so much as a swat on the rump with a wet noodle. "Kids like you never get paddled," he sneered.

These three passages have several things in common. All three were written in response to assignments in freshman English. All three are introductory paragraphs. All three reflect an earnest desire for self-expression. And all three were written to be read to an audience of fellow students. These last two similarities are particularly important.

The desire for self-expression gave the students a personal reason for writing. The author of passage 1 had been a member of the college marching band and had seen troubling signs of financial extravagance in the football program. The author of passage 2 was an English major with a slightly guilty conscience about her fondness for romances. And the author of passage 3 felt a personal urge to share what it is like to have always been seen as the "teacher's pet."

These personal reasons for writing, however, do not explain the appeal of the paragraphs to other readers. In each case the author carefully considered the purposes of readers and attempted to respond to those purposes. Almost uniformly, readers demand to be persuaded, informed, and entertained. Thus, Keith Martin decided to **persuade** his readers that the athletic program wastes money, but in doing so he provided factual information through entertaining anecdotes. In contrast, Debbie Chappel's primary purpose in "So You Want to Read a Romance?" is to **inform** readers about the steps to take in selecting a romance. Conscious, however, that her topic might not appeal to all readers, Debbie used an entertaining statement by Germaine Greer to "hook" her readers. She then presented a wry but persuasive argument that romances do indeed offer "vicarious fulfillment of the need for romance and semi-challenging reading material for the semi-literate." Ken Neely's essay "A Taste of Blood" is a personal narrative of his youthful misadventures. His goal then is to **entertain** his readers, and no doubt many of his peers enjoy the subtle humor in this account of a trip to the principal's office. But the essay ultimately succeeds because Ken combines his humor with an effort to inform us about the human character.

The purposes of most prose involve some such combination of the intents to entertain, inform, and persuade, and they usually grow out of a writer's desire for self-expression. These four purposes predominate in good writing for clear-cut reasons. A written essay involves four components: the writer, the reader, the subject, and the language, as shown in the accompanying figure.

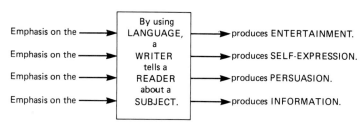

The Writing Process and the Written Product

An essay dominated by the writer's preoccupations and interests will be self-expressive, as was Jan Simpson's account of the rest home. An essay focusing almost exclusively on the subject, without paying any particular attention to the writer, the reader, or the language, is likely to be informative. A description of the symptoms of AIDS is an example of such informative writing. An essay focusing on the reader, such as an editorial urging a calm response to the AIDS epidemic, will be persuasive. And an essay focusing on the humorous or amusing possibilities of language, like a piece by Art Buchwald or Mark Twain, will be entertaining. Most writing, however, involves a conscious combination of these purposes to increase the chances of getting and holding a reader's attention.

The structure of this text is governed by our conviction that writers need to understand their purposes and combine them effectively in appealing to readers. By studying the writing strategies of able students and professionals, you should be able to improve your own writing. Each of the strategies you will study in the coming chapters involves a different mix of the four general purposes of writing. When the emphasis is on self-expression (often to discover ideas for an essay), you will write diary entries, journal entries, lists, and other forms of brainstorming. Thus, this text begins with two chapters in which you will learn about and practice the techniques of self-expression and invention. The bulk of the text, however, is concerned with writing for readers, where the purposes are best combined but where the emphasis varies from entertaining to informing to persuading. Let us examine briefly how such shifts in emphasis influence the strategies of writers.

Entertainment

A few unusual individuals actually seem to enjoy boring things, like *Sesame Street*'s Burt who fondles his paper clip collection, breathlessly awaits each segment of "Pigeons in the News," and delights in dining on oatmeal. The rest of us, though, struggle during the greater part of our daily lives to avoid dullness, and when we read, our primary purpose is often to banish boredom. In writing for others, therefore, the first rule must be to enliven the subject in order to entertain the reader. That is, of course, much more easily said than done.

As usual there are exceptions to this rule: the *Shop Manual for the 1986 Pontiac Fiero* need provide only information about the specifications, repair, and maintenance of the automobile. We would not expect —nor would we want—anything else in exchange for our $18.95. Similarly, ever since the days of Samuel Johnson (who in 1755 defined *lexicographer* as "a writer of dictionaries, a harmless drudge"), no lexicographer has felt the need to make definitions the least bit entertaining. Nevertheless, entertainment does play a central role in the sale of most books and articles—so much so that even best-selling cookbooks like *The Joy of Cooking* are fun to read as well as informative. Perhaps more to the point, your English teacher is so rarely entertained by the themes he or she must grade that your essay is almost certain to stand out if it provides amusement while meeting the other criteria of the assignment. We do not wish to imply, however, that all of your essays should be funny. Indeed, although wit and humor are wonderful additions to some essays, they might be quite inappropriate in others—in a research paper on child abuse, for example. But any essay can be made more enthralling by the use of dramatic examples and specific, image-producing details.

Fiction is by far the most common form of written entertainment. Thus, if we wish to make our own writing more lively, we might start by examining the techniques of novelists and short-story writers. The study of fiction is itself the focus of many a college course, and the subject is much too complex to be examined fully here. However, fiction entertains largely as a result of the power of narration, and good narration requires action, dialogue, and description. As we will see, essayists sometimes use narration to develop an entire essay, as Langston Hughes does in "Salvation." Often, especially in professional journalism, dialogue provides the substance for an entire piece, as in the transcripts of interviews or in John Leo's "Fire Belles in the Night." Similarly, description dominates an essay like Annie Dillard's "On Seeing" as easily as it does an advertisement in the Sears catalogue. Frequently, however, brief narrative anecdotes, fragments of conversation, and descriptions of characters or locales are used as illustrations and examples in essays developed according to other rhetorical strategies. In Chapters 6 and 7 on **description** and **narration** we explore the ways in which these two strategies can be used either in paragraphs or in entire essays to achieve the entertainment that characterizes most successful writing.

Information

How many beautiful virgins slept with the Persian king Ahasuerus before he selected Esther as his queen? Exactly what will an embalmer eventually do to your frail flesh? How were comets explained before

Newton described the laws of cometary motion? If you are like most readers, you are interested in finding out the answers to such questions. It follows that one way to interest your readers is to provide them with information.

Intriguing information is often useless trivia, like the knowledge that Ahasuerus entertained at least a thousand virgins before finding Esther to his liking (see *Esther* 1–2 in the Bible). Often, too, information is of no immediate practical value to the reader, as with Bertrand Russell's explanations in "On Comets" of the early superstitions surrounding their appearance. Frequently, however, essayists seek to provide information useful to the reader; Jessica Mitford's essay on "The Embalmer's Art" informs readers about the process of embalming so that they can decide whether they wish to continue to pay the price (which she believes is clearly exorbitant and unnecessary) for that service. In each case, however, the information provided is likely to be new to most readers. Indeed, once information has lost its newness, it ceases to be either informative or interesting. This is why most of us use yesterday's newspaper only to carry out the garbage.

Thus, when you seek to inform your readers, you must first discover something that you know and they don't. Then, you must present that information in an appropriate and interesting form. Sometimes essayists present intriguing information through **exemplification**, as when Roger Rosenblatt in "Oops! How's That Again?" uses copious examples to illustrate the range and hilarity of slips of the tongue. Elsewhere the essayist may provide information about a **process**, as Jessica Mitford does in writing about embalming. Still other essayists use **classification** to organize, categorize, and define ideas, as Darrell Huff does in examining "How to Lie with Statistics."

Although exemplification, process analysis, and classification are sensible and straightforward means of organizing and presenting factual information, other rhetorical patterns are frequently used with good results. A description, for example, may be entirely imaginative in fiction, but it may also be factual and informative as in the advertisement for "The 100 Greatest Books Ever Written." Similarly, the rhetorical patterns most closely associated with persuasion (casual analysis, comparison and contrast, and argumentation) almost inevitably require the presentation of much information.

Persuasion

The urge to persuade others to share your heartfelt views on a given subject is perhaps the most compelling reason for writing. That urge guides antinuclear advocates like Paul Ehrlich in "North America after the War" as they present the dangers of nuclear war. And it guides representatives for animal rights like David Stone and Linda Koebner in their essay entitled "Do Chimps Share Human Rights?" But the tools of persuasion are powerful and are not employed solely by people with honest and deep convictions. They are misappropriated daily by advertisers seeking to show off the glories of the Cut-Rite Vegematic, hack writers pandering the latest "proofs" of a conspiracy to kill John F. Kennedy, and con artists preaching the virtues of Uncle Ebenezer's Corn Elixir:

> a marvelous cure for what ails you: more wholesome than mother's milk, more invigorating than a carrot cocktail; a little dab of Corn Elixir will remove the mustache from an old maid's lip; a bit more will eat away all the calluses on a sailor's palm; one little sip will embolden a beggar to brave "the slings and arrows of outrageous fortune"; two jolts will lay him so contentedly low that most of those arrows pass unnoticed overhead. Yes, buy Uncle Ebenezer's Corn Elixir—the cure for all that ails you!

In constructing a persuasive essay, **comparison and contrast** is often the most useful structure. By comparing the arguments for opposing views, you clarify the issues involved, present them in a systematic and fair-minded fashion, and enable readers either to join in your conclusions or to reach their own. Indeed, one purpose of a liberal education is to teach students to abandon prejudices and evaluate both sides of any controversy.

Sometimes, however, the implications of a position or phenomenon are not so much controversial as simply unexplored. In such cases an essayist may wish to use **cause and effect**. One need not argue, for example, that a nuclear war would be a catastrophe, but few of us are sufficiently aware of the long-term biological effects of a nuclear war. Paul Ehrlich in "North America after the War" presents a specific and detailed chain of causes and effects in order to persuade us that nuclear warfare is too barbarous to retain as a defensive strategy.

Persuasion can also take a variety of other forms that generally involve a combination of rhetorical strategies. We group these complex combinations under the heading **argumentation**. In principle, most of us aspire to create the kinds of logical arguments forged by Thomas Jefferson in *The Declaration of Independence*. In practice, feelings often prevail over pure reasoning; thus, the poetic emotion of a speech like Martin Luther King's "I Have a Dream" is often more moving and persuasive than a strictly logical argument.

In various combinations these eight rhetorical approaches (narration, description, exemplification, process, classification, comparison and contrast, cause and effect, and argumentation) govern the development of virtually all essays. Yet essayists rarely commence the writing process by selecting a rhetorical strategy; rarely, for example, does one set out to write a process analysis without first deciding on a topic and a purpose. These rhetorical patterns are tools to be used by writers in achieving their purposes; their use is not a goal in itself, but a means to a goal. Thus Paul Roberts wrote "How to Say Nothing in Five Hundred Words" not to show off his mastery of process analysis, but instead to entertain students through a satire of the typical freshman composition, to inform them about the common errors that mar much student writing, and finally to persuade them that they can write better simply by avoiding those errors. As you practice these eight rhetorical strategies, by all means imitate Roberts's emphasis on entertaining, informing, and persuading the reader.

PUTTING PURPOSE IN YOUR OWN WRITING

By studying the models of student and professional writing contained in this text, you will be able to increase your awareness of what makes writing purposeful and effective. It is one thing, however, to perceive the purposes in the writing of others and entirely another thing to write purposeful prose — especially while responding to the demands of a classroom assignment. Nonetheless, it *is* possible to take direct action to make your writing more purposeful. Some suggestions follow:

1. **Share your writing.** Some instructors make it easy for students to share their writing by scheduling periodic peer group sessions or seminar meetings (during which six to eight students meet with their instructor to read and comment on each other's work). If such peer groups or seminar groups are not a formal part of your English course (and in many cases scheduling problems make formal seminar groups impossible), you can obtain the same experience on your own. Try to get together for a weekly lunch with some of your classmates to read each other's work, or work out similar arrangements with your roommates and suitemates, or share your essays with your family. The important thing is to *have* an audience and to write with that audience firmly in mind. The practice of writing for an audience (real or imaginary) will force you do develop a more purposeful and persuasive style.

2. If you are able to take part in a seminar group, here are three recommendations: if possible, **read your essays aloud to your audience; provide each member of the group with a photocopy of your paper; and share your essay with others before the final version is due.** Reading aloud forces you to consider both the sound and the sense of your words; moreover, it helps you to concentrate on the actual words you have written and their effect on your audience. Often, the simple process of reading aloud helps you to discover just what you need to revise. The reactions of a sympathetic and attentive audience normally serve to confirm what you already sensed, but they also help you to appreciate the *strengths* in your writing. By providing readers with a photocopy of your text, you make it possible for them to examine your essay carefully and to suggest thoughtful revisions. Your readers should be encouraged — as editors — to annotate your paper freely with comments and suggestions. Finally, by sharing your work before it is due, you give yourself an opportunity to see how it affects others, and you can then make final changes on the basis of your audience's responses.

3. **Explicitly consider the audience of each essay you write.** Ask yourself what audience it is intended for and what effect it should have on that audience. Even if your audience is purely imaginary (as it must be during actual composition), you will strengthen your writing by considering how your essay can meet that audience's needs.

4. **Combine purposes.** As the model essays in this text demonstrate, most good writing strives to entertain, inform, and persuade. Emphasize one of these purposes, but try to achieve them all in some measure. During revision, reexamine each paragraph to be certain that it contributes to the fulfillment of at least one of these purposes.

5. **Make truthful self-expression a part of all your writing.** Good writing is writing that *matters* to the author. Strive to strengthen and clarify your own values through your writing. In a sense, make yourself your own audience. That way, your writing will have a personal purpose, and you will be able to write forcefully because you feel strongly. Do not, however, allow self-expression to become your only goal. Remember that an essay is a means of communicating with others and therefore that the informing, persuading, and entertaining of your audience must take precedence over pure self-expression.

Chapter 2

THE READING PROCESS

It is said that 93 percent of a human being is water. Mind, heart, and soul are all confined within the rubbery skin of a body that is little more than a water balloon. When that skin is pierced by blade or bullet, our fluids drain, and with them life ebbs. Perhaps our souls survive in some form, but all that remains of us on earth are the works of mind and hand—the houses we have built, the artifacts we have made, and most especially the words we have written.

By writing we achieve a limited form of immortality. A certain portion of what we have thought and felt is captured, however imperfectly, on paper. As Lord Byron noted in 1821,

> . . . *words are things, and a small drop of ink,*
> *Falling like dew, upon a thought, produces*
> *That which makes thousands, perhaps millions, think.*
> *'Tis strange, the shortest letter which man uses*
> *Instead of speech, may form a lasting link*
> *Of ages; to what straits old Time reduces*
> *Frail man, when paper—even a rag like this,*
> *Survives himself, his tomb, and all that's his.*

In this sense writing is an egotistical act of self-preservation, but reading is quite the opposite. In reading we charitably open ourselves to the thoughts of others. Yet it is a mistake to think of reading as a passive and purely receptive activity. No, a reader is almost a god, resurrecting the dead and summoning the distant. When we read that stanza by Byron, a bit of him lives again, but *we* are in control of the process. We make of him what we wish and we put him aside when we will. No monarch has ruled a subject more imperiously than *every reader* rules an author. The greatest of thinkers from Einstein to Aristotle are as much

15

at our command as are the most unassuming of humorists. Our goal in this chapter is to help you to exercise even more control over your reading process, taking in more of that rich lode of ideas that the writers in any book offer you as tribute.

It is useful to divide the reading process into four steps:

1. **Consider the context of the piece you are reading.**   Before even beginning to read an essay or a story, look at the title and the author's name. Often the title gives direct clues to the content, tone, or thesis of the essay. For example, we can infer from the title "The Grass Is Always Greener on the Football Field" that Keith Martin's essay will take a critical and somewhat cynical look at football. After all, the old aphorism about the greenness of the grass on the other side of the fence is itself wryly cynical. At the very least, an essay's title can help you to identify its topic, as in the case of "Salutation Displays," "The Politics of Food," and "Japanese and American Workers: Two Casts of Mind."

The author's name may provide other important clues. In some cases that name will be familiar — Thomas Jefferson, Martin Luther King, Ernest Hemingway. More often, you will have to pick up whatever knowledge you can from the headnote preceding the essay. Once you know that Robin Lakoff is a professor of linguistics it becomes easy to deduce that her essay entitled "You Are What You Say" will examine the ways in which words themselves often mold personalities and opinions. After you learn (or are reminded) that Gloria Steinem is a prominent feminist, you can quickly guess that her essay on "The Politics of Food" will focus on the way food can become a weapon in the war between the sexes.

You should also take note of the date and source of original publication. This information could give you important clues about the characteristics and expectations of the audience, as well as the style and tone of the essay itself. Sometimes, of course, you will know little about that audience. But if a particular piece was originally published in *Ms.*, you can anticipate that it will be written from the feminist perspective. If, however, it first appeared in *Time* or *Newsweek* or *The New York Times*, you know little more than that most of the readers were expected to be college educated and interested in significant contemporary issues. Similarly, a piece first published in the mid-nineteenth century (one by Thoreau or Hawthorne, for example) can be expected to be more formal in style than one from the 1970s by Tom Wolfe.

2. **Read the entire selection slowly for pleasure.**   Some observers of society contend that part of the problem in America in recent years has been the tendency to reject the leisurely pleasure of craftsmanship in the pursuit of productivity and wealth. The result has been that in industry we build cars too quickly with too little concern for quality. As college students we drive those cars to class too fast and with too little concern for safety. We try to get a four-year college degree in three years without caring how much or how well we learn. And we take courses in speed-reading without thinking about what we lose in enjoy-

ment and understanding by racing through our reading as we race through our lives.

During the 1976 presidential campaign, one of the cruel little clichés hurled at Gerald Ford (along with the one about being unable to walk and chew gum at the same time) was that he is the kind of person who moves his lips while he reads. Perhaps the slur is revealing in an unintended way, for as a congressman, vice president, and president, Ford was distinguished by his thoroughness and understanding. Reading carefully and savoring every word are good tactics in approaching any work that has been crafted with care. Printed texts are mere patterns of symbols on a page, much like the magnetic charges on an audiotape. As readers, we must listen to the music of the words if we are to recapture the author's thinking in high fidelity.

To read well you should be comfortable, but not too comfortable. If reading in bed makes you drowsy, don't do it—at least not when you want full comprehension. If noise interferes with your concentration, find a place that is free from boom-boxes and babble. If you get sleepy after dinner, do your serious reading *before* dinner. But don't make yourself a martyr. Part of your goal should be to enjoy reading essays and stories that, at least in this book, were selected *because* most students find them enjoyable as well as thought-provoking. As you read, relax and let yourself enter the world of the writer. Let the people, places, and things rise up as mental images. Listen to the cadence of the language. React mentally to the writer's challenges and assertions. At the end of this first, careful reading, check your comprehension by trying to answer the "Questions on Content" that follow the selections. You should be able to answer most or all of these questions after a single thorough reading, but don't worry unduly if you are stumped by one or two. Merely mark those questions to remind yourself to return to them later.

3. **Read the selection again, this time underlining important passages and writing marginal comments or queries.** Reading is an activity of the mind, and nothing focuses that activity as effectively as keeping a pencil at hand and using it often to record *your* reactions, opinions, and judgments. Sometimes these notes to yourself might be little more than an occasional underlined sentence that you find particularly interesting or important, but often you should include marginal commentary as well. Try to note where you agree with the author and where you disagree, and briefly indicate why. Be bold and assertive, stating your feelings bluntly: "Nonsense! Fear is debilitating, not stimulating." "Give me a break. It's no crime to desire success." "I like that. Thin people *do* need watching. Too often hungry, on edge, devious— they need a good meal and a nap." At the very least mark for future attention those sentences that reveal the writer's thesis, and pay particular attention to any topic sentences in individual paragraphs.

Both before and after rereading the selection, it is wise to consider the "Questions on Thesis, Purpose, and Structure" and "Questions on Style and Diction." By reading these questions before rereading the essay, you can keep them in the back of your mind as you read, noting your answers both consciously and subconsciously. By explicitly considering each question after your second reading, you can discover much about the writer's tactics and achievement.

4. **Finally, skim the entire piece one more time in an effort to formulate your opinions about its strengths and weaknesses.** Having read an essay or story twice, you should have a good grasp of its content, but skimming can give you a quick overview of its structure and help you synthesize your reactions. At this point we think you should pay particular attention to questions of purpose. What motivated the author to write? What reasons does the author give *you* for reading? Is the piece entertaining? Informative? Persuasive? Is it some combination of these? Could it have been a stronger piece of writing if it had fulfilled some of these purposes more effectively?

This four-stage reading process may at first seem excessive. Clearly, you would not choose to use it for everything you read. A person who started the day by prereading, reading, rereading, and skimming each story in the morning newspaper might go to bed at night without having finished the classified ads. However, this is a method of study, and we recommend it for the essays, stories, and advertisements in this book because you are embarking on a course of study. By engaging fully with the writing in this text, you can learn much about what makes that writing effective. When you have done so, you should be able to apply some of what you have learned in making your own writing more effective.

Fire Belles in the Night
John Leo

For many years a senior writer for *Time* magazine, John Leo has written comic dialogues between the ultraconservative Ralph and his feminist wife, Wanda, that have become a well-established form of commentary on the perennial battle of the sexes. This essay appeared in *Time* on April 5, 1982.

1 Wanda: Ralph, what do you think of women fire fighters?
2 Ralph: Not much, my sweet. It's a bit like using partially blind people as umpires.
3 Wanda: Why did I ask?
4 Ralph: Perhaps to depict me as a sputtering sexist, my own true love. Alas, in this case, your unvoiced criticism is wide of the mark. Even Alan Alda knows that the best women can't compete with the best men in feats of strength and stamina. Upper-body strength, you know. This may be why there are no women in pro football. I don't see why standards should be any lower in pro fire fighting.
5 Wanda: Right, Ralph. All the fire fighters just have to be male, just like all the doctors, lawyers and alchemists were male when you were growing up in the 9th century.

Ralph: I didn't invent biology, dear love, and as far as I know, none of   6
my friends did either. Who do you want dragging you out of a fire, a
brute or a firelady with correct feminist principles?

Wanda: Anybody who can pass a fair test. Why do you think Atlanta,   7
San Diego, Seattle and a dozen or so other cities have hired women
for their fire departments?

Ralph: Normal pressure-group politics. Once all the lobbies win their   8
nonnegotiable demands, your local fire department will probably
have three women, one creationist, a couple of joggers, a native
American, a Moonie who survived deprogramming and one self-actualized bisexual vegetarian. The town will burn down, but what the
hell, that's a small price to pay for a truly trendy department.

Wanda: Ralph, the veins are standing out in your neck. Look, women   9
don't want quotas or special preferences, just a fair shot at the jobs.
It's not written in stone that only men can extinguish flames.

Ralph: That sounds good, but it doesn't work out that way. Look at   10
what happened in New York. The city has 13,000 males and no
females in its fire department. So the women say, "Just give us a fair
chance at passing the test." Eighty women take the physical test,
and — guess what — all 80 fail. Do the women say, "Gee, it takes
more strength than I thought to be a fireman"? No, they decide the
test was sexist: they sue. And they win.

Wanda: Hold on, Ralph. There were real problems with the city test.   11
In the handgrip test, nobody told the women that you could adjust
the machine for smaller hand size. They couldn't get leverage, and
they all did poorly. A candidate is supposed to run the mile in 4 min.
50 sec. What's that got to do with being a good fire fighter? And the
part where you have to carry a 120-lb. dummy up a flight of stairs —
the dummy was canvas-covered and cylindrical, so people with
shorter arms couldn't quite grasp it right. How often do you have to
plunge into a burning building to rescue a slippery cylinder? Some
of these tests are dopey, and the rest are created by and for males.

Ralph: You mean the tests were created by pros, and now they'll be   12
adjusted by and for amateurs. I hope they don't invent a test for
women eye surgeons that a high-school graduate can pass after a
week of home study.

Wanda: Ralph, I'm not wild about your analogies.   13

Ralph: They're not that wild, Wanda dearest. The goodhearted federal   14
judge in the New York City case made one of those stupefying
rulings. The city has to hire 45 women as fire fighters — here we go
with quotas — and the department was ordered to devise a test
women could pass. Terrific. That's how we ruined our schools, by
designing trick tests that anybody with a heartbeat could pass. This
is worse — lives are at stake here. With all due respect to the judiciary, I think the judge has a goodly portion of pudding between his
ears. You could use the same logic to force the NBA to lower its
baskets 5 ft. and accept a quota of dwarfs. By the way, last week
there was talk that those 45 women the city has to hire could get

$40,000 on their first working day—imaginary back pay for the time they would have worked if they could have passed the tests. Alice in Wonderland stuff, Wanda.

15   **Wanda:**   Calm yourself, Ralph. I'm not going to bother reasoning with you about how good women might be if they were offered the kind of training programs, support and encouragement that men get routinely. Anyway, did you really think, after all these years of feminism, that fire fighting was going to be left blissfully alone as an all-male profession? There are only a couple hundred women on the job now, but in a few years it will be thousands, so get used to the idea.

16   **Ralph:**   I'm used to the idea right now. From now on, all the fires in this house will be on the first floor, right near the door, where even a court-appointed woman can put them out. And if I'm ever trapped under a beam or something, I'll nod knowingly if a firelady stops by and says, "Sorry, I can't lift 120 lbs. The judge said that I could save three 40-lb. people instead."

17   **Wanda:**   Just look at Nancy Sweeney, who jogged, lifted weights, did push-ups and carried her kids up and down three fights of stairs to get in shape. She not only passed the Indianapolis fire department test, she was named 1981 Rookie of the Year. Betsy Powell, a paramedic in the Dallas fire department, could also pull you out from under a beam, where maybe you belong. She admits that men in the department have greater upper-body strength, but she's learned to compensate by using her legs more in lifting. She's in great shape, she's served as engine foreman, and her captain says she is "exceptionally good" at what she does. He says she's not strong enough to pull down a shiplap ceiling, whatever that is, so he has someone else do that. Big deal. There are always some people in every department who can't do certain things, the older guys, for instance. But they are all valuable, so will you please shut up.

18   **Ralph:**   Well, if the women take orders, and stay out of the way, maybe each department could carry a firelady or two without messing up.

19   **Wanda:**   Even if they are slippery and cylindrical. Say good night, Ralph.

Questions on Content

1. What major cities had already hired women for their fire departments when this essay was written?
2. What happened in New York when women tried to become firefighters?
3. What evidence indicates that women are not qualified to become firefighters?
4. What evidence indicates that women can make excellent firefighters?
5. How would you describe the personalities of Ralph and Wanda? What general views in society do they represent?

Questions on Thesis, Purpose, and Structure

1. This essay was originally published in *Time*, a major newsmagazine. Does it present newsworthy information?
2. Suppose the essay were rewritten as a straight news story. How much shorter

could it be? What is lost in the condensation? Would you be more or less likely to read and remember the condensed news story?

3. Does the conflict between Ralph and Wanda add anything besides entertaining drama? How are the conflicting positions that they represent also part of the "story" that John Leo is reporting?

4. Clearly, both Ralph and Wanda are attempting to present their points of view persuasively, but does John Leo himself take sides? That is, does the essay as a whole reflect any bias on his part?

5. How would you state the thesis of the essay? What sentence (or sentences) in the essay comes closest to a statement of the thesis?

Questions on Style and Diction

1. Explain the pun in the title. How is the pun related to the content of the essay?

2. Explain the allusion to Alan Alda in paragraph 4. What point is Ralph trying to make through the allusion?

3. Leo frequently uses sentence fragments. Why are these sentence fragments acceptable and appropriate in this essay, but perhaps not in a straight news story?

4. When Wanda says in paragraph 5, "Right, Ralph. All the fire fighters just have to be male, just like all the doctors, lawyers and alchemists were male when you were growing up in the 9th century," does she mean it? How can we tell that she is being sarcastic and means the opposite of what she actually says?

5. Consider Ralph's use of analogies. Are the analogies fair and logically persuasive? Do they reflect Ralph's personality, interests, and prejudices?

Ideas for Essays

1. Rewrite this essay as a straight news story. Concentrate on presenting factual information in a neutral and unbiased fashion.

2. Write a dialogue between Ralph and Wanda on some other issue. Some possible topics are abortion, coed dormitories on college campuses, women in the ministry, girls in Little League baseball or football, males on cheerleading squads.

3. In an analytical essay discuss the extent to which John Leo combines purposes (entertainment, information, persuasion). Is the balance of purposes that Leo achieves appropriate for his audience (*Time* readers) and thesis? Why or why not?

How to Spell
John Irving

In recent years the International Paper Company has sponsored a series of essay/advertisements on subjects related to reading and writing. These essays, each of which is written by a prominent author, are published as two-page advertisements in major national magazines like *Time* and *Newsweek*. Among the other titles in this series have been "How to Read Faster" by Bill Cosby,

(Continued on p. 24.)

How to spell

By John Irving

International Paper asked John Irving, author of "The World According to Garp," "The Hotel New Hampshire," and "Setting Free the Bears," among other novels—and once a hopelessly bad speller himself—to teach you how to improve your spelling.

Let's begin with the bad news.

If you're a bad speller, you probably think you always will be. There are exceptions to every spelling rule, and the rules themselves are easy to forget. George Bernard Shaw demonstrated how ridiculous some spelling rules are. By following the rules, he said, we could spell fish this way: ghoti. The "f" as it sounds in enough, the "i" as it sounds in women, and the "sh" as it sounds in fiction.

With such rules to follow, no one should feel stupid for being a bad speller. But there are ways to improve. Start by acknowledging the mess that English spelling is in—but have sympathy: English spelling changed with foreign influences. Chaucer wrote "gesse," but "guess," imported earlier by the Norman invaders, finally replaced it. Most early printers in England came from Holland; they brought "ghost" and "gherkin" with them.

If you'd like to intimidate yourself—and remain a bad speller forever—just try to remember the 13 different ways the sound "sh" can be written:

shoe	suspicion
sugar	nauseous
ocean	conscious
issue	chaperone
nation	mansion
schist	fuchsia
pshaw	

Now the good news

The good news is that 90 percent of all writing consists of 1,000 basic words. There is, also, a method to most English spelling and a great number of how-to-spell books. Remarkably, all these books propose learning the same rules! Not surprisingly, most of these books are humorless.

Just keep this in mind: If you're familiar with the words you use, you'll probably spell them correctly—and you shouldn't be writing words you're unfamiliar with anyway. USE a word—out loud, and more than once—before you try writing it, and make sure (with a new word) that you know what it means before you use it. This means you'll have to look it up in a dictionary, where you'll not only learn what it means, but you'll see how it's spelled. Choose a dictionary you enjoy browsing in, and guard it as you would a diary. You wouldn't lend a diary, would you?

A tip on looking it up

Beside every word I look up in my dictionary, I make a mark.

Beside every word I look up more than once, I write a note to myself—about WHY I looked it up. I have looked up "strictly" 14 times since 1964. I prefer to spell it with a k as in "stricktly." I have looked up "ubiquitous" a dozen times. I can't remember what it means.

Another good way to use your dictionary: When you have to look up a word, for any reason, learn—and learn to spell—a new word at the same time. It can be any useful word on the same page as the word you looked up. Put the date beside this new word and see how quickly, or in what way, you forget it. Eventually, you'll learn it.

Almost as important as knowing what a word means (in order to spell it) is knowing how it's pronounced. It's government, not goverment. It's February, not Febuary. And if you know that anti- means against, you should know how to spell antidote and antibiotic and antifreeze. If you know that ante- means before, you shouldn't have trouble spelling antechamber or antecedent.

Some rules, exceptions, and two tricks

I don't have room to touch on all the rules here. It would take a book to do that. But I can share a few that help me most:

What about -ary or -ery? When a word has a primary accent on the first syllable and a secondary accent on the next-to-last syllable (sec're-tar'y), it usually ends in -ary. Only six important words like this end in -ery:

"Love your dictionary"

cemetery   monastery
millinery   confectionery
distillery   stationery
                         (as in pap<u>er</u>)

Here's another easy rule. Only four words end in -<u>efy</u>. Most people misspell them–with -<u>ify</u>, which is usually correct. Just memorize these, too, and use -<u>ify</u> for all the rest.

stupefy   putrefy
liquefy   rarefy

As a former bad speller, I have learned a few valuable tricks. Any good how-to-spell book will teach you more than these two, but these two are my favorites. Of the 800,000 words in the English language, the most frequently misspelled is <u>alright</u>; just remember that <u>alright</u> is <u>all wrong</u>. You wouldn't write <u>alwrong</u>, would you? That's how you know you should write <u>all right</u>.

The other trick is for the truly *worst* spellers. I mean those of you who spell so badly that you can't get close enough to the right way to spell a word in order to even FIND it in the dictionary. The word you're looking for is there, of course, but you won't find it the way you're trying to spell it. What to do is look up a synonym–another word that means the same thing. Chances are good that you'll find the word you're looking for under the definition of the synonym.

Demon words and bugbears

Everyone has a few demon words–they never look right, even when they're spelled correctly. Three of my demons are <u>medieval</u>, <u>ecstasy</u>, and <u>rhythm</u>. I have learned to hate these words, but I have not learned to spell them; I have to look them up every time.

And everyone has a spelling rule that's a bugbear–it's either too difficult to learn or it's impossible to remember. My personal bugbear among the rules is the one governing whether you add -<u>able</u> or -<u>ible</u>. I can teach it to you, but I can't

remember it myself.

You add -<u>able</u> to a full word: adapt, adaptable; work, workable. You add -<u>able</u> to words that end in <u>e</u>–just remember to drop the final <u>e</u>: love, lovable. But if the word ends in two <u>e</u>'s, like agree, you keep them both: agreeable.

You add -<u>ible</u> if the base is not a full word that can stand on its own: credible, tangible, horrible, terrible. You add -<u>ible</u> if the root word ends in -<u>ns</u>: responsible. You add -<u>ible</u> if the root word ends in -miss: permissible. You add -<u>ible</u> if the root word ends in a soft <u>c</u>

"This is one of the longest English words in common use. But don't let the length of a word frighten you. There's a rule for how to spell this one, and you can learn it."

(but remember to drop the final <u>e</u>!): force, forcible.

Got that? I don't have it, and I was introduced to that rule in prep school; with that rule, I still learn one word at a time.

Poor President Jackson

You must remember that it is permis<u>ible</u> for spelling to drive you crazy. Spelling had this effect on Andrew Jackson, who once blew his stack while trying to write a Presidential paper. "It's a damn poor mind that can think of only one way to spell a word!" the President cried.

When you have trouble, think of poor Andrew Jackson and know that you're not alone.

What's really important

And remember what's really important about good writing is not good spelling. If you spell badly but write well, you should hold your head up. As the poet T.S. Eliot recommended, "Write for as large and miscellaneous an audience as possible"–and don't be overly concerned if you can't spell "miscellaneous."

Also remember that you can spell correctly and write well and still be misunderstood. Hold your head up about that, too.

As good old G.C. Lichtenberg said, "A book is a mirror: if an ass peers into it, you can't expect an apostle to look out"–whether you spell "apostle" correctly or not.

John Irving

Reprinted by permission of International Paper Company.

"How to Enjoy Poetry" by James Dickey, "How to Make a Speech" by George Plimpton, "How to Use a Library" by James A. Michener, and "How to Write with Style" by Kurt Vonnegut. John Irving, the author of "How to Spell," was born and raised in Exeter, New Hampshire, and educated at the universities of Pittsburgh, Vienna, New Hampshire, and Iowa, before beginning a teaching and writing career at Massachusetts' Mount Holyoke College in 1975. Irving's flamboyant fiction — which includes the best-selling novels *The World According to Garp* (1978), *The Hotel New Hampshire* (1981), and *The Cider House Rules* (1985) — has earned him considerable acclaim and the distinction of being one of only a handful of contemporary writers whose works have successfully bridged the gap between serious and popular fiction.

Questions on Content

1. Why is English spelling particularly difficult to master?
2. How many words are used in the basic vocabulary of 90 percent of all writing?
3. What special techniques does Irving recommend in using a dictionary?
4. What two rules about spelling does Irving single out for attention?
5. What is the most frequently misspelled word in the English language?
6. How can you look up the spelling of a word if you don't know how to spell it?

Questions on Thesis, Purpose, and Structure

1. What basic purpose is indicated by the title of the essay? Is the essay as a whole designed primarily to entertain, to inform, or to persuade?
2. One might expect an essay on how to spell to be dull. What does Irving do to make his discussion of spelling lively and entertaining? Identify specific passages and attempt to explain what makes them interesting.
3. Is the audience for this essay more apt to be composed of strong or weak spellers? What does Irving do to put weak spellers at ease?
4. What points are made by Irving's concluding quotations from Andrew Jackson, T. S. Eliot, and G. C. Lichtenberg? Are these points related to the thesis of the essay? How would you state that thesis?
5. This essay was published as an advertisement by the International Paper Company. Is the company more interested in creating goodwill or in trying to persuade you to use and purchase products made by International Paper? Support your point of view with reasonable arguments and evidence drawn from the advertisement.

Questions on Style and Diction

1. Normally, writers try to avoid paragraphs composed of only one sentence. Why does Irving begin his essay with a one-sentence paragraph?
2. Consider the connotations of the word *fish*. Why is that a particularly good word to use in demonstrating the ridiculousness of English spelling?
3. What is a "bugbear"? Why does Irving use the words *demon* and *bugbear* instead of more formal words?
4. Throughout his essay Irving writes in the first person ("I") and addresses the reader directly ("you"). What is the effect of these choices in point of view?

Ideas for Essays

1. Assume that you are a marketing expert for International Paper and that you thought of the "Power of the Printed Word" advertising strategy. Write a memo to your supervisor in which you try to persuade him or her that a series of "How to" essays about reading and writing represent a wise use of International Paper's advertising dollars. Keep in mind that full-page advertisements in major magazines are quite costly—and these advertisements will require two full pages! Note also that the direct mention of International Paper is confined to a small box at the end of the second page.

2. In an analytical essay discuss the extent to which John Irving combines purposes (entertainment, information, persuasion). Is the balance of purposes that Irving achieves appropriate for his audience (readers of popular magazines) and thesis? Why or why not?

Birthday Party
Katharine Brush

After earning a bachelor's degree from Centenary College, Katharine Brush (1900–1952) became a successful novelist and short-story writer, publishing ten novels and two collections of her stories, as well as frequently placing stories in magazines like *Cosmopolitan, Good Housekeeping,* and *The New Yorker.* "Birthday Party," originally published in *The New Yorker* in 1946, is an excellent example of how good writers make every word count.

They were a couple in their late thirties, and they looked unmistak-   1
ably married. They sat on the banquette opposite us in a little narrow restaurant, having dinner. The man had a round, self-satisfied face, with glasses on it; the woman was fadingly pretty, in a big hat. There was nothing conspicuous about them, nothing particularly noticeable, until the end of their meal, when it suddenly became obvious that this was an Occasion—in fact, the husband's birthday, and the wife had planned a little surprise for him.

It arrived, in the form of a small but glossy birthday cake, with one   2
pink candle burning in the center. The headwaiter brought it in and placed it before the husband, and meanwhile the violin-and-piano orchestra played "Happy Birthday to You" and the wife beamed with shy pride over her little surprise, and such few people as there were in the restaurant tried to help out with a pattering of applause. It became clear at once that help was needed, because the husband was not pleased. Instead he was hotly embarrassed, and indignant at his wife for embarrassing him.

You looked at him and you saw this and you thought, "Oh, now,   3
don't *be* like that!" But he was like that, and as soon as the little cake had been deposited on the table, and the orchestra had finished the birthday piece, and the general attention had shifted from the man and the woman, I saw him say something to her under his breath—some punishing thing, quick and curt and unkind. I couldn't bear to look at the woman then, so I stared at my plate and waited for quite a long time. Not

long enough, though. She was still crying when I finally glanced over there again. Crying quietly and heartbrokenly and hopelessly, all to herself, under the gay big brim of her best hat.

Questions on Content

1. What is the Occasion mentioned in paragraph 1 and what is the wife's "little surprise"?
2. Why does the husband react as he does to the wife's surprise?

Questions on Thesis, Purpose, and Structure

1. Short stories are normally intended to entertain a reader. Is there any sense in which this little episode entertains?
2. To what extent does this story inform the reader about typical human reactions?
3. What are the narrator's attitudes toward the husband and the wife? How does she persuade you that one spouse is more deserving of sympathy than the other?
4. What is the implied thesis of the story?

Questions on Style and Diction

1. Consider the description of the man in paragraph 1. What can you conclude about the man and the narrator's attitude toward the man? Suppose Brush had written, "The man had a round, self-satisfied face, and wore glasses." What would be lost in the revision?
2. Consider the description of the woman in paragraph 1. What does the detail of the big hat indicate? Why does Brush mention it again at the end of paragraph 3?
3. Why does Brush capitalize the word *Occasion* in paragraph 1? What details in the story serve to diminish this occasion by emphasizing littleness or cheapness?
4. Describe the narrative point of view in paragraphs 1 and 2. How involved is the narrator in the action? How does the narrative point of view change in paragraph 3? Why does the narrator's involvement increase?

Ideas for Essays

1. Rewrite "Birthday Party" from the point of view of the husband. Try to see events through his eyes and therefore to justify his actions, even though he may realize that he will later come to regret them.
2. Write a three-paragraph short story of your own. As in "Birthday Party" focus on the emotional interactions and implications of some fairly ordinary event. As in "Birthday Party" sharply limit the amount of time you attempt to cover in your story. And finally, let your own thesis about the events be clearly implied by the story's end.
3. In an analytical essay discuss the extent to which Katharine Brush combines purposes (entertainment, information, persuasion). Is the balance of purposes that Brush achieves appropriate for her audience (the elite readers of *The New Yorker*) and thesis? Why or why not?

◇◇◇

Chapter 3

THE WRITING PROCESS

To some extent writing is a skill that varies from one individual to another, but every writer can improve through diligence and practice. Happily, most writers' skills ripen naturally through years of practice, trial and error, and the normal process of personal growth. However, this natural maturation can be speeded up through inspiration, perspiration, and faith in one's own ability to learn. Often the only difference between a good writer and a mediocre one is that the former is more willing than the latter to take pains and spend time at writing. Beginning writers often greatly underestimate the complexity of the writing process and the amount of time that must be devoted to it. The pages that follow call explicit attention to the various stages in the composing process and offer concrete advice about strategies for effective and efficient writing. Although we have presented these stages of the writing process in a sequential order (prewriting — writing — revision), in practice they often overlap one another in keeping with the unpredictable shifts and leaps of the writer's thought.

PREWRITING

1. **Understand the writing assignment.** As soon as a writing assignment is given, you should ask enough questions so that you understand exactly what is expected. This is no time to be reticent; in all likelihood the questions you wish to ask, but feel reluctant about, are the very questions that are also going unanswered in the minds of your classmates.

If your subject is assigned, you need to analyze it carefully to make certain that you fully understand its implications and possibilities, as well as its limitations. If, on the other hand, the topic is one of your own choosing, you need to leave ample time to identify a topic that interests you and that you are capable of developing to meet the stated expectations of your instructor.

In either case, be sure to consider the audience for whom you are writing. If, for example, you are writing about your experiences in registering for college classes, your tone, your vocabulary, your supporting examples, and even your thesis may depend on your audience. In writing to a close friend you might use an informal tone in describing the variety of faces and body types that you see in line around you — demure, oval-faced Malaysian women in traditional caftans; "good old boys" sporting boots, blue jeans, and sheepskin jackets; serious-minded young Republicans wearing wing-tips, dress slacks, button-down shirts, and striped ties. However, in writing to the registrar to recommend improvements in the registration procedure, you might wish to make your tone more formal while emphasizing the annoyance of long lines, the need for clearer written directions for registering, and the advisability of having some registration workers circulating among the students to answer their many questions.

2. **Get started early and use time efficiently.**   On out-of-class assignments it is best to begin planning and writing your essay as soon as possible. Such early planning allows you to raise questions about the assignment in class or in conference and assures ample time for writing and revision. On in-class assignments the need to use time efficiently is even more important, because every minute lost reduces the length and (potentially) the quality of the essay.

3. **Gather information in an effort to discover new ideas and new approaches to the topic.**   Good writing does not emerge from a vacuum, nor should a writer rehash stale ideas. Paul Roberts (see "How to Say Nothing in Five Hundred Words") suggests that on receiving an assignment students should jot down their first thoughts as quickly as possible and then *throw those notes away!* What springs immediately to one person's mind is very likely to spring immediately to every mind and, therefore, to give rise to an essay filled with boring commonplaces. Roberts, of course, is exaggerating to make a point. There is no reason to throw away a *good* idea just because it occurs to you immediately. Still, many first ideas are *just* first ideas and deserve to be discarded as you think more deeply.

How, then, can you find original and intriguing ideas? Often, you need only rediscover what you already know. Listing, free association, free writing, and journal writing are all powerful means of unlocking a wealth of experiences in every student. Some topics, however, require the discovery of new knowledge. In such cases library research, brainstorming, journalistic inquiry, or Aristotelian invention may prove helpful. Such techniques of invention and problem solving are extremely important to the success of many writing assignments and, therefore, are discussed in some detail in the early chapters of this book. Yet even if you use no formal methods of invention and discovery, by beginning early and planning your essay over several days, you will find that many of the problems presented by the assignment are solved subconsciously during the intervals between working periods.

Exercise 3-1

Choose one of the following topics and then follow Paul Roberts's advice: Write down your first thoughts as rapidly as possible. After five minutes or so, stop, begin again, and make a new list of ideas for your essay, trying to avoid using the ideas that first occurred to you.

Topics
1. Why family members sometimes can't get along together despite their love for one another.
2. Why sports are important.
3. The qualities of a natural leader.
4. The reasons why you are considering (or would never consider) becoming a teacher (doctor, lawyer, minister).
5. Why people love their pets.

Exercise 3-2

Using the topic chosen in exercise 3-1, write briefly on the ways in which your essay might change for different audiences. How, for example, would the thesis, tone, and supporting examples be different if you were writing for a six-year-old child instead of an audience of college students? How would your essay differ if written for an administrator or a public official?

4. **Form a thesis and keep it in mind throughout the essay.**   A thesis is the assertion that unifies and controls the entire essay. Each paragraph — and each sentence in each paragraph — should help to prove, clarify, or illustrate the thesis. For example, the thesis of this brief guide to writing and revision is that you can improve your essay by understanding the assignment, using time efficiently, discovering new ideas, forming a thesis, imposing order, composing a rough draft, revising in stages, making a clean copy, and proofreading the completed essay. Although the thesis need not always be stated explicitly in the essay, it is usually wise to include it and even to place it emphatically in the introductory paragraph. By formulating a thesis and sticking to it, you will increase the clarity of your essay and more easily avoid irrelevancies.

5. **Write with a purpose and a plan.**   It may at first seem obvious that an essay with a thesis must also have a purpose — if only to prove that thesis — but many a freshman essay has been based on an assertion that can't be proven or needn't be! Consider the following theses from recent submissions: "The universe was created exactly as de-

scribed in Genesis." "The Republicans will inevitably lead us into nuclear war." "Heroin addiction can blight a student's bright future."

Such issues are inherently unpromising topics for essays. The first, like many religious contentions, is better preserved as a matter for faith than selected as a topic for persuasion. The second, like most political predictions, may sometimes be a matter of heated debate, but in the absence of specific information about the future, it is mainly a matter of political prejudice (or conjecture). The third, like all platitudes, is so obvious and so widely publicized as to be almost impossible to treat with originality.

In contrast, the successful essay develops its thesis in a way that is informative, persuasive, or entertaining—or, better yet, some combination of these purposes. Its assertions may be unusual and bold, but they are also potentially demonstrable. Consider the following theses:

"Christianity shows many similarities with early Orphic rituals."

"Both Republicans, by serving the needs of the rich, and Democrats, by relying on the votes of the poor, contribute to the proliferation of America's underprivileged classes."

"'Private vices lead to public benefits!' That outrageous statement remains as true today as it was in 1714 when Bernard Mandeville first made the claim."

Clearly, the first of these theses must be supported by valid historical information. The second requires both factual information and persuasive argumentation; it may also generate some humorous pessimism about American political parties. The third requires persuasive and presumably humorous examples to back it up. In each case the forcefully stated thesis provides the writer with a sense of direction and the essay with a destination.

The preparation of a carefully developed outline adds a method of organization and offers the writer control over the subject. Some writers prefer to make an outline before even beginning a rough draft; others like to write their ideas down as rapidly and as fully as possible before attempting to impose order on them. Either way, formal or informal outlining at some point during the writing process can help you to make your writing more logical and understandable. Readers are like motorists in an unfamiliar town. If the streets are winding and unmarked, the motorist will become hopelessly lost no matter how picturesque the community. But if the streets are well marked and arranged in some orderly pattern, or if a good map is at hand, even a newcomer can navigate with ease. In the same way, to prevent meandering, the writer's sentences need to be marked off by paragraphs into orderly blocks. In general, these blocks should be labeled with clear signposts: topic sentences that announce to the reader the main topic of each paragraph and its relationship to the thesis. The thesis and the topic sentences thus form a map of the entire essay, allowing the reader to remain on course.

By clearly outlining the route to the essay's destination, they allow the reader to relax and enjoy the scenery.

Do remember, however, that outlines and other planning strategies are servants, not masters, of the writing process. There is always the danger of becoming so wedded to an outline that it impedes rather than enhances the writing of purposeful prose. Writing is a complex, problem-solving activity. As we write and then revise, we often discover new ways of organizing and arranging our material, and we must always retain the option to modify or even abandon our original design in light of new ideas. To return to the earlier metaphor, maps are fine and practical devices for getting us where we want to go, but the most reliable maps are those that undergo periodic revision to reflect the growing and changing environment.

Exercise 3-3

Evaluate each of the following theses. Is the thesis sufficiently unified and assertive? Does each thesis present opportunities for originality? Does each thesis present opportunities to inform, persuade, and entertain an audience of college students?

Theses
1. The best fishermen study the habits of fish, the signs of change in the weather, and the fastest routes to take in driving to the fishing hole.
2. Driving while intoxicated is dangerous and illegal.
3. I can tell you from personal experience that e. e. cummings was wrong when he claimed that "nobody loses all the time."
4. Personal computers have revolutionized the writing process and they can often help build the self-confidence of young programmers.
5. Sadly, Shakespeare was correct when he wrote that "the evil that men do lives after them, / the good is oft interred with their bones."

Exercise 3-4

Formulate a thesis and a brief outline for the topic you chose in exercise 3-1 and for the audience you prefer in exercise 3-2. Write a paragraph or two on the opportunities you see in your topic for informing, persuading, and entertaining your chosen audience.

WRITING

6. **Press ahead with a rough draft.** Experts on composition theorize that two conflicting psychological states govern the process of composing. One of these states is like a gas pedal; it is a creative, nonjudgmental force that manifests itself in a sudden, enthusiastic rush of words. The other state is like a brake pedal; it is a reflective censor

that demands perfection through continual changes. When both pedals are pressed simultaneously no motion occurs despite thunderous throbbings and groanings; the urge to create is blocked by the need to perfect, and the result is an incapacitating misery called writer's block. All writers must find their own ways to cope with this wrenching internal battle. It is helpful to realize, however, that the misery of writer's block is normal and that these two forces are each essential to the composing process, just as both a brake and an accelerator are essential to a car. They simply need to be used in alternation for productive writing to proceed. Some writers achieve this alternation by deliberately setting aside half-hour periods for continuous writing, without revision. Others prefer more rapid alternation and tend to rewrite each sentence as they proceed through the first draft. Still others may use continuous writing on some occasions and stop-and-go writing on others. The key is to recognize the importance of both forces, to use them without being paralyzed by them, and to push ahead to a complete rough draft in either one or two sessions of continuous writing or through a series of stop-and-go stages. Once you realize that your first vision is usually followed by "re-vision," that the first draft of any essay is simply a first draft, and that you aren't expected to write perfectly the first time through, you will have taken a concrete step toward overcoming the anxiety-provoking desire for perfection that causes writer's block. Writer's block, like all forms of anxiety, is self-imposed. Its only permanent "cure" is increased experience with the writing process itself.

REVISION

According to composition specialist Donald M. Murray, revision is "the process of seeing what you've said to discover what you have to say." To the extent that revision substantially changes what we have written, and thus allows us to discover what we really meant to say, it can be viewed as an extension of the process of exploration and discovery that began with our earliest prewriting decisions. As we revise, new possibilities emerge that cause us to alter, or perhaps even abandon, our original plan. We discover where our arguments are weak and need focus or additional support; where our materials need to be expanded, condensed, or rearranged or the sake of logic, clarity, emphasis, or effect; and where individual sentences and paragraphs need to be strengthened. Successful revision is essential to successful writing, and most successful writers confess not only that they spend more time rewriting than they do writing, but also that the opportunity offered by revision is sometimes the most creative, exciting, and rewarding part of the entire writing process. So enticing is revision that the novelist H. G. Wells once remarked ruefully (no doubt with editors in mind) that, "No passion in the world is equal to the passion to alter someone else's draft."

Important as they are, the processes of revision are difficult to isolate and describe in ways that are immediately applicable to every writer. For most writers, in fact, revision is not a totally separate stage of the writing process, occurring only *after* the completion of a new draft. Writing and rewriting often take place concurrently through a process of trial and error in which we pause to reread, assess, and then revise what we have written before moving on. To make room for these changes, by the way, many writers prefer to write their rough drafts on every other line. Sometimes, in fact, good writers revise so much while drafting an essay that it becomes virtually impossible in retrospect to identify a first draft. Similarly, how much revision actually occurs between one draft and the next is directly related to just how much revision has already occurred. Conceived of in this way, the task of revision is never totally over. No matter how long or how hard we work, no piece of writing is ever perfect. Thus, writing becomes very much the sort of adventure described by Winston Churchill:

> Writing . . . is an adventure. To begin with it is a toy and an amusement. Then it becomes a mistress, then it becomes a master, then it becomes a tyrant. The last phase is that just as you are about to be reconciled to your servitude, you kill the monster and fling him to the public.

Successful revision demands, above all, that we adopt the critical perspective of a detached and objective reader and place ourselves imaginatively in the position of our audience. Conversely, the inability to revise successfully almost always results from the inability to evaluate objectively what we have already written or to understand the evaluation of others. Achieving such psychic distance is by no means easy, for there is always the possibility, having completed the first draft and reduced our experience or ideas to words, that we will feel wedded to those first words. Successful writers coldly divorce themselves even from the words they most admire and actively search out new phrases to love. As in true divorce, the surest way to gain at least a measure of detachment is to allow time for passion to be replaced by judgment. A week, a day, or even an hour between drafts can help greatly. Another method of gaining detachment is to share your writing with someone whose judgment you trust and who can help to identify the problems in your essay.

7. **Revise in stages.**   Because of the importance and complexity of revision, it makes sense, whenever time permits, to review the essay separately for each of the following key elements of composition:

Logic.   If the essay has a clear thesis and follows an outline, it is less likely to be marred by serious errors in logic. Still, it is wise to reread the essay critically, as if hostile to its thesis. Does it limit its claims sufficiently and avoid logical fallacies? Does it provide convincing support for its assertions? Are there gaps in the argument or unsupported assumptions?

Purpose.   A good thesis should assure an overall sense of purpose (to inform, to persuade, or to entertain), but the best writing achieves a smoother and richer texture by blending all three purposes wherever possible. During revision, reexamine each paragraph to be certain that it contributes to the fulfillment of at least one of these basic purposes of prose.

Detail.   Strong, clear writing requires muscle over the bare bones of an argument. Prose is strengthened through the use of specific examples, precise analogies, and imagistic language. An essay need not be so packed with examples as to become grotesquely muscle-bound—there is room in language as in life for slim beauty—but healthy prose should avoid the pallor of pure abstraction.

Diction.   The effective choice of words is the basis of sound writing. As a general rule, prefer short words to long ones, and few words to many. A sharp kick with hard, short words more quickly focuses the reader's attention then a leisurely but overblown "circumlocution." These rules do *not* require that each word be monosyllabic, or that each sentence be short, but only that each bubble of hot air be pricked with a pen point in revision.

8. **Edit for errors in grammar, punctuation, and spelling.** Revision does not end the writing process; we still need to edit and proofread what we have written and to prepare a clean final copy. Careless errors in grammar, usage, punctuation, and spelling should be corrected as soon as they are noticed at any stage in revision, but some writers make the same errors over and over again. Once these writers learn from corrections on their early essays that they have a weakness in punctuation, for example, they should revise each new essay with punctuation in mind, checking proper usage in the appropriate section of an English handbook. This is also the time to check any constructions that seem awkward and any words whose spelling or meaning may be unfamiliar. It is usually also wise to read the essay aloud and, if possible, ask a friend to read it too. Frequently, awkward expressions and outright errors are more easily detected when spoken than when read silently.

9. **Make a clean copy.**   Every essay submitted in a college course should be neat, easy to read, and in an acceptable format. Instructors may have personal preferences about format; ask about these preferences and follow them. In most cases instructors will refer you to a handbook in which detailed advice about handwritten and typed formats is supplied. (At the very least be sure that your name appears on each page and that your pages are numbered.) When you have a choice between submitting handwritten or typed essays, typing is always preferable. A typed, double-spaced essay is easier to read; therefore it is easier to understand, and therefore it is more apt to be rewarded with a high grade. Many experienced writers, incidentally, find it helpful to revise and edit from typed copy as well, stressing that seeing their words in type rather than in their own handwriting (or solely on a computer screen) provides an additional measure of the objectivity that is so essential to the process of revision.

10. **Proofread the completed essay.**   Some errors inevitably creep into an essay while it is being typed or neatly handwritten. Thus, the last task before submission is careful proofreading. Typographical errors are often the most difficult to catch, simply because in reading what we ourselves have written we often see what we want to see rather than what is actually there. As you proofread, you should proceed slowly, line by line and word by word, perhaps with the aid of a ruler to increase your concentration. It is usually permissible to correct minor errors in ink at this point, but if the changes become too numerous or too significant, it is best to retype or rewrite those pages. Some common proofreading symbols are reproduced in the accompanying table.

11. **Make certain that you fully understand your instructor's comments.**   The writing process should not end when your instructor returns your essay with marginal comments and a grade. Indeed, if the essay truly meant something to you — that is, if you had a clear purpose and envisioned a real audience, and if you devoted time and effort to the process of composition and revision — then you will want to make changes based on your instructor's comments. Such comments, in most cases, are designed to help you see where your paper is particularly successful as well as where it doesn't "work," where the writing becomes confused, and where the paper has failed to fulfill its purpose and possibilities. If your writing is to improve, then this feedback must be carefully considered when you write your next essay. When comments are unclear, or when you are uncertain what to do about them, make an appointment with your instructor. Most writing teachers are eager to help students who demonstrate that they take their education seriously and genuinely wish to learn.

Common Proofreading Symbols

Symbol	Meaning	Example
ℯ	delete	A curled pig's tail means to delete.
⌒	close up	Horizontal parentheses mean close up.
¶	paragraph	You don't always have to retype your entire essay to correct an error in paragraphing. ¶ Teachers do have hearts.
∧	insert	A missing word or letter can be inserted using a caret.
∼	transpose	Reversed letters or words are also possible to correct without retyping.
≡	capitalize	three lines under a lowercase letter mean that it should be capitalized.
/	lowercase	A single slash through a letter indicates that it should be lowercase.
#	space	Insert a space using a caret and the space symbol.

Exercise 3-5

If you have been working the earlier exercises in this chapter, now is the time to write an essay on the topic you have chosen to explore. Write your first draft in a way that comes naturally, but also force yourself to complete that draft fairly rapidly. An hour or two of concerted effort should see you through to a complete draft. Once you have such a draft, practice your revision skills by reviewing the entire essay separately for its use of logic, its combination of purposes, its richness of supporting details, and its clarity of word choice.

Exercise 3-6

The paragraphs that follow come from an essay entitled "Nothing Personal" by Deborah Chappel, a freshman at Arkansas State University. In the full essay Debbie vividly describes the reactions of her classmates in the fourth grade when a previously unobtrusive girl, who had been "inspected by her peers and found unworthy of remark," suddenly appears before them wearing a pale pink dress, "a cheap garment of chiffon ruffles obviously purchased on the sale rack at the local five-and-dime. . . . the sort of dress mothers might laugh at but very young girls, unaware of the niceties of style, might admire."

Carefully consider the changes Debbie makes between her drafts. Why do you think she struck out so many words and images in revision? Do the additions and revisions improve the paragraph? To what extent do these revisions help the essay achieve its stated purpose? That purpose is "To raise the level of the readers' awareness of how they treat others and to make them more conscious of the feelings of those who are excluded from social groups."

STUDENT ESSAY _____

FIRST DRAFT

from "NOTHING PERSONAL"

by Deborah Chappel

I remember ~~being~~ _her face_ so clearly — the eagerness, the hope. Surprised, I thought, "Why, she's been unhappy all this time. ~~It's really~~ She wants ~~to~~ us to like her." And, when the derisive comments and laughter were hurled at her like _sharp_ stones, I saw her flinch, saw her shoulders hunch with despair and her face take on a ~~flat~~ blank, cornered expression. She became for me, in that moment, a human being, and ~~I it seemed I wanted to leap up turn~~ I was conscious of a sudden desire to snap and force them to back away. ~~I~~ Instead, I was very quiet. ~~and simply watched her square her resignedly making her way to the back of the room. For~~ _a few_ ~~two or three days, enraged at my friends playmates without really understanding why, I sought Gwen out during recess, sat staunchly beside her at lunch, and took her home with me to play. She moved away soon but we were not really suited to one another and soon drifted apart. She moved away shortly thereafter, still unaware~~ _that she had_ ~~of the~~ ~~caused me to understand another human beings feelings~~ ~~profound effect she'd had on my life.~~ _independence, for the first time, of my own._

SECOND DRAFT

I can still remember her face clearly — the eagerness, the hope _mirrored_ _there. With sudden insight,_ ~~Surprised,~~ I thought, "Why, she's been unhappy all this time. She wants us to really like her." ~~And,~~ When the derisive comments and laughter were hurled at her like sharp stones, I saw her flinch, saw her shoulders hunch with despair and her face took on a blank, cornered expression. That momentary vitality which had transformed her face that morning seemed to seep out of her like _air from an inflatable toy_ ~~water from a leaking cup~~, leaving her _in that moment_ once more listless, quiet, a trifle sulky. She became for me, a human being, and I was conscious of a sudden desire to ~~snap at my classmates~~ ~~like a wild animal, to face~~ them ~~and snarl and force them to back~~ ~~away. Instead, I was very quiet.~~ protect her, and to somehow force my classmates to feel shame for our treatment of her. Instead, I was very quiet.

FINAL DRAFT

from "NOTHING PERSONAL"

by Deborah Chappel

I can still remember her face clearly — the eagerness, the hope mirrored there. With sudden insight, I thought, "Why, she's been unhappy all this time. She wants us to really like her." When the derisive comments and laughter were hurled at her like sharp stones, I saw her flinch, saw her shoulders hunch with despair. The momentary vitality which had so transformed her face that morning seemed to seep out of her like air from an inflatable toy, leaving her once more listless, quiet, a trifle sulky. She became for me, in that moment, a human being, and I was conscious of a sudden desire to protect her, to somehow force my classmates to feel shame for our treatment of her. Instead, I was very quiet.

PART II

WRITING FOR ONESELF

Chapter 4

DIARIES AND JOURNALS

SELF-EXPRESSIVE WRITING

It happens to everyone!

Your boss calls you into the office and fires you when you were expecting a raise. Or your best friend goes to the drive-in with your sweetheart. Or your history professor says that the essay on Napoleon you poured your soul into is trivial and boring.

You sit down at your desk, gnash your teeth, and begin to write:

You snivelling sod! You warty, sack-shaped clod! You parody of a person with your face as wrinkled as a hippo's hip, your snaggle-toothed smile, and your cold, little catfish mouth. What a challenge some mortician will find in laboring to make *you* appear life-like! Why even your breath has the fish-bait smell of dead, caged craw-dads. And when you walk, you emanate an odor of tepid ditch-water. In your presence diligent housewives ache to spray Lysol on your jeans, and public health officials ponder the measures to take against plague. . . .

After a few more lines of abuse and perhaps a few threats, you rapidly scrawl your signature. You may even go so far as to address, stamp, and seal an envelope, but if you are lucky, that corrosive little note will seem to scorch your fingertips as you trudge toward the post office; you will realize that you wrote it to purge yourself of your passions and that it would be foolish to complicate your life by mailing it.

Almost all of us at certain times feel a need to write simply to express our feelings. Occasionally we find such self-expression in fur-ious letters that we never mail. However, it is safer and ultimately more fulfilling to indulge in self-expression by keeping a diary or journal on a regular basis. Such self-expressive writing allows us an outlet for our passions and a means of discovering and recording our ideas. Indeed, a great many successful people in business, letters, and science keep journals — at least in part to hone their skills at analyzing themselves and their peers. A journal can also become a rich repository of memories about college, career, and family. Whereas a photo album allows you only to see yourself as others saw you, a journal will help you to relive earlier joys, sorrows, and meditations. The keeping of a journal can even help you build those lively habits of mind that make daily life more meaningful, more worthy of being recorded, and more amusing when reread. If nothing else, a journal gives you a place to rage at your roommate or to glory in a good grade — a place to reflect on the brilliance of your history professor's analysis of Alexander the Great or to sneer at his hasty appraisal of your essay on Napoleon. As an outlet for such emotions, it can often prevent the embarrassment that attends the mailing of those passionately abusive letters.

Even those of us who rarely put our tempestuous feelings into words and who never seem able to find the time to keep a journal often engage in self-expressive writing, for self-expression is a means of discovering the thoughts that we wish to communicate to others. For example, suppose that your world literature professor asks you to write a review of the next of Shakespeare's plays to be shown on the Public Broadcasting System. If you approach the assignment seriously, you will certainly wish to take notes as you watch the play. Those notes allow you to express and record fleeting questions and ideas in a form that is probably meaningful only to you. They will be the raw material out of which your review of the play will finally emerge. Similarly, you might begin your next freshman English assignment ("How to Enjoy the Opera") by listing your first thoughts about the topic:

Three and a half hours of tedium
Ornate Italian oratorios
Florid movements by fat sopranos
Monocles, tuxedos, and canes
Wigs, waddles, and corsets
Ceremony and cigars
Lechery and love

Although such a list of frankly personal reactions may at first seem hopelessly unintellectual and unpromising, it may in fact lead to an amusing satire on the characters, conventions, and connoisseurs of the opera. Such notes and lists are common forms of self-expression and self-discovery. In Chapter 5, "Invention Techniques," we will consider these and other methods of generating ideas for essays.

As the preceding paragraphs have suggested, writing for oneself encourages introspection, analysis, and creativity. The clarity and structure that are so important in writing for others are less important in writing for oneself. Indeed, self-expressive writing is often most fascinating and revealing when it seems to arise directly from the subconscious as in an account of a dream. Writing for others is strictly controlled; writing for oneself is fluid and formless. Writing for others is revised and rewritten; writing for oneself is spontaneous and free. Writing for others is smooth and fully developed; writing for oneself is digressive and abbreviated. Writing for others is groomed, like one's appearance at an important interview; writing for oneself is as honest and revealing as one's naked image in a mirror.

DIARIES VERSUS JOURNALS

Both diaries and journals seek to make more permanent the fleeting events of our lives, and both demand the discipline of daily writing. But in practice a fine distinction exists between the two. A diary tends to be a fairly mundane and practical record of daily activities. Entry after entry is apt to record where you went in the morning, who joined you for lunch, what problems arose at work in the afternoon, and how you spent the evening. Like the grains of sand outside an ant hill, diary entries accumulate rapidly but are easily scattered and forgotten. Many people, of course, enjoy the routine of keeping a diary. Moreover, in time their diaries become for them a treasured record of factual information on which they can later draw to stimulate memories and occasionally gain insight into their own motives and personalities.

In contrast, a journal is primarily a place for reflection, experimentation, and self-discovery. A journal writer rarely focuses on the ordinary events in life — unless the writer wishes to record some sudden insight about the nature or importance of a seemingly ordinary event. The following entry by freshman Cody Pendergist is a good example of the way a journal writer can sometimes find significance in mundane observations.

"DORM ROOM"

by Cody Pendergist

Jane loves John forever on the ceiling.

It was written with a broom handle. . . .

What a lasting covenant!

Faded stickers and the sticky

of stickers that are now gone

Still haunt the bookcase.

The history of others decorates

my room through the caked dust on the baseboards

to nail holes in the wall.

Their names are plastered on the door

and their taste in art—

like prehistoric man—

is colored on the closet door.

A diary is a bit like a loyal and hard-working sheep dog, but a journal is like a barn cat: domestic, yet untamable; satisfying, yet unpredictable; a creature of the night side of life. Indeed, a description of a dream sometimes makes an interesting journal entry, as in the following example by freshman Jan Simpson.

"DREAM"

by Jan Simpson

I can't believe it's 2 a.m., it's quiet in the dorm, AND I CAN'T SLEEP! I'll be dead-on-my-feet tomorrow. I just had a short nap today, nothing like the 6 hour naps I've been taking! I did have a terrible dream though. I can't remember all of it, but innocent people were dying horrible, horrible deaths. I dreamt my sister just expanded and expanded until she blew up, and Melanie just withered into nothing. Emil drowned in his own sweat as he labored over something—I can't remember what. In a way I'm glad I can't remember more than that. It disturbs me.

As in the two examples just cited, a journal is a record of what one has felt and thought, not just of what one has done. It is a place to record beliefs and ideas, likes and dislikes, goals and ambitions, observations and insights. It is a place for recording those sights, sounds, smells, tastes, and feelings that make our world a sensuous delight. It is a place for recording those experiences that make us feel most fully alive. If, as Plato insisted, the unexamined life is not worth living, then a journal is a virtual necessity, for it is preeminently a place for examining life and preserving all one can learn from and about life.

Despite the obvious differences between diaries and journals, both help one to learn about oneself. Both allow one to record ideas and experiences worth remembering. Both help one to achieve fluency with words through the discipline of daily writing. Both sharpen the mind by forcing vague feelings to take shape in words and by encouraging concentration on sense impressions. Indeed, the differences between diaries and journals begin to fade away if both are written with energy and intelligence. Rightly conceived, journals and diaries are like letters written to one's future self. Whereas the diary emphasize actions, the journal emphasizes reflections, but each may serve to reveal the personality of the writer and stimulate self-expression.

KEEPING A JOURNAL

If you are asked to keep a journal during your composition course, or if you decide to keep one on your own initiative, you will gain the most from the experience by trying to be both diligent and prolific. **Establish a habit of writing in your journal for ten to twenty minutes during a time of your own choosing,** perhaps before going to bed. The discipline of daily writing, like that of daily running, will improve your speed, your vigor, and your mental health.

In addition, **keep your journal with you as much of the time as possible.** Often your best ideas will occur at odd and unpredictable moments. That brilliant idea that sparkles within your imagination as you slosh through the snow to class may fizzle out entirely and be lost forever if you don't write it down before returning home.

Keep your journal in a spiral notebook, an artist's sketch book, or something equally permanent. There may be times when your journal isn't handy and you must jot down an idea on an envelope, a sales receipt, or any available scrap of paper. Such entries can always be pasted into your journal later. Still, the journal itself should be sturdy and bound somehow. Separate sheets of paper in a file or a looseleaf notebook are easily lost; moreover, the blank pages of a bound journal may seem to exert a subtle but firm pressure on you to push on, to complete the volume you have begun.

If you find yourself having difficulty deciding what to write in your journal on a given occasion, **begin writing on anything that interests you at the moment and trust that the process of writing itself will lead you to important ideas.** Before long, you will discover that writing is a means of thinking.

Although you *should* write thoughtfully, remember that one function of the journal is to increase your fluency and your familiarity with the written word. **Don't get bogged down.** Instead move confidently from one idea to the next, letting your mind play with language as a child plays with blocks — creating settings to be peopled by the imagination; rooms, towers, cities, and labyrinths to explore; places you have seen and those you'd like to see; people you once knew and those you'd like to know; things you have done and those you'd like to do; books you have read and those you'd like to read. Set yourself free to wander in your own personal wonderland. And by all means try the techniques of invention that serve as gateways and maps to the mind.

Consider using your journal as a writing log. Writing an essay is a process made up of a number of overlapping stages, each of which demands care and attention. As with other human activities, what works for one person may not work for another. Each of us, over time, develops his or her own writing habits, employs different strategies for generating ideas, and invests varying amounts of effort in revising and editing. A journal, used as a writing log, provides a convenient place to learn about your own writing habits.

When you finish an essay, spend some time with your journal, jotting down as much as you can recall about the actual process just completed. Consider such questions as the following: How many identifiable stages did your writing process entail? Where did the emphasis fall, in terms of both time and effort? What difficulties did you encounter getting started? Where did your best ideas come from? What strategies of invention did you employ and which seemed to work the best? What stages of the writing process gave you the most trouble? Which came most easily? In each case, do you know why? What conclusions about your own writing process can you reach? A series of such entries kept throughout the semester may help you learn much about how you actually write—and how you can help yourself to write better.

STUDENT JOURNAL ENTRY _____

"ONE WOMAN'S AWAKENING"

by Wanda Yopp

Why are women expected to work from daylight to bedtime? Who made these rules we all live by?

I see and hear of so many men who work eight hours a day, five days a week. Then they go home and relax because they are tired.

I used to work like a horse twenty years ago. I hope I never forget what a typical day was like. That will help me to make sure I never fall into that routine again. I would get up at 5 a.m. I was quiet so everyone else could sleep. I wonder why they needed more sleep than I did? Why did I go along with this?

I would prepare breakfast. Usually bacon, eggs, biscuits, coffee, and juice. Then I would get my husband up and his sister (who lived with us); then I would wake up my son.

After breakfast everyone got cleaned up and dressed. I got myself and my son ready to go. I washed the dishes and cleaned the kitchen and bathroom while they had another cup of coffee. I made the beds after they left for work. Then I took the baby to the daycare center and went to work.

After working on my feet all day in a warehouse, lifting boxes and loading trucks, I picked up the baby and went home. We all got there about the same time. My husband and his sister went to the living room, put their feet up and hollered for a coke because "they were tired." I fixed it for them and began preparing the evening meal. Always a big meal with meat, vegetables, salad, and dessert.

I could hear them laughing at something funny on TV. I remember thinking how nice it would be to sit down after work. But I was a wife and couldn't. If only I'd been born a male or stayed single I could enjoy TV too. But I didn't get mad or tell them how I felt. Why didn't I look at it differently? How silly to wish I'd been born a male so I'd be able to rest.

After the evening meal they all watched TV while I did the dishes, mopped the kitchen and bathroom, fixed all lunches for the next day, did any mending or laundry that needed doing—then bathed the baby and put him to bed. My husband and his sister got ready for bed while I cleaned their mess up in the living room and turned down their beds. After everyone was in bed, I'd get my bath and clean anything I'd left undone, and then go to bed myself.

On the weekend I did the shopping, cut hair, trimmed nails, vacuumed, cleaned curtains, windows, porches, cars, and anything else anyone wanted cleaned. I almost forgot; I ironed for all of them too. What a big job!

If the house was ever anything other than perfect, I was in trouble. He was the master and I was the servant. On payday I turned my paycheck over to my husband. If I wanted to spend any money, I had to ask for it and account for every penny and give him the change.

I really had it made compared to some of my friends. One of my friends, Pat, had four children, wasn't allowed to work or leave the house and her husband would run the streets. When he got ready to come home, he would be drunk and come in mad. He usually hit her a few times. She wasn't allowed to cut her hair or get a permanent in it.

I got tired of being a slave. But I didn't know what to do. It took five years to change and everyone around me has changed. My husband wouldn't change so I changed husbands. Now I am a free person and I intend to stay that way.

Hateful Things and Rare Things
Sei Shōnagon

Sei Shōnagon (c. 966–1013), herself the daughter of a poet, entered the service of the Japanese empress in 991. That same year she began to keep the diary called the *Pillow Book* (apparently because she kept it under her pillow for safekeeping). In this journal she recorded in a witty and original style her experiences and impressions as well as a great deal of information about contemporary court life.

HATEFUL THINGS

1   One is in a hurry to leave, but one's visitor keeps chattering away. If it is someone of no importance, one can get rid of him by saying, "You must tell me all about it next time"; but, should it be the sort of visitor whose presence commands one's best behavior, the situation is hateful indeed.

2   One finds that a hair has got caught in the stone on which one is rubbing one's inkstick, or again that gravel is lodged in the inkstick, making a nasty, grating sound.

3   One is just about to be told some interesting piece of news when a baby starts crying.

4   A flight of crows circle about with loud caws.

5   An admirer has come on a clandestine visit, but a dog catches sight of him and starts barking. One feels like killing the beast.

6   One has gone to bed and is about to doze off when a mosquito appears, announcing himself in a reedy voice. One can actually feel the wind made by his wings and, slight though it is, one finds it hateful in the extreme.

One is telling a story about old times when someone breaks in with 7
a little detail that he happens to know, implying that one's own version
is inaccurate — disgusting behavior!

Very hateful is a mouse that scurries all over the place.   8

Some children have called at one's house. One makes a great fuss of 9
them and gives them toys to play with. The children become accustomed to this treatment and start to come regularly, forcing their way
into one's inner rooms and scattering one's furnishings and possessions.
Hateful!

A man with whom one is having an affair keeps singing the praises 10
of some woman he used to know. Even if it is a thing of the past, this can
be very annoying. How much more so if he is still seeing the woman!
(Yet sometimes I find that it is not as unpleasant as all that.)

A lover who is leaving at dawn announces that he has to find his fan 11
and his paper. "I know I put them somewhere last night," he says. Since
it is pitch dark, he gropes about the room, bumping into the furniture
and muttering, "Strange! Where on earth can they be?" Finally he dis-
covers the objects. He thrusts the paper into the breast of his robe with a
great rustling sound; then he snaps open his fan and busily fans away
with it. Only now is he ready to take his leave. What charmless behavior!
"Hateful" is an understatement.

Equally disagreeable is the man who, when leaving in the middle of 12
the night, takes care to fasten the cord of his headdress. This is quite
unnecessary; he could perfectly well put it gently on his head without
tying the cord. And why must he spend time adjusting his cloak or
hunting costume? Does he really think someone may see him at this
time of night and criticize him for not being impeccably dressed?

A good lover will behave as elegantly at dawn as at any other time. 13
He drags himself out of bed with a look of dismay on his face. The lady
urges him on: "Come, my friend, it's getting light. You don't want
anyone to find you here." He gives a deep sigh, as if to say that the night
has not been nearly long enough and that it is agony to leave. Once up,
he does not instantly pull on his trousers. Instead he comes close to the
lady and whispers whatever was left unsaid during the night. Even when
he is dressed, he still lingers, vaguely pretending to be fastening his
sash.

Presently he raises the lattice, and the two lovers stand together by 14
the side door while he tells her how he dreads the coming day, which
will keep them apart; then he slips away. The lady watches him go, and
this moment of parting will remain among her most charming
memories.

Indeed, one's attachment to a man depends largely on the elegance 15
of his leave-taking. When he jumps out of bed, scurries about the room,
tightly fastens his trouser-sash, rolls up the sleeves of his Court cloak,
overrobe, or hunting costume, stuffs his belongings into the breast of his
robe and then briskly secures the outer sash — one really begins to hate
him.

RARE THINGS

16   People who live together and still manage to behave with reserve towards each other. However much these people may try to hide their weaknesses, they usually fail.

17   To avoid getting ink stains on the notebook into which one is copying stories, poems, or the like. If it is a very fine notebook, one takes the greatest care not to make a blot; yet somehow one never seems to succeed.

18   One has given some silk to the fuller and, when he sends it back, it is so beautiful that one cries out in admiration.

Diary Entries

Samuel Pepys

Samuel Pepys (1633–1703), the son of a London tailor, rose through the ranks of the British civil service on the basis of merit to become secretary of the Admiralty and a member of Parliament. He also became one of the great diarists in the English language. For some nine years, from 1660 to 1669, when failing eyesight forced him to quit, Pepys religiously kept a day-by-day diary in which he recorded in simple, unadorned prose both the details of his own life, public and private, and the political, historical, cultural, and social events that defined Restoration England. Writing in shorthand and sometimes in secret code, Pepys seemed to find no event unworthy of his curiosity and notice, from the great fire which destroyed four fifths of London in 1666 to his own casual flirtations in church.

1   August 18, 1667 (Lord's day).   I walked towards White Hall, but, being wearied, turned into St. Dunstan's Church, where I heard an able sermon of the minister of the place; and stood by a pretty, modest maid, whom I did labour to take by the hand and the body; but she would not, but got further and further from me; and, at last, I could perceive her to take pins out of her pocket to prick me if I should touch her again— which seeing I did forbear, and was glad I did spy her design. And then I fell to gaze upon another pretty maid in a pew close to me, and she on me; and I did go about to take her hand, which she suffered a little and then withdrew. So the sermon ended, and the church broke up, and my amours ended also, and so took coach and home, and there took my wife, and to Islington with her.

2   October 10, 1667.   Waked in the morning with great pain or the collique, by cold taken yesterday, I believe, with going up and down in my shirt, but with rubbing my belly, keeping of it warm, I did at last

come to some ease, and rose, and up to walk up and down the garden with my father, to talk of all our concernments: about a husband for my sister, whereof there is at present no appearance; but we must endeavour to find her one now, for she grows old and ugly: then for my brother; and resolve he shall stay here this winter, and then I will either send him to Cambridge for a year, till I get him some church promotion, or send him to sea as a chaplain, where he may study, and earn his living. My father and I, with a dark lantern, it being now night, into the garden with my wife, and there went about our great work to dig up my gold. But, Lord! what a tosse I was for some time in, that they could not justly tell where it was; that I begun heartily to sweat, and be angry, that they should not agree better upon the place, and at last to fear that it was gone: but by and by poking with a spit, we found it, and then begun with a spudd to lift up the ground. But, good God! to see how silly they did it, not half a foot underground, and in the sight of the world from a hundred places, if any body by accident were near hand, and within sight of a neighbour's window, and their hearing also, being close by: only my father says that he saw them all gone to church before he begun the work, when he laid the money, but that do not excuse it to me. But I was out of my wits almost, and the more from that, upon lifting up the earth with the spudd, I did discern that I had scattered the pieces of gold round about the ground among the grass and loose earth; and taking up the iron head-pieces wherein they were put, I perceive the earth was got among the gold, and wet, so that the bags were all rotten, and all the notes, that I could not tell what in the world to say to it, not knowing how to judge what was wanting, or what had been lost by Gibson in his coming down: which, all put together, did make me mad; and at last was forced to take up the head-pieces, dirt and all, and as many of the scattered pieces as I could with the dirt discern by the candle-light, and carry them up into my brother's chamber, and there locke them up till I had eat a little supper: and then, all people going to bed, W. Hewer and I did all alone, with several pails of water and basins, at last wash the dirt off of the pieces, and parted the pieces and the dirt, and then begun to tell [them]; and by a note which I had of the value of the whole in my pocket, do find that there was short above a hundred pieces, which did make me mad; so W. Hewer and I out again about midnight, for it was now grown so late, and there by candle-light did make shift to gather forty-five pieces more. And so in, and to cleanse them: and by this time it was past two in the morning; and so to bed, with my mind pretty quiet to think that I have recovered so many.

October 11, 1667.   Rose and called W. Hewer, and he and I, with   3 pails and a sieve, did lock ourselves into the garden, and there gather all the earth about the place into pails, and then sift those pails in one of the summer-houses, just as they do for dyamonds in other parts of the world; and there, to our great content, did with much trouble by nine o'clock (and by the time we emptied several pails and could not find one), we did make the last night's forty-five up seventy-nine: so that we are come to about twenty or thirty of what I think the true number should be; and perhaps within less; and of them I may reasonably think that Mr. Gibson might lose some: so I am pretty well satisfied that my loss is not great, and do bless God that it is so well, and do leave my father to make a second examination of the dirt, which he promises he will do, and, poor man, is mightily troubled for this accident, but I declared myself well satisfied, and so indeed I am.

Journal Entry

Anaïs Nin

Anaïs Nin (1903–1977)—literary critic, short-story writer, novelist, and practicing psychoanalyst—kept a detailed private diary from the age of ten onward as a means of exploring and understanding her own unfolding inner life. These diaries, which her friend and fellow writer Henry Miller correctly described as "a woman's journey of self-discovery," were published in seven volumes between 1966 and 1978. Their publication, late in Nin's life, earned her an international reputation and brought her invitations to speak and lecture, particularly from women's groups, which saw in Nin's sixty-year inner struggle toward growth and self-fulfillment the affirmation of their own. The feminist appeal of her diaries was not lost on Nin. "Sometimes," she noted in 1971, "I feel like I have about ten million daughters."

1   The nurses begin to talk again. I say, "Let me alone." I place my two hands on my stomach and very slowly, very softly, with the tips of my fingers I drum, drum, drum on my stomach, in circles. Round and round, softly, with eyes open in great serenity. The doctor comes near and looks with amazement. The nurses are silent. Drum drum drum drum drum in soft circles, in soft quiet circles. "Like a savage," they whisper. The mystery.

2   Eyes open, nerves quiet, I drum gently on my stomach for a long while. The nurses begin to quiver. A mysterious agitation runs through them. I hear the ticking of the clock. It ticks inexorably, separately. The little nerves awaken, stir. I say, "I can push now!" and I push violently. They are shouting, "A little more! Just a little more!"

3   Will the ice come, and the darkness, before I am through? At the end of the dark tunnel, a knife gleams. I hear the clock and my heart. I say, "Stop!" The doctor holds the instrument, and he is leaning over. I sit up and shout at him. He is afraid again. "Let me alone, all of you!"

4   I lie back so quietly. I hear the ticking. Softly I drum, drum, drum. I feel my womb stirring, dilating. My hands are so weary, they will fall off. They will fall off, and I will lie there in darkness. The womb is stirring and dilating. Drum drum drum drum drum. "I am ready!" The nurse puts her knee on my stomach. There is blood in my eyes. A tunnel. I

push into this tunnel. I bite my lips and push. There is fire, flesh ripping and no air. Out of the tunnel! All my blood is spilling out. "Push! Push! It is coming! It is coming!" I feel the slipperiness, the sudden deliverance, the weight is gone. Darkness.

I hear voices. I open my eyes. I hear them saying, "It was a little girl. Better not show it to her." All my strength is coming back. I sit up. The doctor shouts, "For God's sake, don't sit up, don't move!"   5

"Show me the child," I say.   6

"Don't show it," says the nurse, "it will be bad for her."   7

The nurses try to make me lie down. My heart is beating so loudly I can hardly hear myself repeating, "Show it to me!" The doctor holds it up. It looks dark, and small, like a diminutive man. But it is a little girl. It has long eyelashes on its closed eyes, it is perfectly made, and all glistening with the waters of the womb. It was like a doll, or like a miniature Indian, about one foot long, skin on bones, no flesh. But completely formed. The doctor told me afterwards that it had hands and feet exactly like mine. The head was bigger than average. As I looked at the dead child, for a moment I hated it for all the pain it had caused me, and it was only later that this flare of anger turned into great sadness.   8

Chapter 5

INVENTION TECHNIQUES

Journals, among their virtues, provide a valuable source of raw material to draw upon for writing on topics of our own choosing. But how do we gather material to deal with topics chosen by others — say, for the essay assigned by our composition teacher, or for the report that our impatient boss demands by Monday morning? How do we get past the all-too-familiar feeling of having nothing to write about, nothing that is really worth saying? Often, we discover that much of what we need is in fact already ours by virtue of our own experience (although at any given moment that experience may be only half remembered). At other times we need to supplement our own experience through investigating the experiences of others. In both cases, invention comes into play.

Most of the techniques of invention used by writers occur naturally during the composing process, but it is helpful to isolate them and to practice them in the same way that one practices skills in the laboratory, shots in tennis, plays in football, or routines in gymnastics. Many writers first come to grips with a topic by **listing** all the ideas they can think of about it (a process sometimes referred to as brainstorming). As the list becomes longer and more complicated, it is natural to begin **grouping** related ideas to discover potential ways of developing the subject. After some preliminary listing and grouping of ideas, many writers start right in on a first draft, often becoming so enthusiastic that uninhibited **free writing** ensues. Thoughts spring up, blossom, and seed more thoughts as word follows uninterrupted word. These periods of free writing also encourage free association of words and ideas, so that new insights can emerge from the arbitrary juxtaposition of old ones, and the writer's initial list of ideas continues to grow. Another natural invention technique involves the use of **dialogue.** Sometimes the best ideas come to us as we debate an issue with a friend or engage in an inner dialogue.

Most writers find these first four invention techniques to be natural components of the composing process, and they use all four repeatedly as their essays move from the first stages to the final drafts. Sometimes, however, these basic techniques are usefully supplemented by more formal ones. **Aristotelian invention,** for example, allows us to consider a topic in light of a series of systematic yet open-ended questions. Similarly, if the topic requires description of something that happened to the writer or to someone else, the most sensible procedure to follow may be the **reporter's questions:** Who? When? What? Where? Why? Finally, during revision most good writers consciously seek to enliven their writing by using specific, image-producing language; such imagery is sometimes sought through a process of **analogy** in an effort to see the topic from different perspectives.

As this brief chronology suggests, invention is not an activity that occurs exclusively before you begin to write. Still, you must discover something to write about before beginning an essay. The seven techniques of invention just defined may help you do so.

Almost inevitably, invention is messy—producing rapid scrawls on numerous sheets, with many arrows, deletions, and marginal insertions. This is as it should be. Just as a scientist's inventiveness usually grows from trial and error in a laboratory, so too a writer's creativity springs from trial and error with words through listing, grouping, free writing, dialogue, Aristotelian invention, reporter's questions, and analogy.

LISTING

Lists are valuable aids to invention, understanding, and memory. Consider a list of grocery items:

> strawberries (fresh, not frozen)
> whipping cream
> cauliflower
> cheddar cheese
> milk
> ground coffee
> French bread
> sirloin steak (with a long, thin bone)
> Burgundy

Such a list is first intended as an aid in planning, in this case planning a single meal on a special occasion—an anniversary, birthday, or holiday. As soon as the planning is complete, however, the list becomes a memory aid at the supermarket, where it may undergo further revision and change.

Writers use lists in much the same manner. First, good writers record their topic in order to avoid confused meandering. Then, working rapidly and usually jotting down words and phrases rather than full sentences, they begin to generate a list of subdivisions, substeps, related concepts, causes, effects, similarities, and differences. The aim here is to become as thoroughly involved with — "tuned into" — the topic as possible, for most writers report that as involvement increases, their ideas become more insightful and useful. Whenever the flow of ideas begins to ebb, it is important to stop, read the list, and think critically about each item in it. This rethinking may lead to the striking out of some ideas and the substitution of others. As revision and expansion of the list take place, most writers begin to recognize the many possibilities offered by any topic; they discover which ideas interest them and which they are best qualified to discuss.

Making a list is a bit like casting for panfish. Each new catch may seem small and insignificant, but if the bites are frequent and if you just keep fishing, you find that before long your bucket is full and you have enough food for a nourishing and tasty meal. Indeed, if your luck is very good, you will throw the small fry back for future fishing and still tote home plenty of food for thought.

The writer — particularly the journal writer — often finds listing an easy and enjoyable means of netting a dazzling assortment of ideas. Our spontaneous enjoyment of lists, both as readers and as writers, is as ancient as the genealogy of the *Old Testament* or the lists of ships in *The Iliad* and as modern as Irving Wallace's recent best-seller, *The Book of Lists.* Indeed, interesting lists are neither rare nor uniquely the work of professional writers. Through the exercise of making a list, all of us may resurrect memories and reveal our own personalities, as Jan Simpson does in this extract from her journal:

"PLEASING THINGS"

by Jan Simpson

Being covered in multiple layers of Grandma's cotton patchwork quilts on cold, frosty mornings, the scent of honeysuckle along a fence row on a balmy afternoon, watching a litter of puppies or kittens nursing, the sensation one gets walking barefoot on a freshly cut St. Augustine lawn, and the sounds of a happy child are all pleasing things. Big fluffy towels with too much Downy in them, the soft feeling of baby powder on one's skin, the unselfish affection given one by a young pup, holding wild baby animals in one's hand, and toasting jumbo marshmallows on hickory limbs over an open fire are also pleasing. Other pleasing things include: the feeling one gets after returning a frightened lost baby bird to its nest, eating hot, steamy corn-on-the-cob that has been smothered with butter and pepper, watching tiny young fish strike at a big, baitless hook, letting one's feet skim across the water's surface as the boat glides across the reservoir, and collapsing on a big, soft bed after a tiring day.

Exercise 5-1 _____

Spend ten uninterrupted minutes making a list like Jan Simpson's list of pleasing things. Do this either as a journal exercise or, if your teacher permits, as part of the invention work for an essay in your composition class. You may list pleasing things, as Jan has done, or you may pick another topic of interest. You might consider making a list of hateful things, memorable individuals, embarrassing moments, humorous situations, idle dissipations, and so forth. Whatever topic you choose, try to make your list as specific as possible. Use words that help you to pin down the actual things you did or saw or heard or tasted or touched or felt.

GROUPING

After making a list of ideas, writers naturally seek to group related ideas and to explore the interrelationships among them. In the process, we often discover new and unexpected relationships among what originally had seemed to be separate, random, and disparate items. Jan Simpson's pleasing things, for example, are readily divided into two categories:

I. Sensory Pleasures

Being covered in layers of quilts on frosty morns
The scent of honeysuckle on a balmy afternoon
Walking barefoot on a new-mown lawn
The sounds of a happy child
The smell of fluffy, freshly washed towels
The soft feeling of baby powder on one's skin
Toasting marshmallows over an open fire
Eating buttery corn-on-the-cob
Letting one's feet skim across the water's surface
Collapsing in bed after a tiring day

II. Emotional Pleasures

Watching a litter of puppies or kittens nursing
The affection given one by a young pup
Holding wild baby animals
Returning a frightened baby bird to its nest
Watching young fish strike a baitless lure

Even such a simple grouping may be stimulating. One notes, for instance, that Jan not only listed images that appeal to each of the five senses, but with the instinct of a fine writer, she often discovered images that appeal to two or three senses at once. Fluffy towels (fresh from the dryer with too much Downy in them) have a distinctive smell, texture, and appearance. Similarly, a new-mown lawn smells fresh, looks trim and green, and feels prickly under bare feet. This combination of differ- ent senses in a single image (called synesthesia) is often cited as a characteristic of excellent poetry. The fact that such images arose sponta- neously as Jan sought to list pleasing things suggests that the combina- tion of senses makes them more memorable and vivid. From this obser- vation an essay about the similarities between poetry and open self-expression might be developed.

The second group of Jan's pleasing things is equally thought-pro- voking. Each emotional pleasure is tied in some way to an obvious interest in children and young animals. Indeed, several of Jan's sensory pleasures are also associated with infancy and youth: the feeling of baby powder, toasting marshmallows, letting one's feet skim on the surface of a lake, and so on. Now it may be that Jan moved from one youthful image to the next as a result of the subconscious processes of free association. In a sense her mind may have been exploring the nature of youthful pleasures, and a good essay on that topic might emerge from her journal entry. Perhaps, however, there is also some wistfulness in this list; perhaps it implies that our most memorable pleasures are experienced during youth and that the adult is sentenced to survive on ever-paler recollections of youthful joy. William Wordsworth, one of the great English Romantic poets, grappled with this possibility in a whole series of wonderful poems. It may also be, however, that Jan's interest in children and young animals is a fundamental part of her own character. Such a self-discovery might change her entire life, influencing her to study child development, pediatrics, or veterinary medicine. Hence, by grouping ideas in her list of pleasurable things, she might be encour- aged to write an essay mapping out her college curriculum and her career plans.

Thus, grouping ideas is a technique of discovery that allows one to map the mind. Imagine that you wish to explore the river of your thoughts. By paddling upstream from the first placid stretches where the river enters the sea of consciousness, you penetrate farther and farther into the wilderness. In this way writers can map out the structure of a general topic and discover relatively unexplored areas of interest. All that is required for the technique to work well is an open and inquisitive mind and a willingness to keep questioning, to keep pushing upstream. Beginning with any topic, one seeks to formulate questions about that topic, and then more questions about each subsequent answer until a rough outline forms, like the map of a river's watershed.

Mapping, like grouping, is an extremely useful tool for exploring, developing, and organizing ideas. Part of its value lies in its flexibility, for a map can be altered and changed in response to new thoughts and ideas. Maps are valuable as well not only because they help organize our ideas visually in ways that make clear their underlying relationships but also because they tell us at a glance just how much subject matter we have generated for development. When that amount of subject matter seems to be insufficient, we can return to our listing exercise to develop still more.

Exercise 5-2

Turn back to the list you made in exercise 5-1. Study the various items in the list and try to discover as many different ways of grouping those items as you can. Whenever you come up with a way to group items, ask yourself questions about that category. What makes that category important? What unifies the items within it? How does such a category explain your own personality or your outlook on the world? How is the category like or unlike the other categories you have discovered? For each of these questions (and any others you can think of) make brief notes about your answers. Then, having grouped the items on your list in as many ways as possible, try to reach some conclusions about the best ways to handle such a list in an essay. What can you prove or demonstrate by referring to the various items on your list?

FREE WRITING

One of the most effective ways of exploring a subject and generating ideas is through free writing. As the name suggests, free writing is the spontaneous act of putting pen to paper and, without stopping, automatically recording everything that comes to mind. There are no constraints or limitations; the only requirement is that you write continuously, without pausing to revise or edit, until the end of your allotted time — usually ten to twenty minutes. The purpose of free writing is to discover and explore your true feelings about the topic at hand and to release an abundant flow of impressions, memories, and ideas. By letting one idea lead to another in a relaxed and uncritical progression, you may be able to generate and record more ideas about your subject than you ever thought you had. It is important, however, not to get bogged down. Do not let an occasional bad idea or awkward phrase, let alone the conventions of grammar, spelling, or punctuation, bring you to a stop. If you wish to tour a museum, you need to move your feet; if you wish to tour your mind, you need to move your pen.

Unfocused free writing, pursued for its own sake, is not unlike the warm-up exercises that professional athletes engage in prior to competition. It helps to limber up both the mind and the hand. Pursued as a journal exercise two or three times a week, unfocused free writing can lead to the discovery of subjects interesting enough to develop into essays at a later date, as the occasion demands. Such exercises provide interesting alternatives to the more premeditated and focused kinds of writing we normally associate with journal entries.

Focused free writing also has its uses and can be employed in a number of different ways. In focused free writing you repeatedly use a simple verbal formula to prime the pump of your imagination and keep up a strong flow of ideas. For example, in one ten-minute session you could try to write as many short paragraphs as possible, beginning each paragraph with the words "I remember." You should try to record a few specific images associated with each memory, but you shouldn't linger too long on any one incident. Instead, you should keep returning to the "I remember" formula in an effort to explore and develop new possibilities. If you run dry of ideas, simply write, "I remember, I remember, I remember . . ." until something comes to mind. Eventually, it will.

The exploration of memories in focused free writing can be informative, psychologically revealing, and fun. At their best these memories spring to life again for the writer, resurrecting an almost forgotten richness of sights, sounds, and sensations. Here, for example, is a delightful paragraph of student writing by Jan Simpson that employs the "I remember" formula:

"I REMEMBER . . ."

by Jan Simpson

I keep thinking of when I was a little girl and of the things I did then. I remember going on long trips with the family. I used to stick my arm out the window and let the air pull it back. I used to pretend that my arm was an airplane wing or that I was a bird gliding along. I remember making chains from wildflowers and wearing them about my neck, pretending to be mischievous little sprite. I remember thinking I could fly like Mary Poppins when I opened an umbrella on a windy day. I remember making mud pies with Norman, the little boy down the street, and decorating them with white rocks from the drive. I remember making sand castles in my sand box. I used to fill my pail with damp sand and turn it over—presto—instant castle. My parents got rid of the sand box when they found the present that the neighbor's kitty left in it. I remember swinging high on my swing set thinking that if I went high enough my feet would touch the sky. I never went that high, though. The swing set shook too much, and I was afraid that I'd fall. I remember having tricycle races with my little sister—I always won. I remember Mama walking me to school in the mornings and being there to walk me home in the afternoon. I remember going down to Grandma and

Grandpa's coloring in my coloring books, and "helping" to feed the chickens and pigs. I remember watching Great Grandpa Walter get angry when he watched Sunday afternoon wrestling on the little black and white television. I remember finding little "pop-balls" around the trees and smashing them with my feet. They made a dull, dry, and dusty little "pop" when I did that. I remember Daddy spanking me for throwing rocks at that man's car—I was only playing, but that apparently didn't matter. I remember so many little things. The little girl seems like another person. It is strange. I can almost reach out and touch the things I saw. It all seems so long ago—and yet—seems as if it happened yesterday.

Other useful formulas for priming the pump include creating a series of sentences beginning with, "I wish" or "I wonder." Or you may use paired sentences consisting of a question and an answer, a possibility ("Either . . .") and an alternative ("Or . . ."), or a recollection ("Once . . .") and a prediction ("Soon . . ."). No limit exists on the number of such devices for stimulating free writing, and each new device carries the writer into a slightly different region of the mind.

As invention strategies, such stimuli to free writing seem to work well because they put us immediately in charge of the writing process, nudge us past the paralysis of writer's block and engage us quickly and fully with the subject at hand. To be sure, the results of any given free writing exercise, at least at first, are a mixture of wheat and chaff that will need to be winnowed in order to discover what is most interesting and valuable. And, of course, even with these raw materials at hand, a great deal of hard work still lies ahead in organizing, revising, and editing what has been originally produced with relative ease. Like most writing strategies worth mastering, free writing demands diligence, concentration, and practice if it is to yield the mind's best work. But results do come and often are accompanied by insights that surprise and delight us precisely because they are both new and unexpected.

Exercise 5-3

Use one of the suggested formulas for focused free writing in an effort to generate ideas for an essay. Keep returning to that formula at the beginnings of your sentences in an effort to stimulate your imagination. Try to write without stopping for at least ten minutes. If you run out of ideas, simply continue writing the formula ("I wish, I wish, I wish . . .") until something comes to you.

Exercise 5-4 _____

Reread the material generated by the focused free writing you have just
done. Underline any ideas that strike you as potentially useful in an essay
written for an audience of fellow students. Then spend at least five
minutes in uninterrupted free writing on each of the underlined ideas.
At the end of this two-stage process you should have enough material for
a short essay. If not, repeat the process of focused free writing one more
time.

DIALOGUE

Most of us enjoy conversation and dialogue. Indeed, most of us prefer
talking to writing precisely because we practice it more. We delight in
discussing last night's party and speculating about exactly what induced
Gene to dance with a hat stand and wear a potted fern as a wig. Similarly,
we become enthralled at the theater while hearing Desdemona plead
with Othello to spare her life. For somewhat the same reasons, many
writers especially enjoy using dialogue as a means of inventing ideas for
a writing assignment.

One means of discovering ideas through dialogue is to discuss an
essay topic with a friend. The free exchange of opinions helps us to see
what questions are most likely to be raised about our topic; it allows us
to test our ideas on another person; and it helps us to generate ideas by
answering the other person's questions.

For a writer, however, internal dialogue is often more flexible and
dependable than actual conversation. Writers can create their mental
dialogues late at night or before rising in the morning when few friends
are eager to consider the disputed merits of, say, abortion on demand or
any of the other topics typically assigned in composition courses. Similarly, an internal dialogue can unfold in the silence of a library or a study
hall where actual conversation is impossible, impolite, or directly forbidden. Finally, there is little chance that an inner debate will digress, as
real conversations are apt to do, into gossip about intrigues at the office
or the hot new movie on HBO. Furthermore, internal dialogue can
achieve many of the same results as actual conversation. It encourages us
to formulate those questions that we consider most important about our
topic, it forces us to consider our ideas from another perspective, it eases
the task of recording our first thoughts, and it encourages careful and
skeptical evaluation of those thoughts.

To use dialogue as a means of invention, you should try to create
characters with radically different personalities and points of view. One
voice may well be your own, but make the second speaker someone who
is entirely different from you. You might choose a character from a
movie, a television series, or a novel as your antagonist. Even better, you
might imagine a debate with your mother, father, sister, or brother since

you probably know exactly what each of them would say about nearly any topic. As you write the dialogue, change speakers frequently in order to challenge as many assumptions as possible, but do develop each speech in enough detail to make the ideas clear. Finally, have fun. Let the personalities of your speakers emerge and let the conversation evolve through the various moods of seriousness, intensity, anger, and humor. New insights about a topic occur as readily through a change of mood as through a change of speaker.

Exercise 5-5

Imagine yourself in the following situation. You have just returned home to visit your parents for the first time in several months. On the morning after your arrival, you slouch down at the breakfast table with your eyelids feeling as heavy as two cinderblocks. Your parents are already on their third cup of coffee apiece and are right in the middle of a heated debate about some well-known person currently in the news. As you settle into your chair, your father is hotly contending that this person " . . . has made a real fool of himself this time!" And your mother is steaming more vigorously than the teakettle. Fill in the blank with some actual person in today's news and then write down the dialogue as you imagine it might occur between your parents. Spend at least twenty minutes on this invention exercise.

ARISTOTELIAN INVENTION

Sometimes the relatively informal methods of invention that we have so far discussed prove inadequate. Perhaps you are writing a research paper on recent changes in the federal income tax and you don't know how to begin. Or perhaps your professor in business management has asked you to propose a way for the Acme Flyswatter Company to double its production of flyswatters without doubling the plant size or operating hours. In confronting such topics, you may wish to use one of the variations of Aristotelian invention. As a problem-solving activity, Aristotelian invention proceeds through a series of questions that force us to think about a particular subject in a systematic and efficient way. The questions themselves are carefully defined and arranged yet sufficiently open-ended that in answering them we are stimulated both to learn more about our subject and to discover anew what we already know.

   Two different sets of questions, both applying the Aristotelian method, follow. The first set of questions is a general one, of the sort that might be used to explore an assigned subject with which we are largely unfamiliar; the second set is a model that has been suggested by Erika Lindemann and Richard Larson (in *A Rhetoric for Writing Teachers*, 1982) for exploring issue-related subjects.

I.   Traditional Aristotelian Invention

1. How is your subject **defined** in the dictionary? What is the history of the word? Where does the word come from and how has its meaning changed? What meaning are you most interested in?
2. What other subjects can you **classify** with yours as part of some more general topic? How can you **subdivide** your subject?
3. What other subjects can you **compare** with yours to show similarities, differences, and degrees of value? What do you learn about your subject through unusual or unlikely comparisons?
4. What are the **causes and effects** of your subject? What comes before it and after it?
5. What is the **history** of your subject? Does it exist now? How did it come to exist? What has happened to it in the past? What is likely to happen to it in the future?
6. What authoritative **testimony** can you discover firsthand by means of personal interviews, surveys or questionnaires, or letters of inquiry; or secondhand through indexed magazines and journals, computerized data bases, reference works (bibliographies, encyclopedias, world almanacs, statistical abstracts, anthologies of famous quotations, etc.), or books and monographs?

II.   A Problem-Solving Approach to Aristotelian Invention

1. What is the problem?
2. Why is the problem indeed a problem?
3. What goals must be served by whatever actions are taken or whatever solutions are proposed?
4. What goals have the highest priority?
5. What can I predict about the consequences of each possible action or solution?
6. How do the various possibilities compare with each other as solutions to the problem?
7. What course of action is best?

In using Aristotelian invention, proceed slowly and thoughtfully and take notes on your responses to each question. Depending on your topic, some questions will be more relevant and productive than others. If a given question doesn't seem to apply, by all means leave it and go on to the next. When you have completed the process, review your notes carefully, underscoring or circling what seems most interesting and promising. Provided you devote sufficient time and attention to the task, you will gain a much better understanding of the range of information available to you, and you will be in a position to limit your essay to those aspects of the topic that are most intriguing and productive.

Aristotelian invention provides a valuable strategy for defining and probing your subject and for gathering and organizing your materials. It will prevent you from beginning the composing process too soon, before you have fully explored your subject, adopted your stance or point of view, and gathered sufficient information. In this sense, Aristotelian invention, although it may at first seem time-consuming, complicated, and perhaps unnecessary, is a way of conserving time and improving writing efficiency. Finally, the questions posed by Aristotelian invention can be returned to once the writing process has actually begun or during the process of revision as a means of providing needed clarification or generating additional materials.

Exercise 5-6

To discover the possibilities of traditional Aristotelian invention, try it out on some topic that you already know a lot about. If you are an expert gardener, apply the questions to the subject of home gardening. If you are an enthusiastic golfer, write about the game and its traditions. Whatever you are expert in, choose that as your topic and see how much Aristotelian invention can help you to discover what you already know. Spend at least an hour on this invention exercise.

Exercise 5-7

Use the questions in the problem-solving approach to generate ideas for an essay on some issue of local concern on your college campus. If parking is a problem, you might focus on it. If the general education requirements are undergoing review, you might try to develop your own view about the proposed changes. If the athletic program is running at a massive deficit, you might focus on that perennial problem.

THE REPORTER'S QUESTIONS

Newspaper reporters, because they face the pressure of a daily deadline, have developed a simple and reliable technique for recording the key elements of a story. If your essay involves describing what has happened to you or someone else, you too can benefit from the reporter's procedure. All that is required is that you ask yourself, "Who? When? What? Where? Why?" Your answers to these questions will provide much of the basic information that must be incorporated into an essay dealing with personal experience or newsworthy events.

This technique is most likely to produce plain, practical writing about factual matters. In addition to serving newswriters, it is also of particular use to students taking essay exams. For example, a student asked to write an in-class essay on Chaucer's *Canterbury Tales* might mentally map out an answer as follows:

> **Who?**   Geoffrey Chaucer, the actual author, makes himself just one among a group of thirty imaginary storytellers from all levels of society.

When?   About 1390, during a fictional pilgrimage to Canterbury.

What?   A splendid collection of medieval stories in all of the popular forms of the time: romance, fabliau, exemplum, fable, allegory, sermon, saint's life, satire.

Where?   Chaucer himself lived in London. The stories in the *Canterbury Tales* are told along the road by the various "pilgrims" accompanying "Chaucer" on a pilgrimage to Canterbury Cathedral, the place of burial of England's most famous saint, Thomas à Becket.

Why?   The pilgrims narrate the tales to occupy their time as they ride, to amuse one another, and to compete for a prize dinner to be awarded by the proprietor of the Tabard Inn to the teller of the best tale. Chaucer's greatest innovation is in the complex interactions between the various pilgrims, who often tell their stories to chide, deride, and mock one another. The various prologues during which Chaucer's characters converse about the tale just told and introduce the one to come are justly famous for their humorous and realistic portrayal of humanity in fourteenth-century England.

In using this technique, beware of two traps: First, the five questions will provide you with basic information that you should include in your essay, but they do not provide a method of organizing your actual essay. Second, beware of answering the questions too rapidly or too superficially. At first thought "Geoffrey Chaucer" might seem to be the only answer to the question "Who?" It is only on reflection that one realizes that Chaucer himself is just one of the many fictional narrators of the tales. Similarly, the question "Why?" takes on different meanings from different perspectives. We first tried to indicate why the pilgrims told their tales, but then we discovered what the most important question is, "Why are the *Canterbury Tales* so interesting, so innovative, and so important in English literary history?" Our sentences on the interaction between the various pilgrims introduce one possible answer, and a good in-class essay would probably go on to develop a detailed analysis of the relationships between a few of the Chaucerian narrators and the tales they tell.

Useful as this device is, it cannot be expected to generate anything more than the key elements of a clear, factual response. Creative approaches, imaginative ideas, and vivid details are more reliably generated by the other invention techniques outlined in this chapter.

Exercise 5-8

The following topics call on you to write an essay based on personal experience. Use the reporter's questions to discover the plain, factual material that should be included in such an essay.

An unforgettable evening
My most embarrassing moment
My favorite way to spend a free hour between classes
The best of my high school teachers
The worst of my high school teachers
How I learned the meaning of true friendship
A moving insight into the meaning of life
A prank gone awry

Exercise 5-9

If you have read an interesting book lately, use the reporter's questions to generate information that you would need to include in an essay explaining to fellow students why they too might enjoy the book.

ANALOGY

Analogies and metaphors are often thought to be the essence of poetry, but they are also essential in vivid prose. Their use enables a writer to state ideas more understandably, more entertainingly, and often more persuasively. Furthermore, the attempt to discover comparisons almost invariably leads to new discoveries about what one wishes to say as well as how best to say it.

Good analogies can sometimes be discovered through idle reverie, but it is more efficient to force the process along. One way to do so is to describe the subject that you are interested in exploring as if it were a tree, mammal, flower, bird, insect, or other member of some general class of things. In drafting the preceding chapter of this textbook, we used this technique to discover ideas about journals and diaries. As part of our prewriting for the chapter, we recorded the following comparisons:

Tree   A journal is a cherry tree — it produces a petal-fall of tiny poems; it nourishes its owner with a harvest of bittersweet fruit; and after many years one might still carve from its trunk the timbers for an important piece of writing.

A diary is a poplar tree — quick to grow but poor fuel in winter.

Mammal   A journal is a cat — domestic, but untamable; satisfying, but unpredictable; a creature of the night side of life.

A diary is like a dog — a reliable, playful daily companion.

Flower   A journal is a morning glory — each day brings forth its new flowers that will fall unnoticed unless enjoyed and recorded as they bloom.

A diary is a daisy—a petal is pulled for each day of love or its loss.

Bird   A journal is like a loon—its mournful call draws one back into reveries of the past.

A diary is like a mockingbird, repeating the same song too often.

Insect   A journal is a honeybee—it pollinates the imagination and stores up nectar for future use.

A diary is an ant—industrious, unimaginative, tasteless.

Clearly, some of these analogies are more appropriate and more effective than others. Some may even be insipid or downright foolish. Hence, only three of the ten eventually found their way into the chapter, but even those we didn't use were helpful in stimulating and clarifying our general ideas on journals and diaries.

The specific classifications you use in forcing your own analogies along are relatively unimportant. Choose categories that you like and that you know something about. A music major, for example, might seek to compare a diary to specific pieces of jazz, rock, country, gospel, and orchestral music. A theater major might seek out comparisons involving characters in stage plays, movies, TV serials, and musicals. The categories you choose and the types of comparisons you use in your writing should (and inevitably will) reflect your interests and idiosyncrasies. Be aware, however, that your goal is not necessarily to create analogies that you will actually use in your essay. Instead, you should concentrate on discovering the *ideas* that you wish to express. As you formulate analogies to fit each separate category, you should continue to discover new facets of your subject, just as an artist continuously rediscovers a piece of sculpture by seeing it in different light and from different vantage points. It follows that you should not attempt to create metaphors and similes too rapidly. It takes time to switch from one basis of comparison to another, time to adjust to the new light in which you are attempting to see your subject.

Remember, too, that creating analogies as a strategy of invention is quite different from using metaphors in poetry. In poetry a good metaphor is rarely explained; it simply *feels* right. When the modern American poet William Carlos Williams wrote, "Your thighs are apple trees, whose blossoms touch the sky," he wisely avoided explaining his meaning too explicitly. To do so might have ruined the poem and offended the sensibilities of some readers. What ambiguity exists in the lines is useful in stimulating the imagination of the reader. Conversely, the composition student who writes enigmatically, "A journal is a honeybee"—and no more—is likely to wonder later how he could ever have imagined that such sugary goo constituted a meaningful insight. The metaphor alone is too barren. Only by attaching additional phrases or sentences can one make pertinent those aspects of the similarity that promoted the comparison during prewriting.

One final piece of advice: use sensory imagery in your comparisons. Your goal is to discover clear, specific ideas about your topic. The best way to do so is to pull your writing down from the clouds by referring to what can be seen, heard, tasted, smelled, or felt. Remember that you have five senses; try to use them all.

Exercise 5-10 _____

Pick one topic from the left column below and then explore it by forcing a comparison based on each of the categories in the right column, for example, "If Bruce Springsteen were a tree, he would be a hickory because . . ."

Topics
    Your favorite musician
    Your favorite automobile
    Your favorite food
    Some politician of note
    An author you admire
    Richard Nixon
    Jimmy Carter
    The space shuttle
    Time magazine
    Prince Charles
    Princess Diana
    Martina Navratilova
    The month of April (or any other month)
    A newborn child
    A computer

Categories
Tree
Mammal
Flower
Bird
Insect

Exercise 5-11 _____

Repeat exercise 5-10, but this time use any topic that you might like to write about and choose five new categories for comparison. Base these categories on your own interests. If you are interested in machines, for example, you might choose as your categories *car, airplane, computer, home appliance*, and *hand tool.* Unusual categories will produce unusual insights, and your goal, of course, is to discover such insights.

Often the analogies you discover through this invention exercise will be directly useful in developing a portion of an essay. Occasionally, in fact, an extended analogy provides the structure for an entire essay. An example is Henry David Thoreau's extended comparison of human warfare and ant warfare in "The Battle of the Ants." There Thoreau satirizes humankind's delusions about the glory of combat by using the grandiose verbiage of military heroism in describing a minuscule massacre among ants.

WHEN INVENTION FAILS

Although the various strategies of invention discussed in this chapter work for most writers if understood and consciously practiced, there are times when such methods don't seem to pay off with the desired results. When invention fails, consider the following possibilities:

1. **You may need to take more time to understand, practice, and master the various strategies of invention.** "One of the chief differences between good and poor writers, and good and poor problem-solvers in general," remarks Professor Linda Flowers, "is the repertory of strategies . . . on which they draw. Good writers not only have a large repertory of powerful strategies, but they have sufficient self-awareness of their own process to draw upon these techniques as they need them."

2. **You haven't fully understood the problem you wish to solve.** Writing is a form of problem solving, involving questions of strategy: how best to communicate something to someone. If you proceed too quickly without identifying the problem being addressed and its various facets, and without having your purpose or purposes clearly in mind, you invariably waste time pursuing unproductive leads, and you may experience a growing sense of frustration, anxiety, or even anger.

3. **You haven't allowed sufficient time for your ideas and problems to incubate.** Often, time itself is the best weapon for problem solving. By deliberately taking time out from the problem you are wrestling with, you may gain enough psychic distance to discover solutions that hadn't occurred to you earlier. Put another way, sometimes invention fails because we haven't allowed our intellect and our imagination sufficient time to engage our subject fully. One of the principal values of employing invention as a prewriting strategy is that it discourages us from prematurely putting pen to paper without fully considering what we mean to say and how we mean to say it.

4. **You are unprepared or unwilling to consider the unexpected.** One of the most interesting, exciting, and valuable things about invention is that its various strategies often result in surprises. Often people dismiss original ideas without a full examination precisely because the ideas are unusual and unexpected. To make invention work, you must consciously open yourself to new ideas.

5. **You consider invention only as a prewriting activity.** Invention can be effectively employed at any time during the composing process, including during the stages of revision and editing. Indeed, throughout the writing process you should maintain a mood of flexibility and preserve a willingness to revise what you have begun in light of the new, the unexpected, and (until fully explored) the unclear.

PART III

WRITING FOR OTHERS

Chapter 6

DESCRIPTION

=====◇◇◇=====

"Describe a friend or acquaintance whom you think others should get to know as you do."

"Describe your favorite campus hangout in such a way that your reader can fully appreciate its attractions."

Such topics as these are common and useful assignments in freshman English. They draw on your personal experiences and convictions, but at the same time they challenge you to use words creatively, as a poet or novelist might. Only through careful and precise language describing what can be seen, heard, smelled, tasted, or touched is it possible to transport your readers vicariously into the pipe-scented presence of the Dean of Science. Only through the use of clear sensory imagery can you set them down amidst the chaos of bells, buzzers, and bomb blasts that characterizes the game room in the Student Union. This reliance on sensory detail makes descriptive writing more specific, more vivid, and more entertaining than most other forms of writing; however, the purposes of descriptive writing are in no way limited by this specificity. As we shall see, descriptions can be—and often are—written to inform and to persuade as well as to entertain.

OBJECTIVE DESCRIPTION

Descriptions are normally categorized as either objective or subjective. **Objective descriptions** are common in scientific writing, technical writing, and news reports, where they communicate information with few emotional overtones. The biochemist writing about the location of microtubules in a cow's brain will *not* describe in great gory detail how he found those microtubules by purchasing the cow's warm and still

Louvre, Paris/Giraudon/Art Resource, NY

L'Absinthe (1880) by Edgar Degas. Although considered one of the French Impressionists, Degas read and was influenced by the meticulously realistic fiction of French novelist Émile Zola. What elements in this painting seem particularly realistic? What elements help to create an impression of the emotions experienced by the man and the woman? How would you **describe** this painting and its effects?

twitching head from the local slaughterhouse; nor will he mention how he wore a blood-splattered lab coat as he laboriously sawed through the skull and ground up the animal's brain in a blender. Instead the scientist will describe the cow's brain and the procedure for processing it in impersonal, unemotional language. Scientific description seeks to state plain facts, shorn of all emotional overtones.

Objective descriptions are common in the fine print of encyclopedias and other reference works. If, for example, you want to learn about the sophisticated microprocessors found in personal computers, you can turn to a variety of dictionaries and encyclopedias specifically designed for owners and users of microcomputers. There you may find such information as the following:

> A microprocessor is the central processing unit or "brain" of a modern binary computer. Within the microprocessor, instructions are called up one by one, information is stored temporarily, and arithmetic or logical operations are carried out. The microprocessor itself is a set of electrical circuits printed on a silicon chip slightly larger than a pinhead. In order to make room for the forty or more tiny wires that connect the microprocessor to the other components of the computer, this chip is embedded in an epoxy and metal package a little smaller than a stick of gum.

Very likely the description will go on to identify and explain the function of each of the different components of a microprocessor. It may also contain sketches or photographs to clarify details of structure or appearance. By providing unadorned, objective details, such a description allows readers with a serious interest in the operation and design of computers to recognize the microprocessor on an actual circuit board and to understand its operation. Note, however, that even this relatively technical description provides sensory details to help the readers visualize a microprocessor. The size of the silicon chip is compared with that of a pinhead and the appearance of the complete microprocessor is likened to a stick of gum. Clarity is the highest priority in objective description; in the pursuit of clarity even scientific writers will sometimes resort to using similes and metaphors.

SUBJECTIVE DESCRIPTION

Subjective descriptions are common in literature, feature writing, and advertising. They focus on the dominant impression created by an object, a place, or a person. Like objective descriptions, they provide readers with useful information, but they normally seek to entertain or persuade as well—hence serving as complex and intriguing writing assignments. Therefore our advice in the remainder of this chapter refers primarily to subjective descriptions.

Most descriptions probably occur in short stories and novels, where their primary purpose is to paint a clear and enthralling picture of a character or setting. Consider James Joyce's "Araby," for example. An alert and sensitive reader easily recognizes that Mangan's teenaged sister is the object of the adolescent narrator's romantic fantasies. This is how the narrator describes Mangan's sister as she stands silhouetted by lamplight on a stairway:

> She held one of the spikes, bowing her head towards me. The light from the lamp opposite our door caught the white curve of her neck, lit up her hair that rested there and, falling, lit up the hand

upon the railing. It fell over one side of her dress and caught the white border of a petticoat, just visible as she stood at ease.

In this lingering description of her neck, her hair, and her body, we sense the narrator's infatuation — his longing to touch her as gently as the soft lamplight does.

This attempt to convey a mood or an impression is what differentiates literary description from the more neutral descriptions in technical prose. The author of the paragraph on microprocessors literally has no thesis. There is no *opinion* about microprocessors that he wishes to communicate — only facts, figures, and diagrams. In contrast, the narrator of "Araby" certainly has a very fervent opinion about the beauty of Mangan's sister.

For yet another example of effective subjective description, consider the following paragraph from *Huckleberry Finn*. Notice how Huck describes his father so vividly that the reader not only sees Pap in his mind's eye, but also picks up Huck's opinion about his father, a fear bordering on loathing:

He was most fifty, and he looked it. His hair was long and tangled and greasy, and hung down, and you could see his eyes shining through like he was behind vines. It was all black, no gray; so was his long, mixed-up whiskers. There warn't no color in his face, where his face showed; it was white; not like another man's white, but a white to make a body sick, a white to make a body's flesh crawl — a tree-toad white, a fish belly white. As for his clothes — just rags, that was all. He had one ankle resting on 'tother knee; the boot on that foot was busted, and two of his toes stuck through, and he worked them now and then. His hat was laying on the floor; an old black slouch with the top caved in, like a lid.

Clearly, Pap is not a dignified member of the working poor. His dissipated slovenliness is an all-too-accurate indicator of his total lack of virtue and respectability. In this instance the writer's thesis, or opinion, about Pap remains entirely unstated and emerges only through images and the connotations of words. Pap's eyes shine behind his tangled hair "like he was behind vines" and make him seem like a jungle predator. Furthermore, Pap is entirely described in black and white — colors that often suggest malevolence and death. The pallor of Pap's skin makes Huck's "flesh crawl." That pallor is "not like another man's white, but a white to make a body sick . . . a tree-toad white, a fish belly white." For Huck, Pap is less a father than an incarnate devil whose appearance has been foreshadowed by signs and portents of evil.

PREWRITING

In writing a description, you will have less difficulty than normal in discovering what to say. In most cases the subject to be described will be either right before your eyes or so familiar that you have no need to see it. If you are describing a painting like Edgar Degas's *L'Absinthe* (see p. 74) you will naturally begin by looking at it very carefully. If you are describing a person — your eighty-nine-year-old great-grandmother or your wacky aunt in Topeka — you will begin by consulting your memory. However, one can look at a person or painting without truly *seeing* it in all of its complexity and detail. In developing ideas for a descriptive essay, you may wish to use two of the established techniques of invention.

Listing specific details about your subject will undoubtedly be the most helpful technique. In listing, make a conscious attempt to be very specific and to appeal to as many different senses as possible. You may even wish to make different lists for sight, sound, taste, touch, and smell, as in the following example:

Prewriting List on Degas's *L'Absinthe*

Sight:	Rumpled man, disheveled woman.
	Slouched postures.
	Dull colors in clothing.
	Forgotten drinks.
	Asymmetrical composition, figures pushed to right.
	Tables at angle to viewer, diagonal lines.
	Muted colors — burgundy not red; gray not white or black.
	Dim, smoky lighting.
	Man looks up and away from the woman; woman looks down and away from the man.
Smell:	Stale wine and beer.
	Cigar and pipe smoke.
	Unwashed bodies.
Taste:	The sharp astringence of cheap wine.
	The licorice-like taste of absinthe.
Sound:	A strained silence if the bar is empty.
	A cacophony of half-heard conversations if the bar is crowded.
Touch:	Gritty film of dirt on tabletop?

Remember that your goal in a subjective description is to develop an interpretation of your subject based on the dominant impression it makes. Clearly a description of a painting like *L'Absinthe* must be visual, but the details on smell, taste, sound, and touch are still relevant. A subjective description records impressions and draws on the imagination. Its goal is to help the reader to imagine the setting, and the best way to do so is to use sensory details.

Listing of details is only one way of recording your impressions — and not always the best way. **Another way to discover your feelings about a subject is to develop comparisons.** You should write down any comparisons that seem apt, but if you are initially at a loss, try forced analogies, again using all five senses:

Prewriting Comparisons on Degas's *L'Absinthe*

It look like . . . two lovers on the verge of separating.
It feels like . . . the oppressive tension one feels just before a
summer thunderstorm.
It smells like . . . the petty, putrid sins of all our yesterdays.
It tastes like . . . flat beer left too long in the sun.
It sounds like . . . the murmurings of mourners at a wake.

Not all of the ideas generated through such lists will be useful in your essay. Indeed, the speculative items, like the half-heard conversations, should be either omitted entirely or, if used, acknowledged as purely speculative. No matter which items are actually used in your essay, the making of the lists will still have served a function by helping you realize what you feel about your subject.

PLANNING AND DRAFTING A DESCRIPTION

After you have gathered some ideas about your topic, you are ready to begin planning and drafting your essay. As you do so, keep in mind the following recommendations:

Give your description a thesis that allows you to focus on an unusual or out-of-the-ordinary impression. A description, like nearly every piece of solid writing, needs a unifying thesis. In most cases that thesis should emerge logically from the mood you seek to create through the details you include in your essay. The potential theses on Degas's *L'Absinthe* are numerous. You might argue that it portrays two lovers at a moment of crisis in their relationship. You might contend that the man and woman are contrasting individuals whom circumstance has somehow yoked together. You might insist that Degas uses form, color, technique, and characterization to communicate a mood of reflective remorse. Any of these theses, along with many others, might lead to a good essay. Remember, however, that your chances of interesting, informing, and persuading your readers will improve if you take a stance that has probably not occurred to them. For that reason you should avoid so obvious a thesis as that the painting is a realistic portrayal of two people in a seedy bar.

Try to recapture the psychological and emotional impact of whatever you are describing. In a subjective description, your goal is to describe not just what you saw but also how it made you (and presumably other viewers) feel. In doing so, you will need to be particularly conscious of the connotations of words. Use emotionally charged language whenever appropriate. Do not write, for example, that the man in Degas's painting is "dressed casually and seated comfortably" when you can turn up the emotional temperature by portraying him as "a disheveled man wearing a drab, crumpled suit and slouching beside a melancholy woman." Nonetheless, avoid bald statements of your feelings. Claiming that Degas's painting depresses you will not convince a reader unless you can accurately describe the depressing features in the painting. And if you can do so, your readers will readily share your mood without overt statements on your part.

Select an organizing pattern that is compatible with your thesis and the dominant impression you seek to convey. Because you are frequently striving to share an emotional reaction through your description, at first it may seem that an organizing scheme is unnecessary. Remember, though, that in many cases your readers will never have seen the object you are describing. In such situations they are even more lost at sea than usual and will need to cling to your organizational framework to avoid sinking beneath a flood of fine writing. Spatial organizations are particularly easy for readers to follow. You might describe a room from front to back or back to front; a painting from left to right (or vice versa); or a person from head to toe. Such a spatial organization was chosen by Mark Twain in creating Huck Finn's description of Pap on page 76. Notice how Huck's description moves progressively from Pap's head to his feet and finally concludes with the black slouch hat on the floor. That simple pattern allows us to construct a mental picture of Pap easily, without struggling for scattered details. Furthermore, the head-to-toe pattern is also a natural one: a man's face is usually the first feature we observe; only later do we notice his clothing and shoes. Spatial organizations are not, however, the only possibilities. A description might logically follow a wide variety of organizing patterns — moving, for example, from what is most prominent to what is least prominent, or from attractive features to unattractive features, or from sight to sound, smell, taste, and touch.

COMBINING PURPOSES

Subjective descriptions usually attempt to entertain. **In striving to make your essay appealing to readers, you should cite very specific details using colorful language.** Readers are always entertained to some extent by specificity, but particularly in descriptions it is helpful to present details that are so concrete that they remain imprinted in the reader's mind. The two toes poking through Pap's boot and wiggling "now and then" are examples of such memorable details. We have also seen how the image of Pap peering through his tangled hair "like he was behind vines" is emotionally evocative. To include such memorable imagery in your own writing, you may wish to return to the lists you made during prewriting and consciously make the details more specific and more directly appealing to your reader's senses of sight, sound, smell, taste, and touch. In our list of observations about Degas's *L'Absinthe,* for example, the "forgotten drinks" might be revised to read: "The woman's goblet of absinthe is untouched and presumably forgotten; the man's half-empty carafe of red wine, which he drinks from a tumbler, suggests that there is something he is trying to forget."

Another way to make your description more entertaining is

to include representative speech or action within it. People enjoy action, and they are often amused by the idiosyncratic quirks in the speech of others. Of course, if you are describing a painting, or something equally static, speech and action can be difficult to include. But in a description of a person or even a place (see Tom Wolfe's essay on Las Vegas on page 89), dialogue and action can play a part. Beware, however, of letting the dialogue and action become dominant. Your assignment is to write a description, not a narration. Nonetheless, even minor actions can animate an otherwise static description. Such is the case when Mark Twain describes how Pap works his toes through the hole in his boot.

Even the most vivid and appealing description may strike your reader as pointless if you fail to make your essay informative or persuasive as well as entertaining. In a character study you might seek to inform your readers about human beings generally or about special classes of people. Pap, for example, is illustrative of a segment of the poor that Twain finds simply irredeemable, despite the well-intentioned efforts of social reformers. If you are describing a place, you can often find a persuasive purpose — arguing, perhaps, for environmental conservation, or for the preservation of the values and lifestyle in rural America. No one can tell you exactly *how* to give your essay an informative or persuasive purpose. You may, however, discover such purposes for yourself if you at least keep in mind the desirability of finding them and combining them with specific, entertaining descriptive imagery.

TIPS ON REVISION

1. **Check to see whether your organizing principle is compatible with your thesis.** For example, Lis Wood's thesis in her description of Degas's *L'Absinthe* (p. 82) is that "Degas uses several compositional devices . . . to create and communicate the mood of reflective remorse." With such a thesis Lis is almost compelled to organize her essay according to compositional devices like form, color, and brush technique. A purely spatial organization (describing the painting, say, from top to bottom) would not be wholly compatible with her thesis.

2. **If you have chosen a spatial method of organization, check to see that you have not overemphasized it.** Remember that your central concern is normally to communicate some dominant impression about your subject. A spatial organization is usually sufficiently clear without dreary pronouncements like "moving down from the pert mouth, we next examine the somewhat saggy jaw" or "the second most easterly feature of town is. . . . " Although transitional devices are useful in most essays, they can quickly become monotonous in a spatial description.

3. **Use a thesaurus to seek out apt and colorful language, but never use a word unless it is part of *your* vocabulary.** A thesaurus can be helpful in reminding you of a wide range of descriptive options,

but the words presented in it are not wholly interchangeable. There is a vast difference between *legal tender* and *filthy lucre* even though both are presented as synonyms for *money.*

IDEAS FOR ESSAYS

In writing on any of the following topics, remember to develop a thesis that is somehow based on an impression or mood. Choose an appropriate organizational scheme.

1. Describe a friend or acquaintance whom you think others should get to know as you do.

2. Describe your favorite campus hangout in such a way that your reader can fully appreciate its attractions.

3. Describe one of your favorite childhood hangouts as it seemed to you then and as it appears to you now.

4. Describe a relative, a close friend, or a national celebrity as he or she looks in a photograph taken several years ago and as he or she appears in a recent photograph. Attach the two photographs to your essay.

5. Describe some public place on campus at several different times of day.

6. Describe your boyfriend, girlfriend, or spouse from your own point of view and then from the point of view of your parents.

7. Describe any of the advertisements that are reproduced in this text.

8. Describe any of the artwork that is reproduced in this text.

STUDENT ESSAY _____

The following student essay was written as an in-class assignment. The topic was to write a subjective, interpretive description of Degas's painting entitled *L'Absinthe*.

FIRST DRAFT

"DEGAS'S L'ABSINTHE"

by Lisbeth Wood

The subject is a print of a ~~famous~~ well-known painting by the famous artist Edgar Degas who lived in the ~~early~~ late 1800's. The painting is typical of Degas in its movement away from ~~the~~ compositional norms, creating his own unique and slightly pessimistic ~~message~~ statement to us.

Degas ~~uses several~~ takes advantage of ~~his artistic~~ several devices to accomplish the mood of remorseful reflection. The first is ~~his use of~~ the ~~was he~~ oddity we notice in ~~that~~ the figures ~~the~~ of the man and woman who would normally be placed in the center ~~of a~~ to give them prominence are instead pushed off to the right of the painting. This creates the odd effect of having come upon the scene by chance. There is no posing ~~of~~ or formality here, we see only a quiet and sad reflection; it is an average ordinary subject. Degas places his two figures behind 3 large gray tables ~~at~~ with their backs against the wall behind them. There is no mistake in the use of rectangular forms throughout the ~~pa~~ work--in the tables and on the wall in background. These forms help create an image of instability.

The second compositional device Degas uses is color. We see a smokey, ashy gray in the tables and wall and in the clothing. The reds used are subdued ~~and~~ with darker browns and blacks to lessen their force. There is no pure use of color--no brightness of white nor solidness of true black. Degas, ~~helps~~ by his use of murky, colorless colors creates the mood through color.

Thirdly, Degas uses his own special "technique" of brush stroke and applying the paint in less soft strokes. Again, to be more bold in his application of paint & technique would confuse the mood he has set up.

Finally, Degas uses the characters themselves to send us the message in their clothing, body language, and especially their expressions. Their clothes are dull and crumpled, their bodies slouched as if the weight of their regret weighs on them. The woman looks with downcast eyes and almost mournful expression to some spot on the floor ahead while the man glances out to the right of the picture to some unimportant event which we cannot know.

All these compositional devices which Degas uses together help to create his mood of somber, regret in his painting L'Absinthe.

Commentary: After reading this essay aloud to her professor and a group of fellow students, Lis realized that she needed to clarify her structure and sharpen her actual description of the painting. During the next class meeting, she rewrote it as follows:

SECOND DRAFT

"DEGAS'S L'ABSINTHE"

by Lisbeth Wood

Thesis: Degas uses several compositional devices in his painting L'Absinthe to create and communicate the mood of reflective remorse.

A. Introduction and objective description of subject.

B. Comp. Device: Form

Figures--pushed to right

Tables--diagonal lines

C. Comp. Device: Color

Subdued, smokey

Lots of gray

D. Comp. Device: Brush stroke and technique

Soft, fuzzy

E. Comp. Device: Characters (expressions)

Clothing

Expressions

Looking away

F. Conclusion--last sentence

The subject is a print of a well-known painting entitled L'Absinthe by the famous artist Edgar Degas who lived in the late 1800's. The painting is set at some neighborhood pub and centers on two people--a young and attractive woman, the focus of the painting, sitting to the right of a dark, bearded, rather disheveled man, who seems to be her opposite. Both figures are located off-center, in the right half of the painting. On the table in front of the odd couple are their drinks, forgotten, as they both seem to be distracted by their own thoughts.

The painting is typical of Degas in its movement away from compositional norms, creating a mood of somber remorse in a slightly pessimistic statement to us. Degas takes advantage of three compositional devices to communicate the mood.

The first compositional device Degas uses is form. We notice that the figures of the man and woman, who would normally be placed in the center to give them prominence, are instead pushed off to the right of the painting. This creates the odd effect of having come upon the scene by chance. There is no pose or formality here; we, as spectators, seem to be seated at an adjacent table. Degas places these two figures behind three large gray tables with their backs against the wall behind them. There is no mistake in his use of diagonal and rectangular forms throughout the work. These uneven forms help create the image of instability, as if we see the scene and catch the mood only by accident.

The second compositional device Degas uses is color. We see a smokey, ashy gray in the tables and wall and in the clothing. The reds used are subdued with darker browns and blacks to lessen their force. There is no pure use of color--no brightness of white nor solidness of true black. Degas, by his use of murky, colorless colors, helps us feel the mood of remorseful reflection.

Thirdly, Degas uses his own special "technique" of brush stroke (the applying of paint) and makes somewhat fuzzy images to contribute to the mood. To be more bold in his application of paint would only confuse the mood he has set up.

Finally, Degas uses the characters themselves to send us his message in their clothing, their body language, and especially their expressions. Their clothes are dull and crumpled, their bodies slouched as if the weight of their reflections weighs heavily on them. The woman looks with downcast eyes and rueful expression to some spot on the floor ahead while the man glances out to the right of the picture to some unimportant event which we cannot know. They are together and yet apart. This crystallizes the emotion for us.

All these compositional devices used together help to create and communicate the mood of somber, reflective remorse in Degas's painting L'Absinthe.

Commentary: This was an in-class, impromptu essay, written in two fifty-minute sessions. As such, it is clearly very successful. Lis effectively combines purposes by informing us of the artistic techniques Degas uses and persuading us that those techniques contribute to the overall impression created by the painting. The descriptions are clear and effective in illustrating the painting's mood of "reflective remorse." We learn from Lis's essay to understand and appreciate the painting more fully.

At the same time, the essay is not flawless. Both the introduction and conclusion are lackluster, failing to capture the reader's interest at the beginning and to underscore the essay's importance at the end. Furthermore, Lis's essay does little to entertain the reader; her analysis is technical, formal, and somewhat "dry." If these are flaws, however, they are, nonetheless, minor flaws in an essay written under pressure and in a limited amount of time.

The Battle of the Ants
Henry David Thoreau

Henry David Thoreau (1817–1862), a lifelong resident of the village of Concord, Massachusetts, took up residence at nearby Walden Pond on July 4, 1845 (Independence Day), in order "to live deliberately, to front only the essentials of life, and see if I could not learn what it had to teach, and not, when I came to die, discover I had not lived." The remarkable account of his two-year and two-month stay in his cabin by the pond initially began as a series of journal entries and was published in 1854 as *Walden*, a book long since recognized as a classic of American literature. One major reason for *Walden*'s success is Thoreau's delightful ability to describe the sights and sounds of the natural world around him in a manner that uses analogy to illuminate the world of men. The following excerpt, which has come to be titled "The Battle of the Ants," is typical of Thoreau's literary style and craftsmanship.

1   One day when I went out to my wood-pile, or rather my pile of stumps, I observed two large ants, the one red, the other much larger, nearly half an inch long, and black, fiercely contending with one another. Having once got hold they never let go, but struggled and wrestled and rolled on the chips incessantly. Looking farther, I was surprised to find that the chips were covered with such combatants, that it was not a *duellum*, but a *bellum*,[1] a war between two races of ants, the red always pitted against the black, and frequently two red ones to one black. The legions of these Myrmidons[2] covered all the hills and vales in my wood-yard, and the ground was already strewn with the dead and dying, both red and black. It was the only battle which I have ever witnessed, the only battle-field I ever trod while the battle was raging; internecine war; the red republicans on the one hand, and the black imperialists on the other. On every side they were engaged in deadly combat, yet without any noise that I could hear, and human soldiers never fought so resolutely. I watched a couple that were fast locked in each other's embraces, in a little sunny valley amid the chips, now at noonday prepared to fight till the sun went down, or life went out. The smaller red champion had fastened himself like a vice to his adversary's front, and through all the tumblings on that field never for an instant ceased to gnaw at one of his feelers near the root, having already caused the other to go by the board; while the stronger black one dashed him from side to side, and, as I saw on looking nearer, had already divested him of several of his members. They fought with more pertinacity than bulldogs. Neither manifested the least disposition to retreat. It was evident that their battle-cry was "Conquer or die." In the meanwhile there came along a single red ant on the hillside of this valley, evidently full of excitement, who either had dispatched his foe, or had not yet taken part in the battle; probably the latter, for he had lost none of his limbs; whose mother had charged him

[1]Not a duel, but a war.
[2]Loyal followers and ferocious warriors.

to return with his shield or upon it. Or perchance he was some Achilles, who had nourished his wrath apart, and had now come to avenge or rescue his Patroclus.[3] He saw this unequal combat from afar—for the blacks were nearly twice the size of the red—he drew near with rapid pace till he stood on his guard within half an inch of the combatants; then, watching his opportunity, he sprang upon the black warrior, and commenced his operations near the root of his right foreleg, leaving the foe to select among his own members; and so there were three united for life, as if a new kind of attraction had been invented which put all other locks and cements to shame. I should not have wondered by this time to find that they had their respective musical bands stationed on some eminent chip, and playing their national airs the while, to excite the slow and cheer the dying combatants. I was myself excited somewhat even as if they had been men. The more you think of it, the less the difference. And certainly there is not the fight recorded in Concord history, at least, if in the history of America, that will bear a moment's comparison with this, whether for the numbers engaged in it, or for the patriotism and heroism displayed. For numbers and for carnage it was an Austerlitz or Dresden.[4] Concord Fight! Two killed on the patriot's side, and Luther Blanchard wounded! Why here every ant was a Buttrick—"Fire! for God's sake fire!"—and thousands shared the fate of Davis and Hosmer.[5] There was not one hireling there. I have no doubt that it was a principle they fought for, as much as our ancestors, and not to avoid a three-penny tax on their tea; and the results of this battle will be as important and memorable to those whom it concerns as those of the battle of Bunker Hill, at least.

I took up the chip on which the three I have particularly described 2 were struggling, carried it into my house, and placed it under a tumbler on my window-sill, in order to see the issue. Holding a microscope to the first-mentioned red ant, I saw that, though he was assiduously gnawing at the near foreleg of his enemy, having severed his remaining feeler, his own breast was all torn away, exposing what vitals he had there to the jaws of the black warrior, whose breastplate was apparently too thick for him to pierce; and the dark carbuncles of the sufferer's eyes shone with ferocity such as war only could excite. They struggled half an hour longer under the tumbler, and when I looked again the black soldier had severed the heads of his foes from their bodies, and the still living heads were hanging on either side of him like ghastly trophies at his saddle-bow, still apparently as firmly fastened as ever, and he was endeavoring with feeble struggles, being without feelers, and with only the remnant of a leg, and I know not how many other wounds, to divest himself of them, which at length, after half an hour more, he accom-

---

[3]In the *Iliad* the Greek hero Achilles was killed while trying to revenge the death of his friend Patroclus.

[4]Major battles during the Napoleonic wars.

[5]Americans who lost their lives at the Battle of Concord Bridge during the early days of the American Revolution.

plished. I raised the glass, and he went off over the window-sill in that crippled state. Whether he finally survived that combat, and spent the remainder of his days in some Hôtel des Invalides,[6] I do not know; but I thought that his industry would not be worth much thereafter. I never learned which party was victorious, nor the cause of the war, but I felt for the rest of that day as if I had my feelings excited and harrowed by witnessing the struggle, the ferocity and carnage, of a human battle before my door.

3   Kirby and Spence tell us that the battles of ants have long been celebrated and the date of them recorded, though they say that Huber[7] is the only modern author who appears to have witnessed them. "Aeneas Sylvius," say they, "after giving a very circumstantial account of one contested with great obstinacy by a great and small species on the trunk of a pear tree," adds that " 'this action was fought in the pontificate of Eugenius the Fourth, in the presence of Nicholas Pistoriensis, an eminent lawyer, who related the whole history of the battle with the greatest fidelity.' A similar engagement between great and small ants is recorded by Olaus Magnus, in which the small ones, being victorious, are said to have buried the bodies of their own soldiers, but left those of their giant enemies a prey to the birds. This event happened previous to the expulsion of the tyrant Christian the Second from Sweden." The battle which I witnessed took place in the Presidency of Polk, five years before the passage of Webster's Fugitive-Slave Bill.

Questions on Content

1. Where does the battle of the ants take place?
2. What are the differences in size and appearance of the combating ants?
3. What does Thoreau speculate were the causes of the battle of the ants?
4. Of the three ants Thoreau observes most closely, only one survives. Which one? What are his wounds? What does Thoreau speculate will become of him?

Questions on Thesis, Purpose, and Structure

1. Where is Thoreau's actual use of description most specific and detailed?
2. Why does Thoreau combine his description of the warring ants with so many comparisons to human warfare?
3. To what extent do these comparisons exaggerate the importance of the battle of the ants? To what extent do they satirize and ridicule human warfare?
4. Are you amused by Thoreau's ironic comparisons between human warfare and ant warfare? Why or why not?
5. What is Thoreau's thesis? Does he ever state it directly?
6. Are you persuaded by the essay that all wars are futile and ultimately ridiculous?
7. In his concluding paragraph Thoreau provides information about historical records of ant warfare. Why does he do so?

----

[6]A home for crippled soldiers in Paris.
[7]Kirby, Spence, and Huber were leading specialists in the study of insects (entomology) during Thoreau's day.

Questions on Style and Diction

1. Find the following words in the essay and determine their definitions in context: internecine war, resolutely, divested, pertinacity, perchance, eminent chip, hireling (paragraph 1); assiduously, carbuncles, saddle-bow, harrowed (paragraph 2); circumstantial, obstinacy, pontificate (paragraph 3).
2. The battle of the ants is fought "between two races of ants" over a "pile of stumps." Is this simply objective description or is Thoreau implying something about the nature of warfare? What are the connotations of a pile of stumps? Why does Thoreau choose to use the word *races* instead of *species*— a word that is more accurate in this instance?
3. At one point in paragraph 1 Thoreau describes the ants as "the red republicans on the one hand, and the black imperialists on the other." To what historical events was he probably alluding? Where else in the essay does he refer to battles between republicans and imperialists? What does Thoreau mean by republicans and imperialists?
4. What is the tone of this essay? Is it sober, angry, lighthearted, reverential, or wry? Defend your answer.

Ideas for Essays

1. Observe ants carefully in some other activity (feeding, cleaning themselves, building their nest) and then write a description of their conduct. Consider using analogies, as Thoreau did, to enliven your writing and clarify your thesis.
2. Observe some other common insect carefully and write an essay describing the insect's behavior and giving your subjective response to the insect.
3. By carefully observing and describing the conflict between a pair of dogs, cats, blue jays, or other common animals, try to reach some conclusions of your own about how human combat differs from combat among animals.

Las Vegas (What?) Las Vegas (Can't Hear You! Too Noisy) Las Vegas!!
Tom Wolfe

Tom Wolfe (1931–   ) was born in Richmond, Virginia, and educated at Washington and Lee University and Yale University, where he earned a Ph.D. in American Studies. He began his career as a reporter for the Springfield, Massachusetts, *Union*, the *Washington Post*, and the New York *Herald-Tribune* and then in the mid-1960s began writing for *New York* magazine, *Harper's*, and *Esquire*, where he developed the colorful, freewheeling writing style that has come to be called "the New Journalism." His books, which study and critique contemporary manners and culture, include among others *The Kandy-Colored Tangerine-Flake Streamline Baby* (1965); *The Electric Kool-Aid Acid Test* (1968) about novelist and cult hero Ken Kesey; *Mauve Gloves & Madmen,*

Clutter & Vine (1976); *The Right Stuff* (1979) about the American space program; and a novel, *The Bonfire of the Vanities* (1987). In his extensive description of Las Vegas from *The Kandy-Colored Tangerine-Flake Streamline Baby*, Wolfe posits that the sensory overkill in Las Vegas is merely an intensification of characteristics that prevail in American culture as a whole.

1   Hernia, hernia, hernia, hernia, hernia, hernia, hernia, hernia, hernia, hernia, hernia, hernia, hernia, HERNia; hernia, HERNia, hernia, hernia, hernia, hernia, HERNia, HERNia, HERNia; hernia, hernia, hernia, hernia, hernia, hernia, hernia, eight is the point, the point is eight; hernia, hernia, HERNia, hernia, hernia, hernia, hernia, all hernia, hernia, HERNia, hernia, hernia, hernia, HERNia, hernia, hernia, hernia, HERNia, hernia, hernia, hernia, hernia

2   "What is all this *hernia hernia* stuff?"

3   This was Raymond talking to the wavy-haired fellow with the stick, the dealer, at the craps table about 3:45 Sunday morning. The stickman had no idea what this big wiseacre was talking about, but he resented the tone. He gave Raymond that patient arch of the eyebrows known as a Red Hook brushoff, which is supposed to convey some such thought as, I am a very tough but cool guy, as you can tell by the way I carry my eyeballs low in the pouches, and if this wasn't such a high-class joint we would take wiseacres like you out back and beat you into jellied madrilene.

4   At this point, however, Raymond was immune to subtle looks.

5   The stickman tried to get the game going again, but every time he would start up his singsong, by easing the words out through the nose, which seems to be the style among craps dealers in Las Vegas — "All right, a new shooter . . . eight is the point, the point is eight" and so on — Raymond would start droning along with him in exactly the same tone of voice, "Hernia, hernia, hernia; hernia, HERNia, HERNia, hernia; hernia, hernia, hernia."

6   Everybody at the craps table was staring in consternation to think that anybody would try to needle a tough, hip, elite *soldat* like a Las Vegas craps dealer. The gold-lamé odalisques of Los Angeles were staring. The Western sports, fifty-eight-year-old men who wear Texas string ties, were staring. The old babes at the slot machines, holding Dixie Cups full of nickels, were staring at the craps tables, but cranking away the whole time.

7   Raymond, who is thirty-four years old and works as an engineer in Phoenix, is big but not terrifying. He has the sort of thatchwork hair that grows so low all along the forehead there is no logical place to part it, but he tries anyway. He has a huge, prognathous jaw, but it is as smooth, soft and round as a melon, so that Raymond's total effect is that of an Episcopal divinity student.

8   The guards were wonderful. They were dressed in cowboy uniforms like Bruce Cabot in *Sundown* and they wore sheriff's stars.

9   "Mister, is there something we can do for you?"

10   "The expression is 'Sir,'" said Raymond. "You said 'Mister.' The expression is 'Sir.' How's your old Cosa Nostra?"

Amazingly, the casino guards were easing Raymond out peaceably, 11
without putting a hand on him. I had never seen the fellow before, but
possibly because I had been following his progress for the last five
minutes, he turned to me and said, "Hey, do you have a car? This wild
stuff is starting again."

The gist of it was that he had left his car somewhere and he wanted 12
to ride up the Strip to the Stardust, one of the big hotel-casinos. I am
describing this big goof Raymond not because he is a typical Las Vegas
tourist, although he has some typical symptoms, but because he is a
good example of the marvelous impact Las Vegas has on the senses.
Raymond's senses were at a high pitch of excitation, the only trouble
being that he was going off his nut. He had been up since Thursday
afternoon, and it was now about 3:45 A.M. Sunday. He had an envelope
full of pep pills—amphetamine—in his left coat pocket and an envelope full of Equanils—meprobamate—in his right pocket, or were the
Equanils in the left and the pep pills in the right? He could tell by
looking, but he wasn't going to look anymore. He didn't care to see how
many were left.

He had been rolling up and down the incredible electric-sign 13
gauntlet of Las Vegas' Strip, U.S. Route 91, where the neon and the par
lamps—bubbling, spiraling, rocketing, and exploding in sunbursts ten
stories high out in the middle of the desert—celebrate one-story casinos. He had been gambling and drinking and eating now and again at
the buffet tables the casinos keep heaped with food day and night, but
mostly hopping himself up with good old amphetamine, cooling himself down with meprobamate, then hooking down more alcohol, until
now, after sixty hours, he was slipping into the symptoms of toxic
schizophrenia.

He was also enjoying what the prophets of hallucinogen call "con- 14
sciousness expansion." The man was psychedelic. He was beginning to
isolate the components of Las Vegas' unique bombardment of the
senses. He was quite right about this *hernia hernia* stuff. Every casino in
Las Vegas is, among the other things, a room full of craps tables with
dealers who keep up a running singsong that sounds as though they are
saying "hernia, hernia, hernia, hernia, hernia" and so on. There they are
day and night, easing a running commentary through their nostrils. What
they have to say contains next to no useful instruction. Its underlying
message is, We are the initiates, riding the crest of chance. That the
accumulated sound comes out "hernia" is merely an unfortunate pho-
netic coincidence. Actually, it is part of something rare and rather grand:
a combination of baroque stimuli that brings to mind the bronze gongs,
no larger than a blue plate, that Louis XIV, his ruff collars larded with the
lint of the foul Old City of Byzantium, personally hunted out in the
bazaars of Asia Minor to provide exotic acoustics for his new palace
outside Paris.

The sounds of the craps dealer will be in, let's say, the middle 15
register. In the lower register will be the sound of the old babes at the
slot machines. Men play the slots too, of course, but one of the indelible
images of Las Vegas is that of the old babes at the row upon row of slot

machines. There they are at six o'clock Sunday morning no less than at three o'clock Tuesday afternoon. Some of them pack their old hummocky shanks into Capri pants, but many of them just put on the old print dress, the same one day after day, and the old hob-heeled shoes, looking like they might be going out to buy eggs in Tupelo, Mississippi. They have a Dixie Cup full of nickels or dimes in the left hand and an Iron Boy work glove on the right hand to keep the callouses from getting sore. Every time they pull the handle, the machine makes a sound much like the sound a cash register makes before the bell rings, then the slot pictures start clattering up from left to right, the oranges, lemons, plums, cherries, bells, bars, buckaroos — the figure of a cowboy riding a bucking bronco. The whole sound keeps churning up over and over again in eccentric series all over the place, like one of those random-sound radio symphonies by John Cage. You can hear it at any hour of the day or night all over Las Vegas. You can walk down Fremont Street at dawn and hear it without even walking in a door, that and the spins of the wheels of fortune, a boring and not very popular sort of simplified roulette, as the tabs flap to a stop. As an overtone, or at times simply as a loud sound, comes the babble of the casino crowds, with an occasional shriek from the craps tables, or, anywhere from 4 P.M. to 6 A.M., the sound of brass instruments or electrified string instruments from the cocktail-lounge shows.

16   The crowd and band sounds are not very extraordinary, of course. But Las Vegas' Muzak is. Muzak pervades Las Vegas from the time you walk into the airport upon landing to the last time you leave the casinos. It is piped out to the swimming pool. It is in the drugstores. It is as if there were a communal fear that someone, somewhere in Las Vegas, was going to be left with a totally vacant minute on his hands.

17   Las Vegas has succeeded in wiring an entire city with this electronic stimulation, day and night, out in the middle of the desert. In the automobile I rented, the radio could not be turned off, no matter which dial you went after. I drove for days in a happy burble of Action Checkpoint News, "Monkey No. 9," "Donna, Donna, the Prima Donna," and picking-and-singing jingles for the Frontier Bank and the Fremont Hotel.

18   One can see the magnitude of the achievement. Las Vegas takes what in other American towns is but a quixotic inflammation of the senses for some poor salary mule in the brief interval between the flagstone rambler and the automatic elevator downtown and magnifies it, foliates it, embellishes it into an institution.

19   For example, Las Vegas is the only town in the world whose skyline is made up neither of buildings, like New York, nor of trees, like Wilbraham, Massachusetts, but signs. One can look at Las Vegas from a mile away on Route 91 and see no buildings, no trees, only signs. But such signs! They tower. They revolve, they oscillate, they soar in shapes before which the existing vocabulary of art history is helpless. I can only attempt to supply names — Boomerang Modern, Palette Curvilinear, Flash Gordon Ming-Alert Spiral, McDonald's Hamburger Parabola, Mint Casino Elliptical, Miami Beach Kidney. Las Vegas' sign makers work so far out beyond the frontiers of conventional studio art that they have no

names themselves for the forms they create. Vaughan Cannon, one of those tall, blond Westerners, the builders of places like Las Vegas and Los Angeles, whose eyes seem to have been bleached by the sun, is in the back shop of the Young Electric Sign Company out on East Charleston Boulevard with Herman Boernge, one of his designers, looking at the model they have prepared for the Lucky Strike Casino sign, and Cannon points to where the sign's two great curving faces meet to form a narrow vertical face and says:

"Well, here we are again — what do we call that?"   20

"I don't know," say Boernge. "It's sort of a nose effect. Call it a   21
nose."

Okay, a nose, but it rises sixteen stories high above a two-story   22
building. In Las Vegas no farseeing entrepreneur buys a sign to fit a building he owns. He rebuilds the building to support the biggest sign he can get up the money for and, if necessary, changes the name. The Lucky Strike Casino today is the Lucky Casino, which fits better when recorded in sixteen stories of flaming peach and incandescent yellow in the middle of the Mojave Desert. In the Young Electric Sign Co. era signs have become the architecture of Las Vegas, and the most whimsical, Yale-seminar-frenzied devices of the two late geniuses of Baroque Modern, Frank Lloyd Wright and Eero Saarinen, seem rather stuffy business, like a jest at a faculty meeting, compared to it. Men like Boernge, Kermit Wayne, Ben Mitchem and Jack Larsen, formerly an artist for Walt Disney, are the designer-sculptor geniuses of Las Vegas, but their motifs have been carried faithfully throughout the town by lesser men, for gasoline stations, motels, funeral parlors, churches, public buildings, flophouses and sauna baths.

Then there is a stimulus that is both visual and sexual — the Las   23
Vegas buttocks décolletage. This is a form of sexually provocative dress seen more and more in the United States, but avoided like Broadway message-embroidered ("Kiss Me, I'm Cold") underwear in the fashion pages, so that the euphemisms have not been established and I have no choice but clinical terms. To achieve buttocks décolletage a woman wears bikini-style shorts that cut across the round fatty masses of the buttocks rather than cupping them from below, so that the outer-lower edges of these fatty masses, or "cheeks," are exposed. I am in the cocktail lounge of the Hacienda Hotel, talking to managing director Dick Taylor about the great success his place has had in attracting family and tour groups, and all around me the waitresses are bobbing on their high heels, bare legs and décolletage-bare backsides, set off by pelvis length lingerie of an uncertain denomination. I stare, but I am new here. At the White Cross Rexall drugstore on the Strip a pregnant brunette walks in off the street wearing black shorts with buttocks décolletage aft and illusion-of-cloth nylon lingerie hanging fore, and not even the old mom's-pie pensioners up near the door are staring. They just crank away at the slot machines. On the streets of Las Vegas, not only the show girls, of which the town has about two hundred fifty, bona fide, in residence, but girls of every sort, including, especially, Las Vegas' little high-school buds, who adorn what locals seeking roots in the sand call "our city of

churches and schools," have taken up the chic of wearing buttocks décolletage step-ins under flesh-tight slacks, with the outline of the undergarment showing through fashionably. Others go them one better. They achieve the effect of having been dipped once, briefly, in Helenca stretch nylon. More and more they look like those wonderful old girls out of Flash Gordon who were wrapped just once over in Baghdad pantaloons of clear polyethylene with only Flash Gordon between them and the insane red-eyed assaults of the minions of Ming. It is as if all the hip young suburban gals of America named Lana, Deborah and Sandra, who gather wherever the arc lights shine and the studs steady their coiffures in the plate-glass reflection, have convened in Las Vegas with their bouffant hair above and anatomically stretch-pant-swathed little bottoms below, here on the new American frontier. But exactly!

Questions on Content

1. What does the essay's title suggest about Las Vegas?
2. Why does Raymond begin his "hernia" chant whenever the stickman starts trying to get the crap game going? What has caused Raymond's distress?
3. Raymond is described in paragraph 7 as resembling an Episcopal divinity student. Does he seem to fit in with the other gamblers? What do they look like?
4. What sounds predominate in Las Vegas?
5. How tall are the signs in front of the casinos? How tall are the casinos?
6. What is Las Vegas buttocks décolletage?

Questions on Thesis, Purpose, and Structure

1. What typifies Las Vegas and differentiates it from other American cities?
2. Wolfe uses both narration and dialogue in paragraphs 1–11, but his emphasis is still on description. How do those first paragraphs help to introduce Wolfe's thesis about the effect of Las Vegas on the senses?
3. What do we learn about the sounds (paragraphs 1–17) and sights (paragraphs 18–23) of Las Vegas?
4. Is Wolfe successful in persuading us that Las Vegas is defined by its assault on the senses? To what extent does he use entertaining information in proving his point?

Questions on Style and Diction

1. Find the following words in the essay and determine their definitions in context: wiseacre, jellied madrilene (paragraph 3); consternation, elite *soldat*, gold-lamé odalisques (paragraph 6); prognathous jaw (paragraph 7); baroque stimuli (paragraph 14); indelible, hummocky shanks (paragraph 15); foliates (paragraph 18); oscillate (paragraph 19); entrepreneur (paragraph 22); décolletage, euphemisms, minions, coiffures (paragraph 23).
2. Wolfe's journalistic style is certainly unique and—some would say—even revolutionary. By carefully examining one paragraph (paragraph 23, for example) try to define the characteristics of that style.

Ideas for Essays

1. Assume that you are a cub reporter who overhears your editor's outraged reaction to Tom Wolfe's essay. "Buttocks décolletage!" he roars. "We can't print a description of buttocks décolletage! It's vulgar and offensive." Write a memo to your editor in which you argue that Wolfe's piece should be published without alteration.

2. Write a description of your own home community or of your college or university community. Be sure to develop some unified subjective impression that can serve as your thesis.

On Seeing

Annie Dillard

Annie Dillard (1945–   ) was born and raised in Pittsburgh and educated at Hollins College in Roanoke, Virginia, where she received a B.A. and an M.A. in English literature. During her years at Hollins, Dillard lived by Tinker Creek in a valley among the Blue Ridge Mountains. While there she began to keep a journal in which she recorded detailed observations of the natural world around her, together with quotations, odds and ends of scientific information, and her own religious speculations. These entries, some 1100 in number, which she ultimately transferred to index cards, became the basis of her highly acclaimed first book, *Pilgrim at Tinker Creek* (1974), for which she earned the Pulitzer Prize for nonfiction in 1975. *Pilgrim at Tinker Creek* clearly owes a debt to Thoreau's *Walden*, a work Dillard had chosen as the subject of her master's thesis. That indebtedness is seen not only in the book's poetic and celebratory descriptions of nature but also in its insistence on seeing the natural world as a reflection or revelation of "a power that is unfathomably secret, holy, and fleet."

When I was six or seven years old, growing up in Pittsburgh, I used to take a penny of my own and hide it for someone else to find. It was a curious compulsion; sadly, I've never been seized by it since. For some reason I always "hid" the penny along the same stretch of sidewalk up the street. I'd cradle it at the roots of a maple, say, or in a hole left by a chipped-off piece of sidewalk. Then I'd take a piece of chalk and, starting at either end of the block, draw huge arrows leading up to the penny from both directions. After I learned to write I labeled the arrows "SURPRISE AHEAD" or "MONEY THIS WAY." I was greatly excited, during all this arrow-drawing, at the thought of the first lucky passerby who would receive in this way, regardless of merit, a free gift from the universe. But I never lurked about. I'd go straight home and not give the matter another thought, until, some months later, I would be gripped by the impulse to hide another penny.

2   There are lots of things to see, unwrapped gifts and free surprises.
The world is fairly studded and strewn with pennies cast broadside from
a generous hand. But—and this is the point—who gets excited by a
mere penny? If you follow one arrow, if you crouch motionless on a
bank to watch a tremulous ripple thrill on the water, and are rewarded by
the sight of a muskrat kit paddling from its den, will you count that sight
a chip of copper only, and go your rueful way? It is very dire poverty
indeed for a man to be so malnourished and fatigued that he won't stoop
to pick up a penny. But if you cultivate a healthy poverty and simplicity,
so that finding a penny will make your day, then, since the world is in
fact planted in pennies, you have with your poverty bought a lifetime of
days. What you see is what you get.

3   Unfortunately, nature is very much a now-you-see-it, now-you-don't
affair. A fish flashes, then dissolves in the water before my eyes like so
much salt. Deer apparently ascend bodily into heaven; the brightest
oriole fades into leaves. These disappearances stun me into stillness and
concentration; they say of nature that it conceals with a grand noncha-
lance, and they say of vision that it is a deliberate gift, the revelation of a
dancer who for my eyes only flings away her seven veils.

4   For nature does reveal as well as conceal: now-you-don't-see-it,
now-you-do. For a week this September migrating red-winged blackbirds were feeding heavily down by Tinker Creek at the back of the
house. One day I went out to investigate the racket; I walked up to a tree,
an Osage orange, and a hundred birds flew away. They simply materialized out of the tree. I saw a tree, then a whisk of color, then a tree again.
I walked closer and another hundred blackbirds took flight. Not a
branch, not a twig budged: the birds were apparently weightless as well
as invisible. Or, it was as if the leaves of the Osage orange had been
freed from a spell in the form of red-winged blackbirds; they flew from
the tree, caught my eye in the sky, and vanished. When I looked again at
the tree, the leaves had reassembled as if nothing had happened. Finally
I walked directly to the trunk of the tree and a final hundred, the real
diehards, appeared, spread, and vanished. How could so many hide in
the tree without my seeing them? The Osage orange, unruffled, looked
just as it has looked from the house, when three hundred red-winged
blackbirds cried from its crown. I looked upstream where they flew, and
they were gone. Searching, I couldn't spot one. I wandered upstream to
force them to play their hand, but they'd crossed the creek and scattered.
One show to a customer. These appearances catch at my throat; they are
the free gifts, the bright coppers at the roots of trees.

5   It's all a matter of keeping my eyes open. Nature is like one of those
line drawings that are puzzles for children: Can you find hidden in the
tree a duck, a house, a boy, a bucket, a giraffe, and a boot? Specialists can
find the most incredibly hidden things. A book I read when I was young
recommended an easy way to find caterpillars: you simply find some
fresh caterpillar droppings, look up, and there's your caterpillar. More
recently an author advised me to set my mind at ease about those piles of
cut stems on the ground in grassy fields. Field mice make them; they cut

the grass down by degrees to reach the seeds at the head. It seems that when the grass is tightly packed, as in a field of ripe grain, the blade won't topple at a single cut through the stem; instead, the cut stem simply drops vertically, held in the crush of grain. The mouse severs the bottom again and again, the stem keeps dropping an inch at a time, and finally the head is low enough for the mouse to reach the seeds. Meanwhile the mouse is positively littering the field with its little piles of cut stems into which, presumably, the author is constantly stumbling.

If I can't see these minutiae, I still try to keep my eyes open. I'm 6 always on the lookout for ant lion traps in sandy soil, monarch pupae near milkweed, skipper larvae in locust leaves. These things are utterly common, and I've not seen one. I bang on hollow trees near water, but so far no flying squirrels have appeared. In flat country I watch every sunset in hopes of seeing the green ray. The green ray is a seldom-seen streak of light that rises from the sun like a spurting fountain at the moment of sunset; it throbs into the sky for two seconds and disappears. One more reason to keep my eyes open. A photography professor at the University of Florida just happened to see a bird die in midflight; it jerked, died, dropped, and smashed on the ground.

I squint at the wind because I read Stewart Edward White: "I have 7 always maintained that if you looked closely enough you could *see* the wind—the dim, hardly-made-out, fine débris fleeing high in the air." White was an excellent observer, and devoted an entire chapter of *The Mountains* to the subject of seeing deer: "As soon as you can forget the naturally obvious and construct an artificial obvious, then you too will see deer."

But the artificial obvious is hard to see. My eyes account for less than 8 1 percent of the weight of my head; I'm bony and dense; I see what I expect. I just don't know what the lover knows; I can't see the artificial obvious that those in the know construct. The herpetologist asks the native, "Are there snakes in the ravine?" "No, sir." And the herpetologist comes home with, yessir, three bags full. Are there butterflies on that mountain? Are the bluets in bloom? Are there arrowheads here, or fossil ferns in the shale?

Peeping through my keyhole I see within the range of only about 9 30 percent of the light that comes from the sun; the rest is infrared and some little ultraviolet, perfectly apparent to many animals, but invisible to me. A nightmare network of ganglia, charged and firing without my knowledge, cuts and splices what I do see, editing it for my brain. Donald E. Carr points out that the sense impressions of one-celled animals are *not* edited for the brain: "This is philosophically interesting in a rather mournful way, since it means that only the simplest animals perceive the universe as it is."

A fog that won't burn away drifts and flows across my field of vision. 10 When you see fog move against a backdrop of deep pines, you don't see the fog itself, but streaks of clearness floating across the air in dark shreds. So I see only tatters of clearness through a pervading obscurity. I can't distinguish the fog from the overcast sky; I can't be sure if the light is direct or reflected. Everywhere darkness and the presence of the unseen appalls. We estimate now that only one atom dances alone in every cubic meter of intergalactic space. I blink and squint. What planet or power yanks Halley's Comet out of orbit? We haven't seen it yet; it's a question of distance, density, and the pallor of reflected light. We rock, cradled in the swaddling band of darkness. Even the simple darkness of night whispers suggestions to the mind. This summer, in August, I stayed at the creek too late.

11   Where Tinker Creek flows under the sycamore log bridge to the tear-shaped island, it is slow and shallow, fringed thinly in cattail marsh. At this spot an astonishing bloom of life supports vast breeding populations of insects, fish, reptiles, birds, and mammals. On windless summer evenings I stalk along the creek bank or straddle the sycamore log in absolute stillness, watching for muskrats. The night I stayed too late I was hunched on the log staring spellbound at spreading, reflected stains of lilac on the water. A cloud in the sky suddenly lighted as if turned on by a switch; its reflection just as suddenly materialized on the water upstream, flat and floating, so that I couldn't see the creek bottom, or life in the water under the cloud. Downstream, away from the cloud on the water, water turtles smooth as beans were gliding down with the current in a series of easy, weightless push-offs, as men bound on the moon. I didn't know whether to trace the progress of one turtle I was sure of, risking sticking my face in one of the bridge's spider webs made invisible by the gathering dark, or take a chance on seeing the carp, or scan the mudbank in hope of seeing a muskrat, or follow the last of the swallows who caught at my heart and trailed it after them like streamers as they appeared from directly below, under the log, flying upstream with their tails forked, so fast.

12   But shadows spread and deepened and stayed. After thousands of years we're still strangers to darkness, fearful aliens in an enemy camp with our arms crossed over our chests. I stirred. A land turtle on the bank, startled, hissed the air from its lungs and withdrew to its shell. An uneasy pink here, an unfathomable blue there, gave great suggestion of lurking beings. Things were going on. I couldn't see whether that rustle I heard was a distant rattle-snake, slit-eyed, or a nearby sparrow kicking in the dry flood debris slung at the foot of a willow. Tremendous action roiled the water everywhere I looked, big action, inexplicable. A tremor welled up beside a gaping muskrat burrow in the bank and I caught my breath, but no muskrat appeared. The ripples continued to fan upstream with a steady, powerful thrust. Night was knitting an eyeless mask over my face, and I still sat transfixed. A distant airplane, a delta wing out of nightmare, made a gliding shadow on the creek's bottom that looked like a stingray cruising upstream. At once a black fin slit the pink cloud on the water, shearing it in two. The two halves merged together and seemed to dissolve before my eyes. Darkness pooled in the cleft of the creek and rose, as water collects in a well. Untamed, dreaming lights flickered over the sky. I saw hints of hulking underwater shadows, two pale splashes out of the water, and round ripples rolling close together from a blackened center.

13   At last I stared upstream where only the deepest violet remained of

the cloud, a cloud so high its underbelly still glowed, its feeble color reflected from a hidden sky lighted in turn by a sun halfway to China. And out of that violet, a sudden enormous black body arced over the water. Head and tail, if there was a head and tail, were both submerged in cloud. I saw only one ebony fling, a headlong dive to darkness; then the waters closed, and the lights went out.

I walked home in a shivering daze, up hill and down. Later I lay   14
openmouthed in bed, my arms flung wide at my sides to steady the whirling darkness. At this latitude I'm spinning 836 miles an hour round the earth's axis; I feel my sweeping fall as a breakneck arc like the dive of dolphins, and the hollow rushing of wind raises the hairs on my neck and the side of my face. In orbit around the sun I'm moving 64,800 miles an hour. The solar system as a whole, like a merry-go-round unhinged, spins, bobs, and blinks at the speed of 43,200 miles an hour along a course set east of Hercules. Someone has piped and we are dancing a tarantella until the sweat pours. I open my eyes and I see dark, muscled forms curl out of water, with flapping gills and flattened eyes. I close my eyes and I see stars, deep stars giving way to deeper stars, deeper stars bowing to deepest stars at the crown of an infinite cone.

"Still," wrote Van Gogh in a letter, "a great deal of light falls on   15
everything." If we are blinded by darkness, we are also blinded by light. Sometimes here in Virginia at sunset low clouds on the southern or northern horizon are completely invisible in the lighted sky. I only know one is there because I can see its reflection in still water. The first time I discovered this mystery I looked from cloud to no cloud in bewilderment, checking my bearings over and over, thinking maybe the ark of the covenant was just passing by south of Dead Man Mountain. Only much later did I learn the explanation: polarized light from the sky is very much weakened by reflection, but the light in clouds isn't polarized. So invisible clouds pass among visible clouds, till all slide over the mountains; so a greater light extinguishes a lesser as though it didn't exist.

In the great meteor shower of August, the Perseid, I wail all day for   16
the shooting stars I miss. They're out there showering down, committing hara-kiri in a flame of fatal attraction, and hissing perhaps at last into the ocean. But at dawn what looks like a blue dome clamps down over me like a lid on a pot. The stars and planets could smash and I'd never know. Only a piece of ashen moon occasionally climbs up or down the inside of the dome, and our local star without surcease explodes on our heads. We have really only that one light, one source for all power, and yet we must turn away from it by universal decree. Nobody here on the planet seems aware of this strange, powerful taboo, that we all walk about carefully averting our faces, this way and that, lest our eyes be blasted forever.

Darkness appalls and light dazzles; the scrap of visible light that   17
doesn't hurt my eyes hurts my brain. What I see sets me swaying. Size and distance and the sudden swelling of meanings confuse me, bowl me over. I straddle the sycamore log bridge over Tinker Creek in the summer. I look at the lighted creek bottom: snail tracks tunnel the mud in

quavering curves. A crayfish jerks, but by the time I absorb what has happened, he's gone in a billowing smoke screen of silt. I look at the water; minnows and shiners. If I'm thinking minnows, a carp will fill my brain till I scream, I look at the water's surface: skaters, bubbles, and leaves sliding down. Suddenly, my own face, reflected, startles me witless. Those snails have been tracking my face! Finally, with a shuddering wrench of the will, I see clouds, cirrus clouds. I'm dizzy, I fall in.

18   This looking business is risky. Once I stood on a humped rock on nearby Purgatory Mountain, watching through binoculars the great autumn hawk migration below, until I discovered that I was in danger of joining the hawks on a vertical migration of my own. I was used to binoculars, but not, apparently, to balancing on humped rocks while looking through them. I reeled. Everything advanced and receded by turns; the world was full of unexplained foreshortenings and depths. A distant huge object, a hawk the size of an elephant, turned out to be the browned bough of a nearby loblolly pine. I followed a sharp-shinned hawk against a featureless sky, rotating my head unawares as it flew, and when I lowered the glass a glimpse of my own looming shoulder sent me staggering. What prevents the men at Palomar[1] from falling, voiceless and blinded, from their tiny, vaulted chairs?

19   I reel in confusion; I don't understand what I see. With the naked eye I can see two million light-years to the Andromeda galaxy. Often I slop some creek water in a jar, and when I get home I dump it in a white china bowl. After the silt settles I return and see tracings of minute snails on the bottom, a planarian or two winding round the rim of water, roundworms shimmying, frantically, and finally, when my eyes have adjusted to these dimensions, amoebae. At first the amoebae look like *muscae volitantes*, those curled moving spots you seem to see in your eyes when you stare at a distant wall. Then I see the amoebae as drops of water congealed, bluish, translucent, like chips of sky in the bowl. At length I choose one individual and give myself over to its idea of an evening. I see it dribble a grainy foot before it on its wet, unfathomable way. Do its unedited sense impressions include the fierce focus of my eyes? Shall I take it outside and show it Andromeda, and blow its little endoplasm? I stir the water with a finger, in case it's running out of oxygen. Maybe I should get a tropical aquarium with motorized bubblers and lights, and keep this one for a pet. Yes, it would tell its fissioned descendants, the universe is two feet by five, and if you listen closely you can hear the buzzing music of the spheres.

20   Oh, it's mysterious, lamplit evenings here in the galaxy, one after the other. It's one of those nights when I wander from window to window, looking for a sign. But I can't see. Terror and a beauty insoluble are a riband of blue woven into the fringe of garments of things both great and small. No culture explains, no bivouac offers real haven or rest. But it could be that we are not seeing something. Galileo thought comets were an optical illusion. This is fertile ground: since we are

---

[1]An astronomical observatory in California.

certain that they're not, we can look at what our scientists have been saying with fresh hope. What if there are *really* gleaming, castellated cities hung up-side-down over the desert sand? What limpid lakes and cool date palms have our caravans always passed untried? Until, one by one, by the blindest of leaps, we light on the road to these places, we must stumble in darkness and hunger. I turn from the window. I'm blind as a bat, sensing only from every direction the echo of my own thin cries.

I chanced on a wonderful book called *Space and Sight*, by Marius   21
Von Senden. When Western surgeons discovered how to perform safe cataract operations, they ranged across Europe and America operating on dozens of men and women of all ages who had been blinded by cataracts since birth. Von Senden collected accounts of such cases; the histories are fascinating. Many doctors had tested their patients' sense percep- tions and ideas of space both before and after the operations. The vast majority of patients, of both sexes and all ages, had, in Von Senden's opinion, no idea of space whatsoever. Form, distance, and size were so many meaningless syllables. A patient "had no idea of depth, confusing it with roundness." Before the operation a doctor would give a blind patient a cube and a sphere; the patient would tongue it or feel it with his hands, and name it correctly. After the operation the doctor would show the same objects to the patient without letting him touch them; now he had no clue whatsoever to what he was seeing. One patient called lemonade "square" because it pricked on his tongue as a square shape pricked on the touch of his hands. Of another postoperative patient the doctor writes, "I have found in her no notion of size, for example, not even within the narrow limits which she might have en- compassed with the aid of touch. Thus when I asked her to show me how big her mother was, she did not stretch out her hands, but set her two index fingers a few inches apart."

For the newly sighted, vision is pure sensation unencumbered by   22
meaning. When a newly sighted girl saw photographs and paintings, she asked " 'Why do they put those dark marks all over them?' 'Those aren't dark marks,' her mother explained, 'those are shadows. That is one of the ways the eye knows that things have shape. If it were not for shadows, many things would look flat,' 'Well, that is how things do look,' Joan answered. 'Everything looks flat with dark patches.' "

In general the newly sighted see the world as a dazzle of "color-   23
patches." They are pleased by the sensation of color, and learn quickly to name the colors, but the rest of seeing is tormentingly difficult. Soon after his operation a patient "generally bumps into one of these colour- patches and observes them to be substantial, since they resist him as tactual objects do. In walking about it also strikes him — or can if he pays attention — that he is continually passing in between the colours he sees, that he can go past a visual object, that a part of it then steadily disappears from view; and that in spite of this, however he twists and turns — whether entering the room from the door, for example, or re- turning back to it — he always has a visual space in front of him. Thus he

gradually comes to realize that there is also a space behind him, which he does not see."

24   The mental effort involved in these reasonings proves overwhelming for many patients. It oppresses them to realize that they have been visible to people all along, perhaps unattractively so, without their knowledge or consent. A disheartening number of them refuse to use their new vision, continuing to go over objects with their tongues, and lapsing into apathy and despair.

25   On the other hand, many newly sighted people speak well of the world, and teach us how dull our own vision is. To one patient, a human hand, unrecognized, is "something bright and then holes." Shown a bunch of grapes, a boy calls out, "It is dark, blue and shiny. . . . It isn't smooth, it has bumps and hollows." A little girl visits a garden. "She is greatly astonished, and can scarcely be persuaded to answer, stands speechless in front of the tree, which she only names on taking hold of it, and then as 'the tree with the lights in it.' " Another patient, a twenty-two-year-old girl, was dazzled by the world's brightness and kept her eyes shut for two weeks. When at the end of that time she opened her eyes again, she did not recognize any objects, but "the more she now directed her gaze upon everything about her, the more it could be seen how an expression of gratification and astonishment overspread her features; she repeatedly exclaimed: 'Oh God! How beautiful!' "

26   I saw color-patches for weeks after I read this wonderful book. It was summer; the peaches were ripe in the valley orchards. When I woke in the morning, color-patches wrapped round my eyes, intricately, leaving not one unfilled spot. All day long I walked among shifting color-patches that parted before me like the Red Sea and closed again in silence, transfigured, wherever I looked back. Some patches swelled and loomed, while others vanished utterly, and dark marks flitted at random over the whole dazzling sweep. But I couldn't sustain the illusion of flatness. I've been around for too long. Form is condemned to an eternal danse macabre with meaning: I couldn't unpeach the peaches. Nor can I remember ever having seen without understanding; the color-patches of infancy are lost. My brain then must have been smooth as any balloon. I'm told I reached for the moon; many babies do. But the color-patches of infancy swelled as meaning filled them; they arrayed themselves in solemn ranks down distance which unrolled and stretched before me like a plain. The moon rocketed away. I live now in a world of shadows that shape and distance color, a world where space makes a kind of terrible sense. What Gnosticism[2] is this, and what physics? The fluttering patch I saw in my nursery window—silver and green and shape-shifting blue—is gone; a row of Lombardy poplars takes its place, mute, across the distant lawn. That humming oblong creature pale as light that stole along the walls of my room at night, stretching exhilaratingly around the corners, is gone, too, gone the night I ate of the bittersweet fruit, put two and two together and puckered

_____

[2]Pretension to esoteric spiritual knowledge.

forever my brain. Martin Buber tells this tale: "Rabbi Mendel once boasted to his teacher Rabbi Elimelekh that evenings he saw the angel who rolls away the light before the darkness, and mornings the angel who rolls away the darkness before the light. 'Yes,' said Rabbi Elimelekh, 'in my youth I saw that too. Later on you don't see these things anymore.'"

27 Why didn't someone hand those newly sighted people paints and brushes from the start, when they still didn't know what anything was? Then maybe we all could see color-patches too, the world unraveled from reason, Eden before Adam gave names. The scales would drop from my eyes; I'd see trees like men walking; I'd run down the road against all orders, hallooing and leaping.

28 Seeing is of course very much a matter of verbalization. Unless I call my attention to what passes before my eyes, I simply won't see it. If Tinker Mountain erupted, I'd be likely to notice. But if I want to notice the lesser cataclysms of valley life, I have to maintain in my head a running description of the present. It's not that I'm observant; it's just that I talk too much. Otherwise, especially in a strange place, I'll never know what's happening. Like a blind man at the ball game, I need a radio.

29 When I see this way I analyze and pry. I hurl over logs and roll away stones; I study the bank a square foot at a time, probing and tilting my head. Some days when a mist covers the mountains, when the muskrats won't show and the microscope's mirror shatters, I want to climb up the blank blue dome as a man would storm the inside of a circus tent, wildly, dangling, and with a steel knife claw a rent in the top, peep, and, if I must, fall.

30 But there is another kind of seeing that involves a letting go. When I see this way I sway transfixed and emptied. The difference between the two ways of seeing is the difference between walking with and without a camera. When I walk with a camera I walk from shot to shot, reading the light on a calibrated meter. When I walk without a camera, my own shutter opens, and the moment's light prints on my own silver gut. When I see this second way I am above all an unscrupulous observer.

31 It was sunny one evening last summer at Tinker Creek; the sun was low in the sky, upstream. I was sitting on the sycamore log bridge with the sunset at my back, watching the shiners the size of minnows who were feeding over the muddy sand in skittery schools. Again and again, one fish, then another, turned for a split second across the current and flash! the sun shot out from its silver side. I couldn't watch for it. It was always just happening somewhere else, and it drew my vision just as it disappeared: flash! like a sudden dazzle of the thinnest blade, a sparking over a dun and olive ground at chance intervals from every direction. Then I noticed white specks, some sort of pale petals, small, floating from under my feet on the creek's surface, very slow and steady. So I blurred my eyes and gazed toward the brim of my hat and saw a new world. I saw the pale white circles roll up, roll up, like the world's turning, mute and perfect, and I saw the linear flashes, gleaming silver,

like stars being born at random down a rolling scroll of time. Something broke and something opened. I filled up like a new wineskin. I breathed an air like light; I saw a light like water. I was the lip of a fountain the creek filled forever; I was ether, the leaf in a zephyr; I was flesh-flake, feather, bone.

32   When I see this way I see truly. As Thoreau says, I return to my senses. I am the man who watches the baseball game in silence in an empty stadium. I see the game purely; I'm abstracted and dazed. When it's all over and the white-suited players lope off the green field to their shadowed dugouts, I leap to my feet, I cheer and cheer.

33   But I can't go out and try to see this way. I'll fail, I'll go mad. All I can do is try to gag the commentator, to hush the noise of useless interior babble that keeps me from seeing just as surely as a newspaper dangled before my eyes. The effort is really a discipline requiring a lifetime of dedicated struggle; it marks the literature of saints and monks of every order east and west, under every rule and no rule, discalced and shod. The world's spiritual geniuses seem to discover universally that the mind's muddy river, this ceaseless flow of trivia and trash, cannot be dammed, and that trying to dam it is a waste of effort that might lead to madness. Instead you must allow the muddy river to flow unheeded in the dim channels of consciousness; you raise your sights; you look along it, mildly, acknowledging its presence without interest and gazing beyond it into the realm of the real where subjects and objects act and rest purely, without utterance. "Launch into the deep," says Jacques Ellul, "and you shall see."

34   The secret of seeing, then, is the pearl of great price. If I thought he could teach me to find it and keep it forever I would stagger barefoot across a hundred deserts after any lunatic at all. But although the pearl may be found, it may not be sought. The literature of illumination reveals this above all: although it comes to those who wait for it, it is always, even to the most practiced and adept, a gift and a total surprise. I return from one walk knowing where the killdeer nests in the field by the creek and the hour the laurel blooms. I return from the same walk a day later scarcely knowing my own name. Litanies hum in my ears; my tongue flaps in my mouth, *Alim non*, alleluia! I cannot cause light; the most I can do is try to put myself in the path of its beam. It is possible, in deep space, to sail on solar wind. Light, be it particle or wave, has force: you rig a giant sail and go. The secret of seeing is to sail on solar wind. Hone and spread your spirit till you yourself are a sail, whetted, translucent, broadside to the merest puff.

35   When her doctor took her bandages off and led her into the garden, the girl who was no longer blind saw "the tree with the lights in it." It was for this tree I searched through the peach orchards of summer, in the forests of fall and down winter and spring for years. Then one day I was walking along Tinker Creek thinking of nothing at all and I saw the tree with the lights in it. I saw the backyard cedar where the mourning doves roost charged and transfigured, each cell buzzing with flame. I stood on the grass with the lights in it, grass that was wholly fire, utterly

focused and utterly dreamed. It was less like seeing than like being for the first time seen, knocked breathless by a powerful glance. The flood of fire abated, but I'm still spending the power. Gradually the lights went out in the cedar, the colors died, the cells unflamed and disappeared. I was still ringing. I had been my whole life a bell, and never knew it until at that moment I was lifted and struck. I have since only very rarely seen the tree with the lights in it. The vision comes and goes, mostly goes, but I live for it, for the moment when the mountains open and a new light roars in spate through the crack, and the mountains slam.

Questions on Content

1. What does Dillard mean when she writes that "vision is a deliberate gift" (paragraph 3)?
2. What does the anecdote about the red-wing blackbirds (paragraph 4) show about the observation of nature? What other anecdotes in the next two paragraphs make the same point?
3. What physical limits on human perception are explored in paragraph 9?
4. What things do we fail to see because of too much light (paragraphs 15–16)?
5. What medical operation has allowed many blind persons suddenly to see again?

Questions on Thesis, Purpose, and Structure

1. How is the introductory anecdote about hiding pennies along the sidewalk related to the essay's topic and thesis?
2. Suppose that you are a copy editor of a magazine and you have been asked to insert the following subheadings as appropriate within Dillard's essay. In what order are these topics discussed and where does each discussion begin? Subheadings: Unwrapped Gifts and Free Surprises, When the Blind Begin to See, Reeling in Confusion, Dazzled by Light, Dazed by Darkness, Analyzing and Experiencing.
3. Dillard's reflections on seeing grew out of a series of journal entries about her life on Tinker Creek. How successful has Dillard been at meeting the needs of an audience? To what extent do these still seem purely personal reminiscences and to what extent are they molded to appeal to readers?

Questions on Style and Diction

1. Find the following words in the essay and determine their definitions in context: compulsion (paragraph 1); tremulous (paragraph 2); minutiae (paragraph 6); herpetologist (paragraph 8); ganglia (paragraph 9); pervading obscurity (paragraph 10); unfathomable, inexplicable, welled up, cleft (paragraph 12); surcease, averting (paragraph 16); planarian, amoebae, endoplasm, fissioned (paragraph 19); bivouac, castellated (paragraph 20); danse macabre (paragraph 26); cataclysms (paragraph 28); unscrupulous (paragraph 30); zephyr (paragraph 31); discalced (paragraph 33); litanies, whetted (paragraph 34).
2. Dillard frequently uses similes and metaphors in this essay. Find three instances of simile or metaphor and discuss their meanings and effects.
3. What is the effect of the details about planetary motion in paragraph 14?

Ideas for Essays

1. Many people remember some moment in life when they were particularly awed by the beauty of nature. If you can remember such an occasion, describe what you saw as vividly as possible.
2. Sight is just one of our five senses. Write an essay about the ways in which we perceive sounds, smells, tastes, or tactile sensations.

The Way to Rainy Mountain
N. Scott Momaday

N. Scott Momaday (1934–   ), a pureblood Kiowa Indian, was born in Lawrence, Oklahoma, and received his early education at Navaho, Apache, and Pueblo reservation schools. He attended the University of New Mexico and earned a Ph.D. in English at Stanford University. He has taught at Stanford and the University of California, Berkeley. His teaching and research interests are the art, history, and culture of the American Indian. His writings include the novel *House of Dawn* (1969), which won the Pulitzer Prize for fiction; a volume of poetry, *Angle of Geese and Other Poems* (1974); and a collection of Kiowa Indian legends, *The Way to Rainy Mountain* (1969). In our excerpt from the last of these, Momaday describes the land of the Kiowas and attempts through that description to explain part of their mythology and their sense of cultural identity.

1   A single knoll rises out of the plain in Oklahoma, north and west of the Wichita Range. For my people, the Kiowas, it is an old landmark, and they gave it the name Rainy Mountain. The hardest weather in the world is there. Winter brings blizzards, hot tornadic winds arise in the spring, and in summer the prairie is an anvil's edge. The grass turns brittle and brown, and it cracks beneath your feet. There are green belts along the rivers and creeks, linear groves of hickory and pecan, willow and witch hazel. At a distance in July or August the steaming foliage seems almost to writhe in fire. Great green and yellow grasshoppers are everywhere in the tall grass, popping up like corn to sting the flesh, and tortoises crawl about on the red earth, going nowhere in the plenty of time. Loneliness is an aspect of the land. All things in the plain are isolate; there is no confusion of objects in the eye, but *one* hill or *one* tree or *one* man. To look upon that landscape in the early morning, with the sun at your back, is to lose the sense of proportion. Your imagination comes to life, and this, you think, is where Creation was begun.

2   I returned to Rainy Mountain in July. My grandmother had died in the spring, and I wanted to be at her grave. She had lived to be very old and at last infirm. Her only living daughter was with her when she died, and I was told that in death her face was that of a child.

I like to think of her as a child. When she was born, the Kiowas were living the last great moment of their history. For more than a hundred years they had controlled the open range from the Smoky Hill River to the Red, from the headwaters of the Canadian to the fork of the Arkansas and Cimarron. In alliance with the Comanches, they had ruled the whole of the southern Plains. War was their sacred business, and they were among the finest horsemen the world has ever known. But warfare for the Kiowas was preeminently a matter of disposition rather than of survival, and they never understood the grim, unrelenting advance of the U.S. Cavalry. When at last, divided and ill-provisioned, they were driven onto the Staked Plains in the cold rains of autumn, they fell into panic. In Palo Duro Canyon they abandoned their crucial stores to pillage and had nothing then but their lives. In order to save themselves, they surrendered to the soldiers at Fort Sill and were imprisoned in the old stone corral that now stands as a military museum. My grandmother was spared the humiliation of those high gray walls by eight or ten years, but she must have known from birth the affliction of defeat, the dark brooding of old warriors. 3

Her name was Aho, and she belonged to the last culture to evolve in North America. Her forebears came down from the high country in western Montana nearly three centuries ago. They were a mountain people, a mysterious tribe of hunters whose language has never been positively classified in any major group. In the late seventeenth century they began a long migration to the south and east. It was a journey toward the dawn, and it led to a golden age. Along the way the Kiowas were befriended by the Crows, who gave them the culture and religion of the Plains. They acquired horses, and their ancient nomadic spirit was suddenly free of the ground. They acquired Tai-me, the sacred Sun Dance doll, from that moment the object and symbol of their worship, and so shared in the divinity of the sun. Not least, they acquired the sense of destiny, therefore courage and pride. When they entered upon the southern Plains they had been transformed. No longer were they slave to the simple necessity of survival; they were a lordly and dangerous society of fighters and thieves, hunters and priests of the sun. According to their origin myth, they entered the world through a hollow log. From one point of view, their migration was the fruit of an old prophecy, for indeed they emerged from a sunless world. 4

Although my grandmother lived out her long life in the shadow of Rainy Mountain, the immense landscape of the continental interior lay like memory in her blood. She could tell of the Crows, whom she had never seen, and of the Black Hills, where she had never been. I wanted to see in reality what she had seen more perfectly in the mind's eye, and traveled fifteen hundred miles to begin my pilgrimage. 5

Yellowstone, it seemed to me, was the top of the world, a region of deep lakes and dark timber, canyons and waterfalls. But, beautiful as it is, one might have the sense of confinement there. The skyline in all directions is close at hand, the high wall of the woods and deep cleavages of shade. There is a perfect freedom in the mountains, but it belongs to the eagle and the elk, the badger and the bear. The Kiowas 6 reckoned their stature by the distance they could see, and they were bent and blind in the wilderness.

7   Descending eastward, the highland meadows are a stairway to the plain. In July the inland slope of the Rockies is luxuriant with flax and buckwheat, stonecrop and larkspur. The earth unfolds and the limit of the land recedes. Clusters of trees, and animals grazing far in the distance, cause the vision to reach away and wonder to build upon the mind. The sun follows a longer course in the day, and the sky is immense beyond all comparison. The great billowing clouds that sail upon it are shadows that move upon the grain like water, dividing light. Farther down, in the land of the Crows and Blackfeet, the plain is yellow. Sweet clover takes hold of the hills and bends upon itself to cover and seal the soil. There the Kiowas paused on their way; they had come to the place where they must change their lives. The sun is at home on the plains. Precisely there does it have the certain character of a god. When the Kiowas came to the land of the Crows, they could see the dark lees of the hills at dawn across the Bighorn River, the profusion of light on the grain shelves, the oldest deity ranging after the solstices. Not yet would they veer southward to the caldron of the land that lay below; they must wean their blood from the northern winter and hold the mountains a while longer in their view. They bore Tai-me in procession to the east.

8   A dark mist lay over the Black Hills, and the land was like iron. At the top of a ridge I caught sight of Devil's Tower upthrust against the gray sky as if in the birth of time the core of the earth had broken through its crust and the motion of the world was begun. There are things in nature that engender an awful quiet in the heart of man; Devil's Tower is one of them. Two centuries ago, because they could not do otherwise, the Kiowas made a legend at the base of the rock. My grandmother said:

> Eight children were there at play, seven sisters and their brother. Suddenly the boy was struck dumb; he trembled and began to run upon his hands and feet. His fingers became claws, and his body was covered with fur. Directly there was a bear where the boy had been. The sisters were terrified; they ran, and the bear after them. They came to the stump of a great tree, and the tree spoke to them. It bade them climb upon it, and as they did so it began to rise into the air. The bear came to kill them, but they were just beyond its reach. It reared against the tree and scored the bark all around with its claws. The seven sisters were borne into the sky, and they became the stars of the Big Dipper.

From that moment, and so long as the legend lives, the Kiowas have kinsmen in the night sky. Whatever they were in the mountains, they could be no more. However tenuous their well-being, however much they had suffered and would suffer again, they had found a way out of the wilderness.

9   My grandmother had a reverence for the sun, a holy regard that now is all but gone out of mankind. There was a wariness in her, and an

ancient awe. She was a Christian in her later years, but she had come a long way about, and she never forgot her birthright. As a child she had been to the Sun Dances; she had taken part in those annual rites, and by them she had learned the restoration of her people in the presence of Tai-me. She was about seven when the last Kiowa Sun Dance was held in 1887 on the Washita River above Rainy Mountain Creek. The buffalo were gone. In order to consummate the ancient sacrifice — to impale the head of a buffalo bull upon the medicine tree — a delegation of old men journeyed into Texas, there to beg and barter for an animal from the Goodnight herd. She was ten when the Kiowas came together for the last time as a living Sun Dance culture. They could find no buffalo; they had to hang an old hide from the sacred tree. Before the dance could begin, a company of soldiers rode out from Fort Sill under orders to disperse the tribe. Forbidden without cause the essential act of their faith, having seen the wild herds slaughtered and left to rot upon the ground, the Kiowas backed away forever from the medicine tree. That was July 20, 1890, at the great bend of the Washita. My grandmother was there. Without bitterness, and for as long as she lived, she bore a vision of deicide.

Now that I can have her only in memory, I see my grandmother in the several postures that were peculiar to her: standing at the wood stove on a winter morning and turning meat in a great iron skillet; sitting at the south window, bent above her beadwork, and afterwards, when her vision failed, looking down for a long time into the fold of her hands; going out upon a cane, very slowly as she did when the weight of age came upon her; praying. I remember her most often at prayer. She made long, rambling prayers out of suffering and hope, having seen many things. I was never sure that I had the right to hear, so exclusive were they of all mere custom and company. The last time I saw her she prayed standing by the side of her bed at night, naked to the waist, the light of a kerosene lamp moving upon her dark skin. Her long, black hair, always drawn and braided in the day, lay upon her shoulders and against her breasts like a shawl. I do not speak Kiowa, and I never understood her prayers, but there was something inherently sad in the sound, some merest hesitation upon the syllables of sorrow. She began in a high and descending pitch, exhausting her breath to silence; then again and again — and always the same intensity of effort, of something that is, and is not, like urgency in the human voice. Transported so in the dancing light among the shadows of her room, she seemed beyond the reach of time. But that was illusion; I think I knew then that I should not see her again.

Houses are like sentinels in the plain, old keepers of the weather watch. There, in a very little while, wood takes on the appearance of great age. All colors wear soon away in the wind and rain, and then the wood is burned gray and the grain appears and the nails turn red with rust. The windowpanes are black and opaque; you imagine there is nothing within, and indeed there are many ghosts, bones given up to the land. They stand here and there against the sky, and you approach them for a longer time than you expect. They belong in the distance; it is their domain.

12   Once there was a lot of sound in my grandmother's house, a lot of coming and going, feasting and talk. The summers there were full of excitement and reunion. The Kiowas are a summer people; they abide the cold and keep to themselves, but when the season turns and the land becomes warm and vital they cannot hold still; an old love of going returns upon them. The aged visitors who came to my grandmother's house when I was a child were made of lean and leather, and they bore themselves upright. They wore great black hats and bright ample shirts that shook in the wind. They rubbed fat upon their hair and wound their braids with strips of colored cloth. Some of them painted their faces and carried the scars of old and cherished enmities. They were an old council of warlords, come to remind and be reminded of who they were. Their wives and daughters served them well. The women might indulge themselves; gossip was at once the mark and compensation of their servitude. They made loud and elaborate talk among themselves, full of jest and gesture, fright and false alarm. They went abroad in fringed and flowered shawls, bright beadwork and German silver. They were at home in the kitchen, and they prepared meals that were banquets.

13   There were frequent prayer meetings, and great nocturnal feasts. When I was a child I played with my cousins outside, where the lamplight fell upon the ground and the singing of the old people rose up around us and carried away into the darkness. There were a lot of good things to eat, a lot of laughter and surprise. And afterwards, when the quiet returned, I lay down with my grandmother and could hear the frogs away by the river and feel the motion of the air.

14   Now there is funeral silence in the rooms, the endless wake of some final word. The walls have closed in upon my grandmother's house. When I returned to it in the mourning, I saw for the first time in my life how small it was. It was late at night, and there was a white moon, nearly full. I sat for a long time on the stone steps by the kitchen door. From there I could see out across the land; I could see the long row of trees by the creek, the low light upon the rolling plains, and the stars of the Big Dipper. Once I looked at the moon and caught sight of a strange thing. A cricket had perched upon the handrail, only a few inches away from me. My line of vision was such that the creature filled the moon like a fossil. It had gone there, I thought, to live and die, for there, of all places, was its small definition made whole and eternal. A warm wind rose up and purled like the longing within me.

15   The next morning I awoke at dawn and went out on the dirt road to Rainy Mountain. It was already hot, and the grasshoppers began to fill the air. Still, it was early in the morning, and the birds sang out of the shadows. The long yellow grass on the mountain shone in the bright light, and a scissortail hied above the land. There, where it ought to be, at the end of a long and legendary way, was my grandmother's grave. Here and there on the dark stone were ancestral names. Looking back once, I saw the mountain and came away.

Questions on Content

1. Why did Momaday return to Rainy Mountain?
2. Where did Momaday's grandmother live out her life?
3. On a map of the western United States, locate the Smoky Hill River (in central Kansas), the Red River (on the Texas–Oklahoma border), the headwaters of the Canadian River (in northeastern New Mexico), and the fork of the Arkansas and Cimarron rivers (in northeastern Oklahoma). Why does Momaday choose to define the range of the Kiowas by naming these rivers instead of mentioning the states involved?
4. Where had the forebears of the Kiowas lived?
5. What factors brought about the "golden age" of the Kiowas, and how long did that golden age last?
6. What was the attitude of the Kiowas toward the sun, and how was that attitude predicated on their descent from the mountains to the plains?
7. Why was the U.S. Cavalry able to defeat the Kiowas, "the finest horsemen the world has ever known"?
8. What two factors caused the failure of the Kiowa's last attempted Sun Dance?
9. Where was Momaday's grandmother buried?

Questions on Thesis, Purpose, and Structure

1. Briefly summarize the history of the Kiowa people on "the way to Rainy Mountain."
2. Briefly summarize the life of Momaday's grandmother on her "way to Rainy Mountain."
3. Why does Momaday interweave the story of the Kiowa people with the story of his grandmother? What are the parallels between the two life histories?
4. Momaday's essay clearly has its narrative elements, but his primary goal is to describe. What is the subject of his description? What is Momaday's main point—or thesis—about the object of his description?
5. Momaday supplies a great deal of information about the culture and history of the Kiowas. How does that information help him to develop his thesis?

Questions on Style and Diction

1. Find the following words in the essay and determine their definitions in context: preeminently, disposition, unrelenting, pillage, affliction (paragraph 3); nomadic (paragraph 4); lees, profusion, solstices, caldron (paragraph 7); engender, tenuous (paragraph 8); consummate, disperse, deicide (paragraph 9); inherently (paragraph 10); sentinels, opaque (paragraph 11); cherished enmities (paragraph 12); nocturnal (paragraph 13); purled (paragraph 14); hied (paragraph 15).
2. How would you describe the mood that is created by Momaday's essay? Is it cheerful or melancholy? Energetic or reflective? Cite details from the essay to support your view.
3. How would you describe Momaday's attitude toward his grandmother's death? Is he deeply stricken with grief and remorse? Or is he calmly contemplative? Cite details to support your view.
4. How would you describe Momaday's style? Is it poetic or prosaic? And is Momaday's style well suited to his goals in the essay? Explain your viewpoint by citing relevant details.

Ideas for Essays

1. Look into your own ethnic, racial, and family background. Then attempt to write an essay, like Momaday's, that describes your "people."
2. Think back to times you spent in your grandmother's home. Then write an essay describing that home and attempting to show how it reflects your grandmother's heritage and individuality.

The Grave

Katherine Anne Porter

Katherine Anne Porter (1890–1980) began her career as a newspaper reporter and free-lance writer before turning her attention to the writing of short fiction. Her first collection, *Flowering Judas and Other Stories*, appeared in 1930 and won immediate critical attention for its rich prose style and technical craftsmanship, its insight into the psychology of human relationships, and its effective use of myth and symbol. A number of her works, including the first six stories of the collection entitled *The Leaning Tower* (1944) and two short novels published together in 1939, *Old Mortality* and *Pale Horse, Pale Rider*, focus on the young, inexperienced girl Miranda and follow her slow and often painful discovery of the uncertain world of adulthood. In "The Grave" (from *The Leaning Tower*), Porter tells of Miranda's growing understanding of the cycle of life from birth to death. Although the story is a narrative, description plays an important part in it. Pay especially close attention to the description of the grave and its treasures, the dead rabbit, and the final scene in the Indian marketplace.

1   The grandfather, dead for more than thirty years, had been twice disturbed in his long repose by the constancy and possessiveness of his widow. She removed his bones first to Louisiana and then to Texas as if she had set out to find her own burial place, knowing well she would never return to the places she had left. In Texas she set up a small cemetery in a corner of her first farm, and as the family connection grew, and oddments of relations came over from Kentucky to settle, it contained at last about twenty graves. After the grandmother's death, part of her land was to be sold for the benefit of certain of her children, and the cemetery happened to lie in the part set aside for sale. It was necessary to take up the bodies and bury them again in the family plot in the big new public cemetery, where the grandmother had been buried. At last her husband was to lie beside her for eternity, as she had planned.

2   The family cemetery had been a pleasant small neglected garden of tangled rose bushes and ragged cedar trees and cypress, the simple flat stones rising out of uncropped sweet-smelling wild grass. The graves

were lying open and empty one burning day when Miranda and her brother Paul, who often went together to hunt rabbits and doves, propped their twenty-two Winchester rifles carefully against the rail fence, climbed over and explored among the graves. She was nine years old and he was twelve.

They peered into the pits all shaped alike with such purposeful 3 accuracy, and looking at each other with pleased adventurous eyes, they said in solemn tones: "These were graves!" trying by words to shape a special, suitable emotion in their minds, but they felt nothing except an agreeable thrill of wonder: they were seeing a new sight, doing something they had not done before. In them both there was also a small disappointment at the entire commonplaceness of the actual spectacle. Even if it had once contained a coffin for years upon years, when the coffin was gone a grave was just a hole in the ground. Miranda leaped into the pit that had held her grandfather's bones. Scratching around aimlessly and pleasurably as any young animal, she scooped up a lump of earth and weighed it in her palm. It had a pleasantly sweet, corrupt smell, being mixed with cedar needles and small leaves, and as the crumbs fell apart, she saw a silver dove no larger than a hazel nut, with spread wings and a neat fan-shaped tail. The breast had a deep round hollow in it. Turning it up to the fierce sunlight, she saw that the inside of the hollow was cut in little whorls. She scrambled out, over the pile of loose earth that had fallen back into one end of the grave, calling to Paul that she had found something, he must guess what . . . His head appeared smiling over the rim of another grave. He waved a closed hand at her. "I've got something too!" They ran to compare treasures, making a game of it, so many guesses each, all wrong, and a final showdown with opened palms. Paul had found a thin wide gold ring carved with intricate flowers and leaves. Miranda was smitten at the sight of the ring and wished to have it. Paul seemed more impressed by the dove. They made a trade, with some little bickering. After he had got the dove in his hand, Paul said, "Don't you know what this is? This is a screw head for a *coffin!* . . . I'll bet nobody else in the world has one like this!"

Miranda glanced at it without covetousness. She had the gold ring 4 on her thumb; it fitted perfectly. "Maybe we ought to go now," she said, "maybe one of the niggers 'll see us and tell somebody." They knew the land had been sold, the cemetery was no longer theirs, and they felt like trespassers. They climbed back over the fence, slung their rifles loosely under their arms—they had been shooting at targets with various kinds of firearms since they were seven years old—and set out to look for the rabbits and doves or whatever small game might happen along. On these expeditions Miranda always followed at Paul's heels along the path, obeying instructions about handling her gun when going through fences; learning how to stand it up properly so it would not slip and fire unexpectedly; how to wait her time for a shot and not just bang away in the air without looking, spoiling shots for Paul, who really could hit things if given a chance. Now and then, in her excitement at seeing birds whizz up suddenly before her face, or a rabbit leap across her very toes, she lost her head, and almost without sighting she flung her rifle up and pulled the trigger. She hardly ever hit any sort of mark. She had no proper sense of hunting at all. Her brother would be often completely disgusted with her. "You don't care whether you get your bird or not," he said. "That's no way to hunt." Miranda could not understand his indignation. She had seen him smash his hat and yell with fury when he had missed his aim. "What I like about shooting," said Miranda, with exasperating inconsequence, "is pulling the trigger and hearing the noise."

5   "Then, by golly," said Paul, "whyn't you go back to the range and shoot at bulls-eyes?"

6   "I'd just as soon," said Miranda, "only like this, we walk around more."

7   "Well, you just stay behind and stop spoiling my shots," said Paul, who, when he made a kill, wanted to be certain he had made it. Miranda, who alone brought down a bird once in twenty rounds, always claimed as her own any game they got when they fired at the same moment. It was tiresome and unfair and her brother was sick of it.

8   "Now, the first dove we see, or the first rabbit, is mine," he told her. "And the next will be yours. Remember that and don't get smarty."

9   "What about snakes?" asked Miranda idly. "Can I have the first snake?"

10   Waving her thumb gently and watching her gold ring glitter, Miranda lost interest in shooting. She was wearing her summer roughing outfit: dark blue overalls, a light blue shirt, a hired-man's straw hat, and thick brown sandals. Her brother had the same outfit except his was a sober hickory-nut color. Ordinarily Miranda preferred her overalls to any other dress, though it was making rather a scandal in the countryside, for the year was 1903, and in the back country the law of female decorum had teeth in it. Her father had been criticized for letting his girls dress like boys and go careering around astride barebacked horses. Big sister Maria, the really independent and fearless one, in spite of her rather affected ways, rode at a dead run with only a rope knotted around her horse's nose. It was said the motherless family was running down, with the Grandmother no longer there to hold it together. It was known that she had discriminated against her son Harry in her will, and that he was in straits about money. Some of his old neighbors reflected with vicious satisfaction that now he would probably not be so stiffnecked, nor have any more high-stepping horses either. Miranda knew this, though she could not say how. She had met along the road old women of the kind who smoked corn-cob pipes, who had treated her grandmother with most sincere respect. They slanted their gummy old eyes side-ways at the granddaughter and said, "Ain't you ashamed of yoself, Missy? It's against the Scriptures to dress like that. Whut yo Pappy thinkin about?" Miranda, with her powerful social sense, which was like a fine set of antennae radiating from every pore of her skin, would feel ashamed because she knew well it was rude and ill-bred to shock anybody, even bad-tempered old crones, though she had faith in her father's judgment and was perfectly comfortable in the clothes. Her father had said,

"They're just what you need, and they'll save your dresses for school . . ." This sounded quite simple and natural to her. She had been brought up in rigorous economy. Wastefulness was vulgar. It was also a sin. These were truths; she had heard them repeated many times and never once disputed.

Now the ring, shining with the serene purity of fine gold on her rather grubby thumb, turned her feelings against her overalls and sockless feet, toes sticking through the thick brown leather straps. She wanted to go back to the farmhouse, take a good cold bath, dust herself with plenty of Maria's violet talcum powder — provided Maria was not present to object, of course — put on the thinnest, most becoming dress she owned, with a big sash, and sit in a wicker chair under the trees . . . These things were not all she wanted, of course; she had vague stirrings of desire for luxury and a grand way of living which could not take precise form in her imagination but were founded on family legend of past wealth and leisure. These immediate comforts were what she could have, and she wanted them at once. She lagged rather far behind Paul, and once she thought of just turning back without a word and going home. She stopped, thinking that Paul would never do that to her, and so she would have to tell him. When a rabbit leaped, she let Paul have it without dispute. He killed it with one shot. 11

When she came up with him, he was already kneeling, examining the wound, the rabbit trailing from his hands. "Right through the head," he said complacently, as if he had aimed for it. He took out his sharp, competent bowie knife and started to skin the body. He did it very cleanly and quickly. Uncle Jimbilly knew how to prepare the skins so that Miranda always had fur coats for her dolls, for though she never cared much for her dolls she liked seeing them in fur coats. The children knelt facing each other over the dead animal. Miranda watched admiringly while her brother stripped the skin away as if he were taking off a glove. The flayed flesh emerged dark scarlet, sleek, firm; Miranda with thumb and finger felt the long fine muscles with the silvery flat strips binding them to the joints. Brother lifted the oddly bloated belly. "Look," he said, in a low amazed voice. "It was going to have young ones." 12

Very carefully he slit the thin flesh from the center ribs to the flanks, and a scarlet bag appeared. He slit again and pulled the bag open, and there lay a bundle a tiny rabbits, each wrapped in a thin scarlet veil. The brother pulled these off and there they were, dark gray, their sleek wet down lying in minute even ripples, like a baby's head just washed, their unbelievably small delicate ears folded close, their little blind faces almost featureless. 13

Miranda said, "Oh, I want to *see*," under her breath. She looked and looked — excited but not frightened, for she was accustomed to the sight of animals killed in hunting — filled with pity and astonishment and a kind of shocked delight in the wonderful little creatures for their own sakes, they were so pretty. She touched one of them ever so carefully, "Ah, there's blood running over them," she said and began to tremble without knowing why. Yet she wanted most deeply to see and to know. 14

Having seen, she felt at once as if she had known all along. The very memory of her former ignorance faded, she had always known just this. No one had ever told her anything outright, she had been rather unobservant of the animal life around her because she was so accustomed to animals. They seemed simply disorderly and unaccountably rude in their habits, but altogether natural and not very interesting. Her brother had spoken as if he had known about everything all along. He may have seen all this before. He had never said a word to her, but she knew now a part at least of what he knew. She understood a little of the secret, formless intuitions in her own mind and body, which had been clearing up, taking form, so gradually and so steadily she had not realized that she was learning what she had to know. Paul said cautiously, as if he were talking about something forbidden: "They were just about ready to be born." His voice dropped on the last word. "I know," said Miranda, "like kittens. I know, like babies." She was quietly and terribly agitated, standing again with her rifle under her arm, looking down at the bloody heap. "I don't want the skin," she said, "I won't have it." Paul buried the young rabbits again in their mother's body, wrapped the skin around her, carried her to a clump of sage bushes, and hid her away. He came out again at once and said to Miranda, with an eager friendliness, a confidential tone quite unusual in him, as if he were taking her into an important secret on equal terms: "Listen now. Now you listen to me, and don't ever forget. Don't you ever tell a living soul that you saw this. Don't tell a soul. Don't tell Dad because I'll get into trouble. He'll say I'm leading you into things you ought not to do. He's always saying that. So now don't you go and forget and blab out sometime the way you're always doing . . . Now, that's a secret. Don't you tell."

15   Miranda never told, she did not wish to tell anybody. She thought about the whole worrisome affair with confused unhappiness for a few days. Then it sank quietly into her mind and was heaped over by accumulated thousands of impressions, for nearly twenty years. One day she was picking her path among the puddles and crushed refuse of a market street in a strange city of a strange country, when without warning, plain and clear in its true colors as if she looked through a frame upon a scene that had not stirred nor changed since the moment it happened, the episode of that far-off day leaped from its burial place before her mind's eye. She was so reasonlessly horrified she halted suddenly staring, the scene before her eyes dimmed by the vision back of them. An Indian vendor had help up before her a tray of dyed sugar sweets, in the shapes of all kinds of small creatures: birds, baby chicks, baby rabbits, lambs, baby pigs. They were in gay colors and smelled of vanilla, maybe. . . . It was a very hot day and the smell in the market, with its piles of raw flesh and wilting flowers, was like the mingled sweetness and corruption she had smelled that other day in the empty cemetery at home: the day she had remembered always until now vaguely as the time she and her brother had found treasure in the open graves. Instantly upon this thought the dreadful vision faded, and she saw clearly her brother, whose childhood face she had forgotten, standing again in the blazing

sunshine, again twelve years old, a pleased sober smile in his eyes, turning the silver dove over and over in his hands.

Questions on Content

1. What do Miranda and Paul find in the open graves?
2. How do Paul and Miranda differ in their attitudes toward hunting?
3. How do Miranda's attitudes toward her clothing change as the story progresses?
4. What do Miranda and Paul discover about the rabbit he shoots? Why doesn't Miranda want the rabbit skin? Why does Paul hide the dead rabbit and swear Miranda to secrecy? What does Miranda learn from the whole episode?
5. What does Miranda see years later that causes "the episode of the far-off day [to leap] from its burial place before her mind's eye"?

Questions on Thesis, Purpose, and Structure

1. How is the episode of the open graves related to the hunting episode, and how are both of these related to Miranda's later memory in India?
2. What kinds of burial are discussed in the story? How is each burial somehow also related to birth and to the cycle of life symbolized by the marriage band?
3. How would you describe Porter's purpose in telling this story? Is she mainly interested in entertaining us with the unique events that happened to Miranda and Paul? Is she interested in informing us about the difference between young boys and girls? Is she interested in portraying a young girl's gradually unfolding sexuality? Is she interested in persuading us of an important connection between birth and burial?

Questions on Style and Diction

1. Find the following words in the story and determine their definitions in context: repose, oddments (paragraph 1); covetousness, exasperating inconsequence (paragraph 4); careering, affected, straits (paragraph 10); complacently (paragraph 12).
2. Where in Porter's story does she make the most extensive use of description? How important are these passages of description to the story that Porter wishes to tell?
3. What are the connotations and symbolic associations of the dove and the ring? What does it show about Miranda that she prefers the ring and about Paul that he prefers the dove?

Ideas for Essays

1. Write an essay in which you argue that the meaning of Porter's story hinges on its passages of description.
2. Write an essay in which you recount your first true recognition of the meaning of death. Be sure to use description heavily in your essay.
3. Write an essay in which you recount your first true recognition of the origin of life. Be sure to use description heavily in your essay.

◇◇◇

"The 100 Greatest Books Ever Written"
"America, We Built It for You:
The Atari 520ST"

Clearly, description is one of the most common elements in advertising. Not only is a product normally pictured in an advertisement, but its composition, appearance, dimensions, and utility are usually also described in words. The Sears and Penney's catalogs amply display this kind of advertising.

The two advertisements reproduced on the following pages make more complex and interesting use of description than is the case in catalogs. The problem for the copywriter of "The 100 Greatest Books Ever Written" was to explain how the quality of these volumes justified their relatively high price ($35 apiece). Hence the advertisement is at least in part governed by the "thesis" in its first subheading: "The volumes themselves are works of art."

In "America, We Built It for You," the copywriter's challenges were quite different. At the time, the price of the Atari 520ST was exceptionally low for a machine of its capabilities; however, the public impression of Atari computers was molded by the company's earlier eight-bit machines and by its video-game units. The copywriter wanted to change that popular impression by demonstrating the state-of-the-art capabilities of the new Atari 520ST. The general technique for doing so was a campaign based on the theme "power without the price," but in this particular advertisement (which appeared during the bicentennial of the American Revolution), the color-graphics capabilities of the machine are highlighted. The advertisement (which we have reproduced only in black and white) is dominated by the red, white, and blue of the American flag—visually emphasizing the computer's color graphics and at the same time suggesting that this is a product made in America.

IDEAS FOR DISCUSSION AND WRITING ABOUT "THE 100 GREATEST BOOKS EVER WRITTEN"

Questions on Content

1. What is being advertised?
2. How much will each item cost?
3. How long can you count on the same price?
4. Why is each item so valuable?

Questions on Thesis, Purpose, and Structure

1. Compared with paperback books, these volumes are quite expensive. What arguments are presented in an effort to persuade you that the books are well worth the price?
2. How fully are the books described? What principle has the writer followed in selecting descriptive details?
3. Consider the various headings and subheadings used in this advertisement. How successful are they in gaining your interest and attention? How successful are they in summarizing the content? How successful are they in persuading you to continue reading?

Questions on Style and Diction

1. How many times does the advertisement mention the "genuine leather bindings" and the use of 22kt gold? Is this repetition necessary? Is it desirable?
2. The advertisement only once mentions the use of "acid-neutral paper." Why is that relatively important aspect of the books almost ignored?

Ideas for Essays

1. This advertisement emphasizes the value and luxuriousness of these books. Try rewriting the advertisement to emphasize their durability instead.
2. Make up an advertisement for a series of the "100 Greatest Books Ever Written" to be offered for sale in an inexpensive paperback series.

IDEAS FOR DISCUSSION AND WRITING ABOUT "AMERICA, WE BUILT IT FOR YOU: THE ATARI 520ST"

Questions on Content

1. What is the Atari 520ST?
2. What standard features are part of the machine?
3. How much does the Atari 520ST cost?

Questions on Thesis, Purpose, and Structure

1. Where is the thesis of the advertisement most clearly stated?
2. Do the various descriptive details in the advertisement support the thesis?
3. Can you discover the organizing pattern that governs the description?
4. Is this advertisement informative? Is it persuasive? Is it entertaining?
5. What sort of person is most likely to pay attention to this advertisement? Do you think that the Atari 520ST itself is well designed to appeal to such a person?

Questions on Style and Diction

1. What words or phrases in the advertisement could be called jargon?
2. Do you think that the frequent use of technical jargon is appropriate or inappropriate? (Note that this advertisement appeared primarily in computer magazines.)
3. How and why does the Atari Corporation attempt to associate the machine with America?

Ideas for Essays

1. Compare three or four advertisements for computers. Based on these advertisements, describe the ideal purchaser of each machine.
2. Write a brief advertisement, filled with high-tech jargon, for a common wood pencil.

It is not difficult to list the world's greatest books. The titles and authors leap quickly to mind. And for good reason. The books that have been recognized as great, generation after generation, are part of the world we live in. They have shaped our lives, our language, our values, our outlook.

These books include novels like Melville's *Moby Dick*, Dickens' *A Tale of Two Cities*, Hawthorne's *Scarlet Letter*, Bronte's *Wuthering Heights*. They include serious—yet highly readable—works of thought like Plato's *Republic*... heroic epics like Homer's *Iliad*...sharp-witted satire like Swift's *Gulliver's Travels*...brilliant poetry like Whitman's *Leaves of Grass*.

On everyone's list would be the great works of Shakespeare, Chaucer, Dante, Darwin, and Twain. These are books you want on your bookshelf. Books you want your children and their children to read. And now you can have them—the ultimate private library.

The Volumes Themselves are Works of Art

Your pride in this collection will be two-fold—arising both from the significance and stature of each literary masterpiece...and from the sheer beauty of each volume. Every volume in this unique private library will exemplify the ultimate in the art of printing, binding, and illustration.

Genuine Leather Bindings

Today it is rare to find books bound in genuine leather. The cost of such bindings and the time required to create them has made the crafting of such bindings an almost vanishing art. **But each book in this collection will be bound in genuine leather!**

Intricate Cover Designs Accented With Real 22kt Gold

Each luxurious leather binding will be deeply inlaid with real gold on the spine and in perfectly-matched golden designs on the front and back covers. Then to bring out the full beauty of each cover design, the pages will be gilded along all three sides with a special golden finish.

Elegant Finishing Touches

Each volume will have beautiful endsheets of rich moiré fabric and a matching ribbon page marker. Each volume will be bound with a "hubbed" spine that is characteristic of only the finest books. In every respect, this is to be a collection which rivals anything seen in the great private libraries of days gone by.

Distinctive cover designs accented with real 22kt gold

"Hubbed" spines in the classic tradition of the bookbinders art.

Handsome, readable type faces individually selected for each volume

Highest-quality, acid-neutral paper will last for generations without turning yellow

Beautiful illustrations capture the essence of each author's work

Gilded page edges provide elegance and protection from dust and moisture

Permanently sewn ribbon page marker

Endsheets of rich moiré fabric

Exciting Diversity

The hallmark of a distinctive library is diversity. Therefore, the volumes in the collection will vary in size, in the leathers used, in the distinctive cover designs, and in the illustrations. Yet the collection as a whole will exhibit an unmistakable harmony, because the volumes will be of consistent quality throughout.

Convenient Acquisition Plan

Because of the extreme care and craftsmanship required in printing and binding, the books in this collection will be issued at the rate of one per month. It will give you great pleasure to see your collection becoming more impressive with each passing month.

Comparable books bound in genu-

ine leather command as much as $75 per volume. However, you will be pleased to learn that the volumes in this collection will be priced at only $35.00 each for the first two full years. Future volumes will be similarly priced subject to minor periodic adjustment to reflect varying material costs.

If you desire, you may return any volume within 30 days for a full refund. Moreover, you may cancel your subscription at any time.

R.S.V.P.

To accept this invitation, you need only complete the Preferred Subscription Reservation and return it to us. This simple step is all that is necessary for you to begin building a private library of your own that is sure to be envied by all who see it.

AMERICA
WE BUILT IT FOR YOU
THE ATARI 520ST

"We promised. We delivered. With pride, determination, and good old ATARI know how." *Sam Tramiel, President, ATARI CORP.*

The 520ST simply obsoletes all current personal systems — even those costing thousands of dollars more.

No other computer we know of has been awaited with such anticipation, has received so much national and trade press, and has been so unanimously acclaimed — as the remarkable 520ST.

And for good reason. Its development represents a bold, new standard in personal computing power.

Beneath its full stroke 94-key keyboard is an operating environment so intelligent that it puts you in command almost at once. It's that easy.

Graphic symbols quickly identify available functions. Menus appear just by aiming the mouse. Point to a specific operation, click the mouse and instantly you are able to develop full color charts, recall files from within folders, and so much more.

And when you combine 524,288 bytes of RAM with ATARI's custom circuits and the horsepower of a 68000 microprocessor, you own a powerful computer that delivers crisp, high-resolution images with incredible speed.

With a monochrome monitor your 520ST displays 640 x 400 pixels of extremely high resolution clarity. Select a color monitor and you are able to create beautiful graphs and diagrams from a palette of 512 vivid colors.

Power to grow. An array of expansion ports allow you to easily customize your 520ST. There are standard serial and parallel interface ports for connecting printers and telecommunications equipment, MIDI connectors to interface with music synthesizers and keyboards, and 3.5 inch floppy disk, cartridge and joystick ports. There is also a hard disk port with the lightning communications speed of 1.33 Megabytes per second. ATARI 520ST systems are available now. *When it comes to state-of-the-art technology ...don't settle for less. And when it comes to price ...don't pay a penny more.*

For the dealer nearest you call 408/745-2367.
Or write to:
ATARI Corp.
Customer Service
1196 Borregas Ave.
Sunnyvale, CA 94086

The New Ⓙ**ATARI**®
Power Without the Price

$799⁹⁵ *plus state and local taxes where applicable.*

SYSTEM INCLUDES: 520ST Personal Computer, Monochrome Monitor, Mouse Controller, 3.5 inch Disk Drive, TOS™ - The Operating System Disk ATARI Logo™ Language Disk With full color monitor: $999.95*

Courtesy of Atari Corporation

Chapter 7

NARRATION

George Shultz, Secretary of State during the Reagan administration, is reputed to be a very cautious man and a poor conversationalist. In the midst of the Falkland Islands dispute in 1982, Shultz flew to London, where he was met at Heathrow Airport by Lord Carrington, his British counterpart. During the lengthy and rather tedious drive into London, Lord Carrington struggled manfully to find topics for polite conversation, with little success. The black sedan glided in silence past bucolic green fields filled with grazing sheep.

Making conversation, Carrington said, "Those sheep have been recently shorn."

Shultz stared thoughtfully at the animals for several moments and then replied, "So it would appear . . . at least on the side facing us."

Narrative anecdotes such as the one recounted above are common in good writing. They are capable of entertaining readers by making people, places, and events "come to life." But they also help to illustrate and animate the ideas that give substance to an essay. Although the anecdote about Shultz is probably apocryphal, if it were verifiable it might be useful in a historical study of the Falkland Islands war. Even with its rather uncertain origin, a feature writer might cite it as a current and rather revealing rumor. In that case the author would rely on the humor of the episode to enliven an otherwise dry narration. It might also be useful in a biographical sketch of Shultz, where it would both amuse the reader and provide an illuminating glimpse of Shultz's character. It might even be useful in an essay on the traits of caution in judgment and speech that are requisite in a modern American Secretary of State. Or it might be useful in a more general essay on the debatable virtue of extreme caution.

We are trying to make two points through this brief discussion. First,

The Vatican Collection/Alinari/Art Resource, NY

Laokoön, carved in the second century B.C. in Pergamum, an ancient city in what is now Turkey. Look up the story of Laokoön in the second book of Virgil's *Aeneid*. How effectively does the sculptor present this story through his sculpture?

unlike many fiction writers, who may be content to carve out a slice of life and present it to their readers without any commentary at all, essayists almost invariably use narration to make a point. Indeed, it is only the ability of narration to develop and support a thesis that justifies its inclusion in this text.

Our second point is that narration is useful in wide variety of essays, ranging from straight narration (the feature story) to exemplification (the virtue of extreme caution) to causal analysis (the Secretary of State's need for caution). In your own writing as a college student, you will frequently use narration or narrative anecdotes. You may use narration in a history exam when you must trace the course of the Glorious Revolution of 1688. You may use narration in a psychology exam when you are told to recount and then analyze one of your recurring dreams. You may use frequent narrative examples in a sociology term paper on the problem of hunger in America. Because you will use narration so often and in so many different kinds of writing, you should practice the skills that lead to effective and purposeful storytelling.

PREWRITING

Although a number of prewriting techniques can help you to find material for a narrative essay, we suggest that you **begin work on your narrative essay through focused free writing**. Start by selecting a general topic you find interesting (as long as it fulfills the assignment your instructor has given). Often an aphorism, a witty observation about life, a well-known quotation, or a dramatic situation can provide a good starting point. A number of such topics are included as *Ideas for Essays* at the end of this chapter.

Once you have provisionally selected a topic, take pen in hand and **write continuously for ten minutes**. Jot down as many incidents as you can remember as long as they have a bearing on your topic. As you write, try to narrate in some detail the most dramatic moments in these incidents. Don't worry, however, about getting events in order or recording every last detail. The purpose of free writing is to stimulate the flow of ideas, not to produce anything approaching a rough draft. Whenever you remember another incident with a bearing on your topic, interrupt whatever else you are doing to scribble enough notes about the new idea so that you can later develop it. Whenever you find yourself at a loss for new ideas, immediately return to one of the ideas you have already listed and continue recording your memories of what was said and done.

At the end of ten minutes, you should have discovered at least one incident in your life that can serve as the basis of your narrative essay. If you have not, repeat the process another time with the same topic or turn to another topic of interest. If you have kept a journal recently, you may wish to reread it in your quest for ideas.

When you have chosen a topic and decided on an incident to use in developing that topic, **use the reporter's questions (Who? When? What? Where? Why?) to be sure that your essay includes all of the relevent narrative facts**. Of course, your narrative essay will not present the answers to those questions directly or consecutively. Yet by noting the essential facts as part of the prewriting process, you will have them more clearly in mind when you actually draft your essay.

PLANNING AND DRAFTING A NARRATIVE

Perhaps the best advice about narrative writing is to **tell your own story in your own way**. If the events you are trying to narrate are sufficiently important to you, you can often produce a good rough draft simply by following your instincts. If you think a detail or a snatch of dialogue is important, include it. Concentrate on the parts of the story that make it meaningful to you.

Generally follow a chronological order in narration. A story records a sequence of events over a fixed period of time. The most natural order for narration (and the easiest for readers to follow) is the sequence of events as they actually happened. Suppose you decide to tell about the "relaxing" canoe trip you took over Memorial Day weekend. You begin with your roommate's initial broaching of the idea: "Hey, Bill, what say we chuck these books for the weekend and take a float trip down the Cossatot River?" You then go on in time sequence to describe the drive to the river and your pleasant reveries about lazily drifting down a meandering stream. Next you mention your first feelings of uneasiness at the sight of the steep-sided hills and deep ravines of the terrain surrounding the river. Finally, you narrate each terrifying event in the plummeting free-fall that your roommate had described as a "float trip."

Don't feel chained to a chronological order. A good deal of what happens during a typical day is just plain dull. If you feel you might lose your readers by the rather languid introduction outlined above, consider beginning with a dramatic predicament and then backing up to explain how you got into that predicament: "The canoe crumpled like a Coke can as it smashed into the boulder. Then the boiling waters of the Cossatot wrenched me from my seat and pinned me underwater against the boulder. I knew I should hold my breath, but I couldn't help gasping in pain."

Sharply limit the amount of time covered in your story. In a brief narrative essay you simply don't have room to tell the entire story of your life. In telling about your float trip, for example, you probably should not go into your previous experiences in canoeing or your special dread of drowning: "When I was but a baby my mother briefly lost me in the bathtub. . . . " You'll be doing well if you can adequately describe the float trip itself. Indeed, the bulk of your narrative should focus on the crucial hours—or minutes—of the episode.

If you generally follow a chronological order and if you limit the time span covered, you will have few problems with this assignment. Narrative writing is strengthened, however, if it includes each of the following elements: description, dialogue, characterization, conflict, and crisis.

Include plenty of descriptive details. In a narrative essay one of your goals is to make your reader share your experiences. In doing so, you should use vivid description of what can be seen, heard, smelled, tasted, and felt. A combination of different sensory images is particularly effective, as in the following paragraph from Ken Neely's "A Taste of Blood" (p. 138):

> The office smelled of musty discarded textbooks, cigars, and cold coffee. The hall had smelled of floor polish, which was almost

agreeable. The gash on my upper lip didn't exactly hurt, but I was conscious of it as Mr. Williams eyed me. Blood covered the front of my shirt and I held a now red-colored cloth to my bleeding mouth.

In these four sentences Ken has combined a variety of sights, smells, and sensations. The result is that we seem to stand with him before Mr. Williams.

Of course, the quantity of description should depend on the length of your narrative and the importance of the scene to it. In telling of a float trip down the Cossatot River, you should certainly describe the river itself in great detail, but you may not need to make your reader experience the smells of sawdust, cinnamon, and motor oil in the country store at which you stopped to buy *Deep Woods Off* and a snakebite kit. Similarly, in a brief anecdote like the one about George Shultz, you must be very selective in your choice of descriptive details. Note, however, that the anecdote does include descriptive details (the bucolic green fields, the grazing sheep, the silence in the black sedan) that help to build toward its punch line. Your narrative, too, should include relevant description at its climactic moments.

Use dialogue frequently — especially in the most crucial parts of your story. Life — real life — is filled with talk. Just as descriptive details help to bring your reader into the story, so too does dialogue. It allows the reader to hear what is said and to experience events almost as if they were happening. Note how much is lost in the anecdote about Secretary of State Shultz if it concludes with indirect discourse instead of actual dialogue: "As the black sedan passed a bucolic green field filled with grazing sheep, Carrington happened to comment that the sheep were newly shorn and Shultz replied that they did appear shorn on one side."

The use of dialogue allowed us to sense the desperation in Lord Carrington's small talk. And the pause within Shultz's actual response gives it a flavor of ludicrous sobriety. Change direct dialogue to summary narration, and all of this is lost.

In using dialogue, start a new paragraph with each change in speaker. Readers expect you to follow that convention in paragraphing, and it makes good common sense: A new paragraph is a clear visual signal to the reader of the change in speaker. (To see exactly how dialogue is handled in an essay, study any of the essays included in this chapter.)

When you do change speakers, identify the new speaker unobtrusively. In most cases it is sufficient to insert *he said, she replied, I asked,* or some similar phrase at a place where the speaker would naturally pause. Be sparing in your use of more descriptive verbs and adverbs (*he gloated smugly, she smirked*). If your dialogue is accurate and convincing, the tone of the speaker will be clear enough without elaborate qualifiers.

Use dialect sparingly. Regional variations in pronunciation and grammar give a great deal of color to American speech. Use such variations at your discretion in creating characters within your story, but remember that dialect is like pepper—a little of it adds a lot of spice. Suppose you decide to reproduce a warning from an Ozark hillbilly in your story about floating the Cossatot. Don't write, "That there river is laik t' a stuck hawg. It spouts an' spews an' roars an' dashes an' is jus' plum' dang'rous till it settles down a mite." Too many misspellings can make the dialogue hard to follow. The regional flavor comes through clearly enough in the speaker's rural images and peculiar word choice: "That there river is like to a stuck hog. It spouts and spews and roars and dashes and is just plumb dangerous till it settles down a mite."

Create "round" characters. Round characters are capable of surprising us in a convincing way. When we think of George Shultz staring at the grazing sheep and then describing them as newly shorn "at least on the side facing us," we are initially startled. On reflection, though, that cautious pronouncement is largely compatible with our mental image of the staid Secretary of State. This capacity to surprise, delight, and convince all at once gives to literary characters a "roundness" and reality that readers find appealing. It is part of the continuing attraction of characters like Tom Sawyer and Huckleberry Finn. And it is glaringly absent in one-dimensional creatures like Nancy Drew or the Hardy boys.

One particularly effective way to create round characters is to make them learn from their experiences. In the story of an ordeal on the Cossatot the narrator could, for example, learn that his will to survive burns brightest when he is dry and warm—and barely flickers when he is damp, depressed, bug-bitten, benighted, and bone-weary. Or he may learn quite the opposite—that his will to survive is so strong that he is capable even of clawing past his best friend in swimming to the comparative safety of an overturned canoe. Resist the temptation, however, to make yourself the hero of your own story. Readers will naturally suspect special pleading if you try to show that your adventures on the Cossatot taught you to have confidence in your own strength and heroism.

Develop some form of conflict. Stories are most interesting if they build an agreeable tension within the reader—a longing to discover what happens next. That tension is usually the result of the conflicts experienced by the main character in the story. Tasty conflicts come in three basic flavors. **Conflict with nature or the environment** is one possibility: the float trip down the Cossatot River pitted you against the rushing torrent, the jagged rocks, and the snake-infested ledges. A second possibility is **conflict with others**: as the hardships of the canoe trip mounted, you and your roommate grew increasingly hostile, lashing out and hissing at each other like the malign water moccasins on the banks of the river. Finally, a story can include **internal conflict**: halfway down the river, when the rapids ahead seemed most treacherous, you crouched on a narrow, protected ledge to consider whether to press ahead or wait for rescuers to find you. As these brief examples indicate, stories sometimes develop all three forms of conflict simultaneously.

Build to a crisis. Nearly every story worth telling involves some crisis scene. At the crisis the various conflicts developed throughout the story reach a peak in emotional intensity. The diverse elements of the story come together—here the carbon, there the saltpeter, and now the flint. The resulting explosion releases the tension that has built throughout the story and allows a resolution and a conclusion. Because the crisis is the culmination of your story, you should make it a scene that supports your thesis and you should develop it very specifically, using both descriptive details and dialogue. This advice also holds for brief anecdotes—note how the anecdote about George Shultz concludes with both description and dialogue.

COMBINING PURPOSES

A story that includes description, dialogue, character, conflict, and crisis almost invariably entertains the reader. Your biggest challenge, then, is somehow to make your story informative or persuasive as well as entertaining. The key step in achieving that goal is to **formulate a thesis even if you never state it directly in your essay**.

Look again at the anecdote about George Shultz at the beginning of this chapter. The first sentence presents the thesis that Shultz "is a very cautious man and a poor conversationalist." The anecdote itself illustrates that thesis. Furthermore, the first sentence identifies Shultz as Ronald Reagan's Secretary of State. Thus the story about Shultz illustrates the characteristics of the man and perhaps the characteristics of a good Secretary of State. It informs us about the person and persuades us that he is suited to his office. To see the difference a good thesis makes, imagine the effect of the anecdote if it didn't refer to any specific person: "Two men were riding in a sedan past a flock of grazing sheep. One man said to the other . . ." There would perhaps still be some humor in the conversation, but there would be no thesis and hence nothing informative or persuasive about the anecdote.

In a narrative essay you will often wish to avoid stating your thesis baldly in the first paragraph. You may wish to be more subtle and let the thesis unfold from the implications of the story itself. Be certain, though, that you know what your thesis is and that it is truly informative or persuasive. Avoid the obvious ("Whitewater canoeing can be dangerous") or the preachy ("Only my faith in God and my trust in human kindness saved me on the Cossatot River"). An obvious thesis doesn't merit development because everyone already believes it. A preachy thesis is difficult to defend because many readers will suspect you of manipulating the narrative in order to support your cause.

TIPS ON REVISION

After completing a draft (or several drafts) of your essay, revise it at least one more time with the following advice in mind:

1. **Prefer nouns and active verbs to adjectives and adverbs.**
2. **Keep your verb tenses consistent.**
3. **Use appropriate transitions.**

Good stories are active. They tell of people doing things. The words naming the people and the things they do are nouns. The words for the "doing" are verbs. Nouns and verbs give to narration heart and muscle and bone. This is not to say that you should avoid all adjectives and adverbs, but if you can make a passive, descriptive sentence more active, you should normally do so. Suppose your first draft includes the following sentence: "At dawn the Cossatot River lay enveloped in fog, but the ominous crash of rapids could be heard in the distance." In your final revision, consider making such a sentence more active: "At dawn we clambered into our canoes. A damp, thick fog swirled around us and fell in droplets from our chins, our noses, our elbows, our hats. As we glided downstream, the deep rumble of approaching rapids drowned out the clatter of our paddles knocking against the sides of the canoe."

Because narration requires describing a sequence of events, verb tenses and transitions are quite important. Verb tenses indicate when things happen and the relationships in time between events. If you choose to tell your story in the past tense, you should stick to the past tense throughout, unless a different verb tense is necessary to reflect the true order of events: "Jack rolled repeatedly as he slid down the mud bank into the river. As he climbed back out again, he was even muddier than he had been at the Sigma Chi Mud Wrestling Championships." Here the past tense is used consistently except when the past-perfect tense is necessary to show that the Mud Wrestling Championships took place *before* the action in the story. Consult a grammar textbook during this stage of revision if you have questions about when to use the various verb tenses.

Finally, use transitional expressions as necessary to underscore the sequence of events. A story can become monotonous if it is composed solely of simple sentences in the past tense: "She smiled . . . He said . . . He grabbed . . . She kicked . . . He howled." An occasional transition can vary the sentence structure and break up the monotony: "After she smiled at him for the third time in as many minutes, he said . . . " Such transitional expressions also give the reader more information about the time sequence than do the verb tenses alone.

IDEAS FOR ESSAYS

1. Write a narrative essay illustrating one of the following aphorisms.
   a. Nothing is more unpleasant than a virtuous person with a mean mind.
      —*Walter Bagehot*
   b. A little sincerity is a dangerous thing, and a great deal of it is absolutely fatal.
      —*Oscar Wilde*
   c. My belief is that to have no wants is divine.
      —*Socrates*
   d. By perseverance the snail reached the ark.
      —*Charles H. Spurgeon*

    e. The mind of the bigot is like the pupil of the eye; the more light you pour upon it, the more it will contract.
       — *Oliver Wendell Holmes, Jr.*

    f. Nothing can bring you peace but the triumph of principles.
       — *Ralph Waldo Emerson*

    g. Power tends to corrupt and absolute power corrupts absolutely.
       — *Lord Acton*

    h. You grow up the day you have the first real laugh — at yourself.
       — *Ethel Barrymore*

    i. Nothing in life is to be feared. It is only to be understood.
       — *Marie Curie*

    j. Success is counted sweetest / By those who ne'er succeed.
       — *Emily Dickinson*

2. Write a narrative essay on one of the following general topics.

    a. Think back to a time when you felt like an outsider or when you were part of a group that ostracized someone else. Write a narrative essay about these experiences and what you learned from them.

    b. Write an essay about someone you know whose language, culture, or customs create a sense of separation from the larger community.

    c. Write about a time in your life when you took part in activities that, on reflection, you know to have been morally wrong. What caused your involvement in these actions, what were the consequences of your failure to live up to your own values, and what can you conclude from the sequence of events?

    d. "Foot-in-mouth disease" is a common human ailment. Write about a time when you made a thoughtless comment that caused you or others unnecessary embarrassment or pain.

    e. Throughout our lives there are moments of sudden understanding of ourselves, others, or the world we share. Examples of such moments are our first true understanding of love or death or greed. James Joyce called these moments "epiphanies." Write about one of these epiphanies in your own life.

STUDENT ESSAY

The following student essay was written out of class in response to the following assignment: "Write a narrative essay about a time in your life when an adult in a position of authority treated you unfairly or unjustly."

FIRST DRAFT

"A TASTE OF BLOOD"

by Kenneth Neely

"Somebody get the teacher," I vaguely remember the fat boy saying as I spit the blood and what was left of a piece of peppermint candy out of my mouth. The kids gathered around and had already decided on what happened. They had seen it happen.

They led us quietly into the principal's office. It smelled of musty old teacher's books and cigars and cold coffee. *and I held a now red cloth to my mouth* The gash on my upper lip ~~hurt~~ didn't exactly hurt but I was very conscious of it. Blood covered the front of my shirt. "Boys," the heavy, balding man said quietly as he leaned forward, *behind a large desk* "I've been told what happened, the eyewitnesses told me, so there's no need for further explanation."

I knew then. What little respect I had gained from the teachers was shattered like a delicate china cup dropped out a fourth-story window.

"Fighting, right in the classroom, like a real-life criminal," they would squeak in their most teacher-like voice. *Strangely,→* This realization actually made me feel better. No longer would I be considered such a goody-goody type *a label* guy, which I never actually deserved.

"Terry, I'm going to give you four licks for this. You've become quite a discipline problem. Won't ~~these~~ this paddling make your eleventh one ~~in a~~ for this year?" Mr.

Williams then turned his long-practiced gaze on me. His face became less stern.

"Well, Kenneth, I'm not going to paddle you. Seeing as how you've never been a trouble-maker and this is your first time here. I was told how Terry here provoked ~~such a~~ your little, ah, disagreement." My lip began to ache when he ~~said~~ lessened our crime from physical fighting to a simple little harmless disagreement.

He cleared his throat. "Now you had better go call your mother, you're going to need a few stitches. Tell her to bring you a nice clean shirt, too." You can leave now, Kenneth, I've matters to attend to with Terry here." His face became stern again as he heard Terry ~~tell me that he was sorry~~ apologize to me.

~~I was almost out the door~~ My lip started bleeding again as I passed through the doorway.

Then "Oh, and Kenneth, I'm sorry that all this had to happen to you." ~~And~~ he actually smiled at me.

As my mother drove me to the doctor's office, I began to cry. I just couldn't help it. That fat old man was going to whitewash the whole episode. Teachers would sympathize with me when I ~~needed~~ *deserved* no sympathy.

I cried for a while longer out of frustration. Why couldn't those stupid, yet well-meaning, administrators and teachers leave me alone. I was in a fight, so what, many kids fight. They should discipline me, not make me into some kind of 8th grade martyr. It takes two to fight, but in their eyes I was a victim. I was a good boy and therefore not responsible.

Commentary: Ken's first draft shows considerable potential. Instead of responding to the assignment with the typical tale of an undeserved paddling, Ken has decided to explain the injustice of *not* getting a paddling when it *is* deserved. Thus, his story immediately grabs our attention. His first draft ably captures the key elements in the incident, but it is still plagued with the kinds of problems that typically mar first drafts. Too many of the paragraphs are short; too many of the sentences are joined loosely with commas. Furthermore, the essay begins at its most dramatic moment with the fight and peters out during the scene in the principal's office. The final paragraphs, which present the thesis, are told in a rather preachy form of summary narration. On reflection, Ken realized that he needed to build up the drama as the story progressed and make the story's crisis reveal the essay's thesis without overt preaching.

SECOND DRAFT

We were led silently into the principal's office. ~~by a rather hairy football Dickie His name~~ Our principal was named Dickie, Dickie Williams. Students loved to call him "ole Dickie" behind his back.

The room smelled of musty old ~~teachers's~~ text books, cigars, and cold coffee. The ~~medium sized~~ gash over my left upper lip didn't exactly hurt, but I became very [*as he looked at me slowly studied me from head to toe.*] conscious of it. Blood covered the front of my shirt and I held a now red ~~cloth white~~ cloth to my mouth.

"Well, boys," the heavy set balding man ~~who was secretly called~~ "~~Ole~~ Dickie," said as he swiveled his plush overstuffed chair in our direction. ~~"Let's~~

I knew then. At that moment I felt surely the image would be broken. I could actually hear the tinkling of glass [*the image were glass and*] as if it had been dropped from some fourth-floor window onto the hard pavement below. No longer would teachers treat me as if I were some ~~painting come to life.~~ They [*innocent incapable of even contemplating evil.*] would now see me for what I was, which was just an ordinary kid who somehow had gotten the label of a goody-goody. I actually smiled behind the cloth and tasted the saltiness of my blood.

After my combatant, Terry, told his side of the story. I told what I remembered, which was ~~a lot~~ little because I had blacked out. My short story agreed with his longer

version ~~one~~ and I ~~really~~ believed what he had said. We were both
actually responsible for the goings-on. We both knew that. Then we
simply sat nervously ~~to~~ await*ed* our fate.
down and

Mr. Williams looked at Terry and said, "Four licks for
you. You're getting to be ~~quite~~ a discipline problem. Eight
trips to this office in one semester. ~~Huh!~~" Then he cleared
his throat loudly.

Turning his well-practiced gaze on me, Mr. Williams'
facial look became softer, as if he were perhaps my
grandfather. "Well, Kenneth, I don't actually consider this

*I know what
kind of a
troublemaker
Terry is.*

you're gonna

any fault of yours. I *also* know you're a good kid and, well,
you'd better go call your mom now. I think ~~you will~~ need
several stitches in that lip."

"But, Mr. Williams, I ~~caused~~ am just as responsible
as . . ." I started to argue. But, deep within, I knew I
deserved it.

"Now, don't try to talk too much," he said. He got up
out of his big chair and began to steer me toward the
door. "Tell your mother to bring you a nice clean shirt
when she comes ~~for you~~." Then he smiled and I just
walked out.

I couldn't believe it. He had actually smiled at me.
That fat stupid man had smiled and had called out fight a
"little disagreement."

I felt like running back to that office and telling him
how stupid he was. I wanted to call him Dickie to his face,
Dickie, Dickie, Dickie.

*Later, as
out a hall
window,*

~~I saw my mother's car arrive.~~ I was looking ~~about 15~~
~~minutes later and~~ I saw my mother drive up to the school.
Before I could leave, though, several teachers in group
stopped me and told me how badly they felt that I had

provoked

been so ~~bullied~~ and mistreated by the boy. They said Mr.
Williams had told them all about it.

sneer

Dickie, you mean, I wanted to ~~say~~ to them, but I
didn't. My lip throbbed harder.

On our way to the doctor's office I started to cry. ~~out of
frustration.~~ I just couldn't help it. I was so frustrated.

*a normal
kid no
better, no
worse than
any other?*

"Why can't people just accept ~~other~~ people ~~as humans
and not want to as~~ Why must people ~~create stupid images
and~~ shove other people into cubbyholes?" I asked my mom.

"People are like that," she answered.

"I'm just as responsible as Terry for the fight, but no

understand

one but me seems to ~~know~~ that."

*Then she
smiled
at me.*

"I know," she answered.

And the throbbing of my lip seemed to lessen then.

Commentary: Ken has made two major changes in this second
draft. First he has begun his story with the trip to the principal's office.
By avoiding all direct description of the fight, Ken has successfully
changed the emphasis from the fight itself to his own disappointment in
the principal's unjust reaction to the fight. The greatly expanded fourth
paragraph is particularly important in explaining Ken's frustration with
the "goody-goody" image that has somehow been pinned on him.

The second major change comes at the end when Ken uses dialogue
with his mother to clarify and develop his thesis. Now his story clearly
lashes out at the injustice of those who "shove other people into cubbyholes." Ken thoughtfully demonstrates that the injustice can be as painful to the stereotyped "good" child as it is to the "bad" child.

Despite these improvements, Ken was not yet ready to move on to a
final draft. The beginning of the essay still troubled him. The idea of
beginning with the trip to the principal's office struck him as solid, but
he recognized that his readers might be confused unless he gave them
some background information about the fight and the other participant
in it. His third draft, therefore, simply involved two separate attempts at
an introduction that provided the necessary background on the fight.

THIRD DRAFT

I looked at the picture of George Washington as we were led
toward the principal's office.

"You ever fought before?" Terry asked. I shook my head to signify no. "I thought you hadn't," he said simply. "I'm sorry about our fight. I've been ~~to in trouble~~ paddled eight times this semester. It's not much, but he probably won't even do anything to you."

I wondered what Terry meant by that until we arrived at the principal's door. Our principal was named Dickie, Dickie Williams, but most students loved to call him "old Dickie" behind his back . . . .

I glanced . . . principal's office. My first fight, I was thinking to myself, my first trip to the office. I guess I could ask Terry what's it like. Everybody knows he has been in trouble eight times this semester.

Just at that moment Terry seemed to answer my thought. He said I probably wouldn't even get so much as a swat on the hand. Kids like me never get paddled, he added.

I knew what he meant by that, but my stomach still quivered when we arrived at the principal's door. Our principal's name was Dickie, . . . his back . . . .

Commentary: The first of these attempts introduces both boys and the differences between them, but Ken rightly determined that the dialogue stretched the introduction out too much and focused too much attention on Terry. In the second attempt we are drawn within Ken's mind and share his turbulent emotions as he makes his first trip to the principal's office. The tone of mixed anticipation and fear is exactly right for the story Ken wishes to tell. Nonetheless, the actual handling of this interior monologue creates some problems for Ken. He mixes direct and indirect discourse in the third sentence: *I guess I could ask Terry what's it like.* That sentence can be corrected by using quotation marks around the direct question: *I guess I could ask Terry: "What's it like?"* But a simpler and clearer alternative is to use indirect discourse throughout: *I guess I could ask Terry what it is like.* A similar problem occurs in the seventh sentence: *Kids like me never get paddled, he added.* The sentence has the structure of direct discourse, and the grammar of indirect discourse. Ken needs to recast it as dialogue: *"Kids like you never get paddled," he added.*

In his final draft Ken made these changes along with other minor improvements in word choice and phrasing.

FINAL DRAFT

"A TASTE OF BLOOD"

by Kenneth Neely

I glanced at the picture of George Washington as Terry and I walked toward the principal's office. My first fight, I thought to myself, my first trip to the principal's office. I suppose I could ask Terry about what it is like. Everybody knows that he has been in trouble at least eight times this semester, I continued to think.

Just then Terry seemed as if he read my thought. He said that I probably wouldn't get so much as a swat on the rump with a wet noodle. "Kids like you never get paddled," he added.

I knew what he meant by that, but my stomach still quivered when we arrived at the principal's door. Our principal was named Dickie, Dickie Williams, but most of the students loved to call him "old Dickie" behind his back.

The office smelled of musty discarded textbooks, cigars, and cold coffee. The hall had smelled of floor polish, which was almost agreeable. The gash on my upper lip didn't exactly hurt, but I was conscious of it as Mr. Williams eyed me. Blood covered the front of my shirt and I held a now red-colored cloth to my bleeding mouth.

"Well, boys," the heavy, balding man said as he swiveled his padded desk chair in our direction.

I realized it then. At that moment I felt surely that I would be stereotyped no longer. I knew my sugary image would be broken. I could actually hear the tinkling of it as if the image were of glass and it had been dropped from some fourth floor window onto the unyielding pavement below. No longer would those teachers treat me as if I were some innocent incapable of even contemplating evil. They would now see me for what I was, which was just an ordinary kid who somehow had gotten the label of a goody-goody and was too timid to put up a fuss about it. With these thoughts, I actually smiled behind the cloth, and the saltiness of my blood tasted good.

After Terry told his side of the event, I told what little I remembered. I had gotten knocked out on a rather hard concrete floor and did not remember anything except the beginning of our fight. My short story agreed with his longer version and I believed the rest of his story. We both knew we shared the responsibility for our crime. Nervously we sat down to await our sentencing.

Mr. Williams turned toward Terry, "Four licks for you. You're getting to be a discipline problem, Terry. Eight trips to this office in one semester just won't do." Then he cleared his throat loudly.

As Mr. Williams turned his well-practiced gaze on me, his expression became softer, as if he were my grandfather. "Well, Kenneth," he began in a mild voice, "I don't actually consider this, uh, little disagreement any fault of yours. I know how Terry is. I also know that you're a good kid and, well, you'd better go call your mom now. You're gonna need several stitches in that lip."

"But, Mr. Williams, I am just as responsible as . . ." I started to argue. It wasn't that I actually wanted punishment. It was that deep within I knew I deserved it.

"Now, don't try to talk too much," he said. He got up out of his chair and began to steer me toward the floor-polish smell. "Tell your mother to bring you a nice clean shirt when she comes." Then I saw his cigar-stained teeth as he smiled at me. I was filled with revulsion and I walked slowly into the hall.

I could not believe it. He had smiled at me. That fat, stupid man had smiled at me and had called our fight a "little disagreement."

I felt like charging back into that office and telling him how stupid he was. I wanted to call him "Dickie" to his face — "Dickie, Dickie, Dickie."

Later, as I stared blankly out a hall window, my mother arrived. Before I could leave, though, a group of teachers saw me. They told me how badly they felt that something like this should happen to such a star pupil. They knew the fight was not any of my fault. Mr. Williams had told them that, they said.

Old Dickie, you mean, I wanted to sneer at them, but I didn't. I felt sorry for them and my lip throbbed harder.

On our way to the doctor's office, I started to cry. I just could not help it. I was so frustrated.

"Why can't people just accept me as a normal kid, no better, no worse, than most others? Why must people shove other people into cute cubbyholes?" My tears burned my lip.

"People are like that," she answered.

"I'm just as responsible as Terry is for that fight, although no one but me seems to understand that," I said.

"I understand," she said. Then she smiled at me.

And the throbbing of my lip seemed to lessen somehow.

Reggie, Rex
Roger Angell

Roger Angell (1920–   ), who as author and editor has been associated for most of his career with *The New Yorker* magazine, has been called baseball's "most articulate fan." Angell's books about America's national pastime include *The Summer Game* (1972), *Five Seasons: A Baseball Companion* (1977), and *Late Innings: A New Baseball Companion* (1982). Angell's account of the final game of the 1977 World Series from *Late Innings* focuses on the performance of Reggie Jackson, who was widely known as "Mr. October" because of his clutch hitting during play-off and World Series games. Angell concludes his narration with the argument that Jackson's stunning performance finally "justified his gigantic salary" and ushered in a new period of frenzied bidding among owners for the services of outstanding free agents.

1   Even before Reggie Jackson took matters in hand, this was a rousing World Series. The Dodgers hit nine home runs, setting a National League Series record, and if they had somehow been able to carry the action into a seventh game there is good reason to think they could have won it. By far the best game, it turned out, was the first, at Yankee Stadium, and the Yankees' coup was undoubtedly the three runs they scored off the suave and redoubtable Don Sutton. The visitors, it will be recalled, bravely tied the game with a run in the ninth, but then ran smack into Sparky Lyle; deep in the unstilly night, the Yanks won it, 4–3,

on a twelfth-inning double by Randolph and a single by Paul Blair. The next evening, Catfish Hunter, who had suffered through a dreary season of injuries and illness, was badly manhandled by the Dodgers, who whacked four homers and won, 6–1. Hunter, a lighthearted hero of many previous Octobers, smiled and shrugged in response to the post-game questions. "The sun don't shine on the same dog's ass all the time," he said.

Out West, within the vast pastel conch of Dodger Stadium, the Yanks now captured two fine, extremely grudging games behind some stout pitching by Torrez and Guidry, who both went the full distance. The Dodgers, apparently determined to win on pure muscle, excited their multitudes with more downtowners, but the Yankees took the first game, 5–3, on two deflected infield singles, and the second, 4–2, on some modest wrong-field hits and a solo homer by Reggie Jackson. Thurman Munson hit a homer in Game Five, and so did Jackson (a homer to be more noticed later on), but only after the Dodgers had whanged out thirteen hits for Don Sutton, who coasted home in a 10–4 laugher.

With the Yankees leading the Series by three games to two, we came back to New York for the extraordinary conclusion. In this game, the Dodgers took an early 3–2 lead on Reggie Smith's home run off Mike Torrez; it was the third round-tripper for Smith, who was beginning to look like the dominant figure in the Series. The other Reggie came up to bat in the fourth inning (he had walked in the second) and instantly pulled Burt Hooton's first delivery into the right-field stands on a low, long parabola, scoring Munson ahead of him and putting the Yankees ahead for the rest of the game and the rest of the year. Jackson stepped up to the plate again in the next inning (Elias Sosa was now pitching for the Dodgers), with two out and Willie Randolph on first, and this time I called the shot. "He's going to hit it out of here on the first pitch," I announced to my neighbors in the press rows, and so he did. It was a lower drive than the first and carried only four or five rows into the same right-field sector, but it was much more resoundingly hit; at first it looked like a double, or even a loud single, but it stayed up there – a swift white message flying out on an invisible wire — and vanished into the turbulent darkness of the crowd.

My call was not pure divination. With the strange insect gaze of his shining eyeglasses, with his ominous Boche-like helmet pulled low, with his massive shoulders, his gauntleted wrists, his high-held bat, and his enormously muscled legs spread wide, Reggie Jackson makes a frightening figure at bat. But he is not a great hitter. Perhaps he is not even a good one. A chronic overstrider and overswinger, he swings through a lot of pitches, and the unchecked flailing power of his immense cut causes his whole body to drop down a foot or more. He often concludes a trip to the plate (and a Yankee inning) with his legs grotesquely twisted and his batting helmet falling over his eyes — and with the ball, flipped underhand by the departing catcher, rolling gently out to the mound. It is this image, taken in conjunction with his salary and his unending publicity in the sports pages, that seems to enrage so many fans. "Munson!" they cry, like classicists citing Aeschylus. "Now, you take Munson — *there's* a hitter!" And they are right. But Reggie Jackson is streaky and excitable. I have an inexpungeable memory of the two violent doubles he hit for the Oakland A's against Tom Seaver in the sixth game of the 1973 World Series, and of the homer he hit the next day against John Matlack to destroy to Mets. I remember the gargantuan, into-the-lights home rum he hit in the All-Star Game of 1971 in Detroit. And so on. Reggie Jackson is the most emotional slugger I have ever seen. Late in a close big game — and with the deep, baying cries from the stands rolling across the field: "Reg-gie! Reg-gie! Reg-gie!" — he strides to the plate and taps it with his bat and settles his batting helmet and gets his feet right and turns his glittery regard toward the pitcher, and we suddenly know that it is a different hitter we are watching now, and a different man. Get *ready*, everybody — it's show time. And, besides, Reggie had been crushing the ball in batting practice and he had hit a homer in each of the last two games against the Dodgers. Hence (to sound very much like Howard Cosell) my call.

5   I did not call the third homer. One does not predict miracles. This one also came on the first ball pitched — a low and much more difficult pitch, I thought, from knuckleballer Charlie Hough. The ball flew out on a higher and slower trajectory — inviting wonder and incredulity — this time toward the unoccupied sector in faraway center field that forms the black background for the hitters at the plate, and even before it struck and caromed once out there and before the showers of paper and the explosions of shouting came out of the crowd, one could almost begin to realize how many things Reggie Jackson had altered on this night. The game was won, of course (it was 8 – 4 in the end), and the Yankees were world champions once again. It was their first championship since 1962, and their twenty-first in all. Jackson's five homers for the Series was a new record, and so were his ten runs and twenty-five total bases. The three home runs in a single Series game had been done before — by Babe Ruth, in 1926 and again in 1928, but neither of Ruth's splurges had come on consecutive at-bats, and neither had been conclusive. Reggie Jackson's homer in the previous game had been hit on his last trip to the plate, and his base on balls in the second inning had been on four straight pitches. This meant that he had hit four home runs on four consecutive swings of the bat — a deed apparently unique in the annals of the game. But Jackson's achievement, to be sure, cannot properly be measured against any of the famous *sustained* one-man performances in World Series history — by Brooks Robinson in 1970, for instance, or by Roberto Clemente in 1971. Reggie's night — a thunderclap — was both less and more. It was *hors concours*. Jackson, in any case, had won this game and this World Series, and he had also, in some extraordinary confirming fashion, won this entire season, reminding us all of its multiple themes and moods and pleasures, which were now culminated in one resounding and unimaginable final chord.

6   Beyond this — or to one side of it, perhaps — Reggie had at last secured his own fame. He had justified his gigantic salary, if it *could* be justified, and in all probability he had suddenly increased the number of

players who will now decide to seek their fortunes as free agents in the next few years. More than that, he had arranged for them all to receive a great deal more money for their services. Even the flintiest traditionalists among the owners — and among the fans, too — must sense that a new time has arrived in baseball. We are in the Jacksonian Era.

Questions on Content

1. What game in the 1977 World Series between the New York Yankees and the Los Angeles Dodgers is the focus of Angell's narration?
2. Why did Angell think that Reggie Jackson would hit a home run on the first pitch when he came up to bat in the fifth inning?
3. What records did Jackson set in the series?
4. What does Angell mean by concluding that we are now in the Jacksonian Era?

Questions on Thesis, Purpose, and Structure

1. What is achieved in the two-paragraph introduction? Why is the first sentence so necessary to that introduction?
2. What is Angell's thesis? Where does he express it most clearly?
3. Why does Angell emphasize Jackson's weaknesses as a hitter? Why are those weaknesses necessary to the essay's drama? How are they related to the essay's thesis?
4. Discuss Angell's purposes. To what extent is he presenting an entertaining drama? To what extent is he informing us about the records Jackson set? To what extent is he persuading us that we have entered the Jacksonian Era?

Questions on Style and Diction

1. Find the following words in the essay and determine their definitions in context: unstilly night (paragraph 1); parabola, resoundingly (paragraph 3); divination, inexpungeable, gargantuan (paragraph 4); *hors concours*, culminated (paragraph 5).
2. Why does Angell make a point of thrice indicating that he "called the shot" when Jackson hit a home run on the first pitch?
3. What are the purpose and effect of the frequent use of similes and metaphors? Consider, for example, the following words and phrases: downtowners (paragraph 2), a swift white message flying out on an invisible wire (paragraph 3), insect gaze (paragraph 4), like classicists citing Aeschylus (paragraph 4), a thunderclap (paragraph 5), final chord (paragraph 5).

Ideas for Essays

1. After attending some athletic competition on your campus, describe what you have seen in a dramatic narrative.
2. Evaluate Angell's thesis that we are now in the Jacksonian Era. Were professional athletics ever in that era? Are they still in it? Or have they entered some subsequent period?

Salvation

Langston Hughes

Langston Hughes (1902–1967) was born in Joplin, Missouri, and moved east to attend New York's Columbia College. He participated in the Harlem Renaissance, a literary movement of the 1920s that helped to gather and solidify an authentic black American cultural tradition. With the publication of his first volume of poems, *The Weary Blues* (1926), and the many poems, plays, stories, histories, and essays that followed, Hughes became the leading black author of his generation and an important figure in twentieth-century American literature. He also published two volumes of autobiography: *The Big Sea* (1940), from which the selection here is taken, and *I Wonder as I Wander* (1956). In "Salvation" Hughes tells the story of a crisis in the development of his religious views.

1   I was saved from sin when I was going on thirteen. But not really saved. It happened like this. There was a big revival at my Auntie Reed's church. Every night for weeks there had been much preaching, singing, praying, and shouting, and some very hardened sinners had been brought to Christ, and the membership of the church had grown by leaps and bounds. Then just before the revival ended, they held a special meeting for children, "to bring the young lambs to the fold." My aunt spoke of it for days ahead. That night I was escorted to the front row and placed on the mourners' bench with all the other young sinners, who had not yet been brought to Jesus.

2   My aunt told me that when you were saved you saw a light, and something happened to you inside! And Jesus came into your life! And God was with you from then on! She said you could see and hear and feel Jesus in your soul. I believed her. I have heard a great many old people say the same things and it seemed to me they ought to know. So I sat there calmly in the hot, crowded church, waiting for Jesus to come to me.

3   The preacher preached a wonderful rhythmical sermon, all moans and shouts and lonely cries and dire pictures of hell, and then he sang a song about the ninety and nine safe in the fold, but one little lamb was left out in the cold. Then he said: "Won't you come? Won't you come to Jesus? Young lambs, won't you come?" And he held out his arms to all us young sinners there on the mourners' bench. And the little girls cried. And some of them jumped up and went to Jesus right away. But most of us just sat there.

4   A great many old people came and knelt around us and prayed, old women with jet-black faces and braided hair, old men with work-gnarled hands. And the church sang a song about the lower lights are burning, some poor sinners to be saved. And the whole building rocked with prayer and song.

5   Still I kept waiting to *see* Jesus.

6   Finally all the young people had gone to the altar and were saved, but one boy and me. He was a rounder's son named Westley. Westley and I were surrounded by sisters and deacons praying. It was very hot in

the church, and getting late now. Finally, Westley said to me in a whisper: "God damn! I'm tired o' sitting here. Let's get up and be saved." So he got up and was saved.

Then I was left all alone on the mourners' bench. My aunt came and knelt at my knees and cried, while prayers and songs swirled all around me in the little church. The whole congregation prayed for me alone, in a mighty wail of moans and voices. And I kept waiting serenely for Jesus, waiting, waiting — but he didn't come. I wanted to see him, but nothing happened to me. Nothing! I wanted something to happen to me, but nothing happened.   7

I heard the songs and the minister saying: "Why don't you come? My dear child, why don't you come to Jesus? Jesus is waiting for you. He wants you. Why don't you come? Sister Reed, what is this child's name?"   8

"Langston," my aunt sobbed.   9

"Langston, why don't you come? Why don't you come and be saved? Oh, Lamb of God! Why don't you come?"   10

Now it was really getting late. I began to be ashamed of myself, holding everything up so long. I began to wonder what God thought about Westley, who certainly hadn't seen Jesus either, but who was now sitting proudly on the platform, swinging his knickerbockered legs and grinning down at me, surrounded by deacons and old women on their knees praying. God had not struck Westley dead for taking his name in vain or for lying in the temple. So I decided that maybe to save further trouble, I'd better lie, too, and say that Jesus had come, and get up and be saved.   11

So I got up.   12

Suddenly the whole room broke into a sea of shouting, as they saw me rise. Waves of rejoicing swept the place. Women leaped in the air. My aunt threw her arms around me. The minister took me by the hand and led me to the platform.   13

When things quieted down, in a hushed silence, punctuated by a few ecstatic "Amens," all the new young lambs were blessed in the name of God. Then joyous singing filled the room.   14

That night, for the last time in my life but one — for I was a big boy twelve years old — I cried. I cried, in bed alone, and couldn't stop. I buried my head under the quilts, but my aunt heard me. She woke up and told my uncle I was crying because the Holy Ghost had come into my life, and because I had seen Jesus. But I was really crying because I couldn't bear to tell her that I had lied, that I had deceived everybody in the church, that I hadn't seen Jesus, and that now I didn't believe there was a Jesus any more, since he didn't come to help me.   15

Questions on Content

1. Explain the concept of salvation as understood by the young Langston Hughes. What does he expect to see and feel? Why does he believe as he does?
2. When during the revival is there a special meeting for children?
3. What is the nature of the preacher's sermon and of his appeal to the children?

4. Why does Westley leave the mourners' bench?

5. Why does Langston eventually leave the mourners' bench?

6. Why does Langston cry alone in his room later that night?

Questions on Thesis, Purpose, and Structure

1. What is Hughes's thesis? What sentences at the beginning and end of the essay come close to stating that thesis directly?

2. How successful is this essay in combining entertainment, information, persuasion, and self-expression? Explain your answer.

3. What is the ostensible purpose of the revival? Does the revival serve any other purposes? Is it beneficial to the preacher, the church, the other members of the congregation, the "saved" themselves?

4. To what extent is Langston's "salvation" (and presumably the salvation of others in his congregation) a result of religious revelation? Dread of damnation? The desire for communal approval? The fear of isolation?

Questions on Style and Diction

1. Find the following words in the essay and determine their definition in context: revival, mourners' bench (paragraph 1); rounder's son (paragraph 6); serenely (paragraph 7); knickerbockered legs (paragraph 11).

2. Discuss the connotations and the implied message to the children of the following phrases: the mourners' bench, the young sinners (paragraph 1); dire pictures of hell, one little lamb . . . left out in the cold (paragraph 3).

3. In the final paragraph Hughes writes, "That night, for the last time in my life but one — for I was a big boy twelve years old — I cried." Does it matter that he doesn't mention the cause of his later tears? What is the effect of this vague allusion to yet another sharp grief?

Ideas for Essays

1. For most adolescents the discovery of the falseness of something that the adults of the community assert as true is one of wrenching and inevitable stages in maturation. Write about an event in your life when you realized that you could no longer believe in something that you had always been told was true.

2. Literature is filled with conversion accounts ranging from St. Paul's conversion on the road to Damascus to Langston Hughes's experiences in "Salvation." If you have ever undergone a religious transformation, write about your experiences in a narrative essay.

◇◇◇

The Arraignment of Martha Cory
Marion Starkey

Marion Starkey (1901–   ) was born in Worcester, Massachusetts, and educated at nearby Boston University and Harvard. Although she worked as a newspaper editor and taught college English for a number of years, Starkey's real vocation has been the researching and writing of books on early American history. Her best-known work, from which the following selection is taken, is *The Devil in Massachusetts: A Modern Enquiry into the Salem Witch Trials* (1949). The persecution of presumed witches, who were burned at the stake or hung if they refused to confess and recant, was relatively common in Europe during the Middle Ages and Renaissance, but the American colonies had been largely spared from the frenzy until a handful of young girls in Salem became fascinated by Reverend Cotton Mather's book *Memorable Providences*, which describes the symptoms of possession. Soon they thought they began experiencing these symptoms themselves and accused a half-Indian, half-Negro slave named Tituba of tormenting them with witchcraft. Once such accusations began, they quickly snowballed until more than two hundred men, women, and children in and around Salem found themselves on trial for their lives. Before the frenzy subsided, five men and fourteen women (including Martha Cory) had been hanged for refusing to confess to witchcraft. Martha's husband, Giles, was pressed to death by the weight of stones piled on his chest as the inquisitors tried to force him to respond to their questions. Fifty-five others saved themselves by pleading guilty and testifying against their neighbors. Our selection from Starkey's book concerns events that took place relatively early in the witchcraft episode. Prior to Martha Cory's arraignment, the accusations had been made only against the traditional victims, outsiders who were generally unattractive, elderly, impoverished women. With the arraignment of Martha Cory, the frenzy began to affect the entire community.

Friday, 11 March, was observed in Salem Village as a day of fasting and prayer. Again the ministers of the North Shore came down to consult with Parris, and to pray with his distressed flock. And so mightily did they wrestle with the angel of the Lord that the eyes of one of the girls were again opened to the invisible world. Ann Putnam saw and named another witch, and people gasped at the name. It was, to everyone's disappointment, not a tall man of Boston, but a local woman, and this time not a tramp or slave but a respectable matron, a member of the congregation in good standing and a tireless attendant of meeting. It was, in fact, Martha Cory. 1

The natural enemies of the feminine teen-agers were, as has been reported, the older matrons and the dowagers. Many of these were stalwart countrywomen, used to lifting heavy loads, to planting their big feet in muck, to assisting in the birthing of cows and the slaughter of pigs. Their buttocks were broad and their hands were coarse, and since they lived close to the sources of life, so on occasion was their speech. The latter-day caricature of your prim, mealy-mouthed Puritan had not yet been invented. There was nothing at all Victorian about the countrywomen of Salem Village. 2

3   Young girls, still on the threshold of the biological experience that these matrons knew so lustily and well, or else, as seems probable from the later record of some of them, getting furtively and sinfully what their elders enjoyed lawfully, shrank from the pitilessly realistic appraisal in the eyes of the latter. "She'll be over it when she takes to wearing clouts." "Get her a man and the wench'll settle down." Such comments were an intolerable invasion of the privacy of the very young. One is never more delicately an individual than in the teens, or more resentful of crude generalizations that ignore the precious individuality.

4   Martha Cory was just such a countrywoman, and she was, to boot, a stout professor of the faith. Though it was only a year since she had been received into the village congregation from her former communion in Salem Town, she was already a personage. But not too popular a personage. Opinionated, outspoken, Martha Cory had the misfortune of being always right, and no one ever forgives that. In this crisis, however, she had at last put herself in the wrong. Her scepticism about the whole course of the witchcraft was said to border on downright heresy. Neighbours had been muttering about her already, and when Ann in a vision clearly identified her as a witch they said, "I told you so."

5   Nevertheless, as an "old professor" and a constant attendant at meeting, Martha Cory had to be given special consideration. Accordingly on the afternoon following the day of fasting, Edward Putnam and Ezekiel Cheever set out to have a private word with her. Before they did so they took a precaution; they asked Ann to take a good look at Martha's spectral shape and tell them what she had on, this being in the interest of correct identification. But not for nothing had Ann been Tituba's disciple. Her tranced eyes strained into nowhere; then she shook her head.

6   "I am blind now; I cannot see." Ann explained that the wily Martha, perfectly aware that she was about to be interviewed and for what purpose, had cast this spell on her.

7   They found Martha alone in the kitchen. She looked up at them from her spinning-wheel and smiled.

8   "I know what you have come for," said she, and there was in her tone and smile that note of mockery that had got her disliked. "You are come to talk to me about being a witch."

9   Martha had always had an annoying trick of taking the words out of one's mouth. Her visitors, who, whatever their suspicions, had come only anxious to be fair, to warn her, and talk things over with her reasonably, wished that this once Martha could have resisted that temptation. After what Ann had told them such a remark was disturbingly like clairvoyance.

10   But in the next breath Martha incriminated herself beyond redemption.

11   "Did she tell you what clothes I have on?" Her visitors could only look at her. "Well, did she tell you?" insisted Martha.

12   Curtly they admitted to the details of their conversation with Ann. Confronted with their damning implications surely an innocent woman would have been stricken. But Martha actually laughed, and then sat

smiling at them "as if," they reported later, "she had showed us a pretty trick."

They had not, however, come to crack jokes with Martha. They 13 brought up their business; sternly they pointed out to her the dishonour that would come upon the church if one of its members were proved a witch. Martha became serious too. She had had her bellyfull of loose talk going on about her, she said, of being put on by malicious gossip. What did they as fellow professors of the faith propose to do to stop the mouths of scandalmongers?

Cheever and Putnam looked at the woman with mounting aversion. 14 All their earlier doubts in her favour were being destroyed by her mockery, by her wicked prescience. Her present display of righteousness they found insufferable. And now, as if this were not enough, Martha gave way to undisguised blasphemy.

"I do not believe that there are witches," she said. 15

She could say that, they asked, when three proved witches had 16 already been taken in the parish?

Martha might have with justice replied that the witchhood of these 17 three had by no means been proved. Legally Tituba and her companions could not be held guilty until the trial had taken place and a jury had found them so. But Martha, for all her intelligence, had no better acquaintance with jurisprudence than any other Puritan. She too confused examination with trial.

"Well, if they are," she said, still with that irritating smile, "I could 18 not blame the devil for making witches of them, for they are idle slothful persons and minded nothing that was good." But what, she demanded, did such people have to do with her, a professor of the faith, a gospel woman?

"Woman, outward profession of faith cannot save you!" 19

Outraged, the visitors left her. It had been worse than they feared, 20 and now they had no compunctions about her. The sooner the body of the church was cleared of this corrupt branch the better. Why, she was worse than Sarah Good, worse than Osburne; they, at least, though unrepentant had not denied the reality of witchcraft. In all Salem Village they knew no one capable of such outright atheism.

On 19 March a warrant was sworn out for Martha's arrest. That day, 21 however, fell on a Saturday, and it was not until Monday that she was actually taken. So it came about that she was able to astound meetings of the Sunday with a prodigious display of her craft.

Deodat Lawson, minister in Salem Village after George Burroughs, 22 preached at both these meetings. He had come down from Boston to observe the plague that had broken out in his former parish and to investigate a report that the girls had information that his wife and daughter, dead these three years, had been done to death by sorcery.

He reached the village early Saturday afternoon, put up at Inger- 23 soll's ordinary, and at once began his investigations. Mary Walcott was there and a witch was biting her. Lawson heard her shriek and on her invitation examined her wrists by candlelight. It was true; he could see the marks plainly. But Lawson was a cautious man, and when he recorded his observation of the toothmarks in the notes he began to take at once, he took pains to insert the word "apparently."

24   During the evening he went to the parsonage for a consultation with Parris. Once in the house, however, it was nearly impossible to do anything but look at Abigail, who was in full possession. He found the child running through the house saying, "Whish! Whish!" and flapping her arms in an attempt to fly.

25   When he thought to settle down with Parris, ignoring the child awhile, there being women to tend her and the fluttering and whishing a comparatively harmless type of diabolism, the child froze his attention upon herself by going into a dramatic and ominous bit of shadow play.

26   A Shape had entered the room. None but the child could see it, though everyone looked to where Abigail's round eyes were focused. And when the child called it by name, Lawson's heart misgave him, for this was not Tituba nor Osburne nor even Goody Cory, but a woman he had admired and even revered for her charity—for her seeming charity.

27   "Do you not see her? Why, there she stands!" shrilled the child. And now Lawson, really aghast, not at all inclined to make mental reservations involving the word "apparently," saw the child strain to push an invisible and dreadful object away from her.

28   "I won't! I won't! Oh, I won't!" yelled Abigail. "I am sure it is none of God's book! It is the devil's book for all I know!"

29   With his own eyes he saw a human soul in the very act of resisting the devil, or anyway the devil's disciple. Heroic little girl, how she fought, and how helpless they were to rescue her from the agonies with which the hellish Shape punished her resistance. How marvellous was God's providence that to a little child it was given to fight for them all, beating off the power of darkness with her own fists.

30   Presently Abigail lost all control of her actions. She ran into the fireplace, came out with firebrands and hurled them about the house. Then she dashed back and tried to fly up the chimney.

31   Lawson came hollow-eyed to the pulpit next morning; he had been on his knees half the night, wrestling with the angel, imploring God's mercy and his blessing on this poor village which the devil had cursed, imploring that God save harmless these little ones, these innocent children who were the commonwealth's sole bulwark against diabolism. "Suffer little children," the Lord had said. How true it was now, and how clear that of such indeed was the Kingdom of Heaven.

32   Part of this prayer was answered, for Abigail came to meeting in the morning holding fast to the hand of her aunt, rosy and cheerful after a sound night's sleep. She walked down the aisle with eyes downcast, ignoring with the modesty of the truly great the looks of awe that her elders were casting her way.

33   But when Lawson strode up to the pulpit, and standing there let his eye rove over the congregation, he saw what appalled him. The Witch Cory had also come to meeting. In full knowledge that on the morrow she would stand here in ignominy facing a hellish charge, the woman had come to church and taken her place among good Christians. That

she should dare so much was an affront to all decency. The congregation could hardly keep its eyes off her; the afflicted girls were all but forgotten in the scandal of her temerity, but not for long. Martha could have come only for the express purpose of defying God before his very altar. Now, before the eyes of the congregation, she began to work on the children. Invisibly of course; all that the naked eye could see was the sturdy bulk of the woman sitting upright and quiet as any decent body; but all the while her incorporeal essence, her Shape, darted among the children, pinching and choking.

The poor girls wailed so piteously that Lawson could hardly get   34
through his first prayer. And after the psalm was sung, Abigail was beside herself.

"Now stand up and name your text!" There was authority in her   35
clear voice. Every face in the congregation turned to gape at her. Martha alone looked straight ahead of her, and even now the woman had the effrontery to smile. The minister, looking tenderly down at Abigail, obeyed her. "It's a long text!" sneered Abigail, or at least the devil in her sneered.

Lawson entered his sermon, but the tricksy sprites released by   36
Martha Cory would not let him preach in peace. He was hardly well launched when the spirit rather unexpectedly descended upon a hitherto inconspicuous young matron, Mrs Gertrude Pope.

"Now there's enough of that!" rapped out the young woman to the   37
parson.

Not even the Quakers had often dared make more disturbance in   38
meeting, and they had been hanged for it. Yet not a hand was laid on the children and the matron. The minister looked at them sorrowfully and went on as best he could. The young people knew not what they did; one could only pray. Perhaps there would be peace at the afternoon service if Martha did not come.

But Martha did come. There was indeed no way of keeping her out.   39
The warrant had not been served and could not be served on a Sabbath, and until it was, whatever the mockery of the situation, Martha had as good a right as any to take her place in meeting. Useless to reason with the woman or appeal to what a witch might have of a sense of propriety. Martha affected to believe that she was doing God and Salem Village a service by her presence here.

"I will open the eyes of the magistrates and the ministers," the   40
woman had retorted when they reminded her that she must return to this place to-morrow to stand before her accusers.

So Witch Cory returned and sat on her bench, square-set and im-   41
movable as a rock, ignoring the children, ignoring the sidelong glances of her neighbours. But she was paid for it this time; she was publicly exposed.

"Look!" rang out the voice of Abigail suddenly. "There sits Goody   42
Cory on the beam suckling a yellow bird betwixt her fingers."

Eyes shifted from the massive substance of Goody Cory on her   43
bench to the beam overhead where her Shape sat swinging its stout legs. As was to be expected, most people saw nothing more incriminating

than a cobweb. The sharp eyes of Ann Putnam picked her up, however, and saw the bird flutter from the beam to the minister's hat hanging on its peg in the pulpit. She whispered this observation to her neighbours and jumped up to make the announcement public. She was pulled down and hushed. A craving for order was beginning to assert itself even among the Putnams. These were subtly aware of the sentiments of people who blamed the disorder less on Goody Cory than on the girls and their parents. In any case not even the inspired Abigail interrupted the parson thereafter.

44   After such a prelude the good people of Salem Village made sure of their seats early Monday morning, and when at noon the magistrates arrived from town, accompanied by Nicholas Noyes, the house was full. The officials took their places and summoned the defendant.

45   Martha, escorted by the constables, came down the aisle and mounted to the bar. There was nothing cowed about this woman; she turned to the magistrates confidently, as if she had actually looked forward to this opportunity of expressing herself about current events. She had every intention of taking the offensive in this examination, and to this end, after the Reverend Nicholas Noyes had opened the meeting with "a very pertinent and pathetic prayer," Martha asked leave to pray too. As every minister knows, a prayer is a superb device for airing an opinion.

46   The magistrates did not fall into the trap; curtly they told her that they were here not to hear her pray but to examine her, and Hathorne went at once to the point. He did not even ask for her plea; what with the girls yelping on the front benches, such a query was superfluous. He simply asked her why she afflicted them.

47   "I don't afflict them," said Martha.

48   "Who doth?"

49   "I do not know. How should I know?"

50   She added, her self-righteousness asserting itself, that what they accused her of would be impossible to her. "I am a gospel woman."

51   "She's a gospel witch!" screamed out one of the children. All the pack took up the cry. "Gospel witch! Gospel witch!" And there was pandemonium and such earsplitting racket that Hathorne waited for it to quiet down. Presently out of the tumult came the clear voice of little Ann Putnam testifying. She herself at her father's house had seen Goody Cory and another praying to the devil. That was where Goody Cory directed her prayers.

52   The girls had fallen quiet to listen. In this rare lull the magistrates turned to Martha and Martha to the magistrates.

53   "Nay," she said to them, "we must not believe these distracted children."

54   The dry reasonableness of the remark affronted Hathorne. Distracted children, he exclaimed; who then distracted them? Let anyone who had eyes look and see. Indeed the answer was only too plain. Even while Martha proclaimed her innocence her devils had not been able to resist devising new tortures for the girls. What Martha did now they all

did. If she shifted her feet they did so too, and fell to stamping with such force as to rock the meeting-house. If she bit her lips, they yelled that she had bitten theirs, and came running up to the magistrates to show how they bled.

"What's the harm in it?" asked Martha when they ordered her to stop biting her lips.   55

Wearied, the prisoner leaned against the minister's seat; the motion sent such a tearing pain through Mrs Pope's bowels that she flung her muff at Martha, and missing, threw her shoe and fetched her a clout on the side of the head.   56

The girls' eyes and ears opened and they saw and heard that which the rest of the assembly shuddered to think about. One saw the Black Man whispering in the ear of Martha. The ears of others picked up the throb of a spectral drum, and when they looked out the window they saw the witches of all Essex County assembling to take their unblessed sacrament before the very meeting-house.   57

"Don't you hear the drum beat?" cried one. "Why don't you go, gospel witch? Why don't you go too?"   58

Good people sat shivering in the audience, hardly daring to let their eyes shift to the windows. The situation was getting frightful past bearing. Though Tituba had referred to witches' sabbaths, she had been vague about the place. Who could have dreamed that it would be here —and now; that the devil had grown so bold that he could marshal his own before a consecrated house at the exact moment when the forces of light were assembled within to give him battle?   59

Yet what was really appalling was the question of who might be out there on the church lawn serving the devil. The witch-hunt had seemed simple enough when it was a question of the three derelicts who had first appeared. Now the problem was assuming incalculable dimensions. No degree of respectability could be proof against suspicion now. Look at Martha Cory there on the platform; outspoken as she was, she had not been liked; yet until now few had connected her with witchcraft. Look at the one whom Ann Putnam had named in court to-day, one outwardly so gentle that it seemed impossible she could be guilty. Perhaps they had heard Ann wrong; perhaps Ann herself had mistaken the Shape.   60

Yet witches rioted on the lawns outside the meeting-house, and they were witches still unnamed and untaken. God guide these magistrates to find them!   61

The magistrates propounded to Martha some questions out of the catechism. Her answer about the godhead struck the attentive Lawson as odd, but a scrupulous man, he remarked afterward that there was "no great thing to be gathered from it."   62

Martha's great blundering husband Giles was called to testify. He faced the judges in unwonted humility; within the year he had been received into Noyes's church in Salem Town, and he took his devotions seriously. Besides, ever since that business of Martha's hiding his saddle to keep him from the examinations, he was inclined to think that there was something in what people said of her. He answered Hathorne carefully, trying his clumsy best to report the exact truth of what he knew   63 of Martha. The truth, however, was unimpressive, unconvincing even, in a setting like this. What it boiled down to was that Giles found it hard to pray when Martha was about and was in turn bothered by her own fluency in prayer. Once he had found her late at night kneeling mysteriously silent on the hearth and could make nothing of it. Neither, when he reported the incident, could the magistrates.

64   Rather contemptuously they dismissed him, and a rustle of speculation went over the house. What was the old man concealing? Might not his very stupidity be a mask for something else?

65   "You can't prove me a witch!" cried Martha before she was led away to prison to be held for trial. But such a statement was beside the point. What she couldn't prove, what no one at all accused of such a thing could prove, was that she wasn't.

66   Martha Cory had hardly time to acquaint herself with her new surroundings and the questionable society of Good, Osburne and Tituba, before she was joined by an uncommonly small witch, Dorcas Good, five-year-old daughter of the pipe-smoking Sarah. Her Shape, it seemed, had been running about the country like a little mad dog, biting the girls in return for what they had done to her mother. So a warrant was duly sworn, the child, a "hale and well looking girl," fetched in from Benjamin Putnam's by Constable Braybrook, and off to prison she went. She would come out of it eventually; five-year-old witches were not hanged, anyway not in Massachusetts, but she would not come out "hale and well looking," or ever be so again.

Questions on Content

1. Why are the young girls naturally hostile to the older matrons in Salem?
2. Why is Martha Cory particularly disliked and vulnerable to accusation?
3. Why do Edward Putnam and Ezekiel Cheever interview Martha Cory? What does she say to disturb and alienate them during that interview?
4. How do Mary Walcott and Abigail Parris demonstrate that they are possessed by devils?
5. Why does Martha Cory ask permission to pray aloud at the beginning of her formal interrogation by the magistrates? Why do the magistrates deny her request?
6. What evidence is there that Martha torments the children even as she is being interrogated? Why doesn't it occur to the magistrates that the children might be tormenting Martha?
7. What evidence does Giles Cory give concerning the charges against his wife?

Questions on Thesis, Purpose, and Structure

1. Part of Starkey's purpose is to present the known facts about the arraignment of Martha Cory. What does Starkey do to make this presentation of facts dramatic and interesting?
2. Although much of Starkey's purpose is to report historical facts, she is also interested in interpreting those facts. Is she persuasive in presenting the psychological motives of the young girls, the ministers, the magistrates, Martha Cory, and her neighbors? Explain your answers.

3. How effective are the opening and closing paragraphs in suggesting the thesis? Does the essay make just one point or several points about accusations of witchcraft?

Questions on Style and Diction

1. Find the following words in the essay and determine their definitions in context: dowagers, stalwart, caricature (paragraph 2); furtively, clouts (paragraph 3); heresy (paragraph 4); spectral, professor (paragraph 5); clairvoyance (paragraph 9); malicious, scandalmongers (paragraph 13); prescience, blasphemy (paragraph 14); compunctions (paragraph 20); prodigious (paragraph 21); ordinary (paragraph 23); possession (paragraph 24); diabolism (paragraph 25); ignominy, affront, temerity (paragraph 33); effrontery (paragraph 35); sprites (paragraph 36); suckling (paragraph 42); cowed (paragraph 45); superfluous (paragraph 46); pandemonium (paragraph 51); unwonted (paragraph 63).
2. Starkey often attempts to present the thinking of the various individuals in the story in a way that indicates how they might reach the conclusions they do, yet to present her thesis she must also subtly indicate how such thinking is flawed. How does she achieve both goals in presenting the views of Putnam and Cheever in paragraphs 5 through 20? How does she do so in presenting Lawson's views (paragraph 22–31)? How does she do so in presenting Hathorne's views (paragraphs 46–54)?

Ideas for Essays

1. Imagine that you are Martha Cory facing the charge of witchcraft. Write a speech in your own defense.
2. Imagine that you are the chief magistrate. Write a judgment in which you explain why you believe there is sufficient evidence to hold Martha Cory for trial.
3. If you have ever seen an episode of irrational mass hysteria (at a rock concert, an athletic event, or the scene of an accident or crime) write a narrative of the events, attempting to provide some psychological insights as you do so.

Shooting an Elephant
George Orwell

Eric Arthur Blair (1903–1950), whose penname was George Orwell, was born in India, the son of an English civil servant, but raised and educated in Britain. Although perhaps best known for his two antitotalitarian novels *Animal Farm* (1945) and *Nineteen Eighty-Four* (1949), both of which have become twentieth-century classics, Orwell was also a skilled essayist. Orwell's essays, no less than his novels, reveal his passionate concern for social justice and his lifelong struggle for what he called "comparative decency." From 1922 to

1927 Orwell served in Burma as a member of the Indian Imperial Police and experienced the events recounted in "Shooting an Elephant" (1950). The moral dilemma posed in this famous essay clearly demonstrates Orwell's feelings about imperialism and the way in which it enslaves and brutalizes both the oppressed and the oppressor.

1   In Moulmein, in lower Burma, I was hated by large numbers of people — the only time in my life that I have been important enough for this to happen to me. I was sub-divisional police officer of the town, and in an aimless, petty kind of way anti-European feeling was very bitter. No one had the guts to raise a riot, but if a European woman went through the bazaars alone somebody would probably spit betel juice[1] over her dress. As a police officer I was an obvious target and was baited whenever it seemed safe to do so. When a nimble Burman tripped me up on the football field and the referee (another Burman) looked the other way, the crowd yelled with hideous laughter. This happened more than once. In the end the sneering yellow faces of young men that met me everywhere, the insults hooted after me when I was at a safe distance, got badly on my nerves. The young Buddhist priests were the worst of all. There were several thousands of them in the town and none of them seemed to have anything to do except stand on street corners and jeer at Europeans.

2   All this was perplexing and upsetting. For at that time I had already made up my mind that imperialism was an evil thing and the sooner I chucked up my job and got out of it the better. Theoretically — and secretly, of course — I was all for the Burmese and all against their oppressors, the British. As for the job I was doing, I hated it more bitterly than I can perhaps make clear. In a job like that you see the dirty work of Empire at close quarters. The wretched prisoners huddling in the stinking cages of the lock-ups, the gray, cowed faces of the long-term convicts, the scarred buttocks of the men who had been flogged with bamboos — all these oppressed me with an intolerable sense of guilt. But I could get nothing into perspective. I was young and ill educated and I had had to think out my problems in the utter silence that is imposed on every Englishman in the East. I did not even know that the British Empire is dying, still less did I know that it is a great deal better than the younger empires that are going to supplant it. All I knew was that I was stuck between my hatred of the empire I served and my rage against the evil-spirited little beasts who tried to make my job impossible. With one part of my mind I thought of the British Raj as an unbreakable tyranny, as something clamped down, in *saecula saeculorum*,[2] upon the will of prostrate peoples; with another part I thought that the greatest joy in the world would be to drive a bayonet into a Buddhist priest's guts. Feelings like these are the normal by-products of imperialism; ask any Anglo-Indian official, if you can catch him off duty.

3   One day something happened which in a roundabout way was

[1]The betel nut is chewed like gum in the Far East.
[2]For ever and ever.

enlightening. It was a tiny incident in itself, but it gave me a better glimpse than I had had before of the real nature of imperialism — the real motives for which despotic governments act. Early one morning the sub-inspector at a police station the other end of the town rang me up on the 'phone and said that an elephant was ravaging the bazaar. Would I please come and do something about it? I did not know what I could do, but I wanted to see what was happening and I got on a pony and started out. I took my rifle, an old .44 Winchester and much too small to kill an elephant, but I thought the noise might be useful *in terrorem*.[3] Various Burmans stopped me on the way and told me about the elephant's doings. It was not, of course, a wild elephant, but a tame one which had gone "must."[4] It had been chained up, as tame elephants always are when their attack of "must" is due, but on the previous night it had broken its chain and escaped. Its mahout,[5] the only person who could manage it when it was in that state, had set out in pursuit, but had taken the wrong direction and was now twelve hours' journey away, and in the morning the elephant had suddenly reappeared in the town. The Burmese population had no weapons and were quite helpless against it. It had already destroyed somebody's bamboo hut, killed a cow and raided some fruit-stalls and devoured the stock; also it had met the municipal rubbish van and, when the driver jumped out and took to his heels, had turned the van over and inflicted violences upon it.

The Burmese sub-inspector and some Indian constables were waiting for me in the quarter where the elephant had been seen. It was a very poor quarter, a labyrinth of squalid bamboo huts, thatched with palm-leaf, winding all over a steep hillside. I remember that it was a cloudy, stuffy morning at the beginning of the rains. We began questioning the people as to where the elephant had gone and, as usual, failed to get any definite information. That is invariably the case in the East; a story always sounds clear enough at a distance, but the nearer you get to the scene of events the vaguer it becomes. Some of the people said that the elephant had gone in one direction, some said that he had gone in another, some professed not even to have heard of any elephant. I had almost made up my mind that the whole story was a pack of lies, when we heard yells a little distance away. There was a loud, scandalized cry of "Go away, child! Go away this instant!" and an old woman with a switch in her hand came round the corner of a hut, violently shooing away a crowd of naked children. Some more women followed, clicking their tongues and exclaiming; evidently there was something that the children ought not to have seen. I rounded the hut and saw a man's dead body sprawling in the mud. He was an Indian, a black Dravidian coolie,[6] almost naked, and he could not have been dead many minutes. The people said that the elephant had come suddenly upon him round the corner of the hut,

[3]In creating fear.
[4]The "heat" period of sexual excitement.
[5]Trainer.
[6]A coolie is an unskilled laborer or porter. The Dravidians are an Australoid race in southern India.

caught him with its trunk, put its foot on his back and ground him into the earth. This was the rainy season and the ground was soft, and his face had scored a trench a foot deep and a couple of yards long. He was lying on his belly with arms crucified and head sharply twisted to one side. His face was coated with mud, the eyes wide open, the teeth bared and grinning with an expression of unendurable agony. (Never tell me, by the way, that the dead look peaceful. Most of the corpses I have seen looked devilish.) The friction of the great beast's foot had stripped the skin from his back as neatly as one skins a rabbit. As soon as I saw the dead man I sent an orderly to a friend's house nearby to borrow an elephant rifle. I had already sent back the pony, not wanting it to go mad with fright and throw me if it smelt the elephant.

5   The orderly came back in a few minutes with a rifle and five car-tridges, and meanwhile some Burmans had arrived and told us that the elephant was in the paddy fields below, only a few hundred yards away. As I started forward practically the whole population of the quarter flocked out of the houses and followed me. They had seen the rifle and were all shouting excitedly that I was going to shoot the elephant. They had not shown much interest in the elephant when he was merely ravaging their homes, but it was different now that he was going to be shot. It was a bit of fun to them, as it would be to an English crowd; besides they wanted the meat. It made me vaguely uneasy. I had no intention of shooting the elephant — I had merely sent for the rifle to defend myself if necessary — and it is always unnerving to have a crowd following you. I marched down the hill, looking and feeling a fool, with the rifle over my shoulder and an ever-growing army of people jostling at my heels. At the bottom, when you got away from the huts, there was a metalled road and beyond that a miry waste of paddy fields a thousand yards across, not yet ploughed but soggy from the first rains and dotted with coarse grass. The elephant was standing eight yards from the road, his left side toward us. He took not the slightest notice of the crowd's approach. He was tearing up bunches of grass, beating them against his knees to clean them, and stuffing them into his mouth.

I had halted on the road. As soon as I saw the elephant I knew with perfect certainty that I ought not to shoot him. It is a serious matter to shoot a working elephant — it is comparable to destroying a huge and costly piece of machinery — and obviously one ought not to do it if it can possibly be avoided. And at that distance, peacefully eating, the elephant looked no more dangerous than a cow. I thought then and I think now that his attack of "must" was already passing off; in which case he would merely wander harmlessly about until the mahout came back and caught him. Moreover, I did not in the least want to shoot him. I decided that I would watch him for a little while to make sure that he did not turn savage again, and then go home.

7   But at that moment I glanced round at the crowd that had followed me. It was an immense crowd, two thousand at the least and growing every minute. It blocked the road for a long distance on either side. I looked at the sea of yellow faces above the garish clothes — faces all happy and excited over this bit of fun, all certain that the elephant was

going to be shot. They were watching me as they would watch a conjurer about to perform a trick. They did not like me, but with the magical rifle in my hands I was momentarily worth watching. And suddenly I realized that I should have to shoot the elephant after all. The people expected it of me and I had got to do it; I could feel their two thousand wills pressing me forward, irresistibly. And it was at this moment, as I stood there with the rifle in my hands, that I first grasped the hollowness, the futility of the white man's dominion in the East. Here was I, the white man with his gun, standing in front of the unarmed native crowd—seemingly the leading actor of the piece; but in reality I was only an absurd puppet pushed to and fro by the will of those yellow faces behind. I perceived in this moment that when the white man turns tyrant it is his own freedom that he destroys. He becomes a sort of hollow, posing dummy, the conventionalized figure of a sahib.[7] For it is the condition of his rule that he shall spend his life in trying to impress the "natives," and so in every crisis he has got to do what the "natives" expect of him. He wears a mask, and his face grows to fit it. I had got to shoot the elephant. I had committed myself to doing it when I sent for the rifle. A sahib has got to act like a sahib; he has got to appear resolute, to know his own mind and do definite things. To come all the way, rifle in hand, with two thousand people marching at my heels, and then to trail feebly away, having done nothing—no, that was impossible. The crowd would laugh at me. And my whole life, every white man's life in the East, was one long struggle not to be laughed at.

But I did not want to shoot the elephant. I watched him beating his   8
bunch of grass against his knees with that preoccupied grandmotherly air that elephants have. It seemed to me that it would be murder to shoot him. At that age I was not squeamish about killing animals, but I had never shot an elephant and never wanted to. (Somehow it always seems worse to kill a *large* animal.) Besides, there was the beast's owner to be considered. Alive, the elephant was worth at least a hundred pounds; dead, he would only be worth the value of his tusks, five pounds, possibly. But I had got to act quickly. I turned to some experienced-looking Burmans who had been there when we arrived, and asked them how the elephant had been behaving. They all said the same thing: he took no notice of you if you left him alone, but he might charge if you went too close to him.

It was perfectly clear to me what I ought to do. I ought to walk up to   9
within, say, twenty-five yards of the elephant and test his behavior. If he charged, I could shoot; if he took no notice of me, it would be safe to leave him until the mahout came back. But also I knew that I was going to do no such thing. I was a poor shot with a rifle and the ground was soft mud into which one would sink at every step. If the elephant charged and I missed him, I should have about as much chance as a toad under a steam-roller. But even then I was not thinking particularly of my own skin, only of the watchful yellow faces behind. For at that moment, with

[7]Master.

the crowd watching me, I was not afraid in the ordinary sense, as I would have been if I had been alone. A white man mustn't be frightened in front of "natives"; and so, in general, he isn't frightened. The sole thought in my mind was that if anything went wrong those two thousand Burmans would see me pursued, caught, trampled on, and reduced to a grinning corpse like that Indian up the hill. And if that happened it was quite probable that some of them would laugh. That would never do. There was only one alternative. I shoved the cartridges into the magazine and lay down on the road to get a better aim.

10   The crowd grew very still, and a deep, low, happy sigh, as of people who see the theater curtain go up at last, breathed from innumerable throats. They were going to have their bit of fun after all. The rifle was a beautiful German thing with cross-hair sights. I did not then know that in shooting an elephant one would shoot to cut an imaginary bar running from ear-hole to ear-hole. I ought, therefore, as the elephant was sideways on, to have aimed straight at his ear-hole; actually I aimed several inches in front of this, thinking the brain would be further forward.

11   When I pulled the trigger I did not hear the bang or feel the kick — one never does when a shot goes home — but I heard the devilish roar of glee that went up from the crowd. In that instant, in too short a time, one would have thought, even for the bullet to get there, a mysterious, terrible change had come over the elephant. He neither stirred nor fell, but every line of his body had altered. He looked suddenly stricken, shrunken, immensely old, as though the frightful impact of the bullet had paralyzed him without knocking him down. At last, after what seemed a long time — it might have been five seconds, I dare say — he sagged flabbily to his knees. His mouth slobbered. An enormous senility seemed to have settled upon him. One could have imagined him thousands of years old. I fired again into the same spot. At the second shot he did not collapse but climbed with desperate slowness to his feet and stood weakly upright, with legs sagging and head drooping. I fired a third time. That was the shot that did for him. You could see the agony of it jolt his whole body and knock the last remnant of strength from his legs. But in falling he seemed for a moment to rise, for as his hind legs collapsed beneath him he seemed to tower upward like a huge rock toppling, his trunk reaching skyward like a tree. He trumpeted, for the first and only time. And then down he came, his belly toward me, with a crash that seemed to shake the ground even where I lay.

12   I got up. The Burmans were already racing past me across the mud. It was obvious that the elephant would never rise again, but he was not dead. He was breathing very rhythmically with long rattling gasps, his great mound of a side painfully rising and falling. His mouth was wide open — I could see far down into caverns of pale pink throat. I waited a long time for him to die, but his breathing did not weaken. Finally I fired my two remaining shots into the spot where I thought his heart must be. The thick blood welled out of him like red velvet, but still he did not die. His body did not even jerk when the shots hit him, the tortured breathing continued without a pause. He was dying, very slowly and in great agony, but in some world remote from me where not even a bullet

could damage him further. I felt that I had got to put an end to that dreadful noise. It seemed dreadful to see the great beast lying there, powerless to move and yet powerless to die, and not even to be able to finish him. I sent back for my small rifle and poured shot after shot into his heart and down his throat. They seemed to make no impression. The tortured gasps continued as steadily as the ticking of a clock.

In the end I could not stand it any longer and went away. I heard 13 later that it took him half an hour to die. Burmans were bringing dahs[8] and baskets even before I left, and I was told they had stripped his body almost to the bones by the afternoon.

Afterward, of course, there were endless discussions about the 14 shooting of the elephant. The owner was furious, but he was only an Indian and could do nothing. Besides, legally I had done the right thing, for a mad elephant has to be killed, like a mad dog, if its owner fails to control it. Among the Europeans opinion was divided. The older men said I was right, the younger men said it was a damn shame to shoot an elephant for killing a coolie, because an elephant was worth more than any damn Coringhee coolie. And afterwards I was very glad that the coolie had been killed; it put me legally in the right and it gave me a sufficient pretext for shooting the elephant. I often wondered whether any of the others grasped that I had done it solely to avoid looking a fool.

Questions on Content

1. At the time of the events described, where did Orwell live, what was his job, and what were his attitudes toward that job and toward the native peoples?
2. Why is the elephant so uncontrollable and destructive?
3. Why does Orwell send for his elephant gun?
4. Why does a crowd gather once they see this gun?
5. What is the elephant doing when Orwell finds it?
6. Why doesn't he approach it?
7. Why does Orwell feel that he *must* shoot the elephant? Why doesn't he want to do so?
8. How many times does Orwell shoot in his effort to kill the elephant?

Questions on Thesis, Purpose, and Structure

1. The first two paragraphs seem to have no direct connection with shooting the elephant. Why are they nonetheless appropriate in introducing the story Orwell wants to tell?
2. What sentences in the essay most directly indicate its thesis?
3. Why does Orwell describe the dead coolie in such detail?
4. How does this episode show Orwell the futility of imperialism?
5. How does imperialism destroy the freedom of both the ruler and subject?
6. How fully do the expectations of the Hindus govern Orwell's conduct as well as their own?
7. How does the summary of attitudes in the concluding paragraph strengthen Orwell's thesis?

[8]Long knives.

Questions on Style and Diction

1. Find the following words in the essay and determine their definitions in context: bazaars (paragraph 1); cowed, flogged, supplant, prostrate (paragraph 2); ravaging (paragraph 3); labyrinth, squalid, professed (paragraph 4); garish clothes, dominion, resolute (paragraph 7); senility, remnant (paragraph 11); pretext (paragraph 14).
2. Is the word *guts* in paragraphs 1 and 2 too informal? What would be the effect of substituting more formal and precise words like *courage* in paragraph 1 and *abdomen* in paragraph 2?
3. How much time is covered by the main events in the story? What is the effect of the close attention to events in a limited time period?
4. In paragraphs 4, 6, 7, and 9 Orwell uses forceful similes. Find these similes and discuss their effectiveness.

Ideas for Essays

1. At one point Orwell writes, "And suddenly I realized that I should have to shoot the elephant after all. The people expected it of me and I had got to do it." Write about a time in your life when you did something you knew was wrong because other people expected you to do it or might laugh at you if you didn't.
2. Orwell's story points out how racism destroys freedom and breeds hatred in both the dominant race and the oppressed race. Write about a situation in your own experience that illustrates Orwell's point.
3. Orwell shot the elephant for a variety of complex (and sometimes conflicting) reasons. In a thoughtful and thorough essay, analyze the causes of Orwell's actions.

A & P

John Updike

John Updike (1932–   ) was graduated from Harvard University *summa cum laude* before pursuing graduate work in art at the Ruskin School of Drawing and Fine Art in Oxford, England. From 1955 through 1957 he wrote the "Talk of the Town" column for *The New Yorker*, but thereafter he devoted himself entirely to free-lance writing. In a very productive career, he has published twelve novels, including *Rabbit Run* (1960), *The Centaur* (which won the National Book Award for 1963), *The Witches of Eastwick* (1984), and most recently *S.* (1988). In addition, his short stories to date have been collected in nine separate volumes, his poems in four volumes, and his essays in two volumes. "A & P" (1962), perhaps his most frequently anthologized story, first appeared in *The New Yorker*.

1   In walks these three girls in nothing but bathing suits. I'm in the third checkout slot, with my back to the door, so I don't see them until they're

over by the bread. The one that caught my eye first was the one in the plaid green two-piece. She was a chunky kid, with a good tan and a sweet broad soft-looking can with those two crescents of white just under it, where the sun never seems to hit, at the top of the backs of her legs. I stood there with my hand on a box of HiHo crackers trying to remember if I rang it up or not. I ring it up again and the customer starts giving me hell. She's one of these cash-register-watchers, a witch about fifty with rouge on her cheekbones and no eyebrows, and I know it made her day to trip me up. She'd been watching cash registers for fifty years and probably never seen a mistake before.

By the time I got her feathers smoothed and her goodies into a bag—she gives me a little snort in passing, if she'd been born at the right time they would have burned her over in Salem—by the time I get her on her way the girls had circled around the bread and were coming back, without a pushcart, back my way along the counters, in the aisle between the checkouts and the Special bins. They didn't even have shoes on. There was this chunky one, with the two-piece—it was bright green and the seams on the bra were still sharp and her belly was still pretty pale so I guessed she just got it (the suit)—there was this one, with one of those chubby berry-faces, the lips all bunched together under her nose, this one, and a tall one, with black hair that hadn't quite frizzed right, and one of these sunburns right across under the eyes, and a chin that was too long—you know, the kind of girl other girls think is very "striking" and "attractive" but never quite makes it, as they very well know, which is why they like her so much—and then the third one, that wasn't quite so tall. She was the queen. She kind of led them, the other two peeking around and making their shoulders round. She didn't look around, not this queen, she just walked straight on slowly, on these long white prima-donna legs. She came down a little hard on her heels, as if she didn't walk in her bare feet that much, putting down her heels and then letting the weight move along to her toes as if she was testing the floor with every step, putting a little deliberate extra action into it. You never know for sure how girls' minds work (do you really think it's a mind in there or just a little buzz like a bee in a glass jar?) but you got the idea she had talked the other two into coming in here with her, and now she was showing them how to do it, walk slow and hold yourself straight.

She had on a kind of dirty-pink—beige maybe, I don't know— bathing suit with a little nubble all over it and, what got me, the straps were down. They were off her shoulders looped loose around the cool tops of her arms, and I guess as a result the suit had slipped a little on her, so all around the top of the cloth there was this shining rim. If it hadn't been there you wouldn't have known there could have been anything whiter than those shoulders. With the straps pushed off, there was nothing between the top of the suit and the top of her head except just *her*, this clean bare plane of the top of her chest down from the shoulder bones like a dented sheet of metal tilted in the light. I mean, it was more than pretty.

She had sort of oaky hair that the sun and salt had bleached, done up

in a bun that was unravelling, and a kind of prim face. Walking into the
A & P with your straps down, I suppose it's the only kind of face you *can*
have. She held her head so high her neck, coming up out of those white
shoulders, looked kind of stretched, but I didn't mind. The longer her
neck was, the more of her there was.

5   She must have felt in the corner of her eye me and over my shoulder
Stokesie in the second slot watching, but she didn't tip. Not this queen.
She kept her eyes moving across the racks, and stopped, and turned
so slow it made my stomach rub the inside of my apron, and buzzed
to the other two, who kind of huddled against her for relief, and then
they all three of them went up the cat-and-dog-food-breakfast-cereal-
macaroni-rice-raisins-seasonings-spreads-spaghetti-soft-drinks-crackers-
and-cookies aisle. From the third slot I look straight up this aisle to the
meat counter, and I watched them all the way. The fat one with the tan
sort of fumbled with the cookies, but on second thought she put the
package back. The sheep pushing their carts down the aisle—the girls
were walking against the usual traffic (not that we have one-way signs or
anything)—were pretty hilarious. You could see them, when Queenie's
white shoulders dawned on them, kind of jerk, or hop, or hiccup, but
their eyes snapped back to their own baskets and on they pushed. I bet
you could set off dynamite in an A & P and the people would by and
large keep reaching and checking oatmeal off their lists and muttering
"Let me see, there was a third thing, began with A, asparagus, no, ah, yes,
applesauce!" or whatever it is they do mutter. But there was no doubt,
this jiggled them. A few houseslaves in pin curlers even looked around
after pushing their carts past to make sure what they had seen was
correct.

6   You know, it's one thing to have a girl in a bathing suit down on the
beach, where what with the glare nobody can look at each other much
anyway, and another thing in the cool of the A & P, under the fluorescent
lights, against all those stacked packages, with her feet paddling along
naked over our checkerboard green-and-cream rubber-tile floor.

7   "Oh Daddy," Stokesie said beside me. "I feel so faint."

8   "Darling," I said. "Hold me tight." Stokesie's married, with two
babies chalked up on his fuselage already, but as far as I can tell that's
the only difference. He's twenty-two, and I was nineteen this April.

9   "Is it done?" he asks, the responsible married man finding his voice.
I forgot to say he thinks he's going to be manager some sunny day,
maybe in 1990 when it's called the Great Alexandrov and Petrooshki Tea
Company or something.

10   What he meant was, our town is five miles from a beach, with a big
summer colony out on the Point, but we're right in the middle of town,
and the women generally put on a shirt or shorts or something before
they get out of the car into the street. And anyway these are usually
women with six children and varicose veins mapping their legs and
nobody, including them, could care less. As I say, we're right in the
middle of town, and if you stand at our front doors you can see two banks
and the Congregational church and the newspaper store and three real-
estate offices and about twenty-seven old freeloaders tearing up Central

Street because the sewer broke again. It's not as if we're on the Cape; we're north of Boston and there's people in this town haven't seen the ocean for twenty years.

The girls had reached the meat counter and were asking McMahon something. He pointed, they pointed, and they shuffled out of sight behind a pyramid of Diet Delight peaches. All that was left for us to see was old McMahon patting his mouth and looking after them sizing up their joints. Poor kids, I began to feel sorry for them, they couldn't help it.

Now here comes the sad part of the story, at least my family says it's   11
sad, but I don't think it's so sad myself. The store's pretty empty, it being Thursday afternoon, so there was nothing much to do except lean on the register and wait for the girls to show up again. The whole store was like a pinball machine and I didn't know which tunnel they'd come out of. After a while they come around out of the far aisle, around the light bulbs, records at discount of the Caribbean Six or Tony Martin Sings or some such gunk you wonder they waste the wax on, sixpacks of candy bars, and plastic toys done up in cellophane that fall apart when a kid looks at them anyway. Around they come, Queenie still leading the way, and holding a little gray jar in her hand. Slots Three through Seven are unmanned and I could see her wondering between Stokes and me, but Stokesie with his usual luck draws an old party in baggy gray pants who stumbles up with four giant cans of pineapple juice (what do these bums *do* with all that pineapple juice? I've often asked myself) so the girls come to me. Queenie puts down the jar and I take it into my fingers icy cold. Kingfish Fancy Herring Snacks in Pure Sour Cream: 49¢. Now her hands are empty, not a ring or a bracelet, bare as God made them, and I wonder where the money's coming from. Still with that prim look she lifts a folded dollar bill out of the hollow at the center of her nubbled pink top. The jar went heavy in my hand. Really, I thought that was so cute.

Then everybody's luck begins to run out. Lengel comes in from   12
haggling with a truck full of cabbages on the lot and is about to scuttle into that door marked MANAGER behind which he hides all day when the girls touch his eye. Lengel's pretty dreary, teaches Sunday school and the rest, but he doesn't miss that much. He comes over and says, "Girls, this isn't the beach."

Queenie blushes, though maybe it's just a brush of sunburn I was   13
noticing for the first time, now that she was so close. "My mother asked me to pick up a jar of herring snacks." Her voice kind of startled me, the way voices do when you see the people first, coming out so flat and dumb yet kind of tony, too, the way it ticked over "pick up" and "snacks." All of a sudden I slid right down her voice into her living room. Her father and the other men were standing around in ice-cream coats and bow ties and the women were in sandals picking up herring snacks on toothpicks off a big glass plate and they were all holding drinks the color of water with olives and sprigs of mint in them. When my parents have somebody over they get lemonade and if it's a real racy

affair Schlitz in tall glasses with "They'll Do It Every Time" cartoons stencilled on.

14   "That's all right," Lengel said. "But this isn't the beach." His repeating this struck me as funny, as if it had just occurred to him, and he had been thinking all these years the A & P was a great big dune and he was the head lifeguard. He didn't like my smiling—as I say he doesn't miss much—but he concentrates on giving the girls that sad Sunday-school-superintendent stare.

15   Queenie's blush is no sunburn now, and the plump one in plaid, that I liked better from the back—a really sweet can—pipes up, "We weren't doing any shopping. We just came in for the one thing."

16   "That makes no difference," Lengel tells her, and I could see from the way his eyes went that he hadn't noticed she was wearing a two-piece before. "We want you decently dressed when you come in here."

17   "We *are* decent," Queenie says suddenly, her lower lip pushing, getting sore now that she remembers her place, a place from which the crowd that runs the A & P must look pretty crummy. Fancy Herring Snacks flashed in her very blue eyes.

18   "Girls, I don't want to argue with you. After this come in here with your shoulders covered. It's our policy." He turns his back. That's policy for you. Policy is what the kingpins want. What the others want is juvenile delinquency.

19   All this while, the customers had been showing up with their carts but, you know, sheep, seeing a scene, they had all bunched up on Stokesie, who shook open a paper bag as gently as peeling a peach, not wanting to miss a word. I could feel in the silence everybody getting nervous, most of all Lengel, who asks me, "Sammy, have you rung up their purchase?"

20   I thought and said "No" but it wasn't about that I was thinking. I go through the punches, 4, 9, GROC, TOT—it's more complicated than you think, and after you do it often enough, it begins to make a little song, that you hear words to, in my case "Hello *(bing)* there, you *(gung)* hap-py *pee*-pul *(splat)*!"—the *splat* being the drawer flying out. I uncrease the bill, tenderly as you may imagine, it just having come from between the two smoothest scoops of vanilla I had ever known were there, and pass a half and a penny into her narrow pink palm, and nestle the herrings in a bag and twist its neck and hand it over, all the time thinking.

21   The girls, and who'd blame them, are in a hurry to get out, so I say "I quit" to Lengel quick enough for them to hear, hoping they'll stop and watch me, their unsuspected hero. They keep right on going, into the electric eye; the door flies open and they flicker across the lot to their car, Queenie and Plaid and Big Tall Goony-Goony (not that as raw material she was so bad), leaving me with Lengel and a kink in his eyebrow.

22   "Did you say something, Sammy?"

23   "I said I quit."

24   "I thought you did."

"You didn't have to embarrass them."   25

"It was they who were embarrassing us."   26

I started to say something that came out "Fiddle-de-doo." It's a   27
saying of my grandmother's, and I know she would have been pleased.

"I don't think you know what you're saying," Lengel said.   28

"I know you don't," I said. "But I do." I pull the bow at the back of   29
my apron and start shrugging it off my shoulders. A couple of customers
that had been heading for my slot begin to knock against each other, like
scared pigs in a chute.

Lengel sighs and begins to look very patient and old and gray. He's   30
been a friend of my parents for years. "Sammy, you don't want to do this
to your Mom and Dad," he tells me. It's true. I don't. But it seems to me
that once you begin a gesture it's fatal not to go through with it. I fold the
apron, "Sammy" stitched in red on the pocket, and put it on the counter,
and drop the bow tie on top of it. The bow tie is theirs, if you've ever
wondered. "You'll feel this for the rest of your life," Lengel says, and I
know that's true, too, but remembering how he made that pretty girl
blush makes me so scrunchy inside I punch the No Sale tab and the
machine whirs "pee-pul" and the drawer splats out. One advantage to
this scene taking place in summer, I can follow this up with a clean exit,
there's no fumbling around getting your coat and galoshes, I just saunter
into the electric eye in my white shirt that my mother ironed the night
before, and the door heaves itself open, and outside the sunshine is
skating around on the asphalt.

I looked around for my girls, but they're gone, of course. There   31
wasn't anybody but some young married screaming with her children
about some candy they didn't get by the door of a powder-blue Falcon
station wagon. Looking back in the big windows, over the bags of peat
moss and aluminum lawn furniture stacked on the pavement, I could see
Lengel in my place in the slot, checking the sheep through. His face was
dark gray and his back stiff, as if he'd just had an injection of iron, and my
stomach kind of fell as I felt how hard the world was going to be to me
hereafter.

Questions on Content

1. What first draws Sammy's attention to the three girls?
2. What do the girls purchase?
3. What does Lengel say to them?
4. What does Sammy do once the girls leave?

Questions on Thesis, Purpose, and Structure

1. What is Sammy's attitude toward the regular patrons of the A & P?
2. What is Sammy's attitude toward the A & P itself?
3. What is Sammy's attitude toward the community in which he lives and
works?
4. What is Sammy's attitude toward his family and the family that he imagines
for Queenie?

5. Sammy initially watches the girls because they are attractive and perhaps he is bored. Why and how does his attitude toward them change?
6. Why does Sammy quit his job? Is he in any sense right to do so?
7. What does Sammy mean to say when, as a final gesture, he pushes the No Sale tab on his cash register?
8. Why does Updike conclude his story as he does in paragraph 31?
9. Where does Updike use dialogue most intensively? Why is that dialogue necessary or desirable?
10. Consider the combination of purposes in Updike's writing. What makes the story entertaining? Does it present any information about society or human behavior? Does it make any persuasive points?

Questions on Style and Diction

1. "A & P" is ostensibly narrated by the nineteen-year-old checkout teller Sammy. How successful is Updike in capturing the characteristics of the language used by a person like Sammy? Pay particular attention to word choice, sentence structure, and imagery.
2. "A & P" is filled with figurative language — simile, metaphor, allusion, ambiguity, understatement, overstatement, and irony. Examine a number of instances of such poetic devices. Is it believable that Sammy would use such expressions? Consider, for example, Sammy's attempt to describe Queenie's beauty:

> With the straps pushed off, there was nothing between the top of the suit and the top of her head except just *her*, this clean bare plane of the top of her chest down from the shoulder bones like a dented sheet of metal tilted in the light. I mean, it was more than pretty.

3. Most of Sammy's similes and metaphors add imagery to his narrative. How much do these comparisons add to the humor in the story? To what extent do they add to the theme by revealing Sammy's attitudes toward his work and the people who shop in the A & P? (Pay particular attention to the comparisons between the shoppers and sheep or pigs.)

Ideas for Essays

1. If you have ever quit a job, write a narrative of the events that led up to your resignation. Do not openly explain your reasons for quitting. Instead try to let your motives and emotions emerge from the description, dialogue, and action in your story.
2. Write about a time in your life when you took a stand on a principle despite opposition from your friends, relatives, or superiors.
3. Analyze Sammy's dramatic gesture. Why did he quit? Was he right or wrong in doing so? What should he do in the days and months to come?

◇◇◇

The Necklace

Guy de Maupassant

Guy de Maupassant (1850–1893) was born in Normandy in northwest France. Although he studied law and spent a decade working in Paris as a clerk in the naval ministry, Maupassant's real love was literature and it was as a writer of fiction that he established a national and international reputation. From 1880 to 1890 Maupassant wrote almost three hundred short stories and six novels. Maupassant's best stories succeed in providing truthful insights into the lives of people caught up in the trials and ironies of everyday existence, like M. and Mme. Loisel in "The Necklace" (1884). In the late 1870s Maupassant began experiencing the first symptoms of syphilis, which was in his day as serious as AIDS is in ours. By 1889 Maupassant's syphilis had begun to infect his brain. After attempting suicide in 1891, he was committed to an asylum, where he remained until he died.

She was one of those pretty, charming young ladies, born, as if through an error of destiny, into a family of clerks. She had no dowry, no hopes, no means of becoming known, appreciated, loved and married by a man either rich or distinguished; and she allowed herself to marry a petty clerk in the office of the Board of Education. 1

She was simple, not being able to adorn herself, but she was unhappy, as one out of her class; for women belong to no caste, no race, their grace, their beauty and their charm serving them in the place of birth and family. Their inborn finesse, their instinctive elegance, their suppleness of wit, are their only aristocracy, making some daughters of the people the equal of great ladies. 2

She suffered incessantly, feeling herself born for all delicacies and luxuries. She suffered from the poverty of her apartment, the shabby walls, the worn chairs and the faded stuffs. All these things, which another woman of her station would not have noticed, tortured and angered her. The sight of the little Breton, who made this humble home, awoke in her sad regrets and desperate dreams. She thought of quiet antechambers with their oriental hangings lighted by high bronze torches and of the two great footmen in short trousers who sleep in the large armchairs, made sleepy by the heavy air from the heating apparatus. She thought of large drawing rooms hung in old silks, of graceful pieces of furniture carrying bric-a-brac of inestimable value and of the little perfumed coquettish apartments made for five o'clock chats with most intimate friends, men known and sought after, whose attention all women envied and desired. 3

When she seated herself for dinner before the round table, where the tablecloth had been used three days, opposite her husband who uncovered the tureen with a delighted air, saying: "Oh! the good potpie! I know nothing better than that," she would think of the elegant dinners, of the shining silver, of the tapestries peopling the walls with ancient personages and rare birds in the midst of fairy forests; she thought of the exquisite food served on marvelous dishes, of the whispered gallantries, 4 listened to with the smile of the Sphinx while eating the rose-colored flesh of the trout or a chicken's wing.

5   She had neither frocks nor jewels, nothing. And she loved only those things. She felt that she was made for them. She had such a desire to please, to be sought after, to be clever and courted.

6   She had a rich friend, a schoolmate at the convent, whom she did not like to visit; she suffered so much when she returned. And she wept for whole days from chagrin, from regret, from despair and disappointment.

7   One evening her husband returned, elated, bearing in his hand a large envelope.

8   "Here," he said, "here is something for you."

9   She quickly tore open the wrapper and drew out a printed card on which were inscribed these words:

10   *The Minister of Public Instruction and Madame George Ramponneau ask the honor of M. and Mme Loisel's company Monday evening, January 18, at the Minister's residence.*

11   Instead of being delighted, as her husband had hoped, she threw the invitation spitefully upon the table, murmuring:

12   "What do you suppose I want with that?"

13   "But, my dearie, I thought it would make you happy. You never go out, and this is an occasion, and a fine one! I had a great deal of trouble to get it. Everybody wishes one, and it is very select; not many are given to employees. You will see the whole official world there."

14   She looked at him with an irritated eye and declared impatiently:

15   "What do you suppose I have to wear to such a thing as that?"

16   He had not thought of that; he stammered:

17   "Why, the dress you wear when we go to the theater. It seems very pretty to me."

18   He was silent, stupefied, in dismay, at the sight of his wife weeping. Two great tears fell slowly from the corners of her eyes toward the corners of her mouth; he stammered:

19   "What is the matter? What is the matter?"

20   By a violent effort she had controlled her vexation and responded in a calm voice, wiping her moist cheeks:

21   "Nothing. Only I have no dress and consequently I cannot go to this affair. Give your card to some colleague whose wife is better fitted out than I."

22   He was grieved but answered:

23   "Let us see, Matilda. How much would a suitable costume cost, something that would serve for other occasions, something very simple?"

24   She reflected for some seconds, making estimates and thinking of a sum that she could ask for without bringing with it an immediate refusal and a frightened exclamation from the economical clerk.

Finally she said in a hesitating voice: 25
"I cannot tell exactly, but it seems to me that four hundred francs   26
ought to cover it."

He turned a little pale, for he had saved just this sum to buy a gun   27
that he might be able to join some hunting parties the next summer, on
the plains at Nanterre, with some friends who went to shoot larks up
there on Sunday. Nevertheless, he answered:

"Very well. I will give you four hundred francs. But try to have a   28
pretty dress."

The day of the ball approached, and Mme Loisel seemed sad, dis-   29
turbed, anxious. Nevertheless, her dress was nearly ready. Her husband
said to her one evening:

"What is the matter with you? You have acted strangely for two or   30
three days."

And she responded: "I am vexed not to have a jewel, not one stone,   31
nothing to adorn myself with. I shall have such a poverty-laden look. I
would prefer not to go to this party."

He replied: "You can wear some natural flowers. At this season they   32
look very chic. For ten francs you can have two or three magnificent
roses."

She was not convinced. "No," she replied, "there is nothing more   33
humiliating than to have a shabby air in the midst of rich women."

Then her husband cried out: "How stupid we are! Go and find your   34
friend Madame Forestier and ask her to lend you her jewels. You are
well enough acquainted with her to do this."

She uttered a cry of joy. "It is true!" she said. "I had not thought of   35
that."

The next day she took herself to her friend's house and related her   36
story of distress. Mme Forestier went to her closet with the glass doors,
took out a large jewel case, brought it, opened it and said: "Choose, my
dear."

She saw at first some bracelets, then a collar of pearls, then a   37
Venetian cross of gold and jewels and of admirable workmanship. She
tried the jewels before the glass, hesitated, but could neither decide to
take them nor leave them. Then she asked:

"Have you nothing more?"   38
"Why, yes. Look for yourself. I do not know what will please you."   39

Suddenly she discovered in a black satin box a superb necklace of   40
diamonds, and her heart beat fast with an immoderate desire. Her hands
trembled as she took them up. She placed them about her throat, against
her dress, and remained in ecstasy before them. Then she asked in a
hesitating voice full of anxiety:

"Could you lend me this? Only this?"   41
"Why, yes, certainly."   42

She fell upon the neck of her friend, embraced her with passion,   43
then went away with her treasure.

The day of the ball arrived. Mme Loisel was a great success. She was   44 the prettiest of all, elegant, gracious, smiling and full of joy. All the men noticed her, asked her name and wanted to be presented. All the members of the Cabinet wished to waltz with her. The minister of education paid her some attention.

45   She danced with enthusiasm, with passion, intoxicated with pleasure, thinking of nothing, in the triumph of her beauty, in the glory of her success, in a kind of cloud of happiness that came of all this homage and all this admiration, of all these awakened desires and this victory so complete and sweet to the heart of woman.

46   She went home toward four o'clock in the morning. Her husband had been half asleep in one of the little salons since midnight with three other gentlemen whose wives were enjoying themselves very much.

47   He threw around her shoulders the wraps they had carried for the coming home, modest garments of everyday wear, whose poverty clashed with the elegance of the ball costume. She felt this and wished to hurry away in order not to be noticed by the other women who were wrapping themselves in rich furs.

48   Loisel detained her. "Wait," said he. "You will catch cold out there. I am going to call a cab."

49   But she would not listen and descended the steps rapidly. When they were in the street they found no carriage, and they began to seek for one, hailing the coachmen whom they saw at a distance.

50   They walked along toward the Seine, hopeless and shivering. Finally they found on the dock one of those old nocturnal coupés that one sees in Paris after nightfall, as if they were ashamed of their misery by day.

51   It took them as far as their door in Martyr Street, and they went wearily up to their apartment. It was all over for her. And on his part he remembered that he would have to be at the office by ten o'clock.

52   She removed the wraps from her shoulders before the glass for a final view of herself in her glory. Suddenly she uttered a cry. Her necklace was not around her neck.

53   Her husband, already half undressed, asked: "What is the matter?"
54   She turned toward him excitedly:
55   "I have — I have — I no longer have Madame Forestier's necklace."
56   He arose in dismay: "What! How is that? It is not possible."
57   And they looked in the folds of the dress, in the folds of the mantle, in the pockets, everywhere. They could not find it.
58   He asked: "You are sure you still had it when we left the house?"
59   "Yes, I felt it in the vestibule as we came out."
60   "But if you had lost it in the street we should have heard it fall. It must be in the cab."
61   "Yes. It is probable. Did you take the number?"
62   "No. And you, did you notice what it was?"
63   "No."
64   They looked at each other, utterly cast down. Finally Loisel dressed himself again.
65   "I am going," said he, "over the track where we went on foot, to see if I can find it."

And he went. She remained in her evening gown, not having the 66
force to go to bed, stretched upon a chair, without ambition or thoughts.

Toward seven o'clock her husband returned. He had found nothing. 67

He went to the police and to the cab offices and put an advertise- 68
ment in the newspapers, offering a reward; he did everything that af-
forded them a suspicion of hope.

She waited all day in a state of bewilderment before this frightful 69
disaster. Loisel returned at evening, with his face harrowed and pale, and
had discovered nothing.

"It will be necessary," said he, "to write to your friend that you have 70
broken the clasp of the necklace and that you will have it repaired. That
will give us time to turn around."

She wrote as he dictated. 71

At the end of a week they had lost all hope. And Loisel, older by five 72
years, declared:

"We must take measures to replace this jewel." 73

The next day they took the box which had inclosed it to the jeweler 74
whose name was on the inside. He consulted his books.

"It is not I, madame," said he, "who sold this necklace; I only 75
furnished the casket."

Then they went from jeweler to jeweler, seeking a necklace like the 76
other one, consulting their memories, and ill, both of them, with chagrin
and anxiety.

In a shop of the Palais-Royal they found a chaplet of diamonds 77
which seemed to them exactly like the one they had lost. It was valued at
forty thousand francs. They could get it for thirty-six thousand.

They begged the jeweler not to sell it for three days. And they made 78
an arrangement by which they might return it for thirty-four thousand
francs if they found the other one before the end of February.

Loisel possessed eighteen thousand francs which his father had left 79
him. He borrowed the rest.

He borrowed it, asking for a thousand francs of one, five hundred of 80
another, five louis of this one and three louis of that one. He gave notes,
made ruinous promises, took money of usurers and the whole race of
lenders. He compromised his whole existence, in fact, risked his signature without even knowing whether he could make it good or not, and,
harrassed by anxiety for the future, by the black misery which surrounded him and by the prospect of all physical privations and moral
torture, he went to get the new necklace, depositing on the merchant's
counter thirty-six thousand francs.

When Mme Loisel took back the jewels to Mme Forestier the latter 81
said to her in a frigid tone:

"You should have returned them to me sooner, for I might have 82
needed them."

She did not open the jewel box as her friend feared she would. If 83
she should perceive the substitution what would she think? What should
she say? Would she take her for a robber?

Mme Loisel now knew the horrible life of necessity. She did her 84 part, however, completely, heroically. It was necessary to pay this frightful debt. She would pay it. They sent away the maid; they changed their lodgings; they rented some rooms under a mansard roof.

85   She learned the heavy cares of a household, the odious work of a kitchen. She washed the dishes, using her rosy nails upon the greasy pots and the bottoms of the stewpans. She washed the soiled linen, the chemises and dishcloths, which she hung on the line to dry; she took down the refuse to the street each morning and brought up the water, stopping at each landing to breathe. And, clothed like a woman of the people, she went to the grocer's, the butcher's and the fruiterer's with her basket on her arm, shopping, haggling to the last sou her miserable money."

86   Every month it was necessary to renew some notes, thus obtaining time, and to pay others.

87   The husband worked evenings, putting the books of some merchants in order, and nights he often did copying at five sous a page.

88   And this life lasted for ten years.

89   At the end of ten years they had restored all, with interest of the usurer, and accumulated interest, besides.

90   Mme Loisel seemed old now. She had become a strong, hard woman, the crude woman of the poor household. Her hair badly dressed, her skirts awry, her hands red, she spoke in a loud tone and washed the floors in large pails of water. But sometimes, when her husband was at the office, she would seat herself before the window and think of that evening party of former times, of that ball where she was so beautiful and so flattered.

91   How would it have been if she had not lost that necklace? Who knows? Who knows? How singular is life and how full of changes! How small a thing will ruin or save one!

92   One Sunday, as she was taking a walk in the Champs Elysées to rid herself of the cares of the week, she suddenly perceived a woman walking with a child. It was Mme Forestier, still young, still pretty, still attractive. Mme Loisel was affected. Should she speak to her? Yes, certainly. And now that she had paid, she would tell her all. Why not?

93   She approached her. "Good morning, Jeanne."

94   Her friend did not recognize her and was astonished to be so familiarly addressed by this common personage. She stammered:

95   "But, madame—I do not know—You must be mistaken."

96   "No, I am Matilda Loisel."

97   Her friend uttered a cry of astonishment: "Oh! my poor Matilda! How you have changed."

98   "Yes, I have had some hard days since I saw you, and some miserable ones—and all because of you."

99   "Because of me? How is that?"

100   "You recall the diamond necklace that you loaned me to wear to the minister's ball?"

101   "Yes, very well."

102   "Well, I lost it."

"How is that, since you returned it to me?" 103

"I returned another to you exactly like it. And it has taken us ten 104
years to pay for it. You can understand that it was not easy for us who
have nothing. But it is finished, and I am decently content."

Mme Forestier stopped short. She said: 105

"You say that you bought a diamond necklace to replace mine?" 106

"Yes. You did not perceive it then? They were just alike." 107

And she smiled with a proud and simple joy. Mme Forestier was 108
touched and took both her hands as she replied:

"Oh, my poor Matilda! Mine were false. They were not worth over 109
five hundred francs!"

Questions on Content

1. What sort of life does Matilda Loisel dream of at the beginning of the story?
   What sort of life does she have?
2. What happens to disrupt the unsatisfying routine of Matilda's life? How does
   she at first react to the opportunity her husband extends to her?
3. What happens to the borrowed necklace?
4. What must the Loisels do in order to replace the necklace?
5. How much had Mme. Forestier's necklace actually been worth?

Questions on Thesis, Purpose, and Structure

1. Consider the character and values of M. and Mme. Loisel. What do we know
   about their values from the way they conduct themselves? How does the
   necklace Mme. Loisel selects symbolize her life and values?
2. Why does Matilda refuse to wait while her husband calls a cab? Why is this
   refusal typical of her? How does it contribute to her downfall?
3. Why do the Loisels decide to replace the necklace without explaining the
   situation to Mme. Forestier? How is this illustrative of the flaws in their
   values?
4. How does Matilda change in personality and appearance over the years? Has
   she changed for better or worse? Has she become lost or saved?
5. Is Matilda's pride in telling Mme. Forestier how hard she worked to replace
   the necklace any different from the pride that led her to borrow it in the first
   place?
6. What statement does the story as a whole make about pride and materialism?

Questions on Style and Diction

1. Find the following words in the essay and determine their definitions in
   context: dowry (paragraph 1); caste, finesse, suppleness (paragraph 2); antechambers, bric-a-brac, coquettish (paragraph 3); tureen, tapestries, gallantries
   (paragraph 4); chagrin (paragraph 6); chic (paragraph 32); homage (paragraph 45); salons (paragraph 46); nocturnal coupés (paragraph 50); vestibule
   (paragraph 59); usurers (paragraph 80); chemises (paragraph 85).
2. In what is called *situational irony*, a set of circumstances turns out to be the
   reverse of what is appropriate or expected. Where is situational irony used in
   this story? How is this use of irony related to the author's main point or
   theme?

Ideas for Essays

1. Write an essay about the causes and effects of Matilda Loisel's misfortune.
2. "How small a thing will ruin or save one," writes de Maupassant. Write a narrative essay based on your own experiences that illustrates Maupassant's observation.
3. M. and Mme. Loisel are good examples of the vain and materialistic members of the middle class in France over a century ago. Compare the Loisels with typical members of today's middle class.

"Are You Ready for an Alfa Romeo?"
"Kawasaki Lets the Good Times Roll."

The use of narration in advertisements is relatively uncommon. A company normally wishes to convince consumers that *they* will find the product useful, but a specific story risks appealing only to those consumers who are similar to the protagonist and either ignoring or alienating others. This difficulty is avoided in "Are you ready for an Alfa Romeo?" by the use of three brief narratives. By presenting three quite different purchasers, the company is obviously attempting to broaden the appeal of the product and the advertisement.

In contrast, the advertisement for Kawasaki motorcycles uses only one anecdote. The appeal of the advertisement is much the same as that of a short story. It includes characters, conflict, and a witty resolution. We read the advertisement not because we see ourselves as being particularly similar to the man on the motorcycle, but because we grow interested in the little drama that plays itself out beside the country road. As we read, of course, we pick up hints about the Kawasaki KE175 — its "new-fangled engine, an' a five-speed transmission" and its usefulness on and off the road. And when we finish we are left with the impression that a Kawasaki motorcycle is a reliable means of transportation, purchased by clever people.

Are you ready for an Alfa Romeo?

Sheila C.

Bill B.

Ray R.

"When I was a young man I dreamed that one day I would own an Alfa Romeo.

"When I was 25 I was really the perfect wife, the perfect mother and the perfect homemaker.

"I drove a great big stationwagon.

"Well, I'm no longer 25 and I'm no longer anyone's wife—my kids are grown and have kids of their own and I have a career.

"And that stationwagon is just a rusted memory.

"You know what I did? I went out and bought myself an Alfa Romeo Spider.

"It's red and it's got a convertible top and sometimes when I pass those ladies in their huge stationwagons full of kids, and dogs, and groceries I wave—and say to myself, there but for the grace of my Alfa go I."

"But then I got married and Jennifer arrived a year later; two years after that, Robert.

"My dream of owning an Alfa gave way to the reality of a mortgage, dentist's bills, and college tuition.

"But now Jennifer is married and has a Jennifer of her own, Robert Junior is through law school.

"And this 50 year old kid went out and bought himself an Alfa Romeo Spider.

"Do I love my Alfa as much as I thought I would? Well, It's a dream come true."

"I limped through college and graduate school with one crummy used car after another.

"But now that I've got a grown up job with grown up responsibility, I thought I'd treat myself to a brand new car.

"Well, at first, I thought the world had passed me by—all those cars were so boring!

"Then I discovered the Alfa Spider. First of all, it's a convertible! And most of all it's an Alfa Romeo.

"What a machine!

"Today when I leave the office after all those meetings, my hair cut short, necktie in place, I'll jump into my very own Alfa Romeo Spider.

"You know, all that college was worth it."

The Alfa Romeo Spider Veloce: $13,995 1980 manufacturer's suggested retail price P.O.E. Inland transportation, dealer preparation, local taxes, and optional equipment not included. For the name of your nearest Alfa Romeo Dealer, call us anytime, toll free at 800-447-4700; in Illinois call 800-322-4400.

Alfa Romeo

Courtesy of Alfa Romeo, Inc.

Ideas for Discussion and Writing

1. Consider the brief life stories of Sheila, Bill, and Ray. How do they differ? In what ways are they alike? What does the Alfa Romeo Spider offer to each?
2. What tensions or conflicts existed in the lives of each character? How does the purchase of the Alfa Romeo Spider help each one to resolve these tensions?
3. What does the advertisement suggest about the age, sex, life situation, and personality of the typical Alpha Romeo owner?
4. How does this advertisement entertain the reader? What information does it provide about the Alfa Romeo Spider? Do you find it persuasive? That is, are you more, or less, likely to desire this car after having read the advertisement? Explain your reasoning.

CITY BOY. Paul spotted him first, just a bouncin' along, an' a grinnin' away like he know'd somethin' everybody else didn't. When he finally got to where we were a settin', Paul winked at me an' ask him real straight-faced, "You lost, city boy?"

"Not necessarily," he smiled.

Bobby ask him what it was that he was ridin', an' city boy said it was a Kawasaki. "A whut?" Bobby said. "A Kawasaki, KE175," city boy told him, real proud. Said it had some kinda new-fangled engine, an' a five-speed transmission, an' all kinds'a other fancy stuff. Said he could ride it just about anywhere he pleased, too...on the road or off — didn't make no difference. Bobby said,"I'll take my palomino any day, he don't get lost." "That's right," Paul said, "horses got brains. Know where they're goin', even if you don't."

City boy just grinned an' said, "Which way's town?"

Well, right away Paul starts ta' pointin' up the road, toward the bunkhouse. An' no sooner'n he had his finger stuck out, an' Bobby was a pointin' up t'other way.

City boy just eyed 'em both for a minute, an' then, with that same grin on his face, he started up his motor-sickle. First kick. Then he pulled out a map an' handed it over ta' Bobby an' said straight-out, "Stick it where your brains are, cowboy...and maybe you'll end up smart as your horse," An' off he rode.

Thought Paul and Bobby's faces were gonna turn redder'n their necks. Good thing that machine didn't stall.

Kawasaki
lets the good times roll.

[1976]

Courtesy of Kawasaki Motors Corp., U.S.A.

Ideas for Discussion and Writing

1. In our earlier comments on narration, we argued that you should include description, dialogue, characterization, conflict, and crisis in your narrations. How successful is this advertisement in including each of these five elements?
2. Why is a regional dialect used in the advertisement? What do you learn about the narrator from the dialect? What are the main features of the dialect? Is it used effectively, or is it overused?
3. How effectively does this advertisement combine purposes? Is it informative? Entertaining? Persuasive? Explain your answers.

Chapter 8

PROCESS

Pity the poor parent assembling Castle Grayskull at midnight on Christmas eve. After all the hours of last-minute shopping and festive decorating, she has had enough problems without confronting an instruction to "Place trap door activator so it will fit over lower lock tab." Trap door activator? Lower lock tab? What *are* these things? And *where* the dickens are they?

The same parent may well begin assembling her daughter's scooter even later in the night. At 2 A.M. the instruction to "Attach handle assembly to frame by inserting hinge pin through hinge bracket and through hinge bushings on frame" might as well be written in Greek.

Such instructions are examples of process analysis at its most vexing. But they are also examples of the nearly inexhaustible need for good process writing. Not only is almost every new product sold with a set of instructions, but many magazine articles and books also describe processes. American cash registers ring merrily from purchases of *How to Make Love to a Man, The Beverly Hills Diet, The One-Minute Manager*, and the *Jane Fonda Exercise Book*. Tennis stars teach us "How to Hit a Drop Shot," and shop manuals tell us how to fix our cars. Intellectuals explain to us how the universe was formed or how the heart pumps blood.

DIRECTIONS AND EXPLANATIONS

As these examples indicate, process analysis has great variety, but it takes two basic forms. One form involves instructions or directions: the how-to-do-it essay. You engage in this form of discourse when you tell a friend how to find your home or when you write down a recipe. The other form of process analysis describes how something happens: how a star evolves, how a snowflake is formed, how a tree captures sunlight,

Castello Sforzesco, Milan/Alinari/Art Resource, NY

The *Rodanini Pieta* (1552–1564) was the third great attempt by Michelangelo to depict the grief of Mary for her son Jesus; it was also the one on which he labored longest and hardest, continuing almost to the day of his death. Note how the figures only partially emerge from the stone. Note, too, the coarse chiseling, the lack of polish, and the roughed-in facial expressions. (You may wish to compare this sculpture with the picture of Michelangelo's *David* in Chapter 11.) What can you tell about the process of carving from this sculpture? Would the sculpture be better if it were "finished"?

how an avalanche begins, how an automobile engine works, how a computer "thinks."

By completing the earlier chapters in this book, you have already learned much of what you need to know in order to write an effective process analysis. Clear description is obviously crucial. Your reader must be able to visualize the "trap door activator" and the "lower lock tab." Sometimes the need for description is reduced by the provision of illustrations and diagrams, but in a writing assignment you may not be allowed to use illustrations or they may be inappropriate. (How would you illustrate an avalanche?) Thus, the ability to use descriptive imagery will serve you well in process analysis.

Skill in narration is also helpful. Like a story, a process records events in time sequence. However, whereas a story emphasizes entertainment, a process emphasizes information. And whereas a story tells of events that may have happened only once, a process describes things that happen the same way (or should be done the same way) every time. You would write a story to recount the particular tragedies that occurred during the avalanche at Val D'Isere in France. You would write a process analysis to explain what transpires during every avalanche.

PREWRITING

Begin planning your essay by thinking through each step in the process. As you do so, make brief notes on each step to consult as you draft your essay.

If time permits, try to explain the process to someone else. During this dialogue, rely only on words to explain the process. Resist the temptation to pick up your tennis racquet and demonstrate the proper forehand grip. Take particular notice of the questions that your partner in this dialogue asks. ("What do you mean when you say 'grip the racquet naturally'? Should I grab it as I would a hammer or should I try to shake hands with it?") The questions and confusions of your partner will let you know where to be most careful and detailed in describing the process. Your notes on this dialogue may also prove invaluable in helping you to discover steps that you skipped over in your first set of notes.

PLANNING AND DRAFTING
A PROCESS PAPER

Early in an instructional essay, devote a paragraph to describing any special tools and materials needed for the process. A list of ingredients is essential in a recipe for pumpkin pie, just as a list of necessary equipment is essential in instructions on learning to windsurf: "The basic needs of a beginning windsurfer are a board, a bathing suit, a *gentle* breeze, and a book to read in case the wind stiffens. The board, of course, has several components. . . ."

Define unfamiliar terminology. To do so, you must consider your audience. If you are writing an essay on windsurfing for members of the Boston Yacht Club, you can probably plunge right into your subject: "To raise the sail, plant your feet shoulder width apart, with one foot just aft of the universal joint and the other just aft of the dagger-board. Grasp the uphaul with your masthand, stand up straight, and apply steady lift by leaning back slightly." But if you are writing for your classmates, you will need to explain your terms:

The *universal joint* connects the mast to the board and allows the mast to tilt freely in any direction.

The *daggerboard* is a thin fiberglass blade about three feet long and six to twelve inches wide. It is inserted in a slot near the center of the board to improve steering and stability.

The *uphaul* is a thick rope attached to the boom where it joins the mast. It is used, as its name suggests, to haul up the sail.

Your *masthand* is the hand that grasps the boom closest to the mast. When the wind is coming from the left as you face the bow (a port tack), your masthand will be your left hand; when the wind is coming from the right (a starboard tack), your masthand will be your right hand.

Follow a strict chronological order. Discuss the steps in a process one at a time, as they actually occur or should be performed. If several events occur at once, try to arrange the events in order of importance: "When you have raised the mast to vertical and the boom is perpendicular to the length of the board, get underway by tilting the entire rig slightly toward the bow, 'sheeting in' the sail, and leaning back slightly against the pull of the sail. To 'sheet in' the sail you must pull in sharply with your 'leeward' hand — that is, with the hand closest to the stern of the board. . . ."

Try to anticipate difficulties by warning your readers of the major tasks ahead: "The beginning windsurfer faces three major problems — lifting the sail from the water, getting underway, and steering the board back to the dock." Such a forewarning actually groups the steps in the process into major subdivisions. These subdivisions help the readers to understand the structure of your essay, but they also give them important guidance in completing the process successfully. By knowing what the problems in the process will be, your readers can concentrate on those problems and more rapidly overcome them.

Another way to anticipate difficulties is to **tell your readers what to do if something goes wrong:** "Once you begin to sail, if you feel yourself falling backwards towards the water, immediately tilt the entire sail toward the front of the board, crouch down, and pull in on the back edge of the sail with your 'leeward' hand."

Don't confine yourself to the sparest possible description of the process. **Pause as necessary to tell your readers how to make the process easier or more enjoyable:** "Since you'll probably spend more time in the water than one the board, consider wearing a wetsuit to conserve body heat — and by all means wear a life jacket."

COMBINING PURPOSES

Process essays are primarily informative, and you may have to struggle a bit to find ways to be entertaining and persuasive as well as informative. **One possibility is to consider a humorous topic or a humorous approach to a serious topic.** This is the solution chosen by Deborah Chappel in her essay "So You Want to Read a Romance" (p. 192). She wishes to give her readers serious advice about how to go about choosing a romance, but she selected the topic at least in part because of the possibilities for humor in it. After all, many college-educated people are a bit embarrassed about having a taste for books with lurid covers and titles like *Sweet Savage Love.* By her choice of topic, Debbie opened up possibilities for self-mockery, satire of the romance genre, and even some gentle ribbing of her readers.

The wry and mildly satirical tone of Debbie's essay is something of a staple in process analysis. Sometimes this humor is most easily attained by describing a process that no one really wants to experience. This is the case in Paul Roberts's "How to Say Nothing in Five Hundred Words" (p. 218) and Jessica Mitford's "The Embalmer's Art" (p. 198).

You should be cautious, however, in your selection of a humorous topic. An essay on "How to Flunk Out of School Without Offending Your Parents" is almost certain to be humorous, but it may not be informative or persuasive in any sensible way. After all, few students really wish to flunk out of school, and few readers will long to master the technique. With such a topic, your best bet is to use irony; by explaining how to flunk out of school, you can warn your readers against making the errors of unsuccessful students. In other words, **try to develop a thesis with a persuasive component**. In writing on the topic "How to Say Nothing in Five Hundred Words," Paul Roberts actually hopes to persuade students to *say something* in their essays. In describing the process of embalming, Jessica Mitford actually hopes to persuade her readers to forego that grisly and costly procedure. In writing an essay on "How to Windsurf," you might develop a variety of persuasive theses:

Windsurfing is excellent exercise for the entire body.
You may not learn to windsurf in just one day, but you will surely improve your swimming.
Don't try windsurfing; you will only be frustrated by failure and confused by terminology.
Windsurfing provides wonderful illustrations of the scientific principles of aerodynamics and leverage.
Windsurfing is an ideal way to enjoy being on a lake without polluting the environment.

TIPS ON REVISION

Indicate time sequence through transitional expressions. Whether you are providing instructions on windsurfing or explaining the formation of snowflakes, your reader will appreciate help in recognizing the major steps and the approximate amount of time each step takes. You may, of course, use explicit indicators like *first, next,* or *then*. But avoid making your readers labor up a flight of stairs; *the first step, the second step, the third step, . . . the twenty-ninth step*. The drudgery of such an approach is all too obvious. Vary the form of your transitions, using occasional time markers like *soon, shortly thereafter, in about three minutes*, and so on.

When you think your draft is as clear as you can make it, **test your work by having a friend read through it**. If you have written a set of instructions, you may wish to have your friend actually perform them. If that is not possible or if you have written a process explanation, encourage your friend to pause frequently to ask questions. You may discover that you have failed to define some crucial term, skipped an important step, or left an ambiguity in an instruction. If you are explaining how to clean and gap a spark plug, you certainly need to define a torque wrench even if you use one daily. Similarly, you may need to revise an instruction to "Use the plug wrench to remove the spark plug." Does one do so by turning the wrench clockwise or counterclockwise? Often the fresh insight of your reader can help you catch minor omissions and ambiguities.

IDEAS FOR ESSAYS

1. Write an instructional (how-to-do-it) process analysis on one of the following topics:

   How to eat pizza (or a taco, or Chinese food)
   How to select a detective novel (or a romance, a science fiction novel, a book of poems, and so on)
   How to enjoy an opera
   How to study for a final exam
   How to borrow your dad's car
   How to borrow money from a friend
   How to win at tennis (or golf, chess, poker, etc.) without actually playing better
   How to tell a fish story
   How to chastise a child
   How to behave on a first date
   How to impress the parents of your boyfriend, girlfriend, or spouse
   How to "break up" gracefully
   How to survive the month of December (or any other month of your choice)
   How to sleep in class without getting caught
   How to flunk out of college without losing the blessings of your parents
   How to sell a clunker
   How to get the perfect schedule during registration

How to watch a football game (or basketball game)
How to die of old age by thirty
How to find a rich husband (or wife)
How to be a backseat driver
How to live on $50 a year
How to let someone else pick up the tab for lunch

Check with your instructor if you wish to modify any of these topics or if you have another good idea for an instructional process analysis.

> 2. Write an explanatory process analysis on one of the following topics. Remember that in this form of essay you tell how something happens, not how to do it:

How people make up their minds while shopping for a new car
How a cat catches a bird
How family vacations go awry
How an author develops a character
How bad habits are acquired
How a fight between good friends is patched up
How people cope with grief
How children win our affection
How rock stars fade into oblivion
How soap operas create addicts

STUDENT ESSAY ─────────────────────────

Deborah Chappel wrote this essay in her freshman English course as an out-of-class response to the topics supplied under "Ideas for Essays" — specifically, the topic "How to choose a detective novel (or a romance, a science fiction novel, a book of poems, and so on)." She began by taking detailed notes about each stage in the process.

FIRST DRAFT

"SO YOU WANT TO READ A ROMANCE NOVEL?"

by Deborah Chappel

I. Decide Whether You Qualify as a Potential Romance Reader

A. Problems you need to escape from

B. Strong sense of the ridiculous to carry you through the ~~truly~~ wretchedly written romance—all dedicated romance readers encounter a few of these. The petite, curvaceous heroine who signs on as cabin boy of a ship bound for an exotic port and captained by a dashing, decidedly chauvinistic rake. If you *undetected* buy the line that she passes, as a boy for several months on a small ship, then you really can't blame the author for trying to convince you that she holds her own in a swordfight and eludes the lustful advances of every male except our hero, the sardonic captain. If you can remain tolerantly amused by the improbable impostures and marriages of convenience, you'll probably make an excellent romance reader.

C. Are you prepared to encounter a certain amount of persecution in the pursuit of your new hobby? You can, of course, minimize this problem by concealing the cover of your book in a specially designed jacket available at most bookstores. Other methods such as hiding your book in a capacious shoulder bag and finding isolated spots for reading can help, but be warned that sometime, somewhere ~~you'll be~~ your crime will be uncovered. You must prepare yourself to humbly accept the ridicule of people who haven't read anything except the back of their cereal boxes since they graduated from high school.

II. If you answered "yes" to all three parts of Question 1 above, then the next issue of interest to you is where to buy your romances.

A. You could, of course, go to the public library. ~~They,~~ It would be unlikely, however, to carry the newest titles and you might not want to give a public institution like this a chance to obtain indelible records of your choice in literature.

B. Bookstores are terrible places to buy romances, since those who shop and work there are often the intellectual types who will eye you with open disdain.

C. Grocery stores and discount variety stores have good selections of romances and are generally good spots to buy your books. The only drawback is that these stores are public gathering places in your community and chances are good that you will meet your boss, physician, or Sunday School teacher while you loiter in front of the paperbacks or wait in the checkout line.

D. The best place to find your romances is a used paperback bookstore. These shops will generally save you money, since the usual policy is that you receive credit of one-fourth of the book's cover price of books you bring to trade and you pay one-half the cover price on books you purchase. Once you have read a few romances, you will find that you welcome this convenient method of getting rid of your discards, as you will encounter few romances worthy of saving for posterity. Used bookstores often have ~~vintage~~ good collections ~~which allow good~~ of vintage authors and series unavailable through any other source. In addition, the owner of the shop is generally a prolific romance reader who can point you toward the most entertaining selections.

III. Now that you have identified yourself as a potential romance reader and decided where to purchase your books, let us turn our attention to the matter of what kinds of books to choose. A quick glance at the shelves of any bookstore selling romance novels reveals a bewildering array *of titles,* and varieties. The type of book you *publishers,* choose is, of course, a matter of personal preference, but a little information on the types of romances currently available may be helpful.

Avon, Ballen, and Pocket Fiction

A. Bestsellers. These books can be easily identified by the titles and covers, since the titles generally include one or more of the following words: "sweet, *lust,* love, savage, flame, heart, desire," or ~~wayward~~ passion," and the cover usually features a half-clothed and well-endowed female reluctantly submitting to the passionate embrace of a dashing male. The majority of these novels ~~ar~~ call themselves historical fiction and a few of them, such as Roberta Gellis' Roselynde Chronicles, really ~~are~~ give the reader interesting background ~~inform~~ on certain periods of history. These books are generally ~~m~~ lengthier and feature more sensuous detail than the other categories listed below. The inevitably beautiful heroine travels from one end of the globe to the other on her improbable but entertaining adventures. She is generally separated by war, death, or disaster from the resources of her wealthy family and must be rescued, generally against her will and often after a rape or two, by the forceful hero. The hero is ~~always~~ inevitably ~~drawn by~~ captured by the heroine's beauty, spirit, and ~~natural~~ untutored sexual prowess, so that the reader has the certain knowledge that every romance of this nature will indeed end happily. Since the titles give ~~no~~ the reader little clue of the book's plot, the informed romance reader will peruse the back cover and the ~~inside~~ blurbs on the first page (it's sometimes helpful to read that the Chattanooga Dispatch found this book "electrifying") before purchasing).

B. Harlequin romances are generally shorter, with less

complicated plots and characters and less sensual detail. Whereas the longer bestseller romance brings the hero and heroine into bed early in the book and focuses on passionate conflicts between the two, Harlequin and other romances of this genre focus on the cat-and-mouse game of courtship. These books are the ultimate in escapism and afford a terrifically easy read, especially since the conclusion is never a surprise. I've known ~~people~~ women who were addicted to Harlequins, greedily consuming ten or more books in a single week.

C. Superromance, Silhouette Desires, Intimate Moments, and Special Editions attempt to merge the most popular components of both Harlequins and bestseller romantic fiction. Hence, the cat-and-mouse of courtship is blended with ~~the~~ sensual detail, ~~of~~ usually resulting in a good bit of frustration for the reader and most especially for the characters. The standard plots used in Harlequins and bestsellers do not generally lend themselves to this type of romance unless the author expects the reader to ~~belief~~ believe some mighty silly stuff, but you may find the occasional entertaining innovation. Try this variety, if a few inconsistencies and some very repetitious love scenes don't bother you, you may find these books enjoyable.

D. At last we come to my personal favorites, Gothics, ~~and~~ Victorians, and Regencies. Don't be at first disappointed if you encounter some exceedingly ~~silly~~ inane works in this field. There are some classics written by entertaining authors, such as Georgette Heyer (~~she writes with~~ you need a sense of humor to appreciate her style) and Victoria Holt. ~~Once you~~

~~find a good author~~ The best books of this type are
hard to find, with the best superior collections in used
bookstores and garage sales.

Commentary: Debbie's free writing in outline format has given
her most of the material that she will need for the final draft of her essay.
However, she clearly needs a catchy introduction to attract readers and
she needs something in her conclusion to persuade her readers that
romances, despite their frequent silliness, really are worth reading.
    In two further drafts (which we have not reproduced) Debbie
worked on her introduction and conclusion while also beefing up her
discussion of the various categories of romance by defining Gothics,
Victorians, and Regencies more fully and by adding lists of recommended reading. In her final draft she included a formal outline as a
check on the organization and logic in the completed essay.

FINAL DRAFT

"SO YOU WANT TO READ A ROMANCE?"

by Deborah Chappel

OUTLINE

I. INTRO—(Thesis: Romances do serve some valuable and constructive
purposes for society.)

II. STEPS IN BECOMING A ROMANCE READER

    A. Are you a potential romance reader?

        1. Have problems?

        2. Strong sense of the ridiculous?

        3. Prepared for persecution?

    B. Where to obtain your romances?

        1. Library

        2. Bookstore

        3. Grocery or discount variety store

        4. Best method—used book store

    C. Types of romances available

        1. Bestsellers

            a. Description

      b. Best way to choose

      c. Recommended authors and titles

  2. Harlequins, First Loves, and Silhouettes

      a. Description

      b. Best way to choose (no need—all the same)

      c. Recommended authors

  3. Superromance, Silhouette Desire, Intimate Moments, etc.

      a. Description—merging of bestseller and Harlequin

      b. Best way to choose

      c. Recommended authors

  4. Victorians, Gothics, Regencies

      a. Description of each type

      b. Best way to choose

      c. Recommended authors

III. CONCLUSION—Restatement of thesis

Several years ago, after reading a quotation from a popular romance depicting a heroine feeling quivers of excitement, chills, and palpitations when the hero kissed her hand, Germaine Greer stated, "Indeed, if hand kissing can produce orgasm, actual intercourse might well bring on epilepsy." That kind of attitude toward romances continues today, partly because it is fun and easy to write disdainful commentary on these works, and partly because some of this disdainful commentary is so richly deserved. Few would dispute the fact that the majority of romances on the shelves at the local grocery store cannot be classified as literature. However, these books do serve valuable and constructive purposes, offering vicarious fulfillment of the need for romance and semi-challenging reading material for the semi-literate.

If you have an interest in sex, you may be a potential romance reader, but not necessarily. There are three basic questions you should ask yourself before proceeding.

1. Do you have problems you would like to escape? If you think your life is just ducky as it is, then escapist romantic fiction probably holds little appeal.

2. Do you have a strong sense of the ridiculous? Half the fun of reading romances is laughing at the truly wretched ones. All dedicated romance readers encounter a few of these, usually featuring a petite but improbably curvaceous heroine who signs on as a cabin boy of a ship bound for an exotic port and captained by a dashing, decidedly chauvinistic male. If you buy the line that she passes undetected as a boy for several months on a small ship, then you really can't blame the author for trying to convince you that she holds her own in a swordfight and eludes the lustful advances of every male except our hero, the sardonic captain. If you can remain tolerantly amused by improbable impostures and unwarranted marriages of convenience, you'll probably make an excellent romance reader.

3. Are you prepared to encounter a certain amount of persecution in the pursuit of your new hobby? You can, of course, minimize this problem by concealing the cover of your book in a specially designed cover available at most bookstores. Other methods, such as hiding your book in a capacious shoulder bag and finding isolated spots to read it surreptitiously, can help, but be forewarned that sometime, somewhere, your guilty secret will be uncovered. You must prepare yourself to humbly accept the ridicule of people who haven't read anything except the back of their cereal boxes since they graduated from high school.

If you still wish to proceed, then the next step is finding a source of good romance. There are four avenues open to you: public libraries, bookstores, grocery or discount stores, and used book stores. You can, of course, find romances in your public library, but libraries are unlikely to carry the newest titles and you may not want to give a public institution permanent records of your choice in literature. Bookstores are terrible places to buy romances, since those who shop and work there are often intellectual types who will eye you with open disdain. Grocery stores and discount variety stores have good selections of romances and are generally good spots to buy your books. Their only drawback is that they are public gathering places in your community, and chances are good that you will meet your boss, physician, or Sunday School teacher as you loiter in front of the paperbacks, a confrontation that might well prove humiliating for all concerned.

The best place to purchase romances is a used paperback book store. These shops will generally save you money, since the usual policy is that you receive credit for one-fourth of the cover price of books you bring to trade and pay one-half of the cover price of books you purchase. Once you have read a few romances, you will find that you welcome this convenient method of ridding yourself of your discards, as you will encounter few romances worthy of adorning the shelves of your home library. Used book stores often have collections of vintage authors and series unavailable through any other source. In addition, the owner of the shop is generally a prolific romance reader who can point you toward the most entertaining selections. You will find a very comfortable conspiracy to preserve each patron's anonymity in used book stores. (I have not included the purchase of Harlequins through the mail among the avenues of supply of romances. Having no personal experience with this method, I hesitate to recommend it, although, if you plan on purchasing Harlequins, having several arrive at your home each month concealed in brown paper must hold some appeal.)

Now that you have identified yourself as a potential romance reader and have considered where to make your purchase, you must next decide what kind of romance you will choose. A quick glance at the shelves of any bookstores selling romances reveals a bewildering array of titles, publishers, and varieties. The type of book you choose is, of course, a matter of personal preference, but a little information on the types of romances currently available may be helpful. Romances fall naturally into four categories:

1. Bestsellers. These books can be easily identified by the titles and covers. The titles generally include one or more of the following words: sweet, love, savage, flame, heart, desire, captive, or passion. And the cover usually features a half-clothed and well-endowed female reluctantly submitting to the passionate embrace of a dashing male. The majority of these novels call themselves historical fiction, and a few of them really are, particularly Roberta Gellis' Roselynde series. Bestseller romantic fiction is generally lengthier and contains more sensuous detail than the other types of romance. The plots generally follow a predictable and juicy pattern, the most common element being that a

beautiful heroine travels from one end of the globe to the other on
entertaining but unlikely adventures. She is typically separated by war,
death, or disaster from the resources of her wealthy family and must be
rescued, usually against her will and often after a rape or two, by the
forceful hero. The hero is inevitably and unwillingly captivated by the
heroine's beauty, spirit, and untutored sexual prowess; thus, the reader
has the certain knowledge from the outset that every romance of this
nature will indeed end happily. Since the titles give the reader little clue
to the book's plot, the informed romance reader will peruse the back
cover and the blurbs on the facing page before purchasing. (It is
sometimes helpful to know that the Chattanooga Dispatch found a book
"electrifying.") Recommended publishers: Avon, Gallen, Pocket Fiction.
Recommended books: Sweet Savage Love by Rosemary Rodgers; The
Wolf and the Dove and The Flame and the Flower, by Kathleen
Woodiwiss; Hummingbird, by Lavyrle Spencer; and the Calder series
and all other books written by Janet Daley.

2. Harlequins, First Loves, and Silhouettes. This variety is generally
shorter, with less complicated plots and characters and less sensual
detail. While the longer bestseller romance brings the hero and heroine
into bed early in the book and focuses on passionate conflicts between
the two thereafter, Harlequins and other romances of this genre focus on
the cat-and-mouse games of courtship. These books are the ultimate in
escapism and afford a terrifically easy read, especially since the
conclusion is never a surprise. The plots are so alike that if you like this
variety, you can read any of the books available with equal enjoyment.
Recommended books: Harlequins by Janet Daley and Ann Mather.

3. Superromance, Silhouette Desire, Candlelight Ecstasy Romance,
Intimate Moments, Special Editions, and Gallen Books. Even the titles in
this category are slightly embarrassing. All of these varieties attempt,
usually unsuccessfully, to merge the most popular components of both the
bestseller and the Harlequin romance. Thus, the cat-and-mouse of
Harlequin is blended with the sensual detail of the bestseller, usually
resulting in a good bit of frustration for the reader and most especially
for the hapless characters. Love scenes and plots get a little tedious and

mighty silly when forced to sustain such high degrees of sexual tension through so many passionate conflicts while avoiding consummation until the bitter, long-awaited end. Again, the back cover and blurbs on the facing page can be helpful, but the best indicators of a really juicy romance are a well-known author or personal recommendation. Recommended publisher divisions: Gallen Books and Silhouette Special Editions. Recommended authors: Jude Devereaux, Carole Halston, and Janet Daley.

4. Gothics, Victorians, and Regencies. At last we come to my personal favorites! Gothics are usually pseudo-mysteries peopled with governesses, paid companions, and lesser nobility, all coming together in a plot which provides the heroine with ample reason to suspect the hero of foul play. True love does, of course, prevail, and some minor character is found to be the villain after all. Victorian romances are prim and often tongue-in-cheek works featuring the coming together of our worthy heroine with a sometimes less-than-worthy hero through the amusing antics of Victorian England's ton. Regencies feature much of the same, with a bit of bawdiness and mystery thrown in for good measure. Good Gothics, Victorians, and Regencies are the most insipid and ridiculous books in existence. The best method of choosing these books is to find an author you like and systematically read everything she has written. The best books of this type are hard to find, with the superior collections in used book stores and garage sales. Recommended authors: Georgette Heyer and Victoria Holt.

English instructors and literary critics will criticize your new form of recreation; however, I doubt that reading romances is any more degenerative or ridiculous than watching cartoons or sitcoms on television. At least reading romances requires some minimal concentration and effort on the reader's part, and, sadly enough, may serve to improve your vocabulary. Reading romances is definitely preferable to reading nothing at all, and varying your romance reading with an occasional honest-to-goodness book will keep your gray matter from turning to total mush. The best a romance can claim to be is good entertainment. A well-written romance accomplishes this purpose quite nicely. After all, Jane Austen's <u>Pride and Prejudice</u> has been doing this for generations.

Commentary: Debbie's rather extensive process of invention, outlining, and revision has obviously helped her to write an essay that is entertaining in its satire of romances, informative about the various classifications of romance and the best authors in each, and persuasive in arguing that the reading of romances is no more "degenerative or ridiculous than watching cartoons or sitcoms on television" and is "definitely preferable to reading nothing at all." In addition to combining purposes, Debbie's essay also combines rhetorical modes. Although it is true that the essay as a whole provides useful advice about the *process* to use in choosing a romance, Debbie also engages in a good bit of classification. Roughly half of the essay is devoted to the classification of the various kinds of romance. As we have argued throughout this text, the combination of purposes and of modes is characteristic of most good writing.

The Embalmer's Art

Jessica Mitford

Jessica Mitford (1917–   ) was born and educated in England and came to the United States in 1939 where she held a series of jobs—bartender, salesperson, government investigator—before launching her writing career in 1945. She is the author of an autobiography, *Daughters and Rebels* (1960); *The Trial of Dr. Spock* (1969); *Kind and Unusual Punishment: The Prison Business* (1973); *Poison Penmanship: The Gentle Art of Muckraking* (1979); and *Faces of Philip: A Memoir of Philip Toynbee* (1984). Our extract is from *The American Way of Death* (1963), a telling exposé of the funeral industry. In it she explains in appalling detail the actual process of embalming.

1   The drama begins to unfold with the arrival of the corpse at the mortuary.

2   Alas, poor Yorick! How surprised he would be to see how his counterpart of today is whisked off to a funeral parlor and is in short order sprayed, sliced, pierced, pickled, trussed, trimmed, creamed, waxed, painted, rouged and neatly dressed—transformed from a common corpse into a Beautiful Memory Picture. This process is known in the trade as embalming and restorative art, and is so universally employed in the United States and Canada that the funeral director does it routinely, without consulting corpse or kin. He regards as eccentric those few who are hardy enough to suggest that it might be dispensed

with. Yet no law requires embalming, no religious doctrine commends it, nor is it dictated by considerations of health, sanitation, or even of personal daintiness. In no part of the world but in Northern America is it widely used. The purpose of embalming is to make the corpse presentable for viewing in a suitably costly container; and here too the funeral director routinely, without first consulting the family, prepares the body for public display.

Is all this legal? The processes to which a dead body may be subjected are after all to some extent circumscribed by law. In most states, for instance, the signature of next of kin must be obtained before an autopsy may be performed, before the deceased may be cremated, before the body may be turned over to a medical school for research purposes; or such provision must be made in the decedent's will. In the case of embalming, no such permission is required nor is it ever sought. A textbook, *The Principles and Practices of Embalming*, comments on this: "There is some question regarding the legality of much that is done within the preparation room." The author points out that it would be most unusual for a responsible member of a bereaved family to instruct the mortician, in so many words, to "*embalm*" the body of a deceased relative. The very term "embalming" is so seldom used that the mortician must rely upon custom in the matter. The author concludes that unless the family specifies otherwise, the act of entrusting the body to the care of a funeral establishment carries with it an implied permission to go ahead and embalm.   3

Embalming is indeed a most extraordinary procedure, and one must wonder at the docility of Americans who each year pay hundreds of millions of dollars for its perpetuation, blissfully ignorant of what it is all about, what is done, how it is done. Not one in ten thousand has any idea of what actually takes place. Books on the subject are extremely hard to come by. They are not to be found in most libraries or bookshops.   4

In an era when huge television audiences watch surgical operations in the comfort of their living rooms, when, thanks to the animated cartoon, the geography of the digestive system has become familiar territory even to the nursery school set, in a land where the satisfaction of curiosity about almost all matters is a national pastime, the secrecy surrounding embalming can, surely, hardly be attributed to the inherent gruesomeness of the subject. Custom in this regard has within this century suffered a complete reversal. In the early days of American embalming, when it was performed in the home of the deceased, it was almost mandatory for some relative to stay by the embalmer's side and witness the procedure. Today, family members who might wish to be in attendance would certainly be dissuaded by the funeral director. All others, except apprentices, are excluded by law from the preparation room.   5

A close look at what does actually take place may explain in large measure the undertaker's intractable reticence concerning a procedure that has become his major *raison d'être*. Is it possible he fears that public information about embalming might lead patrons to wonder if they really want this service? If the funeral men are loath to discuss the   6 subject outside the trade, the reader may, understandably, be equally loath to go on reading at this point. For those who have the stomach for it, let us part the formaldehyde curtain . . . .

7   The body is first laid out in the undertaker's morgue — or rather, Mr. Jones is reposing in the preparation room — to be readied to bid the world farewell.

8   The preparation room in any of the better funeral establishments has the tiled and sterile look of a surgery, and indeed the embalmer-restorative artist who does his chores there is beginning to adopt the term "dermasurgeon" (appropriately corrupted by some mortician-writers as "demi-surgeon") to describe his calling. His equipment, consisting of scalpels, scissors, augers, forceps, clamps, needles, pumps, tubes, bowls and basins, is crudely imitative of the surgeon's, as is his technique, acquired in a nine- or twelve-month post-high-school course in an embalming school. He is supplied by an advanced chemical industry with a bewildering array of fluids, sprays, pastes, oils, powders, creams, to fix or soften tissue, shrink or distend it as needed, dry it here, restore the moisture there. There are cosmetics, waxes and paints to fill and cover features, even plaster of Paris to replace entire limbs. There are ingenious aids to prop and stabilize the cadaver: a Vari-Pose Head Rest, the Edwards Arm and Hand Positioner, the Repose Block (to support the shoulders during the embalming), and the Throop Foot Positioner, which resembles an old-fashioned stocks.

9   Mr. John H. Eckels, president of the Eckels College of Mortuary Science, thus describes the first part of the embalming procedure: "In the hands of a skilled practitioner, this work may be done in a comparatively short time and without mutilating the body other than by slight incision — so slight that it scarcely would cause serious inconvenience if made upon a living person. It is necessary to remove the blood, and doing this not only helps in the disinfecting, but removes the principal cause of disfigurement due to discoloration."

10   Another textbook discusses the all-important time element: "The earlier this is done, the better, for every hour that elapses between death and embalming will add to the problems and complications encountered . . . ." Just how soon should one get going on the embalming? The author tells us, "On the basis of such scanty information made available to this profession through its rudimentary and haphazard system of technical research, we must conclude that the best results are to be obtained if the subject is embalmed before life is completely extinct — that is, before cellular death has occurred. In the average case, this would mean within an hour after somatic death." For those who feel that there is something a little rudimentary, not to say haphazard, about this advice, a comforting thought is offered by another writer. Speaking of fears entertained in early days of premature burial, he points out, "One of the effects of embalming by chemical injection, however, has been to dispel fears of live burial." How true; once the blood is removed, chances of live burial are indeed remote.

11   To return to Mr. Jones, the blood is drained out through the veins and replaced by embalming fluid pumped in through the arteries. As

noted in *The Principles and Practices of Embalming*, "every operator has a favorite injection and drainage point — a fact which becomes a handicap only if he fails or refuses to forsake his favorites when conditions demand it." Typical favorites are the carotid artery, femoral artery, jugular vein, subclavian vein. There are various choices of embalming fluid. If Flextone is used, it will produce a "mild, flexible rigidity. The skin retains a velvety softness, the tissues are rubbery and pliable. Ideal for women and children." It may be blended with B. and G. Products Company's Lyf-Lyk tint, which is guaranteed to reproduce "nature's own skin texture . . . the velvety appearance of living tissue." Suntone comes in three separate tints: Suntan; Special Cosmetic Tint, a pink shade "especially indicated for young female subjects"; and Regular Cosmetic Tint, moderately pink.

About three to six gallons of a dyed and perfumed solution of   12
formaldehyde, glycerin, borax, phenol, alcohol and water is soon circulating through Mr. Jones, whose mouth has been sewn together with a "needle directed upward between the upper lip and gum and brought out through the left nostril," with the corners raised slightly "for a more pleasant expression." If he should be bucktoothed, his teeth are cleaned with Bon Ami and coated with colorless nail polish. His eyes, meanwhile, are closed with flesh-tinted eye caps and eye cement.

The next step is to have at Mr. Jones with a thing called a trocar. This   13
is a long, hollow needle attached to a tube. It is jabbed into the abdomen, poked around the entrails and chest cavity, the contents of which are pumped out and replaced with "cavity fluid." This done, and the hole in the abdomen sewn up, Mr. Jones's face is heavily creamed (to protect the skin from burns which may be caused by leakage of the chemicals), and he is covered with a sheet and left unmolested for a while. But not for long — there is more, much more, in store for him. He has been embalmed, but not yet restored, and the best time to start the restorative work is eight to ten hours after embalming, when the tissues have become firm and dry.

The object of all this attention to the corpse, it must be remem-   14
bered, is to make it presentable for viewing in an attitude of healthy repose. "Our customs require the presentation of our dead in the semblance of normality . . . unmarred by the ravages of illness, disease or mutilation," says Mr. J. Sheridan Mayer in his *Restorative Art*. This is rather a large order since few people die in the full bloom of health, unravaged by illness and unmarked by some disfigurement. The funeral industry is equal to the challenge: "In some cases the gruesome appearance of a mutilated or disease-ridden subject may be quite discouraging. The task of restoration may seem impossible and shake the confidence of the embalmer. This is the time for intestinal fortitude and determination. Once the formative work is begun and affected tissues are cleaned or removed, all doubts of success vanish. It is surprising and gratifying to discover the results which may be obtained."

The embalmer, having allowed an appropriate interval to elapse,   15
returns to the attack, but now he brings into play the skill and equipment of sculptor and cosmetician. Is a hand missing? Casting one in plaster of

Paris is a simple matter. "For replacement purposes, only a cast of the back of the hand is necessary; this is within the ability of the average operator and is quite adequate." If a lip or two, a nose or an ear should be missing, the embalmer has at hand a variety of restorative waxes with which to model replacements. Pores and skin texture are simulated by stippling with a little brush, and over this cosmetics are laid on. Head off? Decapitation cases are rather routinely handled. Ragged edges are trimmed, and head joined to torso with a series of splints, wires and sutures. It is a good idea to have a little something at the neck — a scarf or a high collar — when time for viewing comes. Swollen mouth? Cut out tissue as needed from inside the lips. If too much is removed, the surface contour can easily be restored by padding with cotton. Swollen necks and cheeks are reduced by removing tissue through vertical incisions made down each side of the neck. "When the deceased is casketed, the pillow will hide the suture incisions . . . as an extra precaution against leakage, the suture may be painted with liquid sealer."

16   The opposite condition is more likely to present itself — that of emaciation. His hypodermic syringe now loaded with massage cream, the embalmer seeks out and fills the hollowed and sunken areas by injection. In this procedure the backs of the hands and fingers and the under-chin area should not be neglected.

17   Positioning the lips is a problem that recurrently challenges the ingenuity of the embalmer. Closed too tightly, they tend to give a stern, even disapproving expression. Ideally, embalmers feel, the lips should give the impression of being ever so slightly parted, the upper lip protruding slightly for a more youthful appearance. This takes some engineering, however, as the lips tend to drift apart. Lip drift can sometimes be remedied by pushing one or two straight pins through the inner margin of the lower lip and then inserting them between the two front upper teeth. If Mr. Jones happens to have no teeth, the pins can just as easily be anchored in his Armstrong Face Former and Denture Replacer. Another method to maintain lip closure is to dislocate the lower jaw, which is then held in its new position by a wire run through holes which have been drilled through the upper and lower jaws at the midline. As the French are fond of saying, *il faut souffrir pour être belle.*[1]

18   If Mr. Jones has died of jaundice, the embalming fluid will very likely turn him green. Does this deter the embalmer? Not if he has intestinal fortitude. Masking pastes and cosmetics are heavily laid on, burial garments and casket interiors are color-correlated with particular care, and Jones is displayed beneath rose-colored lights. Friends will say "How *well* he looks." Death by carbon monoxide, on the other hand, can be rather a good thing from the embalmer's viewpoint: "One advantage is the fact that this type of discoloration is an exaggerated form of a natural pink coloration." This is nice because the healthy glow is already present and needs but little attention.

19   The patching and filling completed, Mr. Jones is now shaved,

[1]You have to suffer to be beautiful.

washed and dressed. Cream-based cosmetic, available in pink, flesh, suntan, brunette and blond, is applied to his hands and face, his hair is shampooed and combed (and, in the case of Mrs. Jones, set), his hands manicured. For the horny-handed son of toil special care must be taken; cream should be applied to remove ingrained grime, and the nails cleaned. "If he were not in the habit of having them manicured in life, trimming and shaping is advised for better appearance — never questioned by kin."

Jones is now ready for casketing (this is the present participle of the verb "to casket"). In this operation his right shoulder should be depressed slightly "to turn the body a bit to the right and soften the appearance of lying flat on the back." Positioning the hands is a matter of importance, and special rubber positioning blocks may be used. The hands should be cupped slightly for a more lifelike, relaxed appearance. Proper placement of the body requires a delicate sense of balance. It should lie as high as possible in the casket, yet not so high that the lid, when lowered, will hit the nose. On the other hand, we are cautioned, placing the body too low "creates the impression that the body is in a box."   20

Jones is next wheeled into the appointed slumber room where a few last touches may be added — his favorite pipe placed in his hand or, if he was a great reader, a book propped into position. (In the case of little Master Jones a Teddy bear may be clutched.) Here he will hold open house for a few days, visiting hours 10 A.M. to 9 P.M.   21

All now being in readiness, the funeral director calls a staff conference to make sure that each assistant knows his precise duties. Mr. Wilber Kriege writes: "This makes your staff feel that they are a part of the team, with a definite assignment that must be properly carried out if the whole plan is to succeed. You never heard of a football coach who failed to talk to his entire team before they go on the field. They have drilled on the plays they are to execute for hours and days, and yet the successful coach knows the importance of making even the bench-warming third-string substitute feel that he is important if the game is to be won." The winning of *this* game is predicated upon glass-smooth handling of the logistics. The funeral director has notified the pallbearers whose names were furnished by the family, has arranged for the presence of clergyman, organist, and soloist, has provided transportation for everybody, has organized and listed the flowers sent by friends. In *Psychology of Funeral Service* Mr. Edward A. Martin points out: "He may not always do as much as the family thinks he is doing, but it is his helpful guidance that they appreciate in knowing they are proceeding as they should. . . . The important thing is how well his services can be used to make the family believe they are giving unlimited expression to their own sentiment."   22

The religious service may be held in a church or in the chapel of the funeral home; the funeral director vastly prefers the latter arrangement, for not only is it more convenient for him but it affords him the opportunity to show off his beautiful facilities to the gathered mourners. After   23 the clergyman has had his say, the mourners queue up to file past the casket for a last look at the deceased. The family is *never* asked whether they want an open-casket ceremony; in the absence of their instruction to the contrary, this is taken for granted. Consequently well over 90 per cent of all American funerals feature the open casket — a custom unknown in other parts of the world. Foreigners are astonished by it. An English woman living in San Francisco described her reaction in a letter to the writer:

> I myself have attended only one funeral here — that of an elderly fellow worker of mine. After the service I could not understand why everyone was walking towards the coffin (sorry, I mean casket), but thought I had better follow the crowd. It shook me rigid to get there and find the casket open and poor old Oscar lying there in his brown tweed suit, wearing a suntan makeup and just the wrong shade of lipstick. If I had not been extremely fond of the old boy, I have a horrible feeling that I might have giggled. Then and there I decided that I could never face another American funeral — even dead.

24   The casket (which has been resting throughout the service on a Classic Beauty Ultra Metal Casket Bier) is now transferred by a hydraulically operated device called Porto-Lift to a balloon-tired, Glide Easy casket carriage which will wheel it to yet another conveyance, the Cadillac Funeral Coach. This may be lavender, cream, light green — anything but black. Interiors, of course, are color-correlated, "for the man who cannot stop short of perfection."

25   At graveside, the casket is lowered into the earth. This office, once the prerogative of friends of the deceased, is now performed by a patented mechanical lowering device. A "Lifetime Green" artificial grass mat is at the ready to conceal the sere earth, and overhead, to conceal the sky, is a portable Steril Chapel Tent ("resists the intense heat and humidity of summer and the terrific storms of winter . . . available in Silver Grey, Rose or Evergreen"). Now is the time for the ritual scattering of earth over the coffin, as the solemn words "earth to earth, ashes to ashes, dust to dust" are pronounced by the officiating cleric. This can today be accomplished "with a mere flick of the wrist with the Gordon Leak-Proof Earth Dispenser. No grasping of a handful of dirt, no soiled fingers. Simple, dignified, beautiful, reverent! The modern way!" The Golden Earth Dispenser (at $5) is of nickel-plated brass construction. It is not only "attractive to the eye and long wearing"; it is also "one of the 'tools' for building better public relations" if presented as "an appropriate non-commercial gift" to the clergyman. It is shaped something like a saltshaker.

26   Untouched by human hand, the coffin and the earth are now united.

27   It is in the function of directing the participants through this maze of gadgetry that the funeral director has assigned to himself his relatively new role of "grief therapist." He has relieved the family of every detail, he has revamped the corpse to look like a living doll, he has arranged for it to nap for a few days in a slumber room, he has put on a well-oiled performance in which the concept of *death* has played no part whatsoever — unless it was inconsiderately mentioned by the clergyman

who conducted the religious service. He has done everything in his power to make the funeral a real pleasure for everybody concerned. He and his team have given their all to score an upset victory over death.

Questions on Content

1. Must the next of kin give permission before embalming can begin?
2. How and why does the funeral industry limit knowledge about the actual process of embalming?
3. From the point of view of the mortician, when should embalming begin?
4. What is one of the unexpected side benefits of embalming?
5. What is the goal of restoration?
6. Why should the body be placed as high as possible in the casket? What is wrong with placing the body low?
7. Are open-casket funerals common in other parts of the world?

Questions on Purpose, Thesis, and Structure

1. What are the main steps in the processes of embalming and restoration?
2. What is Mitford's opinion of embalming and restoration? What techniques does she use to reveal her opinion and to indicate her views about the proper way to treat the dead?
3. Which portions of the essay present process analysis? Which portions analyze causes and effects? Which portions present examples?
4. What balance does Mitford strike in informing, persuading, and entertaining the reader?

Questions on Style and Diction

1. Find the following words in the essay and determine their definitions in context: circumscribed, bereaved (paragraph 3); docility, perpetuation (paragraph 6); gruesomeness, dissuaded (paragraph 5); intractable reticence, *raison d'être* (paragraph 6); reposing (paragraph 18); queue (paragraph 23); prerogative, sere (paragraph 25).
2. Explain the allusion to Yorick in paragraph 2. (You may need to read or reread *Hamlet*, Act V, Scene i.)
3. Mitford names a number of specialized tools and products used in embalming and restoration: the Vari-Pose Head Rest, the Edwards Arm and Hand Positioner, the Troop Foot Positioner, Lyf-Lyk tint, and so on. What effect does she achieve by doing so?
4. What are the purposes and effects of Mitford's quotations from textbooks on embalming?
5. What is the effect of the football analogy in paragraphs 22 and 27?

Ideas for Essays

1. Write a defense of the funeral industry. In doing so, attempt to refute as many of Mitford's arguments as possible.
2. Write a satirical analysis of one of the other processes to which we human beings submit almost without question. Some possibilities are circumcision of male infants, civil and religious marriage ceremonies, natural childbirth procedures, graduation ceremonies, and retirement parties.

The Peter Principle
Laurence J. Peter and Raymond Hull

Laurence J. Peter (1919–   ), a Canadian by birth, was educated at Washington State University and has pursued a career as an educational psychologist, author, and consultant at the University of British Vancouver and the University of Southern California. His collaborator, Raymond Hull (1919–1985), an Englishman who moved to British Columbia in 1947, was the author of more than two dozen books and plays. Peter and Hull are the authors of the humorous best-seller *The Peter Principle: Why Things Always Go Wrong* (1969) and its sequels, *The Peter Prescription and How to Make Things Go Right* (1972), *The Peter Plan: A Proposal for Survival* (1975), and *Why Things Go Wrong: or The Peter Principle Revisited* (1985). Our excerpt from the first of these establishes and explores as "the key to an understanding of all hierarchal systems, and therefore to an understanding of the whole structure of civilization" the principle that "In a hierarchy every employee tends to rise to his level of incompetence." Note how Peter and Hull use examples to illustrate the process of rising to one's level of incompetence.

1   When I was a boy I was taught that the men upstairs knew what they were doing. I was told, "Peter, the more you know, the further you go." So I stayed in school until I graduated from college and then went forth into the world clutching firmly these ideas and my new teaching certificate. During the first year of teaching I was upset to find that a number of teachers, school principals, supervisors and superintendents appeared to be unaware of their professional responsibilities and incompetent in executing their duties. For example my principal's main concerns were that all window shades be at the same level, that classrooms should be quiet and that no one step on or near the rose beds. The superintendent's main concerns were that no minority group, no matter how fanatical, should ever be offended and that all official forms be submitted on time. The children's education appeared farthest from the administrator's mind.

2   At first I thought this was a special weakness of the school system in which I taught so I applied for certification in another province. I filled out the special forms, enclosed the required documents and complied willingly with all the red tape. Several weeks later, back came my application and all the documents!

3   No, there was nothing wrong with my credentials; the forms were correctly filled out; an official departmental stamp showed that they had been received in good order. But an accompanying letter said, "The new regulations require that such forms cannot be accepted by the Department of Education unless they have been registered at the Post Office to ensure safe delivery. Will you please remail the forms to the Department, making sure to register them this time?"

4   I began to suspect that the local school system did not have a monopoly on incompetence.

5   As I looked further afield, I saw that every organization contained a number of persons who could not do their jobs.

A UNIVERSAL PHENOMENON

Occupational incompetence is everywhere. Have you noticed it? Probably we all have noticed it.   6

We see indecisive politicians posing as resolute statesmen and the "authoritative source" who blames his misinformation on "situational imponderables." Limitless are the public servants who are indolent and insolent; military commanders whose behavioral timidity belies their dreadnought rhetoric, and governors whose innate servility prevents their actually governing. In our sophistication, we virtually shrug aside the immoral cleric, corrupt judge, incoherent attorney, author who cannot write and English teacher who cannot spell. At universities we see proclamations authored by administrators whose own office communications are hopelessly muddled, and droning lectures from inaudible or incomprehensible instructors.   7

Seeing incompetence at all levels of every hierarchy—political, legal, educational and industrial—I hypothesized that the cause was some inherent feature of the rules governing the placement of employees. Thus began my serious study of the ways in which employees move upward through a hierarchy, and of what happens to them after promotion.   8

For my scientific data hundreds of case histories were collected. Here are three typical examples.   9

Municipal Government File, Case No. 17

J. S. Minion[1] was a maintenance foreman in the public works department of Excelsior City. He was a favorite of the senior officials at City Hall. They all praised his unfailing affability.   10

"I like Minion," said the superintendent of works. "He has good judgment and is always pleasant and agreeable."   11

This behavior was appropriate for Minion's position: he was not supposed to make policy, so he had no need to disagree with his superiors.   12

The superintendent of works retired and Minion succeeded him. Minion continued to agree with everyone. He passed to his foreman every suggestion that came from above. The resulting conflicts in policy, and the continual changing of plans, soon demoralized the department. Complaints poured in from the Mayor and other officials, from taxpayers and from the maintenance-workers' union.   13

Minion still says "Yes" to everyone, and carries messages briskly back and forth between his superiors and his subordinates. Nominally a superintendent, he actually does the work of a messenger. The maintenance department regularly exceeds its budget, yet fails to fulfill its program of work. In short, Minion, a competent foreman, became an incompetent superintendent.   14

---

[1]Some names have been changed, in order to protect the guilty.

Service Industries File, Case No. 3

15   E. Tinker was exceptionally zealous and intelligent as an apprentice at G. Reece Auto Repair Inc., and soon rose to journeyman mechanic. In this job he showed outstanding ability in diagnosing obscure faults, and endless patience in correcting them. He was promoted to foreman of the repair shop.

16   But here his love of things mechanical and his perfectionism became liabilities. He will undertake any job that he thinks looks interesting, no matter how busy the shop may be. "We'll work it in somehow," he says.

17   He will not let a job go until he is fully satisfied with it.

18   He meddles constantly. He is seldom to be found at his desk. He is usually up to his elbows in a dismantled motor and while the man who should be doing the work stands watching, other workmen sit around waiting to be assigned new tasks. As a result the shop is always overcrowded with work, always in a muddle, and delivery times are often missed.

19   Tinker cannot understand that the average customer cares little about perfection — he wants his car back on time! He cannot understand that most of his men are less interested in motors than in their pay checks. So Tinker cannot get on with his customers or with his subordinates. He was a competent mechanic, but is now an incompetent foreman.

Military File, Case No. 8

20   Consider the case of the late renowned General A. Goodwin. His hearty, informal manner, his racy style of speech, his scorn for petty regulations and his undoubted personal bravery made him the idol of his men. He led them to many well-deserved victories.

21   When Goodwin was promoted to field marshal he had to deal, not with ordinary soldiers, but with politicians and allied generalissimos.

22   He would not conform to the necessary protocol. He could not turn his tongue to the conventional courtesies and flatteries. He quarreled with all the dignitaries and took to lying for days at a time, drunk and sulking, in his trailer. The conduct of the war slipped out of his hands into those of his subordinates. He had been promoted to a position that he was incompetent to fill.

AN IMPORTANT CLUE!

23   In time I saw that all such cases had a common feature. The employee had been promoted from a position of competence to a position of incompetence. I saw that, sooner or later, this could happen to every employee in every hierarchy.

Hypothetical Case File, Case No. 1

Suppose you own a pill-rolling factory, Perfect Pill Incorporated. Your   24
foreman pill roller dies of a perforated ulcer. You need a replacement.
You naturally look among your rank-and-file pill rollers.

Miss Oval, Mrs. Cylinder, Mr. Ellipse and Mr. Cube all show various   25
degrees of incompetence. They will naturally be ineligible for promotion. You will choose — other things being equal — your most competent pill roller, Mr. Sphere, and promote him to foreman.

Now suppose Mr. Sphere proves competent as foreman. Later, when   26
your general foreman, Legree, moves up to Works Manager, Sphere will
be eligible to take his place.

If, on the other hand, Sphere is an incompetent foreman, he will get   27
no more promotion. He has reached what I call his "level of incompetence." He will stay there till the end of his career.

Some employees, like Ellipse and Cube, reach a level of incompe-   28
tence in the lowest grade and are never promoted. Some, like Sphere
(assuming he is not a satisfactory foreman), reach it after one promotion.

E. Tinker, the automobile repair-shop foreman, reached his level of   29
incompetence on the third stage of the hierarchy. General Goodwin
reached his level of incompetence at the very top of the hierarchy.

So my analysis of hundreds of cases of occupational incompetence   30
led me on to formulate *The Peter Principle*:

In a Hierarchy Every Employee Tends
to Rise to His Level of Incompetence

A NEW SCIENCE!

Having formulated the Principle, I discovered that I had inadvertently   31
founded a new science, hierarchiology, the study of hierarchies.

The term "hierarchy" was originally used to describe the system of   32
church government by priests graded into ranks. The contemporary
meaning includes any organization whose members or employees are
arranged in order of rank, grade or class.

Hierarchiology, although a relatively recent discipline, appears to   33
have great applicability to the fields of public and private administration.

THIS MEANS YOU!

My Principle is the key to an understanding of all hierarchal systems, and   34
therefore to an understanding of the whole structure of civilization. A
few eccentrics try to avoid getting involved with hierarchies, but everyone in business, industry, trade-unionism, politics, government, the
armed forces, religion and education is so involved. All of them are
controlled by the Peter Principle.

Many of them, to be sure, may win a promotion or two, moving from   35 one level of competence to a higher level of competence. But competence in that new position qualifies them for still another promotion. For each individual, for *you*, for *me*, the final promotion is from a level of competence to a level of incompetence.

36   So, given enough time—and assuming the existence of enough ranks in the hierarchy—each employee rises to, and remains at, his level of incompetence. Peter's Corollary states:

37   *In time, every post tends to be occupied by an employee who is incompetent to carry out its duties.*

WHO TURNS THE WHEELS?

38   You will rarely find, of course, a system in which *every* employee has reached his level of incompetence. In most instances, something is being done to further the ostensible purposes for which the hierarchy exists.

39   *Work is accomplished by those employees who have not yet reached their level of incompetence.*

Questions on Content

1. What incidents in his personal life first convinced Peter that every organization contains a number of people who cannot do their jobs?
2. What is the Peter Principle?
3. What was the original meaning of the word *hierarchy*?
4. What is Peter's Corollary?
5. How can any work be accomplished if all hierarchies are dominated by the Peter Principle?

Questions on Purpose, Thesis, and Structure

1. How many examples of the Peter Principle do Peter and Hull cite? How do the virtues of lower-level employees become weaknesses in supervisors? What are the stages in the process described by Peter and Hull?
2. The examples used by Peter and Hull are either hypothetical or impossible to verify because the names of the parties were changed. Does this make the examples unconvincing? Explain your answer.

Questions on Style and Diction

1. Find the following words in the essay and determine their definitions in context: imponderables, indolent, insolent, dreadnought, servility, proclamations, droning (paragraph 7); hierarchy, hypothesized (paragraph 8); affability (paragraph 10); zealous, obscure (paragraph 15); renowned, idol (paragraph 20); generalissimo (paragraph 21); protocol (paragraph 22); perforated (paragraph 24); ineligible (paragraph 25).
2. How effective (and how correct) is the grammatical parallelism in paragraph 7?
3. Consider the use of fictional names in this essay. Are these names clever and witty or crude and corny?

Ideas for Essays

1. If you have worked in some business or bureaucracy long enough to see one or more of your co-workers promoted, evaluate the Peter Principle by considering your own personal experiences.

2. Assume that you are an executive in a major corporation. Write a memo to the various managers under your supervision warning them about the danger of the Peter Principle. In this memo outline the procedures you wish to them to use to reduce the risk of promoting workers in your corporation to their levels of incompetence.

Colonizing the Heavens

Isaac Asimov

Isaac Asimov (1920–   ), one of America's leading science and science fiction writers, was born in Russia but raised in Brooklyn, New York. Although he completed a Ph.D. in chemistry at Columbia University and for a time taught at Boston University, Asimov's real vocation has been as a writer. His published output since 1950, which includes not only science fiction novels and short stories but books on topics as diverse as man's discoveries in the universe, Shakespeare, and the Bible, has been prodigious. Much of Asimov's writing attempts to make the reader more aware of the potential and achievements of science. In "Colonizing the Heavens" (1975), Asimov discusses the feasibility of creating huge, self-supporting space stations. Note that Asimov discusses both the way in which such a space station could be constructed (a how-to-do-it process analysis) and the way in which the space station would then support human life (how-it-works process analysis).

The population bomb ticks on steadily . . .   1

We are 4 billion now, in 1975. Barring catastrophes, we shall be 5   2
billion in 1986 and 6 billion in 1995 and 7 billion in 2002 and 8 billion in . . . What do we do with all of ourselves when already, with our puny 4 billion, we find that the effort to feed and power the population is destroying the planet that feeds and powers us? We must reduce the birthrate and lower the population, but that will take time. What do we do meanwhile?

One answer is that we do as we have done before. We must take up   3
the trek again and move on to new lands. Since there are no new lands on earth worth the taking, we must move to new worlds and colonize the heavens.

No, not the moon. Prof. Gerard O' Neill of the physics department   4
of Princeton University suggests two other places to begin with — places as far from earth as the moon is, but not the moon. Imagine the moon at zenith, exactly overhead. Trace a line due eastward from the moon down

to the horizon. Two-thirds of the way along that line, one-third of the way up from the horizon, is one of those places. Trace another line westward from the moon down to the horizon. Two-thirds of the way along that line, one-third of the way up from the horizon, is another of those places.

5   Put an object in either place, and it will form an equilateral triangle with the moon and earth. It is 237,000 miles from earth to the moon. It is also 237,000 miles from earth to that place, and from the moon to that place.

6   What is so special about those places? Back in 1772 the astronomer Joseph Louis Lagrange showed that in those places any object remained stationary with respect to the moon. As the moon moved about the earth, any object in either of those places would also move about the earth in such a way as to keep perfect step with the moon. The competing gravities of earth and the moon would keep it where it was. If anything happened to push it out of place, it would promptly move back, wobbling back and forth a bit ("librating") as it did so. The two places ideally are merely points in space and are called "Lagrangian points," or "libration points."

7   Lagrange discovered five such points altogether, but three of them are of no importance because they don't represent stable conditions. An object in those three points, once pushed out of place, would continue to drift outward and would never return. The two points in which an object remains stable are called "L4" and "L5." L4 is the one that lies toward the eastern horizon, and L5 the one that lies toward the western.

8   Professor O'Neill wants to take advantage of that gravitational lock and suggests the building of space colonies there, colonies that would become permanent parts of the earth-moon system. He envisions long cylinders designed to hold human beings plus a complex life-support system, facilities for growing food, maintaining atmospheres, recycling wastes, and so on.

9   Such concepts have been used in science fiction. The most memorable example is Robert A. Heinlein's story "Universe," published in 1941, in which a large ship, supporting thousands of people through indefinite numbers of generations, is making its slow way to the stars. The men aboard have forgotten the original purpose of the voyage and consider the ship to be the entire universe (hence the title). A lineal descendant of the story, translated to television, was the recent ill-fated series, "The Starlost."

10   In science fiction, though, such enormous, self-contained ships are *ships*, thickly spaced with decks, utterly enclosed with walls — the equivalent of many-layered caverns. O'Neill's vision is of another kind. He sees hollow cylinders with human beings living on the inner surface, a surface that is designed and contoured into a familiar world with all the accoutrements and accompaniments of earth. The cylinder would be composed of long, alternating strips of opaque and transparent material — aluminum and tough plastic. Sunshine, reflected by long mirrors, would enter and illuminate the cylinder and turn what would otherwise be a cave into a daylit world. The entry of light could be controlled by mirror-shifting to allow for alternating day and night.

The inner surface of the opaque portions of the cylinder would be   11
spread with soil, which could be used for agriculture and, eventually,
animal husbandry. All the artificial works of man — his buildings and
machines — would be there, too.

What makes this concept plausible and lifts the vision out of the   12
realm of science fiction is the careful manner in which O'Neill has
analyzed the masses of material necessary, the details of design, the
thicknesses and strengths of materials required, the manner of lifting
and assembly, and the cost of it all. The conclusion is that the establishment of such space colonies is possible and even practical in terms of
present-day technology.

It would be expensive, of course, and getting the process started   13
would require an input equivalent to that spent on the Apollo program.
But O'Neill demonstrates clearly that the expense would decline rapidly
after that. As the colonies increase in number, they could be expected to
grow larger and more elaborate, too. O'Neill conceives the first space
colonies (Model 1) to be only as large as is required to be workable —
two spinning cylinders, each 3,280 feet long and 328 feet wide, supporting a total of 10,000 people.

The two cylinders, each spinning about its long axis, would turn in   14
opposite directions. When they were held together, the total system
would have virtually no spin and the cylinders could be designed in
such a way as to have one end of the structure point constantly toward
the sun in the course of the orbit about the earth.

It is from the sun that the colony would obtain its energy — a   15
copious, endless, easily handled, non-polluting form of energy. It would
be used to smelt the ores, power the factories, grow the food, recycle the
wastes. It would serve to start the cylinders spinning and increase the
rate of spin to the point where there would be a centrifugal effect
sufficient to hold everything within to all parts of the inner surface with
the apparent pull of normal gravity. For a cylinder 328 feet wide, this
would require a spin of three revolutions a minute.

O'Neill envisions larger cylinder-pairs, too, and has calculated the   16
requirements for some as large as 20 miles long and 2 miles wide
(Model 4), spinning once in two minutes. Each cylinder of a pair like
that would be as wide as Manhattan and half again as long, would have a
total inner surface 10 times as great as that of Manhattan, and could
support up to 20 million people if it were exploited to the full, though 5
to 10 million might be a more comfortable population.

With so great a width, the cylinder would have a sufficient depth of   17
air within to allow a blue sky and to support clouds. In a Model 4 colony
the end caps of the cylinders could be modeled into mountainous
territory — full-sized mountains, not just bas-reliefs.

But where are we to get all the material for the construction of these   18
space colonies? Our groaning planet, sagging under it weight of humanity, with its supply of key resources sputtering and giving out, couldn't
possibly afford to give up the colossal quantities of supplies needed for
it all. (Over half a million tons of construction is needed for each Model
1, probably a thousand times as much for a Model 4.)

But earth is lucky, for virtually none of the material need come from   19 our planet. As it happens, we are supplied with a moon, an empty and dead world that is one-eightieth the size of the earth. It is close enough for us to reach—we have already reached it over and over—and it is free to be used as a quarry. Lunar material will yield the aluminum, glass, concrete, and other substances needed for constructing the colony. Lunar soil will be spread over the interior surface, and on it agriculture will be practiced. Not only is all that material present on the moon in virtually unlimited quantities, but lifting it off the moon against that body's weak gravity would require only one-twentieth the effort necessary for lifting it off earth. All the smelting and other chemical work would, of course, be done in space. But the lunar material is not perfectly adapted to human needs. It is low in volatile elements, those that vaporize easily when heated. The most serious lack is the volatile element hydrogen (an essential component of water).

20   O'Neill calculates that setting up a Model 1 colony would require some 5,400 metric tons of liquid hydrogen, and that would have to come from earth. Fortunately, earth can spare that much. We can get it from sea water, and there is an embarrassing oversupply of sea water on earth. We live in comfort only because so much of earth's water supply is tied up in the ice caps of Greenland and Antarctica. If these ever melt, the sea level will rise 200 feet and drown our population-packed coastal areas. Extracting hydrogen from a little of our oversupply and giving it away will do us no harm.

21   As colonies multiply, of course, the quantity of hydrogen we would have to give up could become a little painful. Once space colonization swings into high gear, however, hydrogen and other volatile elements of which the moon has insufficient supply can be obtained from farther out. They can come from some of the asteroids or from the occasional comet that blunders past the earth-moon system on its way to wheel about the sun.

22   The first space colony would be by far the most expensive, even if it were small, for we would have to supply not only the advanced equipment, the machinery, the various life forms, the basic food supply and energy, but even some 2 percent of the raw materials. After that, there would be leap-frogging. Each space colony would help to build up the next, while the facilities for mining, smelting, shipping, and constructing would be ever improving. In the end, new colonies might be formed with no more trouble than it now takes to put up a new row of houses in the suburbs.

23   O'Neill thinks that if all were to go optimally, the first space colony could be floating in space by the late Eighties and that several hundred more elaborate colonies would be there by the mid-twenty-first century. These would be comfortable worlds, not, like earth, taken as found, but carefully designed to meet human needs. The temperature and weather would be controlled; energy would be free and non-polluting; weeds, vermin, and pathogenic bacteria would be left back on earth.

24   Dangers? Difficulties? Yes, some.

25   The possibility of a meteor strike exists, but that is not very strong. The space of the earth-moon system is full of meteoric dust, which is not

likely to be bothersome, and pinhead meteors may pit the aluminum and craze the plastic, but that would be a minor annoyance. A meteorite large enough to cause serious damage to a colony is so rare that the time between strikes could be counted in the millions of years per colony. As the colonies grow more numerous, the chances that *one* will be hit increases—but mankind can live with that. We now live with the knowledge that there is a finite chance that at any moment a large meteorite, or a major earthquake, may strike and demolish a city on earth.

Energetic solar radiation is dangerous but would not be a problem   26
in a cylinder protected by aluminum, plastic, and soil. Cosmic rays are much more serious. They are ever present and ever dangerous and very penetrating. There is some question as to whether O'Neill's original design offered sufficient protection. At the most recent scientific conference held on the subject (at Princeton on May 7–9, 1975) this subject was among those discussed.

Then, too, the centrifugal effect of the cylinder spin does not per-   27
fectly duplicate earth's gravitation. On earth the gravitational pull is not perceptibly altered as we rise from the surface. Inside a spinning cylinder the effect weakens rapidly as one rises from the inner surface, falling to zero at the long axis. Is a fluctuating gravitational effect dangerous to the human body in the long run? We have no way of knowing as yet, but if not, a gravitational pull that lessens with height can have its advantages.

The small distances on the space colonies would make it unneces-   28
sary to use high-energy systems for transportation. Bicycles would be ideal for the ground, and with the lowering gravity, gliders would be perfect for air transport—and amusement.

Mountain climbing on the larger colonies would have comforts   29
unknown on earth. As one climbed higher, the downward pull would weaken, it would become easier to climb farther, and, of course, the air would grow neither thinner nor colder. In carefully enclosed areas on the mountaintops, people could fly by their own muscle power when they were outfitted with plastic wings on light frames. Shades of Icarus!

As the space colonies increased in number, the room available for   30
human beings would increase, too, and at an exponential rate. Within a century there could be room for a billion people on the space colonies, and by 2150, perhaps, there would be more people in space than on earth.

This prospect does not obviate the need to lower our birthrate in the   31
long run, for if human beings continue to multiply at their present rate, the total mass of flesh and blood will equal the total mass of the known universe in 6,700 years. Long before then the building of space colonies would not be able to keep up under any conceivable conditions.

The colonies could act as a safety valve; however, that would give   32
humanity a somewhat longer time to accomplish the turnabout without absolute disaster.

It may be that finally, when a stable population is attained (or at very   33
worst, one that is growing only as fast as can be handled by additional colonies), the earth itself will be only thinly populated. It will, perhaps,

be devoted, then, to carefully preserved wilderness and part areas. It may serve as a monument to man's origin and to the pre-human ecology, and it would be supported largely by tourism.

34   Tourism would also exist among the multiplying colonies (which would eventually expand out of the Lagrangian points and take up other and somewhat more difficult-to-handle orbits). Because each colony would have no intrinsic gravitational field to speak of and all are likely to be at about the same distance from the sun, travel from one to another would consume surprisingly little energy. And because each colony is likely to be unique in its way, the result would be worth the effort.

35   After all, almost as important as the basic fact that room would be found for humanity is the additional fact that it would be found in thousands of different, isolated, and culturally independent places. Each colony would have its own way of life, and some might be quite a distance off the norm. Among the offbeat colonies we could imagine puritanical ones and hedonistic ones, libertarian ones and authoritarian ones, Orthodox Jewish ones and hard-shell Baptist ones.

36   You could choose where you wanted to go; and if you were born on one, you might choose to try another—or at least visit one. Human culture would explode in variety, with each colony having its own styles in clothing, music, art, literature. The options for creativity in general and for scientific advance in particular would be unbounded.

37   Yet though the advantages of space colonies can be drawn up in a thoroughly lyrical fashion, one has to admit that the chances that the program will be started are, perhaps, not bright.

38   These are difficult times. The Apollo program, by its very success, seems to have taken the shine off space ventures; the economy teeters; there is widespread disillusionment with glowing dreams—particularly in the United States (which would have to supply the major portion of what would have to be a global effort) caught in the wake of the Vietnam failure.

39   But perhaps mankind will answer to the lure of immediate and high-visibility profit. With that in mind, perhaps, O'Neill is carefully working out the details of an ancillary idea—the practical economics of establishing a structure designed to be a "Satellite Solar Power Station" (SSPS), one that will absorb sunlight and convert it into microwave energy that can be beamed to earth for use as direct electrical current.

40   Earth could, in this way, be supplied with copious, nearly pollution-free energy. The amount of land that would have to be devoted to microwave reception would be, by O'Neill's calculations, as little as 5 percent of that required for direct solar-energy reception, because the inefficient part of the operation would be kept out in space.

41   The development of power stations at the Lagrangian points is as practical as the development of space colonies, and the benefits of the former to mankind are sure to be seen as more immediately desirable by the public generally. Yet once power stations are built at the Lagrangian points, the expertise and facilities used for that can also be used to build other industrial systems—and space colonies, too. The basic investments having been made, the additional expense will be almost trivial. Why not go on, then?

It is the energy crisis, then, that may be offering us the opportunity. 42
It is solar energy by way of space that may serve as the bribe. And, if the
opportunity is seized and the bribe is accepted, space colonies could
follow almost inevitably. With that *might* come the salvation of humanity
and its entry into a new and larger scene with overall changes as momentous as those that followed the discovery of fire.

Questions on Content

1. What is special about Lagrangian points and where are they located?
2. According to Professor O'Neill, what is the smallest workable size for his
   cylindrical space stations, and about how many people would they support?
3. Where would we get most of the raw materials needed in constructing the
   space stations?
4. What are some of the dangers and drawbacks of O'Neill's plan?
5. How might the proliferation of space colonies benefit the ecology of the
   earth? How might they increase cultural diversity and human liberty?
6. How could the energy crisis be an unexpected boon in the long-term goal of
   establishing space colonies?

Questions on Thesis, Purpose, and Structure

1. Why does Asimov begin his essay with population predictions?
2. What are the contrasts between the huge space stations of science fiction and
   the cylindrical space stations proposed by O'Neill?
3. Does Asimov present how-to-do-it process analysis or how-it-happens analysis? In what paragraphs is process analysis most prevalent? What are the stages
   in the process?
4. What forms of evidence does Asimov cite in trying to persuade the reader that
   these space stations are possible, practical, and worthwhile?
5. Where in the essay does Asimov explore the effects of establishing space
   colonies? What are those effects?

Questions on Style and Diction

1. Find the following words in the essay and determine their definitions in
   context: catastrophes (paragraph 2); trek (paragraph 3); zenith (paragraph 4);
   librating (paragraph 6); lineal (paragraph 9); accoutrements, opaque (paragraph 10); copious, smelt (paragraph 15); bas-reliefs (paragraph 17); colossal
   (paragraph 18); volatile (paragraph 19); intrinsic (paragraph 34); hedonistic,
   libertarian (paragraph 35); ancillary (paragraph 39).
2. Note that many of Asimov's paragraphs are short—only a sentence or two in
   length. Is this a stylistic strength or weakness in his essay? Explain your
   reasoning.

Ideas for Essays

1. Imagine that you are a colonist on one of O'Neill's space stations. Write a
   narrative about a day in your life within the cylinder.
2. Asimov creates a strong argument for the practicality and desirability of
   self-supporting cylindrical space colonies, but this concept has obviously not
   been wholly convincing to NASA, which is pursuing more limited plans for a
   space station. Write a critique of the Asimov/O'Neill proposal.

How to Say Nothing in Five Hundred Words

Paul Roberts

Paul Roberts (1917–1967) was born in San Luis Obispo, California, and was educated at San Jose State College and the University of California at Berkeley, where he earned a Ph.D. in English in 1948. His teaching career as a professor of English and linguistics was spent at San Jose State College (now University), at Cornell University, and at the Rome Center for American Studies. Roberts authored a number of influential textbooks for high school and college students, including *Understanding Grammar* (1954), *Patterns of English* (1956), *Understanding English* (1958), and *English Sentences* (1962). His essay on the five-hundred-word theme from *Understanding English* has become a modern classic and is often reprinted. In it Roberts uses several of the organizational patterns discussed in this text. The essay begins with a narrative anecdote summarizing the process by which many a weak theme has been written. In the remainder of the extract Roberts classifies the most common errors in weak writing and gives useful advice for avoiding those errors.

1   It's Friday afternoon, and you have almost survived another week of classes. You are just looking forward dreamily to the week end when the English instructor says: "For Monday you will turn in a five-hundred-word composition on college football."

2   Well, that puts a good big hole in the week end. You don't have any strong views on college football one way or the other. You get rather excited during the season and go to all the home games and find it rather more fun than not. On the other hand, the class has been reading Robert Hutchins in the anthology and perhaps Shaw's "Eighty-Yard Run," and from the class discussion you have got the idea that the instructor thinks college football is for the birds. You are no fool. You can figure out what side to take.

3   After dinner you get out the portable typewriter that you got for high school graduation. You might as well get it over with and enjoy Saturday and Sunday. Five hundred words is about two double-spaced pages with normal margins. You put in a sheet of paper, think up a title, and you're off:

Why College Football Should Be Abolished

4   College football should be abolished because it's bad for the school and also bad for the players. The players are so busy practicing that they don't have any time for their studies.

This, you feel, is a mighty good start. The only trouble is that it's only thirty-two words. You still have four hundred and sixty-eight to go, and you've pretty well exhausted the subject. It comes to you that you do your best thinking in the morning so you put away the typewriter and go to the movies. But the next morning you have to do your washing and some math problems, and in the afternoon you go to the game. The English instructor turns up too, and you wonder if you've taken the right side after all. Saturday night you have a date, and Sunday morning you have to go to church. (You can't let English assignments interfere with your religion.) What with one thing and another, it's ten o'clock Sunday night before you get out the typewriter again. You make a pot of coffee and start to fill out your views on college football. Put a little meat on the bones.

Why College Football Should Be Abolished

In my opinion, it seems to me that college football should be abolished. The reason why I think this to be true is because I feel that football is bad for the colleges in nearly every respect. As Robert Hutchins says in his article in our anthology in which he discusses college football, it would be better if the colleges had race horses and had races with one another, because then the horses would not have to attend classes. I firmly agree with Mr. Hutchins on this point, and I am sure that many other students would agree too.   5

One reason why it seems to me that college football is bad is that it has become too commercial. In the olden times when people played football just for the fun of it, maybe college football was all right, but they do not play football just for the fun of it now as they used to in the old days. Nowadays college football is what you might call a big business. Maybe this is not true at all schools, and I don't think it is especially true here at State, but certainly this is the case at most colleges and universities in America nowadays, as Mr. Hutchins points out in his very interesting article. Actually the coaches and alumni go around to the high schools and offer the high school stars large salaries to come to their colleges and play football for them. There was one case where a high school star was offered a convertible if he would play football for a certain college.   6

Another reason for abolishing college football is that it is bad for the players. They do not have time to get a college education, because they are so busy playing football. A football player has to practice every afternoon from three to six and then he is so tired that he can't concentrate on his studies. He just feels like dropping off to sleep after dinner, and then the next day he goes to his classes without having studied and maybe he fails the test.   7

(Good ripe stuff so far, but you're still a hundred and fifty-one words from home. One more push.)

Also I think college football is bad for the colleges and the universities because not very many students get to participate in it. Out of a college of ten thousand students only seventy-five or a hundred play football, if that many. Football is what you might call a spectator sport. That means that most people go to watch it but do not play it themselves.   8

(Four hundred and fifteen. Well, you still have the conclusion, and when you retype it, you can make the margins a little wider.)

These are the reasons why I agree with Mr. Hutchins that college football should be abolished in American colleges and universities.   9

10   On Monday you turn it in, moderately hopeful, and on Friday it comes back marked "weak in content" and sporting a big "D."

11   This essay is exaggerated a little, not much. The English instructor will recognize it as reasonably typical of what an assignment on college football will bring in. He knows that nearly half of the class will contrive in five hundred words to say that college football is too commercial and bad for the players. Most of the other half will inform him that college football builds character and prepares one for life and brings prestige to the school. As he reads paper after paper all saying the same thing in almost the same words, all bloodless, five hundred words dripping out of nothing, he wonders how he allowed himself to get trapped into teaching English when he might have had a happy and interesting life as an electrician or a confidence man.

12   Well, you may ask, what can you do about it? The subject is one on which you have few convictions and little information. Can you be expected to make a dull subject interesting? As a matter of fact, this is precisely what you are expected to do. This is the writer's essential task. All subjects, except sex, are dull until somebody makes them interesting. The writer's job is to find the argument, the approach, the angle, the wording that will take the reader with him. This is seldom easy, and it is particularly hard in subjects that have been much discussed: College Football, Fraternities, Popular Music, Is Chivalry Dead?, and the like. You will feel that there is nothing you can do with such subjects except repeat the old bromides. But there are some things you can do which will make your papers, if not throbbingly alive, at least less insufferably tedious than they might otherwise be.

AVOID THE OBVIOUS CONTENT

13   Say the assignment is college football. Say that you've decided to be against it. Begin by putting down the arguments that come to your mind: it is too commercial, it takes the students' minds off their studies, it is hard on the players, it makes the university a kind of circus instead of an intellectual center, for most schools it is financially ruinous. Can you think of any more arguments, just off hand? All right. Now when you write your paper, *make sure that you don't use any of the material on this list.* If these are the points that leap to your mind, they will leap to everyone else's too, and whether you get a "C" or a "D" may depend on whether the instructor reads your paper early when he is fresh and tolerant or late, when the sentence "In my opinion, college football has become too commercial," inexorably repeated, has brought him to the brink of lunacy.

14   Be against college football for some reason or reasons of your own. If they are keen and perceptive ones, that's splendid. But even if they are trivial or foolish or indefensible, you are still ahead so long as they are not everybody else's reasons too. Be against it because the colleges don't spend enough money on it to make it worthwhile, because it is bad for the characters of the spectators, because the players are forced to

attend classes, because the football stars hog all the beautiful women, because it competes with baseball and is therefore un-American and possibly Communist inspired. There are lots of more or less unused reasons for being against college football.

Sometimes it is a good idea to sum up and dispose of the trite and 15 conventional points before going on to your own. This has the advantage of indicating to the reader that you are going to be neither trite nor conventional. Something like this:

> We are often told that college football should be abolished be- 16 cause it has become too commercial or because it is bad for the players. These arguments are no doubt very cogent, but they don't really go to the heart of the matter.

Then you go the heart of the matter.

TAKE THE LESS USUAL SIDE

One rather simple way of getting into your paper is to take the side of 17 the argument that most of the citizens will want to avoid. If the assignment is an essay on dogs, you can, if you choose, explain that dogs are faithful and lovable companions, intelligent, useful as guardians of the house and protectors of children, indispensable in police work—in short, when all is said and done, man's best friend. Or you can suggest that those big brown eyes conceal, more often than not, a vacuity of mind and an inconstancy of purpose; that the dogs you have known most intimately have been mangy, ill-tempered brutes, incapable of instruction; and that only your nobility of mind and fear of arrest prevent you from kicking the flea-ridden animals when you pass them on the street.

Naturally personal convictions will sometimes dictate your ap- 18 proach. If the assigned subject is "Is Methodism Rewarding to the Individual?" and you are a pious Methodist, you have really no choice. But few assigned subjects, if any, will fall in this category. Most of them will lie in broad areas of discussion with much to be said on both sides. They are intellectual exercises, and it is legitimate to argue now one way and now another, as debaters do in similar circumstances. Always take the side that looks to you hardest, least defensible. It will almost always turn out to be easier to write interestingly on that side.

This general advice applies where you have a choice of subjects. If 19 you are to choose among "The Value of Fraternities" and "My Favorite High School Teacher" and "What I Think About Beetles," by all means plump for the beetles. By the time the instructor gets to your paper, he will be up to his ears in tedious tales about the French teacher at Bloombury High and assertions about how fraternities build character and prepare one for life. Your views on beetles, whatever they are, are bound to be a refreshing change.

Don't worry too much about figuring out what the instructor thinks 20 about the subject so that you can cuddle up with him. Chances are his views are no stronger than yours. If he does have convictions and you oppose him, his problem is to keep from grading you higher than you deserve in order to show he is not biased. This doesn't mean that you should always cantankerously dissent from what the instructor says; that gets tiresome too. And if the subject assigned is "My Pet Peeve," do not begin, "My pet peeve is the English instructor who assigns papers on 'my pet peeve.'" This was still funny during the War of 1812, but it has sort of lost its edge since then. It is in general good manners to void personalities.

SLIP OUT OF ABSTRACTION

21   If you will study the essay on college football [near the beginning of this essay], you will perceive that one reason for its appalling dullness is that it never gets down to particulars. It is just a series of not very glittering generalities: "football is bad for the colleges," "it has become too commercial," "football is a big business," "it is bad for the players," and so on. Such round phrases thudding against the reader's brain are unlikely to convince him, though they may well render him unconscious.

22   If you want the reader to believe that college football is bad for the players, you have to do more than say so. You have to display the evil. Take your roommate, Alfred Simkins, the second-string center. Picture poor old Alfy coming home from football practice every evening, bruised and aching, agonizingly tired, scarcely able to shovel the mashed potatoes into his mouth. Let us see him staggering up to the room, getting out his econ textbook, peering desperately at it with his good eye, falling asleep and failing the test in the morning. Let us share his unbearable tension as Saturday draws near. Will he fall, be demoted, lose his monthly allowance, be forced to return to the coal mines? And if he succeeds, what will be his reward? Perhaps a slight ripple of applause when the third-string center replaces him, a moment of elation in the locker room if the team wins, of despair if it loses. What will he look back on when he graduates from college? Toil and torn ligaments. And what will be his future? He is not good enough for pro football, and he is too obscure and weak in econ to succeed in stocks and bonds. College football is tearing the heart from Alfy Simkins and, when it finishes with him, will callously toss aside the shattered hulk.

23   This is no doubt a weak enough argument for the abolition of college football, but it is a sight better than saying, in three or four variations, that college football (in your opinion) is bad for the players.

24   Look at the work of any professional writer and notice how constantly he is moving from the generality, the abstract statement, to the concrete example, the facts and figures, the illustration. If he is writing on juvenile delinquency, he does not just tell you that juveniles are (it seems to him) delinquent and that (in his opinion) something should be done about it. He shows you juveniles being delinquent, tearing up movie theatres in Buffalo, stabbing high school principals in Dallas, smoking marijuana in Palo Alto. And more than likely he is moving toward some specific remedy, not just a general wringing of the hands.

It is no doubt possible to be *too* concrete, too illustrative or anecdo-   25
tal, but few inexperienced writers err this way. For most the soundest
advice is to be seeking always for the picture, to be always turning
general remarks into seeable examples. Don't say, "Sororities teach girls
the social graces." Say, "Sorority life teaches a girl how to carry on a
conversation while pouring tea, without sloshing the tea into the
saucer." Don't say, "I like certain kinds of popular music very much."
Say "Whenever I hear Gerber Sprinklittle play 'Mississippi Man' on the
trombone, my socks creek up my ankles."

GET RID OF OBVIOUS PADDING

The student toiling away at his weekly English theme is too often   26
tormented by a figure: five hundred words. How, he asks himself, is he
to achieve this staggering total? Obviously by never using one word
when he can somehow work in ten.

He is therefore seldom content with a plain statement like "Fast   27
driving is dangerous." This has only four words in it. He takes thought,
and the sentence becomes:

In my opinion, fast driving is dangerous.

Better, but he can do better still:

In my opinion, fast driving would seem to be rather dangerous.

If he is really adept, it may come out:

In my humble opinion, though I do not claim to be an expert on
this complicated subject, fast driving, in most circumstances, would
seem to be rather dangerous in many respects, or at least so it would
seem to me.

Thus four words have been turned into forty, and not an iota of content
has been added.

Now this is a way to go about reaching five hundred words, and if   28
you are content with a "D" grade, it is as good a way as any. But if you
aim higher, you must work differently. Instead of stuffing your sentences
with straw, you must try steadily to get rid of the padding, to make your
sentences lean and tough. If you are really working at it, your first draft
will greatly exceed the required total, and then you will work it down,
thus:

It is thought in some quarters that fraternities do not contribute as   29
much as might be expected to campus life.
Some people think that fraternities contribute little to campus
life.
The average doctor who practices in small towns or in the country   30
must toil night and day to heal the sick.
Most country doctors work long hours.

31   When I was a little girl, I suffered from shyness and embarrassment in the presence of others.
        I was a shy little girl.

32   It is absolutely necessary for the person employed as a marine
fireman to give the matter of steam pressure his undivided attention at
all times.
        The fireman has to keep his eye on the steam gauge.

33   You may ask how you can arrive at five hundred words at this rate.
Simple. You dig up more real content. Instead of taking a couple of
obvious points off the surface of the topic and then circling warily
around them for six paragraphs, you work in and explore, figure out the
details. You illustrate. You say that fast driving is dangerous, and then
you prove it. How long does it take to stop a car at forty and at eighty?
How far can you see at night? What happens when a tire blows? What
happens in a head-on collision at fifty miles an hour? Pretty soon your
paper will be full of broken glass and blood and headless torsos, and
reaching five hundred words will not really be a problem.

CALL A FOOL A FOOL

34   Some of the padding in freshman themes is to be blamed not on anxiety
about the word minimum but on excessive timidity. The student writes,
"In my opinion, the principal of my high school acted in ways that I
believe every unbiased person would have to call foolish." This isn't
exactly what he means. What he means is, "My high school principal was
a fool." If he was a fool, call him a fool. Hedging the thing about with
"in-my-opinion's" and "it-seems-to-me's" and "as-I-see-it's" and "at-
least-from-my-point-of-view's" gains you nothing. Delete these phrases
whenever they creep into your paper.

35   The student's tendency to hedge stems from a modesty that in other
circumstances would be commendable. He is, he realizes, young and
inexperienced, and he half suspects that he is dopey and fuzzy-minded
beyond the average. Probably only too true. But it doesn't help to
announce your incompetence six times in every paragraph. Decide what
you want to say and say it as vigorously as possible, without apology and
in plain words.

36   Linguistic diffidence can take various forms. One is what we call
euphemism. This is the tendency to call a spade "a certain garden
implement" or women's underwear "unmentionables." It is stronger in
some eras than others and in some people than others but it always
operates more or less in subjects that are touchy or taboo: death, sex,
madness, and so on. Thus we shrink from saying "He died last night" but
say instead "passed away," "left us," "joined his Maker," "went to his
reward." Or we try to take off the tension with a lighter cliché: "kicked
the bucket," "cashed in his chips," "handed in his dinner pail." We have
found all sorts of ways to avoid saying *mad*: "mentally ill," "touched,"
"not quite right upstairs," "feeble-minded," "innocent," "simple," "off

his trolley," "not in his right mind." Even such a now plain word as *insane* began as a euphemism with the meaning "not healthy."

Modern science, particularly psychology, contributes many polysyl- **37** lables in which we can wrap our thoughts and blunt their force. To many writers there is no such thing as a bad schoolboy. Schoolboys are malad-justed or unoriented or misunderstood or in the need of guidance or lacking in continued success toward satisfactory integration of the per-sonality as a social unit, but they are never bad. Psychology no doubt makes us better men and women, more sympathetic and tolerant, but it doesn't make writing any easier. Had Shakespeare been confronted with psychology, "To be or not to be" might have come out, "To continue as a social unit or not to do so. That is the personality problem. Whether 'tis a better sign of integration at the conscious level to display a psychic tolerance toward the maladjustments and repressions induced by one's lack of orientation in one's environment or—" But Hamlet would never have finished the soliloquy.

Writing in the modern world, you cannot altogether avoid modern **38** jargon. Nor, in an effort to get away from euphemism, should you salt your paper with four-letter words. But you can do much if you will mount guard against those roundabout phrases, those echoing polysylla-bles that tend to slip into your writing to rob it of its crispness and force.

BEWARE OF PAT EXPRESSIONS

Other things being equal, avoid phrases like "other things being equal." **39** Those sentences that come to you whole, or in two or three doughy lumps, are sure to be bad sentences. They are no creation of yours but pieces of common thought floating in the community soup.

Pat expressions are hard, often impossible, to avoid, because they **40** come too easily to be noticed and seem too necessary to be dispensed with. No writer avoids them altogether, but good writers avoid them more often than poor writers.

By "pat expressions" we mean such tags as "to all practical intents **41** and purposes," "the pure and simple truth," "from where I sit," "the time of his life," "to the ends of the earth," "in the twinkling of an eye," "as sure as you're born," "over my dead body," "under cover of dark-ness," "took the easy way out," "when all is said and done," "told him time and time again," "parted the best of friends," "stand up and be counted," "gave him the best years of her life," "worked her fingers to the bone." Like other clichés, these expressions were once forceful. Now we should use them only when we can't possibly think of anything else.

Some pat expressions stand like a wall between the writer and **42** thought. Such a one is "the American way of life." Many student writers feel that when they have said that something accords with the American way of life or does not they have exhausted the subject. Actually, they have stopped at the highest level of abstraction. The American way of life is the complicated set of bonds between a hundred and eighty million ways. All of us know this when we think about it, but the tag phrase too often keeps us from thinking about it.

43   So with many another phrase dear to the politician: "this great land of ours," "the man in the street," "our national heritage." These may prove our patriotism or give a clue to our political beliefs, but otherwise they add nothing to the paper except words.

COLORFUL WORDS

44   The writer builds with words, and no builder uses a raw material more slippery and elusive and treacherous. A writer's work is a constant struggle to get the right word in the right place, to find that particular word that will convey his meaning exactly, that will persuade the reader or soothe him or startle or amuse him. He never succeeds altogether — sometimes he feels that he scarcely succeeds at all — but such successes as he has are what make the thing worth doing.

45   There is no book of rules for this game. One progresses through everlasting experiment on the basis of ever-widening experience. There are few useful generalizations that one can make about words as words, but there are perhaps a few.

46   Some words are what we call "colorful." By this we mean that they are calculated to produce a picture or induce an emotion. They are dressy instead of plain, specific instead of general, loud instead of soft. Thus, in place of "Her heart beat," we may write, "Her heart *pounded, throbbed, fluttered, danced.*" Instead of "He sat in his chair," we may say, "He *lounged, sprawled, coiled.*" Instead of "It was hot," we may say, "It was *blistering, sultry, muggy, suffocating, steamy, wilting.*"

47   However, it should not be supposed that the fancy word is always better. Often it is as well to write "Her heart beat" or "It was hot" if that is all it did or all it was. Ages differ in how they like their prose. The nineteenth century liked it rich and smoky. The twentieth has usually preferred it lean and cool. The twentieth century writer, like all writers, is forever seeking the exact word, but he is wary of sounding feverish. He tends to pitch it low, to understate it, to throw it away. He knows that if he gets too colorful, the audience is likely to giggle.

48   See how this strikes you: "As the rich, golden glow of the sunset died away along the eternal western hills, Angela's limpid blue eyes looked softly and trustingly into Montague's flashing brown ones, and her heart pounded like a drum in time with the joyous song surging in her soul." Some people like that sort of thing, but most modern readers would say, "Good grief," and turn on the television.

COLORED WORDS

49   Some words we would call not so much colorful as colored — that is, loaded with associations, good or bad. All words — except perhaps

structure words — have associations of some sort. We have said that the meaning of a word is the sum of the contexts in which it occurs. When we hear a word, we hear with it an echo of all the situations in which we have heard it before.

In some words, these echoes are obvious and discussable. The word 50 *mother*, for example, has, for most people, agreeable associations. When you hear *mother* you probably think of home, safety, love, food, and various other pleasant things. If one writes, "She was like a mother to me," he gets an effect which he would not get in "She was like an aunt to me." The advertiser makes use of the associations of *mother* by working it in when he talks about his product. The politician works it in when he talks about himself.

So also with such words as *home, liberty, fireside, contentment,* 51 *patriot, tenderness, sacrifice, childlike, manly, bluff, limpid.* All of these words are loaded with associations that would be rather hard to indicate in a straightforward definition. There is more than a literal difference between "They sat around the fireside" and "They sat around the stove." They might have been equally warm and happy around the stove, but *fireside* suggests leisure, grace, quiet tradition, congenial company, and *stove* does not.

Conversely, some words have bad associations. *Mother* suggests 52 pleasant things, but *mother-in-law* does not. Many mothers-in-law are heroically lovable and some mothers drink gin all day and beat their children insensible, but these facts of life are beside the point. The point is that *mother* sounds good and *mother-in-law* does not.

Or consider the word *intellectual.* This would seem to be a compli- 53 mentary term, but in point of fact it is not, for it has picked up associations of impracticality and ineffectuality and general dopiness. So also such words as *liberal, reactionary, Communist, socialist, capitalist, radical, schoolteacher, truck driver, undertaker, operator, salesman, huckster, speculator.* These convey meaning on the literal level, but beyond that — sometimes, in some places — they convey contempt on the part of the speaker.

The question of whether to use loaded words or not depends on 54 what is being written. The scientist, the scholar, try to avoid them; for the poet, the advertising writer, the public speaker, they are standard equipment. But every writer should take care that they do not substitute for thought. If you write, "Anyone who thinks that is nothing but a Socialist (or Communist or capitalist)" you have said nothing except that you don't like people who think that, and such remarks are effective only with the most naïve readers. It is always a bad mistake to think your readers more naïve than they really are.

COLORLESS WORDS

But probably most student writers come to grief not with words that are 55 colorful or those that are colored but with those that have no color at all. A pet example is *nice*, a word we would find it hard to dispense with in casual conversation but which is no longer capable of adding much to a description. Colorless words are those of such general meaning that in a particular sentence they mean nothing. Slang adjectives like *cool* ("That's real cool") tend to explode all over the language. They are applied to everything, lose their original force, and quickly die.

56   Beware also of nouns of very general meaning, like *circumstances, cases, instances, aspects, factors, relationships, attitudes, eventualities,* etc. In most circumstances you will find that those cases of writing which contain too many instances of words like these will in this and other aspects have factors leading to unsatisfactory relationships with the reader resulting in unfavorable attitudes on his part and perhaps other eventualities, like a grade of "D." Notice also what "etc." means. It means "I'd like to make this list longer, but I can't think of any more examples."

Questions on Content

1. What are the typical stages in writing a "D" paper?
2. What are the steps in the process of writing a good essay?

Questions on Thesis, Purpose, and Structure

1. What rhetorical pattern does Roberts use in explaining how the "D" paper on college football is written?
2. Does Roberts use process analysis, classification, or some combination of the two in explaining how one *should* write a college essay?
3. Composition theorists now often speak of prewriting, writing, and revision. Does the advice given by Roberts fit into such a process?
4. Is Roberts's essay informative, persuasive, and entertaining? What makes it so?

Questions on Style and Diction

1. Find the following words in the essay and determine their definitions in context: bromides, insufferably tedious (paragraph 12); inexorably (paragraph 13); keen (paragraph 14); trite (paragraph 15); cogent (paragraph 16); vacuity, inconstancy (paragraph 17); plump (paragraph 19); cantankerously, dissent (paragraph 20); callously (paragraph 22); iota (paragraph 27); diffidence, taboo (paragraph 36); polysyllables, soliloquy (paragraph 37); limpid (paragraph 48); congenial (paragraph 51).
2. Roberts fills his essay with informal slang phrases—for example, "for the birds" (paragraph 2), "a little meat on the bones" (paragraph 4), "good ripe stuff" (paragraph 7), "hog all the beautiful women" (paragraph 14). What is the effect of this informality, especially when coming from a writing instructor?
3. Consider each major piece of advice about writing in this essay. Does Roberts follow that advice in his own writing?
4. Roberts published this essay in 1958, before the feminist movement had heightened sensitivity to the potentially sexist implications of some conventions of standard English. Discuss the use of masculine pronouns in this essay (for example, in paragraphs 11 and 20). How could you rewrite those paragraphs in a way that avoids any possibility of sexism?

Ideas for Essays

1. Write two five-hundred-word essays on a topic of your own choosing. In one of the essays try to write the lousiest essay you can by doing just the opposite of what Roberts recommends. Use only the most obvious content, take the usual side of any controversial issues, write as abstractly as you can, and so on. In the second essay write on the same topic, but this time take pains to follow Roberts's advice to the best of your ability.

2. Write a practical essay of advice to fellow students dealing with some other aspect of college life. You might write, for example, on how to study for an essay exam, how to pick good college classes, or how to get the most for your money on the cafeteria meal plan.

The Purloined Letter
Edgar Allan Poe

Edgar Allan Poe (1809–1849) was born in Boston to theatrical parents. Poe's life was a troubled one, punctuated by bitter literary and personal quarrels, poverty, the lingering illness and death of his teen-aged wife, and his own physical and psychological instabilities. His talents and achievements as a writer were nevertheless unmistakable. Although most often associated with exotic tales of horror and terror, Poe was also an adept writer of satire, burlesque, and hoax, as well as a sensitive lyric poet. With his tales of C. Auguste Dupin, the eccentric Parisian detective, Poe also became the father of the modern detective story. Several processes play a part in "The Purloined Letter" (1845). There is, first of all, the methodical process by which the police search for the missing letter; then there is the process by which Dupin deduces the whereabouts of the letter; and finally there is the process by which the letter was concealed in the first place.

> Nil sapientiae odiosius acumine nimio.[1]
> *SENECA*

At Paris, just after dark one gusty evening in the autumn of 18—, I was 1
enjoying the twofold luxury of meditation and a meerschaum, in company with my friend C. Auguste Dupin, in his little back library, or book-closet, *au troisième, No. 33, Rue Dunôt, Faubourg St. Germain.* For one hour at least we had maintained a profound silence; while each, to any casual observer, might have seemed intently and exclusively occupied with the curling eddies of smoke that oppressed the atmosphere of the chamber. For myself, however, I was mentally discussing

---

[1]"Nothing is more hateful to wisdom than too much cunning."

certain topics which had formed matter for conversation between us at an earlier period of the evening; I mean the affair of the Rue Morgue, and the mystery attending the murder of Marie Rogêt.[2] I looked upon it, therefore, as something of a coincidence, when the door of our apartment was thrown open and admitted our old acquaintance. Monsieur G——, the Prefect of the Parisian police.

2   We gave him a hearty welcome; for there was nearly half as much of the entertaining as of the contemptible about the man, and we had not seen him for several years. We had been sitting in the dark, and Dupin now arose for the purpose of lighting a lamp, but sat down again, without doing so, upon G.'s saying that he had called to consult us, or rather to ask the opinion of my friend, about some official business which had occasioned a great deal of trouble.

3   "If it is any point requiring reflection," observed Dupin, as he forbore to enkindle the wick, "we shall examine it to better purpose in the dark."

4   "That is another of your odd notions," said the Prefect, who had a fashion of calling every thing "odd" that was beyond his comprehension, and thus lived amid an absolute legion of "oddities."

5   "Very true," said Dupin, as he supplied his visiter with a pipe, and rolled towards him a comfortable chair.

6   "And what is the difficulty now?" I asked. "Nothing more in the assassination way, I hope?"

7   "Oh no; nothing of that nature. The fact is, the business is *very* simple indeed, and I make no doubt that we can manage it sufficiently well ourselves; but then I thought Dupin would like to hear the details of it, because it is so excessively *odd*."

8   "Simple and odd," said Dupin.

9   "Why, yes; and not exactly that, either. The fact is, we have all been a good deal puzzled because the affair *is* so simple, and yet baffles us altogether."

10   "Perhaps it is the very simplicity of the thing which puts you at fault," said my friend.

11   "What nonsense you *do* talk!" replied the Prefect, laughing heartily.

12   "Perhaps the mystery is a little *too* plain," said Dupin.

13   "Oh, good heavens! who ever heard of such an idea?"

14   "A little *too* self-evident."

15   "Ha! ha! ha! — ha! ha! ha! — ho! ho! ho!" — roared our visiter, profoundly amused, "oh, Dupin, you will be the death of me yet!"

16   "And what, after all, *is* the matter on hand?" I asked.

17   "Why, I will tell you," replied the Prefect, as he gave a long, steady, and contemplative puff, and settled himself in his chair. "I will tell you in a few words; but, before I begin, let me caution you that this is an affair demanding the greatest secrecy, and that I should most probably lose the position I now hold, were it known that I confided it to any one."

18   "Proceed," said I.

[2]The allusion is to Poe's first two detective stories, "The Murders in the Rue Morgue" (1841) and "The Mystery of Marie Rogêt" (1842).

"Or not," said Dupin. 19

"Well, then; I have received personal information, from a very high 20
quarter, that a certain document of the last importance, has been purloined from the royal apartments. The individual who purloined it is
known; this beyond a doubt; he was seen to take it. It is known, also, that
it still remains in his possession."

"How is this known?" asked Dupin. 21

"It is clearly inferred," replied the Prefect, "from the nature of the 22
document, and from the non-appearance of certain results which would
at once arise from its passing *out* of the robber's possession;—that is to
say, from his employing it as he must design in the end to employ it."

"Be a little more explicit," I said. 23

"Well, I may venture so far as to say that the paper gives its holder a 24
certain power in a certain quarter where such power is immensely
valuable." The Prefect was fond of the cant of diplomacy.

"Still I do not quite understand," said Dupin. 25

"No? Well; the disclosure of the document to a third person, who 26
shall be nameless, would bring in question the honor of a personage of
most exalted station; and this fact gives the holder of the document an
ascendancy over the illustrious personage whose honor and peace are so
jeopardized."

"But this ascendancy," I interposed, "would depend upon the rob- 27
ber's knowledge of the loser's knowledge of the robber. Who would
dare—"

"The thief," said G., "is the Minister D——, who dares all things, 28
those unbecoming as well as those becoming a man. The method of the
theft was not less ingenious than bold. The document in question—a
letter, to be frank—had been received by the personage robbed while
alone in the royal *boudoir*. During its perusal she was suddenly interrupted by the entrance of the other exalted personage from whom
especially it was her wish to conceal it. After a hurried and vain endeavor
to thrust it in a drawer, she was forced to place it, open as it was, upon a
table. The address, however, was uppermost, and, the contents thus
unexposed, the letter escaped notice. At this juncture enters the Minister
D——. His lynx eye immediately perceives the paper, recognises the
handwriting of the address, observes the confusion of the personage
addressed, and fathoms her secret. After some business transactions,
hurried through in his ordinary manner, he produces a letter somewhat
similar to the one in question, opens it, pretends to read it, and then
places it in close juxtaposition to the other. Again he converses, for some
fifteen minutes, upon the public affairs. At length, in taking leave, he
takes also from the table the letter to which he had no claim. Its rightful
owner saw, but, of course, dared not call attention to the act, in the
presence of the third personage who stood at her elbow. The minister
decamped; leaving his own letter—one of no importance—upon the
table."

"Here, then," said Dupin to me, "you have precisely what you 29
demand to make the ascendancy complete—the robber's knowledge of
the loser's knowledge of the robber."

"Yes," replied the Prefect; "and the power thus attained has, for 30 some months past, been wielded, for political purposes, to a very dangerous extent. The personage robbed is more thoroughly convinced, every day, of the necessity of reclaiming her letter. But this, of course, cannot be done openly. In fine, driven to despair, she had committed the matter to me."

31   "Than whom," said Dupin, amid a perfect whirlwind of smoke, "no more sagacious agent could, I suppose, be desired, or even imagined."

32   "You flatter me," replied the Prefect; "but it is possible that some such opinion may have been entertained."

33   "It is clear," said I, "as you observe, that the letter is still in possession of the minister; since it is in this possession, and not any employment of the letter, which bestows the power. With the employment the power departs."

34   "True," said G.; "and upon this conviction I proceeded. My first care was to make thorough search of the minister's hotel;³ and here my chief embarrassment lay in the necessity of searching without his knowledge. Beyond all things, I have been warned of the danger which would result from giving him reason to suspect our design."

35   "But," said I, "you are quite *au fait*⁴ in these investigations. The Parisian police have done this thing often before."

36   "O yes; and for this reason I did not despair. The habits of the minister gave me, too, a great advantage. He is frequently absent from home all night. His servants are by no means numerous. They sleep at a distance from their master's apartment, and, being chiefly Neapolitans, are readily made drunk. I have keys, as you know, with which I can open any chamber or cabinet in Paris. For three months a night has not passed, during the greater part of which I have not been engaged, personally, in ransacking the D—— Hôtel. My honor is interested, and, to mention a great secret, the reward is enormous. So I did not abandon the search until I had become fully satisfied that the thief is a more astute man than myself. I fancy that I have investigated every nook and corner of the premises in which it is possible that the paper can be concealed."

37   "But is it not possible," I suggested, "that although the letter may be in possession of the minister, as it unquestionably is, he may have concealed it elsewhere than upon his own premises?"

38   "This is barely possible," said Dupin. "The present peculiar condition of affairs at court, and especially of those intrigues in which D—— is known to be involved, would render the instant availability of the document—its susceptibility of being produced at a moment's notice —a point of nearly equal importance with its possession."

39   "Its susceptibility of being produced?" said I.

40   "That is to say, of being *destroyed*," said Dupin.

41   "True," I observed; "the paper is clearly then upon the premises. As for its being upon the person of the minister, we may consider that as out of the question."

42   "Entirely," said the Prefect. "He has been twice waylaid, as if by

³Mansion or townhouse.
⁴Skilled.

footpads,[5] and his person rigorously searched under my own inspection."

"You might have spared yourself this trouble," said Dupin. "D——, 43 I presume, is not altogether a fool, and, if not, must have anticipated these waylayings, as a matter of course."

"Not *altogether* a fool," said G., "but then he's a poet, which I take 44 to be only one remove from a fool."

"True," said Dupin, after a long and thoughtful whiff from his 45 meerschaum, "although I have been guilty of certain doggerel myself."

"Suppose you detail," said I, "the particulars of your search." 46

"Why the fact is, we took our time, and we searched *every where*. I 47 have had long experience in these affairs. I took the entire building, room by room; devoting the nights of a whole week to each. We examined, first, the furniture of each apartment. We opened every possible drawer; and I presume you know that, to a properly trained police agent, such a thing as a *secret* drawer is impossible. Any man is a dolt who permits a 'secret' drawer to escape him in a search of this kind. The thing is *so* plain. There is a certain amount of bulk—of space—to be accounted for in every cabinet. Then we have accurate rules. The fiftieth part of a line could not escape us. After the cabinets we took the chairs. The cushions we probed with the fine long needles you have seen me employ. From the tables we removed the tops."

"Why so?" 48

"Sometimes the top of a table, or other similarly arranged piece of 49 furniture, is removed by the person wishing to conceal an article; then the leg is excavated, the article deposited within the cavity, and the top replaced. The bottoms and tops of bed-posts are employed in the same way."

"But could not the cavity be detected by sounding?" I asked. 50

"By no means, if, when the article is deposited, a sufficient wadding 51 of cotton be placed around it. Besides, in our case, we were obliged to proceed without noise."

"But you could not have removed—you could not have taken to 52 pieces *all* articles of furniture in which it would have been possible to make a deposit in the manner you mention. A letter may be compressed into a thin spiral roll, not differing much in shape or bulk from a large knitting-needle, and in this form it might be inserted into the rung of a chair, for example. You did not take to pieces all the chairs?"

"Certainly not; but we did better—we examined the rungs of every 53 chair in the hotel, and, indeed, the jointings of every description of furniture, by the aid of a most powerful microscope.[6] Had there been any traces of recent disturbance we should not have failed to detect it instantly. A single grain of gimlet-dust, for example, would have been as obvious as an apple. Any disorder in the glueing—any unusual gaping in the joints—would have sufficed to insure detection."

"I presume you looked to the mirrors, between the boards and the 54

[5]Highwaymen who prey on pedestrians.
[6]A magnifying glass.

plates, and you probed the beds and the bed-clothes, at well as the curtains and carpets."

55   "That of course; and when we had absolutely completed every particle of the furniture in this way, then we examined the house itself. We divided its entire surface into compartments, which we numbered, so that none might be missed; then we scrutinized each individual square inch throughout the premises, including the two houses immediately adjoining, with the microscope, as before."

56   "The two houses adjoining!" I exclaimed; "you must have had a great deal of trouble."

57   "We had; but the reward offered is prodigious."

58   "You include the *grounds* about the houses?"

59   "All the grounds are paved with brick. They gave us comparatively little trouble. We examined the moss between the bricks, and found it undisturbed."

60   "You looked among D——'s papers, of course, and into the books of the library?"

61   "Certainly; we opened every package and parcel; we not only opened every book, but we turned over every leaf in each volume, not contenting ourselves with a mere shake, according to the fashion of some of our police officers. We also measured the thickness of every book-*cover*, with the most accurate admeasurement, and applied to each the most jealous scrutiny of the microscope. Had any of the bindings been recently meddled with, it would have been utterly impossible that the fact should have escaped observation. Some five or six volumes, just from the hands of the binder, we carefully probed, longitudinally, with the needles."

62   "You explored the floors beneath the carpets?"

63   "Beyond doubt. We removed every carpet, and examined the boards with the microscope."

64   "And the paper on the walls?"

65   "Yes."

66   "You looked into the cellars?"

67   "We did."

68   "Then," I said, "you have been making a miscalculation, and the letter is *not* upon the premises, as you suppose."

69   "I fear you are right there," said the Prefect." And now, Dupin, what would you advise me to do?"

70   "To make a thorough re-search of the premises."

71   "That is absolutely needless," replied G——. "I am not more sure that I breathe than I am that the letter is not at the Hôtel."

72   "I have no better advice to give you," said Dupin. "You have, of course, an accurate description of the letter?"

73   "Oh yes!"—And here the Prefect, producing a memorandum-book, proceeded to read aloud a minute account of the internal, and especially of the external appearance of the missing document. Soon after finishing the perusal of this description, he took his departure, more entirely depressed in spirits than I had ever known the good gentleman before.

In about a month afterwards he paid us another visit, and found us 74
occupied very nearly as before. He took a pipe and a chair and entered
into some ordinary conversation. At length I said,—

"Well, but G——, what of the purloined letter? I presume you have 75
at last made up your mind that there is no such thing as overreaching the
Minister?"

"Confound him, say I—yes; I made the re-examination, however, 76
as Dupin suggested—but it was all labor lost, as I knew it would be."

"How much was the reward offered, did you say?" asked Dupin. 77

"Why, a very great deal—a *very* liberal reward—I don't like to say 78
how much, precisely; but one thing I *will* say, that I wouldn't mind
giving my individual check for fifty thousand francs to any one who
could obtain me that letter. The fact is, it is becoming of more and more
importance every day; and the reward has been lately doubled. If it were
trebled, however, I could do no more than I have done."

"Why, yes," said Dupin, drawlingly, between the whiffs of his 79
meerschaum, "I really—think, G——, you have not exerted yourself—
to the utmost in this matter. You might—do a little more. I think, eh?"

"How?—in what way?" 80

"Why—puff, puff—you might—puff, puff—employ counsel in 81
the matter, eh?—puff, puff, puff. Do you remember the story they tell of
Abernethy?"

"No; hang Abernethy!" 82

"To be sure! hang him and welcome. But, once upon a time, a 83
certain rich miser conceived the design of spunging upon this Abernethy
for a medical opinion. Getting up, for this purpose, an ordinary conversation in a private company, he insinuated his case to the physician, as
that of an imaginary individual.

"'We will suppose,' said the miser, 'that his symptoms are such and 84
such; now, doctor, what would *you* have directed him to take?'"

"'Take!' said Abernethy,[7] 'why, take *advice*, to be sure.'" 85

"But," said the Prefect, a little discomposed, "I am *perfectly* willing 86
to take advice, and to pay for it. I would *really* give fifty thousand francs
to any one who would aid me in the matter."

"In that case," replied Dupin, opening a drawer, and producing a 87
checkbook, "you may as well fill me up a check for the amount mentioned. When you have signed it, I will hand you the letter."

I was astounded. The Prefect appeared absolutely thunder-stricken. 88
For some minutes he remained speechless and motionless, looking
incredulously at my friend with open mouth, and eyes that seemed
starting from their sockets; then, apparently recovering himself in some
measure, he seized a pen, and after several pauses and vacant stares,
finally filled up and signed a check for fifty thousand francs, and handed
it across the table to Dupin. The latter examined it carefully and deposited it in his pocketbook; then, unlocking an *escritoire*,[8] took thence a

---

[7]John Abernethy (1764–1831), a famous English surgeon.
[8]A writing desk.

letter and gave it to the Prefect. This functionary grasped it in a perfect agony of joy, opened it with a trembling hand, cast a rapid glance at its contents, and then, scrambling and struggling to the door, rushed at length unceremoniously from the room and from the house, without having uttered a syllable since Dupin had requested him to fill up the check.

89   When he had gone, my friend entered into some explanations.

90   "The Parisian police," he said, "are exceedingly able in their way. They are persevering, ingenious, cunning, and thoroughly versed in the knowledge which their duties seem chiefly to demand. Thus, when G—— detailed to us his mode of searching the premises at the Hôtel D——, I felt entire confidence in his having made a satisfactory investigation—so far as his labors extended."

91   "So far as his labors extended?" said I.

92   "Yes," said Dupin. "The measures adopted were not only the best of their kind, but carried out to absolute perfection. Had the letter been deposited within the range of their search, these fellows would, beyond a question, have found it."

93   I merely laughed—but he seemed quite serious in all that he said.

94   "The measures, then," he continued, "were good in their kind, and well executed; their defect lay in their being inapplicable to the case, and to the man. A certain set of highly ingenious resources are, with the Prefect, a sort of Procrustean bed,[9] to which he forcibly adapts his designs. But he perpetually errs by being too deep or too shallow, for the matter in hand; and many a schoolboy is a better reasoner than he. I knew one about eight years of age, whose success at guessing in the game of 'even and odd' attracted universal admiration. This game is simple, and is played with marbles. One player holds in his hand a number of these toys, and demands of another whether that number is even or odd. If the guess is right, the guesser wins one; if wrong, he loses one. The boy to whom I allude won all the marbles of the school. Of course he had some principle of guessing; and this lay in mere observation and admeasurement of the astuteness of his opponents. For example, an arrant simpleton is his opponent, and, holding up his closed hand, asks, 'are they even or odd?' Our schoolboy replies, 'odd,' and loses; but upon the second trial he wins, for he then says to himself, 'the simpleton had them even upon the first trial, and his amount of cunning is just sufficient to make him have them odd upon the second; I will therefore guess odd;'—he guesses odd, and wins. Now, with a simpleton a degree above the first, he would have reasoned thus: 'This fellow finds that in the first instance I guessed odd, and, in the second, he will propose to himself upon the first impulse, a simple variation from even to odd, as did the first simpleton; but then a second thought will suggest that this is too simple a variation, and finally he will decide upon putting it even as before. I will therefore guess even;'—he guesses

---

[9]Procrustes was a legendary Greek robber who fitted his victims to his bed by either stretching their legs or cutting them off.

even, and wins. Now this mode of reasoning in the schoolboy, whom his fellows termed 'lucky,' — what, in its last analysis, is it?"

"It is merely," I said, "an identification of the reasoner's intellect   95
with that of his opponent."

"It is," said Dupin; "and, upon inquiring of the boy by what means   96
he effected the *thorough* identification in which his success consisted, I received answer as follows: 'When I wish to find out how wise, or how stupid, or how good, or how wicked is any one, or what are his thoughts at the moment, I fashion the expression of my face, as accurately as possible, in accordance with the expression of his, and then wait to see what thoughts or sentiments arise in my mind or heart, as if to match or correspond with the expression.' This response of the schoolboy lies at the bottom of all the spurious profundity which has been attributed to Rochefoucauld, to La Bougive, to Machiavelli, and to Campanella."[10]

"And the identification," I said, "of the reasoner's intellect with that   97
of his opponent, depends, if I understand you aright, upon the accuracy with which the opponent's intellect is admeasured."

"For its practical value it depends upon this," replied Dupin; "and   98
the Prefect and his cohort fail so frequently, first, by default of this identification, and, secondly, by ill-admeasurement, or rather through non-admeasurement, of the intellect with which they are engaged. They consider only their *own* ideas of ingenuity; and, in searching for anything hidden, advert only to the modes in which *they* would have hidden it. They are right in this much — that their own ingenuity is a faithful representative of that of *the mass*; but when the cunning of the individual felon is diverse in character from their own, the felon foils them, of course. This always happens when it is above their own, and very usually when it is below. They have no variation of principle in their investigations; at best, when urged by some unusual emergency — by some extraordinary reward — they extend or exaggerate their old modes of *practice*, without touching their principles. What, for example, in this case of D——, has been done to vary the principle of action? What is all this boring, and probing, and sounding, and scrutinizing with the microscope, and dividing the surface of the building into registered square inches — what is it all but an exaggeration *of the application* of the one principle or set of principles of search, which are based upon the one set of notions regarding human ingenuity, to which the Prefect, in the long routine of his duty, has been accustomed? Do you not see he has taken it for granted that *all* men proceed to conceal a letter, — not exactly in a gimlet-hole bored in a chair-leg — but, at least, in *some* out-of-the-way hole or corner suggested by the same tenor of thought which would

---

[10]François de La Rochefoucauld (1613–1680) was the French author of *Moral Maxims and Reflections* (1665); Niccolò Machiavelli (1460–1527), an Italian, was the author of *The Prince* (1513), the classic treatise on the art of statecraft; Tommaso Campanella (1568–1639) was an Italian philosopher; "La Bougive," it has been suggested, is the result of an error in transcription — Poe intended an allusion to Jean de la Bruyère (1645–1696), the French author of *Characters* (1688), a study of human manners. All these writers saw selfishness as the chief motive for human behavior.

urge a man to secrete a letter in a gimlet-hole bored in a chair-leg? And do you not see also, that such *recherchés*[11] nooks for concealment are adapted only for ordinary occasions, and would be adopted only by ordinary intellects; for, in all cases of concealment, a disposal of the article concealed — a disposal of it in this *recherché*[12] manner, — is, in the very first instance, presumable and presumed; and thus its discovery depends, not at all upon the acumen, but altogether upon the mere care, patience, and determination of the seekers; and where the case is of importance — or, what amounts to the same thing in the political eyes, when the reward is of magnitude, — the qualities in question have *never* been known to fail. You will now understand what I meant in suggesting that, had the purloined letter been hidden any where within the limits of the Prefect's examination — in other words, had the principles of its concealment been comprehended within the principles of the Prefect — its discovery would have been a matter altogether beyond question. This functionary, however, has been thoroughly mystified; and the remote source of his defeat lies in the supposition that the Minister is a fool, because he has acquired renown as a poet. All fools are poets; this the Prefect *feels*; and he is merely guilty of a *non distributio medii*[13] in thence inferring that all poets are fools."

99   "But is this really the poet?" I asked. "There are two brothers, I know; and both have attained reputation in letters. The Minister I believe has written learnedly on the Differential Calculus. He is a mathematician, and no poet."

100   "You are mistaken; I know him well; he is both. As poet *and* mathematician, he would reason well; as mere mathematician, he could not have reasoned at all, and thus would have been at the mercy of the Prefect."

101   "You surprise me," I said, "by these opinions, which have been contradicted by the voice of the world. You do not mean to set at naught the well-digested idea of centuries. The mathematical reason has long been regarded as *the* reason *par excellence.*"

102   "'*Il y a à parier*,'" replied Dupin, quoting from Chamfort, "'*que toute idée publique, toute convention reçue, est une sottise, car elle a convenu au plus grand nombre.*'[14] The mathematicians, I grant you, have done their best to promulgate the popular error to which you allude, and which is none the less an error for its promulgation as truth. With an art worthy a better cause, for example, they have insinuated the term, 'analysis' into application to algebra. The French are the originators of this particular deception; but if a term is of any importance — if words derive any value from applicability — then 'analysis' conveys 'algebra' about as much as, in Latin, '*ambitus*' implies 'ambition,' '*religio*' 'religion,' or '*homines honesti*,' a set of *honorable* men."

---

[11]Out of the way.

[12]Clever.

[13]In logic the "undistributed middle" is a syllogistic fallacy yielding a false conclusion.

[14]"The chances are that every popular idea, every accepted convention, is nonsense, since it is acceptable to the majority."

"You have a quarrel on hand, I see," said I, "with some of the   103
algebraists of Paris; but proceed."

"I dispute the availability, and thus the value, of that reason which is   104
cultivated in any especial form other than the abstractly logical. I dispute, in particular, the reason educed by mathematical study. The mathematics are the science of form and quantity; mathematical reasoning is
merely logic applied to observation upon form and quantity. The great
error lies in supposing that even the truths of what is called *pure* algebra,
are abstract or general truths. And this error is so egregious that I am
confounded at the universality with which it has been received. Mathematical axioms are *not* axioms of general truth. What is true of *relation*
—of form and quantity—is often grossly false in regard to morals, for
example. In this latter science it is very usually *un*true that the aggre-
gated parts are equal to the whole. In chemistry also the axiom fails. In
the consideration of motive it fails; for two motives, each of a given
value, have not, necessarily, a value when united, equal to the sum of
their values apart. There are numerous other mathematical truths which
are only truths within the limits of *relation*. But the mathematician
argues, from his *finite truths*, through habit, as if they were of an absolutely general applicability—as the world indeed imagines them to be.
Bryant, in his very learned 'Mythology,'[15] mentions an analogous source
of error, when he says that 'although the Pagan fables are not believed,
yet we forget ouselves continually, and make inferences from them as
existing realities.' With the algebraists, however, who are Pagans themselves, the 'Pagan fables' *are* believed, and the inferences are made, not
so much through lapse of memory, as through an unaccountable addling
of the brains. In short, I never yet encountered the mere mathematician
who could be trusted out of equal roots, or one who did not clandestin-
ely hold it as a point of his faith that $x^2 + px$ was absolutely and uncon-
ditionally equal to q. Say to one of these gentlemen, by way of experiment, if you please, that you believe occasions may occur where $x^2 + px$
is *not* altogether equal to q, and, having made him understand what you
mean, get out of his reach as speedily as convenient, for, beyond doubt,
he will endeavor to knock you down.

"I mean to say," continued Dupin, while I merely laughed at his last   105
observations, "that if the Minister had been no more than a mathematician, the Prefect would have been under no necessity of giving me this
check. I knew him, however, as both mathematician and poet, and my
measures were adapted to his capacity, with reference to the circumstances by which he was surrounded. I knew him as a courtier, too, and
as a bold *intriguant*.[16] Such a man, I considered, could not fail to be
aware of the ordinary policial modes of action. He could not have failed
to anticipate—and events have proved that he did not fail to anticipate
—the waylayings to which he was subjected. He must have foreseen, I
reflected, the secret investigations of his premises. His frequent ab-
sences from home at night, which were hailed by the Prefect as certain

---

[15]Jacob Bryant (1715–1804), the English author of *A New System or Analysis of
Ancient Mythology* (1774–1776).
[16]Schemer.

aids to his success, I regarded only as *ruses*, to afford opportunity for thorough search to the police, and thus the sooner to impress them with the conviction to which G——, in fact, did finally arrive — the conviction that the letter was not upon the premises. I felt, also, that the whole train of thought, which I was at some pains in detailing to you just now, concerning the invariable principle of policial action in searches for articles concealed — I felt that this whole train of thought would necessarily pass through the mind of the Minister. It would imperatively lead him to despise all the ordinary *nooks* of concealment. *He* could not, I reflected, be so weak as not to see that the most intricate and remote recess of his hotel would be as open as his commonest closets to the eyes, to the probes, to the gimlets, and to the microscopes of the Prefect. I saw, in fine, that he would be driven, as a matter of course, to *simplicity*, if not deliberately induced to it as a matter of choice. You will remember, perhaps, how desperately the Prefect laughed when I suggested, upon our first interview, that it was just possible this mystery troubled him so much on account of its being so *very* self-evident."

106   "Yes," said I, "I remember his merriment well. I really thought he would have fallen into convulsions."

107   "The material world," continued Dupin, "abounds with very strict analogies to the immaterial; and thus some color of truth has been given to the rhetorical dogma, that metaphor, or simile, may be made to strengthen an argument, as well as to embellish a description. The principle of the *vis inertiae*,[17] for example, seems to be identical in physics and metaphysics. It is not more true in the former, that a large body is with more difficulty set in motion than a smaller one, and that its subsequent *momentum* is commensurate with this difficulty, than it is, in the latter, that intellects of the vaster capacity, while more forcible, more constant, and more eventful in their movements than those of inferior grade, are yet the less readily moved, and more embarrassed and full of hesitation in the first few steps of their progress. Again: have you ever noticed which of the street signs, over the shop doors, are the most attractive of attention?"

108   "I have never given the matter a thought," I said.

109   "There is a game of puzzles," he resumed, "which is played upon a map. One party playing, requires another to find a given word — the name of town, river, state or empire — any word, in short, upon the motley and perplexed surface of the chart. A novice in the game generally seeks to embarrass his opponents by giving them the most minutely lettered names; but the adept selects such words as stretch, in large characters, from one end of the chart to the other. These, like the over-largely lettered signs and placards of the street, escape observation by dint of being excessively obvious; and here the physical oversight is precisely analogous with the moral inapprehension by which the intellect suffers to pass unnoticed those considerations which are too obtrusively and too palpably self-evident. But this is a point, it appears,

[17]The power of inertia.

somewhat above or beneath the understanding of the Prefect. He never once thought it probable, or possible, that the Minister had deposited the letter immediately beneath the nose of the whole world, by way of best preventing any portion of that world from perceiving it.

"But the more I reflected upon the daring, dashing, and discriminat-   110
ing ingenuity of D——; upon the fact that the document must always have been *at hand*, if he intended to use it to good purpose; and upon the decisive evidence, obtained by the Prefect, that it was not hidden within the limits of that dignitary's ordinary search — the more satisfied I became that, to conceal this letter, the Minister had resorted to the comprehensive and sagacious expedient of not attempting to conceal it at all.

"Full of these ideas, I prepared myself with a pair of green specta-   111
cles, and called one fine morning, quite by accident, at the Ministerial hotel. I found D—— at home, yawning, lounging, and dawdling, as usual, and pretending to be in the last extremity of *ennui*. He is, per-haps, the most really energetic human being now alive — but that is only when nobody sees him.

"To be even with him, I complained of my weak eyes, and lamented   112
the necessity of the spectacles, under cover of which I cautiously and thoroughly surveyed the apartment, while seemingly intent only upon the conversation of my host.

"I paid special attention to a large writing-table near which he sat,   113
and upon which lay confusedly, some miscellaneous letters and other papers, with one or two musical instruments and a few books. Here, however, after a long and very deliberate scrutiny, I saw nothing to excite particular suspicion.

"At length my eyes, in going the circuit of the room, fell upon a   114
trumpery fillagree card-rack of paste-board, that hung dangling by a dirty blue ribbon, from a little brass knob just beneath the middle of the mantel-piece. In this rack, which had three or four compartments, were five or six visiting cards and a solitary letter. This last was much soiled and crumpled. It was torn nearly in two, across the middle — as if a design, in the first instance, to tear it entirely up as worthless, had been altered, or stayed, in the second. It had a large black seal, bearing the D—— cipher *very* conspicuously, and was addressed, in a diminutive female hand, to D——, the minister, himself. It was thrust carelessly, and even, as it seemed, contemptuously, into one of the upper divisions of the rack.

"No sooner had I glanced at this letter, than I concluded it to be that   115
of which I was in search. To be sure, it was, to all appearance, radically different from the one of which the Prefect had read us so minute a description. Here the seal was large and black, with the D—— cipher; there it was small and red, with the ducal arms of the S—— family. Here, the address, to the Minister, was dimunitive and feminine; there the superscription, to a certain royal personage, was markedly bold and decided; the size alone formed a point of correspondence. But, then, the *radicalness* of these differences, which was excessive; the dirt; the

soiled and torn condition of the paper, so inconsistent with the *true* methodical habits of D——, and so suggestive of a design to delude the beholder into an idea of the worthlessness of the document; these things, together with the hyperobtrusive situation of this document, full in the view of every visiter, and thus exactly in accordance with the conclusions to which I had previously arrived; these things, I say, were strongly corroborative of suspicion, in one who came with the intention to suspect.

116   "I protracted my visit as long as possible, and, while I maintained a most animated discussion with the Minister, on a topic which I knew well had never failed to interest and excite him, I kept my attention really riveted upon the letter. In this examination, I committed to memory its external appearance and arrangement in the rack; and also fell, at length, upon a discovery which set at rest whatever trivial doubt I might have entertained. In scrutinizing the edges of the paper, I observed them to be more *chafted* than seemed necessary. They presented the *broken* appearance which is manifested when a stiff paper, having been once folded and pressed with a folder, is refolded in a reversed direction, in the same creases or edges which had formed the original fold. This discovery was sufficient. It was clear to me that the letter had been turned, as a glove, inside out, re-directed, and re-sealed, I bade the Minister good morning, and took my departure at once, leaving a gold snuff-box upon the table.

117   "The next morning I called for the snuff-box, when we resumed, quite eagerly, the conversation of the preceding day. While thus engaged, however, a loud report, as if of a pistol, was heard immediately beneath the windows of the hotel, and was succeeded by a series of fearful screams, and the shoutings of a mob. D—— rushed to a casement, threw it open, and looked out. In the meantime, I stepped to the card-rack, took the letter, put it in my pocket, and replaced it by a *fac-simile*, (so far as regards externals,) which I had carefully prepared at my lodgings; imitating the D—— cipher, very readily, by means of a seal formed of bread.

118   "The disturbance in the street had been occasioned by the frantic behavior of a man with a musket. He had fired it among a crowd of women and children. It proved, however, to have been without ball, and the fellow was suffered to go his way as a lunatic or a drunkard. When he had gone, D—— came from the window, whither I had followed him immediately upon securing the object in view. Soon afterwards I bade him farewell. The pretended lunatic was a man in my own pay."

119   "But what purpose had you," I asked, "in replacing the letter by a *fac-simile*? Would it not have been better, at the first visit, to have seized it openly, and departed?"

120   "D——," replied Dupin, "is a desperate man, and a man of nerve. His hotel, too, is not without attendants devoted to his interests. Had I made the wild attempt you suggest, I might never have left the Ministerial presence alive. The good people of Paris might have heard of me no

more. But I had an object apart from these considerations. You know my political prepossessions. In this matter, I act as a partisan of the lady concerned. For eighteen months the Minister has had her in his power. She has now him in hers; since being unaware that the letter is not in his possession, he will proceed with his exactions as if it was. Thus will he inevitably commit himself, at once, to his political destruction. His downfall, too, will not be more precipitate than awkward. It is all very well to talk about the *facilis descensus Averni*;[18] but in all kinds of climbing, as Catalani[19] said of singing, it is far more easy to get up than to come down. In the present instance I have no sympathy—at least no pity—for him who descends. He is that *monstrum horrendum*,[20] an unprincipled man of genius. I confess, however, that I should like very well to know the precise character of his thoughts, when, being defied by her whom the Prefect terms 'a certain personage,' he is reduced to opening the letter which I left for him in the card-rack."

"How? did you put any thing particular in it?"

"Why—it did not seem altogether right to leave the interior blank —that would have been insulting. D——, at Vienna once, did me an evil turn, which I told him, quite good-humoredly, that I should remember. So, as I knew he would feel some curiosity in regard to the identity of the person who had outwitted him. I thought it a pity not to give him a clue. He is well acquainted with my MS., and I just copied into the middle of the blank sheet the words—

—— Un dessein si funeste,
S'il n'est digne d'Atrée, est digne de Thyeste.[21]

They are to be found in Crébillon's 'Atrée.'"

Questions on Content

1. Why does the Prefect of Police consult Dupin? Explain the case that puzzles the Prefect as fully as you can.
2. How does the Prefect assure himself that Minister D—— does not conceal the purloined letter "upon his person"?
3. After hearing the full details of the Prefect's fruitless search, what does Dupin suggest that the Prefect do? Why does he suggest nothing else?
4. Why is it significant that the thief, Minister D——, is *both* a poet and a mathematician?
5. How does Dupin recognize the purloined letter when he first sees it in the Minister's residence?

[18]"Easy is the descent to Hell"—Vergil's *Aeneid*.
[19]Angelica Catalini (1780–1849), a well-known Italian opera singer.
[20]Horrible monster.
[21]"A design so deadly, if unworthy of Atreus, is quite worthy of Thyestes." The lines are quoted from Crébillion's eighteenth-century French tragedy, *Atrée et Thyeste* (1707), in reference to Atreus, King of Mycenae, who murdered his nephews and served them up as a meal to their father Thyestes. Thyestes had previously seduced Atreus' wife and placed a curse on the house of Atreus.

Questions on Thesis, Purpose, and Structure

1. Early in the story Dupin observes that "Perhaps it is the very simplicity of the thing which puts you at fault." To what extent does that sentence serve as the thesis of the story? Explain.
2. What process does the Prefect follow in attempting to find the purloined letter? How carefully does he perform each stage in the process?
3. What process does Dupin follow in deducing the likely whereabouts of the letter? Describe each step.
4. This story is obviously entertaining, but is it also persuasive? What argument does it create about the nature of a detective's work?

Questions on Style and Diction

1. Find the following words in the story and determine their denotations in context: meerschaum (paragraph 1); contemptible (paragraph 2); purloined (paragraph 20); exalted, ascendancy, illustrious (paragraph 26); *boudoir*, perusal, juncture, fathoms, juxtaposition, decamped (paragraph 28); sagacious (paragraph 31); astute (paragraph 36); gimlet-dust (paragraph 53); prodigious (paragraph 57); perusal (paragraph 73); insinuated (paragraph 83); functionary (paragraph 88); arrant (paragraph 94); profundity (paragraph 96); cohort, acumen (paragraph 98); promulgate (paragraph 102); educed, egregious (paragraph 104); *ruses* (paragraph 105); obtrusively, palpably (paragraph 109); *ennui* (paragraph 111), trumpery, cipher (paragraph 114); *facsimile* (paragraph 117); partisan, exactions (paragraph 120).
2. In describing the circumstances surrounding the theft of the letter, the Prefect speaks in abstract and roundabout terms. Why does he do so? What is the effect of this abstraction? Can you decipher the Prefect's "code" and determine the nature of the letter, the title of the recipient, the recipient's relationship with the letter's author, and her reasons for fearing a public revelation of the theft?

Ideas for Essays

1. Dupin favors what might be called a psychological approach to solving crimes, while the Prefect of Police admires technology. Write a defense of the Prefect's point of view, using for support examples of how modern technology has contributed to detection.
2. Poe obviously intends for the reader to admire Dupin's powers of deduction, but for the sake of argument, analyze Dupin's process of detection, trying wherever possible to point out actual or potential flaws in his methods.

◇◇◇

Mousetrap
Michael Crichton

Michael Crichton (1942–   ) was born in Chicago and educated at Harvard University. While a medical student at Harvard in the 1960s, Crichton began to write thrillers, and although he completed his degree, he soon gave up medicine to pursue a career as a writer and film director. Crichton's best-selling novels, most of which explore the world of science (often science that has run amok), are notable for their carefully created plausibility and verisimilitude. They include *The Andromeda Strain* (1969), *The Terminal Man* (1972), *The Great Train Robbery* (1975), and *Congo* (1980). In Crichton's "Mousetrap" (1984), see if you can figure out what process Harry Waters devises as a "mousetrap" to catch computer thieves.

"No offense," Bobby Vincent said, setting a microtape recorder on the bar. "But tell me again, O.K.?"   1

"Tell you what?" the lawyer said. They were in Eli McFly's in Silicon Valley, sitting beneath the glowing sexy robots that decorated the bar. It was lunchtime, and the place was crowded with young people who worked at nearby computer companies. Nobody was paying attention to them.   2

Bobby pointed to the tape recorder. "Just tell me."   3

"My name is Ted Winslow. I'm a lawyer."   4

"And you're not FBI, and you don't work for the company. . . ." Bobby prompted.   5

"Of course not." Ted Winslow frowned at the tape recorder. "You worried about entrapment?"   6

"I'm not worried about anything," Bobby said. "I'm just careful. Now say what you want me to do."   7

"My client wants you to obtain a copy of the microcode for the System 550 disk operating system."   8

"Your client knows the 550 microcode is confidential information?"   9

"My client knows you work for the company and you wrote the security program for the System 550. So my client thinks you will be able to obtain the microcode."   10

Bobby drummed his finger on the table. "In other words, your client wants me to steal it?"   11

The lawyer hesitated. "Yes."   12

"O.K.," Bobby said. "I'll steal it. Fifty thousand dollars for a first look at the partial code, paid into a Cayman Islands bank account. Fifty thousand dollars for the complete final code."   13

"Thirty and thirty."   14

Bobby clicked the tape recorder off. "You got a deal."   15

They shook hands. "This calls for a drink," the lawyer said. He was sweating.   16

"I can't drink," Bobby said. "I won't be twenty-one until next year." He pushed away from the bar. "Let's get out of here."   17

18   In the parking lot, the lawyer blinked in the bright sunshine. "Cayman Islands bank account?"

19   "I took a vacation there last spring." His account at the George Town Commercial Trust on Grand Cayman allowed deposits and withdrawals to be made remotely by computer.

20   "You're very professional."

21   Bobby put on his sunglasses. "What do you think, I'm some hacker from the Milwaukee 414s? We're not talking teenage fun and games. We're talking a major crime. They catch me, I won't be able to stand in front of congressmen and say, 'Gee whiz, I didn't know it was illegal.'"

22   They came to Bobby's car, a black Porsche 928. It was new; it still had temporary registration and paper license plates. "Nice car," the lawyer said.

23   "Thanks," Bobby said. He unlocked the door. "I'm very proud of this car. I bought it with the bonus the company paid me—for designing the security on the System 550." He grinned.

24   Driving back to his office, Bobby thought it over. The System 550 was the new generation of computers, destined to become the industry standard for at least five years. The microcode for the disk operating system was a crucial design aspect of the 550 computer—for anyone who wanted to make a duplicate machine, a compatible machine. A competing machine.

25   The client was almost certainly Japanese. The money, $60,000, was almost certainly too cheap, even though Bobby's own salary the year before was $25,000. But he would handle the details later. Right now, he had to figure out how to break through the System 550 security program —a program he had designed.

26   Bobby had been a summer trainee at the company during his first year in college. He had stayed on after Murphy, the head of programming, offered him the chance to write the entire security program for the forthcoming System 550.

27   "You're the best young programmer I've seen in a decade," Murphy said. "Brilliant, fast, good. I want you to do this job all by yourself."

28   Bobby couldn't say no. It was every programmer's dream to do a major piece of work on a major machine—to be able to say for years to come, I did that. I wrote that sucker, it's mine.

29   "I have other reasons for my offer," Murphy went on. "Security is not a team sport; I don't want a floor of programmers writing sensitive code. Plus, you know the machine, you're familiar with the 550 architecture. Plus, you're fast. Plus, you're not thirty years old with a wife and two kids and car payments."

30   "True," Bobby said. He was only 18 at the time.

31   "Because," Murphy said, "sooner or later somebody will make you an offer to break into the 550 system. But I'm a good judge of character. I think when that offer is made, you'll report it to us. And let us nail the bastards."

32   'Yes, sir," Bobby had said. "You can count on me."

Bobby turned into the company parking lot and parked in his space.   33
He patted his beautiful black car on the fender. And he went inside the
building to begin robbing the System 550.

Bobby's security program was called Watchdog. It was literally that—a   34
watchdog for the System 550. Watchdog resided permanently in memory, 24 hours a day. It watched who signed on and what they did once
inside the system. It accomplished this by checking users very rapidly—
1,000 individual checks every second—and keeping track of their behavior. If a user couldn't remember his password, if he tried to move to
an unauthorized level, if he tried to get into somebody else's file.
Watchdog saw it and cut him out of the system.

Bobby had turned Watchdog over to the company nearly six months   35
ago. By now the program might have been modified to keep him out. At
the terminal in his office, he logged on the system. The screen blinked:

LOGON: NAME?
  He typed BOBBY VINCENT
PASSWORD?
  He typed his password, WHIZKID
WELCOME TO SYSTEM 550,
BOBBY VINCENT
WHERE DO YOU WANT TO GO?
  He typed COMMAND LEVEL and waited.

Ordinary users weren't allowed to go to the Command Level of a big   36
computer. The Command Level contained control programs for the
entire computer system; it held the Security and Utility programs; it was
the place where tampering could be done most easily. But as a high-
level security programmer, Bobby had access to the Command Level.
The screen flashed:

YOU ARE AT COMMAND LEVEL: S,U,M,R

Bobby looked at the line. The single letters were prompts to remind   37
the user what to do next. These prompts weren't explained, because it
was assumed that anyone at Command Level knew what he was doing.
Bobby typed S for Security.

SYSTEM 550 SECURITY
FILE	AUTHOR	KB
WATCHDOG	(ROBERT VINCENT)	1109
MOUSETRAP	(HAROLD WATERS)	30

"Uh, oh," Bobby said. Watchdog hadn't been changed much, judging   38
from the file size. But there was now a second security file. Mousetrap.
He stared at the screen, drummed his fingers on the desk. This wasn't
going to be as easy as he had thought. Bobby was pretty sure he could
fool Watchdog. But he didn't know anything about Mousetrap.

39   It was his own damn fault that he didn't. He thought ruefully about old Harry Waters, the programmer with an office just down the hall. He remembered one time Harry had come into Bobby's office, wheezing—Harry was fat, and he had asthma or something—and he had said, "Hey, I have a cute idea for something called Mousetrap. Want to hear about it?"

40   "Harry, I'm really busy. . . ."

41   "Sure, sure," Harry said. "Maybe another time."

42   The truth was, Bobby was disdainful of Harry Waters. Bobby was the bright young kid, Harry was the fat old man. Harry was from another era, really; he lived in a different world. Harry never got into the architecture of the machines; he only talked about the users. "I'm a humanist at heart," he used to say. "I care about people." Everybody knew he was out of touch.

43   He had spent his last few years designing keyboards and glare-proof screens and junk like that. His work had a fancy name, ergonomics, but it was really just foolishness as far as Bobby was concerned. Bobby worked with the machines, and he lived in the heart of the beast. It was the machines that counted.

44   Another time Harry came in and said, "Hey, I sold Murphy on my Mousetrap program."

45   And Bobby had said, "That's great, Harry that's really great." And he had thought, Murphy's just being nice to him, waiting for the old fart to retire.

46   "Want to hear about it?" Harry had asked.

47   "Is it co-resident with my program? You need memory allocations or something?"

48   "No, no, it has nothing to do with your Watchdog." Harry had smiled. "Whole separate thing."

49   "Another time, maybe," Bobby had said. "I'm behind."

50   "Sure," Harry had said. "Sure, kid." But he never mentioned Mousetrap again.

```
SYSTEM 550 SECURITY
FILE            AUTHOR              KB
WATCHDOG        (ROBERT VINCENT)   1109
MOUSETRAP       (HAROLD WATERS)      30
```

51   The screen taunted him. Mousetrap stood between him and $60,000. He stared at the file size—it was tiny, only 30 kilobytes. The equivalent of six typed sheets of paper. What could such a little program do? He was tempted to ignore it but he didn't dare. He had to find out about Mousetrap.

52   "Harry's on vacation this month," his secretary, Alice, said. Bobby managed to run into her in the company cafeteria. "Was there something I can help with?"

53   "I just had some questions about Mousetrap."

54   She smiled. "That's Harry's pride and joy."

"You know much about it?"   55
"Just a little. Because of the typing."   56
"The typing . . ."   57
"Yes, for a week Harry was videotaping me, and everyone else in   58
the office, typing. Then he ran the videotapes at very slow speed."
"What was that for?"   59
"I don't know, something about the fingers. He eventually went to   60
typing schools and did more testing. But that wasn't the worst part."
"What was the worst part?"   61
"The handwriting experts! The graphologists. They are weirdos!"   62
"Harry talked to handwriting experts?"   63
"Lots of them. Finding out how they could tell a signature. Harry   64
kept talking about people's 'signature,' even when they typed."
"This was all for Mousetrap?"   65
"Oh, yes. Harry worked hard on Mousetrap. He says it's the crown-   66
ing point of his career."

Typing schools . . . graphologists . . . signatures? It didn't make   67
sense. Bobby couldn't imagine what Mousetrap was about. What did it
do?

Maybe the name was a clue. A "mouse" was a device to move the   68
cursor on a computer, a little box you pushed around the desk. But not
everybody used a mouse so . . . So what? He shook his head.

Knowing that Alice was still in the cafeteria, he dropped by Harry's   69
office. It was chaotic as usual, papers scattered around the terminal, cigar
butts, pictures of his wife, grandchildren. . . . Bobby shook his head as
he looked at the mess. Harry was sloppy, fat and sloppy.

Amid the mess, he noticed that there were three brands of mouse   70
and also many input devices—game paddles, joysticks, track balls. But
what did that mean?

He saw the stack of interoffice memos to one side, unopened,   71
unread. Harry was famous for not following procedure. Bobby remembered how they kept trying to get him to change his password. Employees were supposed to change their password every couple of weeks,
but Harry couldn't be bothered. For years his password had remained
the same, and everybody knew that it . . .

Of course! Bobby snapped his fingers and hurried back to his own   72
office.

```
LOGON: NAME?
HARRY WATERS
PASSWORD?
KEYBOARD
WELCOME TO SYSTEM 550.
HARRY WATERS
WHERE DO YOU WANT TO GO?
```

Bobby smiled. Child's play. "Shoulda changed your password,   73
Harry." He typed MYFILES, to call the user's personal files.

```
MYFILES DIRECTORY OR GET A
SPECIFIC FILE?
GET MOUSETRAP
```

74   The screen cleared again. The computer was responding very fast, without the usual delay of a second or two. There must be relatively few users on the system. He checked his watch; no, it was 2:15, and most people would be back from lunch by now. He shrugged and forgot about the speed as he saw:

```
MOUSETRAP IS A SECURITY FILE
DO YOU WANT:
AUTHOR
PROJECT HISTORY
SOURCE CODE
OBJECT CODE
INTERRUPTS
DISABLE COMMANDS
```

75   "Beautiful." He clapped his hands. There was a complete menu, access to the entire file. Even the history of the project! Very sloppy of Harry to leave this in. . . . He typed PROJECT HISTORY.

```
PROJECT HISTORY NOT AVAILABLE
```

76   The answer came back very fast. And it was an odd answer too. Why wasn't it available? Never mind, he could figure it out from the Source Code, which was the actual program Harry had written. He typed SOURCE CODE.

```
SOURCE CODE NOT AVAILABLE
```

77   Bobby frowned. What was this? The menu didn't go anywhere. He typed OBJECT CODE.

```
OBJECT CODE NOT AVAILABLE
INTERRUPTS
INTERRUPTS NOT AVAILABLE
Finally, frustrated, he typed DISABLE COMMANDS.
And he hit pay dirt. The screen showed:
TO DISABLE MOUSETRAP PROGRAM:
1. AT SYSTEM LEVEL: DISMOUSESYS
2. FOR INDIVIDUAL USER:
DISMOUSEUSE
3. AT SPECIFIC TIME: DISMOUSETIM
```

78   "Hot damn." Bobby said. It didn't matter anymore what Mousetrap did—because he knew how to shut it off. He wrote down the code, Dismouseuse, and exited the system.

79   He was now ready to fool both Watchdog and Mousetrap. Or rather, to have a new employee do it.

"Caught me red-handed!" Carol, the secretary in personnel, tucked the

80

bag of cookies back into her desk. "Not on my diet. What can I do for you, Bobby?"

Bobby moved around the desk, leaned on her console. "I wanted to set up a racquet ball game with Jim." 81

"Jim's in Houston at that conference. He won't be back until Friday," she said, wiping crumbs from her lips. 82

"I'll come back later." Bobby said. "Thanks." He strolled off down the hall. 83

Good old Carol. She never changed. She was always dieting and always breaking her diet. And she was never able to remember her password. That's why she wrote it on a file card pinned to the wall beside her terminal. 84

"Cookie," he thought, how appropriate. 85

He called the lawyer. "I'll have the stuff for you tonight." 86

"Tonight? So fast?" 87

"I got lucky," Bobby said. 88

Paying cash and using the name Jack Ramsay, Bobby took a room in the Sheraton Hotel in Sunnyvale, right in the heart of Silicon Valley. His suitcase contained only his personal computer, bundled in a towel. From his hotel room, he used the computer to tie into the System 550 over a telephone modem. 89

The screen blinked LOGON:NAME? 90

He typed CAROL BANDALINI
PASSWORD?
COOKIE
WELCOME TO SYSTEM 550,
CAROL BANDALINI
WHERE DO YOU WANT TO GO?

As Carol Bandalini, he went directly to Personnel Files and hired a new employee named Xurxes Xynen. The name was obviously phony, but Carol only reviewed new employee listings once a week. And Bobby would be long gone by then. 91

He assigned Xurxes Xynen the password Crackerjack and logged off. He went down the hall to get a Coke from the soft-drink machine. 92

In theory, his plan should work fine. Even though the company had probably modified Watchdog, there was one part of the program that they wouldn't touch—because it concerned speed. 93

Speed was the classic problem for internal monitoring programs. Such programs had been proposed back in the late 1960s, long before computer crime became a problem. But even in the '70s, nobody bothered to write monitoring programs because they slowed down the machines too much. 94

Banks, airlines and hospitals didn't want unauthorized users getting into their systems. But they also didn't want to wait three minutes for a 95 reply at terminal because the computer power was busy with monitoring programs. If internal security programs were to be acceptable, they had to be transparent to users—which meant they had to be fast.

Of course computers were more powerful now, but speed was still a problem. While writing Watchdog, Bobby had employed several speedup tricks. One was to instruct the machine to ignore unlikely user names. For example, nobody had a name that began with the letters XU or XY. To go faster, Watchdog skipped such impossible letter combinations. That meant that once Xurxes Xynen was logged on and verified, Watchdog would proceed to ignore him. It would still sample 1,000 times a second, but it wouldn't sample anything that began XU or XY. Thus as Xurxes Xynen, Bobby would be free to move through the System 550 without Watchdog supervision.

97   At least that was the idea.

98   Back in his room, he sat down at his computer again and dialed into the system. He figured it would take 20 minutes to do the robbery.

> LOGON:NAME?
> XURXES XYNEN
> PASSWORD?
> CRACKERJACK

99   There was a momentary pause, Bobby bit his lip. This was actually the only dangerous part. If anybody watching a terminal in personnel or security had noticed the hiring of Xurxes Xynen, they would have spotted it as phony. And now, somewhere in the system the security people would be waiting for him to come back on. But there was only a short delay before:

> WELCOME TO SYSTEM 550,
> XURXES XYNEN
> WHERE DO YOU WANT TO GO?
>   He was in! Bobby typed COMMAND LEVEL
> YOU ARE AT COMMAND LEVEL:S,U,M,R

100   He typed R to Revise Employee Status. Bobby was satisfied that he had already beaten his own program—according to the System 550, Xurxes Xynen was only cleared for regular user levels, yet Xurxes Xynen had already moved to the Command Level without trouble.

101   He proceeded to give Xurxes Xynen Command Level clearance and a Command Level password: Worldbeater. This additional user password was required for certain functions within the Command Level itself.

102   Of course, an employee was never allowed to revise his own status —but again, since Watchdog didn't monitor anyone named Xurxes Xynen in the first place, it wasn't watching any revisions by Xurxes Xynen of anything, including his own record.

103   He felt a surge of adrenaline. He was now only minutes away from finishing. The only thing still in his way now was Mousetrap. He typed:

```
DISMOUSEUSE
MOUSETRAP PROGRAM DISABLED FOR
USER XURXES XYNEN
```

"Ta da!" he shouted. "Got you, Harry!" He typed U.   104

```
SYSTEM 550 UTILITIES
MICROCODE PR
MICROCODE BUF
MICROCODE DOS
MICROCODE HS
MICROCODE UDR
```

The microcode for the disk operating system was right there: he   105
typed DUMP MICROCODE DOS

```
THAT IS A CONFIDENTIAL FILE
COMMAND-LEVEL PASSWORD?
WORLDBEATER
VERIFYING PASSWORD NOW
```

There was a pause while the System 550 went to the Command   106
Level and checked to see that Xurxes Xynen had the authorization to
receive confidential dump and that Xurxes Xynen's password was indeed Worldbeater. The machine came back:

```
PASSWORD VERIFIED
DUMPING FILE NOW
TRANSMISSION TIME: 9.2 MIN.
```

In the hotel room, the disk drives on his personal computer began   107
to whir as the microcode for the operating system was transferred from
the central system onto his own floppy disk, a communication between
computers that would take about 10 minutes. Bobby went down the hall
and got another Coke; he looked at the kids splashing in the swimming
pool. When he came back, the drives had stopped. He now had a copy of
the code.

It was time to get the hell out.   108
He went to the Command Level and erased all passwords for Xurxes   109
Xynen. He went to the Personnel File and erased any record of hiring
Xurxes Xynen. Then he logged off the system and copied the disk,
erasing half the file from one disk. He disconnected his personal com-
puter, packed up and checked out of the hotel.

"What is this, a pickup place?" the lawyer sniffed. They were in the   110
Rodeo Bar at midnight; the music was blasting.
"Why not, you're picking up," Bobby said, and showed him a disk.   111
"Where's the money?"
The money had been transferred by computer to Bobby's account in   112
the Cayman Islands. "Thirty thousand smackers, kid," Ted said.

113   Bobby gave him the disk. "Here's the first half of the code."

114   "My client will have it verified. Nice doing business with you," Ted said. "This is gonna make you the richest twenty-year-old in the valley."

115   "Not by a long shot," Bobby said.

116   "Yeah, but you're on your way, kid."

117   Ted said it would take the client several days to carry out the code verification. In the meantime, Bobby went to the office as usual. Everything seemed to be fine; there were no rumors in the company cafeteria, no whispers in the company gym as there had been a year ago, when Tim Johnson set up a dummy payroll account or when Betsy Marshall stole one of the Alpha code books and sold it to an FBI undercover woman.

118   One evening as he was leaving, Bobby ran into Harry in the parking lot.

119   "You're back," Bobby said, surprised. "I thought you were on vacation for a month."

120   "Something came up," Harry said. "You know, problems at the office . . . Nice car," Harry said, admiring the Porsche. Harry drove a battered Datsun. "Wish I could afford a car like that."

121   Bobby bit his lip. He didn't like it that Harry had come back. He didn't like it at all. "Hope the problems aren't too serious."

122   "No, no," Harry said, walking down the row of cars to his own sedan. "Just the usual. Nothing too pressing. I'm in a great mood. I tell you, I'm in a crackerjack mood." He laughed.

123   Bobby felt a chill.

124   The telephone in his apartment rang that night. "It's me," Ted said. "I gotta see you right away."

125   "Listen, I have a date tonight."

126   *"Right away."*

127   "O.K., O.K."

128   "I'll come there," Ted said and hung up. He arrived an hour later. He was not alone. "This is Kano," he said, referring to a glowering mountain of solid flesh. "Kano is Samoan."

129   Kano was so big that he had to turn sideways to come through the door. "Hello," Bobby said.

130   Kano grunted.

131   Bobby said, "What's the matter?"

132   "I'll tell you what's the matter," the lawyer said. "The microcode. It's wrong!"

133   "It can't be wrong; it's a straight dump from 550 Utility files."

134   "Well, their experts went over it, and they say it's garbage — it's graphics."

135   "Graphics?"

136   "Did you look at the original disk? No? Look at it now."

137   Bobby crossed the room, turned on his computer and put the disk in. The disk whirred in the drive, and the screen filled with a series of pictures. Harry Waters, his wife, his grandchildren . . .

138   "Uh, oh," Bobby said.

"They want the money back," Ted said, wiping the sweat from his 139
forehead. "That's why they sent Kano. We are in deep trouble. Are you
listening to me?"

"I'm listening," Bobby said. "You can have the money back. I'll get 140
it now. "He dialed the bank account in the Cayman Islands.

The screen glowed ACCOUNT CLOSED. 141

"Jesus," Ted said. "Where's the money, Bobby?" 142

Kano walked over to the light beside the computer. He tore the 143
shade off and gripped the hot glowing bulb in one giant brown hand.
Smiling at Bobby, he crushed the bulb. It exploded like a gunshot. "Get
the money, kid," he said.

"I will," Bobby said. "I will." 144

"Hi, Bobby," Alice said the next morning. "Harry's in his office with Mr. 145
Murphy. They're expecting you."

"They're expecting me?" 146

"Well, they said they were." She saw him hesitate. "You can go right 147
in."

Bobby went in. 148

"Sit down, Bobby," Murphy said. "You look like you're waiting for 149
the firing squad."

"You mean I'm not?" 150

"Well, *we* won't shoot you. Somebody else may, but we won't. It's 151
against company policy to punish people for doing what we want them
to do."

"I don't get it." 152

"I told you when I hired you, Bobby," Murphy said. "I'm a good 153
judge of character. I figured you were smart. I also figured you were an
unprincipled little sneak who'd jump at the first offer he got. I had to
know how vulnerable our system really was—and who better to test
security than the genius who designed it? If you couldn't get in, then
nobody could get in." Murphy smiled broadly. "And you couldn't get
in."

Bobby felt dizzy. He gripped the arms of the chair. "You *wanted* me 154
to break in?"

"I had my hopes. Especially after you took your vacation in the 155
Caymans . . ."

"Is that how you caught me?" 156

"Oh, no. You were mousetrapped," Murphy said. "With Mouse- 157
trap."

"I disabled Mousetrap. The computer said so." 158

"Sure," Harry said. "Because Mousetrap only works in the first 159
twenty seconds while a user logs on. After that it's automatically disabled, code word or not."

Harry smiled. "Just a little idea of mine," he said. "I prefer to work 160
with people, not machines. You see machines can always be broken
into. You broke in very well. Because machines can't really know who
you are, whether you're Bobby Vincent or Xey Yey or whatever the hell
you called yourself. The machine can't tell who's typing.

"And then I thought, maybe a machine *could* tell. Maybe people 161 had identifiable typing rhythms, like voice rhythms. And I found that the way people typed, or used a mouse, or touched a track ball was as uniquely theirs as a fingerprint. Type any nine-letter word—like mousetrap—and I can identify the typist exactly. So you see, we knew who you were every step of the way. The minute the computer saw your typing rhythm didn't match the name you logged on with, it cut you out of the system."

162   "But I was in the system."

163   "You were in a dummy system. You never had access to real files, only to fake files we made up. That was why the system responded so fast."

164   "I wondered about that."

165   "You should have more than wondered, kid. You should have known you'd been cut out and dropped into a special section of memory."

166   Bobby shifted uneasily in the chair. "Who has the money?"

167   "We do," Murphy said, smiling.

168   "Thirty thousand dollars," Harry said, smiling.

169   "They want it back."

170   "I'm sure they do," Murphy said.

171   "Well, I don't have the money, and I've got to come up with it."

172   "That's a problem," Harry said. "What're you gonna do?"

173   "I don't know."

174   "Well, we certainly don't know," Murphy said.

175   "Listen," Bobby said. "This isn't a joke. I need the money."

176   Murphy shrugged. "Guess you gotta sell your car, huh, kid? It's a nice car. It oughta be worth thirty grand, don't you think?"

177   Bobby groaned.

178   "Expensive lesson, kid," Harry said, "but better than jail."

179   "Better than a lot of things," Murphy said. "You should be damned grateful to us, Bobby. Just think: We might have assembled a real-appearing microcode for you to give them—one they'd use for a year before they found out it was fake. But we figured that after a wasted year, they'd send the Samoans to kill you. They use Samoans from Hawaii as enforcers, you know."

180   "I heard that," Bobby said. He was sweating.

181   "We did you a big favor, Bobby," Harry said. "We kept you alive."

182   "And we're keeping you on the job too," Murphy said. "At reduced pay, of course. Say fifteen thou a year?"

183   "Fifteen? That's what secretaries get in this company."

184   "Yes, but you won't be doing security work; we'll find something less demanding."

185   "You're telling me I'm your slave."

186   Murphy spread his hands. "Not at all, Bobby. You do whatever you want. But the thing is, your new employer won't like the letter of recommendation from us right now. Maybe in five years . . ."

187   "When you've matured," Harry said.

188   "That's right, when you've matured."

"Meantime," Harry said, "you take my advice and pay more atten- 189
tion to people and less to machines. Because a machine didn't catch you.
A person did." And Harry smiled.

Questions on Content

1. What is Bobby Vincent asked to steal? Why is it valuable?
2. How does the Watchdog system work?
3. Why does Bobby Vincent create a new employee named Xurxes Xyncn?
4. Why does Harry Waters suddenly return from his vacation?
5. What do you learn by the end of the story about the reasons why Murphy initially hired Bobby Vincent?

Questions on Thesis, Purpose, and Structure

1. What are the steps in the process Bobby Vincent employs in attempting to steal the System 550 Disk Operating System?
2. What process does the Mousetrap program use in catching computer thieves?
3. What do you know about the lifestyle, character, and abilities of Bobby Vincent? What do you know about Harry Waters? How are the contrasts between the two related to the thesis and theme of the story?
4. Discuss the combination of entertainment, information, and persuasion in Crichton's short story. What specific elements of the story contribute to fulfilling each purpose?

Questions on Style and Diction

1. Find the following words in the story and determine their definitions in context: entrapment (paragraph 6), ergonomics (paragraph 43), graphologists (paragraph 62), mouse (paragraph 68), chaotic (paragraph 69), Source Code (paragraph 76), modem (paragraph 89), LOGON (paragraph 90).
2. Crichton uses quite a bit of computer jargon in this story. Why is that terminology necessary?
3. What does Crichton do to keep the computer jargon from confusing or repelling his readers?
4. If you have the expertise to do so, evaluate the precision with which Crichton uses technical terminology.

Ideas for Essays

1. Computers now play some role in all of our lives. Write a narrative essay about your own adventures or misadventures in coping with a computerized society.
2. Compare the process Harry Waters uses in catching a thief with the process used by Dupin in "The Purloined Letter."

Mousetrap (Computer Program)

Michael Crichton

1 In a recent short story about a computer crime, I suggested that one could identify users on a computer system from their typing patterns: that the way a person types is as distinctive and individual as his fingerprint.

2 One reason to write fiction is that you're not obliged to be truthful or accurate; still, I found myself wondering whether the program I described, called Mousetrap, was feasible. An hour at the keyboard convinced me that it was.

3 The following program measures the interval between individual keystrokes as you type your name. A simple, empirically derived algorithm determines whether a second entry of the name has been typed by the same or a different person. Of course, there are highly sophisticated techniques of multivariate analysis to perform the discrimination with elegance, if anyone wanted to take this proposition seriously.

4 But this simple listing is fun to experiment with. Type in your name, step aside, and let somebody else type the same name. And see whether the machine believes it.

Listing 1. Mousetrap for Apple

```
10    REM APPLE MOUSETRAP
20    REM
30    REM BY MICHAEL CRICHTON
40    REM 10/25/83
50    REM
60    REM START ------------------
70    DIM N1(30),N2(30)
80    I = 768:OK = 2.25:NG = 1.5
90    HOME : PRINT "ACCEPTANCE
      LEVEL = ";OK:
      PRINT: PRINT
100   PRINT "LOGON:NAME? ";:
      GOSUB 380
110   T = 1
120   FOR X = 768 TO I
130   N1 (T) = PEEK (X):T = T + 1
140   NEXT : PRINT :N1$ = N$
150   REM AGAIN ------------------
160   I = 768:T = 1
170   PRINT : PRINT "LOGON:NAME?
      ";: GOSUB 380
180   FOR X = 768 TO I
190   N2(T) = PEEK (X):T = T + 1
200   NEXT : PRINT :N2$ = N$
210   REM CHECKER ------------------
220   PRINT
230   IF N1$ < > N2$ THEN PRINT
360   "SORRY, NO MATCH": GOTO
```

Listing 2. Mousetrap for IBM

```
10    REM IBM MOUSETRAP
20    REM
30    REM BY MICHAEL CRICHTON
40    REM 10/15/83
50    REM
60    DIM N1(30),N2(30),D(30)
70    T=1:REM TABLE VALUE
80    OK=1!: REM ACCEPTANCE
      LEVEL
90    NG = 2! : REM REJECTION
      LEVEL PRINT : PRINT
100   CLS:PRINT "ACCEPTANCE
      LEVEL = ";OK;
      REJECTION LEVEL = ";NG
110   PRINT:PRINT
120   PRINT "LOGON:NAME?
      ";:GOSUB 420
130   FOR X=1 TO T
140   N1 (X) = D(X)
150   NEXT
160   N1$=N$
170   REM ---- REPEAT ----
180   T=1
190   PRINT:PRINT
200   PRINT "LOGON:NAME?
      ";:GOSUB 420
210   FOR X=1 TO T
220   N2(X)=D(X)
```

```
240  FOR X = 2 TO LEN (N$) + 1
250  Z = ABS (N1(X) − N2(X))
260  SZ = 3 − Z:SC = SC + SZ
270  NEXT
280  PRINT
290  L = LEN (N$):SF = SC / L
300  SF$ = STR$ (SF):SF$ = LEFT$
     (SF$,3)
310  PRINT SF$;" ";
320  IF SF < NG THEN 350
330  IF SF > NG AND SF < OK
     THEN PRINT ''IDENTITY
     UNSURE BUT ACCEPTED":
     GOTO 360
340  IF SF > OK THEN PRINT
     "IDENTITY CONFIRMED": GOTO
     360
350  PRINT "YOU ARE A FAKE!"
360  END
370  REM MOUSETRAP ITSELF
     -----------
380  N$ = ""
390  CT = 0
400  KB = PEEK ( − 16384): IF KB >
     127 THEN 440
410  INVERSE : PRINT " ";: NORMAL
     : PRINT CHR$ (8);: PRINT "";:
     PRINT CHR$ (8);
420  CT = CT + 1: GOTO 400
430  REM KEYBOARD WAS
     PRESSED
440  POKE − 16368,0
450  POKE I,CT
460  KB = KB − 128:A$ = CHR$
     (KB): PRINT A$;:
     IF A$ = CHR$ (13) THEN
     RETURN
470  N$ = N$ + A$:I = I + 1: GOTO
     390
```

```
230  NEXT
240  N2$=N$
250  REM ----- CHECKER ---
260  PRINT
270  IF N1$ <> N2$ THEN PRINT
     "SORRY, NO MATCH": GOTO
     400
280  FOR X=2 TO LEN (N1$)+1
290  Z = ABS(N1(X)−N2(X))
300  SZ=3−Z:SC=SC+SZ
310  NEXT
320  PRINT
330  L = LEN(N$):SF=ABS (SC/L)
340  SF$=STR$(SF)
350  PRINT USING "\ \";SF$;"";
360  IF SF > NG THEN 390
370  IF SF < NG AND SF > OK
     THEN PRINT "IDENTITY
     UNSURE BUT
     ACCEPTED":GOTO 400
380  IF SF < OK THEN PRINT
     "IDENTITY CONFIRMED": GOTO
     400
390  PRINT "YOU ARE A FAKE!"
400  END
410  REM ----- MOUSETRAP ITSELF
     -----
420  N$ = ""
430  CT=0:REM RESET COUNTER
440  K$=INKEY$:IF K$="" THEN
     CT=CT+1:GOTO 440
450  REM KEYSTROKE OCCURRED
460  D(T)=CT
470  A$=K$:PRINT K$;: IF
     K$=CHR$(13) THEN RETURN
480  N$=N$+A$:T=T+1:GOTO 430
```

Ideas for Discussion and Writing

1. Compare the Mousetrap program as described in Crichton's short story with the program described (and reproduced) here. What features does Harry Waters's program include that are not included in the listing? Why are those features necessary to the plot of the story and useful in catching a computer thief?

2. If you have access to an Apple or IBM-compatible computer and if you are interested in computer programming, type in the Mousetrap program and evaluate it in operation. Test it by logging on yourself and then by having a friend or two log on as well. How well does the program catch imposters? What are its limitations? Can you suggest any ways to improve the program?

3. A computer program is nothing more than a set of instructions that allow the computer to perform some process. If you have experience with programming, discuss the similarities and differences between a good process essay and a good computer program.

"With My Cooking, the Army That Travels on Its Stomach Is Facing a Pretty Bumpy Road"
"How to Turn a Hilton into a Hometel"

Many products have a purpose only within the context of some application. They assist in some process or group of processes. Food processors, power tools of all kinds, and packaged foods or spices (like Hamburger Helper or taco sauce) are examples of such products. In the first of the two advertisements that follows ("With My Cooking . . ."), process analysis is obviously useful. The advertisement begins by setting up a comic situation: an Army cook whose hamburgers taste "like hockey pucks" needs help in salvaging his career. His salvation is a sloppy joes recipe for six thousand involving the use of McCormick/Schilling's Sloppy Joes Mix.

The second advertisement, "How to Turn a Hilton into a Hometel," uses process analysis as a way of highlighting the special attractions of staying in a Hometel instead of a hotel. In studying this advertisement, try to decide whether it describes the process of changing a hotel into a Hometel or the process by which a stay in a Hometel is made "homey."

With my cooking, the army that travels on its stomach is facing a pretty bumpy road.

As far as being a rookie cook goes, I was as green as the guys who ate what I cooked.

They said my hamburgers tasted like hockey pucks.

They said my chipped beef stuck to their ribs, permanently.

And what they said about my sloppy joes could have gotten them all arrested.

I finally had to face up to it. No one could stomach my cooking. And my brilliant military career would have gone down the drain then and there if it wasn't for McCormick/Schilling.

They're the experts on spice and flavor. And they make all kinds of sauces, seasonings and gravies that can really make things taste good. Even the stuff I cook.

So, I tried their sloppy joes mix. All I had to do was brown 1,000 pounds of ground beef, mix in the McCormick/Schilling seasoning; add tomato paste and 150 gallons of water.

And in no time, I had enough to feed an army.

It was easy. And more important, it was good.

Guys were standing in line for seconds. (Before, they never stuck around for firsts).

Matter of fact, they stopped griping about my cooking long enough for me to finally get my stripes.

And I owe it all to McCormick/Schilling.

I guess you could say that when it comes to cooking, they turned me into a seasoned veteran.

My sloppy joes recipe for 6,000:

Brown 1,000 lbs. of ground beef. Mix in 1,000 packages of McCormick/Schilling Sloppy Joes Mix and blend thoroughly. Stir in 1,000 6-ounce cans of tomato paste and 1,250 cups of water. Bring to a boil. Then reduce heat and simmer 10 minutes, stirring occasionally. Spoon over hamburger buns. Makes 6,000 ½-cup servings. (To get 6 servings, divide by 1,000).

McCormick/Schilling flavor makes all the difference in the world.

McCormick/Schilling

[1976]

Ideas for Discussion and Writing

1. What can you conclude about the speaker from his appearance in the picture and from the way he writes?
2. Consider the speaker's use of figurative language—particularly his metaphors and similes. What does the figurative language add to the characterization of the speaker? What does it add to your enjoyment of the writing? Does the speaker use clichés too frequently, or do the clichés themselves tell you something about the speaker?
3. Which portions of this advertisement use narration? What purposes (information, persuasion, entertainment) are served by the narration?
4. Which portions of this advertisement use process analysis? What purposes are served by the process analysis?
5. How effective is the advertisement in persuading you to consider buying McCormick/Schilling's Sloppy Joes Mix?

HOW TO TURN A HILTON INTO A HOMETEL.

Demolition of the Abe Lincoln Hotel in Springfield, Illinois. December 17, 1979. (UPI Photo)

(1) Start over. Get rid of traditional hotel architecture like the old Abe Lincoln Hotel, shown above. Demolish all those single rooms off those long hallways. Eliminate the usual coffee shops, bars and lounges.

(2) Then, do what we do. Replace traditional thinking with an entirely new concept in hotel design. A huge, wide-open, beautifully landscaped interior courtyard—surrounded by floor upon floor of two-room suites and nothing but.

(3) Design the suites with a private bedroom and tv, a separate living room with *its* own tv, a conference-dining table, a queen-size hide-a-bed, plus a galley with refrigerator, oven and wet bar.

(4) Serve every guest a free, full

American breakfast in the courtyard each morning. Eggs cooked to order, bacon, sausage, hash browns, toast. Hotcakes, fresh fruits, cereals, sweet rolls, juice, coffee, tea and milk. No limit, no check, no tipping.

(5) Host a two-hour, open-bar cocktail party in the courtyard for all adult guests (and their guests) every evening. Again, with no check, no tipping.

(6) Finally, price it—suite, breakfast, cocktails and all—about the same as a deluxe, single room only in a traditional hotel.

That's the Granada Royale[SM] concept. We originated it. And if others really wanted to copy it, they could.

But they'd have to start from the ground up.

GRANADA ROYALE HOMETEL

Welcome to the Suite Life.[SM]

For toll-free reservations: (800) 528-1445. In Arizona: (602) 957-9767 collect. **ARIZONA:** Phoenix (5), Scottsdale, Tempe, Tucson (2) **CALIFORNIA:** Buena Park, Covina **COLORADO:** Denver **MINNESOTA:** Bloomington, St. Paul **MISSOURI:** Kansas City **NEBRASKA:** Omaha **TEXAS:** Dallas, El Paso, Houston, Lubbock, San Antonio
© 1983 Hometels® of America Franchising, Inc. For information, write our Marketing Department at 450 Newport Center Drive, Newport Beach, CA 92660.

Questions on Thesis, Purpose, and Structure

1. What are the steps in transforming a Hilton into a Hometel?
2. Is the purpose of this advertisement to tell the reader how to bring about this transformation or to persuade travelers to consider staying in a Granada Royale Hometel? Explain your answer.
3. Consider the opening and closing paragraphs. How do these paragraphs both play off the photographs of the Abe Lincoln Hotel and give the advertisement a sense of roundness and completion?

Questions on Style and Diction

1. Evaluate the title. What is the effect of the alliterating "h" sounds? What are the connotations of the word *Hilton?* What connotations are evoked by the word *Hometel,* and later by the full title *Granada Royale Hometel?* What, by implication, is the quality of a Hometel if a Hilton must be condemned to make way for it?
2. Evaluate the pun in Hometel's signature line, "Welcome to the Suite Life."

Ideas for Discussion and Writing

1. Imagine that you are an executive in an advertising agency and that one of your junior copywriters has just presented this advertisement to you for the big Hometel account. Write an evaluation and critique of this advertising copy and conclude with a recommendation either to go ahead with the advertisement, to send it back for revision, or to abandon the whole concept.
2. Imagine some unique set of circumstances as a result of which you spend a weekend in a Granada Royale Hometel. Furthermore, imagine that for some reasons, no matter how peculiar, all of the pleasant, luxurious features of the Hometel go awry. Write a letter of complaint to the management describing your misfortunes and demanding a refund.
3. Imagine that you are the manager of a Granada Royale Hometel and that you have received a letter of the sort described just above. Write a cordial, kindly, and very specific reply to your disgruntled customer. (Feel free to make up the customer's specific mishaps and complaints.) In your reply you must try to preserve the reputation of your hotel while still smoothing the customer's ruffled feathers.

Chapter 9

EXEMPLIFICATION

Dedicated and successful students usually have one thing in common: the ability to adopt the cast of mind characteristic of their discipline. Consider, for example, the purported reactions of three graduate students stranded on a desert island as a tidal wave loomed on the horizon. The first, a divinity student, began to examine his conscience and beg forgiveness for his sins. The second, a law student, immediately started scribbling his last will and testament to be set adrift in a bottle. The third, a business student, sat silent for a moment; then he turned to the others and said, "Listen, guys. For only ten bucks apiece I'll give you lessons in breathing underwater."

Examples, like those in the preceding paragraph, invigorate writing. A writer's ideas often begin as broad generalizations: "successful students . . . have in common . . . the ability to adopt the cast of mind characteristic of their discipline." But such generalizations remain quite vague until they are given color and clarity by the use of examples. Examples serve a number of important functions. Like descriptive details, examples usually **entertain** the reader with vivid sensory images:

> Mardi Gras in New Orleans is a time of excitement, color, and extravagance: picture the gay paraders snaking through the French Quarter dressed as devils, 'gators, crawdads, and witches; picture the formal cotillion with its shy debutantes, its proud, tuxedoed papas, its bejeweled matrons, its champagne, and its oyster dip; picture the collegiate bacchanals with the spewing kegs, the chugging contests, and the rocking sound of Bruce Springsteen on the stereo.

Examples also **inform** the reader by clarifying and illustrating the meaning of a generalization:

265

The Metropolitan Museum of Art, Bequest of Benjamin Altman, 1913.
The *Intoxication of Wine* by Claude Michel Clodion. To what extent does Clodion's sculpture serve, as its title suggests, to exemplify intoxication? Can you imagine other, or better, ways of representing intoxication through sculpture?

The powers of the President are substantial. Among them are the powers to veto legislation; to act as commander in chief of the armed forces; and to appoint ambassadors, agency heads, and Supreme Court justices.

Finally, well-chosen examples may **persuade** the reader that a generalization is valid:

The United States has begun to lose its lead in science and technology. The Soviet Union with its new space station has taken the lead in space technology — a phenomenon underscored by the explosion in 1986 of the Challenger shuttle and several unmanned rockets. The Japanese with their Hondas, their Toyotas, and their

Subarus make many of the world's most advanced automobiles. The Japanese also dominate the new technology in computers, cameras, video equipment, and stereos. Perhaps only in military technology does the United States still retain a commanding lead, but even there the Russians are joined by the French, the Israelis, and the British in competing with the United States for international sales of guns, bombs, jets, tanks, and other engines of destruction.

Writers more frequently use exemplification to develop a paragraph or sequence of paragraphs than to organize an entire essay. Thus, exemplification is just one component of Roger Rosenblatt's fairly lengthy essay on slips of the tongue entitled "Oops, How's That Again?" (p. 284). In Bertrand Russell's much shorter essay "On Comets," however, exemplification governs the essay's entire structure (p. 279). In the paragraphs that follow, we will focus on using exemplification to develop a brief essay like Russell's. We do so, however, with the conviction that, by stuffing one or two essays full of examples, you will become better able to include occasional paragraphs of exemplification in *all* of your writing.

PREWRITING

In writing an essay based on exemplification, your first task is to **select an appropriate topic**. As we have already indicated, the topics most appropriate for exemplification involve generalizations that can be supported by examples. Not all general statements are appropriate. Because an example is by definition "one instance out of many possibilities," you would not choose to use exemplification to develop a topic that calls for only one instance. Consider the topic: "Abraham Lincoln wisely timed the issuance of the Emancipation Proclamation." In developing such an assertion, you have only the one instance to work with — the issuance of the Emancipation Proclamation on September 23, 1862 — and your task is to explain why the release of that proclamation just after the battle of Antietam was wise. Although you may use causal analysis to develop such an essay, you cannot use exemplification with only one instance.

If, on the other hand, you choose to write on the topic "Abraham Lincoln ruled wisely during the Civil War," you might use the Emancipation Proclamation, the Second Inaugural Address, and the promotion of Ulysses S. Grant to general in chief of the Union armies as examples of Lincoln's wisdom. But would three examples really suffice? On such a topic you might need to cite a dozen or more major instances of sound leadership to sustain your thesis, and a full development of those examples might lead you to write an essay of great length.

Perhaps your best bet would be to limit yourself to some reasonably narrow aspect of Lincoln's presidency: "Abraham Lincoln's policy toward slavery was wise." Because this is a restricted aspect of Lincoln's presidency, you should be able to handle it by citing four or five clear examples. Thus, **when making a generalization, be sure to limit**

your thesis through appropriate qualifications. Often you can achieve this by adding a single word or a brief phrase:

Too Broad: Students think textbooks are intended only as coasters for the drinks of their choice.

Limited: *Some* students think textbooks are intended only as coasters for the drinks of their choice.

Too Broad: Machines have minds of their own.

Limited: Machines *can* have minds of their own.

Too Broad: Those who make the best first impression don't make the best friends.

Limited: Those who make the best first impression *don't always* make the best friends.

Once you have chosen an appropriate generalization to write on, **list all the examples you can think of that might help you illustrate that generalization.** Suppose, for example, that you decide to write on the thesis, "Many famous people have turned a blemish or physical imperfection into a virtual trademark." Your preliminary list might include the following items:

Princess Diana's sizable nose (which is difficult to shade even by the wide-brimmed hats she wears).
Prince Charles's prominent ears. (Some say they are the consequence of old-fashioned punishment at the hands of his vexed tutors.)
Richard Nixon's jowls (something like the gray, flapping ears of an elephant).
Brooke Shields's bushy eyebrows (rather like two woolly worms on a tree trunk).
Alfred Hitchcock's girth (which he demonstrated so proudly at the beginning and end of his television mystery show *Alfred Hitchcock Presents*).
The sturdy squatness of Mary Lou Retton. (Some claim that her picture need not be reduced to fit on a Wheaties box.)

If you can think of a half-dozen useful examples in your first fifteen or twenty minutes of concentrated effort, then you have probably chosen a workable topic. But wait! Don't begin your essay yet (unless, of course, you are writing an in-class essay). Try to expand your list by talking with friends. If time permits, spend an afternoon in the library using such reference tools as the *Readers' Guide to Periodical Literature* and the subject catalogue to look up essays on well-known celebrities. Or page through a few popular magazines like *Time, People,* and *Seventeen.*

Through discussion and research, your list on the physical flaws of famous people might grow to include:

The long, craning neck of ballet star Suzanne Farrell.
Jimmy Stewart's stutter.
Mae West's prominent mole.
Bob Hope's ski-jump nose.
Sophia Loren's large mouth.
Jimmy Carter's smile (rather like that of the Cheshire cat).
Meryl Streep's eyes (which are so large that they seem to have originated in a cow).
Linda Evans's shoulders (which might do honor to a full-back).
Former Dodger third baseman Ron Cey's legs. (Even his admirers claimed that he looked a little like a penguin in pinstripes.)

PLANNING AND DRAFTING AN EXEMPLIFICATION ESSAY

Having selected and narrowed your topic and having made a list of potential examples, you should be ready to begin writing the first draft of your essay. **Try to begin and end your essay with particularly effective examples.** Suppose that you have decided to write on the thesis that "Under the right conditions, many people will be caught up in mass hysteria." If your best examples are the annual excess of the Super Bowl, the Salem witchcraft frenzy in 1692, and the widespread accusations of child abuse in Jordan, Minnesota, in 1983, then your opening paragraph might read:

> There is a deadly quirk in human nature such that villages, townships, and even entire cities or nations sometimes go suddenly and uncontrollably berserk. Let us call it mass hysteria. This quirk causes the poor folks of whatever city happens to win the Super Bowl to begin celebrating by pouring the contents of the handiest bottle over the head of the handiest fellow citizen and to end their celebration by overturning cars and pillaging liquor stores. Mass hysteria is also what caused the sober Puritans of Salem, Massachusetts, in 1692 to accept as irrefutable evidence the testimony of a clique of young girls and to hang as witches 14 women, 5 men, and 2 dogs.

In your middle paragraphs you would then develop further examples, perhaps including the mass extermination of Jews, Poles, and resistance fighters by the Nazis; the search for communists in the military (the so-called "Red scare") led by Senator Joseph McCarthy during the 1950s; the Cultural Revolution in China during the 1960s; and the mass suicide in Jonestown, Guyana, in 1978. Finally, your essay might conclude with your strongest (or at least most recent and therefore most frightening) example:

Despite the annual affront of Super Bowl Sunday, we twentieth-century Americans are inclined to reassure ourselves that "It can't happen here; it can't happen now." Yet as recently as 1983, 24 citizens of Jordan, Minnesota, found themselves deprived of the custody of their children, accused of child sexual abuse, jailed and arraigned for trial—all because County Attorney Kathleen Morris accepted as irrefutable evidence the testimony of 37 little boys and girls. After months of legal persecution, all charges against the adults were dropped when investigators discovered that the testimony of many of the children had been fabricated (if not coached and coerced by Ms. Morris) and that the objective evidence pointed to only one perpetrator of child sexual abuse in the entire town. It *can* happen here. It *does* happen now.

This strategy of beginning and ending with your strongest examples is analogous to the tactic used in an Olympic relay race. In track events it is traditional to have your second fastest runner begin the race. He or she is followed by the two weakest runners in no particular order. The team's fastest runner finishes the race. Just as the track coach hopes to build the team's confidence at the beginning of the race and to spur on the best athlete at the end, so it is with writers. By beginning with one of your best examples, you predispose your reader to accept the truth of your contention. The reader is apt to think, "That was really convincing; this essay is *good*." By concluding with your strongest example, you leave your reader persuaded that what you have said is true.

If your topic can be adequately developed with no more than four or five examples, those examples can be organized just like runners in a relay race. But **if you wish to cite a dozen or more examples to illustrate your thesis, you may need to combine exemplification with classification or causal analysis.** If, for example, you decide to write on the physical imperfections in some of the world's most famous people, you might classify those imperfections by location—imperfections of the eyes, the nose, the lips, the teeth, and so on. Alternatively, you might attempt causal analysis by speculating on the reasons why the fame of some people transcends an apparent flaw. (Some, like Jimmy Stewart, are so skilled as performers that we overlook—or even come to love—their flaws; some turn an imperfection into a strength, as gymnast Mary Lou Retton does with her compact frame; and some, like Mae West or Princess Diana, use their imperfections as beauty marks, almost like photographic signatures.)

TIPS ON REVISION

One problem you will certainly encounter is that of deciding how fully to present each example. In the essay on the physical flaws in famous people, must you describe each person in great detail or simply allude to that person by name? In the essay on Abraham Lincoln's policies toward slavery, can you simply name the various proclamations and pieces of legislation, or must you carefully describe Lincoln's role in each act? Unfortunately, there is no uniform answer to such questions, and in your first draft you should probably ignore whatever anxieties you might have and press on toward your conclusion. During the process of revision, however, you should confront such issues head-on. The best advice we have is to **consider how much your audience will know about each example.**

If you expect that most members of your audience will have seen pictures of Princess Diana, you can probably satisfy them with a few well-chosen words about her height and the size of her nose. On the other hand, many fewer of your readers will have seen a movie featuring Mae West, so that you may need to explain her popularity and describe her appearance in several sentences. If you are writing for a group of fellow students, few (if any) of them will have much specific knowledge about the presidency of Abraham Lincoln. Thus, you would probably need to devote at least a paragraph to the discussion of each of his major actions concerning the southern slaves.

Your second major area of concern during revision should be to **check to see that you have adequately supported your thesis**. One possibility is that the examples you have chosen may be insufficient. Suppose, for example, that you wish to argue that handguns pose many dangers and have no useful purpose. If all of your examples demonstrate the dangers posed by handguns in the home, in revision you should either narrow your thesis or seek out additional examples of the uselessness and danger of owning handguns for hunting, self-protection on the streets, and target practice.

A second possibility is that you may have gotten so involved in discussing one of your examples that you have drifted away from your thesis. The best safeguard against this danger is to **include a topic sentence in each paragraph**. During revision it is a good idea to underline these topic sentences and to consider carefully their relationship with your thesis. Your thesis and topic sentences should constitute a logical outline of your essay. In the essay on the dangers of handguns, that outline might look something like this:

Thesis: Handguns are too dangerous to be stored in the home.

Topic Sentence 1: Far from providing protection against intruders, they are more apt to be used by intruders against the hapless homeowner.

Topic Sentence 2: Accidents while cleaning handguns cause many injuries.

Topic Sentence 3: Ready access to handguns is responsible for many suicides and domestic homicides.

Topic Sentence 4: The most tragic accidents involving handguns are caused by children playing with "unloaded" weapons.

The essay itself (which combines causal analysis with exemplification) will be powerful and convincing if it combines appropriate statistics with specific examples of tragedies involving handguns in the home.

IDEAS FOR ESSAYS

Use exemplification in an essay developing one of the following generalizations.

1. Private vices sometimes contribute to the public welfare.
2. The best teachers are those with a sense of humor.
3. Sports stars at _____ (your school) receive too much (or too little) recognition.
4. College students need a stronger moral character.
5. This year's new television shows are worse than ever.
6. Children's television shows do have some redeeming features.
7. Clothes make the man or woman.
8. Our "leaders" today are really only followers with access to the best pollsters.
9. Fast-food places are all the same.
10. There are still some heroes (or saints) in American society.
11. Some books belong on every student's bookshelf.
12. Most of our pleasures are signs of selfishness.
13. In today's movies, sex has destroyed romance.
14. The strongest nations in the world are also the most ruthless.
15. Loneliness is misery, but togetherness is an illusion.

STUDENT ESSAY _____

Brian wrote "Force of Habit" as an out-of-class essay. The assignment called for an essay filled with examples on the topic "private vices can lead to public benefits."

"FORCE OF HABIT"

by Brian Griffith

Prewriting Invention

1. Chew fingernail (nail taste good stuff)
2. Smoking (tobacco farmers, cigarette manufacturing workers, taxes)
3. Drinking (grain farmers, brewery workers, barrel makers, timber cutters)
4. Bad driving habits (hospitals, new car makers, body shops)
5. Shopping binges
6. Overeating (restaurants, fast-food places, weight-loss clinics, clothing stores)
7. Unfaithfulness (lawyers, marriage counselors, hotels, nightclubs, herpes control force)

FIRST DRAFT

"Mommy said, don't do that!" "Does your finger taste good?" Most of us heard these and many other phrases, when we were growing up to correct our improper behavior, but inevitably, some of us develop bad habits just the same anyway. All these bad habits, though, are only "bad" for the individual who has them, and many people profit from the quest of habituals to either correct or satisfy their addictions.

A great number of institutions have developed to aid people with problems varying from nail-biting, to wife beating, to insomnia. There are a multitude of psychiatric

examiners, lovingly referred to as "shrinks," gainfully
employed and receiving healthy pay for helping people
with their problems. Many government mental health
organizations exist, not to mention literature and clubs
available to people for self-help groups, self-hypnosis,
biofeedback, or some other hocus-pocus of pills, diets or
formulas.

But the big money deals with people who take their
habits to an excess. The drinking of alcoholic beverages
employs a vast field of workers including the farmers that
produce the grain ~~yeast~~ or grapes and sugarcane for
sugar, the brewery workers. A great deal of transportation
and delivery, all the way down to the timber man who
cuts bolts of wood, later shaped into staves to make aging
and fermentation barrels. Smoking and dipping, too,
involve the tobacco farmer, marketer, packaging cigarette
and cigar factory workers. And as an added boost to the
economy, sizable taxes are levied on these commodities.
Even the illegal drug industry creates jobs, not only with the
people involved but also for police, federal agents and
other government employees.

There are also the ones whose habits are not what
they consume but what they do. We're all familiar with the
old, tobacco drooling geezer in a beat up truck or the
dizzy blonde in a new 300ZX who think they are the only
ones on the road and never even heard of a "turn signal."
Poor driving habits turn dents into dough for the man with
the wrecker and the man at the bodyshop. In some cases,
probably even the new car market.

~~Then there are a group of people who go on shopping
binges to relieve tension or cure depression.~~

Even the man who cannot resist cheating on his wife is
helping the hotel chains, and if he has a suspicious wife, a
private detective may receive employment. If the unfaithful

[handwritten margin note:] Grocery stores, the clothing industry, candy factories, fast-food joints, and weight clinics all benefit from the overeater.

is caught, marriage counseling may be sought, but more often than not, it's a divorce lawyer instead.

As one can easily see, there is an endless chain of people who directly or indirectly gain from another's bad habit, and while the habit is bad for the afflicted, it's a boon to the economy.

Commentary: Brian's first draft shows considerable potential, but that potential is largely unfulfilled. Although Brian recognizes the variety of ways in which bad habits stimulate economic activity, the examples in this first draft are often abstract or poorly phrased. Thus, Brian's major goal in his second draft was to increase the number of examples and make them more specific.

SECOND DRAFT

"FORCE OF HABIT"

by Brian Griffith

"Mommy said, don't do that!" "Does your finger taste good?" Most of us heard these and other phrases while we were growing up to correct our improper behavior, but inevitably, some of us develop bad habits anyway. All of these bad habits, though, are only "bad" for the individual who has them, and many people profit from the quest of habituals to either correct or satisfy their addictions.

The greatest trickle-down of money occurs with people whose habits consist of addictions ~~who take their habits to an excess.~~ From the barrel-bellied sports nut, who drinks a case of beer watching Monday Night Football, to the sloppy, decrepit drunk in an alley off Bourbon Street, the heavy drinker can easily spends hundreds of dollars a year on his habit. From the brewery to the liquor store, many people are employed; for instance, the workers and management personnel in the many ~~beer~~ breweries, distilleries and wineries, not to mention the ~~management and~~ salespersons, ~~and the~~ distributors, and

truck drivers who get the product to the consumer. To
produce the ~various~ beverages, the factories need grain or grapes,
sugar, yeast and many other ingredients, thereby creating
opportunity for farmers, vineyard keepers, and the
suppliers of the other components. ~There is a whole lot of~
~businesses involved in~ *Even* the production of aging and
fermentation barrels, *involves several different businesses.*

Visualize in your mind a nervous secretary, closing down two packs of ciga-
The use of tobacco products opens a whole avenue of *rettes a*
opportunities. There are many companies producing *day, or an*
old cowboy,
cigarettes, cigars, packaged tobacco and snuff products, *with a*
golf-ball
employing many ~*workers*~ and supporting the tobacco farmer. Even *sized wad*
of dip in
the government profits from the sizable taxes levied on *his lip.*
these commodities. *From the coke-snorting Hollywood agent,* ~The~ illegal drug industry is very *to the Harlem*
which
profitable for the hoods involved and indirectly creates *heroin*
addict, the
jobs for the police, federal agents and other government *habitual*
drug user
employees. *supports*

exists, ranging
⌐ A seemingly endless list of bad habits from shopping
| binges to overeating, from nailbiting to insomnia, and from
move | *governmental and private*
to | kleptomania to wife beating. A multitude of institutions
① | *been*
have developed to aid people with their problems,
engaging the services of
~employing~ many counselors and psychiatric examiners,
lovingly referred to as "shrinks." The field has blossomed to
include weight loss centers, health clubs, self-help groups
and fly-by-night organizations, the later offering literature
on self-hypnosis, biofeedback, or some other hocus-pocus of
⌐ pills, diets or formulas.

are
We're all familiar with the old, tobacco drooling
geezer in a beat-up truck, or the dizzy blonde in a new
300ZX, who think they are the only ones on the road and
never have even heard of a "turn-signal." Poor driving
habits turn dents into dough for the wrecker service and
the man at the body shop. When a car is wrecked beyond
repair, it even helps the new car market.

Even the man who cannot resist cheating on his wife is

helping the hotel chains, and if he has a suspicious wife, a

private detective may receive employment. If the unfaithful *spouse*

is caught, marriage counseling may be sought, but more

there is work for a

insert   often than not, ~~it's a~~ divorce lawyer instead.

① from   *after touching on only a few examples,*

previous   ~~As~~ one can easily see, there is an endless chain of

page   *opportunists*   *that*   *person's*

~~people~~ who directly or indirectly gain from another's bad

is

habit, and while the habit is bad for the afflicted, it's a

boon to the economy.

Commentary: Note how Brian makes his examples much more
specific and imagistic in this second draft. Instead of discussing only the
range of jobs supported by heavy drinkers, Brian creates vivid pictures of
the drinkers themselves: "From the barrel-bellied sports nut, who drinks
a case of beer watching Monday Night Football, to the sloppy, decrepit
drunk in an alley off Bourbon Street." He creates similar images of the
nervously smoking secretary, the tobacco-dipping cowboy, the coke-
snorting Hollywood agent, and the Harlem heroin addict. Each of these
examples helps to make the essay more entertaining while also helping
to persuade us of the pervasive impact of bad habits on the economy.
This combination of entertainment and persuasion is a large contributor
to the success of Brian's essay.

Note also the many minor changes in wording that Brian makes in
his penciled-in revisions. Closely evaluate a few of these changes. Do
they always help to make the writing more clear and precise, or do they
sometimes merely add unnecessary words?

FINAL DRAFT

"FORCE OF HABIT"

by Brian Griffith

"Mommy said, don't do that!" "Does your finger taste good?" Most

of us heard these and other phrases while we were growing up to

correct our improper behavior, but inevitably, some of us developed

bad habits anyway. All of these bad habits, though, are only "bad" for

the individual who has them, and many people profit from the quest of

habituals to either correct or satisfy their addictions.

The greatest trickle-down of money occurs with people whose habits become addictions. From the barrel-bellied sports nut who drinks a case of beer watching Monday Night Football to the sloppy, decrepit drunk in an alley off Bourbon Street, the heavy drinker can easily spend hundreds of dollars a year on his habit. From the brewery to the liquor store, many people are employed; for instance, the workers and management personnel in the many breweries, distilleries and wineries; not to mention the salespersons, distributors and truck drivers who get the product to the consumer. To produce the beverages, the factories need grain or grapes, sugar, yeast and many other ingredients, thereby creating opportunity for farmers, vineyard keepers, and the suppliers of the other components. Even the production of aging and fermentation barrels involves several different businesses.

Visualize in your mind a nervous secretary, choking down two packs of cigarettes a day, or an old cowboy, with a golf-ball-sized wad of dip in his lip. The habitual use of tobacco products also opens a whole avenue of opportunities. There are many companies producing cigarettes, cigars, packaged tobacco and snuff products, employing many workers and supporting the tobacco farmer. Even the government profits from the sizable taxes levied on these commodities. From the coke-snorting Hollywood agent, to the Harlem heroin addict, the habitual drug user supports the illegal drug industry, which is very profitable for the hoods involved and indirectly creates jobs for the police, federal agents and other government employees.

We are all familiar with the old, tobacco drooling geezer in a beat-up truck, or the dizzy blonde in a new 300ZX, who think they are the only ones on the road and never have even heard of a "turn-signal." Poor driving habits turn dents into dough for the wrecker service and the man at the body shop. When a car is wrecked beyond repair, it even helps the new car market.

Even the man who cannot resist cheating on his wife is helping the hotel chains, and if he has a suspicious wife, a private detective may receive employment. If the unfaithful spouse is caught, marriage counseling may be sought, but more often than not, there is work for a divorce lawyer instead.

A seemingly endless list of bad habits exists ranging from binge shopping to overeating, from nailbiting to insomnia, and from kleptomania to wife beating. A multitude of governmental and private institutions have been developed to aid people with their problems, engaging the services of many counselors and psychiatric examiners, lovingly referred to as "shrinks." The field has blossomed to include weight-loss centers, health clubs, self-help groups and fly-by-night organizations, the later offering literature on self-hypnosis, biofeedback, or some other hocus-pocus of pills, diets or formulas.

After touching on only a few examples, one can easily see that there is an endless chain of people who directly or indirectly gain from another's bad habit, and while the habit is bad for the afflicted, it's a boon to the economy.

On Comets
Bertrand Russell

Bertrand Russell (1872–1970) was one of the great original thinkers of the twentieth century. Born in Wales, Russell was educated at Trinity College, Cambridge, where he distinguished himself by his brilliance in mathematics and philosophy and where he became a fellow in 1895. His early work on the newly developing field of set theory was published in *The Principles of Mathematics* (1903) and was followed by the monumental treatise *Principia Mathematica* (1910–1913, in collaboration with Alfred North Whitehead). Among philosophers and mathematicians, this work is celebrated for demonstrating how the concepts of arithmetic and algebra can be defined through logical deduction; nonmathematicians, however, tend to be amused that it isn't until page 302 that Russell deduces that $1 + 1 = 2$. A genuine intellectual who published works in many fields, Russell spoke his mind on important social and political issues, including the need for less puritanical attitudes toward sex and the need for nuclear disarmament, but he also wrote comic and satiric essays like the following piece, "On Comets," from *In Praise of Idleness* (1935).

If I were a comet, I should consider the men of our present age a   1
degenerate breed.

In former times, the respect for comets was universal and profound.   2
One of them foreshadowed the death of Caesar; another was regarded as

indicating the approaching death of the Emperor Vespasian. He himself was a strong-minded man, and maintained that the comet must have some other significance, since it was hairy and he was bald; but there were few who shared this extreme of rationalism. The Venerable Bede said that "comets portend revolutions of kingdoms, pestilence, war, winds, or heat." John Knox regarded comets as evidences of divine anger, and other Scottish Protestants thought them "a warning to the King to extirpate the Papists."

3   America, and especially New England, came in for a due share of cometary attention. In 1652 a comet appeared just at the moment when the eminent Mr. Cotton fell ill, and disappeared at his death. Only ten years later, the wicked inhabitants of Boston were warned by a new comet to abstain from "voluptuousness and abuse of the good creatures of God by licentiousness in drinking and fashions in apparel." Increase Mather, the eminent divine, considered that comets and eclipses had portended the deaths of Presidents of Harvard and Colonial Governors, and instructed his flock to pray to the Lord that he would not "take away stars and send comets to succeed them."

4   All this superstition was gradually dispelled by Halley's discovery that one comet, at least, went round the sun in an orderly ellipse, just like a sensible planet, and by Newton's proof that comets obey the law of gravitation. For some time, Professors in the more old-fashioned universities were forbidden to mention these discoveries, but in the long run the truth could not be concealed.

5   In our day, it is difficult to imagine a world in which everybody, high and low, educated and uneducated, was preoccupied with comets, and filled with terror whenever one appeared. Most of us have never seen a comet. I have seen two, but they were far less impressive than I had expected them to be. The cause of the change in our attitude is not merely rationalism, but artificial lighting. In the streets of a modern city the night sky is invisible; in rural districts, we move in cars with bright headlights. We have blotted out the heavens, and only a few scientists remain aware of stars and planets, meteorites and comets. The world of our daily life is more man-made than at any previous epoch. In this there is loss as well as gain: Man, in the security of his dominion, is becoming trivial, arrogant, and a little mad. But I do not think a comet would now produce the wholesome moral effect which it produced in Boston in 1662; a stronger medicine would now be needed.

Questions on Content

1. What examples does Russell cite of the past "respect for comets"?
2. Were comets more apt to be seen as portents of the future or warnings not to repeat past mishaps? Support your answer.
3. According to Russell, what discovery "gradually dispelled" the superstition about comets?
4. Why are comets less impressive sights than they were in the past?

Questions on Thesis, Purpose, and Structure

1. Which paragraphs in Russell's essay make the most use of exemplification?
2. Which paragraphs in Russell's essay explore causes and effects?
3. What use does Russell make of chronology in organizing his essay?
4. In what sense does Russell's opening sentence serve as the thesis of his essay? How would you rephrase that sentence in order to make it a more explicit and precise thesis?
5. Which features of Russell's essay make it entertaining? Informative? Persuasive?

Questions on Style and Diction

1. Find the following words in the essay and determine their definitions in context: degenerate (paragraph 1); profound, rationalism, portend, pestilence, extirpate, Papists (paragraph 2); eminent, abstain, voluptuousness, licentiousness (paragraph 3); dispelled (paragraph 4); arrogant (paragraph 5).
2. Many writing instructors discourage the use of single-sentence paragraphs. Should Russell's one-sentence introductory paragraph be welcomed as an exception? Why or why not?
3. Russell's essay has a formal—possibly even stuffy—tone. What features of style and diction contribute to that tone? Is that tone appropriate in this essay?

Ideas for Essays

1. Consider some other natural or human phenomenon about which ideas have changed over time. Some examples might be old age, plumpness, cats, working mothers, masculinity, and femininity. In an essay filled with examples, try to explain the early attitudes, the modern attitudes, and the reasons for the change.
2. Write a narrative essay about your own experiences during the last appearance of Halley's comet in 1987.

Angels on a Pin
Alexander Calandra

Alexander Calandra (1911–   ) was educated at Brooklyn College, Columbia University, and New York University and for many years was a member of the physics faculty at Washington University in St. Louis, Missouri. The following essay was first published in *Saturday Review* in 1968. Note how the physics student uses examples to mock the narrow-minded thinking of his professor.

Some time ago, I received a call from a colleague who asked if I would   1
be the referee on the grading of an examination question. He was about

to give a student a zero for his answer to a physics question, while the student claimed he should receive a perfect score and would if the system were not set up against the student. The instructor and the student agreed to submit this to an impartial arbiter, and I was selected.

2   I went to my colleague's office and read the examination question: "Show how it is possible to determine the height of a tall building with the aid of a barometer."

3   The student had answered: "Take the barometer to the top of the building, attach a long rope to it, lower the barometer to the street, and then bring it up, measuring the length of the rope. The length of the rope is the height of the building."

4   I pointed out that the student really had a strong case for full credit, since he had answered the question completely and correctly. On the other hand, if full credit were given, it could well contribute to a high grade for the student in his physics course. A high grade is supposed to certify competence in physics, but the answer did not confirm this. I suggested that the student have another try at answering the question. I was not surprised that my colleague agreed, but I was surprised that the student did.

5   I gave the student six minutes to answer the question, with the warning that his answer should show some knowledge of physics. At the end of five minutes, he had not written anything. I asked if he wished to give up, but he said no. He had many answers to this problem; he was just thinking of the best one. I excused myself for interrupting him, and asked him to please go on. In the next minute, he dashed off his answer, which read:

6   "Take the barometer to the top of the building and lean over the edge of the roof. Drop the barometer, timing its fall with a stopwatch. Then, using the formula $S = \frac{1}{2}at^2$, calculate the height of the building."

7   At this point, I asked my colleague if *he* would give up. He conceded, and I gave the student almost full credit.

8   In leaving my colleague's office, I recalled that the student had said he had other answers to the problem, so I asked him what they were. "Oh, yes," said the student. "There are many ways of getting the height of a tall building with the aid of a barometer. For example, you could take the barometer out on a sunny day and measure the height of the barometer, the length of its shadow, and the length of the shadow of the building, and by the use of a simple proportion, determine the height of the building."

9   "Fine," I said. "And the others?"

10   "Yes," said the student. "There is a very basic measurement method that you will like. In this method, you take the barometer and begin to walk up the stairs. As you climb the stairs, you mark off the length of the barometer along the wall. You then count the number of marks, and this will give you the height of the building in barometer units. A very direct method.

11   "Of course, if you want a more sophisticated method, you can tie the barometer to the end of a string, swing it as a pendulum, and determine the value of 'g' at the street level and at the top of the

building. From the difference between the two values of 'g,' the height of the building can, in principle, be calculated."

Finally he concluded, there are many other ways of solving the   12
problem. "Probably the best," he said, "is to take the barometer to the basement and knock on the superintendent's door. When the superintendent answers, you speak to him as follows: 'Mr. Superintendent, here I have a fine barometer. If you will tell me the height of this building, I will give you this barometer.'"

At this point, I asked the student if he really did not know the   13
conventional answer to this question. He admitted that he did, but said that he was fed up with high school and college instructors trying to teach him how to think, to use the "scientific method," and to explore the deep inner logic of the subject in a pedantic way, as is often done in the new mathematics, rather than teaching him the structure of the subject. With this in mind, he decided to revive scholasticism as an academic lark to challenge the Sputnik-panicked classrooms of America.

Questions on Content

1. What was the nature of the dispute between the physics student and his instructor?
2. Why does Calandra offer the student another chance to answer the question? Why is he surprised when the student accepts?
3. Does the student know the answer that his teacher was seeking? That answer is never explicitly given, but can you figure it out?

Questions on Thesis, Purpose, and Structure

1. Consider each of the student's answers to the physics question. Which answer do you find most amusing? Which is the most practical? Which shows the most sophisticated understanding of physics?
2. What do the student's answers collectively show about his personality, his intelligence, and his approach to education?
3. The particular order in which the student presents his answers often causes us to change our impressions about him. Trace these changes and consider the rhetorical impact created by this particular progression of examples. How would the essay be changed if the examples were presented in different sequences?
4. What is the thesis of the essay? Where in the essay is it most clearly expressed?

Questions on Style and Diction

1. Find the following words in the essay and determine their definitions in context: arbiter (paragraph 1); competence (paragraph 4); pedantic, scholasticism, lark (paragraph 13).
2. The title of the essay is based on an allusion. Explain the allusion and its relevance to this essay.
3. What is the tone of the student's comments to the professors? What features in his speech create this tone?

Ideas for Essays

1. At some point nearly every student has been involved in an argument with a teacher. Write an essay recounting a number of the disputes you have observed or taken part in. Be sure to give your essay some unifying thesis.
2. Calandra's essay uses examples to satirize the attitudes toward scientific education during the days of "the Sputnik-panicked classrooms of America." Today, the central issues concerning education are different. Write an essay filled with examples in which you indicate how your teachers or your fellow students have responded to modern catchwords like *back to the basics, cultural illiteracy,* or *accountability.*

Oops! How's That Again?
Roger Rosenblatt

Roger Rosenblatt (1940–   ) was born in New York City and educated at New York University and Harvard University, where he earned his Ph.D. in 1968. Rosenblatt taught until 1973. Then he went to work briefly for the National Endowment for the Humanities before becoming literary editor of *The New Republic* and a columnist and editorial writer for the *Washington Post.* Currently a senior editor at *Time,* Rosenblatt also contributes essays to such magazines as *Harper's* and the *Saturday Review* and writes occasional essays for the *MacNeil/Lehrer Newshour* on PBS. Not only is "Oops! How's That Again?" (first published in *Time* in 1981) packed with examples, it also attempts to define the different categories of slips of the tongue and to speculate on the causes of our laughter.

> "That is not what I meant at all. That is not it, at all."
> —*T.S. ELIOT, "The Love Song of J. Alfred Prufrock"*

1   At a royal luncheon in Glasgow last month, Businessman Peter Balfour turned to the just-engaged Prince Charles and wished him long life and conjugal happiness with Lady Jane. The effect of the sentiment was compromised both by the fact that the Prince's betrothed is Lady Diana (Spencer) and that Lady Jane (Wellesley) is one of his former flames. "I feel a perfect fool," said Balfour, who was unnecessarily contrite. Slips of the tongue occur all the time. In Chicago recently, Governor James Thompson was introduced as "the mayor of Illinois," which was a step down from the time he was introduced as "the Governor of the United States." Not all such fluffs are so easy to take, however. During the primaries, Nancy Reagan telephoned her husband as her audience listened in, to say how delighted she was to be looking at all "the beautiful white people." And France's Prime Minister Raymond Barre, who has a reputation for putting his *pied* in his *bouche,* described last October's

bombing of a Paris synagogue as "this odious attack that was aimed at Jews and that struck at innocent Frenchmen"—a crack that not only implied Jews were neither innocent nor French but also suggested that the attack would have been less odious had it been more limited.

One hesitates to call Barre sinister, but the fact is that verbal errors   2 can have a devastating effect on those who hear them and on those who make them as well. Jimmy Carter never fully recovered from his reference to Polish lusts for the future in a mistranslated speech in 1977, nor was Chicago's Mayor Daley ever quite the same after assuring the public that "the policeman isn't there to create disorder, the policeman is there to preserve disorder." Dwight Eisenhower, John Kennedy, Spiro Agnew, Gerald Ford, all made terrible gaffes, with Ford perhaps making the most unusual ("Whenever I can I always watch the Detroit Tigers on radio"). Yet this is no modern phenomenon. The term *faux pas* goes back at least as far as the seventeenth century, having originally referred to a woman's lapse from virtue. Not that women lapse more than men in this regard. Even Marie Antoinette's fatal remark about cake and the public, if true, was due to poor translation.

In fact, mistranslation accounts for a great share of verbal errors. The   3 slogan "Come Alive with Pepsi" failed understandably in German when it was translated: "Come Alive out of the Grave with Pepsi." Elsewhere it was translated with more precision: "Pepsi Brings Your Ancestors Back from the Grave." In 1965, prior to a reception for Queen Elizabeth II outside Bonn, Germany's President Heinrich Lübke, attempting an English translation of *"Gleich geht et los"* (It will soon begin), told the Queen: "Equal goes it loose." The Queen took the news well, but no better than the President of India, who was greeted at an airport in 1962 by Lübke, who, intending to ask, "How are you?" instead said: "Who are you?" To which his guest answered responsibly: "I am the President of India."

The most prodigious collector of modern slips was Kermit Schafer,   4 whose "blooper" records of mistakes made on radio and television consisted largely of toilet jokes, but were nonetheless a great hit in the 1950s. Schafer was an avid self-promoter and something of a blooper himself, but he did have an ear for such things as the introduction by Radio Announcer Harry von Zell of President "Hoobert Heever," as well as the interesting message: "This portion of *Women on the Run* is brought to you by Phillips' Milk of Magnesia." Bloopers are the lowlife of verbal error, but spoonerisms are a different fettle of kitsch. In the early 1900s the Rev. William Archibald Spooner caused a stir at New College, Oxford, with his famous spoonerisms, most of which were either deliberate or apocryphal. But a real one—his giving out a hymn in chapel as "Kinquering Kongs Their Titles Take"—is said to have brought down the house of worship, and to have kicked off the genre. After that, spoonerisms got quite elaborate. Spooner once reportedly chided a student: "You have hissed all my mystery lectures. In fact, you have tasted the whole worm, and must leave by the first town drain."

Such missteps, while often howlingly funny to ignorami like us, are   5 deadly serious concerns to psychologists and linguists. Victoria Fromkin of the linguistics department at U.C.L.A. regards slips of the tongue as clues to how the brain stores and articulates language. She believes that thought is placed by the brain into a grammatical framework before it is expressed — this in spite of the fact that she works with college students. A grammatical framework was part of Walter Annenberg's trouble when, as the newly appointed U.S. Ambassador to Britain, he was asked by the Queen how he was settling in to his London residence. Annenberg admitted to "some discomfiture as a result of a need for elements of refurbishing." Either he was overwhelmed by the circumstance or he was losing his mind.

6   When you get to that sort of error, you are nearing a psychological abyss. It was Freud who first removed the element of accident from language with his explanation of "slips," but lately others have extended his theories. Psychiatrist Richard Yazmajian, for example, suggests that there are some incorrect words that exist in associative chains with the correct ones for which they are substituted, implying a kind of "dream pair" of elements in the speaker's psyche. The nun who poured tea for the Irish bishop and asked, "How many lords, my lump?" might therefore have been asking a profound theological question.

7   On another front, Psychoanalyst Ludwig Eidelberg made Freud's work seem childishly simple when he suggested that a slip of the tongue involves the entire network of id, ego and superego. He offers the case of the young man who entered a restaurant with his girlfriend and ordered a room instead of a table. You probably think that you understand that error. But just listen to Eidelberg: "All the wishes connected with the word 'room' represented a countercathexis mobilized as a defense. The word 'table' had to be omitted, because it would have been used for infantile gratification of a repressed oral, aggressive and scopophilic wish connected with identification with the preoedipal mother." Clearly, this is no laughing matter.

8   Why then do we hoot at these mistakes? For one thing, it may be that we simply find conventional discourse so predictable and boring that any deviation comes as a delightful relief. In his deeply unfunny *Essay on Laughter* the philosopher Henri Bergson theorized that the act of laughter is caused by any interruption of normal human fluidity or momentum (a pie in the face, a mask, a pun). Slips of the tongue, therefore, are like slips on banana peels; we crave their occurrence if only to break the monotonies. The monotonies run to substance. When that announcer introduced Hoobert Heever, he may also have been saying that the nation had had enough of Herbert Hoover.

9   Then too there is the element of pure meanness in such laughter, both the meanness of enjoyment in watching an embarrassed misspeaker's eyes roll upward as if in prayer — his hue turn magenta, his hands like homing larks fluttering to his mouth — and the mean joy of discovering his hidden base motives and critical intent. At the 1980 Democratic National Convention, Jimmy Carter took a lot of heat for referring to Hubert Humphrey as Hubert Horatio Hornblower because it was instantly recognized that Carter thought Humphrey a windbag.

David Hartman of *Good Morning America* left little doubt about his feelings for a sponsor when he announced: "We'll be right back after this word from General Fools." At a conference in Berlin in 1954, France's Foreign Minister Georges Bidault was hailed as "that fine little French tiger, Georges Bidet," thus belittling the tiger by the tail. When we laugh at such stuff, it is the harsh and bitter laugh, the laugh at the disclosure of inner condemning truth.

Yet there is also a more kindly laugh that occurs when a blunderer   10
does not reveal his worst inner thoughts, but his most charitable or optimistic. Gerald Ford's famous error in the 1976 presidential debate, in which he said that Poland was not under Soviet domination, for instance. In a way, that turned out to contain a grain of truth, thanks to Lech Walesa and the strikes; in any case it was a nice thing to wish. As was U.N. Ambassador Warren Austin's suggestion in 1948 that Jews and Arabs resolve their differences "in a true Christian spirit." Similarly, Nebraska's former Senator Kenneth Wherry might have been thinking dreamily when, in an hour-long speech on a country in Southeast Asia, he referred throughout to "Indigo-China." One has to be in the mood for such a speech.

Of course, the most interesting laugh is the one elicited by the truly   11
bizarre mistake, because such a mistake seems to disclose a whole new world of logic and possibility, a deranged double for the life that is. What Lewis Carroll displayed through the looking glass, verbal error also often displays by conjuring up ideas so supremely nutty that the laughter it evokes is sublime. The idea that Pepsi might actually bring one back from the grave encourages an entirely new view of experience. In such a view it is perfectly possible to lust after the Polish future, to watch the Tigers on the radio, to say "Equal goes it loose" with resounding clarity.

Still, beyond all this is another laugh entirely, that neither con-   12
demns, praises, ridicules nor conspires, but sees into the essential nature of a slip of the tongue and consequently sympathizes. After all, most human endeavor results in a slip of the something—the best-laid plans gone suddenly haywire by natural blunder: the chair, cake or painting that turns out not exactly as one imagined; the kiss or party that falls flat; the life that is not quite what one had in mind. Nothing is ever as dreamed.

So we laugh at each other, perfect fools all, flustered by the mistake   13
of our mortality.

Questions on Content

1. What different kinds of slips of the tongue does Rosenblatt identify?
2. What are the most common explanations of the causes of slips of the tongue? How seriously does Rosenblatt take those explanations?
3. What are some of the reasons we laugh at slips of the tongue?

Questions on Thesis, Purpose, and Structure

1. Rosenblatt gives structure and clarity to his essay by making plentiful and effective use of topic sentences. Find and underline the topic sentence in as many paragraphs as you can. (Note that some of the longer paragraphs may include two topic sentences.)

2. Which paragraphs in the essay are devoted to defining the varieties of verbal slips? Which paragraphs attempt to explain the causes of verbal slips? Which paragraphs attempt to explain why we laugh at slips of the tongue? How logical is the overall structure of the essay?

3. Evaluate the essay's introduction and conclusion. What does Rosenblatt do to capture the reader's attention and interest in the opening paragraph? How does Rosenblatt attempt to open up the thought-provoking implications of his topic in the final two paragraphs?

4. What makes Rosenblatt's essay entertaining? What information does the essay include? Does the essay attempt to persuade you of anything? If so, what?

Questions on Style and Diction

1. Find the following words in the essay and determine their definitions in context: conjugal, betrothed, contrite, odious (paragraph 1); gaffes, *faux pas* (paragraph 2); prodigious, blooper, spoonerisms, apocryphal, chided (paragraph 3); discomfiture, refurbishing (paragraph 5); disclosure (paragraph 9); elicited (paragraph 11).

2. Explain the pun that opens the second paragraph.

3. What does Rosenblatt mean when he calls spoonerisms a "different fettle of kitsch"? How does this example help to define a spoonerism?

4. Explain the humor in mistakenly referring to George Bidault as Georges Bidet and in Rosenblatt's comment that this belittles "the tiger by the tail."

5. What effect is achieved by the shift to a first-person-plural point of view in the essay's closing sentence?

Ideas for Essays

1. Can you think of any causes of slips of the tongue that Rosenblatt has failed to mention? If so, write an essay in which you explain those causes and illustrate them with examples.

2. Write an essay about the impact of verbal slips in contemporary politics.

3. "Putting your foot in your mouth" is a common enough human condition. Write an essay on how gracefully to handle those situations in which you yourself or one of your companions commits an embarrassing verbal *faux pas.*

Gimpel the Fool

Issac Bashevis Singer

Issac Bashevis Singer (1904–   ) was born, raised, and educated in Poland and had successfully launched a career as a serious writer before coming to the United States to live in 1935. Since the early 1940s Singer has been recognized as one of America's major writers for his many novels, short stories, and essays dealing with the events, traditions, and themes of Jewish life. Singer has been awarded the National Book Award on two occasions and in 1978 won the Nobel Prize in Literature. In "Gimpel the Fool" (1953; translated by Saul Bellow) Singer presents many examples of conduct that others see as foolish. In doing so, he leads us slowly to recognize that Gimpel's unquestioning credulity is a sign of his goodness, not his foolishness.

I

I am Gimpel the fool. I don't think myself a fool. On the contrary. But that's what folks call me. They gave me the name while I was still in school. I had seven names in all: imbecile, donkey, flax-head, dope, glump, ninny, and fool. The last name stuck. What did my foolishness consist of? I was easy to take in. They said "Gimpel, you know the rabbi's wife has been brought to childbed?" So I skipped school. Well, it turned out to be a lie. How was I supposed to know? She hadn't had a big belly. But I never looked at her belly. Was that really so foolish? The gang laughed and hee-hawed, stomped and danced and chanted a good-night prayer. And instead of the raisins they give when a woman's lying in, they stuffed my hand full of goat turds. I was no weakling. If I slapped someone he'd see all the way to Cracow. But I'm really not a slugger by nature. I think to myself: Let it pass. So they take advantage of me. 1

I was coming home from school and heard a dog barking. I'm not afraid of dogs, but of course I never want to start up with them. One of them may be mad, and if he bites there's not a Tartar in the world who can help you. So I made tracks. Then I looked around and saw the whole market-place wild with laughter. It was no dog at all but Wolf-Leib the Thief. How was I supposed to know it was he? It sounded like a howling bitch. 2

When the pranksters and leg-pullers found that I was easy to fool, every one of them tried his luck with me. "Gimpel, the Czar is coming to Frampol; Gimpel, the moon fell down in Turbeen; Gimpel, little Hodel Furpiece found a treasure behind the bathhouse." And I like a golem[1] believed everyone. In the first place, everything is possible, as it is written in the Wisdom of the Fathers, I've forgotten just how. Second, I had to believe when the whole town came down on me! If I ever dared to say, "Ah, you're kidding!" there was trouble. People got angry. "What do you mean! You want to call everyone a liar?" What was I to do? I believed them, and I hope at least that did them some good. 3

[1]Golem: a dunce or blockhead.

4   I was an orphan. My grandfather who brought me up was already bent toward the grave. So they turned me over to a baker, and what a time they gave me there! Every woman or girl who came to bake a batch of noodles had to fool me at least once. "Gimpel, there's a fair in heaven; Gimpel, the rabbi gave birth to a calf in the seventh month; Gimpel, a cow flew over the roof and laid brass eggs." A student from the yeshiva[2] came once to buy a roll, and he said. "You, Gimpel, while you stand here scraping with your baker's shovel the Messiah has come. The dead have arisen." "What do you mean?" I said. "I heard no one blowing the ram's horn!" He said, "Are you deaf?" And all began to cry, "We heard it, we heard!" Then in came Rietze the Candle-dipper and called out in her hoarse voice, "Gimpel, your father and mother have stood up from the grave. They're looking for you."

5   To tell the truth, I knew very well that nothing of the sort had happened, but all the same, as folks were talking, I threw on my wool vest and went out. Maybe something had happened. What did I stand to lose by looking? Well, what a cat music went up! And then I took a vow to believe nothing more. But that was no go either. They confused me so that I didn't know the big end from the small.

6   I went to the rabbi to get some advice. He said, "It is written, better to be a fool all your days than for one hour to be evil. You are not a fool. They are the fools. For he who causes his neighbor to feel shame loses Paradise himself." Nevertheless the rabbi's daughter took me in. As I left the rabbinical court she said, "Have you kissed the wall yet?" I said, "No; what for?" She answered, "It's the law; you've got to do it after every visit." Well, there didn't seem to be any harm in it. And she burst out laughing. It was a fine trick. She put one over on me all right.

7   I wanted to go off to another town, but then everyone got busy matchmaking, and they were after me so they nearly tore my coat tails off. They talked at me and talked until I got water on the ear. She was no chaste maiden, but they told me she was a virgin pure. She had a limp, and they said it was deliberate, from coyness. She had a bastard, and they told me the child was her little brother. I cried, "You're wasting your time. I'll never marry that whore." But they said indignantly, "What a way to talk! Aren't you ashamed of yourself? We can take you to the rabbi and have you fined for giving her a bad name." I saw then that I wouldn't escape them so easily and I thought: They're set on making me their butt. But when you're married the husband's the master, and if that's all right with her it's agreeable to me too. Besides, you can't pass through life unscathed, nor expect to.

8   I went to her clay house, which was built on the sand, and the whole gang, hollering and chorusing, came after me. They acted like bear-baiters. When we came to the well they stopped all the same. They were afraid to start anything with Elka. Her mouth would open as if it were on a hinge, and she had a fierce tongue. I entered the house. Lines were strung from wall to wall and clothes were drying. Barefoot she stood by the tub, doing the wash. She was dressed in a worn hand-me-down gown

---

[2]Yeshiva: a seminary for rabbis.

of plush. She had her hair up in braids and pinned across her head. It took my breath away, almost, the reek of it all.

Evidently she knew who I was. She took a look at me and said, 9 "Look who's here! He's come, the drip. Grab a seat."

I told her all; I denied nothing. "Tell me the truth," I said, "are you 10 really a virgin, and is that mischievous Yechiel actually your little brother? Don't be deceitful with me, for I'm an orphan.".

"I'm an orphan myself," she answered, "and whoever tries to twist 11 you up, may the end of his nose take a twist. But don't let them think they can take advantage of me. I want a dowry of fifty guilders, and let them take up a collection besides. Otherwise they can kiss my you-know-what." She was very plainspoken. I said, "It's the bride and not the groom who gives a dowry." Then she said, "Don't bargain with me. Either a flat 'yes' or a flat 'no' — Go back where you came from."

I thought: No bread will ever be baked from *this* dough. But ours is 12 not a poor town. They consented to everything and proceeded with the wedding. It so happened that there was a dysentery epidemic at the time. The ceremony was held at the cemetery gates, near the little corpse-washing hut. The fellows got drunk. While the marriage contract was being drawn up I heard the most pious high rabbi ask, "Is the bride a widow or a divorced woman?" And the sexton's wife answered for her, "Both a widow and divorced." It was a black moment for me. But what was I to do, run away from under the marriage canopy?

There was singing and dancing. An old granny danced opposite me, 13 hugging a braided white *chalah*.[3] The master of revels made a "God 'a mercy" in memory of the bride's parents. The schoolboys threw burrs, as on Tishe b'Av[4] fast day. There were a lot of gifts after the sermon: a noodle board, a kneading trough, a bucket, brooms, ladles, household articles galore. Then I took a look and saw two strapping young men carrying a crib. "What do we need this for?" I asked. So they said, "Don't rack your brains about it. It's all right, it'll come in handy." I realized I was going to be rooked. Take it another way though, what did I stand to lose? I reflected: "I'll see what comes of it. A whole town can't go altogether crazy."

II

At night I came where my wife lay, but she wouldn't let me in. "Say, look 14 here, is this what they married us for?" I said. And she said, "My monthly has come." "But yesterday they took you to the ritual bath, and that's afterward, isn't it supposed to be?" Today isn't yesterday," said she, "and yesterday's not today. You can beat it if you don't like it." In short, I waited.

Not four months later she was in childbed. The townsfolk hid their 15

[3]*Chalah:* a loaf of bread eaten on the Sabbath.
[4]Tishe b'Av: a holiday commemorating the Roman destruction of the Second Temple in A.D. 70.

laughter with their knuckles. But what could I do? She suffered intolerable pains and clawed at the walls. "Gimpel," she cried, "I'm going. Forgive me!" The house filled with women. They were boiling pans of water. The screams rose to the welkin.

16   The thing to do was to go to the House of Prayer to repeat Psalms, and that was what I did.

17   The townsfolk liked that, all right. I stood in a corner saying Psalms and prayers, and they shook their heads at me. "Pray, pray!" they told me. "Prayer never made any woman pregnant." One of the congregation put a straw to my mouth and said, "Hay for the cows." There was something to that too, by God!

18   She gave birth to a boy. Friday at the synagogue the sexton stood up before the Ark, pounded on the reading table, and announced, "The wealthy Reb Gimpel invites the congregation to a feast in honor of the birth of a son." The whole House of Prayer rang with laughter. My face was flaming. But there was nothing I could do. After all, I *was* the one responsible for the circumcision honors and rituals.

19   Half the town came running. You couldn't wedge another soul in. Women brought peppered chick-peas, and there was a keg of beer from the tavern. I ate and drank as much as anyone, and they all congratulated me. Then there was a circumcision, and I named the boy after my father, may he rest in peace. When all were gone and I was left with my wife alone, she thrust her head through the bed-curtain and called me to her.

20   "Gimpel," said she, "why are you silent? Has your ship gone and sunk?"

21   "What shall I say?" I answered. "A fine thing you've done to me! If my mother had known of it she'd have died a second time."

22   She said, "Are you crazy, or what?"

23   "How can you make such a fool," I said, "of one who should be the lord and master?"

24   "What's the matter with you?" she said. "What have you taken it into your head to imagine?"

25   I saw that I must speak bluntly and openly. "Do you think this is the way to use an orphan?" I said. "You have borne a bastard."

26   She answered, "Drive this foolishness out of your head. The child is yours."

27   "How can he be mine?" I argued. "He was born seventeen weeks after the wedding."

28   She told me then that he was premature. I said, "Isn't he a little too premature?" She said she had had a grandmother who carried just as short a time and she resembled this grandmother of hers as one drop of water does another. She swore to it with such oaths that you would have believed a peasant at the fair if he had used them. To tell the plain truth, I didn't believe her; but when I talked it over next day with the schoolmaster he told me that the very same thing had happened to Adam and Eve. Two they went up to bed, and four they descended.

29   "There isn't a woman in the world who is not the granddaughter of Eve," he said.

30   That was how it was; they argued me dumb. But then, who really knows how such things are?

I began to forget my sorrow. I loved the child madly, and he loved   31
me too. As soon as he saw me he'd wave his little hands and want me to
pick him up, and when he was colicky I was the only one who could
pacify him. I bought him a little bone teething ring and a little gilded
cap. He was forever catching the evil eye from someone, and then I had
to run to get one of those abracadabras for him that would get him out of
it. I worked like an ox. You know how expenses go up when there's an
infant in the house. I don't want to lie about it; I didn't dislike Elka
either, for that matter. She swore at me and cursed, and I couldn't get
enough of her. What strength she had! One of her looks could rob you of
the power of speech. And her orations! Pitch and sulphur, that's what
they were full of, and yet somehow also full of charm. I adored her every
word. She gave me bloody wounds though.

In the evening I brought her a white loaf as well as a dark one, and   32
also poppyseed rolls I baked myself. I thieved because of her and
swiped everything I could lay hands on: macaroons, raisins, almonds,
cakes. I hope I may be forgiven for stealing from the Saturday pots the
women left to warm in the baker's oven. I would take out scraps of meat,
a chunk of pudding, a chicken leg or head, a piece of tripe, whatever I
could nip quickly. She ate and became fat and handsome.

I had to sleep away from home all during the week, at the bakery.   33
On Friday nights when I got home she always made an excuse of some
sort. Either she had heartburn, or a stitch in the side, or hiccups, or
headaches. You know what women's excuses are. I had a bitter time of it.
It was rough. To add to it, this little brother of hers, the bastard, was
growing bigger. He'd put lumps on me, and when I wanted to hit back
she'd open her mouth and curse so powerfully I saw a green haze
floating before my eyes. Ten times a day she threatened to divorce me.
Another man in my place would have taken French leave and disappeared. But I'm the type that bears it and says nothing. What's one to do?
Shoulders are from God, and burdens too.

One night there was a calamity in the bakery; the oven burst, and we   34
almost had a fire. There was nothing to do but go home, so I went home.
Let me, I thought, also taste the joy of sleeping in bed in mid-week. I
didn't want to wake the sleeping mite and tiptoed into the house.
Coming in, it seemed to me that I heard not the snoring of one but, as it
were, a double snore, one a thin enough snore and the other like the
snoring of a slaughtered ox. Oh, I didn't like that! I didn't like it at all. I
went up to the bed, and things suddenly turned black. Next to Elka lay a
man's form. Another in my place would have made an uproar, and
enough noise to rouse the whole town, but the thought occurred to me
that I might wake the child. A little thing like that—why frighten a little
swallow, I thought. All right then, I went back to the bakery and
stretched out on a sack of flour and till morning I never shut an eye. I
shivered as if I had had malaria. "Enough of being a donkey," I said to
myself. "Gimpel isn't going to be a sucker all his life. There's a limit
even to the foolishness of a fool like Gimpel."

In the morning I went to the rabbi to get advice, and it made a great   35
commotion in the town. They sent the beadle for Elka right away. She
came, carrying the child. And what do you think she did? She denied it,

denied everything, bone and stone! "He's out of his head," she said. "I know nothing of dreams or divinations." They yelled at her, warned her, hammered on the table, but she stuck to her guns; it was a false accusation, she said.

36   The butchers and the horse-traders took her part. One of the lads from the slaughterhouse came by and said to me, "We've got our eye on you, you're a marked man." Meanwhile the child started to bear down and soiled itself. In the rabbinical court there was an Ark of the Covenant, and they couldn't allow that, so they sent Elka away.

37   I said to the rabbi, "What shall I do?"

38   "You must divorce her at once," said he.

39   "And what if she refuses?" I asked.

40   He said, "You must serve the divorce. That's all you have to do."

41   I said, "Well, all right, Rabbi. Let me think about it."

42   "There's nothing to think about," said he. "You mustn't remain under the same roof with her."

43   "And if I want to see the child?" I asked.

44   "Let her go, the harlot," said he, "and her brood of bastards with her."

45   The verdict he gave was that I mustn't even cross her threshold — never again, as long as I should live.

46   During the day it didn't bother me so much. I thought: It was bound to happen, the abscess had to burst. But at night when I stretched out upon the sacks I felt it all very bitterly. A longing took me, for her and for the child. I wanted to be angry, but that's my misfortune exactly, I don't have it in me to be really angry. In the first place — this was how my thoughts went — there's bound to be a slip sometimes. You can't live without errors. Probably that lad who was with her led her on and gave her presents and what not, and women are often long on hair and short on sense, and so he got around her. And then since she denies it so, maybe I was only seeing things? Hallucinations do happen. You see a figure or a mannikin or something, but when you come up closer it's nothing, there's not a thing there. And if that's so, I'm doing her an injustice. And when I got so far in my thoughts I started to weep. I sobbed so that I wet the flour where I lay. In the morning I went to the rabbi and told him that I had made a mistake. The rabbi wrote on with his quill, and he said that if that were so he would have to reconsider the whole case. Until he had finished I wasn't to go near my wife, but I might send her bread and money by messenger.

III

47   Nine months passed before all the rabbis could come to an agreement. Letters went back and forth. I hadn't realized that there could be so much erudition about a matter like this.

48   Meanwhile Elka gave birth to still another child, a girl this time. On the Sabbath I went to the synagogue and invoked a blessing on her. They called me up to the Torah, and I named the child for my mother-in-law

—may she rest in peace. The louts and loudmouths of the town who came into the bakery gave me a going over. All Frampol refreshed its spirits because of my trouble and grief. However, I resolved that I would always believe what I was told. What's the good of *not* believing? Today it's your wife you don't believe; tomorrow it's God Himself you won't take stock in.

By an apprentice who was her neighbor I sent daily a corn or a   49
wheat loaf, or a piece of pastry, rolls or bagels, or, when I got the chance, a slab of pudding, a slice of honeycake, or wedding strudel—whatever came my way. The apprentice was a goodhearted lad, and more than once he added something on his own. He had formerly annoyed me a lot, plucking my nose and digging me in the ribs, but when he started to be a visitor to my house he became kind and friendly. "Hey, you, Gimpel," he said to me, "you have a very decent little wife and two fine kids. You don't deserve them."

"But the things people say about her," I said.   50
"Well, they have long tongues," he said, "and nothing to do with   51
them but babble. Ignore it as you ignore the cold of last winter.

One day the rabbi sent for me and said, "Are you certain, Gimpel,   52
that you were wrong about your wife?"

I said, "I'm certain."   53
"Why, but look here! You yourself saw it."   54
"It must have been a shadow," I said.   55
"The shadow of what?"   56
"Just one of the beams, I think."   57
"You can go home then. You owe thanks to the Yanover rabbi. He   58
found an obscure reference in Maimonides that favored you."

I seized the rabbi's hand and kissed it.   59
I wanted to run home immediately. It's no small thing to be sepa-   60
rated for so long a time from wife and child. Then I reflected: I'd better go back to work now, and go home in the evening. I said nothing to anyone, although as far as my heart was concerned it was like one of the Holy Days. The women teased and twitted me as they did every day, but my thought was: Go on, with your loose talk. The truth is out, like the oil upon the water. Maimonides says it's right, and therefore it is right!

At night, when I had covered the dough to let it rise, I took my share   61
of bread and a little sack of flour and started homeward. The moon was full and the stars were glistening, something to terrify the soul. I hurried onward, and before me darted a long shadow. It was winter, and a fresh snow had fallen. I had a mind to sing, but it was growing late and I didn't want to wake the householders. Then I felt like whistling, but I remembered that you don't whistle at night because it brings the demons out. So I was silent and walked as fast as I could.

Dogs in the Christian yards barked at me when I passed, but I   62
thought: Bark your teeth out! What are you but mere dogs? Whereas I am a man, the husband of a fine wife, the father of promising children.

As I approached the house my heart started to pound as though it   63
were the heart of a criminal. I felt no fear, but my heart with thump! thump! Well, no drawing back. I quietly lifted the latch and went in. Elka

was asleep. I looked at the infant's cradle. The shutter was closed, but the moon forced its way through the cracks. I saw the newborn child's face and loved it as soon as I saw it — immediately — each tiny bone.

64   Then I came nearer to the bed. And what did I see but the apprentice lying there beside Elka. The moon went out all at once. It was utterly black, and I trembled. My teeth chattered. The bread fell from my hands, and my wife waked and said, "Who is that, ah?"

65   I muttered, "It's me."

66   "Gimpel?" she asked. "How come you're here? I thought it was forbidden."

67   "The rabbi said," I answered and shook as with a fever.

68   "Listen to me, Gimpel," she said, "go out to the shed and see if the goat's all right. It seems she's been sick." I have forgotten to say that we had a goat. When I heard she was unwell I went into the yard. The nannygoat was a good little creature. I had a nearly human feeling for her.

69   With hesitant steps I went up to the shed and opened the door. The goat stood there on her four feet. I felt her everywhere, drew her by the horns, examined her udders, and found nothing wrong. She had probably eaten too much bark. "Good night, little goat," I said. "Keep well." And the little beast answered with a "Maa" as though to thank me for the good will.

70   I went back. The apprentice had vanished.

71   "Where," I asked, "is the lad?"

72   "What lad?" my wife answered.

73   "What do you mean?" I said. "The apprentice. You were sleeping with him."

74   "The things I have dreamed this night and the night before," she said, "may they come true and lay you low, body and soul! An evil spirit has taken root in you and dazzles your sight." She screamed out, "You hateful creature! You moon calf! You spook! You uncouth man! Get out, or I'll scream all Frampol out of bed!"

75   Before I could move, her brother sprang out from behind the oven and struck me a blow on the back of the head. I thought he had broken my neck. I felt that something about me was deeply wrong, and I said, "Don't make a scandal. All that's needed now is that people should accuse me of raising spooks and *dybbuks*."[5] For that was what she had meant. "No one will touch bread of my baking."

76   In short, I somehow calmed her.

77   "Well," she said, "that's enough. Lie down, and be shattered by wheels."

78   Next morning I called the apprentice aside. "Listen here, brother!" I said. And so on and so forth. "What do you say?" He stared at me as though I had dropped from the roof or something.

79   "I swear," he said, "you'd better go to an herb doctor or some healer. I'm afraid you have a screw loose, but I'll hush it up for you." And that's how the thing stood.

---

[5] *Dybbuks:* according to legend condemned souls which seek to escape their punishment by entering the bodies of religious persons.

To make a long story short, I lived twenty years with my wife. She   80
bore me six children, four daughters and two sons. All kinds of things
happened, but I neither saw nor heard. I believed, and that's all. The
rabbi recently said to me, "Belief in itself is beneficial. It is written that a
good man lives by his faith."

Suddenly my wife took sick. It began with a trifle, a little growth   81
upon the breast. But she evidently was not destined to live long; she had
no years. I spent a fortune on her. I have forgotten to say that by this time
I had a bakery of my own and in Frampol was considered to be something of a rich man. Daily the healer came, and every witch doctor in the
neighborhood was brought. They decided to use leeches, and after that
to try cupping. They even called a doctor from Lublin, but it was too late.
Before she died she called me to her bed and said, "Forgive me,
Gimpel."

I said, "What is there to forgive? You have been a good and faithful   82
wife."

"Woe, Gimpel!" she said. "It was ugly how I deceived you all these   83
years. I want to go clean to my Maker, and so I have to tell you that the
children are not yours."

If I had been clouted on the head with a piece of wood it couldn't   84
have bewildered me more.

"Whose are they?" I asked.   85

"I don't know," she said. "There were a lot . . . but they're not   86
yours." And as she spoke she tossed her head to the side, her eyes
turned glassy, and it was all up with Elka. On her whitened lips there
remained a smile.

I imagined that, dead as she was, she was saying, "I deceived   87
Gimpel. That was the meaning of my brief life."

IV

One night, when the period of mourning was done, as I lay dreaming on   88
the flour sacks, there came the Spirit of Evil himself and said to me,
"Gimpel, why do you sleep?"

I said, "What should I be doing? Eating *kreplach*?"[6]   89

"The whole world deceives you," he said, "and you ought to de-   90
ceive the world in your turn."

"How can I deceive all the world?" I asked him.   91

He answered, "You might accumulate a bucket of urine every day   92
and at night pour it into the dough. Let the sages of Frampol eat filth."

"What about the judgment in the world to come?" I said.   93

"There is no world to come," he said. "They've sold you a bill of   94
goods and talked you into believing you carried a cat in your belly. What
nonsense!"

"Well then," I said, "and is there a God?"   95

He answered, "There is no God either."   96

---

[6]*Kreplach:* a pastry containing chopped meat.

97   "What," I said, "*is* there, then?"

98   "A thick mire."

99   He stood before my eyes with a goatish beard and horn, long-toothed, and with a tail. Hearing such words, I wanted to snatch him by the tail, but I tumbled from the flour sacks and nearly broke a rib. Then it happened that I had to answer the call of nature, and, passing, I saw the risen dough, which seemed to say to me, "Do it." In brief, I let myself be persuaded.

100   At dawn the apprentice came. We kneaded the bread, scattered caraway seeds on it, and set it to bake. Then the apprentice went away, and I was left sitting in the little trench by the oven on a pile of rags. Well, Gimpel, I thought, you've revenged yourself on them for all the shame they've put on you. Outside the frost glittered, but it was warm beside the oven. The flames heated my face. I bent my head and fell into a doze.

101   I saw in a dream at once, Elka in her shroud. She called to me, "What have you done, Gimpel?"

102   I said to her, "It's all your fault," and started to cry.

103   "You fool!' she said. "You fool! Because I was false is everything false too? I never deceived anyone but myself. I'm paying for it all, Gimpel. They spare you nothing here."

104   I looked at her face. It was black; I was startled and waked, and remained sitting dumb. I sensed that everything hung in the balance. A false step now and I'd lose Eternal Life. But God gave me His help. I seized the long shovel and took out the loaves, carried them into the yard, and started to dig a hole in the frozen earth.

105   My apprentice came back as I was doing it. "What are you doing boss?" he said, and grew pale as a corpse.

106   "I know what I'm doing," I said, and I buried it all before his very eyes.

107   Then I went home, and took my hoard from its hiding place, and divided it among the children. "I saw your mother tonight," I said. "She's turning black, poor thing.

108   They were so astounded they couldn't speak a word.

109   "Be well," I said, "and forget that such a one as Gimpel ever existed." I put on my short coat, a pair of boots, took the bag that held my prayer shawl in one hand, my stock in the other, and kissed the *mezzuzah*.[7] When people saw me in the street they were greatly surprised.

110   "Where are you going?" they said.

111   I answered, "Into the world." And so I departed from Frampol.

112   I wandered over the land, and good people did not neglect me. After many years I became old and white; I heard a great deal, many lies and falsehoods, but the longer I lived the more I understood that there were really no lies. Whatever doesn't really happen is dreamed at night.

---

[7]*Mezzuzah:* a piece of parchment inscribed on one side with the texts of Deut. vi. 4–9 and xi. 13–21 and on the other with the name of God, enclosed in a case and attached to a doorpost to ward off evil.

It happens to one if it doesn't happen to another, tomorrow if not today, or a century hence if not next year. What difference can it make? Often I heard tales of which I said, "Now this is a thing that cannot happen." But before a year had elapsed I heard that it actually had come to pass somewhere.

Going from place to place, eating at strange tables, it often happens   113
that I spin yarns—improbable things that could never have happened —about devils, magicians, windmills, and the like. The children run after me, calling, "Grandfather, tell us a story." Sometimes they ask for particular stories, and I try to please them. A fat young boy once said to me, "Grandfather, it's the same story you told us before." The little rogue, he was right.

So it is with dreams too. It is many years since I left Frampol, but as   114
soon as I shut my eyes I am there again. And whom do you think I see? Elka. She is standing by the washtub, as at our first encounter, but her face is shining and her eyes are as radiant as the eyes of a saint, and she speaks outlandish words to me, strange things. When I wake I have forgotten it all. But while the dream lasts I am comforted. She answers all my queries, and what comes out is that all is right. I weep and implore, "Let me be with you." And she consoles me and tells me to be patient. The time is nearer than it is far. Sometimes she strokes and kisses me and weeps upon my face. When I awaken I feel her lips and taste the salt of her tears.

No doubt the world is entirely an imaginary world, but it is only   115
once removed from the true world. At the door of the hovel where I lie, there stands the plank on which the dead are taken away. The gravedigger Jew has his spade ready. The grave waits and the worms are hungry; the shrouds are prepared—I carry them in my beggar's sack. Another *shnorrer*[8] is waiting to inherit my bed of straw. When the time comes I will go joyfully. Whatever may be there, it will be real, without complication, without ridicule, without deception. God be praised: there even Gimpel cannot be deceived.

Questions on Content

1. How does the Rabbi console Gimpel when he expresses concern about being known as a fool? What is the immediate result of this consultation?
2. What made Gimpel's marriage ceremony a black moment for him?
3. What was married life like for Gimpel?
4. Why doesn't Gimpel raise a ruckus when he first finds another man sleeping with his wife? How is that a turning point for Gimpel?
5. After the death of his wife, how and why does Gimpel start to revenge himself upon the people of Frampol? Why doesn't he carry through with his plan?

Questions on Thesis, Purpose, and Structure

1. Why do the people of Frampol call Gimpel a fool? Examine a few specific examples of his "foolishness" and explain Gimpel's reasons for letting people take him in and make fun of him.

[8]*Shnorrer:* a shameless beggar.

2. Gimpel is "fooled" into accepting another man's son as his own. How does his life become more fulfilling as a result of this joke on him?
3. At one point Gimpel says, "What's one to do? Shoulders are from God, and burdens too." To what extent does that statement serve as a thesis for the story? Is it the statement of a philosopher or a fool? Explain.
4. At another point Gimpel says, "Today it's your wife you don't believe; tomorrow it's God Himself you won't take stock in." How much of Singer's thesis is conveyed in *that* statement?
5. What information about Orthodox Jewish life is conveyed in this story? What makes the story entertaining? Does it have any persuasive purpose?

Questions on Style and Diction

1. Singer makes Gimpel the teller of his own tale. Analyze the tone, sentence structure, and word choice in a few paragraphs of the story. How does Gimpel's way of speaking contribute to his characterization and to the theme of the story?
2. Singer is noted as a major Jewish writer. How do the sentence patterns, word choices, and allusions contribute to our sense of the Jewishness of this story?

Ideas for Essays

1. By drawing on "Gimpel the Fool" for supporting examples, write an extended definition of a "wise fool."
2. Again by drawing on "Gimpel the Fool" for supporting examples, analyze the reasons why some people try to make fools of others.
3. Every age has its saints. In an essay filled with examples, write a character sketch of someone you have known whom you would call in some sense a "modern saint."

Goodbye to Goodbye
Stephen Dixon

Stephen Dixon (1936–   ) was born and educated in New York City. He is currently teaching in the Writing Program at Johns Hopkins University. His short stories have appeared in *Harper's, Viva, Playboy, Paris Review, American Review, The Atlantic,* and several collections including *No Relief* (1976), *Quite Contrary* (1979), *Fourteen Stories* (1980), *Movies: Seventeen Stories* (1983), and *Time to Go* (1984). In "Goodbye to Goodbye" (1984) Dixon retells the same basic story several different times in order to exemplify the complex psychological processes by which the mind sometimes struggles to come to terms with separation and loss.

1   "Goodbye," and she goes. I stay there, holding the gift I was about to give her. Had told her I was giving her. This afternoon, on the phone. I said "I'd like to come over with something for you." She said "How

come?'' I said "Your birthday.'' She said "You know I don't like to be reminded of those, but come ahead if you want, around seven, okay?'' I came. She answered the door. From the door I could see a man sitting on a couch in the living room. She said "Come in.'' I came in, gave her my coat, had the gift in a shopping bag the woman's store had put it in. "I have a friend here, I hope you don't mind,'' she said. "Me? Mind? Don't be silly—but how good a friend?'' "My business,'' she said, "do you mind?'' "No, of course not, why should I? Because you're right, it is your business.'' We went into the living room. The man got up. "Don't get up,'' I said. "It's no bother,'' he said. "How do you do? Mike Sliven,'' and he stuck out his hand. "Jules Dorsey,'' and I stuck out mine. "Like a drink, Jules?'' she said, as we shook hands, and I said "Yes, what do you have?'' "Beer, wine, a little brandy, but I'd like to save that if you don't mind.'' "Why should I mind? Though something hard is what I think I'd like. Beer.'' "Light or dark?'' she said. "Whatever you have most of,'' I said. "I have six-packs of both.'' "Then . . . dark,'' I said. "I feel like a dark. Suddenly feel very dark. Only kidding, of course,'' I said to Mike and then turned to her so she'd also see I was only kidding. She went to the kitchen. Mike said "Now I remember your name. Arlene's spoken of you.'' "I'm sure she had only the very best things to say of me too.'' "She did and she didn't,'' he said, "but you're kidding again, no doubt.'' "Oh, I'm kidding, all right, or maybe I'm not. Say, who the hell are you anyway and what the hell are you doing here? I thought Arlene was still only seeing me,'' and I grabbed him off the couch. He was much bigger than I, but didn't protest. "Where's your coat and hat?'' I said and he said "I didn't come with a hat and my coat's over there, in the closet.'' "Then we're going to get it and you're going to leave with it.'' I clutched his elbow and started walking him to the closet. Arlene came into the living room and said "Jules, what are you doing?—and where are you going, Mike?'' "I think out,'' he said. "Out,'' I said. "I came over to give you a gift and take you to dinner for your birthday and later to spend the night with you here or at my place or even at a great hotel if you wish, and goddamnit that's what I'm going to do.'' "What is it with you, Jules?— I've never heard you talk like that before.'' "Do you mind?'' I said. "No, I kind of like it. And Mike. Are you going to leave when someone tells you to, just like that?'' "I think I have to,'' he said, "since if there's one thing I don't like to do in life it's to get into or even put up a fight, especially when I see there's no chance of winning it.'' I opened the closet. He got his coat. I opened the front door and he left. I locked the door. Bolted it, just in case he already had the keys. Then I turned around. Arlene was standing in the living room holding my glass of beer. She came into the foyer with it. I didn't move, just let her come. "You still want this?'' she said. "No, the cognac,'' I said. "It's brandy but good imported brandy.'' "Then the brandy,'' I said. "How do you want it?'' "With ice.'' "Coming right up,'' and she went back into the kitchen. I followed her. She was reaching for the brandy on a cupboard shelf above her, had her back to me. I got up behind her—she didn't seem to know I was there—put my arms around her, pressed into her. She turned her head around, kissed me. We kissed. I started to undress her right there.

That's not the way it happened, of course. The way it happened was   2 like this. I did come over with a gift, it wasn't her birthday, a man named Mike was there when I thought she'd be alone, she said he was a good friend, "In fact, the man I'm sleeping with now." "Oh," I said. "Well, I still have this gift for you so you might as well take it." She said "Really, it wouldn't be fair." Mike came into the foyer, introduced himself. "Mike Ivory," he said. "Jules Dorsey," I said. "Maybe I shouldn't stay." "No, Jules, come in and have a drink. What'll you have?" "What do you got?" I said. "I don't know. What do we have?" he said to Arlene. She said "Beer—light and dark—wine—red and white—scotch, vodka, rye, bourbon, gin, brandy and I think there's a little of that cognac left, and all the mixers to go with them, besides other nonalcoholic stuff if you're suddenly into that." "Come on, Jules drinks his share," Mike said, "or at least will with us here." "I drink, all right," I said, "though not that much. But tonight I'd like a double of that cognac you said you have, if you've enough for a double." "Why not—right, Arlene? Want me to get it?" "It's okay, I'll get it," she said, "but what's a double?" "Just double whatever you normally pour," he said. "If there's so little in the bottle that you don't have enough to double what you normally pour, empty the whole thing in his glass." "I just usually pour, I don't know how much," she said. "So do it that way," he said, " but double it." "Fill half a regular juice glass," I said, "and then put some ice in it, if you don't mind?" "Ice in one of the best cognacs there is?" he said. "No way, sir. Sorry." "Then make it your worst cognac," I said, "but ice in it, please? I feel like a cognac and I feel like a double and I feel like I want that double cognac ice-cold." "Sorry—really," he said. "We only have one cognac and it's one of the rarest there is. Gin, vodka, bourbon, scotch, even the beer, light or dark, I'll put ice in for you, and the wine, either one, too. But not that cognac or even the brandy. They're both too good. I'm telling you the truth when I say I couldn't sleep right tonight if I knew I was instrumental or helpful in any way or even allowed it, just stood by and allowed ice in cognac or brandy when I knew that just by saying something I might be able to stop it." "Listen, you," I said and grabbed his neck with one hand. He swung at me. I ducked and hit him in the stomach, he fell forward and I clipped him on the back. He went down. I put my foot under his chest and nudged him with it and he turned himself over on his back. I looked at Arlene. Her hands covered her eyes but she seemed to be peeking through the finger cracks. I said to Mike "Probably Arlene won't like this but I'm going to give you to ten to get your coat and hat and—" "I didn't come with a coat and hat," he said. "Then ten just to get the hell out of here." "Jules, this is awful," Arlene said, not looking alarmed or frightened or really upset or anything like that. "I don't care. It's what I suddenly felt like doing even if I didn't feel that right about doing it so that's what I did. Now get, buddy," I said to Mike. "One, two, three . . ." He got up, held his stomach as he went to the front door. By the count of eight he was out of the apartment. She said "I hate it when anyone does that to people, but I think deep inside I loved it when you did it to him. Not because it was Mike. He's very nice. It's just that you were, well—I've never seen you like that before. I don't know what that makes me, but come here, you rat." I came to her. She mussed my hair, with her other hand slipped off one and then the other of her shoes. "Shall we do it here or in the bedroom?" "Here," I said, "or the opening part of it, but first let me lock the front door."

That's not the way it happened either. It happened like this. Ar- 3 lene's my wife. We've been married for three years. We lived together for two years before that. We have a nine-month-old son. During dinner Arlene said she wanted a divorce. Our son was asleep in his room. I'd just put the main dish and side courses on the table. I dropped my fork. I was in what could be called a state of shock. I don't like that term but for now it'll have to do. Figuratively and maybe in some way literally— technically, scientifically—I was in a state of shock. I didn't move for I don't know how long. A minute, two, three. Just stared at my fork on my plate. Till the moment she told me this I thought that though we had some problems in our marriage, they were manageable and correctable and not untypical and that we were serious at working them out. All in all I felt we were very compatible in most ways and that the marriage was a successful one and getting better all the time. Arlene had said it several times — many times — too. About once a month she used to tell me that she loved me and loved being married to me, and about once a month, and not just after she told me this, I'd tell her the same thing. I meant it and felt she meant it. I had no reason to believe she didn't mean it. This is the truth. Sometimes out of the blue she'd say "I love you, Jules." Sometimes I'd answer "You do?" and she'd say "Truly love you." We could be in a taxi and she'd turn to me and say it. Or walking to a movie theater or in front of a theater during the intermission of a play and she'd break off whatever either of us was saying to say it. At that dinner, which I cooked—it was a good dinner, a chicken dish, rice cooked to perfection—something she taught me how to do—a baked zucchini dish, a great salad, a good bottle of wine, crabmeat cocktail to begin with, two drinks with cheese on crackers before we sat down, we had made love the previous night and we both said later on that it was one of the best acts of lovemaking we'd ever had, our son was wonderful and we loved being parents though admitted it was tough and tiring at times, both of us were making a pretty good income for the first time in our relationship so as a family we were financially sound, nothing was wrong or just about nothing, everything or just about everything was right, so that's why I say I was suddenly in a state of shock. "You want a divorce?" I finally said after she said "So what do you have to say about what I said before?" "Yes," she said, "a divorce." "Whatever for?" "Because I don't love you anymore," she said. "But just last week or the week before that you said you loved me more than you ever have, or as much as you ever have, you said." "I was lying," she said. "You wouldn't lie about some-thing like that." "I'm telling you, I was lying," she said. "Why don't you love me anymore?" "Because I love someone else." "You love someone else?" "That's what I just said, I love someone else." "Since when?" I said. "Since months." "And you stopped loving me the minute you started loving him?" "No, a couple of months earlier." "Why?" "I don't know. I asked myself the same thing lots of times and all I could come up with was that I felt rather than knew why. You fall in, you fall out. You fall out, you fall in. Though this time I'm sure I've fallen in forever, since the feeling has never been stronger." "I can't believe it," I said. "Believe it. I've been having the most intense affair possible with a man I met at work—someone you don't know—and he's married but will get a divorce to be with me, just as I'm going to get a divorce to be with him." "But the children, I mean, the child," I said. "We'll work it out. We were always good at working things out in the past that most other couples never could, and we'll work this out too. I'll take Kenneth for the time being and when he's completely weaned you can have him whenever you like for as long as you like so long as it doesn't disrupt his life too much." "But just leaving me, divorcing me, breaking up this family, will disrupt his life," I said. "I'm sorry, I didn't want to, I in fact tried not to, but the force of the feeling I have for this man and he for me—" "What's his name?" "What's the difference?" "Just tell me his name? Maybe I do know him." "Even if you did, which you don't, nothing you could do or say—" "His name, please, his name? I just want to know what and whom I'm up against." "What could you know by just his name? If it was Butch or Spike or Mike, would it make you feel more or less confident that I'm not very much in love with him and that I'm not going to divorce you to marry him?" "Is it Mike?" "It isn't but you know that wasn't my point. All right, it is Mike," when I continued to stare at her as if I'd caught her fibbing, "but so what? Mickey, Michael or Mike, it's just a given name." "Mike what?" I said. "Now that's enough, Jules. I don't want you starting trouble." "I won't start anything. I just want to know the man's full name. That way I can begin saying to myself you're leaving and divorcing me and breaking up our family for Mike So-and-So and not just a shadow. I'm not sure why, but it'll make it seem realer to me and so will be much easier to work out in my head." "Spiniker," she said. "Mike Spiniker." "With an *i, a* or *e* or even a *u* on the second half of his last name?" "Now you're going too far," she said. "Anyway, good—I have enough." I got up, got the phone book off the phone stand in the living room. "What are you doing?" she said. "Can't be too many Mike Spinikers in the book, with an *a, e, u* or second *i.*" I looked up his name. "One, a Michael, with two *i*'s, on Third Avenue." I dialed him. "Stop that" she said. "He lives in another city, commutes here." A woman answered. "Is Michael Spiniker in?" I said. "Who's speaking?" the woman said. "Lionel Messer. I'm his stocks and bonds man." "Mike has stocks and bonds? That's news to me." "He has a huge portfolio of them and I've something very urgent to tell him about them if he doesn't want to go broke by midnight tonight." "I'll get him, hold on." She put down the phone. "Stop wasting your time," Arlene said on the bedroom extension. "Hang up. It can't be Mike. I'm telling you, he lives fifty miles from here." "Hey, what's this about stocks and bonds?" Mike said. "Hello, Mr. Spiniker. Do you know Arlene Dorsey? Arlene Chernoff Dorsey—she goes professionally by Chernoff." "Sure I do. We work in the same office building. But anything wrong? Because I thought this was about some stocks and bonds I don't have." "You seem very concerned about Ms. Chernoff. Are you?" "Sure I'm concerned. By your tone, who wouldn't be? What's happened?" "You sound as if you're in love with Ms. Chernoff, Mr. Spiniker. Are you?" "Listen, who is this? And what kind of jerky call is this? You either dialed the wrong Spiniker or you're crazy and not making any sense, but I'll have to hang up." "This is her husband, wise guy, and you better stop seeing her or I'm going to break your neck with my bare hands. If that doesn't work, I'll put a bullet through your broken neck. I have the means. And I don't just mean a weapon or two or people to do it for me — I'll do it myself gladly. I can. I have. Now do you read me?" "I read you, brother. Okay, fine. You have the right number and you're not crazy and you're probably right on target in everything you said, so my deepest apologies for getting excited at you. But let's say there must be two Michael Spinikers in this city, because I have no stocks and bonds broker and after what you just told me, I don't ever plan to do anything with my money but keep it in the bank, okay?" "Got you," I said and hung up. Arlene came running back to the living room. "You'd do that for me? You'd really go that far?" "I wasn't just threatening for effect or because I knew you were on the line. The way I see our marriage is that until it's clearly impossible to stay together, we're stuck together for life. Of course I only feel this way because of the kid." "I bet. You know, awful as this must seem about me, I think my feelings have come around another hundred and eighty degrees. What a husband I now realize I have. And what a weakling and pig that guy was for taking it the way he did, even if you weren't all bluff, after all he swore just the other day about how he'd stand with me against you and his wife when it finally came down to this. I'm sorry, Jules. So sorry, I want to beat my brains in against this chair. If my saying I love you very much isn't enough, what else can I say or do to prove what I just said is true and that I never want to stop being married to you?" "You can take my clothes off and carry me to bed." "Will do if I can." She put her arms around my waist and tried to lift me. "Oof, what a load. Instead of carrying you, which I no can do, what would you say to my just taking your clothes off and we do whatever your want us to right here on the floor or couch?" "Fine by me," I said and she grabbed my shirt by the two collar ends and tore it off me.

That's ridiculous also and never happened. Why not say what really 4 did happen and be done with it? It was all very simple and fast. We were eating dinner when she said she was leaving me for a man named Mike. We had no child, we'd been married for eight years. I said I wouldn't try to stop her. I could see it'd be useless and I did only want her to be happy. If she couldn't be happy with me, I was glad she was with someone she could be happy with. She said she was thankful I was taking it so well and in such a decent, civilized way. I asked about him. She said he worked in a law office on the same floor as hers. They'd been carrying on for six months. He was divorced, had two children. That night Arlene and I slept in separate rooms for the first time in our marriage, or for the first time when one of us wasn't very angry at the other or wasn't so ill that he or she needed to sleep alone. We just thought it best to sleep separately till she moved out. They rented a new apartment together the following month. I helped her pack and bring her belongings to the van she rented and drove. I told her I wouldn't mind if Mike came and helped, since she had several vanfuls of stuff to move. She said she felt I shouldn't meet him till much later on; when they were married, perhaps; maybe a year into their marriage when I could come by with my new woman who she said she knew I'd have by then. "You'll be as much in love with someone else in a few months as I am now with Mike." I said "I hope you're right. It'll certainly be what I want." So she was gone. I thought I was taking it well but I wasn't. I couldn't take it, in fact. Every night I'd get drunk thinking about her. I read her old adoring notes and letters to me and looked at her photos and would slam the wall or table with my fists and shout and cry. I couldn't stand thinking of her being with another man, kissing him, whispering to him, making love with him, doing all those private things with him, confiding to him, telling him what happened to her at the store that day, asking him if he'd like to see such and such movie or play that week, meeting him for lunch, going away with him some weekend, visiting friends, et cetera, maybe even planning to have a child. It also distressed me that they were in the same profession. I knew that'd make them even closer, all those professional matters they could discuss and look up and share. A month after she left me I showed up in front of their office building at around the time I knew they'd be finished for the day. They walked out of the building fifteen minutes later, holding hands, chatting animatedly. I had a wrench with me. I pulled it out of my jacket, ran up to him and screamed "Meet Jules, her husband, you bastard" and hit him in the hand he threw up to protect his head from the wrench. He grabbed that hand, turned to run and I hit him in the back of the head with the wrench. He went down. I kept yelling "I'll never let her be with anyone else, you bastard, never. I love her too much. I'll love her forever," and swung the wrench over his face but didn't hit him again. The police came. I didn't try to get away. I don't know what Arlene was doing at the time. I was arrested. Mike was taken away in an ambulance. Later he pressed charges against me. I pleaded guilty and was sentenced to five years. That means I'll serve around three and a half years if I don't cause any trouble in prison. Arlene visits me every day she's allowed to and stays the maximum time. It's six hours by bus for her round trip but she says she doesn't mind. Twice in my first half year here we were allowed to walk around the prison garden for an hour. She broke off with Mike and he's already moved in with another woman. "So much for his professed eternal devotion," Arlene said, "not that I would want it now." She's said several times that she'll never again be with another man but me. She hated my hitting Mike with the wrench but sees now it was probably the only way I could ever get through to her how much I loved her and wanted to get her back. "In some oddball way," she said, "it made me fall for you all over again. Maybe also because what I did and the way I did it forced you to lose control and try to kill him and I'm trying to make up for that too. But it'll all be different from now on. I can't wait to be back home with you, my arms around you, in bed with you, I can't wait." At certain designated spots in the garden we're allowed to hug and kiss for a half-minute, which we always did past the time limit until one of the guards ordered us to stop.

That's not it. This is it. There wasn't a wrench. There is a Mike. My   5
wife fell in love with him and told me this at breakfast, not dinner. She
said she didn't want to tell me at night because she wanted to give me
plenty of time to adjust to it before I went to bed and also time for her to
get her things out of the apartment and move in with a friend. We have
no child. We tried for a while but couldn't. Then I had a corrective
operation and we could have a child, but she said the marriage wasn't as
good as it used to be and she wanted to be sure it was a very good
marriage before we had a child. That was three years ago. She's had
several affairs since then. She told me about them while she was having
them. I didn't like her having them but put up with it because I didn't
want her to leave me. I don't know why I mentioned anything about a
gift. Maybe because her birthday's in two weeks and I've been thinking
recently about what to get her. A bracelet, I thought. Or earrings. But
that's out. This morning she said she realizes this is the third or fourth
serious affair she's had in three years. She's had one or two others but
they were quick and not so serious. She doesn't want to continue having
affairs while she's married or at least still living with me. It isn't fair to
me, she said. She also said I shouldn't put up with it and shouldn't have
in the past. Not that if I had told her to stop she would have, she said. But
I should tell her to get the hell out of the house and should have two to
three years ago. Since I won't, she'll have to leave me. That means
divorce, she said. The marriage isn't working out. What's she talking
about? she said. The marriage is so bad that she doesn't think it'll ever
work out — it never will, that's all, never. And because she wants to have
children, maybe two, maybe three, but with someone she's very much in
love with, she'll have to end our marriage and eventually get married to
someone else. Maybe it'll be with Mike but she doubts it. He's married,
though about to separate from his wife, and has indicated he never wants
to marry again. He also has two children from a previous marriage and
has expressed no interest in having more. Anyway, she said, it's fairer if I
stay here and she goes, since she's the one breaking up the marriage. Of
course, if I want to leave, she said, then she'll be more than happy to
stay, since it's a great apartment and one she can afford and she'll never
be able to get anything like it at twice the rent. "If you don't mind," I
said, "I think I'd like to keep the apartment. Losing you and also having
to find a new place might be a little too much for me." "I don't mind,"
she said, "why should I mind? I already said the apartment's yours if you
want. So, do you mind if I start to pack up now to go?" "No, go right
ahead. I'd love for you to stay forever, naturally, but what could I do to
stop you from going? Nothing, I guess, right?" "Right." She went to the
bedroom. I brought the dishes into the kitchen, washed them, sat down
at the small table there and looked at the river. She came into the living
room an hour later with two suitcases and a duffel bag. "This ought to do
it for now," she said. "If it's okay with you. I'll arrange with a friend to
come by for the rest of my stuff some other time." "Sure," I said. "You
moving in with this Mike?" "No, I told you, he's married, still living with
his wife. I'll be staying with Elena for now. If you want to reach me for
anything, you can get me there or at work. You have her number?" "I can
look it up." "But you won't call me at either place for very personal

reasons, will you? Such as saying how much you miss me or things like that and you want me back? Because I've definitely made up my mind, Jules. The marriage is finished." "I understand that. I mean, I don't understand why it's so definitely finished, but I do understand that you definitely feel it is. But I can't make just one more pitch? There's nothing I can do or say or promise to help you change your mind?" "Nothing." "Then goodbye," I said. "I'll miss you terribly. I love you tremendously. I'll be as sad as any man can be over a thing like this for I don't know how long. But that's my problem, not yours, I guess, and eventually I'll work it out." "I'm glad you're taking it like this. Not that you'll be sad—I don't want you to be like that—but at least that you see the situation for what it is and that in the long run you'll be able to handle it. Because it'll make it much easier—it already is—for both of us. You'll see. You'll get over me before you know it." "Not on your life," I said. "Yes you will." "I'm telling you. Never." "No, I know you will. Good-bye." She opened the door, put the suitcases right outside it, said "I'll be back for these in a minute," and carried the duffel bag downstairs. "I'll help you with the suitcases," I yelled down the stairs. "No need to," she said. "It'd actually be better if you closed the door so we won't have to say goodbye again." I shut the door.

Questions on Content

1. How many times does the narrator, Jules Dorsey, retell the story of discovering Arlene's relationship with Mike?
2. What are the facts about Jules's relationship with Arlene and his reaction to discovering her affair with Mike?

Questions on Thesis, Purpose, and Structure

1. How many paragraphs does Dixon use in telling his story? What guides him in the decision to begin a new paragraph?
2. Compare the events in the different versions of the story. What remains basically the same in each version? What are the principal differences between the versions? Is there any systematic change in the narrator's portrayal of himself, his actions, and his relationship with Arlene? If so, describe what guides the changes.
3. Clearly, Dixon's story explores the discrepancy between events as we would have liked them to happen and the sad reality. Try to formulate in a sentence or two Dixon's apparent opinion about this discrepancy. In other words, try to formulate an appropriate thesis for the story.
4. To what extent does this story make use of exemplification?
5. Do you find the story entertaining? Why or why not? Is Dixon trying to persuade you of anything? If so, what?

Questions on Style and Diction

1. Dixon—or rather his narrator—obviously deviates from many of the conventions of standard grammar, punctuation, and paragraphing. Make a list of the narrator's "errors" and then try to decide if there are defensible reasons for his rejection of standard English.
2. Many of the narrator's sentences are quite short—sometimes even fragmen-

tary. What is the effect of these short, choppy sentences? How do they help to convey the narrator's personality and state of mind?

Ideas for Essays

1. At some point in life probably all of us have handled a crisis or conflict badly—and longed in retrospect to be able to relive those moments and respond differently. Write about such a crisis or conflict in your own life, exploring the various outcomes you can imagine.
2. Jules Dorsey claims that the final version of his story is the true one. But he had also made a similar claim for each earlier version. In an analytical essay explore the questions about truth, reality, and imagination raised in Dixon's story. Can you prove that the final version is the true one? Conversely, can you prove that each version is equally subjective and equally true (or untrue)?

"Prehistoric Sea Creature?"
"United States Patent 4,378,627
Is in Good Company"

Because an example is one instance out of many possibilities, the use of examples can help a company suggest the quality, variety, and attraction of its products or activities. An example tells us something specific, but it also suggests that other, equivalent examples could also be cited. Thus, when the magazine *Science 82* displays a tantalizing picture of something that could be a prehistoric sea creature before explaining that it is actually an organism living in the follicle of the human eyelash, we are encouraged to think that if we subscribe to the magazine, we will learn about many such mysteries of science. In this case a single example suggests a range of similar possibilities.

The advertisement by IBM relies instead on overwhelming the reader with numerous examples. The basic advertisement is a two-page display of the titles of patents issued to IBM in less than five months (11/9/82–4/5/83). The text of the advertisement goes on to emphasize the eleven thousand patents awarded to IBM over the past twenty-five years as a means of convincing the reader that IBM has been and continues to be on the cutting edge of modern technology.

PREHISTORIC SEA CREATURE?

No, it's very likely alive and well and living in your eyelashes!

It goes by the fancy name of demodex folliculorum. It lives in the follicle of the human eyelash—and nobody knows where it comes from . . . or even why it's there!

Fact is, there are scientific mysteries that surround and confound us every day. And every month, there is one magazine that unveils them in a way that makes the whole world of science come alive. Science 82.

Today, that means seeing through the eyes of a satellite the universe that lies beyond our solar system as much as probing through a microscope the myriad worlds that live within us. It's the discovery of a cancer created to fight cancer and the

revelations of the 4th dimension . . . constructed by a computer.

Science 82 You can read it for the drama of breakthroughs in genetics, in solar power, in physics and medicine . . . you can read it for the beauty of its photography and illustration. Best of all, you and your family can enjoy it all—because it's all written to be understood.

Science 82. Find out why more than 2 million readers every month let Science 82 open up their lives to the wonder of it all. Join them today. Cut out the coupon on this page, fill it out and send it in to the listed address. We'll rush your first copy to you upon receipt of your coupon.

Reprinted by permission from *Science '82* by the American Association for the Advancement of Science.

Questions on Thesis, Purpose, and Structure

1. What sentences in this advertisement come closest to expressing its thesis?
2. What examples are used to support the thesis?
3. How do the examples chosen by the author help to show the range and diversity of the issues discussed in *Science 82*? What contrasts are used and how effective are those contrasts?
4. What factual information is included in this advertisement? How successful is the advertisement in persuading you to fill out the coupon for a subscription to *Science 82*? Why is it successful or unsuccessful?

Questions on Style and Diction

1. Consider the picture, the captions, and the opening paragraph. What is the effect of the sudden shift in time and place from the prehistoric past and the oceanic depths to the present moment in the human eyelash? Is this general effect repeated elsewhere in the advertisement?
2. Consider the imagery (of veils and mysteries, seeing and understanding). Why is that imagery effective and how is it related to the thesis and purpose of the advertisement?

Ideas for Discussion and Writing

1. In a short essay of two or three paragraphs, analyze the visual impact of this advertisement. Consider such topics as the use of curves, lines, and boxes; the comparative size of the typefaces; and the visual associations of the pictured objects.
2. Go to your college library and look up a number of back issues of this magazine. Write an essay explaining why you feel that the magazine either exceeds, meets, or fails to meet the expectations raised by this advertisement.

United States Patent 4,378,627 is in good company.

4,379,218 – FLUXLESS ION BEAM SOLDERING PROCESS – 4/5/83

4,379,022 – METHOD FOR MASKLESS CHEMICAL MACHINING – 4/5/83

4,379,005 – SEMICONDUCTOR DEVICE FABRICATION – 4/5/83

4,378,630 – PROCESS FOR FABRICATING A HIGH PERFORMANCE PNP AND NPN STRUCTURE – 4/5/83

4,378,627 – SELF-ALIGNED METAL PROCESS FOR FIELD EFFECT TRANSISTOR INTEGRATED CIRCUITS USING POLYCRYSTALLINE SILICON GATE ELECTRODES – 4/5/83

4,378,589 – UNIDIRECTIONAL LOOPED BUS MICROCOMPUTER ARCHITECTURE – 3/29/83

4,378,421 – CLEANING METHOD AND APPARATUS FOR AN ELECTROGRAPHIC SYSTEM – 3/29/83

4,378,383 – METHOD OF MAKING CONDUCTIVE PATHS THROUGH A LAMINA IN A SEMICONDUCTOR DEVICE – 3/29/83

4,377,854 – SUBSTRATE FOR MAGNETIC DOMAIN DEVICE – 3/22/83

4,377,849 – MACRO ASSEMBLER PROCESS FOR AUTOMATED CIRCUIT DESIGN – 3/22/83

4,377,845 – OPTIONAL MACHINE INHIBITION FOR FEATURE MALFUNCTION – 3/22/83

4,377,842 – FLYBACK VOLTAGE CONTROL – 3/22/83

4,377,806 – PARALLEL TO SERIAL CONVERTER – 3/22/83

4,377,803 – ALGORITHM FOR THE SEGMENTATION OF PRINTED FIXED PITCH DOCUMENTS – 3/22/83

4,377,633 – METHODS OF SIMULTANEOUS CONTACT AND METAL LITHOGRAPHY PATTERNING – 3/22/83

4,377,338 – METHOD AND APPARATUS FOR COPIER QUALITY MONITORING AND CONTROL – 3/22/83

4,376,963 – COMPOSITE MAGNETIC RECORDING DISK – 3/15/83

4,376,960 – FLEXIBLE DISK STABILIZING STRUCTURE – 3/15/83

4,376,943 – RECORD CARRIER FOR AN ELECTRO-EROSION PRINTER AND METHOD FOR MAKING SAME – 3/15/83

4,376,932 – MULTI-REGISTRATION IN CHARACTER RECOGNITION – 3/15/83

4,376,897 – LOW VOLTAGE SERIAL TO PARALLEL TO SERIAL CHARGE COUPLED DEVICE – 3/15/83

4,376,588 – BI-DIRECTIONAL SERIAL PRINTER WITH LOOK-AHEAD – 3/15/83

4,376,587 – PRINT RIBBON PROTECTION – 3/15/83

4,376,569 – ELECTROLYTE FOR AN ELECTROCHROMIC DISPLAY – 3/15/83

4,376,411 – PRINT HAMMER LIMIT CONTROL – 3/15/83

4,376,252 – BOOTSTRAPPED DRIVER CIRCUIT – 3/8/83

4,376,249 – VARIABLE AXIS ELECTRON BEAM PROJECTION SYSTEM – 3/8/83

4,376,057 – ETCHANT COMPOSITION AND USE THEREOF – 3/8/83

4,375,657 – MAGNETIC HEAD ASSEMBLY – 3/1/83

4,375,656 – MAGNETIC HEAD ASSEMBLY WITH ASYMMETRIC SLOTTED CONFIGURATION – 3/1/83

4,375,652 – FACSIMILE VECTOR DATA COMPRESSION – 3/1/83

4,375,652 – HIGH-SPEED TIME DELAY AND INTEGRATION SOLID STATE SCANNER – 3/1/83

4,375,600 – SENSE AMPLIFIER FOR INTEGRATED MEMORY ARRAY – 3/1/83

4,375,592 – INCREMENTAL ROTARY ENCODER – 3/1/83

4,375,390 – THIN FILM TECHNIQUES FOR FABRICATING NARROW TRACK FERRITE HEADS – 3/1/83

4,375,339 – ELECTRICALLY CONDUCTIVE RIBBON BREAK DETECTOR FOR PRINTERS – 3/1/83

4,375,390 – THIN FILM TECHNIQUES FOR FABRICATING NARROW TRACK FERRITE HEADS – 3/1/83

4,375,103 – METHOD AND APPARATUS OF SIGNALLING REQUEST TO SEND CLEAR TO SEND DELAY – 2/22/83

4,375,085 – DENSE ELECTRICALLY ALTERABLE READ ONLY MEMORY – 2/22/83

4,375,079 – DIGITAL DATA DISPLAY SYSTEM – 2/22/83

4,375,072 – SELF-CALIBRATING OVERCURRENT DETECTOR – 2/22/83

4,375,062 – ASPIRATOR FOR AN INK JET PRINTER – 2/22/83

4,374,911 – PHOTO METHOD OF MAKING TRI-LEVEL DENSITY PHOTOMASK – 2/22/83

4,374,626 – ERASING TYPEWRITER WITH AUTOMATIC/MANUAL SELECTION – 2/22/83

4,374,625 – TEXT RECORDER WITH AUTOMATIC WORD ENDING – 2/22/83

4,374,618 – MICROFILM CAMERA HAVING A MOVING LENS – 2/22/83

4,374,586 – DOCUMENT FEED SHEET ALIGNER – 2/22/83

4,374,429 – INFORMATION TRANSFER SYSTEM WHEREIN BIDIRECTIONAL TRANSFER IS EFFECTED UTILIZING UNIDIRECTIONAL BUS IN CONJUNCTION WITH KEY DEPRESSION SIGNAL LINE – 2/15/83

4,374,415 – HOST CONTROL OF SUSPENSION AND RESUMPTION OF CHANNEL PROGRAM EXECUTION – 2/15/83

4,374,386 – FORCE-TEMPERATURE STABILIZATION OF AN ELECTROMAGNETIC DEVICE – 2/15/83

4,374,383 – CAPACITIVE TRANSDUCER FOR SENSING A HOME POSITION – 2/15/83

4,374,321 – AUTOMATIC TEMPERATURE CONTROLLER FOR AN ELECTRO-PHOTOGRAPHIC APPARATUS FUSER AND METHOD THEREFOR – 2/15/83

4,374,007 – TRIVALENT CHROMIUM ELECTROPLATING SOLUTION AND PROCESS – 2/15/83

4,374,001 – ELECTROLYTIC PRINTING – 2/15/83

4,373,966 – FORMING SCHOTTKY BARRIER DIODES BY DEPOSITING ALUMINUM SILICON AND COPPER OR BINARY ALLOYS THEREOF AND ALLOY-SINTERING – 2/15/83

4,373,778 – CONNECTOR IMPLEMENTED WITH FIBER OPTIC MEANS AND SITE THEREIN FOR INTEGRATED CIRCUIT CHIPS – 2/15/83

4,373,194 – FULL PAGE REPRESENTATION THROUGH DYNAMIC MODE SWITCHING – 2/8/83

4,373,183 – BUS INTERFACE UNITS SHARING A COMMON BUS USING DISTRIBUTED CONTROL FOR ALLOCATION OF THE BUS – 2/8/83

4,373,173 – MULTI-ELEMENT HEAD ASSEMBLY – 2/8/83

4,373,166 – SCHOTTKY BARRIER DIODE WITH CONTROLLED CHARACTERISTICS – 2/8/83

4,372,699 – SHEET FEEDER FOR TYPEWRITERS – 2/8/83

4,372,697 – RIBBON DRIVE ARRANGEMENT FOR A PRINTER – 2/8/83

4,372,672 – SELF-TRIGGERING QUALITY CONTROL SENSOR – 2/8/83

4,372,671 – SHOCK ABSORBING CARRIAGE DRIVE COUPLING FOR COPIER – 2/8/83

4,371,933 – BI-DIRECTIONAL DISPLAY OF CIRCULAR ARCS – 2/1/83

4,371,932 – I/O CONTROLLER FOR TRANSFERRING DATA BETWEEN A HOST PROCESSOR AND MULTIPLE I/O UNITS – 2/1/83

4,371,929 – MULTIPROCESSOR SYSTEM WITH HIGH DENSITY MEMORY SET ARCHITECTURE INCLUDING PARTITIONABLE CACHE STORE INTERFACE TO SHARED DISK DRIVE MEMORY – 2/1/83

4,371,902 – DISK INITIALIZATION METHOD – 2/1/83

4,371,857 – ELECTROMAGNETICALLY OPERABLE RAM ACTUATOR IN PARTICULAR FOR IMPACT PRINTERS – 2/1/83

4,371,565 – PROCESS FOR ADHERING AN ORGANIC RESIN TO A SUBSTRATE BY MEANS OF PLASMA POLYMERIZED PHOSPHINES – 2/1/83

4,371,273 – ELECTROCHEMICAL PRINTHEAD – 2/1/83

4,371,157 – COMPACT ENVELOPE HANDLING DEVICE – 2/1/83

4,370,732 – SKEWED MATRIX ADDRESS GENERATOR – 1/25/83

4,370,651 – ADVANCED PLASMA PANEL TECHNOLOGY – 1/25/83

4,370,641 – ELECTRONIC CONTROL SYSTEM – 1/25/83

4,370,197 – PROCESS FOR ETCHING CHROME – 1/25/83

4,369,501 – DUAL CYCLE DATA DETECTION SYSTEM AND METHOD FOR BUBBLE MEMORIES – 1/18/83

4,369,463 – GRAY SCALE IMAGE DATA COMPRESSION WITH CODE WORDS A FUNCTION OF IMAGE HISTORY – 1/18/83

4,369,396 – COLOR CATHODE RAY TUBE APPARATUS WITH SHADOW MASK – 1/18/83

4,369,271 – LACQUER FOR RECORD CARRIERS AND PROCESS FOR ITS PRODUCTION – 1/18/83

4,369,154 – PROCESS FOR PRODUCING SMOOTHER CERAMIC SURFACES – 1/18/83

4,369,072 – METHOD FOR FORMING IGFET DEVICES HAVING IMPROVED DRAIN VOLTAGE CHARACTERISTICS – 1/18/83

4,368,977 – DOCUMENT EJECTOR APPARATUS AND METHOD USEFUL FOR COPIERS – 1/18/83

4,368,538 – SPOT FOCUS FLASH X-RAY SOURCE – 1/11/83

4,368,513 – PARTIAL ROLL-MODE TRANSFER FOR CYCLIC BULK MEMORY – 1/11/83

4,368,466 – DISPLAY REFRESH MEMORY WITH VARIABLE LINE START ADDRESSING – 1/11/83

4,368,220 – PASSIVATION OF RIE PATTERNED AL-BASED ALLOY FILMS BY ETCHING TO REMOVE CONTAMINANTS AND SURFACE OXIDE FOLLOWED BY OXIDATION – 1/11/83

4,367,947 – DOCUMENT FEEDER FOR MOVING BED MACHINES SUCH AS COPIERS – 1/11/83

4,367,549 – METHOD AND APPARATUS FOR MULTIPLEXING A DATA SIGNAL AND SECONDARY SIGNALS – 1/4/83

4,367,503 – HERMETICALLY SEALED DISK FILE – 1/4/83

4,367,119 – PLANAR MULTI-LEVEL METAL PROCESS WITH BUILT-IN ETCH STOP – 1/4/83

4,367,052 – FLAT RATE SPRING PARTICULARLY ADAPTED FOR TYPEWRITER CARTRIDGES – 1/4/83

4,367,044 – SITU RATE AND DEPTH MONITOR FOR SILICON ETCHING – 1/4/83

4,366,613 – METHOD OF FABRICATING AN MOS DYNAMIC RAM WITH LIGHTLY DOPED DRAIN – 1/4/83

4,366,540 – CYCLE CONTROL FOR A MICROPROCESSOR WITH MULTI-SPEED CONTROL STORES – 12/28/82

4,366,537 – AUTHORIZATION MECHANISM FOR TRANSFER OF PROGRAM CONTROL OR DATA BETWEEN DIFFERENT ADDRESS SPACES HAVING DIFFERENT STORAGE PROTECT KEYS – 12/28/82

4,366,518 – MULTI-TRACK HEAD ASSEMBLY – 12/28/82

4,366,493 – SEMICONDUCTOR BALLISTIC TRANSPORT DEVICE – 12/28/82

4,365,779 – TILT AND ROTATE APPARATUS FOR A DISPLAY MONITOR – 12/28/82

4,365,318 – TWO-SPEED RECIRCULATING MEMORY SYSTEM USING PARTIALLY GOOD COMPONENTS – 12/21/82

4,365,317 – SUPERCONDUCTIVE LATCH CIRCUIT – 12/21/82

4,365,296 – SYSTEM FOR CONTROLLING THE DURATION OF THE TIME INTERVAL BETWEEN BLOCKS OF DATA IN A COMPUTER-TO-COMPUTER COMMUNICATION SYSTEM – 12/21/82

4,365,235 – CHINESE/KANJI ON-LINE RECOGNITION SYSTEM – 12/21/82

4,365,163 – PATTERN INSPECTION TOOL – METHOD AND APPARATUS – 12/21/82

4,364,683 – PAPER FEED ROLLER ASSEMBLY FOR A TYPEWRITER OR PRINTER – 12/21/82

4,364,166 – SEMICONDUCTOR INTEGRATED CIRCUIT INTERCONNECTIONS – 12/21/82

4,364,100 – MULTI-LAYERED METALLIZED SILICON MATRIX SUBSTRATE – 12/14/82

4,364,074 – V-MOS DEVICE WITH SELF-ALIGNED MULTIPLE ELECTRODES – 12/14/82

4,364,024 – SIGNATURE PRES METHOD AND APPARATUS –

4,363,919 – HETEROFULVALE GEMINAL DITHIOLATE COM AND THEIR SELENIUM AND TELLURIUM ANALOGS AND OF FABRICATING THE SAM

4,363,828 – METHOD FOR DI SILICON FILMS AND RELAT MATERIALS BY A GLOW DIS IN A DISILANE OR HIGHER SILANE GAS – 12/14/82

4,363,549 – ELECTROMECHA OPERATED FUSER ROLL CLOSURE – 12/14/82

4,363,125 – MEMORY READB CHECK METHOD AND APPARATUS – 12/7/82

4,363,124 – RECIRCULATING MEMORY ARRAY TESTER – I

4,363,110 – NON-VOLATILE D RAM CELL – 12/7/82

4,363,093 – PROCESSOR INTERCOMMUNICATION SYSTEM – 12/7/82

4,363,057 – RECIRCULATING DUCT DESIGN – 12/7/82

4,363,044 – TRAY FOR MAGN DRIVE MACHINE – 12/7/82

4,362,977 – METHOD AND A FOR CALIBRATING A ROBO COMPENSATE FOR INACCU THE ROBOT – 12/7/82

4,362,843 – PROCESS FOR P A POLYMERIZED, HEAT-RES LACQUER – 12/7/82

4,362,798 – HYDRAZONE AN PYRAZOLINE OR ACETOSO CONTAINING CHARGE TRAN LAYER PHOTOCONDUCTOR ELECTROPHOTOGRAPHIC USING THE SAME – 12/7/82

4,362,662 – HETEROFULVALE GEMINAL DITHIOLATE COM AND THEIR SELENIUM AND TELLURIUM ANALOGS AND OF FABRICATING THE SAM

4,362,611 – QUADRUPOLE R. SPUTTERING SYSTEM HAVI ANODE/CATHODE SHIELD FLOATING TARGET SHIELD

4,362,596 – ETCH END POIN DETECTOR USING GAS FLO CHANGES – 12/7/82

4,362,486 – AUTOMATIC MUL CERAMIC (MLC) SCREENIN MACHINE – 12/7/82

4,362,406 – DOT MATRIX PR HEAD – 12/7/82

4,361,845 – DEVICE FOR PRE THE CONTAMINATION OF I COMPONENTS – 11/30/82

4,361,781 – MULTIPLE ELECT CATHODE RAY TUBE – 11/30

4,361,768 – SUPERCONDUCTING SOLITON DEVICES – 11/30/82

4,360,898 – PROGRAMMABLE LOGIC ARRAY SYSTEM INCORPORATING JOSEPHSON DEVICES – 11/23/82

4,360,870 – PROGRAMMABLE I/O DEVICE IDENTIFICATION – 11/23/82

4,360,768 – HIGH CURRENT ACCELERATION SERVO MOTOR DRIVER – 11/23/82

4,360,583 – HIGH RESOLUTION VIDEO STORAGE DISK – 11/23/82

4,360,289 – PIN FOR BRAZING TO A

INTERCONNECTION CAPABLE OF SUSTAINED HIGH POWER LEVELS BETWEEN A SEMICONDUCTOR DEVICE AND A SUPPORTING SUBSTRATE – 11/23/82

4,359,937 – DOT MATRIX PRINTER – 11/23/82

4,359,816 – SELF-ALIGNED METAL PROCESS FOR FIELD EFFECT TRANSISTOR INTEGRATED CIRCUITS – 11/23/82

4,359,772 – DUAL FUNCTION ERROR CORRECTING SYSTEM – 11/16/82

ON THE SURFACE OF A RECORD CARRIER – 11/16/82

4,359,288 – SINGLE PASS RIBBON CARTRIDGE FOR IMPACT PRINTERS HAVING MEANS TO PREVENT INCORRECT INSERTION – 11/16/82

4,359,286 – CHARACTER SET EXPANSION – 11/16/82

4,358,890 – PROCESS FOR MAKING A DUAL IMPLANTED DRAIN EXTENSION FOR BUCKET BRIGADE DEVICE TERTRODE STRUCTURE – 11/16/82

4,358,848 – DUAL FUNCTION ECC SYSTEM WITH BLOCK CHECK BYTE – 11/9/82

STORAGE ORGANIZED ON A WORD BASIS – 11/9/82

4,358,824 – OFFICE CORRESPONDENCE STORAGE AND RETRIEVAL SYSTEM – 11/9/82

U.S. Patent 4,378,627 was one of five issued to IBM on Tuesday, April 5. This invention will provide faster circuits for computers through increased density.

But as the latest addition to this partial list of IBM achievements in technology and science, it represents something larger: the creativity of IBM inventors.

Over the last 25 years, they've been granted more than 11,000 patents.

Their innovations and discoveries helped IBM make contributions to all aspects of the information processing industry — from typewriters to our largest computers.

For instance, our most advanced disk file transfers data at 3 million characters per second, the fastest rate available in a production unit. Our experimental 288,000-bit memory chip has the largest capacity yet reported for a chip produced on a manufacturing line. And the circuit packaging in our larger computers is the densest in the industry.

Each achievement, no matter how small (or how large), contributes to making IBM products faster, less expensive, easier to use and more reliable.

It's all part of IBM's worldwide commitment to research and development.

And that's the patent truth.

Courtesy of International Business Machines Corporation

Questions on Content

1. Look closely at the list of inventions that forms a background to the boxed text. Estimate the number of patents by IBM listed on the two pages of the advertisement.
2. How many months are spanned in the patents by IBM listed in this advertisement?
3. What five patents were issued to IBM on April 5, 1983?

Questions on Thesis, Purpose, and Structure

1. This advertisement relies heavily on the presentation of factual information. Glance over some of the patents listed in the background and compare them with the ones emphasized in the boxed section. What implicit point is made by the examples that IBM chooses to highlight?
2. Put the thesis of this advertisement into your own words. Do any of the sentences in the advertisement come close to expressing that thesis?
3. This advertisement mentions no specific product and makes no transparent appeal to purchasers. Is it then devoid of all persuasive purpose? What is the benefit to the company of such an advertisement?

Questions on Style and Diction

1. Explain the pun in the caption: "United States Patent 4,378,627 is in good company." Why does that make an effective introduction?
2. Explain the pun in the final sentence of the boxed area. Why is that an effective conclusion?

Ideas for Discussion and Writing

1. Compare this advertisement by IBM with the advertisement by the Atari Corporation on p. 122. Write an essay about how the different tactics in each advertisement are related to the nature of the company's products and its potential customers.
2. If you have any firsthand experience with IBM products, write a brief essay about your impression of those products and the extent to which your impressions correspond with the expectations raised by this advertisement.

Chapter 10

DIVISION AND CLASSIFICATION

At the beginning of this book is a table of contents that divides the text into four parts, which are further subdivided into chapters. In Parts II and III these chapters are subdivided yet again into an introduction to a particular mode of composition and a number of readings illustrating that mode. Whenever you take one thing—be it a book, a bicycle, or a loaf of bread—and slice it into various pieces, you have used the process of **division**. You may develop an essay using division in exactly the same way as a book, by taking one subject and carving it into components.

In **classification** you start with a large number of things and sort them into groups. Your college or university librarian, for example, sorts the thousands of new acquisitions each year by subject or title or author's name. In the widely used Library of Congress classification system, a book's content provides the primary basis of classification. The first letter in the call number of any book reflects its general content according to the following categories of classification:

A	General Works
B	Philosophy and Religion
C	History and Auxiliary Sciences
D	Universal History and Topography
E – F	American History
G	Geography, Anthropology, Folklore
H	Social Sciences
J	Political Sciences
K	Law
L	Education
M	Music
N	Fine Arts

Woodcut illustration of Dante's *Inferno* by Gustave Doré. In *The Inferno* Dante attempts to classify those condemned to Hell. The clothed figures in the center of the illustration are Dante and his guide Virgil, the author of the *Aeneid*. Surrounding them are seven groups of the damned. What major sin do you think is represented by each grouping? Feel encouraged to develop your own definitions and classifications of sin.

P	Language and Literature
Q	Science
R	Medicine
S	Agriculture
T	Technology
U	Military Science
V	Naval Science
Z	Library Science and Bibliography

Subclasses within each of these broad areas are indicated by a second letter: HB, for example, indicates a book on economic theory, and HC indicates a book on economic history. Still other subclassifications (based on content, author, and title) are indicated by the numbers that follow the two initial letters. At the end of a rather complex process of classification, each book receives a unique call number.

Although division and classification at first seem quite different, the differences are more apparent than real. From one perspective, a library is one large building subdivided into various floors. The floors are subdivided into alcoves; each alcove contains bookshelves; each bookshelf contains books. Ultimately, the subdivision of a library shows the exact arrangement of books on the shelves. Thus, division, like classification, may illustrate the Library of Congress classification system. Both division and classification are essentially the same, the primary difference being whether we start with one thing (the library) or many things (the books in the library). Because of the close, reciprocal relationship between division and classification, most of our comments in the remainder of this chapter will refer to classification, with the understanding that our advice usually applies just as well to division.

PREWRITING

You will find a variety of different invention techniques useful as you plan an essay using division or classification. **If you are using division, mapping** (see p. 58) **is a natural invention strategy.** You commence with one thing—your income, for instance—and you begin to map out the various expenditures of your income as shown in the accompanying figure. Another possibility might be to map out the sources of your income as shown in the accompanying figure.

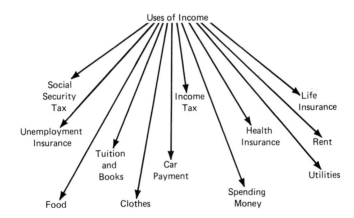

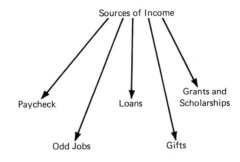

The difficulty with division, as both of these invention exercises illustrate, is that the ideas it generates often seem self-evident and therefore uninteresting. Topics for classification usually offer more flexibility. Suppose, for example, that you decide to write an essay classifying your favorite rock musicians. **The natural way to begin a classification essay is by listing**—in this case by listing the musicians you prefer:

Stevie Ray Vaughn	Bruce Springsteen
Jimi Hendrix	The Rolling Stones
White Snake	Twisted Sister
The Doors	Jimmy Buffet
Linda Ronstadt	Buddy Holly
Def Leppard	Bon Jovi
The Beach Boys	Rod Stewart
Janis Joplin	B. B. King
Van Halen	Madonna
Jerry Lee Lewis	Jefferson Airplane
David Bowie	David Bromberg
Pink Floyd	Chuck Berry
Bonnie Raitt	Elton John
The Temptations	The Supremes
Iron Maiden	Metallica

After five or ten minutes of thoughtful listing, **your next step is to decide on a classifying principle**. A number of different possibilities will probably occur to you here. You might classify rock musicians, for example, on the basis of the style of music they play (straight rock and roll, Motown, heavy metal, rhythm and blues) or the audience for their songs (gospel rock, teeny-bopper rock, California beach music, acid rock, punk rock) or the mood each musician ordinarily creates (kick-out-the-jams rock, mellow music, cry-in-your-beer blues, turn-the-lights-down-low love songs). As you try out each classifying principle, you should go back to your initial list of musicians, sorting them into the appropriate groups, and adding to the list as the names of additional musicians occur to you.

PLANNING AND DRAFTING
A CLASSIFICATION ESSAY

The classifications or subdivisions that you developed during the process of invention provide your essay with a ready-made structure. In most cases you will need to do nothing more than **follow the outline suggested by your notes**. Remember to begin your essay with something that will get the reader's attention, use plenty of examples in developing a paragraph for each major subheading, and build to your most interesting or persuasive points as your essay nears its conclusion.

In addition, keep three other points in mind:

1. **Be consistent. Use only one classifying principle in a short essay.** Suppose you are writing on the embarrassments of first dates. Your reader will find your essay easy to follow if you approach the topic chronologically: embarrassments involved in making contact, arranging a date, meeting the parents or roommates, being out on the date itself, and saying good night. Your reader will also find your essay easy to follow if you focus on progressively more embarrassing moments: mildly embarrassing moments, moderately embarrassing moments, excruciatingly embarrassing moments. A mixture of these two classifying principles, however, is apt to produce confusion. What is your reader to conclude from a series of paragraphs dealing with making contact, arranging a date, mildly embarrassing moments, excruciatingly embarrassing moments, and saying good night?

2. **Be complete. Make sure that your classifying scheme includes all significant possibilities.** Suppose you decide to classify different kinds of pets according to their desirability. You might start with "excellent pets": cats, dogs, horses, guppies, even denatured skunks. A second category of "adequate pets" would include hamsters, goats, boa constrictors, perhaps even iguanas. You would need yet a third category for "truly terrible pets": rattlesnakes, lions, elephants, black widow spiders, adolescent children. Note that only your *categories* need to be complete. In an essay on pets, no one expects you to name and classify all of the thousands of species of animals. If your topic seems to splinter off into so many tiny categories that completeness eludes you, try narrowing the topic. It is easier to classify the "major trends" in contemporary rock music than to discuss thoroughly every fleeting fashion.

3. **Avoid overlapping categories.** In a classification of popular movies, you would not want separate categories for "science fiction movies" and "alien creature movies." A movie about an invasion of giant slugs from Mars is just as much a science fiction movie as one in which Luke Skywalker saves Princess Leia by doing battle with Darth Vader. Indeed, the use of alien creatures is more likely to be a component of science fiction movies than a separate category; the leonine Chubacca and the cuddly Ewoks may play subordinate parts in the Star Wars movies, but such creatures are present in these as in most other science fiction movies.

COMBINING PURPOSES

Division and classification are primarily techniques for conveying information. Indeed, much scientific information is made manageable and comprehensible by the process of classification. In 1735 Carolus Linneaus published his *Systema Natura* outlining the modern scientific system for classifying all forms of life according to species, genus, family, order, class, and phylum. When we consult the *Peterson Guide to Atlantic Shorebirds* or the Golden Press *Guide to the Trees of North America*, we use methods of scientific classification to help us assimilate our own observations of nature. In much the same way, chess masters classify the various gambits for opening and closing a chess match. Similarly, chemists use Dimitri Mendeleev's periodic table (1869) to classify and understand the properties of the basic chemical elements.

The usefulness of classification in organizing information does not assure that anyone will find that information particularly interesting. After all, few of us turn to the periodic table of elements or a manual of chess openings when we want a little entertainment after dinner. Therefore, part of your challenge in writing an essay using division or classification is to find a way to make it appeal to readers. Perhaps the best response to that challenge is to **discover a highly original and convincing basis for classification**. Desmond Morris does this repeatedly in his essay on "Salutation Displays" (p. 339). Most of us take marked delight in coming to a conscious understanding of behavior that we have always followed subconsciously. That is what happens when Morris analyzes the various inconvenience displays that all humans use to take note of arrivals and departures: we signal our great delight in the arrival of comic Uncle Charlie by rushing out of the house to meet him as he pulls into the driveway. On the other hand, the moocher who lives across the street doesn't even merit a greeting at the doorway; we simply shout "come in" over the din of the baseball game and grunt in acceptance when he asks to borrow the lawn mower.

Sadly, few of us add significantly to the store of human understanding when we use division or classification in an essay. We can and should expect ourselves to discover *something* new and interesting in the classifications or subdivisions we devise. If that is not the case, we should return to the prewriting stage and continue to explore new topics or new ways of classifying the information at hand. Still, in most instances we may have to content ourselves with a simpler goal than that of being profound. We may need to **look for opportunities for humor and wit.** Fortunately, classification lends itself readily to humorous approaches. Humor is implied — if not indispensable — in such topics as "Six Ways to Torment Your Sister," "Four Stumbling Blocks on First Dates," "Useful Excuses for Cutting Class," and "Foolish Fads in Footware."

If the quest for humor is inappropriate or leads nowhere, you can still please an audience if you **use lots of specific, sensuous details and examples**. Any topic for classification necessarily abounds with examples. Your task is to choose the best examples at your disposal and to make them as appealing as possible. Suppose you are attempting to classify excuses for cutting class. It is certainly true that every instructor gets a dose of phony funeral excuses from students who want to skip class. However, you need to animate your discussion of that classification by citing a few examples:

> Twice a semester most college instructors have a vague intuition that in some mystifying, inexplicable way, the mere giving

of exams causes death at a distance. Twice a semester the remote kin of many a hapless college student begin to drop like flies in a fog of RAID: granddad in Tallahassee felled by a wayward eighteen-wheeler; the cousin on the construction crew beaned by a plummeting lunch pail; the aunt in Topeka whose festering foot gives way to septicemia. All of these sad departures—and hundreds more like them—are instances of the modern student's ingenious Funereal Fantasies.

Finally, the most important factor in writing a successful essay is to **develop a persuasive thesis**. It is, of course, possible to classify items without expressing any opinion about the items or the value of the classifications. An essay on contemporary rock music, for example, might simply explain the different musical styles used by today's musicians. The same essay would probably be more interesting, however, if it attempted to present a thesis. It might argue that by evolving away from rock's original bluesy beat, many of today's top-forty hits have lost the ability to get blood pumping, toes tapping, and bodies swaying. Alternatively, an essay using virtually the same classifications might present the viewpoint that over the past thirty years rock lyrics (at least by major musicians) have become more mature and intellectual; the "Shoo-be-do-be-oh-ahs" of the fifties have been replaced by the sophisticated balladry of Bruce Springsteen and Rod Stewart. Even a well-reasoned statement of your preferences (that, for example, gospel rock is an encouraging new combination of religious morality with rock's raw emotion) will add purpose to your writing and keep your readers interested in either agreeing or disagreeing with you.

TIPS ON REVISION

To be useful at all, an essay using division or classification must present information in an orderly fashion. If you have used an outline in developing your ideas, your draft should be fairly well organized. In revising that draft you can help your reader see the basis of your organization.

Your essay will seem more structured and orderly if you **develop equal categories equally**, treating each at roughly the same length and with the same degree of specificity. Of course, you should never pad a category with meaningless words simply to achieve this parallelism. Still, readers are apt to think that a category described in detail is more important than one that is mentioned only briefly. Because the bulk of your essay should deal with important categories, you may need to beef up some sections or trim down others during revision.

Another way to emphasize the structure of your essay is to **use parallel designations for each category**. If your essay is fairly short —five hundred words or so—you can best achieve this through your topic sentences. Simply use similar phrasing in announcing each new classification:

> The common excuses for cutting class fall into four basic categories: the first category is The Commuting Catastrophe. . . .

The second category is The Sudden Illness Incident. . . .

The third category is The Hospitalized Kinsman Caper. . . .

The final category involves The Funereal Fantasy. . . .

The risk of monotony in such parallel phrasing is reduced by the fact that these sentences are separated from one another by a least a paragraph of varied details and examples. The result is that the parallelism effectively reinforces the essay's purpose in classifying information.

In an essay of several thousand words, you may wish to **add formal subheadings to make the major classifications clear at a glance**. Subheadings are especially useful when you plan to develop each category for several paragraphs or several pages.

IDEAS FOR ESSAYS

1. Use division in analyzing one of the following topics. Remember that in using division you divide one thing into its component parts. Do not use narration or process analysis. Explain or describe each subdivision in detail.
   a. A particular poem, short story, play, or film.
   b. A typical joke (that is, the elements in every joke, not one particular joke).
   c. The elements of a "tall tale" (a fishing story, for example).
   d. The components of a typical gospel song (or country ballad or rock narrative).
   e. The components of a typical soap opera (or situation comedy, spy novel, or news broadcast).

2. Use classification in analyzing one of the following topics.
   a. Teachers.
   b. Popular musicians.
   c. Novels on the best-seller list.
   d. College students.
   e. Athletes.
   f. Unforgettable characters.
   g. Types of love, hate, jealousy, or sloth.
   h. Attitudes toward good students (or bad students).
   i. Types of courtship.
   j. Obnoxious new products.
   k. Commercials or advertisements.
   l. Rock musicians.
   m. Types of good students (or bad students).
   n. Vacations.
   o. Summer jobs.
   p. Obnoxious people.
   q. Acquaintances.
   r. People waiting in line.
   s. Ways to get even.
   t. Ways to make up after a fight.

STUDENT ESSAY _____

The following essay by Judy Perrin was written as an in-class assignment in two fifty minute sessions of her Freshman English class. She was presented with a list of options similar to the "Ideas for Essays" in this chapter.

FIRST DRAFT

"SPEEDY, SLOWPOKE, GROUCHY, AND ME"

by Judy Perrin

People Waiting in Line

Principle of classification–Rude people in check-out lines

Shopping happens to be one of my favorite pastimes, much to my husband's dismay. Often as I'm waiting in a check-out line my eyes tend to wander, and I find myself engrossed in another favorite pastime ~~of mine~~: people-watching. I could spend hours gazing at people, ~~taking~~ *take* in every little movement and quirk, reading the lines in their faces, ~~and~~ *while* trying to guess ~~the~~ *their* personality *is* ~~of each person my eyes fall upon.~~ Very often I have noticed how rude people are ~~as~~ *while* they are waiting in ~~a~~ check-out lines. Generally this rudeness occurs during the Christmas season. Lines are often long and slow-moving during this time so I am able to pick out these rude people easily.

People Who Take Their Time

Usually there is always at least one of these people, standing in line. You've seen ~~these people~~ *her* before. ~~They are~~ *She is* the one~~s~~ who ~~are~~ *is* undecided about ~~some item in their~~ *a pair of gloves in her* shopping cart. ~~They pick this item up and examine it, put it~~ *She picks the gloves up and examines them* ~~down, then shake their head, pick it up again and~~ *Carefully. She places them back in her cart, shakes her head, picks them up again and proceeds to return them* ~~proceed to return it to its proper place. They leave their~~ *to the shelf. She leaves her* shopping cart in line and disappears. You can't move ~~their~~ *her* cart out of line~~.~~ for That would be rude, so everyone waits for ~~the person~~ her to return. Finally ~~they~~ she arrives with a different ~~item and they have~~ pair of gloves she has also acquired a friend along the way. Now the slowpoke and the friend are engaged in deep conversation, not noticing the ~~check-out girl is~~ cashier clearing her throat and tapping on the counter ~~waiting~~ as she waits to check them out. Finally ~~they~~ slowpoke get~~s~~ the message and begin~~s~~ to unload the items from ~~the~~ her cart onto the counter. The check-out girl informs the customer that an item ~~they have~~ she is purchasing is on sale today~~.~~: two for the price of one. So slow-poke wanders off to get the extra item, leaving distressed looks on the faces of the other people in line. After a long absence ~~they~~ she return~~s~~, and everyone is praying that nothing else she is purchasing is on sale. The amount is rung up and slow-poke begins to go through ~~their~~ her wallet~~,~~ and much to ~~their~~ her dismay, ~~they don't~~ she doesn't have enough cash on hand. Now ~~they'll~~ she'll have to write a check if ~~they~~ she can find ~~their~~ her checkbook. After a thorough search (which can mean dumping the entire contents of ~~their~~ her purse onto the counter)~~,~~ ~~they~~ she finally locate~~s~~ it, and very ~~carefully and~~ slowly make~~s~~ out the check while the rest of the people in line are silently cheering.

People in a Hurry

   Woe to anyone who happens to be in front of the person ~~who is~~ in a hurry. For some reason ~~they~~ he tend~~s~~ to use ~~their~~ his shopping cart as a battering ram. ~~They~~ He want~~s~~ to hurry everyone along, so very gently ~~they~~ he nudge~~s~~ the person in front of ~~them~~ him, moving ~~them~~ her up an inch or so. A chain reaction occurs and everyone in line has been moved up a ~~tiny bit, but they are~~ couple of inches; but he is in a hurry, and one little nudge won't do it, ~~so they back up their cart~~ ⊙ He proceeds to back his cart up and ram the ~~person~~ lady ahead of them again, clipping ~~their~~ her heels this time. Usually ~~they~~ speedy receive~~s~~ a dirty look which is a sign to "cut it out!"

If you've ever noticed, these people, ~~they~~ are constantly tapping their fingers on the handle of shopping carts, looking at their watch *es every few minutes,* shifting from one foot to the other, and making little noises that sound as though they're gasping for air. As they finally reach the ~~check-out girl~~ *cashier,* they exclaim, "Well it's about time!" Then they proceed to show everyone how quick checking-out can be. It always tickles me when an item they're purchasing doesn't have a price marked on it, and old speedy has to wait until someone can price it.

People Who Are Grouches

These people are easy to spot. They have deep furrows in their forehead from frowning all the time. They never have a nice word to say to anyone. Often these people are mothers who have a handfull of children with them. Children will be children, but these people are not in the mood for the antics of children while standing in line. So they proceed to scream warnings to the little ones in very unladylike language, disregarding everyone else in line. *When all else fails, next comes the swatting of little hands, legs, and bottoms, and more threats.*

Often these people are husbands who have decided *to* ~~that they would~~ help their *wives* ~~wife~~ with the shopping. They stand in line and grouch and grumble about the price of everything, the crowds, the rudeness of the sales personnel, and the long line they're standing in. The ~~wife is~~ *wives are* embarrassed because of *their* ~~his~~ rude, loud mouth, the people in line feel sorry for the *wives* ~~wife~~, and the ~~check-out girl~~ *cashier* is feeling sorry for herself because she gets the pleasure of checking out *these* ~~this~~ old grouch. *Many times the grouch has a bone to pick with the cashier. She is either dissatisfied with the service or some item she is returning. She proceeds to give the cashier a piece of her mind, and when that isn't sufficient she demands to see the manager.*

As my daughter and I are waiting to be checked out, I can't help noticing all these rude people standing around us. I am quick to point out these characteristics to her, and she in turn informs me of one other class of people who tend to be very rude. ~~It's a shame people have to be so rude while waiting in check-out lines. My daughter informed me of one other class of people who tend to be very rude.~~

People Who Stare

These people have a habit of standing in line, eyes fixed upon someone, giving them the once-over. Their eyes move up and down the person taking in every *little* movement and quirk, reading the lines in their faces and trying to guess their personality.

"Mom," my daughter says quietly, "you're staring again, and that's rude."

Commentary: Judy has made three major kinds of revision by her penciled-in changes: First, she has made her examples more specific and therefore more interesting. Instead of referring vaguely to "some item" that the slowpoke examines and then decides to return to the shelf, Judy refers specifically to a pair of gloves. Similarly, she adds two more examples to illustrate the behavior of grouches: they tend to swat their children in public and they tend to bicker with the sales personnel.

A second important change is the improved transition to the witty conclusion in which Judy uses herself as an example of the final category of rude shoppers: people who stare.

A third category of changes involves Judy's effort to achieve consistent agreement between her pronouns and their antecedents. In ordinary speech we often use indefinite pronouns as if they were plural: "Everyone has their own opinion about politics." Actually such a sentence poses two problems in agreement. By convention indefinite pronouns like *everyone, anyone, one,* and *each* are conceived to be singular. Thus, one should write, "Everyone has his own opinion about politics." Increasingly, however, the masculine possessive pronoun *his* is thought to be sexist, so some writers substitute the phrase "his or her" for "his." More and more, however, such sentences are recast in the plural: "All people have their own opinion about politics." But if the people are now plural, shouldn't there be more than one "opinion"? That is, shouldn't the agreement problems finally be resolved by a thoroughly consistent use of either singular nouns and pronouns or plural nouns and pronouns? One way to do so is to revise the sentence to read: "All people have their own opinions about politics." The problems of agreement that we have just described can be complex and difficult to resolve, and many of Judy's changes in her rough draft result from her awareness of these difficulties and her attempts to resolve them.

FINAL DRAFT

"SPEEDY, SLOWPOKE, GROUCHY, AND ME"

by Judy Perrin

Outline

Division and Classification

Topic — People waiting in line

Principle of classification – Rude people waiting in check-out lines

Thesis — One can encounter four types of rude people waiting in check-out lines.

Classification of rude people

1. People who take their time

   Characteristics: slow-moving, unconcerned about others.

2. People who are grouches

   Characteristics: discourteous, running over others, impatient.

3. People who are grouches

   Characteristics: frowners, mothers with children, grumpy or bored husbands.

4. People who stare

   Characteristics: me pursuing my pastime — staring.

Shopping happens to be one of my favorite pastimes, much to my husband's dismay. Often as I'm waiting in a check-out line my eyes tend to wander, and I find myself engrossed in another favorite pastime: people-watching. I could spend hours gazing at people. I take in every little movement and quirk, reading the lines in their faces, while trying to guess their personalities. Very often I have noticed how rude people are while they are waiting in check-out lines. Generally this rudeness occurs during the Christmas season. Lines are often long and slow moving during this time so I am able to pick out these rude people easily.

People Who Take Their Time

Usually there is always at least one of these people standing in line. You've seen her before. She is the one who is undecided about a pair of gloves in her shopping cart. She picks the gloves up and examines them carefully. She places them back in her cart, shakes her head, picks them up again and proceeds to return them to the shelf. She leaves her shopping cart in line and disappears. You can't move her cart out of line for that would be rude, so everyone waits for her to return. Finally she arrives with a different pair of gloves and she has also acquired a friend along the way. Now the slowpoke and the friend are engaged in a deep conversation, not noticing the cashier clearing her throat and tapping on the counter as she waits to check them out. Slowpoke finally gets the message and begins to unload the items from her cart onto the counter. The check-out girl informs the customer that an item she is purchasing is on sale today: two for the price of one. So Slowpoke wanders off to get the extra item, leaving distressed looks on the faces of the other people in line. After a long absence she returns, and everyone is praying that nothing else she is purchasing is on sale. The amount is rung up and Slowpoke begins to go through her wallet. Much to her dismay, she doesn't have enough cash on hand. Now she'll have to write a check if she can find her checkbook. After a thorough search (which can mean dumping the entire contents of her purse onto the counter) she finally locates it, and very slowly makes out the check while the rest of the people in line are silently cheering.

People in a Hurry

Woe to anyone who happens to be in front of the person in a hurry. For some reason he tends to use his shopping cart as a battering ram. He wants to hurry everyone along, so very gently he nudges the person in front of him, moving her up an inch or so. A chain reaction occurs and everyone in line has been moved up a couple of inches; but he is in a hurry, and one little nudge won't do it, so he backs his cart up and rams the person ahead of him again, clipping her heels this time.

Usually Speedy receives a dirty look, which is a sign to "cut it out!"

If you've ever noticed, these people are constantly tapping their fingers on the handles of shopping carts, looking at their watches every few minutes, shifting from one foot to the other, and making little noises that sound as though they're gasping for air. As they finally reach the cashier, they exclaim, "Well it's about time!" Then they proceed to show everyone how quick checking-out can be. It always tickles me when an item they're purchasing doesn't have a price marked on it, and they have to wait until someone can price it.

People Who Are Grouches

These people are easy to spot. They have deep furrows in their foreheads from frowning all the time. They never have a nice word to say to anyone. Often these people are mothers who have a handful of children with them. Children will be children, but these people are not in the mood for the antics of children while standing in line. They proceed to scream warnings to the little ones in very unladylike language, disregarding everyone else in line. When all else fails, next comes the swatting of little hands, legs, and bottoms—and more threats.

Many times the grouch has a bone to pick with the cashier. She is either dissatisfied with the service or some item she is returning. She proceeds to give the cashier a piece of her mind, and when that isn't sufficient, she demands to see the manager. After expounding her views, she stomps off with her nose in the air.

Often these people are husbands who have decided to help their wives with the shopping. They stand in line and grouch and grumble about the price of everything, the crowds, the rudeness of the sales personnel, and the long line they're standing in. The wives are embarrassed because of their husbands' rude blustering, the people in line feel sorry for the wives, and the cashier feels sorry for herself because she gets the pleasure of checking out these old grouches.

As my daughter and I are waiting to be checked out, I can't help noticing all these rude people standing around us. I am quick to point out these characteristics to her, and she in turn informs me of one other class of people who tend to be very rude.

People Who Stare

These people have a habit of standing in line, eyes fixed upon someone, giving them the once-over. Their eyes move up and down the person taking in every movement and quirk, reading the lines in their faces and trying to guess their personalities.

"Mom," my daughter says quietly, "you're staring again, and that's rude."

How to Lie with Statistics
Darrell Huff

Darrell Huff (1913–   ) was born in Guthrie, Iowa, and educated at the University of Iowa in Iowa City. He began his career in 1936, before graduation, as a reporter for the Clinton, Iowa, *Herald* and then went on to hold a series of editing jobs with increasing responsibility with *Look* magazine, the D. C. Cook Publishing Company, and *Better Homes and Gardens* magazine, before turning exclusively to free-lance writing. Although best known for his book *How to Lie with Statistics* (1954), Huff has also written *Twenty Careers of Tomorrow* (1945), *How to Take a Chance* (1959), *Cycles in Your Life* (1964), and *Complete Book of Home Improvement* (1970). Note the use of headings in this excerpt to identify the various classifications of misuse of statistics.

1   "The average Yaleman, Class of '24," *Time* magazine noted once, commenting on something in the New York *Sun*, "makes $25,111 a year."

2   Well, good for him!

3   But wait a minute. What does this improbably precise and salubrious figure mean? Is it, as it appears to be, evidence that if you send your boy to Yale you won't have to work in your old age and neither will he? Is this average a mean or is it a median? What kind of sample is it based on? You could lump one Texas oilman with two hundred hungry free-lance writers and report *their* average income as $25,000-odd a year. The arithmetic is impeccable, the figure is convincingly precise, and the amount of meaning there is in it you could put in your eye.

4   In just such ways is the secret language of statistics, so appealing in a fact-minded culture, being used to sensationalize, inflate, confuse, and

oversimplify. Statistical terms are necessary in reporting the mass data of social and economic trends, business conditions, "opinion" polls, this year's census. But without writers who use the words with honesty and understanding and readers who know what they mean, the result can only be semantic nonsense.

In popular writing on scientific research, the abused statistic is   5 almost crowding out the picture of the white-jacketed hero laboring overtime without time-and-a-half in an ill-lit laboratory. Like the "little dash of powder, little pot of paint," statistics are making many an important fact "look like what she ain't." Here are some of the ways it is done.

THE SAMPLE WITH THE BUILT-IN BIAS

Our Yalemen, as they say in the Time-Life building, belong to this   6 flourishing group. The exaggerated estimate of their income is not based on all members of the class nor on a random or representative sample of them. At least two interesting categories of 1924-model Yale men have been excluded.

First there are those whose present addresses are unknown to their   7 classmates. Wouldn't you bet that these lost sheep are earning less than the boys from prominent families and the others who can be handily reached from a Wall Street office?

There are those who chucked the questionnaire into the nearest   8 wastebasket. Maybe they didn't answer because they were not making enough money to brag about. Like the fellow who found a note clipped to his first paycheck suggesting that he consider the amount of his salary confidential: "Don't worry," he told the boss. "I'm just as ashamed of it as you are."

Omitted from our sample then are just two groups most likely to   9 depress the average. The $25,111 figure is beginning to account for itself. It may indeed be a true figure for those of the Class of '24 whose addresses are known and who are willing to stand up and tell how much they earn. But even that requires a possibly dangerous assumption that the gentlemen are telling the truth.

To be dependable to any useful degree at all, a sampling study must   10 use a representative sample (which can lead to trouble too) or a truly random one. If *all* the Class of '24 is included, that's all right. If every tenth name on a complete list is used, that is all right too, and so is drawing an adequate number of names out of a hat. The test is this: Does every name in the group have an equal chance to be in the sample?

This leads to a moral: You can prove about anything you want to by   11 letting your sample bias itself. As a consumer of statistical data—a reader, for example, of a news magazine—remember that no statistical conclusion can rise above the quality of the sample it is based upon. In the absence of information about the procedures behind it, you are not warranted in giving any credence at all to the result.

THE TRUNCATED, OR GEE-WHIZ, GRAPH

12   If you want to show some statistical information quickly and clearly, draw a picture of it. Graphic presentation is the thing today. If you don't mind misleading the hasty looker, or if you quite clearly *want* to deceive him, you can save some space by chopping the bottom off many kinds of graphs.

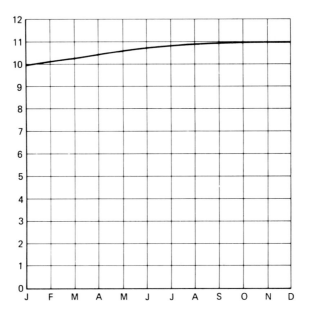

13   Suppose you are showing the upward trend of national income month by month for a year. The total rise, as in one recent year, is 10 percent. It looks like the graph above. That is clear enough. Anybody can see that the trend is slightly upward. You are showing a 10 percent increase and that is exactly what it looks like.

14   But it lacks schmaltz. So you chop off the bottom, this way:

The figures are the same and so is the curve. It is the same graph. Nothing has been falsified—except the impression that it gives. But what the hasty reader sees now is a national-income line that has climbed halfway up the paper in twelve months, all because most of the chart isn't there any more. Like the missing parts of speech in sentences that you met in grammar classes, it is "understood." Of course, the eye doesn't "understand" what isn't there, and a small rise has become, visually, a big one.

THE SOUPED-UP GRAPH

Sometimes truncating is not enough. The trifling rise in something or 15 other still looks almost as insignificant as it is. You can make that 10 percent look livelier than 100 percent ordinarily does. Simply change the proportion between the ordinate and the abscissa. There's no rule against it, and it does give your graph a prettier shape. All you have to do is let each mark up the side stand for only one-tenth as many dollars as before. That *is* impressive, isn't it? Anyone looking at it can just feel prosperity throbbing in the arteries of the country. It is a subtler equivalent of editing "National income rose 10 percent" into ". . . climbed a whopping 10 percent." It is vastly more effective, however, because it contains no adjectives or adverbs to spoil the illusion of objectivity. There's nothing anyone can pin on you.

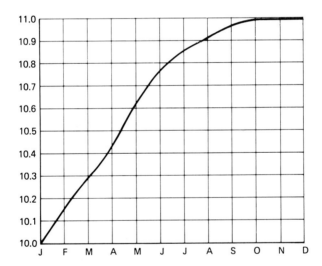

THE WELL-CHOSEN AVERAGE

I live near a country neighborhood for which I can report an average 16 income of $15,000. I could also report it as $3,500.

If I should want to sell real estate hereabouts to people having a 17 high snobbery content, the first figure would be handy. The second figure, however, is one to use in an argument against raising taxes, or the local bus fare.

Both are legitimate averages, legally arrived at. Yet it is obvious that 18 at least one of them must be as misleading as an out-and-out lie. The $15,000 figure is a mean, the arithmetic average of the incomes of all the families in the community. The smaller figure is a median; it might be called the income of the average family in the group. It indicates that half the families have less than $3,500 a year and half have more.

19   Here is where some of the confusion about averages comes from. Many human characteristics have the grace to fall into what is called the "normal" distribution. If you draw a picture of it, you get a curve that is shaped like a bell. Mean and median fall at about the same point, so it doesn't make very much difference which you use.

20   But some things refuse to follow this neat curve. Income is one of them. Incomes for most large areas will range from under $1,000 a year to upward of $50,000. Almost everybody will be under $10,000, way over on the left-hand side of that curve.

21   One of the things that made the income figure for the "average Yaleman" meaningless is that we are not told whether it is a mean or a median. It is not that one type of average is invariably better than the other; it depends upon what you are talking about. But neither gives you any real information—and either may be highly misleading—unless you know which of those kinds of average it is.

22   In the country neighborhood I mentioned, almost everyone has less than the average—the mean, that is—of $15,000. These people are all small farmers, except for a trio of millionaire weekenders who bring up the mean enormously.

23   You can be pretty sure that when an income average is given in the form of a mean nearly everybody has less than that.

THE INSIGNIFICANT DIFFERENCE
OR THE ELUSIVE ERROR

24 Your two children Peter and Linda (we might as well give them modish names while we're about it) take intelligence tests. Peter's I.Q., you learn, is 98 and Linda's is 101. Aha! Linda is your brighter child.

25   Is she? An intelligence test is, or purports to be, a sampling of intellect. An I.Q., like other products of sampling, is a figure with a statistical error, which expresses the precision of reliability of the figure. The size of this probable error can be calculated. For their test the makers of the much-used Revised Stanford-Binet have found it to be about 3 percent. So Peter's indicated I.Q. of 98 really means only that there is an even chance that it falls between 95 and 101. There is an equal probability that it falls somewhere else—below 95 or above 101. Similarly, Linda's has no better than a fifty-fifty chance of being within the fairly sizable range of 98 to 104.

26   You can work out some comparisons from that. One is that there is rather better than one chance in four that Peter, with his lower I.Q. rating, is really at least three points smarter than Linda. A statistician doesn't like to consider a difference significant unless you can hand him odds a lot longer than that.

27   Ignoring the error in a sampling study leads to all kinds of silly conclusions. There are magazine editors to whom readership surveys are

gospel; with a 40 percent readership reported for one article and a 35 percent for another, they demand more like the first. I've seen even smaller differences given tremendous weight, because statistics are a mystery and numbers are impressive. The same thing goes for market surveys and so-called public opinion polls. The rule is that you cannot make a valid comparison between two such figures unless you know the deviations. And unless the difference between the figures is many times greater than the probable error of each, you have only a guess that the one appearing greater really is.

Otherwise you are like the man choosing a camp site from a report   28 of mean temperature alone. One place in California with a mean annual temperature of 61 is San Nicolas Island on the south coast, where it always stays in the comfortable range between 47 and 87. Another with a mean of 61 is in the inland desert, where the thermometer hops around from 15 to 104. The deviation from the mean marks the difference, and you can freeze or roast if you ignore it.

THE ONE-DIMENSIONAL PICTURE

Suppose you have just two or three figures to compare — say the average   29 weekly wage of carpenters in the United States and another country. The sums might be $60 and $30. An ordinary bar chart makes the difference graphic. That is an honest picture. It looks good for American carpenters, but perhaps it does not have quite the oomph you are after. Can't you make that difference appear overwhelming and at the same time give it what I am afraid is known as eye appeal? Of course you can. Following tradition, you represent these sums by pictures of money bags. If the $30 bag is one inch high, you draw the $60 bag two inches high. That's in proportion, isn't it?

The catch is, of course, that the American's money bag, being twice   30 as tall as that of the $30 man, covers an area on your page four times as great. And since your two-dimensional picture represents an object that would in fact have three dimensions, the money bags actually would differ much more than that. The volumes of any two similar solids vary as

the cubes of their heights. If the unfortunate foreigner's bag holds $30 worth of dimes, the American's would hold not $60 but a neat $240.

31   You didn't say that, though, did you? And you can't be blamed; you're only doing it the way practically everybody else does.

THE EVER-IMPRESSIVE DECIMAL

32   For a spurious air of precision that will lend all kinds of weight to the most disreputable statistics, consider the decimal.

33   Ask a hundred citizens how many hours they slept last night. Come out with a total of, say 7.813. Your data are far from precise to begin with. Most people will miss their guess by fifteen minutes or more and some will recall five sleepless minutes as half a night of tossing insomnia.

34   But go ahead, do your arithmetic, announce that people sleep an average of 7.813 hours a night. You will sound as if you knew precisely what you are talking about. If you were foolish enough to say 7.8 (or "almost 8") hours it would sound like what it was — an approximation.

THE SEMIATTACHED FIGURE

35   If you can't prove what you want to prove, demonstrate something else and pretend that they are the same thing. In the daze that follows the collision of statistics with the human mind, hardly anybody will notice that difference. The semiattached figure is a durable device guaranteed to stand you in good stead. It always has.

36   If you can't prove that your nostrum cures colds, publish a sworn laboratory report that the stuff killed 31,108 germs in a test tube in eleven seconds. There may be no connection at all between assorted germs in a test tube and the whatever-it-is that produces colds, but people aren't going to reason that sharply, especially while sniffling.

Maybe that one is too obvious and people are beginning to catch on. 37
Here is a trickier version.

Let us say that in a period when race prejudice is growing it is to 38
your advantage to "prove" otherwise. You will not find it a difficult
assignment.

Ask that usual cross section of the population if they think Negroes 39
have as good a chance as white people to get jobs. Ask again a few
months later. As Princeton's Office of Public Opinion Research has
found out, people who are most unsympathetic to Negroes are the ones
most likely to answer yes to this question.

As prejudice increases in a country, the percentage of affirmative 40
answers you will get to this question will become large. What looks on
the face of it like growing opportunity for Negroes actually is mounting
prejudice and nothing else. You have achieved something rather remarkable: the worse things get, the better your survey makes them look.

THE UNWARRANTED ASSUMPTION, OR *POST HOC* RIDES AGAIN

The interrelation of cause and effect, so often obscure anyway, can be 41
most neatly hidden in statistical data.

Somebody once went to a good deal of trouble to find out if ciga- 42
rette smokers make lower college grades than nonsmokers. They did.
This naturally pleased many people, and they made much of it.

The unwarranted assumption, of course, was that smoking had pro- 43
duced dull minds. It seemed vaguely reasonable on the face of it, so it
was quite widely accepted. But it really proved nothing of the sort, any
more than it proved that poor grades drive students to the solace of
tobacco. Maybe the relationship worked in one direction, maybe in the
other. And maybe all this is only an indication that the sociable sort of
fellow who is likely to take his books less than seriously is also likely to
sit around and smoke many cigarettes.

Permitting statistical treatment to befog causal relationships is little 44
better than superstition. It is like the conviction among the people of the
Hebrides that body lice produce good health. Observation over the
centuries had taught them that people in good health had lice and sick
people often did not. *Ergo*, lice made a man healthy. Everybody should
have them.

Scantier evidence, treated statistically at the expense of common 45
sense, has made many a medical fortune and many a medical article in
magazines, including professional ones. More sophisticated observers
finally got things straightened out in the Hebrides. As it turned out,
almost everybody in those circles has lice most of the time. But when a
man took a fever (quite possibly carried to him by those same lice) and
his body became hot, the lice left.

Here you have cause and effect not only reversed but intermingled. 46

There you have a primer in some ways to use statistics to deceive. A 47
well-wrapped statistic is better than Hitler's "big lie": it misleads, yet it
can't be pinned onto you.

48   Is this little list altogether too much like a manual for swindlers? Perhaps I can justify it in the manner of the retired burglar whose published reminiscences amounted to a graduate course in how to pick a lock and muffle a footfall: The crooks already know these tricks. Honest men must learn them in self-defense.

Questions on Content

1. What does Huff demonstrate through the statistic that "[t]he average Yaleman, Class of '24, . . . makes $25,111 a year"?
2. What conclusion does Huff reach about the use of a biased sample?
3. How can a reader be misled by graphs that actually present accurate information?
4. How can the average annual income in a particular neighborhood be *both* $15,000 and $3,500? What do you need to know in order to make sense of these averages?
5. When comparing two statistics, why is it essential to have some measure of standard deviation?
6. How does Huff defend himself against the charge that his essay is "altogether too much like a manual for swindlers"?

Questions on Thesis, Purpose, and Structure

1. Consider the headings in this essay. What do those headings indicate about the structure of Huff's essay? Is he providing a process analysis about "how to lie with statistics" or is he attempting to classify the various forms of misleading statistics?
2. What techniques does Huff use to clarify and develop each of his classifications? What does he do to make each category both entertaining and informative?
3. Does Huff follow any clear-cut, logical order in presenting his categories? Can you create other logical ways of ordering the classifications?

Questions on Style and Diction

1. Find the following words in the essay and determine their definitions in context: salubrious, mean, median, impeccable (paragraph 3); semantic (paragraph 4); credence (paragraph 11); truncating (paragraph 15); spurious (paragraph 32); nostrum (paragraph 36).
2. When we first see the word *statistics* in Huff's title, our spirits may sink a bit in anticipation of a dreary technical essay. How does Huff make his essay more interesting through his choices in diction and imagery?

Ideas for Essays

1. Analyze the use of statistics in a single issue of some popular newsmagazine. Does the magazine use statistics fairly and accurately or does it abuse them in many of the ways outlined in Huff's article?
2. Conduct an informal survey among your classmates on some issue of particular interest to you. Then write a brief report about the results of your survey, using the manipulative techniques outlined by Huff. Finally, rewrite your report, being careful to indicate all the limitations, inaccuracies, and potential distortions of your survey results.

◇◇◇

Salutation Displays
Desmond Morris

Desmond Morris (1928–   ) was born in a rural county in the southern part of England and educated at Birmingham University and Oxford University. A zoologist by training, Morris began his career by studying animal behavior as a member of the staff of the London Zoo and then as curator of mammals for the Zoological Society of London. His interest in animal behavior, which led him to consider human behavior as well, has resulted in such books as *The Naked Ape: A Zoologist's Study of the Human Animal* (1967), *The Human Zoo* (1970), *Manwatching: A Field Guide to Human Behavior* (1977), and *Gestures: Their Origins and Distributions* (1979). Much of Morris's success results from his ability to make science accessible to a general reading audience. In "Salutation Displays," from *Manwatching*, Morris classifies human signals of greeting and departure and explains the nonverbal messages carried by these displays.

A Salutation Display demonstrates that we wish people well, or, at the very least, that we wish them no harm. It transmits signals of friendliness or the absence of hostility. It does this at peak moments — when people are arriving on the scene, departing from it, or dramatically changing their social role. We salute their comings, their goings and their transformations, and we do it with rituals of greeting, farewell and celebration. 1

Whenever two friends meet after a long separation, they go through a special Greeting Ritual. During the first moments of the reunion they amplify their friendly signals to super-friendly signals. They smile and touch, often embrace and kiss, and generally behave more intimately and expansively than usual. They do this because they have to make up for lost time — lost friendship time. While they have been apart it has been impossible for them to send the hundreds of small, minute-by-minute friendly signals to each other that their relationship requires, and they have, so to speak, built up a backlog of these signals. 2

This backlog amounts to a gestural debt that must be repaid without delay, as an assurance that the bond of friendship has not waned but has survived the passage of time spent apart — hence the gushing ceremonies of the reunion scene, which must try to pay off this debt in a single outburst of activity. 3

Once the Greeting Ritual is over, the old relationship between the friends is now re-established and they can continue with their amicable interactions as before. Eventually, if they have to part for another long spell, there will be a Separation Ritual in which the super-friendly signals will once again be displayed. This time they have the function of leaving both partners with a powerful dose of befriendedness, to last them through the isolated times to come. 4

In a similar way, if people undergo a major change in social role, we again offer them a massive outpouring of friendliness, because we are simultaneously saying farewell to their old self and greeting their new self. We do this when boy and girl become man and wife, when man and wife become father and mother, when prince becomes king, when candidate becomes president, and when competitor becomes champion. 5

6   We have many formal procedures for celebrating these occasions, both the physical arrivals and departures and the symbolic comings and goings of the social transformations. We celebrate birthdays, christenings, comings-of-age, weddings, coronations, anniversaries, inaugurations, presentations, and retirements. We give house-warmings, welcoming parties, farewell dinners, and funerals. In all these cases we are, in essence, performing Salutation Displays.

7   The grander the occasion, the more rigid and institutional are the procedures. But even our more modest, private, two-person rituals follow distinct sets of rules. We seem to be almost incapable of beginning or ending any kind of encounter without performing some type of salutation. This is even true when we write a letter to someone. We begin with "Dear Mr. Smith" and end "Yours faithfully," and the rules of salutation are so compelling that we do this even when Mr. Smith is far from dear to us and we have little faith in him.

8   Similarly we shake hands with unwelcome guests and express regret at their departure, although we are glad to see the back of them. All the more reason, then, that our genuine greetings and farewells should be excessively demonstrative.

9   Social greetings that are planned and anticipated have a distinctive structure and fall into four separate phases:

10   1. The Inconvenience Display. To show the strength of our friendliness, we "put ourselves out" to varying degrees. We demonstrate that we are taking trouble. For both host and guest, this may mean "dressing up." For the guest it may mean a long journey. For the host it also entails a bodily shift from the center of his home territory. The stronger the greeting, the greater the inconvenience. The Head of State drives to the airport to meet the important arrival. The brother drives to the airport to greet his sister returning from abroad. This is the maximum form of bodily displacement that a host can offer. From this extreme there is a declining scale of inconvenience, as the distance traveled by the host decreases. He may only go as far as the local station or bus depot. Or he may move no farther than his front drive, emerging from his front door after watching through the window for the moment of arrival. Or he may wait for the bell to ring and then only displace himself as far as his doorway or front hall. Or he may allow a child or servant to answer the door and remain in his room, the very center of his territory, awaiting the guest who is then ushered into his presence. The minimal Inconvenience Display he can offer is to stand up when the guest enters the room, displacing himself vertically but not horizontally. Only if he remains seated as the guest enters and approaches him, can he be said to be totally omitting Phase One of a planned social greeting. Such omissions are extremely rare today and some degree of voluntary inconvenience is nearly always demonstrated. If, because of some accident or delay, it is unavoidably omitted, there are profuse apologies for its absence when the meeting finally takes place.

11   At the time of farewell, the Inconvenience Display is repeated in much the same form. "You know your own way out" is the lowest level of expression here. Beyond that, there is an increasing displacement

from territorial base, with the usual social level being "I will see you to the door." A slightly more intense form involves going outside the house and waiting there until the departing figures have vanished from sight. And so on, with the full expression being an accompaniment to the station or airport.

2. The Distant Display. The main moment of greeting is when body contact is made, but before this comes the moment of first sighting. As soon as host and guest have identified each other, they signify this fact with a recognition response. Doorstep meetings tend to curtail this phase, because contact can be made almost immediately the door is opened, but in most other greeting situations the Distance Display is prominently demonstrated. It consists of six visual elements: (1) the Smile; (2) the Eyebrow Flash; (3) the Head Tilt; (4) the Hail; (5) the Wave; and (6) the Intention Embrace.

The first three of these almost always occur, and they are performed simultaneously. At the moment of recognition, the head tilts back, the eyebrows arch up, and the face breaks into a large smile. The Head Tilt and the Eyebrow Flash may be very brief. They are elements of surprise. Combined with the smile, they signal a "pleasant surprise" at seeing the friend. This basic pattern may or may not be augmented by an arm movement. The simplest such action is the Hail—the raising of one hand. A more intense version, typical of long-distance greetings, is the Wave, and a still more intense expression is the Intention Embrace, in which the arms are stretched out towards the friend, as if the greeter cannot wait to perform the contact-embrace that is about to take place. A flamboyant specialty sometimes added is the Thrown or Blown Kiss, again anticipating the contact to come.

As before, the same actions are repeated during the farewell Separation Ritual, but with Intention Embraces less likely and Thrown or Blown Kisses more likely.

Of these Distant Displays, the Smile, Head Tilt, and Eyebrow Flash appear to be worldwide. They have been observed in remote native tribes that had never previously encountered white men. The raising of an arm in some form of Hail or Wave salute is also extremely widespread. The exact form of the arm movement may vary from culture to culture, but the existence of *some* kind of arm action appears to be global for mankind. The action seems to stem, like the Intention Embrace, from an urge to reach out and touch the other person. In the Hail, the arm is raised up rather than reached out, because this makes it more conspicuous from a distance, but the movement is essentially a stylized version of touching the distant friend. More "historical" explanations, such as that the hand is raised to show it is empty of weapons or that it is thrust up to mime the action of offering the owner's sword, and therefore his allegiance, may be true in certain specific contexts, but the action is too widespread and too general for this interpretation to stand for all cases of Hailing.

The Wave takes three main forms: the Vertical Wave, the Hidden-palm Wave, and the Lateral Wave. In the Vertical Wave, the palm faces the friend and the hand moves repeatedly up and down. This appears to

12

13

14

15

16

be the "primitive" form of waving. In origin, it seems to be a vacuum patting action, the hand patting the friend's body at a distance, again in anticipation of the friendly embrace to come. The Hidden-palm Wave, seen mainly in Italy, is also a patting action, but with the hand moving repeatedly towards the waver himself. To non-Italians, this looks rather like beckoning, but it is basically another form of vacuum embracing. The Lateral Wave, common all over the world, consists of showing the palm to the friend and then moving it rhythmically from side to side. This appears to be an improved form of the other waves. The modification is essentially one of increasing the visibility and conspicuousness of the patting action. In turning it into a lateral movement, it loses its embracing quality, but gains dramatically in visual impact from a distance. It can be further exaggerated by extending it to full arm-waving, or even double-arm-waving.

17   3. The Close Display. As soon as the Distant Display has been performed, there is an approach interval and then the key moment of actual body contact. At full intensity this consists of a total embrace, bringing both arms around the friend's body, with frontal trunk contact and head contact. There is much hugging, squeezing, patting, cheek-pressing, and kissing. This may be followed by intense eye contact at close range, cheek-clasping, mouth-kissing, hair-stroking, laughing, even weeping, and, of course, continued smiling.

18   From this uninhibited display, there is a whole range of body-contacts of decreasing strength, right down to the formal handshake. The precise intensity will depend on: (1) the depth of the prior relationship; (2) the length of the separation; (3) the privacy of the greeting context; (4) the local, cultural display-rules and traditions; and (5) the changes that have taken place during the separation.

19   Most of these conditions are obvious enough, but the last deserves comment. If the friend is known to have been through some major emotional experience—an ordeal such as imprisonment, illness, or disaster, or a great success such as an award, a victory, or an honor— there will be a much more intense greeting and stronger embracing. This is because the Salutation Display is simultaneously a greeting and a celebration and is, in effect, double-strength.

20   Different cultures have formalized the close greeting performance in different ways. In all cases, the basis of the display is the full embrace, but when this is simplified, different parts of it are retained in different places. In some cultures, the head-to-head element becomes nose-rubbing, cheek-mouthing, or face-pressing. In others, there is a stylized mutual cheek-kiss, with the lips stopping short of contact. In others again, there is kissing between men—in France and Russia, for example—while in many cultures, male-to-male kissing is omitted as supposedly effeminate.

21   While these cultural variations are, of course, of interest, they should not be allowed to obscure the fact that they are all variations on a basic theme—the body embrace. This is the fundamental, global, human contact action, the one we all know as babies, infants, and growing children, and to which we return whenever the rules permit

and we wish to demonstrate feelings of attachment for another individual.

4. The "Grooming" Display. Following the initial body contacts, we move into the final stage of the greeting ceremony, which is similar to the social grooming performances of monkeys and apes. We do not pick at one another's fur, but instead we display "Grooming Talk"— inane comments that mean very little in themselves, but which demonstrate vocally our pleasure at the meeting. "How are you?" "How nice of you to come," "Did you have a good journey?" "You are looking so well," "Let me take your coat," and so on. The answers are barely heard. All that is important is to pay compliments and to receive them. To show concern and to show pleasure. The precise verbal content and the intelligence of the questions is almost irrelevant. This Grooming Display is sometimes augmented by helping with clothing, taking off coats, and generally fussing with creature comforts. On occasion there is an additional Gift Display on the part of the guest, who brings some small offering as a further, material form of salutation.

After the Grooming Display is over, the friends leave the special site of the greeting and move on to resume their old, familiar, social interactions. The Salutation Display is complete and has performed its important task.

By contrast, unplanned greetings are far less elaborate. When we see a friend in the street, or somewhere away from home, we give the typical Distant Display—a smile and a wave—and perhaps no more. Or we approach and add a Close Display, usually a rather abbreviated embrace, but more usually a mere handshake. As we part, we again display, often turning for a final Distant Signal, as we move off.

Introductory Greetings take yet another form. If we are meeting someone for the first time, we omit the Distant Display, simply because we are not recognizing an old friend. We do, however, offer a minor form of Close Display, nearly always a handshake, and we smile at the new acquaintance and offer him a Grooming Display of friendly chatter and concern. We treat him, in fact, as though he were a friend already, not a close one but a friend none the less, and in so doing we bring him into our orbit and initiate a social relationship with him.

As a species of primate, we are remarkably rich in greetings and farewells. Other primates do show some simple greeting rituals, but we exceed them all, and we also show farewell displays which they seem to lack entirely. Looking back into our ancestry, there seems to have been a good reason for this development. Most primates move around in a fairly close-knit group. Occasionally, they may drift apart and then, on reuniting, will give small gestures of greeting. But they rarely part deliberately, in a purposeful way, so they have no use for Separation Displays. Early man established himself as a hunting species, with the male hunting group leaving for a specific purpose at a specific time, and then returning to the home base with the kill. For millions of years, therefore, we have needed Salutation Displays, both in the form of farewells, as the group split up in its major division-of-labor, and in the form of greetings, when they came together again. And the importance of success or failure on the hunt meant that these were not trivial, but vital moments in the communal life of the primeval tribe. Little wonder that today we are such a salutatory species.

Questions on Content

1. What is the purpose of the salutation display, and what are the three basic occasions that evoke it?
2. Why do people engage in a greeting ritual?
3. What does Morris mean by an inconvenience display?
4. What is the distant display, and what are its main components?
5. What are the three main forms of the wave?
6. What is the close display, and what factors cause it to vary in intensity?
7. What is the "grooming" display in humans, and how is it like similar behavior in monkeys and apes?
8. What are the similarities and differences between planned and unplanned greetings?

Questions on Thesis, Purpose, and Structure

1. Examine the structure of the essay. Where does Morris use classification and subclassification? What is the principle of classification? How complete is the system of classification? Does Morris also use division? If so, where? What other patterns of development can you find in this essay?
2. What is Morris's thesis about salutation displays? How important is the final paragraph in both revealing and proving that thesis?
3. Discuss the combination of purposes in this essay. What makes the essay so informative? What makes it persuasive? Are any parts of it entertaining?

Questions on Style and Diction

1. Find the following words in the essay and determine their definitions in context: salutation (paragraph 1); expansively (paragraph 2); gestural, waned (paragraph 3); amicable (paragraph 4); entails, profuse (paragraph 10); curtail (paragraph 12); flamboyant (paragraph 13); beckoning (paragraph 16); inane (paragraph 22).
2. Why does Morris deviate from standard procedures in capitalization?
3. What level of education and sophistication does Morris seem to expect in his audience? Support your answer with arguments based on the essay's tone, diction, and style.

Ideas for Essays

1. Write an essay using classification or division about the rituals of human behavior in some other common circumstance. For example, you might consider human behavior at a football game, a fraternity party, a funeral, or a used car lot.
2. In this essay and in many of his other books, Morris frequently compares human behavior with that of other animals, particularly other primates. Are such comparisons generally valid and useful or demeaning and potentially harmful? Write an essay expressing and supporting your opinion on this issue.

You Are What You Say

Robin Lakoff

Robin Lakoff (1942–   ) was born in Brooklyn, New York, and attended Radcliffe College, Indiana University, and Harvard University. Following the receipt of a Ph.D. in linguistics from Harvard in 1967, Lakoff joined the faculty of the University of Michigan. She has since taught at Stanford University and the University of California at Berkeley. She has published *Abstract Syntax and Latin Complementation* (1968) and *Language and Woman's Place* (1975), the latter being an exploration of the ways in which language, including the language that women themselves use, reveals and reinforces society's attitudes towards women. This, of course, is also the subject of "You Are What You Say," an essay first published in *Ms.* magazine. In this essay she categorizes the various attributes of "feminine" speech. Note that Lakoff also analyzes the implications of our choice of words in referring to men and women.

"Women's language" is that pleasant (dainty?), euphemistic, never-aggressive way of talking we learned as little girls. Cultural bias was built into the language we were allowed to speak, the subjects we were allowed to speak about, and the ways we were spoken of. Having learned our linguistic lesson well, we go out in the world, only to discover that we are communicative cripples—dammed if we do, and dammed if we don't.   1

If we refuse to talk "like a lady," we are ridiculed and criticized for being unfeminine. ("She thinks like a man" is, at best, a left-handed compliment.) If we do learn all the fuzzy-headed, unassertive language of our sex, we are ridiculed for being unable to think clearly, unable to take part in a serious discussion, and therefore unfit to hold a position of power.   2

It doesn't take much of this for a woman to begin feeling she deserves such treatment because of inadequacies in her own intelligence and education.   3

"Women's language" shows up in all levels of English. For example, women are encouraged and allowed to make far more precise discriminations in naming colors than men do. Words like *mauve, beige, ecru, acquamarine, lavender,* and so on, are unremarkable in a woman's active vocabulary, but largely absent from that of most men. I know of no evidence suggesting that women actually see a wider range of colors than men do. It is simply that fine discriminations of this sort are relevant to women's vocabularies, but not to men's; to men, who control most of the interesting affairs of the world, such distinctions are trivial—irrelevant.   4

In the area of syntax, we find similar gender-related peculiarities of speech. There is one construction, in particular, that women use conversationally far more than men: the tag-question. A tag is midway between an outright statement and a yes-no question; it is less assertive than the former, but more confident than the latter.   5

A *flat statement* indicates confidence in the speaker's knowledge and is fairly certain to be believed; a question indicates a lack of knowl-   6 edge on some point and implies that the gap in the speaker's knowledge can and will be remedied by an answer. For example, if, at a Little League game, I have had my glasses off, I can legitimately ask someone else: "Was the player out at third?" A *tag question*, being intermediate between statement and question, is used when the speaker is stating a claim, but lacks full confidence in the truth of that claim. So if I say, "Is Joan here?" I will probably not be surprised if my respondent answers "no"; but if I say, "Joan is here, isn't she?" instead, chances are I am already biased in favor of a positive answer, wanting only confirmation. I still want a response, but I have enough knowledge (or think I have) to predict that response. A tag question, then, might be thought of as a statement that doesn't demand to be believed by anyone but the speaker, a way of giving leeway, of not forcing the addressee to go along with the views of the speaker.

7   Another common use of tag-question is in small talk when the speaker is trying to elicit conversation: "Sure is hot here, isn't it?"

8   But in discussing personal feelings or opinions, only the speaker normally has any way of knowing the correct answer. Sentences such as "I have a headache, don't I" are clearly ridiculous. But there are other examples where it is the speaker's opinions, rather than perceptions, for which corroboration is sought, as in "The situation in Southeast Asia is terrible, isn't it?"

9   While there are, of course, other possible interpretations of a sentence like this, one possibility is that the speaker has a particular answer in mind — "yes" or "no" — but is reluctant to state it baldly. This sort of tag question is much more apt to be used by women than by men in conversation. Why is this the case?

10   The tag question allows a speaker to avoid commitment, and thereby avoid conflict with the addressee. The problem is that, by so doing, speakers may also give the impression of not really being sure of themselves, or looking to the addressee for confirmation of their views. This uncertainty is reinforced in more subliminal ways, too. There is a peculiar sentence intonation-pattern, used almost exclusively by women, as far as I know, which changes a declarative answer into a question. The effect of using the rising inflection typical of a yes-no question is to imply that the speaker is seeking confirmation, even though the speaker is clearly the only one who has the requisite information, which is why the question was put to her in the first place:

(Q)   When will dinner be ready?
(A)   Oh . . . around six o'clock . . . ?

It is as though the second speaker were saying, "Six o'clock — if that's okay with you, if you agree." The person being addressed is put in the position of having to provide confirmation. One likely consequence of this sort of speech-pattern in a woman is that, often unbeknownst to herself, the speaker builds a reputation of tentativeness, and others will refrain from taking her seriously or trusting her with any real responsibilities since she "can't make up her mind," and "isn't sure of herself."

Such idiosyncrasies may explain why women's language sounds   11
much more "polite" than men's. It is polite to leave a decision open, not
impose your mind, or views, or claims, on anyone else. So a tag-question
is a kind of polite statement, in that it does not force agreement or belief
on the addressee. In the same way a request is a polite command, in that
it does not force obedience on the addressee, but rather suggests something to be done as a favor to the speaker. A clearly stated order implies a
threat of certain consequences if it is not followed, and — even more
impolite — implies that the speaker is in a superior position and able to
enforce the order. By couching wishes in the form of a request, on the
other hand, a speaker implies that if the request is not carried out, only
the speaker will suffer; noncompliance cannot harm the addressee. So
the decision is really up to the addressee. The distinction becomes clear
in these examples:

Close the door.
Please close the door.
Will you close the door?
Will you please close the door?
Won't you close the door?

In the same ways as words and speech patterns used *by* women   12
undermine her image, those used to *describe* women make matters even
worse. Often a word may be used of both men and women (and perhaps
of things as well); but when it is applied to women, it assumes a special
meaning that, by implication rather than outright assertion, is derogatory
to women as a group.

The use of euphemisms has this effect. A euphemism is a substitute   13
for a word that has acquired a bad connotation by association with
something unpleasant or embarrassing. But almost as soon as the new
word comes into common usage, it takes on the same old bad connotations, since feelings about the things or people referred to are not
altered by a change of name: thus new euphemisms must be constantly
found.

There is one euphemism for *woman* still very much alive. The   14
word, of course, is *lady*. *Lady* has a masculine counterpart, namely
gentleman, occasionally shortened to *gent*. But for some reason *lady* is
very much commoner than *gent(leman)*. The decision to use *lady* rather
than *woman*, or vice versa, may considerably alter the sense of a sentence, as the following examples show:

(a) A woman (lady) I know is a dean at Berkeley.   15
(b) A woman (lady) I know makes amazing things out of shoelaces   16
and old boxes.

The use of *lady* in (a) imparts a frivolous, or nonserious, tone to the   17
sentence: the matter under discussion is not one of great moment.
Similarly, in (b), using *lady* here would suggest that the speaker considered the "amazing things" not to be serious art, but merely a hobby or an
aberration. If *woman* is used, she might be a serious sculptor. To say
lady doctor is very condescending, since no one ever says *gentleman
doctor* or even *man doctor*. For example, mention in the San Francisco
Chronicle of January 31, 1972, of Madalyn Murray O'Hair as the *lady*

atheist reduces her position to that of scatterbrained eccentric. Even *woman atheist* is scarcely defensible: sex is irrelevant to her philosophical position.

18   Many women argue that, on the other hand, *lady* carries with it overtones recalling the age of chivalry: conferring exalted stature on the person so referred to. This makes the term seem polite at first, but we must also remember that these implications are perilous: they suggest that a "lady" is helpless, and cannot do things by herself.

19   *Lady* can also be used to imply frivolousness, as in titles of organizations. Those that have a serious purpose (not merely that of enabling "the ladies" to spend time with one another) cannot use the word *lady* in their titles, but less serious ones may. Compare the *Ladies' Auxiliary* of a men's group, or the *Thursday Evening Ladies' Browning and Garden Society* with *Ladies' Liberation* or *Ladies' Strike for Peace*. What is curious about this split is that *lady* is in origin a euphemism—a substitute that puts a better face on something people find uncomfortable—for *woman*. What kind of euphemism is it that subtly denigrates the people to whom it refers? Perhaps *lady* functions as a euphemism for *woman* because it does not contain the sexual implications present in *woman*; it is not "embarrassing" in that way. If this is so, we may expect that, in the future, *lady* will replace woman as the primary word for the human female, since *woman* will have become too blatantly sexual. That this distinction is already made in some contexts at least is shown in the following examples, where you can try replacing *woman* with *lady*.

20   (a) She's only twelve, but she's already a woman.
21   (b) After ten years in jail, Harry wanted to find a woman.
22   (c) She's my woman, see, so don't mess around with her.

23   Another common substitute for *woman* is *girl*. One seldom hears a man past the age of adolescence referred to as a boy, save in expressions like "going out with the boys," which are meant to suggest an air of adolescent frivolity and irresponsibility. But women of all ages are "girls": one can have a man—not a boy—Friday, but only a girl—never a woman or even a lady—Friday; women have girlfriends, but men do not—in a nonsexual sense—have boyfriends. It may be that this use of *girl* is euphemistic in the same way the use of *lady* is; in stressing the idea of immaturity, it removes the sexual connotations lurking in *woman*. *Girl* brings to mind irresponsibility; you don't send a girl to do a woman's errand (or even, for that matter, a boy's errand). She is a person who is both too immature and too far from real life to be entrusted with responsibilities or with decisions of any serious or important nature.

24   Now let's take a pair of words which, in terms of the possible relationships in an earlier society, were simple male-female equivalents, analogous to *bull: cow*. Suppose we find that, for independent reasons, society has changed in such a way that the original meanings now are irrelevant. Yet the words have not been discarded, but have acquired new meanings, metaphorically related to their original senses. But suppose these new metaphorical uses are no longer parallel to each other. By seeing where the parallelism breaks down, we discover something

about the different roles played by men and women in this culture. One good example of such a divergence through time is found in the pair, *master: mistress*. Once used with reference to one's power over servants, these words have become unusable today in their original master-servant sense as the relationship has become less prevalent in our society. But the words are still common.

Unless used with reference to animals, *master* now generally refers   25
to a man who has acquired consummate ability in some field, normally nonsexual. But its feminine counterpart cannot be used this way. It is practically restricted to its sexual sense of "paramour." We start out with two terms, both roughly paraphrasable as "one who has power over another." But the masculine form, once one person is no longer able to have absolute power over another, becomes usable metaphorically in the sense of "having power over *something*." *Master* requires as its object only the name of some activity, something inanimate and abstract. But *mistress* requires a masculine noun in the possessive to precede it. One cannot say: "Rhonda is a mistress." One must be *someone's* mistress. A man is defined by what he does, a woman by her sexuality, that is, in terms of one particular aspect of her relationship to men. It is one thing to be an *old master* like Hans Holbein, and another to be an *old mistress*. The same is true of the words *spinster* and *bachelor*—gender words for "one who is not married." The resemblance ends with the definition. While *bachelor* is a neuter term often used as a compliment, *spinster* normally is used pejoratively, with connotations of prissiness, fussiness, and so on. To be a bachelor implies that one has the choice of marrying or not, and this is what makes the idea of a bachelor existence attractive, in the popular literature. He has been pursued and has successfully eluded his pursuers. But a spinster is one who has not been pursued, or at least not seriously. She is old, unwanted goods. The metaphorical connotations of *bachelor* generally suggest sexual freedom; of *spinster*, puritanism or celibacy.

These examples could be multiplied. It is generally considered a   26
faux pas, in society, to congratulate a woman on her engagement, while it is correct to congratulate her fiancé. Why is this? The reason seems to be that it is impolite to remind people of things that may be uncomfortable to them. To congratulate a woman on her engagement is really to say, "Thank goodness! You had a close call!" For the man, on the other hand, there was no such danger. His choosing to marry is viewed as a good thing, but not something essential.

The linguistic double standard holds throughout the life of the   27
relationship. After marriage, bachelor and spinster become man and wife, not man and woman. The woman whose husband dies remains "John's widow"; John, however, is never "Mary's widower."

Finally, why is it that salesclerks and others are so quick to call   28
women customers "dear," "honey," and other terms of endearment they really have no business using? A male customer would never put up with it. But women, like children, are supposed to enjoy these endearments, rather than being offended by them.

In more ways than one, it's time to speak up.   29

Questions on Content

1. What point does Lakoff make about the fine distinctions in the names of colors that are part of "women's language"? Can you think of other implications that could be drawn from the same observation?
2. What is a tag-question and what does the frequent use of tag-questions reveal about women's roles?
3. How can intonation be used to create a question out of a statement? What impression is created by the use of such questions?
4. Why does Lakoff object to the use of the word *lady* in many circumstances?
5. What points does Lakoff make about the common habit of referring to grown women as girls?
6. How have the meanings of the words *master* and *mistress* changed? What does this change suggest about the perceptions of women?

Questions on Thesis, Purpose, and Structure

1. In her opening paragraph Lakoff asserts that as a result of cultural bias, women become "communicative cripples—damned if we do, and damned if we don't." Why is that assertion useful in her introduction? What, exactly, does Lakoff mean by it? Does she prove her point by the end of the essay?
2. Why does Lakoff contrast the implications of statements, questions, and tag-questions?
3. Lakoff creates two major classifications in this essay and then creates several subclassifications under each main heading. Create an outline revealing these classifications and subclassifications. How logical is the structure of the essay? How complete is the system of classification and subclassification?
4. How would you describe the balance of purposes in Lakoff's essay? How much emphasis does she place on informing the reader? Persuading the reading? Entertaining the reader?

Questions on Style and Diction

1. Find the following words in the essay and determine their definitions in context: euphemistic (paragraph 1); mauve, ecru, lavender (paragraph 4); elicit (paragraph 7); corroboration (paragraph 8); subliminal (paragraph 10); noncompliance (paragraph 11); derogatory (paragraph 12); aberration, condescending (paragraph 17); denigrates (paragraph 19); paramour, pejoratively (paragraph 25).
2. Occasionally, Lakoff's essay bogs down in phrases of scholarly precision. Identify a few sentences that strike you as too labored and rewrite them more informally. Do you think that what is lost in precision is compensated for by the gain in simplicity?

Ideas For Essays

1. Write an imitation (or parody) of the forms of linguistic analysis used by Lakoff. You might try to argue, for example, that our habits in speaking to and about children demonstrate our scorn for them as thinking, worthwhile human beings. Or you might analyze the characteristics of speech referring to pets, pests, cars, computers, or virtually anything else.
2. Write a careful critique of Lakoff's prose style. In doing so be sure to use a logical system of subdivision by examining, for example, her diction, imagery, tone, and sentence structure.

◇◇◇

Thinking as a Hobby
William Golding

William Golding (1911–   ) was born in Cornwall on the southwestern coast
of England and educated at Oxford. Although best known for his novel *Lord of
the Flies* (1954), the dark and somber account of the savagery that overtakes a
group of English schoolboys abandoned on a desert island during a global war,
Golding is also an accomplished writer of short stories, poems, plays, and
essays. These cumulative achievements earned Golding the Nobel Prize for
Literature in 1983. Although "Thinking as a Hobby" (1961) is primarily a
narrative essay, note the way Golding defines three categories of thinkers in
the course of his story.

1　　While I was still a boy, I came to the conclusion that there were
three grades of thinking; and since I was later to claim thinking as my
hobby, I came to an even stranger conclusion—namely, that I myself
could not think at all.

2　　I must have been an unsatisfactory child for grownups to deal with. I
remember how incomprehensible they appeared to me at first, but not,
of course, how I appeared to them. It was the headmaster of my grammar
school who first brought the subject of thinking before me—though
neither in the way, nor with the result he intended. He had some
statuettes in his study. They stood on a high cupboard behind his desk.
One was a lady wearing nothing but a bath towel. She seemed frozen in
an eternal panic lest the bath towel slip down any farther; and since she
had no arms, she was in an unfortunate position to pull the towel up
again. Next to her, crouched the statuette of a leopard, ready to spring
down at the top drawer of a filing cabinet labeled A-AH. My innocence
interpreted this as the victim's last, despairing cry. Beyond the leopard
was a naked, muscular gentleman, who sat, looking down, with his chin
on his fist and his elbow on his knee. He seemed utterly miserable.

3　　Some time later, I learned about these statuettes. The headmaster
had placed them where they would face delinquent children, because
they symbolized to him the whole of life. The naked lady was the Venus
of Milo. She was Love. She was not worried about the towel. She was just
busy being beautiful. The leopard was Nature, and he was being natural.
The naked, muscular gentleman was not miserable. He was Rodin's
Thinker, an image of pure thought. It is easy to buy small plaster models
of what you think life is like.

4　　I had better explain that I was a frequent visitor to the headmaster's
study, because of the latest thing I had done or left undone. As we now
say, I was not integrated. I was, if anything, disintegrated; and I was
puzzled. Grownups never made sense. Whenever I found myself in a
penal position before the headmaster's desk, with the statuettes glimmering whitely above him, I would sink my head, clasp my hands
behind my back and writhe one shoe over the other.

5　　The headmaster would look opaquely at me through flashing
spectacles.

6　　"What are we going to do with you?"

7　　Well, what *were* they going to do with me? I would writhe my shoe
some more and stare down at the worn rug.

8   "Look up, boy! Can't you look up?"

9   Then I would look up at the cupboard, where the naked lady was frozen in her panic and the muscular gentleman contemplated the hind-quarters of the leopard in endless gloom. I had nothing to say to the headmaster. His spectacles caught the light so that you could see nothing human behind them. There was no possibility of communication.

10   "Don't you ever think at all?"

11   No, I didn't think, wasn't thinking, couldn't think—I was simply waiting in anguish for the interview to stop.

12   "Then you'd better learn—hadn't you?"

13   On one occasion the headmaster leaped to his feet, reached up and plonked Rodin's masterpiece on the desk before me.

14   "That's what a man looks like when he's really thinking."

15   I surveyed the gentleman without interest or comprehension.

16   "Go back to your class."

17   Clearly there was something missing in me. Nature had endowed the rest of the human race with a sixth sense and left me out. This must be so, I mused, on my way back to the class, since whether I had broken a window, or failed to remember Boyle's Law, or been late for school, my teachers produced me one, adult answer: "Why can't you think?"

18   As I saw the case, I had broken the window because I had tried to hit Jack Arney with a cricket ball and missed him; I could not remember Boyle's Law because I had never bothered to learn it; and I was late for school because I preferred looking over the bridge into the river. In fact, I was wicked. Were my teachers, perhaps, so good that they could not understand the depths of my depravity? Were they clear, untormented people who could direct their every action by this mysterious business of thinking? The whole thing was incomprehensible. In my earlier years, I found even the statuette of the Thinker confusing. I did not believe any of my teachers were naked, ever. Like someone born deaf, but bitterly determined to find out about sound, I watched my teachers to find out about thought.

19   There was Mr. Houghton. He was always telling me to think. With a modest satisfaction, he would tell me that he had thought a bit himself. Then why did he spend so much time drinking? Or was there more sense in drinking than there appeared to be? But if not, and if drinking were in fact ruinous to health—and Mr. Houghton was ruined, there was no doubt about that—why was he always talking about the clean life and the virtues of fresh air? He would spread his arms wide with the action of a man who habitually spent his time striding along mountain ridges.

20   "Open air does me good, boys—I know it!"

21   Sometimes, exalted by his own oratory, he would leap from his desk and hustle us outside into a hideous wind.

22   "Now boys! Deep breaths! Feel it right down inside you—huge draughts of God's good air!"

23   He would stand before us, rejoicing in his perfect health, an open-air man. He would put his hands on his waist and take a tremendous breath. You could hear the wind, trapped in the cavern of his chest and struggling with all the unnatural impediments. His body would reel with

shock and his ruined face go white at the unaccustomed visitation. He would stagger back to his desk and collapse there, useless for the rest of the morning.

Mr. Houghton was given to high-minded monologues about the good life, sexless and full of duty. Yet in the middle of one of these monologues, if a girl passed the window, tapping along on her neat little feet, he would interrupt his discourse, his neck would turn of itself and he would watch her out of sight. In this instance, he seemed to me ruled not by thought but by an invisible and irresistible spring in his nape. 24

His neck was an object of great interest to me. Normally it bulged a bit over his collar. But Mr. Houghton had fought in the First World War alongside both Americans and French, and had come—by who knows what illogic?—to a settled detestation of both countries. If either country happened to be prominent in current affairs, no argument could make Mr. Houghton think well of it. He would bang the desk, his neck would bulge still further and go red. "You can say what you like," he would cry, "but I've thought about this—and I know what I think!" 25

Mr. Houghton thought with his neck. 26

There was Miss Parsons. She assured us that her dearest wish was our welfare, but I knew even then, with the mysterious clairvoyance of childhood, that what she wanted most was the husband she never got. There was Mr. Hands—and so on. 27

I have dealt at length with my teachers because this was my introduction to the nature of what is commonly called thought. Through them I discovered that thought is often full of unconscious prejudice, ignorance and hypocrisy. It will lecture on disinterested purity while its neck is being remorselessly twisted toward a skirt. Technically, it is about as proficient as most businessmen's golf, as honest as most politicians' intentions, or—to come near my own preoccupation—as coherent as most books that get written. It is what I came to call grade-three thinking, though more properly, it is feeling, rather than thought. 28

True, often there is a kind of innocence in prejudices, but in those days I viewed grade-three thinking with an intolerant contempt and an incautious mockery. I delighted to confront a pious lady who hated the Germans with the proposition that we should love our enemies. She taught me a great truth in dealing with grade-three thinkers; because of her, I no longer dismiss lightly a mental process which for nine-tenths of the population is the nearest they will ever get to thought. They have immense solidarity. We had better respect them, for we are outnumbered and surrounded. A crowd of grade-three thinkers, all shouting the same thing, all warming their hands at the fire of their own prejudices, will not thank you for pointing out the contradictions in their beliefs. Man is a gregarious animal, and enjoys agreement as cows will graze all the same way on the side of a hill. 29

Grade-two thinking is the detection of contradictions. I reached grade two when I trapped the poor, pious lady. Grade-two thinkers do not stampede easily, though often they fall into the other fault and lag behind. Grade-two thinking is a withdrawal, with eyes and ears open. It 30 became my hobby and brought satisfaction and loneliness in either hand. For grade-two thinking destroys without having the power to create. It set me watching the crowds cheering His Majesty and King and asking myself what all the fuss was about, without giving me anything positive to put in the place of that heady patriotism. But there were compensations. To hear people justify their habit of hunting foxes and tearing them to pieces by claiming that the foxes liked it. To hear our Prime Minister talk about the great benefit we conferred on India by jailing people like Pandit Nehru and Gandhi. To hear American politicians talk about peace in one sentence and refuse to join the League of Nations in the next. Yes, there were moments of delight.

31   But I was growing toward adolescence and had to admit that Mr. Houghton was not the only one with an irresistible spring in his neck. I, too, felt the compulsive hand of nature and began to find that pointing out contradiction could be costly as well as fun. There was Ruth, for example, a serious and attractive girl. I was an atheist at the time. Grade-two thinking is a menace to religion and knocks down sects like skittles. I put myself in a position to be converted by her with an hypocrisy worthy of grade three. She was a Methodist—or at least, her parents were, and Ruth had to follow suit. But, alas, instead of relying on the Holy Spirit to convert me, Ruth was foolish enough to open her pretty mouth in argument. She claimed that the Bible (King James Version) was literally inspired. I countered by saying that the Catholics believed in the literal inspiration of Saint Jerome's *Vulgate*, and the two books were different. Argument flagged.

32   At last she remarked that there were an awful lot of Methodists, and they couldn't be wrong, could they—not all those million? That was too easy, said I restively (for the nearer you were to Ruth, the nicer she was to be near to) since there were more Roman Catholics than Methodists anyway; and they couldn't be wrong, could they—not all those hundreds of millions? An awful flicker of doubt appeared in her eyes. I slid my arm around her waist and murmured breathlessly that if we were counting heads, the Buddhists were the boys for my money. But Ruth had *really* wanted to do me good, because I was so nice. She fled. The combination of my arm and those countless Buddhists was too much for her.

33   That night her father visited my father and left, red-cheeked and indignant. I was given the third degree to find out what had happened. It was lucky we were both of us only fourteen. I lost Ruth and gained an undeserved reputation as a potential libertine.

34   So grade-two thinking could be dangerous. It was in this knowledge, at the age of fifteen, that I remember making a comment from the heights of grade two, on the limitations of grade three. One evening I found myself alone in the school hall, preparing it for a party. The door of the headmaster's study was open. I went in. The headmaster had ceased to thump Rodin's Thinker down on the desk as an example to the young. Perhaps he had not found any more candidates, but the statuettes were still there, glimmering and gathering dust on top of the cupboard. I stood on a chair and rearranged them. I stood Venus in her bath towel on

the filing cabinet, so that now the top drawer caught its breath in a gasp of sexy excitement. "A-ah!" The portentous Thinker I placed on the edge of the cupboard so that he looked down at the bath towel and waited for it to slip.

Grade-two thinking, though it filled life with fun and excitement, did not make for content. To find out the deficiencies of our elders bolsters the young ego but does not make for personal security. I found that grade two was not only the power to point out contradictions. It took the swimmer some distance from the shore and left him there, out of his depth. I decided that Pontius Pilate was a typical grade-two thinker. "What is truth?" he said, a very common grade-two thought, but one that is used always as the end of an argument instead of the beginning. There is still a higher grade of thought which says, "What is truth?" and sets out to find it.   35

But these grade-one thinkers were few and far between. They did not visit my grammar school in the flesh though they were there in books. I aspired to them, partly because I was ambitious and partly because I now saw my hobby as an unsatisfactory thing if it went no further. If you set out to climb a mountain, however high you climb, you have failed if you cannot reach the top.   36

I *did* meet an undeniably grade-one thinker in my first year at Oxford. I was looking over a small bridge in Magdalen Deer Park, and a tiny mustached and hatted figure came and stood by my side. He was a German who had just fled from the Nazis to Oxford as a temporary refuge. He name was Einstein.   37

But Professor Einstein knew no English at that time and I knew only two words of German. I beamed at him, trying wordlessly to convey by my bearing all the affection and respect that the English felt for him. It is possible—and I have to make the admission—that I felt here were two grade-one thinkers standing side by side; yet I doubt if my face conveyed more than a formless awe. I would have given my Greek and Latin and French and a good slice of my English for enough German to communicate. But we were divided; he was as inscrutable as my headmaster. For perhaps five minutes we stood together on the bridge, undeniable grade-one thinker and breathless aspirant. With true greatness, Professor Einstein realized that any contact was better than none. He pointed to a trout wavering in midstream.   38

He spoke: "*Fisch.*"   39

My brain reeled. Here I was, mingling with the great, and yet helpless as the veriest grade-three thinker. Desperately I sought for some sign by which I might convey that I, too, revered pure reason. I nodded vehemently. In a brilliant flash I used up half of my German vocabulary.   40

"*Fisch. Ja Ja.*"   41

For perhaps another five minutes we stood side by side. Then Professor Einstein, his whole figure still conveying good will and amiability, drifted away out of sight.   42

I, too, would be a grade-one thinker. I was irreverent at the best of times. Political and religious systems, social customs, loyalties and tradi-   43 tions, they all came tumbling down like so many rotten apples off a tree. This was a fine hobby and a sensible substitute for cricket, since you could play it all the year round. I came up in the end with what must always remain the justification for grade-one thinking, its sign, seal and charter. I devised a coherent system for living. It was a moral system, which was wholly logical. Of course, as I readily admitted, conversion of the world to my way of thinking might be difficult, since my system did away with a number of trifles, such as big business, centralized government, armies, marriage. . . .

44   It was Ruth all over again. I had some very good friends who stood by me, and still do. But my acquaintances vanished, taking the girls with them. Young women seemed oddly contented with the world as it was. They valued the meaningless ceremony with a ring. Young men, while willing to concede the chaining sordidness of marriage, were hesitant about abandoning the organizations which they hoped would give them a career. A young man on the first rung of the Royal Navy, while perfectly agreeable to doing away with big business and marriage, got as red-necked as Mr. Houghton when I proposed a world without any battle-ships in it.

45   Had the game gone too far? Was it a game any longer? In those prewar days, I stood to lose a great deal, for the sake of a hobby.

46   Now you are expecting me to describe how I saw the folly of my ways and came back to the warm nest, where prejudices are so often called loyalties, where pointless actions are hallowed into custom by repetition, where we are content to say we think when all we do is feel.

47   But you would be wrong. I dropped my hobby and turned professional.

48   If I were to go back to the headmaster's study and find the dusty statuettes still there, I would arrange them differently. I would dust Venus and put her aside, for I have come to love her and know her for the fair thing she is. But I would put the Thinker, sunk in his desperate thought, where there were shadows before him—and at his back, I would put the leopard, crouched and ready to spring.

Questions on Content

1. What kind of thinking was typical of Golding's early teachers—the people who harped most relentlessly about the need for clear thought?
2. What kind of thinker does Golding become in response to his schoolmasters?
3. Who is the grade-one thinker that Golding meets and what is the nature of their interaction?

Questions on Thesis, Purpose, and Structure

1. Golding's essay focuses on episodes from three broad periods in his life. How does he differ as a thinker in each of these periods?
2. What is the symbolic significance, if any, of Golding's inability to communicate with Einstein, the only indisputably grade-one thinker he had ever encountered?
3. Golding describes three different arrangements of the statuettes at different

points in the essay. How is each arrangement (or Golding's interpretation of it) indicative of his own evolving thinking processes?
4. Should this be called a narrative essay or a classification essay? Defend your opinion.

Questions on Style and Diction

1. Find the following words in the essay and determine their definitions in context: incomprehensible (paragraph 2); integrated, disintegrated, penal (paragraph 4); opaquely (paragraph 5); depravity (paragraph 18); impediments (paragraph 23), detestation (paragraph 25); clairvoyance (paragraph 27); remorselessly (paragraph 28); solidarity, gregarious (paragraph 29); restively (paragraph 32); aspirant (paragraph 38); amiability (paragraph 42).
2. Examine the diction in the two paragraphs on Ruth (paragraphs 31 and 32). Is Golding guilty of holding sexist attitudes? If so, is that sexism an intentional part of his argument or a thoughtless but revealing indication of his true beliefs?
3. Both Golding and the headmaster use the statuettes as symbols. Discuss the meanings of those symbols and of any others that you find in the essay.

Ideas for Essays

1. Use Golding's classification system as the framework for an essay on a particular group of contemporary thinkers. Some groups to consider are the following: novelists, politicians, musicians, poets, scientists, clergymen, news reporters, commentators, and so on.
2. Can you think of any subcategories of Golding's three categories? Are there, for example, different classifications of people who think with their necks? If so, write an essay in which you describe these different subclasses, illustrating each with specific examples.

Young Goodman Brown
Nathaniel Hawthorne

Nathaniel Hawthorne (1804–1864) was born in Salem, Massachusetts, into a family that could trace its roots far back into New England's past and included one of the judges who had presided over the famous Salem witch trials of 1692 and 1693. Following his graduation from Bowdoin College in 1825, Hawthorne returned to Salem and for years underwent a period of comparative seclusion during which he began to write the first of his richly allegorical and symbolic short stories dealing with questions of moral responsibility and human guilt. He later expanded on these themes in his famous novels *The Scarlet Letter* (1850), *The House of the Seven Gables* (1851), and *The Blithedale Romance* (1852). In "Young Goodman Brown" (1835), the central concerns of the story involve distinguishing between people who are committed to good and those who are committed to evil.

1   Young Goodman[1] Brown came forth at sunset, into the street of Salem village,[2] but put his head back, after crossing the threshold, to exchange a parting kiss with his young wife. And Faith, as the wife was aptly named, thrust her own pretty head into the street, letting the wind play with the pink ribbons of her cap, while she called to Goodman Brown.

2   "Dearest heart," whispered she, softly and rather sadly, when her lips were close to his ear, "prithee, put off your journey until sunrise, and sleep in your own bed to-night. A lone women is troubled with such dreams and such thoughts that she's afeard of herself sometimes. Pray, tarry with me this night, dear husband, of all nights in the year!"

3   "My love and my Faith," replied young Goodman Brown, "of all nights in the year, this one night must I tarry away from thee. My journey, as thou callest it, forth and back again, must needs be done 'twixt now and sunrise. What, my sweet, pretty wife, dost thou doubt me already, and we but three months married!"

4   "Then God bless you" said Faith with the pink ribbons, "and may you find all well, when you come back."

5   "Amen!" cried Goodman Brown. "Say thy prayers, dear Faith, and go to bed at dusk, and no harm will come to thee."

6   So they parted; and the young man pursued his way until, being about to turn the corner by the meeting-house, he looked back and saw the head of Faith still peeping after him, with a melancholy air, in spite of her pink ribbons.

7   "Poor little Faith!" thought he, for his heart smote him. "What a wretch am I, to leave her on such an errand! She talks of dreams, too. Methought, as she spoke, there was trouble in her face, as if a dream had warned her what work is to be done to-night. But no, no! 't would kill her to think it. Well; she's a blessed angel on earth; and after this one night, I'll cling to her skirts and follow her to Heaven."

8   With this excellent resolve for the future, Goodman Brown felt himself justified in making more haste on his present evil purpose. He had taken a dreary road, darkened by all the gloomiest trees of the forest, which barely stood aside to let the narrow path creep through, and closed immediately behind. It was as lonely as could be; and there is this peculiarity in such a solitude, that the traveller knows not who may be concealed by the innumerable trunks and the thick boughs overhead; so that, with lonely footsteps, he may yet be passing through an unseen multitude.

9   "There may be a devilish Indian behind every tree," said Goodman Brown to himself; and he glanced fearfully behind him, as he added, "What if the devil himself should be at my very elbow!"

10   His head being turned back, he passed a crook of the road, and looking forward again, beheld the figure of a man, in grave and decent

[1]A respectful title of address for individuals not of gentle birth.

[2]Located some sixteen miles northeast of Boston, the Puritan village of Salem, first settled in 1626, was the site of the famous witchcraft hysteria of 1691–1692. John Hathorne, one of Nathaniel Hawthorne's ancestors, presided over the Salem witch trials as a judge. The author himself was born in Salem in 1804.

attire, seated at the foot of an old tree. He arose at Goodman Brown's approach, and walked onward, side by side with him.

"You are late, Goodman Brown," said he. "The clock of the Old   11
South[3] was striking, as I came though Boston; and that is full fifteen minutes agone."

"Faith kept me back awhile," replied the young man, with a tremor   12
in his voice, caused by the sudden appearance of his companion, though not wholly unexpected.

It was now deep dusk in the forest, and deepest in that part of it   13
where these two were journeying. As nearly as could be discerned, the second traveller was about fifty years old, apparently in the same rank of life as Goodman Brown, and bearing a considerable resemblance to him, though perhaps more in expression than features. Still, they might have been taken for father and son. And yet, though the elder person was as simply clad as the younger, and as simple in manner too, he had an indescribable air of one who knew the world, and would not have felt abashed at the governor's dinner-table, or in King William's court,[4] were it possible that his affairs should call him thither. But the only thing about him that could be fixed upon as remarkable, was his staff, which bore the likeness of a great black snake, so curiously wrought, that it might almost be seen to twist and wriggle itself like a living serpent. This, of course, must have been an ocular deception, assisted by the uncertain light.

"Come, Goodman Brown!" cried his fellow-traveller. "This is a dull   14
pace for the beginning of a journey. Take my staff, if you are so soon weary."

"Friend," said the other, exchanging his slow pace for a full stop,   15
"having kept covenant by meeting thee here, it is my purpose now to return whence I came. I have scruples, touching the matter thou wot'st of."

"Sayest thou so?" replied he of the serpent, smiling apart. "Let us   16
walk on, nevertheless, reasoning as we go, and if I convince thee not, thou shalt turn back. We are but a little way in the forest, yet."

"Too far, too far!" exclaimed the goodman, unconsciously resum-   17
ing his walk. "My father never went into the woods on such an errand, nor his father before him. We have been a race of honest men and good Christians, since the days of the martyrs.[5] And shall I be the first of the name of Brown that ever took this path and kept—"

"Such company, thou wouldst say," observed the elder person,   18
interrupting his pause. "Well said, Goodman Brown! I have been as well acquainted with your family as with ever a one among the Puritans; and that's no trifle to say. I helped your grandfather, the constable, when he lashed the Quaker woman so smartly through the streets of Salem. And it was I that brought your father a pitchpine knot, kindled at my own

[3]Old South, the Third Church of Boston, was established in 1669.
[4]William of Orange (1650–1702) who together with Queen Mary II ruled England from 1689 until 1702.
[5]That is, since the period when Mary Tudor, the Catholic queen who ruled England from 1553 until 1558, systematically persecuted Protestants.

hearth, to set fire to an Indian village, in King Phillip's war.[6] They were my good friends, both; and many a pleasant walk have we had along this path, and returned merrily after midnight. I would fain be friends with you, for their sake."

19   "If it be as thou sayest," replied Goodman Brown, "I marvel they never spoke of these matters. Or, verily, I marvel not, seeing that the least rumor of the sort would have driven them from New England. We are a people of prayer and good works to boot, and abide no such wickedness."

20   "Wickedness or not," said the traveller with the twisted staff, "I have a very general acquaintance here in New England. The deacons of many a church have drunk the communion wine with me; the select-men, of divers towns, make me their chairman; and a majority of the Great and General Court[7] are firm supporters of my interest. The governor and I, too—but these are state secrets."

21   "Can this be so!" cried Goodman Brown, with a stare of amazement at his undisturbed companion. "Howbeit, I have nothing to do with the governor and council; they have their own ways, and are no rule for a simple husbandman[8] like me. But, were I to go on with thee, how should I meet the eye of that good old man, our minister, at Salem village? Oh, his voice would make me tremble, both Sabbath-day and lecture-day!"[9]

22   Thus far, the elder traveller had listened with due gravity, but now burst into a fit of irrepressible mirth, shaking himself so violently, that his snakelike staff actually seemed to wriggle in sympathy.

23   "Ha, ha, ha!" shouted he, again and again; then composing himself, "Well, go on, Goodman Brown, go on; but, prithee, don't kill me with laughing!"

24   "Well, then, to end the matter at once," said Goodman Brown, considerably nettled, "there is my wife, Faith. It would break her dear little heart; and I'd rather break my own!"

25   "Nay, if that be the case," answered the other, "e'en[10] go thy ways, Goodman Brown. I would not, for twenty old women like the one hobbling before us, that Faith should come to any harm."

26   As he spoke, he pointed his staff at a female figure on the path, in whom Goodman Brown recognized a very pious and exemplary dame, who had taught him his catechism in youth, and was still his moral and spiritual adviser, jointly with the minister and Deacon Gookin.

27   "A marvel, truly, that Goody[11] Cloyse should be so far in the wilderness, at nightfall!" said he. "But, with your leave, friend, I shall take a

---

[6]The Wampanoag Indians led by Metacom or King Philip waged a short-lived uprising against the New England colonists (1675–1676).

[7]Massachusetts' colonial legislature.

[8]Farmer; but here used in the sense of an ordinary citizen.

[9]New England Puritans set aside two days during the week for the preaching and hearing of sermons or lectures: the Sabbath, or Sunday, and lecture day, usually Wednesday or Thursday.

[10]Just.

[11]Short for "goodwife," the female equivalent of "goodman."

cut[12] through the woods, until we have left this Christian woman behind. Being a stranger to you, she might ask whom I was consorting with, and whither I was going."

"Be it so," said his fellow-traveller. "Betake you to the woods, and 28 let me keep the path."

Accordingly, the young man turned aside, but took care to watch his 29 companion, who advanced softly along the road, until he had come within a staff's length of the old dame. She, meanwhile, was making the best of her way, with singular speed for so aged a woman, and mumbling some indistinct words, a prayer, doubtless, as she went. The traveller put forth his staff, and touched her withered neck with what seemed the serpent's tail.

"The devil!" screamed the pious old lady. 30

"Then Goody Cloyse knows her old friend?" observed the traveller, 31 confronting her, and leaning on his writhing stick.

"Ah, forsooth, and is it your worship, indeed?" cried the good 32 dame. "Yea, truly is it, and in the very image of my old gossip,[13] Goodman Brown, the grandfather of the silly fellow that now is. But, would your worship believe it? my broomstick hath strangely disappeared, stolen, as I suspect, by that unhanged witch, Goody Cory,[14] and that, too, when I was all anointed with the juice of smallage and cinque-foil and wolf's-bane — "[15]

"Mingled with fine wheat and the fat of a new-born babe," said the 33 shape of old Goodman Brown.

"Ah, your worship knows the recipe," cried the old lady, cackling 34 aloud. "So, as I was saying, being all ready for the meeting, and no horse to ride on, I made up my mind to foot it; for they tell me there is a nice young man to be taken into communion to-night. But now your good worship will lend me your arm, and we shall be there in a twinkling."

"That can hardly be," answered her friend. "I may not spare you my 35 arm, Goody Gloyse, but here is my staff, if you will."

So saying, he threw it down at her feet, where, perhaps, it assumed 36 life, being one of the rods which its owner had formerly lent to the Egyptian Magi.[16] Of this fact, however, Goodman Brown could not take cognizance. He had cast his eyes in astonishment, and looking down again, beheld neither Goody Cloyse nor the serpentine staff, but his fellow-traveller alone, who waited for him as calmly as if nothing had happened.

[12]Short cut.

[13]Friend.

[14]Martha Cory, a member in good standing of the church at Salem, was accused, tried, and hung for witchcraft on September 22, 1692; her husband, Giles, was pressed to death with stones three days earlier for failing to plead guilty or not guilty to charges of wizardry. Sarah Cloyse (above) was jailed for witchcraft but later released. Both she and Martha Cory are referred to in contemporary court records as "Goody."

[15]Plants associated with the practice of witchcraft.

[16]The allusion is to the story of Aaron's rod, which when cast at the feet of Egypt's Pharaoh turns into a serpent. Summoning his magicians, pharoah orders them to follow Aaron's example: "For every man cast down his rod, and they became serpents. But Aaron's rod swallowed up their rods." See *Exodus* 7:8–12.

37   "That old woman taught me my catechism!" said the young man; and there was a world of meaning in this simple comment.

38   They continued to walk onward, while the elder traveller exhorted his companion to make good speed and persevere in the path, discoursing so aptly, that his arguments seemed rather to spring up in the bosom of his auditor, than to be suggested by himself. As they went he plucked a branch of maple, to serve for a walking-stick, and began to strip it of the twigs and little boughs, which were wet with evening dew. The moment his fingers touched them, they became strangely withered and dried up, as with a week's sunshine. Thus the pair proceeded, at a good free pace, until suddenly, in a gloomy hollow of the road, Goodman Brown sat himself down on the stump of a tree, and refused to go any farther.

39   "Friend," said he, stubbornly, "my mind is made up. Not another step will I budge on this errand. What if a wretched old woman do choose to got to the devil, when I thought she was going to Heaven! Is that any reason why I should quit my dear Faith, and go after her?"

40   "You will think better of this by and by," said his acquaintance, composedly. "Sit here and rest yourself awhile; and when you feel like moving again, there is my staff to help you along."

41   Without more words, he threw his companion the maple stick, and was as speedily out of sight as if he had vanished into the deepening gloom. The young man sat a few moments by the roadside, applauding himself greatly, and thinking with how clear a conscience he should meet the minister, in his morning walk, nor shrink from the eye of good old Deacon Gookin. And what calm sleep would be his, that very night, which was to have been spent so wickedly, but purely and sweetly now, in the arms of Faith! Amidst these pleasant and praiseworthy meditations, Goodman Brown heard the tramp of horses along the road, and deemed it advisable to conceal himself within the verge of the forest, conscious of the guilty purpose that had brought him thither, though now so happily turned from it.

42   On came the hoof-tramps and the voices of the riders, two grave old voices, conversing soberly as they drew near. These mingled sounds appeared to pass along the road, within a few yards of the young man's hiding-place; but owing, doubtless, to the depth of the gloom at that particular spot, neither the travellers nor their steeds were visible. Though their figures brushed the small boughs by the wayside, it could not be seen that they intercepted, even for a moment, the faint gleam from the strip of bright sky, athwart which they must have passed. Goodman Brown alternately crouched and stood on tiptoe, pulling aside the branches and thrusting forth his head as far as he durst, without discerning so much as a shadow. It vexed him the more, because he could have sworn, were such a thing possible, that he recognized the voices of the minister and Deacon Gookin, jogging along quietly, as they were wont to do, when bound to some ordination or ecclesiastical council. While yet within hearing, one of the riders stopped to pluck a switch.

43   "Of the two, reverend Sir," said the voice like the deacon's, "I had rather miss an ordination dinner than to-night's meeting. They tell me

that some of our community are to be here from Falmouth[17] and beyond, and others from Connecticut and Rhode Island; besides several of the Indian powwows,[18] who, after their fashion, know almost as much deviltry as the best of us. Moreover, there is a goodly young woman to be taken into communion."

"Mighty well, Deacon Goodkin!" replied the solemn old tones of the minister. "Spur up, or we shall be late. Nothing can be done, you know, until I get on the ground."   44

The hoofs clattered again, and the voices, talking so strangely in the empty air, passed on through the forest, where no church had ever been gathered, nor solitary Christian prayed. Whither, then, could these holy men be journeying, so deep into the heathen wilderness? Young Goodman Brown caught hold of a tree, for support, being ready to sink down on the ground, faint and over-burthened with the heavy sickness of his heart. He looked up to the sky, doubting whether there really was a Heaven above him. Yet, there was the blue arch, and the stars brightening in it.   45

"With Heaven above, and Faith below, I will yet stand firm against the devil!" cried Goodman Brown.   46

While he still gazed upward, into the deep arch of the firmament, and had lifted his hands to pray, a cloud, though no wind was stirring, hurried across the zenith, and hid the brightening stars. The blue sky was still visible, except directly overhead, where this black mass of cloud was sweeping swiftly northward. Aloft in the air, as if from the depths of the cloud, came a confused and doubtful sound of voices. Once, the listener fancied that he could distinguish the accents of townspeople of his own, men and women, both pious and ungodly, many of whom he had met at the communion table, and had seen others rioting at the tavern. The next moment, so indistinct were the sounds, he doubted whether he had heard aught but the murmur of the old forest, whispering without a wind. Then came a stronger swell of those familiar tones, heard daily in the sunshine, at Salem village, but never, until now, from a cloud at night. There was one voice, of a young woman, uttering lamentations, yet with an uncertain sorrow, and entreating for some favor, which, perhaps, it would grieve her to obtain. And all the unseen multitude, both saints and sinners, seemed to encourage her onward.   47

"Faith!" shouted Goodman Brown, in a voice of agony and desperation; and the echoes of the forest mocked him, crying—"Faith! Faith!" as if bewildered wretches were seeking her, all through the wilderness.   48

The cry of grief, rage, and terror was yet piercing the night, when the unhappy husband held his breath for a response. There was a scream, drowned immediately in a louder murmur of voices fading into far-off laughter, as the dark cloud swept away, leaving the clear and silent sky above Goodman Brown. But something fluttered lightly down through the air, and caught on the branch of a tree. The young man seized it and beheld a pink ribbon.   49

[17]Massachusetts seaport town on Cape Cod, located southeast of Boston and some seventy miles from Salem.
[18]Medicine men.

50   "My Faith is gone!" cried he, after one stupefied moment. "There is no good on earth, and sin is but a name. Come, devil! for to thee is this world given."

51   And maddened with despair, so that he laughed loud and long, did Goodman Brown grasp his staff and set forth again, at such a rate, that he seemed to fly along the forest path, rather than to walk or run. The road grew wilder and drearier, and more faintly traced, and vanished at length, leaving him in the heart of the dark wilderness, still rushing onward, with the instinct that guides mortal man to evil. The whole forest was peopled with frightful sounds: the creaking of the trees, the howling of wild beasts, and the yell of Indians; while, sometimes, the wind tolled like a distant church bell, and sometimes gave a broad roar around the traveller, as if all Nature was laughing him to scorn. But he was himself the chief horror of the scene, and shrank not from its other horrors.

52   "Ha! ha! ha!" roared Goodman Brown, when the wind laughed at him. "Let us hear which will laugh loudest! Think not to frighten me with your deviltry! Come witch, come wizard, come Indian powwow, come devil himself! and here comes Goodman Brown. You may as well fear him as he fear you!"

53   In truth, all through the haunted forest, there could be nothing more frightful than the figure of Goodman Brown. On he flew, among the black pines, brandishing his staff with frenzied gestures, now giving vent to an inspiration of horrid blasphemy, and now shouting forth such laughter, as set all the echoes of the forest laughing like demons around him. The fiend in his own shape is less hideous, than when he rages in the breast of man. Thus sped the demoniac on his course, until, quivering among the trees he saw a red light before him, as when the felled trunks and branches of a clearing have been set on fire, and throw up their lurid blaze against the sky, at the hour of midnight. He paused, in a lull of the tempest that had driven him onward, and heard the swell of what seemed a hymn, rolling solemnly from a distance, with the weight of many voices. He knew the tune. It was a familiar one in the choir of the village meeting-house. The verse died heavily away, and was lengthened by a chorus, not of human voices, but of all the sounds of the benighted wilderness, pealing in awful harmony together. Goodman Brown cried out; and his cry was lost to his own ear, by its unison with the cry of the desert.

54   In the interval of silence, he stole forward, until the light glared full upon his eyes. At one extremity of an open space, hemmed in by the dark wall of the forest, arose a rock, bearing some rude, natural resemblance either to an altar or a pulpit, and surrounded by four blazing pines their tops aflame, their stems untouched, like candles at an evening meeting. The mass of foliage, that had overgrown the summit of the rock, was all on fire, blazing high into the night, and fitfully illuminating the whole field. Each pendent twig and leafy festoon was in a blaze. As the red light arose and fell, a numerous congregation alternately shone forth, then disappeared in shadow, and again grew, as it were, out of the darkness, peopling the heart of the solitary woods at once.

"A grave and dark-clad company!" quoth Goodman Brown.   55

In truth, they were such. Among them, quivering to-and-fro, be-   56
tween gloom and splendor, appeared faces that would be seen, next day,
at the councilboard[19] of the province, and others which, Sabbath after
Sabbath, looked devoutly heavenward, and benignantly over the
crowded pews, from the holiest pulpits in the land. Some affirm, that the
lady of the governor[20] was there. At least, there were high dames well
known to her, and wives of honored husbands, and widows a great
multitude, and ancient maidens, all of excellent repute, and fair young
girls, who trembled lest their mothers should espy them. Either the
sudden gleams of light, flashing over the obscure field, bedazzled
Goodman Brown, or he recognized a score of the church members of
Salem village, famous for their especial sanctity. Good old Deacon
Gookin had arrived, and waited at the skirts of that venerable saint, his
revered pastor. But, irreverently consorting with these grave, reputable,
and pious people, these elders of the church, these chaste dames and
dewy virgins, there were men of dissolute lives and women of spotted
fame, wretches given over to all mean and filthy vice, and suspected
even of horrid crimes. It was strange to see, that the good shrank not
from the wicked, nor were the sinners abashed by the saints. Scattered,
also, among their pale-faced enemies, were the Indian priests, or powwows, who had often scared their native forest with more hideous
incantations than any known to English witchcraft.

"But, where is Faith?" thought Goodman Brown; and, as hope came   57
into his heart, he trembled.

Another verse of the hymn arose, a slow and mournful strain, such as   58
the pious love, but joined to words which expressed all that our nature
can conceive of sin, and darkly hinted at far more. Unfathomable to mere
mortals is the lore of fiends. Verse after verse was sung, and still the
chorus of the desert swelled between, like the deepest tone of a mighty
organ. And, with the final peal of that dreadful anthem, there came a
sound, as if the roaring wind, the rushing streams, the howling beasts,
and every other voice of the unconverted wilderness were mingling and
according with the voice of guilty man, in homage to the prince of all.
The four blazing pines threw up a loftier flame, and obscurely discovered shapes and visages of horror on the smokewreaths, above the
impious assembly. At the same moment, the fire on the rock shot redly
forth, and formed a glowing arch above its base, where now appeared a
figure. With reverence be it spoken, the apparition bore no slight simili-
tude, both in garb and manner, to some grave divine of the New England
churches.

"Bring forth the converts!" cried a voice, that echoed through the   59
field and rolled into the forest.

At the word, Goodman Brown stepped forth from the shadow of the   60
trees, and approached the congregation, with whom he felt a loathful

[19]The Governor's Council.

[20]The wife of Sir William Phips (1651–1695), Governor of Massachusetts, had been
accused of withchraft during the Salem hysteria.

brotherhood, by the sympathy of all that was wicked in his heart. He could have well-nigh sworn, that the shape of his own dead father beckoned him to advance, looking downward from a smoke-wreath, while a woman, with dim features of despair, threw out her hand to warn him back. Was it his mother? But he had no power to retreat one step, nor to resist, even in thought, when the minister and good old Deacon Gookin seized his arms, and led him to the blazing rock. Thither came also the slender form of a veiled female, led between Goody Cloyse, that pious teacher of the catechism, and Martha Carrier, who had received the devil's promise to be queen of hell.[21] A rampant hag was she! And there stood the proselytes, beneath the canopy of fire.

61   "Welcome, my children," said the dark figure, "to the communion of your race! Ye have found, thus young, your nature and your destiny. My children, look behind you!"

62   They turned; and flashing forth, as it were, in a sheet of flame, the fiendworshippers were seen; the smile of welcome gleamed darkly on every visage.

63   "There," resumed the same form, "are all whom ye have reverenced from youth. Ye deemed them holier than yourselves, and shrank from your own sin, contrasting it with their lives of righteousness and prayerful aspirations heavenward. Yet, here are they all, in my worshipping assembly! This night it shall be granted you to know their secret deeds; how hoary-bearded elders of the church have whispered wanton words to the young maids of their households; how many a woman, eager for widow's weeds, has given her husband a drink at bedtime, and let him sleep his last sleep in her bosom; how beardless youths have made haste to inherit their father's wealth; and how fair damsels — blush not, sweet ones! — have dug little graves in the garden, and bidden me, the sole guest, to an infant's funeral. By the sympathy of your human hearts for sin, ye shall scent out all the places — whether in church, bed-chamber, street, field, or forest — where crime has been committed, and shall exult to behold the whole earth one stain of guilt, one mighty blood-spot. Far more than this! It shall be yours to penetrate, in every bosom, the deep mystery of sin, the fountain of all wicked arts, and which inexhaustibly supplies more evil impulses than human power — than my power, at its utmost! — can make manifest in deeds. And now, my children, look upon each other."

64   They did so; and, by the blaze of the hell-kindled torches, the wretched man beheld his Faith, and the wife her husband, trembling before that unhallowed altar.

65   "Lo! there ye stand, my children," said the figure, in a deep and solemn tone, almost sad, with its despairing awfulness, as if his once

[21]Martha Carrier was another of the accused Salem witches. Cotton Mather (1663–1728), the famous Puritan minister who took an active role in the witchcraft controversies at Salem, concludes his account of her trial of August 2, 1692 in his *Wonders of the Invisible World* (1693) as follows: "this rampant hag . . . was the person of whom the confessions of the witches, and of her own children among the rest, agreed that the devil had promised her, she should be queen of hell." Martha Carrier was executed by hanging on Gallows Hill on August 19, 1692.

angelic nature could yet mourn for our miserable race. "Depending upon one another's hearts, ye had still hoped that virtue were not all a dream! Now are ye undeceived!—Evil is the nature of mankind. Evil must be your only happiness. Welcome, again, my children, to the communion of your race!"

"Welcome!" repeated the fiend-worshippers, in one cry of despair   66
and triumph.

And there they stood, the only pair, as it seemed, who were yet   67
hesitating on the verge of wickedness, in this dark world. A basin was hollowed, naturally, in the rock. Did it contain water, reddened by the lurid light? or was it blood? or, perchance a liquid flame? Herein did the Shape of Evil dip his hand, and prepare to lay the mark of baptism upon their foreheads, that they might be partakers of the mystery of sin, more conscious of the secret guilt of others, both in deed and thought, than they could now be of their own. The husband cast one look at his pale wife, and Faith at him. What polluted wretches would the next glance show them to each other, shuddering alike at what they disclosed and what they saw!

"Faith! Faith!" cried the husband, "Look up to heaven, and resist the   68
Wicked One!"

Whether Faith obeyed, he knew not. Hardly had he spoken, when   69
he found himself amid calm night and solitude, listening to a roar of the wind, which died heavily away through the forest. He staggered against the rock, and felt it chill and damp, while a hanging twig, that had been all on fire, besprinkled his cheek with the coldest dew.

The next morning, young Goodman Brown came slowly into the   70
street of Salem village staring around him like a bewildered man. The good old minister was taking a walk along the grave-yard, to get an appetite for breakfast and meditate his sermon, and bestowed a blessing, as he passed, on Goodman Brown. He shrank from the venerable saint, as if to avoid an anathema.[22] Old Deacon Gookin was at domestic worship, and the holy words of his prayer were heard through the open window. "What God doth the wizard pray to?" quoth Goodman Brown. Goody Cloyse, that excellent old Christian, stood in the early sunshine, at her own lattice, catechising a little girl, who had brought her a pint of morning's milk. Goodman Brown snatched away the child, as from the grasp of the fiend himself. Turning the corner by the meeting-house, he spied the head of Faith, with the pink ribbons, gazing anxiously forth, and bursting into such joy at sight of him that she skipt along the street, and almost kissed her husband before the whole village. But Goodman Brown looked sternly and sadly into her face, and passed on without a greeting.

Had Goodman Brown fallen asleep in the forest, and only dreamed   71
a wild dream of a witch-meeting?

Be it so, if you will. But, alas! it was a dream of evil omen for young   72
Goodman Brown. A stern, a sad, a darkly meditative, a distrustful, if not a desperate man did he become, from the night of that fearful dream. On

---

[22]Curse.

the Sabbath day, when the congregation was singing a holy psalm, he could not list, because an anthem of sin rushed loudly upon his ear, and drowned all the blessed strain. When the minister spoke from the pulpit, with power and fervid eloquence, and with his hand on the open Bible, of the sacred truths of our religion, and of saint-like lives and triumphant deaths, and of future bliss or misery unutterable, then did Goodman Brown turn pale, dreading lest the roof should thunder down upon the gray blasphemer and his hearers. Often, awaking suddenly at midnight, he shrank from the bosom of Faith, and at morning or eventide, when the family knelt down at prayer, he scowled, and muttered to himself, and gazed sternly at his wife, and turned away. And when he had lived long, and was borne to his grave, a hoary corpse, followed by Faith, an aged woman, and children and grand-children, a goodly procession, besides neighbors not a few, they carved no hopeful verse upon his tombstone; for his dying hour was gloom.

Questions on Content

1. What is the name of Goodman Brown's wife? Why is she "aptly named"? How long has she been married?
2. What is peculiar about the staff carried by the traveller who meets Goodman Brown shortly after he enters the woods? What does this staff suggest about the traveller?
3. Why does Goodman Brown at first think that Goody Cloyse is a good Christian woman? What does he learn about her from her conversation with the man with the staff?
4. What meeting has Goodman Brown promised to attend? Why is he reluctant to keep that promise?
5. What events persuade him to keep the appointment after all?
6. What happens when Goodman Brown urges Faith to "look up to heaven, and resist the wicked one"?

Questions on Thesis, Purpose, and Structure

1. Discuss the names of the characters. Which names have symbolic significance? Which names have historical significance? What thematic concerns are raised by these names?
2. Nearly every detail in the story has some symbolic or allegorical meaning in addition to its direct role in the action. Discuss, for example, the symbolic significance of the descriptions of the various settings in the story.
3. What are the promised benefits of communion with the devil? Judging from Goodman Brown's later life, does he reap those benefits? Does Goodman Brown successfully resist the temptation of the devil?
4. What are the main classification of people within this story? What is the result of allowing oneself to make (or even speculate on) such classifications?

Questions on Style and Diction

1. Find the following words in the story and determine their definitions in context: discerned, ocular (paragraph 13); covenant (paragraph 15); irrepressible (paragraph 22); nettled (paragraph 24); cognizance (paragraph 36);

pendent, festoon (paragraph 54); benignantly, affirm, dissolute, incantations (paragraph 56); proselytes (paragraph 60).
2. Closely study the wording of the final two paragraphs in the story. Does Hawthorne use irony in those paragraphs and, if so, what does that irony achieve?

Ideas for Essay

1. A fundamental premise of this text has been that readers wish to be informed, persuaded, or entertained—and that the best writing usually fulfills some combination of these needs. Write a detailed, analytical essay about the extent to which "Young Goodman Brown" informs, persuades, and entertains.
2. By the end of the story Goodman Brown believes that his own society is thoroughly corrupt and hypocritical. What about our society? Write an essay comparing the characters in Hawthorne's story with a selection of religious and political hypocrits of our own day. What can you conclude from such comparisons?

"It's Time to Celebrate Your Vacation. In Bermuda" "Tiga."

Classification and division are methods of organizing information and presenting it coherently. At times, as in the first of these advertisements, classification can be combined with causal analysis. In "It's Time to Celebrate . . ." the copywriter has attempted to classify the attractions of a vacation in Bermuda. These attractions are, of course, also the reasons why we might wish to go to Bermuda.

The second advertisement is an example of division. In first looking at the advertisement, we see a windsurfer planing toward us at high speed, amid much splash and spray—as if about to burst from the confines of the printed page. The text of the advertisement then subdivides the components of this exciting visual display into "the challenge," "the sailor," "the conditions," "the board," and "the company."

It's time to celebrate your vacation. In Bermuda.

Chances are, you've worked too hard and waited too long for your vacation for it to be anything less than extraordinary. So you deserve nothing less than Bermuda. Where the beaches are pink and beautiful. The golf greens are lush. And people are friendly, and speak your language.

1. Our beaches are so beautiful, they blush.
You may have expected to find lovely beaches on our island, but they're more than that. They're legendary—with sand as soft and pink as a bride's cheek, and water that's a most improbable crystal-line jewel-blue (which makes it perfect for scuba-diving, snorkeling, sailing, swimming, and all sorts of water sports).

2. Our greens are emerald gems.
Did you know we have more golf-per-acre in Bermuda than anywhere else in the world? Each of our seven courses has the lush-est greens, the fairest fairways, and breathtaking scenery.
And if golf's not your game, how about a set of tennis on a court ringed by oleander? Or taking off on a motorbike to take in the sights, from historic St. George's to the world's smallest drawbridge.

3. Not all our treasure is sunken.
Diving among the old shipwrecks around Bermuda is for the adventurous. Diving into our shops is for everyone.
And what finds you'll find—from all over the world: French perfumes. Swiss watches. German and Japanese cameras. Irish linens and Scottish cashmeres, to name but a few.
And while they may be treasures, they're not a fortune.

4. A little night magic.
How a Bermuda night dazzles! Start it at sunset, with Rum Swizzles sipped on a terrace. Then a fabulous dinner in one of our world-renowned restaurants. (The Continental cuisine is superb—but don't miss our Bermudian fare, such as Rockfish Chowder with Sherry Peppers.) And dance the rest of the night away under a Bermuda Moongate.

5. The sun isn't the only thing that keeps you warm.
Our sunny skies are outshone only by our sunny smiles. And we'll make you smile, too, when you see our exquisite accommodations—from deluxe hotels, to charming guest houses, to traditional Bermudian cottage colonies.
We're even close by—a mere 600 miles from North Carolina in the Atlantic. And never more than 2½ jet hours from your major East Coast cities, with convenient airline schedules. Send for our colour brochure or contact your Travel Agent today.

Couldn't you use a little Bermuda right now?

Bermuda

For a free Bermuda brochure, address your nearest Bermuda office.

Bermuda Department of Tourism
Suite 646, 630 5th Ave., New York, NY 10111
Suite 1010, 44 School St., Boston, MA 02108
Suite 1150, 300 North State St.,
Chicago, IL 60610
Suite 2008, 235 Peachtree St. N.E.,
Atlanta, GA 30303

Name _____
                          (please print)
Address _____
City _____
State _____ Zip _____

Courtesy of the Bermuda Department of Tourism and Foote, Cone & Belding

Ideas for Discussion and Writing

1. Consider the five numbered paragraphs. To what extent do these paragraphs classify the various appealing features of the Bermudas? To what extent do they provide a causal analysis of the reasons why you should consider a vacation in Bermuda? How persuasive is the advertisement?
2. What useful information about Bermuda is presented in this advertisement?
3. Consider the imagery and especially the similes and metaphors in the advertisement. Is that imagery sensually and emotionally appealing? Why?
4. Consider the visual impression made by the three photographs of island settings. How do the photographs cleverly demonstrate that Bermuda is just right for people of all ages? How do they contribute to the emphasis in the text on the range of activities for vacationers in Bermuda?
5. Note that the paragraph on Bermuda's proximity to the East Coast does not have much to do with "sunny skies" and "sunny smiles." Why do you think that the paragraph is included and placed in the important conclusive position even though it doesn't fit in with the heading?

The challenge.
   Offer "custom board" design, components
and performance at a very un-custom price.
The sailor.
   TIGA race team champion Alex Aguera for one. Or the novice
who wouldn't feel motivated by a board with "beginner" written all
over it.
   For anybody who wants a very fast, very powerful ride. And knows you
can get a premium board without paying a premium price.
The conditions.
   In heavy air, a controlled responsiveness. In competition, a pulse-pounding
acceleration. In the learning stage, a forgiving confidence builder. This board makes
you a little better on each trip. No matter how good you are.
The board.
   Arnaud DeRosnay design (from a prototype he sailed 110 miles from Key West to Cuba).
Double concave hull for quick planing, speed and exceptional pointing ability.
Vertical-cut, high-clew sail with lots of fat-head power. Adjustable
mast track.
   Every inch of this high-quality, high tech performer says, "this board
means business."
The company.
   AMF Alcort Sailboats, P.O. Box 1345, Waterbury, Connecticut 06725.
Write us for a full-color brochure and specs. For your nearest TIGA dealer,
call 1-800-223-1416.   Circle Reader Service No. 2

**AMF
Alcort
Sailboats**   © AMF Incorporated 1984

Courtesy of Funsport

Ideas for Discussion and Writing

1. Discuss the visual impact of this advertisement. What is the effect of the camera angle? What is achieved by letting the sailboard and its spray intrude into the white space of the text?
2. Discuss the five headings in the text. To what extent do these headings serve as subdivisions of the general situation portrayed in the advertisement (the announcement of a new sailboard)?
3. What subdivisions of *the sailor* and *the conditions* are considered in the text of the advertisement?
4. Examine the supporting details presented beneath each heading. What do they tell you about the quality and the price of the board?
5. Examine the diction in the advertisement. Is the advertisement pitched to the novice windsurfer or to someone who already knows a good deal about the sport? Support your opinion.

Chapter 11

COMPARISON AND CONTRAST

On Tuesdays you have four classes: political science, criminology, English composition, and history. During your 8:00 A.M. political science class, the instructor compares the foreign policy goals of the Carter administration and those of the Reagan administration. At 9:30 your criminology professor introduces a police officer and a trial lawyer who proceed to debate whether capital punishment or life imprisonment serves as a better deterrent to crime. In your English class at 12:30 you meet in groups to begin brainstorming on the topic, "Is it preferable to live in a small town or a large city?" Finally, at 2:00 P.M. in world history class you write an in-class essay on the topic, "Discuss the similarities and differences between the American Revolution and the overthrow of Philippine President Marcos in 1985."

What do these four class meetings have in common? Each involved comparisons. Throughout your college career and indeed throughout your life, you will repeatedly draw comparisons and reflect on them. When you dress in the morning you may need to choose which of several pairs of shoes to wear. At breakfast in the cafeteria you may confront dismaying choices: rubbery eggs or cold flapjacks? Warm orange juice or a squishy apple? Watery tea or the dregs of the coffee pot? If you watch the morning news, you may see a debate between two experts with contrasting views on South Africa. As you make your way to class, perhaps you choose to walk instead of taking the bus. Life is packed with unavoidable choices, and in the process of making the most important choices we are wise to draw comparisons.

The formal process of written comparison is our subject in this chapter. Note first that any two items under comparison will demonstrate both similarities and differences: Both rubbery eggs and cold flapjacks will fill your belly, but the eggs are greasier and slide down your gullet more easily. The balance you strike in your essay between comparisons and contrasts depends entirely on the nature of your sub-

Accademia, Florence/Alinari/Art Resource, NY

David (1440 – 1443) by Donatello (p. 376) and *David* (1503 – 1504) by Michel-angelo (above). Look up the story of David and Goliath in the Bible and then compare these two artistic representations of David. How are they alike? How do they differ? What different conceptions of David are displayed in each one? Which one seems to fit the biblical story better? Why?

Museo Nazionele del Bargello, Florence/Alinari/Art Resource, NY

ject and your assignment. You will rarely focus only on comparisons or only on contrasts.

Your primary purpose in developing a comparison will usually be to **persuade** your audience that one of the subjects being compared is somehow better than the other. (You may, of course, compare more than two subjects in an essay. Such comparisons are necessarily more complex and more difficult to manage than a straightforward comparison of two subjects.) In a simple dual comparison you may, for example, conclude that greasy eggs are easy to swallow, but the cold, barely digestible pancakes are a better choice because they'll allow you to economize by skipping lunch. After listening to the police officer and the lawyer debate capital punishment, you may write an essay in which you acknowledge that some crimes seem so heinous as to demand punishment by execution; nonetheless, you conclude that life imprisonment is better because it is less drastic, less expensive (given the costly review procedures when execution is contemplated), more humane, and more just to minorities.

Not all comparisons, however, have a strong persuasive content. Some are intended primarily to **inform.** In the history exam, for example, the point of comparing the American Revolution and the overthrow of Marcos is not to determine which revolution was more noble, more justifiable, or more praiseworthy. Instead, such a comparison helps readers to see the general patterns in many popular revolts and therefore to understand all revolutions more fully. Likewise, in comparing the foreign policy goals of the Carter and Reagan administrations, your professor was probably less interested in judging the two presidents than in demonstrating how their goals are related to the broader political philosophies of Democrats and Republicans.

Although comparison is usually a technique of informing and persuading, it can also serve as the basis of a very entertaining essay. When Suzanne Britt compares fat people and thin people in "That Lean and Hungry Look" (p. 388), she may wish to satirize our national preoccupation with weight, but her main purpose is evidently to giggle and to make giggle. The following paragraph is typical of her essay and a fine example of the possibilities for humor in comparisons:

> Thin people make me tired. They've got speedy little metabolisms that cause them to bustle briskly. They're forever rubbing their bony hands together and eyeing new problems to "tackle." I like to surround myself with sluggish, inert, easygoing fat people, the kind who believe that if you clean it up today, it'll just get dirty again tomorrow.

PREWRITING

Having selected (or been assigned) a topic for comparison, **try to observe with care the two items being compared.** If, for example, you wish to compare your parents as they are today and as they were in the past, you might begin by closely comparing a current photograph of them with one taken five years ago. The changes in their faces, their expressions, their posture, and their clothing will give you much direct material for your essay. More importantly, such changes will help you to remember the events that brought them about and how those changes in appearance reflect changes in lifestyle or personality.

Of course, not all topics allow such direct observation. If you wish to compare high school with college, you must necessarily rely on memory as well as current experiences. To stimulate your memory, **list as many categories for comparison as possible.** Your initial list would probably include such categories as social life, cost, convenience, amount of independence, hours of study, size of student body, quality of teaching, difficulty of courses, size of classes, living conditions, and so on. The point of making such a list is not necessarily to determine the categories you will actually use in your essay. Instead your goal at the moment is simply to set your mental gears a-spinning. You need to remind yourself in a general way of what you know about each item under comparison before you can begin to decide on a purpose and a thesis.

Having begun to get a feel for the topic through observation and listing of categories, next **establish the purpose of your essay.** A short essay of five hundred to a thousand words certainly cannot explore *all* of the similarities and differences between high school and college. Nor is it likely that many readers will be interested in an exhaustive (but relatively purposeless) essay on the subject. If, however, you decide that you wish to use your comparison to *persuade* high school students that college is worth attending, a number of ideas for a thesis should begin to occur to you.

The most important stage in prewriting is to decide on a basis for comparison and a thesis. If your first thought is to compare high school and college as educational institutions, you might argue that college offers better and more varied learning opportunities than high school. The problem with such a thesis is that most readers will already be convinced of it and know the evidence supporting it as well as you do. Hence you have very little chance of being informative, persuasive, or entertaining.

If you are insistent on exploring well-worn territory (such as the differences between high school and college), **your best chance of writing an interesting essay is to take an unconventional point of view.** You might argue, for example, that high school offers *better* opportunities for learning than college: the classes are often smaller; the teachers have known you for years; the courses last longer. Beware, however, of letting your quest for an unconventional thesis push you into an untenable or even silly thesis. Don't argue, for instance, that college makes students more ignorant and immature than they were during high school. Granted, such a thesis might get your reader's attention. Also granted, irresponsible beer binges and experimentation with drugs are common signs of immaturity in college students. Nonetheless, your readers will quickly see the flimsiness of your argument and object that the irresponsibility of some college students is an outgrowth of their relative freedom after high school and is a stage that many pass through in developing increasing maturity.

Another way to interest readers is to seek out an unusual basis for comparison. You might compare high school and college as settings for a romance. You might contrast high school and college as sources of future business contacts. You might look at the ways in which high school and college affect your relationship with your parents. In each case you would use that basis of comparison to *persuade* your readers that college is worth the sacrifices one makes to attend it (or is not worth those sacrifices). Once again, however, avoid choosing a basis of comparison that is too fanciful, cute, or trivial. An essay comparing high school and college classes as locales for reading comic books is almost certain to get a poor grade.

Remember always that if you are truly to inform and persuade an audience, you yourself must be capable of believing in the truth and importance of your thesis.

PLANNING AND DRAFTING A COMPARISON

Before beginning your first rough draft, you should **choose an appropriate structure for your essay.** Essays based on comparison generally follow one of two organizational patterns: subject by subject or category by category. In a subject-by-subject pattern, you divide your essay roughly in half, with the first half devoted to one of the subjects of comparison (high school, for example) and the second half devoted to the other (college). In a category-by-category pattern, you identify several categories for comparison, and within each category you examine both of the subjects before moving on to the next category.

If you were writing an essay on the thesis that college provides a better setting for romance than high school, a subject-by-subject outline might look like this:

Subject-by-Subject Outline

Topic: Comparing high school with college.

Purpose: To help persuade the reader that college is worth attending.

Thesis: College provides a better setting for romance than high school.

 I. High school
   A. Supervision by parents
   B. Few activities for dating couples
   C. Few private places for getting acquainted
 II. College
   A. Supervision by resident assistants
   B. Many activities for dating couples
   C. Many private places for getting acquainted

For short essays of only a paragraph or two, the subject-by-subject structure is sensible. There is always the risk, however, that you will seem to have written separate essays on each of the subjects of comparison. The longer your essay, the more difficult it becomes for the reader to see the connections between the two parts. Thus, in the outline provided above, the reader may have forgotten exactly what you had to say about the romantic haunts of high school students by the time he or she reads about those of college students. For that reason, the category-by-category structure is a safer choice for essays of four or more paragraphs.

A category-by-category comparison alternates from one subject to the other as each new category for comparison is discussed. Here is a representative outline:

Category-by-Category Outline

Topic: Comparing high school with college.

Purpose: To help persuade the reader that college is worth attending.

Thesis: College provides a better setting for romance than high school.

Introduction: Example of a big night out in Plainfield, Illinois, compared with one at Northwestern University.

    I. Supervision
       A. In high school: parents who are sometimes intrusive and difficult to confide in
       B. In college: resident assistants who are friends but also careful advisors
    II. Activities for couples
       A. In high school
          1. Cruising
          2. Movies
          3. Fast food drive-ins
       B. In college
          1. Concerts, plays, movies
          2. Walks through a park-like campus
          3. College pubs and restaurants
          4. Fraternity and sorority parties
   III. Private places for getting acquainted
       A. In high school
          1. The front porch
          2. The basement rec room
          3. The back seat of the car
       B. In college
          1. The dorm lounge
          2. Secluded benches scattered around campus
          3. Dorm room during visitation hours

Conclusion: Is it any wonder that kids in high school get into trouble? To escape the prying eyes of Mom and Dad, they drift into boring activities ranging from cruising to bowling. The simple human need for entertainment leads all too many of them to the dangerous diversions of the back seat. In contrast, college offers couples opportunities for independence, cultural growth, sharing, and mutual understanding. College may not top the Love Boat, but it always has been and still remains a great place for romance.

A third possible structure is the combination of the subject-by-subject and category-by-category structures. You may, for example, wish to start your essay on high school and college with a number of brief comparisons before going on to develop your main arguments in greater detail. In that case you might wish to use the subject-by-subject structure for the brief introductory comparisons and the category-by-category structure for the more substantial ones.

Whether you choose a subject-by-subject structure, a category-by-category structure, or some combination of the two, keep the following points in mind:

1. **Discuss the same categories for both subjects.**   There is no comparison at all if the first half of your essay discusses the high school student's problems with acne and younger brothers, and the second half examines the romantically stifling pressures of college finals and keeping up with car payments. If you want to complain about parental supervision in high school, you must also say something about the supervision of college students.

2. **Arrange your points of comparison in order of increasing importance.**   Whenever you wish to be persuasive, it is a good idea to put your best arguments last. That way they'll be fresh and clearly in mind as your readers attempt to reach their own conclusions.

COMBINING PURPOSES

Essays based on comparison usually strive to persuade and inform. Success in achieving those purposes depends largely on your essay's originality. How can you make your writing more original? Sadly, there is no broad, well-marked fairway leading to originality. Here, however, are two suggestions that might help you to avoid nasty sand traps into which unwary students often fall. The first rule is **downplay the obvious.** If, as a student at New Mexico Highlands University, you decide to compare your school's basketball team with that of the University of New Mexico Lobos, it makes no sense at all to point out that both squads have only five starting players. Because a Highlands team has never been nationally prominent, you might mention briefly the obvious fact that the revenue provided by ticket sales at UNM gives the Lobos many advantages in equipment and facilities. Your best points, however, will be based on comparisons that are not so obvious — perhaps a much larger percentage of your varsity players graduate in four years, or perhaps their income ten years after graduation is higher. Even well-documented facts about the obvious advantages a nationally prominent team has in recruitment will strike few readers as informative. You may need to cite such facts if your goal is to persuade readers that the NCAA should make changes to equalize competition, but the bulk of your essay should develop comparisons that are not obvious at first glance.

A second useful guideline is to **avoid the unimportant.** Suppose once again that you are comparing your basketball team with the team from UNM and you wish to argue for a set of changes in NCAA rules. Wouldn't it be unimportant to note that your school has higher admission standards if they are routinely waived for athletes? Wouldn't it also be unimportant to observe that the UNM coach has an advantage in recruiting players who prefer the excitement of a big city like Albuquerque to the tame diversions of New Mexico Highlands? Could any sane change in recruiting rules reduce UNM's advantage in recruiting players that prefer big-city life? Many readers would legitimately object to your wasting their time with comparisons that are insignificant or irrelevant.

As you attempt to write informatively and persuasively, continue to **look for opportunities to entertain your readers.** Even in serious essays, most readers enjoy an occasional tidbit of wit, humor, scandal, or gossip. At the very least, make your essay entertaining by making it as concrete and specific as possible. It is not enough to observe that many prominent universities have records blackened by violations of NCAA rules. It is somewhat better to be more specific about those violations, which in recent years have included under-the-table payments, forged transcripts, drug abuse, and point shaving. Even better still is an outrageous example:

> Typical of the unrepentant immorality in high-powered college athletics is the case of Norm Ellenberger, the head coach of the UNM Lobos from 1972 to 1979. Not long after being convicted on 21 counts ranging from filing false travel vouchers and doctoring transcripts to fraud and felony, Ellenberger wrote, ". . . I watch Saturday afternoon college football on television, and I see the NCAA's thirty- or sixty-second spot at halftime, where the virtues of football and basketball are expounded as if they were like motherhood, apple pie, and the flag. And I giggle. It just ain't there. Sports are the way they are because of the almighty dollar. We have to make money."

TIPS ON REVISION

Don't be a hypnotist. Nothing is duller than the kind of comparison that resembles the pendular motion of a hypnotist's watch—back and forth, back and forth, monotonously swinging from one subject to the other. Before long your reader is either enraged or asleep. **To avoid monotony, vary your sentence structures, the length of your paragraphs, and your transitions.** Just because you have written six sentences on the problem of recruiting violations at UNM, don't feel that you must devote another six sentences to the lack of recruiting violations at your school. Your obligation to use the same categories for each subject does not oblige you to bestow on each an identical number of words.

Similarly, your obligation to make your comparisons and contrasts clear does not oblige you to use the same transitional constructions repeatedly throughout your essay. An ample number of transitional expressions directly indicate comparison and contrast:

> *Comparison:* similarly, likewise, equally, every bit as, correspondingly, analogously, in like manner, just as, even as
>
> *Contrast:* in contrast, on the contrary, still, nevertheless, on the other hand, even so, notwithstanding, for all that, nonetheless, however, and yet, although this may be true

Fortunately, writers are also endowed with a virtually limitless range of options in defining the exact nature of likeness or difference. The following examples can only begin to illustrate the range of possibilities:

> Although UNM has unsurpassed training equipment, Highlands U has . . .
>
> Gate receipts at UNM are fully five times as large as . . .
>
> Instead of pushing varsity athletes toward careers in professional sports, Highland U . . .
>
> Thus, mighty UNM continues to battle doggedly against the rule changes that Highland U has embraced.
>
> Today UNM emphasizes . . . but just ten years ago . . .
>
> The average forward at UNM is fully six inches taller than his counterpart at . . .

Appropriate variations in content and style give texture to writing and help readers retain a sense of contact with the varied terrain of reality itself.

IDEAS FOR ESSAYS

Write an essay on one of the following topics using either the subject-by-subject or the category-by-category method of comparison.

1. Women and men as athletes
2. Women and men as shoppers
3. City life versus country life
4. Two television personalities (e.g., two actors, two news commentators, two game-show hosts)
5. The job you have versus the job you hope to get after graduation
6. Japanese and American cars
7. Television today and television when you were a child
8. Two different kinds of vacation
9. Two contrasting approaches to a controversial issue such as censorship of pornography, handgun laws, prayer in public schools, and so on
10. Good teachers and bad teachers
11. Your attitudes now versus your attitudes as a child toward your parents, religion, politics, and so on
12. Good dates and bad dates
13. Buying a new car versus buying a used car
13. Two (or more) different brands of a costly product (e.g., stereo systems, tennis racquets, video-cassette recorders, motorbikes)
15. The abilities of humans and those of animals
16. Love and lust
17. True friends and false friends
18. Admiration and envy
19. Being married and going steady
20. Cleverness and genius

STUDENT ESSAY ⎯⎯⎯⎯⎯⎯⎯⎯⎯⎯⎯⎯⎯⎯⎯

Cindy Burton wrote "No More Fairly Tales" as an in-class essay in response to the "Ideas for Essays" in this chapter. Her first draft was developed in one fifty-minute session. Then she shared her essay with a group of her peers and used their suggestions in revising her essay during another class period.

FIRST DRAFT

"NO MORE FAIRY TALES"

by Cindy Burton

OUTLINE

THESIS: Being married and going steady are like living in two different worlds.

  I. Making an impression

    A. Going steady--hair, make-up, dressed up

    B. Being married--just home, just got up

  II. Dining

    A. Going steady--nice restaurant

    B. Being married--eating T.V. dinners

  III. Receiving presents

    A. Going steady--flowers, candy, jewelry

    B. Being married--kitchen appliances, slicer dicers, house shoes

  IV. Going to the Movies

    A. Going steady--*Love Story, The Way We Were*

    B. Being married--Clint Eastwood

  V. Conclusion--some things do improve in marriage

     When I was going steady, I thought marriage would just be more of a good thing. I didn't realize that things change dramatically when you live with someone 365 days a year. Of course, I should have gotten a clue from watching other married people, but they were all old (in their 30's at least) and we would never act like them! We would always be the center of each other's lives. Things don't always change for the worse, but they always change.

For instance, when I was going steady, I spent hours getting ready for my dates. It always makes me think of some ancient ceremony where they prepare the sacrificial virgin. Boys spend all afternoon washing and waxing their cars, getting the chariot ready for Cinderella. But when they get married, they see each other stripped of all their adornments. Few girls look gorgeous when they first wake up in the morning. The boy who comes home from work only vaguely resembles that knight in shining armor.

And isn't he supposed to rescue the damsel in distress? Take her out for a nice relaxing dinner? Instead they end up eating frozen food on a tray in front of the T.V.

Most florists make their living from men going steady. They go to great lengths to gain a young woman's favor--flowers, candy, even jewels. After marriage this changes to slicer-dicers, tea pots, and houseshoes. The most upset my mother ever got was when she received a whistling tea pot for Christmas. She paid Dad back by getting him an ice cream maker for his birthday. For some strange reason, men seem to think women want *practical* gifts after they're married.

Even the types of movies married couples see changes. No more romantic films! Now it's Clint Eastwood blowing people away.

Everything that changes isn't bad. I realize that my husband still loves me even if I look like Phyllis Diller in the mornings. He won't leave me if we have hamburgers three nights in a row. And I've decided it doesn't kill me to get a kitchen gadget for Christmas. My husband might help me with dinner just to play with our new ging-sin knives. And those awful houseshoes do keep my feet warm, even if I do look like a granny with them on. Life does change when you get married, but a lot of the changes are good. Relationships are often like wine, they improve with age.

Commentary: Cindy's first draft presents a fairly well-organized set of contrasts between going steady and being married, but it is far from a polished essay. In addition to the problems in diction and grammar that are nearly universal in early rough drafts, Cindy's essay lacks fully developed comparisons. The essay might also benefit from a more logical structure and a more consistent use of analogies.

Consider the second paragraph, for example. It begins with Cindy's observations about the way she herself used to spend hours preparing for her dates. The analogy to the preparation of a sacrificial virgin is both apt and amusing; however, Cindy then switches rather startlingly to imagery that compares boys' cars to chariots being prepared for Cinderella. Since when does Cinderella ride in a chariot instead of a carriage? What has become of our sacrificial virgin? And why have we switched from Cindy's personal experiences to the generalized experiences of all young men and women?

The second half of the paragraph presents the contrasting behavior of married couples, but instead of continuing with the subject of how couples prepare to go out for the evening, Cindy observes that "Few girls look gorgeous when they first wake up in the morning." Then, instead of describing how married men appear in the morning, Cindy asserts that the husband who "comes home from work only vaguely resembles that knight in shining armor." Clearly, Cindy is drawing useful contrasts between courting couples, who make sure that they are only seen when looking their best, and married couples, who see each other at their worst moments. But it is also clear that these contrasts could be sharpened by a more consistent pattern of imagery and greater parallelism in the situations under comparison.

The students who read Cindy's rough draft pointed out these and other similar flaws, which Cindy attempted to correct in her final draft.

FINAL DRAFT

"NO MORE FAIRY TALES"

by Cindy Burton

When I was going steady, I dreamed of getting married. I knew marriage would be even more exciting and romantic than dating, more of a good thing, so to speak. I didn't realize how difficult it is to keep the romance alive 365 days a year. I should have caught on from watching the married people around me, but they were all so old--in their thirties at least! I knew we would never act like them! Well, as you get older, you finally realize that everything changes, not always for the worse, but things always change.

For instance, when girls are getting ready for a date, they take hours to get ready. Their make-up, clothes, and hair must be perfect. They would give anything to have a fairy-godmother to wave her wand and perform a miracle. The boys have different rituals, but they are equally complicated. They spend all Saturday afternoon washing and waxing their cars. The local car wash is the busiest place in town on Saturdays. The pumpkins have to be transformed into carriages (or Corvettes) for Cinderella to go to the ball (or drive-in). But when these courting couples get married, fairy tales change to reality. Few women look fantastic when they first wake up. The man who comes home dirty and tired from work is hard to recognize as Prince Charming.

And isn't Prince Charming supposed to rescue Cinderella from the dreary duties of a perpetual housemaid? He should take her out for dinner and a movie at least. A little candlelight and wine would do wonders to soothe her nerves after a terrible day. Instead, if he is feeling merciful, he may wash the breakfast dishes while she prepares dinner. Eating hamburgers on a T.V. tray doesn't fit that vision of wedded bliss that they both had when they were dating.

Another drastic change takes place in the gifts women receive after marriage. Young men often spend a fortune on candy and flowers for their girlfriends. Some love-struck men even shower jewels on their ladies. For some strange reason married men think their wives want practical gifts. Slicer-dicers, tea pots, and houseshoes replace those sentimental love tokens they used to receive.

Going steady and being married are totally different. All the changes aren't bad, though. The husband that bought those awful houseshoes is going to love you, even if you look like a granny in them. Marriages are often like wine; they improve with age.

That Lean and Hungry Look
Suzanne Britt

Suzanne Britt earned a B.A. in English and Latin from Salem College in Win-
ston-Salem, North Carolina, and an M.A. in English from Washington University in St. Louis, Missouri. She has taught English at North Carolina State
University, the Divinity School at Duke University, and Meredith College. She
is the author of three books: *Skinny People Are Dull and Crunchy Like Carrots*
(1982), *Show and Tell* (1983), and *A Writer's Rhetoric* (1988). Britt's essays
have appeared in a variety of newspapers and magazines — among them, *The
New York Times*, *Newsday*, and *Newsweek*, which published "That Lean and
Hungry Look" in October of 1978. Although Britt's comparisons between fat
people and thin people are amusing, there is an undercurrent of seriousness as
well. How well does her criticism of thin people and endorsement of fat people
hold up when measured against your own experiences?

1   Caesar was right. Thin people need watching. I've been watching them
for most of my adult life, and I don't like what I see. When these narrow
fellows spring at me, I quiver to my toes. Thin people come in all
personalities, most of them menacing. You've got your "together" thin
person, your mechanical thin person, your condescending thin person,
your tsk-tsk thin person, your efficiency-expert thin person. All of them
are dangerous.

2   In the first place, thin people aren't fun. They don't know how to
goof off, at least in the best, fat sense of the word. They've always got to
be adoing. Give them a coffee break, and they'll jog around the block.
Supply them with a quiet evening at home, and they'll fix the screen
door and lick S&H green stamps. They say things like "there aren't
enough hours in the day." Fat people never say that. Fat people think the
day is too damn long already.

3   Thin people make me tired. They've got speedy little metabolisms
that cause them to bustle briskly. They're forever rubbing their bony
hands together and eyeing new problems to "tackle." I like to surround
myself with sluggish, inert, easygoing fat people, the kind who believe
that if you clean it up today, it'll just get dirty again tomorrow.

4   Some people say the business about the jolly fat person is a myth,
that all of us chubbies are neurotic, sick, sad people. I disagree. Fat
people may not be chortling all day long, but they're a hell of a lot *nicer*
than the wizened and shriveled. Thin people turn surly, mean, and hard
at a young age because they never learn the value of a hot-fudge sundae
for easing tension. Thin people don't like gooey soft things because they
themselves are neither gooey nor soft. They are crunchy and dull, like
carrots. They go straight to the heart of the matter while fat people let
things stay all blurry and hazy and vague, the way things actually are.
Thin people want to face the truth. Fat people know there is no truth.
One of my thin friends is always staring at complex, unsolvable problems and saying, "The key thing is. . . ." Fat people never say that.
They know there isn't any such thing as the key thing about anything.

5   Thin people believe in logic. Fat people see all sides. The sides fat

people see are rounded blobs, usually gray, always nebulous and truly not worth worrying about. But the thin person persists. "If you consume more calories than you burn," says one of my thin friends, "you will gain weight. It's that simple." Fat people always grin when they hear statements like that. They know better.

[Fat people realize that life is illogical and unfair. They know very 6 well that God is not in his heaven and all is not right with the world. If God was up there, fat people could have two doughnuts and a big orange drink anytime they wanted it.]

Thin people have a long list of logical things they are always spout- 7 ing off to me. They hold up one finger at a time as they reel off these things, so I won't lose track. They speak slowly as if to a young child. The list is long and full of holes. It contains tidbits like "get a grip on yourself," "cigarettes kill," "cholesterol clogs," "fit as a fiddle," "ducks in a row," "organize," and "sound fiscal management." Phrases like that.

They think these 2,000-point plans lead to happiness. Fat people 8 know happiness is elusive at best and even if they could get the kind thin people talk about, they wouldn't want it. Wisely, fat people see that such programs are too dull, too hard, too off the mark. They are never better than a whole cheesecake.

Fat people know all about the mystery of life. They are the ones 9 acquainted with the night, with luck, with fate, with playing it by ear. One thin person I know once suggested that we arrange all the parts of a jigsaw puzzle into groups according to size, shape, and color. He figures this would cut the time needed to complete the puzzle by at least 50 percent. I said I wouldn't do it. One, I like to muddle through. Two, what good would it do to finish early? Three, the jigsaw puzzle isn't the important thing. The important thing is the fun of four people (one thin person included) sitting around a card table, working a jigsaw puzzle. My thin friend had no use for my list. Instead of joining us, he went outside and mulched the boxwoods. The three remaining fat people finished the puzzle and made chocolate, double-fudged brownies to celebrate.

The main problem with thin people is they oppress. Their good 10 intentions, bony torsos, tight ships, neat corners, cerebral machinations, and pat solutions loom like dark clouds over the loose, comfortable, spread-out, soft world of the fat. Long after fat people have removed their coats and shoes and put their feet up on the coffee table, thin people are still sitting on the edge of the sofa, looking neat as a pin, discussing rutabagas. Fat people are heavily into fits of laughter, slapping their thighs and whooping it up, while thin people are still politely waiting for the punch line.

Thin people are downers. They like math and morality and rea- 11 soned evaluation of the limitations of human beings. They have their skinny little acts together. They expound, prognose, probe, and prick.

Fat people are convivial. They will like you even if you're irregular 12 and have acne. They will come up with a good reason why you never wrote the great American novel. They will cry in your beer with you. They will put your name in the pot. They will let you off the hook. Fat people will gab, giggle, guffaw, gallumph, gyrate, and gossip. They are generous, giving, and gallant. They are gluttonous and goodly and great. What you want when you're down is soft and jiggly, not muscled and stable. Fat people know this. Fat people have plenty of room. Fat people will take you in.

Questions on Content

1. What are the different kinds of thin people that Britt singles out as dangerous?
2. What reasons does Britt cite for preferring fat people to thin people?
3. What happens when Britt sits down to work a jigsaw puzzle with two fat friends and one thin friend?

Questions on Thesis, Purpose, and Structure

1. Britt adds imagery to her essay by making frequent reference to foods. Which foods are associated with fat people and thin people, respectively?
2. How often and how effectively does Britt use topic sentences in this essay?
3. Outline Britt's essay. How structured are her comparisons? Are these comparisons arranged effectively in building to her conclusion?
4. How seriously do you think Britt takes her own arguments? Is her essay intended *just* to be entertaining, or does it have a persuasive purpose? How convincing do you find her arguments?

Questions on Style and Diction

1. Are you familiar with the lines from Shakespeare to which Britt alludes in her title and first paragraph? If not, look up the lines in *Julius Caesar*, Act 1, Scene 2, 192–95. Why is the allusion effective in making thin people seem menacing?
2. Read Robert Frost's poem "Acquainted with the Night." Then reread paragraph 9. Does Britt's allusion add anything to the meaning or impact of her essay?
3. Consider the exuberant alliteration of "g" sounds in paragraph 12 and the parallel sentence structures throughout that paragraph. Also consider the final veiled allusion to room at the inn. What do these techniques add to the effect of the conclusion?
4. Is Britt's frequent use of clichés irritating or amusing? Explain.

Ideas for Essays

1. Write a rebuttal to this essay from the point of view of a thin person.
2. Write a witty, satirical essay about two other contrasting types. You might, for example, compare mothers and mothers-in-law, kittens and cats, or dreams and daydreams.

Childhood and the Garden of Eden

Marie Winn

Marie Winn (1937–   ) was born in Prague, Czechoslovakia, and came to the United States with her parents in 1939. Educated at Radcliffe and Columbia, Winn is the author and editor of numerous books for and about children. She has also contributed articles to such periodicals as *The New York Times Magazine*, *Parade*, and *The Village Voice*. Winn is best known, however, for her studies *The Plug-In Drug: Television, Children and Family* (1977, revised 1985) and *Children Without Childhood* (1983), from which we have drawn the following essay. Winn's comparisons between the biblical story of the Garden of Eden and the universal experience of childhood innocence and its loss are both stimulating and provocative.

Why do creation myths in so many cultures begin with a paradise so soon   1
to be lost? Why does the story not start right off with the original couple discovering human existence to be the sort of mixed bag of happiness and sorrow that life on earth was in the beginning and is now and probably ever shall be? Perhaps because the makers of the myths understood that human life does indeed begin in a Garden of Eden of sorts, where every need is taken care of and every desire fulfilled — childhood. And yet it is a finite paradise, which must end when the child grows up.

But more than describing a reality — that human life begins with   2
childhood — the major creation myth of our culture, the story of Adam and Eve and their expulsion from the Garden of Eden, contains within it an illumination of the meaning of childhood and its purpose in human life. That the Garden of Eden tale is a metaphor not only for the Childhood of Mankind at its creation but for the childhood of individual men and women is supported by a close examination of the story itself. Each detail of the spare but densely meaningful tale may be related to an aspect of childhood.

Consider the sole condition on which Adam and Eve's term in   3
Paradise depends: it is not that they be good, or that they work hard, or that they be clever, the usual requirements for success in fairy tales or in real life. It is simply that they remain innocent: "Of the tree of knowledge of good and evil, thou shalt not eat of it" is their only injunction from the Lord. As long as they desist from sampling the forbidden fruit, they may remain in the happy Garden, protected from all harm, free of all care. Just so, children are loved and nourished whether or not they behave well or pick up their toys or get A's on their report cards. But their optimal care is as contingent on their childlike innocence as the first Man and Woman's stay in Eden was contingent on theirs. Once children are allowed to discover the complex secrets of the adult world, their days in Paradise are numbered; the dependable protection they once enjoyed is soon transformed into a hardening process that is to prepare them for a difficult life.

What exactly happened when Adam and Eve took the fatal step and   4 ate the forbidden apple? What gave them away? Oddly enough, though it was the fruit of the Tree of Knowledge they had ingested, it did not cause them suddenly to exhibit great wisdom, to declaim learned aphorisms or spout algebraic formulas or engage in pithy dialectics. A simple thing betrayed them: they became self-conscious. Though they were naked from the moment of their creation in Paradise, in their original innocence they had been completely unashamed. Now they tried to hide their nakedness from the Lord. "Who told thee that thou wast naked?" the Lord asked, knowing immediately that they had disobeyed. It was their very awareness of being naked that revealed a new consciousness and defined the end of their innocence.

5   Children, too, lose that natural and unselfconscious ability to enjoy life directly as they learn early the bewildering secrets of the adult world. In biological terms, however, that childlike unawareness of self is one of those neotenic traits specific to the young and programmed to elicit protectiveness from adults. Childhood may thus remain safe and secure — in a word, Paradise.

6   Why, in fact, did Adam and Eve have to pass through that perfectly innocent and happy state on their way to fulfill their human destiny? Did that period of innocence and safety serve a purpose in their post-Edenic existence? And what, by the same token, might a happy and protected childhood provide for humans in their later life? Clearly, everyone has a childhood of some sort. But for some it is longer than for others, and for some it is close to a heaven. Does it make a great difference, as the myth suggests?

7   It is in the nature of that particular unselfconsciousness preceding the Fall that we must seek the first great purpose of childhood. For if we consider that ineffable part of Man which often allows him to endure the bitter sufferings that follow his Fall and to live with the unbearable knowledge of his own morality — the mysterious creative, artistic drive — we may see that its wellsprings lie within that special sensibility of childhood.

8   Many have observed that certain artists have a rare ability to recapture the spontaneous, fresh way of experiencing life that children enjoy. A century ago the German poet and playwright Schiller defined such artists as "naïve" — those who produce their art directly from their own being, without ratiocination or self-analysis. Such artists are as harmoniously integrated with their art as children are in their direct involvement with life. Schiller compared these with a different artistic sensibility that he called "sentimental." This other sort of artist, in Schiller's dichotomy, can only look at that harmony between sense and thinking as an ideal. Self-consciously, such artists search to recapture that vanished world that was once part of them and strive to re-create it in their imagination. The first type of artist, who has somehow remained a child even as an adult, is rare indeed. Most adults have access to their childhood experience only through that second, indirect means. But the "naïve" and the "sentimental" forms of artistic expression have a common ground that unites them: each is informed by the special consciousness of childhood. If childhood is early infiltrated — contaminated, one might go so

far as to say — by adult ways of thinking and behaving, there is a danger that a loss will be felt by generations to come whose artistic reserves will be low, or perhaps nonexistent.

But why prolong childhood? Perhaps even a brief spell in Paradise   9 will provide enough inspiration for future Shakespeares and Homers. The story of Adam and Eve provides yet another clue to yet another purpose of childhood. We observe an odd exception to the carefree and irresponsible life the original couple were given to live in the Garden of Eden: Adam was assigned a particular task, that of giving a name to every living creature in the newly created world, "to all cattle, and to the fowl of the air, and to every beast of the field." A sizable job, when you stop to think of it. But in the Biblical story this taxonomic enterprise is clearly distinguished from the dangerous understanding that resides in the Tree of Knowledge. That alone is forbidden; other forms of knowledge, evidently, are encouraged.

Children too have a task of childhood, not so unlike Adam's task: to   10 systematically accumulate information, to learn, to go to school. Though they must not eat of the Tree of Knowledge if they are to remain children, this other sort of intellectual nourishment is necessary.

We have seen that in other historical times and in other cultures   11 childhood ended far earlier than it does in modern times. But those were simpler times, the childhood of civilization, in a sense. The adults of the Middle Ages, it appears, were themselves more childlike in their ways of thinking and behaving than adults are today, and perhaps more childlike than not a few of today's children. But the more highly developed the species becomes and the more complex the civilization, the lengthier a childhood is required. There is just that much more learning to assimilate. And childhood *is* that time when the human organism has the leisure to lay a solid intellectual foundation upon which it may in later years build a structure of some sort, one that might possibly have significance for the species as a whole. The long childhood hours, if childhood remains an Eden of stability and safety, may be occupied by the slow, methodical accumulation of cultural material culled from the great efforts of thinkers of the past. Like Adam, that original Linnaeus, children can apply themselves to an understanding of all living creatures, their names, their histories, their biology and chemistry. Steadily, under the conditions of dependence with all questions of survival taken care of by others, children may learn how to learn.

The final purpose of childhood is exemplified by the very inevitabil-   12 ity of the Fall itself, in chapter 3 of Genesis. Although Adam and Eve are censured for their weakness in giving way to temptation and are held responsible for all the sufferings that make human life so far from paradisiacal, there was in fact a grand purpose to their eating of the fruit of knowledge. They *had* to leave Paradise, to grow up in another sense, in order to start the human race. "And Adam knew his wife; and she conceived, and bare Cain," begins the next chapter of the story, after the expulsion from Eden. The fateful primal pair made their trade-off, losing blissful dependence to gain wisdom and sexual maturity for a reason: the future of humankind depended on it.

13   Like Adam and Eve, each child must lose his place in Paradise to grow up. Each child must learn the bitter and yet thrilling secrets of adulthood, must face the dangers of the world of capricious natural phenomena and unpredictable human relations, and confront the terrors of morality, in order to survive as an adult, to live independently, to fulfill his particular mission on the earth, whatever it might be. And above all, to become a successful parent, thus continuing the task of Adam and Eve. But it is in the carrying out of that very task that the deepest purpose of childhood lies. Only through the lengthy experience of being a child, of being dependent, of being totally protected and nurtured by loving parents, does the child gain the ability to be a successful, protective, nurturing parent himself.

14   The connection between one's childhood and one's subsequent outcome as an adult has been demonstrated again and again by negative studies: a miserable childhood leads to a troubled adulthood. Battered children grow up to become battering parents. The connection between a long, happy childhood and a rich, fulfilled adulthood, between the quality of one's childhood and one's ability to be a good, loving parent, is harder to pin down. Nevertheless we have our myths of Paradise to teach us the truth about childhood. There must be an Eden at the beginning, just as there is in every creation myth. The future of human-kind still depends on it.

Questions on Content

1. What is "the sole condition on which Adam and Eve's term in Paradise depends," and how is that condition related to childhood?
2. How did Adam and Eve change after eating from the Tree of Knowledge, and how is their change related to growth out of childhood?
3. What characterizes a "naive" artist according to the German poet Schiller? What characterizes a "sentimental" artist?
4. What task does God give Adam in the Garden of Eden? What similar task is given to children?
5. According to Winn, why was the Fall of Adam and Eve both inevitable and essential? Why must children, too, fall from innocence?

Questions on Thesis, Purpose, and Structure

1. What do the first two paragraphs of the essay indicate about Winn's thesis and the comparisons she intends to develop?
2. Why does Winn discuss "Schiller's dichotomy" between "naive" artists and "sentimental" artists? How does this discussion help her develop her case for the importance of childhood? How is this discussion related to the Fall of Adam and Eve?
3. What are the main points Winn makes about the function of a prolonged childhood?
4. In what ways should childhood be like Adam and Eve's residence in the Garden of Eden?
5. What are the implicit threats to childhood in today's society?

Questions on Style and Diction

1. Find the following words in the essay and determine their definitions in context: desist, optimal, contingent (paragraph 3); ingested, aphorisms, dialectics (paragraph 4); neotenic, elicit (paragraph 5); ineffable (paragraph 7); ratiocination, dichotomy (paragraph 8); taxonomic (paragraph 9); assimilate (paragraph 11); censured (paragraph 12); capricious (paragraph 13).
2. Winn makes frequent use of questions in her essay. What are the purposes and effects of including so many questions in a relatively brief essay?
3. Winn makes frequent use of negative constructions. (See, for example, the second sentence in paragraph 1, the first sentence in paragraph 3, and the third sentence in paragraph 4.) What is the rhetorical impact of these sentences about what is *not* true and what did *not* happen?

Ideas for Essays

1. At the heart of Winn's argument is the notion that myths often explore universal elements in the human experience. In this sense the mythological narrative can be seen as an allegorical exploration of common psychological experiences. In an essay using comparisons like Winn's, attempt to develop your own interpretation of a common myth or fairy tale.
2. Look back over your own childhood and write an essay comparing your experiences with those of Adam and Eve in the Garden of Eden. This essay will probably be most interesting if you can show both similarities *and* differences.

Japanese and American Workers: Two Casts of Mind
William Ouchi

William Ouchi (1943–   ) received an M.B.A. from Stanford University and a Ph.D. in business administration from the University of Chicago. A member of the faculty of the Graduate School of Management at UCLA, Ouchi has become well known in recent years for his comparisons of Japanese and American business and how productivity is decisively influenced by the way businesses manage people. He is the author of *Theory Z: How American Business Can Meet the Japanese Challenge* (1981) and *The M-Form Society: How American Teamwork Can Recapture the Competition* (1984), both of which are aimed at restoring the competitive advantage of American business in a world economy. In this extract from *Theory Z*, Ouchi compares the work ethic in Japan and the United States and speculates about the historical causes of the very different viewpoints of East and West.

COLLECTIVE VALUES

1   Perhaps the most difficult aspect of the Japanese for Westerners to comprehend is the strong orientation to collective values, particularly a collective sense of responsibility. Let me illustrate with an anecdote about a visit to a new factory in Japan owned and operated by an American electronics company. The American company, a particularly creative firm, frequently attracts attention within the business community for its novel approaches to planning, organizational design, and management systems. As a consequence of this corporate style, the parent company determined to make a thorough study of Japanese workers and to design a plant that would combine the best of East and West. In their study they discovered that Japanese firms almost never make use of individual work incentives, such as piecework or even individual performance appraisal tied to salary increases. They concluded that rewarding individual achievement and individual ability is always a good thing.

2   In the final assembly area of their new plant long lines of young Japanese women wired together electronic products on a piece-rate system: the more you wired, the more you got paid. About two months after opening, the head foreladies approached the plant manager. "Honorable plant manager," they said humbly as they bowed, "we are embarrassed to be so forward, but we must speak to you because all of the girls have threatened to quit work this Friday." (To have this happen, of course, would be a great disaster for all concerned.) "Why," they wanted to know, "can't our plant have the same compensation system as other Japanese companies? When you hire a new girl, her starting wage should be fixed by her age. An eighteen-year-old should be paid more than a sixteen-year-old. Every year on her birthday, she should receive an automatic increase in pay. The idea that any one of us can be more productive than another must be wrong, because none of us in final assembly could make a thing unless all of the other people in the plant had done their jobs right first. To single one person out as being more productive is wrong and is also personally humiliating to us." The company changed its compensation system to the Japanese model.

3   Another American company in Japan had installed a suggestion system much as we have in the United States. Individual workers were encouraged to place suggestions to improve productivity into special boxes. For an accepted idea the individual received a bonus amounting to some fraction of the productivity savings realized from his or her suggestion. After a period of six months, not a single suggestion had been submitted. The American managers were puzzled. They had heard many stories of the inventiveness, the commitment, and the loyalty of Japanese workers, yet not one suggestion to improve productivity had appeared.

4   The managers approached some of the workers and asked why the suggestion system had not been used. The answer: "No one can come up with a work improvement idea alone. We work together, and any ideas that one of us may have are actually developed by watching others

and talking to others. If one of us was singled out for being responsible for such an idea, it would embarrass all of us." The company changed to a group suggestion system, in which workers collectively submitted suggestions. Bonuses were paid to groups which would save bonus money until the end of the year for a party at a restaurant or, if there was enough money, for family vacations together. The suggestions and productivity improvements rained down on the plant.

One can interpret these examples in two quite different ways. Perhaps the Japanese commitment to collective values is an anachronism that does not fit with modern industrialism but brings economic success despite that collectivism. Collectivism seems to be inimical to the kind of maverick creativity exemplified in Benjamin Franklin, Thomas Edison, and John D. Rockefeller. Collectivism does not seem to provide the individual incentive to excel which has made a great success of American enterprise. Entirely apart from its economic effects, collectivism implies a loss of individuality, a loss of the freedom to be different, to hold fundamentally different values from others.

The second interpretation of the examples is that the Japanese collectivism is economically efficient. It causes people to work well together and to encourage one another to better efforts. Industrial life requires interdependence of one person on another. But a less obvious but far-reaching implication of the Japanese collectivism for economic performance has to do with accountability.

In the Japanese mind, collectivism is neither a corporate or individual goal to strive for nor a slogan to pursue. Rather, the nature of things operates so that nothing of consequence occurs as a result of individual effort. Everything important in life happens as a result of teamwork or collective effort. Therefore, to attempt to assign individual credit or blame to results is unfounded. A Japanese professor of accounting, a brilliant scholar trained at Carnegie-Mellon University who teaches now in Tokyo, remarked that the status of accounting systems in Japanese industry is primitive compared to those in the United States. Profit centers, transfer prices, and computerized information systems are barely known even in the largest Japanese companies, whereas they are a commonplace in even small United States organizations. Though not at all surprised at the difference in accounting systems, I was not at all sure that the Japanese were primitive. In fact, I thought their system a good deal more efficient than ours.

Most American companies have basically two accounting systems. One system summarizes the overall financial state to inform stockholders, bankers, and other outsiders. That system is not of interest here. The other system, called the managerial or cost accounting system, exists for an entirely different reason. It measures in detail all of the particulars of transactions between departments, divisions, and key individuals in the organization, for the purpose of untangling the interdependencies between people. When, for example, two departments share one truck for deliveries, the cost accounting system charges each department for part of the cost of maintaining the truck and driver, so that at the end of the year, the performance of each department can be individually assessed, and the better department's manager can receive a larger raise. Of course, all of this information processing costs money, and furthermore may lead to arguments between the departments over whether the costs charged to each are fair.

9   In a Japanese company a short-run assessment of individual performance is not wanted, so the company can save the considerable expense of collecting and processing all of that information. Companies still keep track of which department uses a truck how often and for what purposes, but like-minded people can interpret some simple numbers for themselves and adjust their behavior accordingly. Those insisting upon clear and precise measurement for the purpose of advancing individual interests must have an elaborate information system. Industrial life, however, is essentially integrated and interdependent. No one builds an automobile alone, no one carries through a banking transaction alone. In a sense the Japanese value of collectivism fits naturally into an industrial setting, whereas the Western individualism provides constant conflicts. The image that comes to mind is of Chaplin's silent film "Modern Times" in which the apparently insignificant hero played by Chaplin successfully fights against the unfeeling machinery of industry. Modern industrial life can be aggravating, even hostile, or natural: all depends on the fit between our culture and our technology.

A DIFFERENCE OF TRADITION

10   The *shinkansen* or "bullet train" speeds across the rural areas of Japan giving a quick view of cluster after cluster of farmhouses surrounded by rice paddies. This particular pattern did not develop purely by chance, but as a consequence of the technology peculiar to the growing of rice, the staple of the Japanese diet. The growing of rice requires the construction and maintenance of an irrigation system, something that takes many hands to build. More importantly, the planting and the harvesting of rice can only be done efficiently with the cooperation of twenty or more people. The "bottom line" is that a single family working alone cannot produce enough rice to survive, but a dozen families working together can produce a surplus. Thus the Japanese have had to develop the capacity to work together in harmony, no matter what the forces of disagreement or social disintegration, in order to survive.

11   Japan is a nation built entirely on the tips of giant, suboceanic volcanoes. Little of the land is flat and suitable for agriculture. Terraced hillsides make use of every available square foot of arable land. Small homes built very close together further conserve the land. Japan also suffers from natural disasters such as earthquakes and hurricanes. Traditionally homes are made of light construction materials, so a house falling down during a disaster will not crush its occupants and also can be quickly and inexpensively rebuilt. During the feudal period until the Meiji restoration of 1868, each feudal lord sought to restrain his subjects from moving from one village to the next for fear that a neighboring lord might amass enough peasants with which to produce a large agricultural

surplus, hire an army and pose a threat. Apparently bridges were not commonly built across rivers and streams until the late nineteenth century, since bridges increased mobility between villages.

Taken all together, this characteristic style of living paints the picture of a nation of people who are homogeneous with respect to race, history, language, religion, and culture. For centuries and generations these people have lived in the same village next door to the same neighbors. Living in close proximity and in dwellings which gave very little privacy, the Japanese survived through their capacity to work together in harmony. In this situation, it was inevitable that the one most central social value which emerged, the one value without which the society could not continue, was that an individual does not matter.   12

To the Western soul this is a chilling picture of society. Subordinating individual tastes to the harmony of the group and knowing that individual needs can never take precedence over the interests of all is repellent to the Western citizen. But a frequent theme of Western philosophers and sociologists is that individual freedom exists only when people willingly subordinate their self-interests to the social interest. A society composed entirely of self-interested individuals is a society in which each person is at war with the other, a society which has no freedom. This issue, constantly at the heart of understanding society, comes up in every century, and in every society, whether the writer be Plato, Hobbes, or B. F. Skinner. The question of understanding which contemporary institutions lie at the heart of the conflict between automatism and totalitarianism remains. In some ages, the kinship group, the central social institution, mediated between these opposing forces to preserve the balance in which freedom was realized; in other times the church or the government was most critical. Perhaps our present age puts the work organization as the central institution.   13

In order to complete the comparison of Japanese and American living situations, consider flight over the United States. Looking out of the window high over the state of Kansas, we see a pattern of a single farmhouse surrounded by fields, followed by another single homestead surrounded by fields. In the early 1800s in the state of Kansas there were no automobiles. Your nearest neighbor was perhaps two miles distant; the winters were long, and the snow was deep. Inevitably, the central social values were self-reliance and independence. Those were the realities of that place and age that children had to learn to value.   14

The key to the industrial revolution was discovering that non-human forms of energy substituted for human forms could increase the wealth of a nation beyond anyone's wildest dreams. But there was a catch. To realize this great wealth, non-human energy needed huge complexes called factories with hundreds, even thousands of workers collected into one factory. Moreover, several factories in one central place made the generation of energy more efficient. Almost overnight, the Western world was transformed from a rural and agricultural country to an urban and industrial state. Our technological advance seems to no longer fit our social structure: in a sense, the Japanese can better cope with modern industrialism. While Americans still busily protect our   15

rather extreme form of individualism, the Japanese hold their individualism in check and emphasize cooperation.

Questions on Content

1. What happens when a leading American electronics firm tries to introduce a
   piece-rate payment system in a Japanese factory? How do the Japanese
   workers prefer to be paid?
2. How do the Japanese workers respond to an American-style suggestion box?
3. How do Japanese and American systems of accounting differ? Which system
   is more primitive? Explain your answer.
4. What does the Japanese landscape look like from a rapidly moving train?
   What does the Kansas landscape look like from an airplane window? What
   does this contrast show?

Questions on Thesis, Purpose, and Structure

1. Consider the first sentence in this essay. Is it a full statement of Ouchi's
   thesis? If not, why not?
2. Why does Ouchi use two narrative anecdotes to introduce his essay? What do
   these examples show about Japanese and American workers?
3. Ouchi argues that collectivism is inherent in the Japanese experience of
   reality, according to which "the nature of things operates so that nothing of
   consequence occurs as a result of individual effort." What evidence does
   Ouchi cite in illustrating and supporting this contention?
4. What are the main contrasts that Ouchi develops in this essay? How does each
   contrast support and develop his thesis?
5. Does Ouchi use category-by-category comparison, subject-by-subject comparison, or some combination of the two?
6. How much information do you learn from this essay? How interesting is that
   information? Is it used to build a persuasive argument?

Questions on Style and Diction

1. Find the following words in the essay and determine their definitions in
   context: incentives (paragraph 1); inimical, maverick (paragraph 5); implication (paragraph 6); proximity (paragraph 12); automatism, totalitarianism,
   mediated (paragraph 13).
2. Note how often Ouchi uses the words *collective* and *collectivism* in this
   essay. (See, for example, paragraphs 5–7.) Is he wise to repeat these words?
   Or should he have sought variety by using synonyms like "collaborative" or
   "communal"?
3. Ouchi clearly sees virtues in the Japanese way of doing business and he also
   sees weaknesses in the American way. Does his preference for the Japanese
   system cause him to be biased against American business or does his treatment of the two systems remain evenhanded? Closely examine the details in
   several paragraphs before reaching your conclusion.

Ideas for Essays

1. Compare Ouchi's essay with the advertisement by Motorola on nearly the
   same subject ("Are Japanese Executives Better People Managers Than American Executives?" p. 500). Your comparison may focus on the different argu-

ments made in the two pieces, but it may also focus on the differences between an essay and an advertisement.

2. Compare your experiences in working collaboratively on projects with your experiences as an individual creator. Which form of creativity do you find more enjoyable, more fulfilling, and more successful?

Do Chimps Share Human Rights?

M. David Stone and
Linda Koebner

As freelance writers, M. David Stone and Linda Koebner demonstrate in the following essay from *Science 82* the issue of animal rights raises important moral and philosophical questions. However, Ms. Koebner's involvement with this issue is more than purely intellectual. As a member of the Lion Country Project beginning in 1974, Ms. Koebner helped to rehabilitate eight laboratory chimpanzees. Here is how Ms. Koebner describes the laboratory living conditions of a chimp named Larry:

> Larry sits in his cage, his eyes vacant, his skin pallid, his muscles atrophied. He repeatedly pulls the hair from his arms. Eleven years old, he has spent nearly all his life in a three-foot-square cubicle. He leaves it only when they come to take blood. . . . On occasion he has seen other chimps, but he has never touched one. In this cage there is little to do. The only light comes in through tiny air holes.
>
> If he survives a normal chimp's life-span, Larry will live another 40 years.

After he was restored to more natural surroundings, Larry slowly recovered from this state of catatonia, progressing through a stage of delayed juvenility until he finally became able to interact with other chimps in a social group.

Kelly-Lynn is two days old, weighing in at just about three pounds. She is, for the moment, the youngest chimpanzee at the Primate Research Institute of New Mexico State University. She lies swaddled in an incubator behind a glass wall. All that shows is a patch of black hair and some tiny pink fingers. 1

In the next room, two chimps share a crib complete with mobiles and toys. Elsewhere, still more chimps, all between six months and a year old, are sleeping in heaps, climbing on a jungle gym, inspecting toys, or playing together. The equipment and the care are superior to that of many preschools. 2

The institute, situated on the grounds of Holloman Air Force Base in Alamogordo, is one of the country's largest breeders and keepers of chimpanzees. It exists to produce human surrogates for medical re- 3 search. Although various groups have been raising chimps at Holloman for many years, the institute itself is new.

4   More than anthropomorphism lies behind the policy of raising infant apes almost as if they were human babies. The chimp is a highly developed, extremely complex, social animal. Chimps make tools, hunt cooperatively, use sticks as weapons, and even learn skills from one another. They possess some rudimentary language abilities and can recognize themselves in a mirror.

5   For many researchers, these facts pose ethical problems. If chimpanzees are so much like people, can they be treated, or mistreated, merely as expendable laboratory tools? Can it ever be justifiable to subject chimpanzees to invasive and often painful experimentation? Is it right to take a baby chimp away from its mother and put it in a sterile environment, subjecting it to experiment after experiment as if it were no more than a convenient blood container? How does one balance the special need of chimps for humane care with the possibility of preventing human suffering?

6   Jim Bowen, an institute veterinarian, worries about the dilemma. "Using chimps in research is justifiable because of their close similarity to man," he says, "but I don't want to see them suffer or be abused. We must treat them as humanely as we can."

7   Bowen's views represent the midpoint of a spectrum of opinions on the morality of exploiting chimps for human benefit. At one end are those who discount the behavioral evidence about chimps and who see no reason beyond the purely practical for treating chimps any better than they have been in the past. Geoffrey Bourne, the retired director of the Yerkes Regional Primate Research Center at Emory University in Atlanta, describes this group as scientists who "look at chimpanzees as test tubes," who see chimps as *just* animals undeserving of special regard.

8   On the other side there are people who contend that behavioral evidence is exactly the point. Some say chimps have demonstrated levels of self-awareness and rationality that are equivalent to those of a normal two-year-old human. Therefore, they argue, chimps deserve equivalent rights. Roger Fouts of Central Washington University in Ellensburg disputes the two-year-old analogy. Fouts is well known for his research with Washoe, the first chimp to learn a sign language of the deaf.

9   "Washoe and I are much closer in cognitive strategy than I am to a two- or a three-year-old child," Fouts says. He prefers to avoid such comparisons because they encourage the idea that chimps are, in some sense, defective human beings rather than normal chimps. Fouts agrees that chimpanzees deserve the same right as humans not to have pain and suffering inflicted on them.

10   Peter Singer, an Australian philosopher and author of the influential book *Animal Liberation,* argues that there is no morally relevant difference between experimenting on humans and any nonhumans. "An experiment cannot be justifiable," he writes, "unless the experiment is so important that the use of a retarded human being would also be justifiable." He contends that the contrary view is "speciesism," a bias he considers morally equivalent to racism.

Singer's views are generally considered extreme, but even those   11
who dispute him are becoming more concerned about the treatment
received by laboratory animals. After long deliberations, a panel appointed by the National Institutes of Health asserted that chimps deserve
humane treatment in the laboratory, but the panel rejected any suggestion that chimps have the same rights as humans. If an animal's resemblance to human beings were a factor, says Terry L. Maple, a Georgia
Institute of Technology psychologist who studies chimps, the way
would be open to justify less humane treatment of species that are less
like people than are chimps. All animals, many people feel, deserve to
be treated as humanely as possible in the laboratory, regardless of how
little they resemble people.

That position goes further than the anticruelty laws on the books in   12
virtually every state. Most states exempt laboratories. Maryland is an
exception, and it was there, last fall, that Edward Taub, head of a laboratory using monkeys, was convicted of mistreating his animals. Taub
maintains the monkeys were getting appropriate care and is appealing
the decision. He contends the overriding issue is the alleviation of
human suffering.

Yet many who agree with Taub when it comes to using other ani-   13
mals will draw the line for chimps. For them, chimpanzees are special,
no matter what government committees may decide.

Questions on Content

1. How are young chimpanzees treated while being raised at the Primate Research Institute?
2. What is the purpose of the Primate Research Institute?
3. How do the cognitive abilities of a chimp compare with those of a human?
4. What is speciesism?
5. Do the laws against cruelty to animals apply to laboratories?

Questions on Thesis, Purpose, and Structure

1. What are the similarities between a young chimp and a human child?
2. What are the similarities between chimp societies and human societies?
3. What are the contrasting opinions about the morality of using chimps in
   medical research?
4. How fair-minded are the authors of this essay in presenting the arguments on
   both sides of the controversy about using chimps in medical research? How
   can you tell which position the authors ultimately advocate?
5. What kinds of information are presented in this essay? Is that information new
   and interesting? What, if any, persuasive purpose in served by the essay?

Questions on Style and Diction

1. Find the following words in the essay and determine their definitions in
   context: anthropomorphism, rudimentary (paragraph 4); exempt, alleviation
   (paragraph 12).
2. What is the effect of giving the newborn chimp a human (not to mention
   trendy) name like Kelly-Lynn? What are the connotations of words like *swaddled, crib, toys,* and *playing*? Do you think the authors are consciously employing such connotations in order to create an effect? Explain your opinion.

3. This essay depends heavily on the testimony of experts. Examine the ways in which Stone and Koebner weave this testimony into their essay. What do they do to put expert testimony into context and to persuade the reader that the testimony is reliable?

Ideas for Essays

1. In an essay of your own take a reasoned, forceful position about the morality of using chimps in medical research.
2. Write an analytical essay about the methods of persuasion used in Stone and Koebner's essay. How do they use factual evidence, testimony, and emotionally charged language in attempting to influence the reader?
3. Write a comparison between humans and some other species in an attempt to prove that speciesism extends beyond our self-centered treatment of chimps.

Astronomer's Wife
Kay Boyle

Kay Boyle (1903–) was born in St. Paul, Minnesota, and studied both architecture and music before deciding to pursue a literary career as a free-lance writer. In 1923 she went to Europe for what was to have been a summer vacation. That vacation became an eighteen-year residence abroad, during which Boyle lived in France, England, Austria, and Germany before returning home as an established novelist in 1941. Despite the fact that she has published many novels, Kay Boyle is most highly regarded as a writer of short stories, the genre that best gives expression to her interest in literary technique, her bold use of language, and her ability to explore the psychology of character. Many of her stories, like "Astronomer's Wife" (1936), deal with the search for love. Note the many contrasts between the aloof, supercilious astronomer and the kindly, down-to-earth plumber.

1   There is an evil moment on awakening when all things seem to pause. But for women, they only falter and may be set in action by a single move: a lifted hand and the pendulum will swing, or the voice raised and through every room the pulse takes up its beating. The astronomer's wife felt the interval gaping and at once filled it to the brim. She fetched up her gentle voice and sent it warily down the stairs for coffee, swung her feet out upon the oval mat, and hailed the morning with her bare arms' quivering flesh drawn taut in rhythmic exercise: left, left, left my wife and fourteen children, right, right, right in the middle of the dusty road.

2   The day would proceed from this, beat by beat, without reflection, like every other day. The astronomer was still asleep, or feigning it, and she, once out of bed, had come into her own possession. Although scarcely ever out of sight of the impenetrable silence of his brow, she

would be absent from him all the day in being clean, busy, kind. He was a man of other things, a dreamer. At times he lay still for hours, at others he sat upon the roof behind his telescope, or wandered down the pathway to the road and out across the mountains. This day, like any other, would go on from the removal of the spot left there from dinner on the astronomer's vest to the severe thrashing of the mayonnaise for lunch. That man might be each time the new arching wave, and woman the undertow that sucked him back, were things she had been told by his silence were so.

In spite of the earliness of the hour, the girl had heard her mistress's voice and was coming up the stairs. At the threshold of the bedroom she paused, and said: "Madame, the plumber is here." 3

The astronomer's wife put on her white and scarlet smock very quickly and buttoned it at the neck. Then she stepped carefully around the motionless spread of water in the hall. 4

"Tell him to come right up," she said. She laid her hands on the bannisters and stood looking down the wooden stairway. "Ah, I am Mrs. Ames," she said softly as she saw him mounting. "I am Mrs. Ames," she said softly, softly down the flight of stairs. "I am Mrs. Ames," spoken soft as a willow weeping. "The professor is still sleeping. Just step this way." 5

The plumber himself looked up and saw Mrs. Ames with her voice hushed, speaking to him. She was a youngish woman, but this she had forgotten. The mystery and silence of her husband's mind lay like a chiding finger on her lips. Her eyes were gray, for the light had been extinguished in them. The strange dim halo of her yellow hair was still uncombed and sideways on her head. 6

For all of his heavy boots, the plumber quieted the sound of his feet, and together they went down the hall, picking their way around the still lake of water that spread as far as the landing and lay docile there. The plumber was a tough, hardy man; but he took off his hat when he spoke to her and looked her fully, almost insolently in the eye. 7

"Does it come from the wash-basin," he said, "or from the other . . . ?" 8

"Oh, from the other," said Mrs. Ames without hesitation. 9

In this place the villas were scattered out few and primitive, and although beauty lay without there was no reflection of her face within. Here all was awkward and unfit; a sense of wrestling with uncouth forces gave everything an austere countenance. Even the plumber, dealing as does a woman with matters under hand, was grave and stately. The mountains round about seemed to have cast them into the shadow of great dignity. 10

Mrs. Ames began speaking of their arrival that summer in the little villa, mourning each event as it followed on the other. 11

"Then, just before going to bed last night," she said, "I noticed something was unusual." 12

The plumber cast down a folded square of sackcloth on the brimming floor and laid his leather apron on it. Then he stepped boldly onto the heart of the island it shaped and looked long into the overflowing bowl. 13

14   "The water should be stopped from the meter in the garden," he said at last.

15   "Oh, I did that," said Mrs. Ames, "the very first thing last night. I turned it off at once, in my nightgown, as soon as I saw what was happening. But all this had already run in."

16   The plumber looked for a moment at her red kid slippers. She was standing just at the edge of the clear, pure-seeming tide.

17   "It's no doubt the soil lines," he said severely. "It may be that something has stopped them, but my opinion is that the water seals aren't working. That's the trouble often enough in such cases. If you had a valve you wouldn't be caught like this."

18   Mrs. Ames did not know how to meet this rebuke. She stood, swaying a little, looking into the plumber's blue relentless eye.

19   "I'm sorry — I'm sorry that my husband," she said, "is still — resting and cannot go into this with you. I'm sure it must be very interesting. √ . ."

20   "You'll probably have to have the traps sealed," said the plumber grimly, and at the sound of this Mrs. Ames' hand flew in dismay to the side of her face. The plumber made no move, but the set of his mouth as he looked at her seemed to soften. "Anyway, I'll have a look from the garden end," he said.

21   "Oh, do," said the astronomer's wife in relief. Here was a man who spoke of action and object as simply as women did! But however hushed her voice had been, it carried clearly to Professor Ames who lay, dreaming and solitary, upon his bed. He heard their footsteps come down the hall, pause, and skip across the pool of overflow.

22   "Katherine!" said the astronomer in a ringing voice. "There's a problem worthy of your mettle!"

23   Mrs. Ames did not turn her head, but led the plumber swiftly down the stairs. When the sun in the garden struck her face, he saw there was a wave of color in it, but this may have been anything but shame.

24   "You see how it is," said the plumber, as if leading her mind away. "The drains run from these houses right down the hill, big enough for a man to stand upright in them, and clean as a whistle too." There they stood in the garden with the vegetation flowering in disorder all about. The plumber looked at the astronomer's wife. "They come out at the torrent[1] on the other side of the forest beyond there," he said.

25   But the words the astronomer had spoken still sounded in her in despair. The mind of man, she knew, made steep and sprightly flights, pursued illusion, took foothold in the nameless things that cannot pass between the thumb and finger. But whenever the astronomer gave voice to the thoughts that soared within him, she returned in gratitude to the long expanses of his silence. Desert-like they stretched behind and before the articulation of his scorn.

26   Life, life is an open sea, she sought to explain it in sorrow, and to survive women cling to the floating débris on the tide. But the plumber

[1]Stream.

had suddenly fallen upon his knees in the grass and had crooked his
fingers through the ring of the drains' trap-door. When she looked down
she saw that he was looking up into her face, and she saw too that his
hair was as light as gold.

"Perhaps Mr. Ames," he said rather bitterly, "would like to come   27
down with me and have a look around?"

"Down?" said Mrs. Ames in wonder.   28

"Into the drains," said the plumber brutally. "They're a study for a   29
man who likes to know what's what."

"Oh, Mr. Ames," said Mrs. Ames in confusion. "He's still—still in   30
bed, you see."

The plumber lifted his strong, weathered face and looked curiously   31
at her. Surely it seemed to him strange for a man to linger in bed, with
the sun pouring yellow as wine all over the place. The astronomer's wife
saw his lean cheeks, his high, rugged bones, and the deep seams in his
brow. His flesh was as firm and clean as wood, stained richly tan with the
climate's rigor. His fingers were blunt, but comprehensible to her,
gripped in the ring and holding the iron door wide. The backs of his
hands were bound round and round with ripe blue veins of blood.

"At any rate," said the astronomer's wife, and the thought of it   32
moved her lips to smile a little, "Mr. Ames would never go down there
alive. He likes going up," she said. And she, in her turn, pointed, but
impudently, towards the heavens. "On the roof. Or on the mountains.
He's been up on the tops of them many times."

"It's matter of habit," said the plumber, and suddenly he went down   33
the trap. Mrs. Ames saw a bright little piece of his hair still shining, like a
star, long after the rest of him had gone. Out of the depths, his voice,
hollow and dark with foreboding, returned to her. "I think something
has stopped the elbow," was what he said.

This was speech that touched her flesh and bone and made her   34
wonder. When her husband spoke of height, having no sense of it, she
could not picture it nor hear. Depth or magic passed her by unless a
name were given. But madness in a daily shape, as elbow stopped, she
saw clearly and well. She sat down on the grasses, bewildered that it
should be a man who had spoken to her so.

She saw the weeds springing up, and she did not move to tear them   35
up from life. She sat powerless, her senses veiled, with no action taking
shape beneath her hands. In this way some men sat for hours on end, she
knew, tracking a single thought back to its origin. The mind of man
could balance and divide, weed out, destroy. She sat on the full, burdened grasses, seeking to think, and dimly waiting for the plumber to
return.

Whereas her husband had always gone up, as the dead go, she knew   36
now that there were others who went down, like the corporeal being of
the dead. That men were then divided into two bodies now seemed
clear to Mrs. Ames. This knowledge stunned her with its simplicity and
took the uneasy motion from her limbs. She could not stir, but sat facing
the mountains' rocky flanks, and harking in silence to lucidity. Her
husband was the mind, this other man the meat, of all mankind.

37   After a little, the plumber emerged from the earth: first the light top of his head, then the burnt brow, and then the blue eyes fringed with whitest lash. He braced his thick hands flat on the pavings of the garden-path and swung himself completely from the pit.

38   "It's the soil lines," he said pleasantly. "The gases," he said as he looked down upon her lifted face, "are backing up the drains."

39   "What in the world are we going to do?" said the astronomer's wife softly. There was a young and strange delight in putting questions to which true answers would be given. Everything the astronomer had ever said to her was a continuous query to which there could be no response.

40   "Ah, come, now," said the plumber, looking down and smiling. "There's a remedy for every ill, you know. Sometimes it may be that," he said as if speaking to a child, "or sometimes the other thing. But there's always a help for everything a-miss."

41   Things come out of herbs and make you young again, he might have been saying to her; or the first good rain will quench any drought; or time of itself will put a broken bone together.

42   "I'm going to follow the ground pipe out right to the torrent," the plumber was saying. "The trouble's between here and there and I'll find it on the way. There's nothing at all that can't be done over for the caring," he was saying, and his eyes were fastened on her face in insolence, or gentleness, or love.

43   The astronomer's wife stood up, fixed a pin in her hair, and turned around towards the kitchen. Even while she was calling the servant's name, the plumber began speaking again.

44   "I once had a cow that lost her cud," the plumber was saying. The girl came out on the kitchen-step and Mrs. Ames stood smiling at her in the sun.

45   "The trouble is very serious, very serious," she said across the garden. "When Mr. Ames gets up, please tell him I've gone down."

46   She pointed briefly to the open door in the pathway, and the plumber hoisted his kit on his arm and put out his hand to help her down.

47   "But I made her another in no time," he was saying, "out of flowers and things and what-not."

48   "Oh," said the astronomer's wife in wonder as she stepped into the heart of the earth. She took his arm, knowing that what he said was true.

Questions on Content

1. What problem confronts Mrs. Ames when she arises?
2. What does the astronomer say when he overhears his wife discussing sewer lines with the plumber? How does she react to his comment?
3. Why does the plumber think that Mr. Ames might like to go down into the drains to "have a look around"?

Questions on Thesis, Purpose, and Structure

1. Describe the astronomer and his way of reacting to his wife. Describe the plumber and his way of reacting to Mrs. Ames. How are these two contrasting

individuals representative of two broad categories of men and illustrative of differing ways of relating to women?

2. How has life with the astronomer changed Mrs. Ames, influencing her self-image, her self-confidence, and her view of a woman's place in the world? What does the plumber do to show her that there are other ways of seeing things?

3. What is implied when the plumber says to Mrs. Ames that "There's nothing at all that can't be done over for the caring" with his eyes "fastened on her face in insolence, or gentleness, or love"?

4. What is the significance of Mrs. Ames's decision to go with the plumber "into the heart of the earth"?

5. What is Boyle saying in this story about the relationships between men and women?

Questions on Style and Diction

1. Find the following words in the story and determine their definitions in context: feigning (paragraph 2); smock (paragraph 4); uncouth (paragraph 10); mettle (paragraph 22); articulation (paragraph 25); rigor (paragraph 31); impudently (paragraph 32); corporeal (paragraph 36); query (paragraph 39); insolence (paragraph 42); hoisted (paragraph 46).

2. What is the effect of the repetition in paragraph five when Mrs. Ames thrice says, "'I am Mrs. Ames,' spoken soft as a willow weeping"? What point does this make about Mrs. Ames?

3. Boyle makes frequent use of imagery (especially through similes and metaphors). Examine a few prominent uses of imagery in the story and attempt to explain how the images help Boyle to develop her thesis about men, women, and their relationships.

Ideas for Essays

1. Write an analytical essay in which you explain how Boyle uses imagery, action, and characterization to build her thesis. You may wish to limit this topic to only one of these three, depending on the length of essay you wish to write.

2. Write a narrative in which you reverse Boyle's situation and have a man confronting two contrasting kinds of women.

Hills Like White Elephants
Ernest Hemingway

Ernest Hemingway (1898–1962) was born and raised in Oak Park, Illinois. Following World War I, during which he was wounded while serving as a volunteer ambulance driver, Hemingway returned to Europe as a foreign correspondent for the Toronto *Star*. While in Paris, he joined the many artists and intellectuals who comprised the so-called lost generation of expatriates. Hemingway's fiction career began in the mid-1920s with the publication of his first collection of short stories, *In Our Time* (1924), and his famous novel of the lost generation, *The Sun Also Rises* (1926). His other major works include *A Farewell to Arms* (1929), *For Whom the Bell Tolls* (1940), and *The Old Man and the Sea* (1952). Hemingway's deceptively simple literary style, with its crisp, "masculine" dialogue, and his insistence on the active, sensuous life made him one of the most popular and widely read of all modern American writers and a legend during his own lifetime. In "Hills Like White Elephants" (1927) Hemingway uses this spare dialogue to develop the contrasting views of a man and a woman toward the "white elephant" of an unwanted pregnancy.

1   The hills across the valley of the Ebro were long and white. On this side there was no shade and no trees and the station was between two lines of rails in the sun. Close against the side of the station there was the warm shadow of the building and a curtain, made of strings of bamboo beads, hung across the open door into the bar, to keep out flies. The American and the girl with him sat at a table in the shade, outside the building. It was very hot and the express from Barcelona would come in forty minutes. It stopped at this junction for two minutes and went on to Madrid.[1]

2   "What should we drink?" the girl asked. She had taken off her hat and put it on the table.

3   "It's pretty hot," the man said.

4   "Let's drink beer."

5   "Dos cervezas," the man said into the curtain.

6   "Big ones?" a woman asked from the doorway.

7   "Yes. Two big ones."

8   The woman brought two glasses of beer and two felt pads. She put the felt pads and the beer glasses on the table and looked at the man and the girl. The girl was looking off at the line of hills. They were white in the sun and the country was brown and dry.

9   "They look like white elephants," she said.

10   "I've never seen one," the man drank his beer.

11   "No, you wouldn't have."

12   "I might have," the man said. "Just because you say I wouldn't have doesn't prove anything."

13   The girl looked at the bead curtain. "They've painted something on it," she said. "What does it say?"

14   "Anis del Toro. It's a drink."

15   "Could we try it?"

16   The man called "Listen" through the curtain. The woman came out from the bar.

17   "Four reales."[2]

18   "We want two Anis del Toro."

19   "With water?"

20   "Do you want it with water?"

---

[1]The references to the Ebro River and the cities of Barcelona and Madrid identify the setting as Spain.

[2]Spanish coins.

"I don't know," the girl said. "Is it good with water?"   21

"It's all right."   22

"You want them with water?" asked the woman.   23

"Yes, with water."   24

"It tastes like licorice," the girl said and put the glass down.   25

"That's the way with everything."   26

"Yes," said the girl. "Everything tastes of licorice. Especially all the   27
things you've waited so long for, like absinthe."

"Oh, cut it out."   28

"You started it," the girl said. "I was being amused. I was having a   29
fine time."

"Well, let's try and have a fine time."   30

"All right. I was trying. I said the mountains looked like white   31
elephants. Wasn't that bright?"

"That was bright."   32

"I wanted to try this new drink. That's all we do, isn't it — look at   33
things and try new drinks?"

"I guess so."   34

The girl looked across at the hills.   35

"They're lovely hills," she said. "They don't really look like white   36
elephants. I just meant the coloring of their skin through the trees."

"Should we have another drink?"   37

"All right."   38

The warm wind blew the bead curtain against the table.   39

"The beer's nice and cool," the man said.   40

"It's lovely," the girl said.   41

"It's really an awfully simple operation, Jig," the man said. "It's not   42
really an operation at all."

The girl looked at the ground the table legs rested on.   43

"I know you wouldn't mind it, Jig. It's really not anything. It's just to   44
let the air in."

The girl did not say anything.   45

"I'll go with you and I'll stay with you all the time. They just let the   46
air in and then it's all perfectly natural."

"Then what will we do afterward?"   47

"We'll be fine afterward. Just like we were before."   48

"What makes you think so?"   49

"That's the only thing that bothers us. It's the only thing that's made   50
us unhappy."

The girl looked at the bead curtain, put her hand out and took hold   51
of two of the strings of beads.

"And you think then we'll be all right and be happy."   52

"I know we will. You don't have to be afraid. I've known lots of   53
people that have done it."

"So have I," said the girl. "And afterward they were all so happy."   54

"Well," the man said, "if you don't want to you don't have to. I   55
wouldn't have you do it if you didn't want to. But I know it's perfectly
simple."

"And you really want to?"   56

57   "I think it's the best thing to do. But I don't want you to do it if you don't really want to."

58   "And if I do it you'll be happy and things will be like they were and you'll love me?"

59   "I love you now. You know I love you."

60   "I know. But if I do it, then it will be nice again if I say things are like white elephants, and you'll like it?"

61   "I'll love it. I love it now but I just can't think about it. You know how I get when I worry."

62   "If I do it you won't ever worry?"

63   "I won't worry about that because it's perfectly simple."

64   "Then I'll do it. Because I don't care about me."

65   "What do you mean?"

66   "I don't care about me."

67   "Well, I care about you."

68   "Oh, yes. But I don't care about me. And I'll do it and then everything will be fine."

69   "I don't want you to do it if you feel that way."

70   The girl stood up and walked to the end of the station. Across, on the other side, were fields of grain and trees along the banks of the Ebro. Far away, beyond the river, were mountains. The shadow of a cloud moved across the field of grain and she saw the river through the trees.

71   "And we could have all this," she said. "And we could have everything and every day we make it more impossible."

72   "What did you say?"

73   "I said we could have everything."

74   "We can have everything."

75   "No, we can't."

76   "We can have the whole world."

77   "No, we can't."

78   "We can go everywhere."

79   "No, we can't. It isn't ours any more."

80   "It's ours."

81   "No, it isn't. And once they take it away, you never get it back."

82   "But they haven't taken it away."

83   "We'll wait and see."

84   "Come on back in the shade," he said. "You mustn't feel that way."

85   "I don't feel any way," the girl said. "I just know things."

86   "I don't want you to do anything that you don't want to do——"

87   "Nor that isn't good for me," she said. "I know. Could we have another beer?"

88   "All right. But you've got to realize——"

89   "I realize," the girl said. "Can't we maybe stop talking?"

90   They sat down at the table and the girl looked across at the hills on the dry side of the valley and the man looked at her and at the table.

91   "You've got to realize," he said, "that I don't want you to do it if you don't want to. I'm perfectly willing to go through with it if it means anything to you."

92   "Doesn't it mean anything to you? We could get along."

"Of course it does. But I don't want anybody but you. I don't want   93
any one else. And I know it's perfectly simple."

"Yes, you know it's perfectly simple."   94

"It's all right for you to say that, but I do know it."   95

"Would you do something for me now?"   96

"I'd do anything for you."   97

"Would you please please please please please please please stop   98
talking?"

He did not say anything but looked at the bags against the wall of   99
the station. There were labels on them from all the hotels where they
had spent nights.

"But I don't want you to," he said, "I don't care anything about it."   100

"I'll scream," the girl said.   101

The woman came out through the curtains with two glasses of beer   102
and put them down on the damp felt pads. "The train comes in five
minutes," she said.

"What did she say?" asked the girl.   103

"That the train is coming in five minutes."   104

The girl smiled brightly at the woman, to thank her.   105

"I'd better take the bags over to the other side of the station," the   106
man said. She smiled at him.

"All right. Then come back and we'll finish the beer."   107

He picked up the two heavy bags and carried them around the   108
station to the other tracks. He looked up the tracks but could not see the
train. Coming back, he walked through the barroom, where people
waiting for the train were drinking. He drank an Anis at the bar and
looked at the people. They were all waiting reasonably for the train. He
went out through the bead curtain. She was sitting at the table and
smiled at him.

"Do you feel better?" he asked.   109

"I feel fine," she said. "There's nothing wrong with me. I feel fine."   110

Questions on Content

1. What are the subjects of conversation between the man and the woman in paragraphs 2–41? What, if anything, can you conclude about them from their conversation?
2. What are the man and woman talking about in paragraphs 42–101? Cite evidence to support your views.
3. What facts do you learn in the course of the story about the man, the woman, their way of life, and their relationship?

Questions on Thesis, Purpose, and Structure

1. How would you describe the relationship between the man and woman? Cite evidence to support your views.
2. Why doesn't Hemingway immediately tell us the names of the man and woman? (We only learn the woman's name in paragraph 42, and we never learn the man's name.)
3. Examine the descriptions of the setting in paragraphs 1, 8, and 70. Is there

any connection between the setting and the situation of the two main characters?

4. Why does Jig ask the man to stop talking in paragraph 98? What does she no longer wish to hear from him? What do you think she would like him to say?

Questions on Style and Diction

1. Why is the story entitled "Hills Like White Elephants"? What is a "white elephant," and how is it related to the situation of the two main characters?

2. Much of this story is told through spare dialogue, with no direct indication of the speaker's tone of voice, facial expression, or attitude. Analyze a portion of this dialogue to see if you can determine how the lines should be spoken.

3. What is implied in paragraph 108 when Hemingway writes that the man "drank an Anis at the bar and looked at the people. They were all waiting reasonably for the train"?

Ideas for Essays

1. Compare the attitudes of the man and woman toward her pregnancy, her planned abortion, the life they are living together, and the future they might have.

2. Write a continuation of the story, providing answers to some of the following questions: Will Jig get on the train? Will she go through with the abortion? What will happen to their relationship if she does? What will happen to their relationship if she refuses to get an abortion?

3. Write an analytic essay comparing the tactics used by men and women when they are arguing.

"When I Grow Up, I'm Going to Be a Judge, or a Senator or Maybe President"
"Everybody Starts at the Bottom"
"Body by Soloflex"

The three advertisements on the pages that follow demonstrate the range in forcefulness and subtlety that is possible in using comparison. The first advertisement, "When I grow up . . . ," draws strong, overt comparisons between a girl's and a boy's chances of growing up to become a judge, a senator, a president, a nurse, a typist, and a schoolteacher. Along the way there are also provocative comparisons between the typical salaries in "men's" and "women's" professions. The advertisement is sponsored by the National Organization of Women (NOW) and its purpose is obviously to persuade the reader that many women are the victims of sexual discrimination.

The second advertisement, "Everybody starts at the bottom," draws a more subtle comparison. In fact, the advertisement actually creates a metaphor, an implied comparison between all of our struggles for success and those of the diver plunging in a perfectly straight line toward the bottom. The text of the advertisement is carefully worded to suggest a number of parallels, concluding with the aphoristic advice to all of us that "the most soaring triumphs are in simply trying again."

The third advertisement, "Body by Soloflex," depends on *simile*—a form of overt comparison using "like," "as," "than," or some similar expression. Here, the human body is praised "As a machine"—intricate, strong, graceful. The wording of the advertisement, however, also encourages us to see the Soloflex body-building machine in the same terms. In fact, the ambiguity of the first three sentences—actually a sentence and two fragments—is probably an intentional effort to make us read the words as applying both to the Soloflex machine and to the human body: "We have been fascinated from the very beginning. By its beauty. The sheer simplicity of line." Once the analogy is suggested in this subtle way, we may perhaps be more willing to think of the machine too as being simple, strong, and beautiful.

© NOW LDEF. Concept & design by Jane Trahey.

"When I grow up, I'm going to be a judge, or a senator or maybe president."

Oh, no you're not little girl!

Your chances of making it into public office are very slim.
Only 23 of 657 FEDERAL JUDGES are women.
Only 2 of 100 SENATORS are women.
No woman has ever been PRESIDENT.
But you do have a 99% chance to be a NURSE.
(You'll earn less than a tree-trimmer.)
Or a 97% chance to be a TYPIST.
(You'll earn less than the janitor.)
Or a 60% chance to be a SCHOOL TEACHER.
(You'll earn less than a zoo-keeper.)

Concerned mamas and daddies are asking how they can help their female children to get an equal crack at vocational training —training that opens doors to non-stereotypical, better paying jobs. Parents want their female children to get the same kind of coaching in sports and physical education as boys do.

Parents want the kind of counseling that will encourage wider career options for girls. (Most young women graduate without the science and math credits they need to exercise full options for higher education.) If your female children attend a federally supported public school in this country you can and should help them get a more equal education.

YOU CAN HELP TO CREATE A BETTER FUTURE.
Write NOW Legal Defense & Education Fund (H) 132 W. 43rd Street, N.Y., N.Y. 10036

Courtesy of NOW LDEF

Ideas for Discussion and Writing

1. How would you describe the little girl's posture and the expression on her face? Does she appear reflective, meditative, melancholy, wistful, concerned, depressed, or some combination of these? Is the expression on her face related to the optimistic and boldly printed words she speaks or to the deflating responses she gets in the "fine print" beneath?
2. How informative and persuasive are the comparisons between career opportunities for men and women? Does it matter that the source of this factual information is not provided?
3. What is implied by the order in which the various careers are mentioned and by the "masculine" jobs mentioned in parentheses after the major career opportunities for women?
4. What is the goal of the advertisement? What response did the copywriter apparently hope to produce in the reader?

Everybody starts at
the bottom.

Real winning comes
in not staying there.
In United States Diving,
young people learn
that it's okay to be afraid,
that there's no shame
in failing. And as they
learn to dazzle the air
and knife the water,
they learn something
much more important.
That the most soaring
triumphs are in simply
trying again.

Phillips Petroleum has sponsored
United States Swimming for eleven
years, and United States Diving for
five, helping with operating costs of
national and international competitions
that lead to the Olympics. We continue
to support them. Because their ideals
touch the lives of everyone.

Courtesy of Phillips Petroleum

Ideas for Discussion and Writing

1. What is shown in the photograph? Describe the picture in some detail.
2. Explain the implied comparisons between living and diving.
3. Although the text for this advertisement is brief, it does make considerable use of imagery focusing on heights and depths. Examine that imagery and its relationship to the concepts of success and failure.
4. In relatively fine print beneath the Phillips 66 logo, there are three final sentences. Why are those sentences in smaller print? Why are they included at all? What benefit can the Phillips Petroleum Corporation expect to get from this advertisement?

We have been fascinated from the very beginning. By its beauty. The sheer simplicity of line. As a machine, the human body remains the supreme invention. While able to perform the most intricate, the most subtle of movements, it is, at the same time, capable of astonishing feats of strength. Strangely enough, the more that we demand of this machine, the more powerful, the more graceful it becomes.

To unlock your body's potential, we proudly offer Soloflex. Twenty-four traditional iron pumping exercises, each correct in form and balance. All on a simple machine that fits in a corner of your home.

For a free Soloflex brochure, call anytime **1-800-453-9000.**

BODY BY SOLOFLEX ®

CALL OUR 24 HR. TOLL-FREE NUMBER

Soloflex, Hillsboro, Oregon 97123.

Courtesy of Soloflex®

Ideas for Discussion and Writing

1. What *two* machines are depicted in this advertisement? What comparisons between the two are suggested by the text of the advertisement?
2. Why is the ambiguity of the first sentence and of the two fragments that follow it useful in encouraging the comparisons that are at the heart of this advertisement?
3. The second paragraph, like the first, contains a sentence followed by two fragments. Discuss the effect of those fragments and their importance in the advertisement.
4. Discuss the combination of purposes in this advertisement. Does it inform? Entertain? Persuade?

Chapter 12

CAUSE AND EFFECT

The gnarled and liver-spotted forefinger jabs shakily at the telephone buttons: *9* (nine electrical blips shoot down the line to the main exchange, and the wire Strowger connector leaps up to the ninth row of contacts); *1* (a single blip nudges another connector at the exchange); *1* (another blip; another connection). A circuit closes, and a distant sound of ringing passes along the wire to the receiver at the old man's ear. He pants into the receiver while the ringing continues—three, four, five, six rings.

Finally, someone answers the line, speaking in a nasal voice heavy with boredom: "This is 911. Will you hold, please?" The soothing tones of Muzak fill the short gaps between the old man's wheezes.

When the operator taps into the line again some moments later, it is dead. The old man has hung up.

Between the old man's first shaky jab at the telephone buttons and the moment of disconnection, we can trace a series of causes and effects. Some of these are obvious and mechanical: a button pushed, a connection made. Others are potentially more interesting. Why did the operator put the old man on hold? Was she in the middle of a snack and unwilling to be bothered? Or was she busy trying to explain the Heimlich maneuver to a panic-stricken mother whose two-year-old child had aspirated a balloon? Why did the old man dial 911 in the first place? Was he suffering from heart failure, trying to report an intruder in his living room, or simply seeking someone to talk to? Finally, why did he hang up? Had he found help elsewhere, grown discouraged, or dropped dead?

When we try to explain why something happened or what were the consequences of something that happened, we engage in causal analysis. As college students, your writing assignments will often require you to use causal analysis. In a history class you may be asked to write on the

422

Museo Nazionale del Bargello, Florence/Alinari/Art Resource, NY

Hercules and Antaeus by Antonio Pollaiuolo. Look up the story of Hercules and Antaeus in some general reference on mythology. How does Pollaiuolo's sculpture reflect the causal relationships that are important in the story of Hercules? Write an analytical description of the sculpture that emphasizes causal relationships.

causes of the American Revolution or the Great Depression. In a literature class you may face an essay question on the motives behind Hamlet's apparent inability to avenge his father's death. In a general science class you may need to analyze the atmospheric causes of a thunderstorm or the effects of a volcanic eruption on world weather patterns.

Beyond being a very practical form of writing, causal analysis is a very important form of reasoning. For that reason alone it deserves attention in the freshman writing course.

PREWRITING

You should have fun discovering the ideas that will eventually go into your causal analysis. After all, reasoning about causes and effects is very much the sort of procedure that a detective follows in solving a crime: What could have caused the peculiar stains on the dead man's fingertips? Are the effects of ingested nightshade compatible with the stains and the symptoms shown by the victim before his demise? Had he shown unusual signs of depression after his wife eloped with her hairdresser? How did he feel about the fact that he lost his job to $1.39 worth of microchips? Do the causes of his behavior and of his death point to murder or suicide?

In thinking about a topic for causal analysis, put yourself in the place of your favorite detective—Sherlock Holmes, Hercule Poirot, Travis McGee, Jane Marple, Jessica Fletcher—and try to develop a chain of reasoning like that of the famous detective. The invention technique to use here is essentially the same as that of making a tree diagram or mapping your ideas (as discussed on pp. 58 and 317). Suppose you want to write about the back-to-the-basics movement in education. You might begin by listing some of the most obvious causes of that movement:

> The declines in SAT scores during the 1970s and '80s
> The increasing conservatism in the nation as a whole
> The perception that courses like "Motion Picture Appreciation" and "Modern Photography" are simply less important than math and English
> The reduced willingness and ability of school boards to fund comprehensive programs

But Sherlock Holmes or Jane Marple would surely not be satisfied with such shallow reasoning. Like them, you need to be subtle and ingenious. Like them, you need to track your way through complexities. Were the declines in SAT scores the result of the many course options presented to students in the 1970s and early 1980s? Or were the declines the result of other factors including some of the following:

> The increasing percentage of high school graduates taking the SAT and going on to college
> Reductions in students' study time as a result of television viewing and part-time jobs
> The shift from an emphasis on academic achievements to an emphasis on sports and extracurricular activities

If the causes of the declines in SAT scores were unrelated to the high school curriculum, will the return to a curriculum of basics be likely to reverse the trend? Are the recent improvements in SAT scores the result of the return to the basics or do they simply indicate that, with reduced levels of financial aid for college students, some marginally qualified students are choosing not to attend college and therefore not to take the SAT?

In striving for subtlety, however, don't ignore plain common sense. Remember that the best detective is often the one who sees the significance of facts that were right under everyone else's nose. If *back to the basics* means a renewed emphasis on English composition and mathematics, then SAT scores, which measure a student's verbal and quantitative aptitudes, should rise.

Focused free writing should also be a useful invention technique for discovering causal relationships. In ten or twenty minutes of nonstop writing, you may discover a host of interrelationships that might not occur to you otherwise. When using focused free writing for this assignment, however, you want to avoid drifting off into idle reverie or unrelated narration. Don't, for example waste ten of your twenty minutes reminiscing fondly about the day when your ninth-grade English teacher, Mr. Hayes, embarrassed himself by repeatedly referring to Supreme Court Justice Sandra Day O'Connor as "Justice Sandra Dee." To avoid digression, draw yourself back to the mode of causal analysis by frequently asking yourself such questions as, "How did Mr. Hayes find new ways to emphasize basic language skills? What are the effects of substituting grammar drills for the sessions of Hangman or Trivial Spelling that once enlivened the classroom?"

Because causal relationships can often be subtle and quite complex, **select and limit your topic carefully.** Clearly, a good essay *can* be written on "The National Effects of the Back-to-the-Basics Movement in High School Education." But an equally good essay can be written on "Getting Back to Basics at Grant High." The narrower topic, dealing with your experiences at your own high school, will likely be easier to develop using entertaining and original anecdotes and examples.

PLANNING AND DRAFTING
A CAUSAL ANALYSIS

Your prewriting exercises should have produced two or three rather jumbled pages of notes—perhaps with arrows pointing off from main points to any number of peripheral causes and effects. Your most pressing task is to impose order on your preliminary notes. To do so, **classify the various kinds of causal relationships that you have discovered.**

The most direct, and often the most useful, classification is called the causal chain. In a causal chain, each event is like a link on a chain, directly tied to its two neighbors: the effect of one cause is the cause of the next effect. The result is that, given the tug of the first event in the chain, the last must follow along. A well-known illustration of the causal chain is the following nursery rhyme:

A Nail, a Shoe, a Horse, and a Rider

For want of a nail the shoe was lost,
For want of a shoe the horse was lost,
For want of a horse the rider was lost,
For want of a rider the battle was lost,
For want of a battle the kingdom was lost—
And all for the want of a nail.

The difficulty with causal chains is that they often contain weak links. It is true that the loss of a nail could easily have caused the horse to throw a shoe. And it is true that the horse may have stumbled and the rider may have broken his neck because of that lost nail and lost shoe. But does it follow that the battle was lost because one rider was involved in an accident? By their very nature, battles involve many injuries and many deaths. Victory or defeat is the result of the cumulative actions of hundreds of men. In ordinary circumstances the actions of no single individual are sufficiently important to determine the outcome directly. Thus, the chain of reasoning in the rhyme breaks down in the fourth line.

Conceivably, however, that weak link could be strengthened. Perhaps the lost rider was bearing a message directing reinforcements to a particular point in the line of battle. In that case the loss of the rider could have meant that hundreds of men did not go where their general expected them to go. The fate of the entire battle and of the kingdom may well have hinged on such a failure of communication.

Causal relationships that are interesting enough to be worth writing about rarely exhibit an unbreakable causal chain. Don't let that fact trouble you. Indeed, the weak link in a causal chain is often the most interesting part of it. After all, your goal is to write a thoughtful essay, not a simple nursery rhyme. For an essayist or a novelist, the whole interest in "A Nail, a Shoe, a Horse, and a Rider" revolves around the mysterious rider and the reasons why his loss might cause the loss of the battle. In your own essays you too will discover that the weakest link in your causal chain usually provides you with your greatest opportunity to interest and inform your reader.

When the direct chain of causes and effects breaks down, you may be able to proceed by attempting to identify immediate causes (or effects) and remote causes (or effects). Suppose you are trying to write an essay explaining the reasons for the recent bankruptcy of your Uncle Ira's farm. If you were to attempt to use a causal chain, you would inevitably oversimplify events and probably end up writing a narrative essay (telling about the sequence of events) instead of a causal analysis (explaining the reasons for the events). In something as complicated as a bankruptcy, a number of different factors usually conspire to bring about the misfortune. An *immediate* cause of the bankruptcy may have been that the market price of corn and soybeans fell below your uncle's cost of production for the third year in a row. Perhaps another immediate cause was that his old 1961 tractor, held together with baling wire and Bondo, finally threw a rod. Without a tractor to harvest his grain, without a market price to make the harvest worthwhile, and with debts as high as his silo, Uncle Ira finally did the sensible thing and sold the farm.

Note that such immediate causes, although affecting and important, may fail to tell the entire story. Perhaps a number of *remote* causes played their parts in the events. The United States policy of farm subsidies, by helping to keep many farmers in business, may be a major factor in the persistent oversupply of farm products and the resulting declines in market prices. The oil embargo of the 1970s, by dramatically increasing the cost of everything from fertilizer to diesel fuel, undoubtedly increased your uncle's cost of production. Maybe, too, he bought up so many parcels of neighboring farm land in the 1970s when land prices were at record highs that he saddled himself with ruinous mortgages.

Another alternative is to classify causes or effects as either primary or secondary. For the sake of illustration, let us consider some of the effects of Uncle Ira's bankruptcy. Among the primary effects are the forced sale of the farm and farm equipment, the family's move to a rented apartment in town, and Uncle Ira's decision to take on work as a cabinetmaker. Some of the secondary effects may have been that Aunt Margaret was much happier because the move took her closer to her grandchildren; Uncle Ira slowly discovered an interest in raising flowers, which he had always been too busy to bother with on the farm; and they both took pleasure in having free weekends for travel or simply lounging around the apartment.

Once you have finished classifying the various causal relationships you have found, you are ready to begin writing your essay. Unless your assignment is to write a lengthy term paper, you should **consider slanting your emphasis toward either causes or effects, not both.** If you decide to write on the *causes* of the recent trend toward studying a foreign language in high school, your introduction should help your reader to see the importance of the topic by dramatically presenting some of the *effects* of that trend: classes in French and Spanish are getting too large for the classrooms; Latin is sometimes actually spoken at toga parties; and in some parts of the country foreign language teachers are courted like prize quarterbacks. With the scope and the significance of the trend toward foreign language study dramatically illustrated, your readers will be more interested in a careful analysis of the causes of the phenomenon.

If, on the other hand, you decide to focus on the *effects* of the reemergence of Latin in the high school curriculum, you should begin your essay by briefly summarizing the *causes* of the trend: the urging of educators who see foreign language study as part of getting back to the basics; the belief of parents that no clique of Latin students is apt to engage in snorting coke or smoking crack; and the intuition of ambitious students that a good foundation in Latin now will ease their transition into medical school later. Once your readers are convinced that the trend has sound causes, they will be more patient with you in your exposition of its effects.

Whether you are writing on causes or effects, your best organizational strategy is to move from what is obvious (but relatively unimportant) to what is subtle (but potentially quite significant). Of course, the higher you build your scaffolding of causal relationships and the farther you get from the solid, earthbound observations that are clear to every dullard, the more speculative you will have to become. Don't worry unduly about the rarified air you are breathing. As we have tried to make clear, the kinds of causal relationships that are the most interesting are usually also the most difficult to prove (or disprove). Your teacher knows this and knows as well that in a brief classroom assignment you can hardly be expected to build a causal argument as solid as one of the great Egyptian pyramids. Your teacher expects plausible reasoning and persuasive supporting examples — a solid framework — but he or she will not demand that your framework be unshakable or that in a matter of a few days you will caulk every window and weatherstrip every doorway. Be a good craftsman, but don't feel that what you build must stand for all the ages.

COMBINING PURPOSES

Be sure that your essay has a persuasive purpose. Causal analysis is primarily a means of persuasion. Irate voters write to the president about the effects of the continuing nuclear arms race in the hope of influencing national policy. Beseeching students often write to their parents about the reasons why they need more money in the hope of receiving a check by return mail. Advertisers write glowingly about the effects of eating Fruit & Fibre cereal or using Crest toothpaste in the hope of selling their products.

To assure yourself that your essay has a persuasive purpose, your thesis should serve as a brief summary of the argument you wish to make. Here are some representative theses for cause-and-effect essays:

A liberal arts education is helpful to students because it teaches them communication skills necessary in any profession, it gives them the cultural knowledge of a literate individual, and it develops the ability to adapt to changes in society and technology.

Students today are choosing business majors in increasing numbers because they perceive that specific business skills are helpful in today's competitive job market, they see a college degree as a passport to wealth rather than a process of education, and they are generally more conservative and pragmatic than the students of years past.

More people should consider kayaking as a recreational sport: the equipment is relatively inexpensive; the sport can be enjoyed alone or in groups; it provides terrific exercise for the upper body (and even the lower body during portages); and it brings one quietly into contact with nature at its most beautiful.

Remember, too, that causal analysis should also be informative and entertaining. Fishermen curiously read articles about the causes and effects of acid rain in the hope of understanding why their stringers are always empty. Homeowners in California read about the causes and effects of earthquakes, perhaps with concern about the adequacy of their insurance coverage. Teachers in Texas read about the back-to-the-basics movement in education to see how changes in curriculum are likely to affect their pupils.

In striving to make your essay informative and entertaining, go beyond simply listing causes and effects. Use examples and narrative anecdotes to get the reader's attention and illustrate your meaning. Note how much better causal analysis becomes when it is developed using vivid details:

> **A Very General Passage on Planning a House** The sun comes up in the east and goes down in the west. This obvious but all-governing fact demands that both kitchen and bathroom be on the east side of house. Such a location as this will also save you money on plumbing.

> **A More Specific Passage on Planning a House** The sun comes up in the east and goes down in the west. Your engineering must begin with this obvious but all-governing fact. If bacon is to be fried by daylight, the kitchen will look southeast. If shaving is to be by daylight, the bathroom will be close by.

> Two vital work areas have been located on your previously blank piece of paper. You spend crucial morning minutes at lavatory and stove, and you make those desparate minutes as warm and cheerful as your own nature may permit. The house, at least, will begin its day pleasantly.

> A cry, "The eggs are boiling," can be heard through the bathroom wall. Your house, while pleasant, is also efficient.

> Since both kitchen and bathroom run on running water, the closer together they are, the shorter the pipes. Your house, already pleasant and efficient, is on its way to being inexpensive.

> —from *Your Engineered House* by Rex Roberts

TIPS ON REVISION

One of your main goals in revising a cause-and-effect essay should be to increase the persuasiveness of your argument. In doing so, keep four thoughts in mind:

1. **Be moderate.** Readers are apt to have scant patience with you if you climb on a soapbox and make unsupported claims about inevitable causes and unavoidable consequences. You will have a much better chance of convincing your readers if you temper your claims. Don't insist that if the United States develops a space-based missile defense system ("Star Wars"), the Soviets will be forced into a preemptive nuclear attack. Your readers will likely recognize that the Soviets' response to the deployment of such a system could take on many forms, most of them falling far short of nuclear war. If you want to raise the spectre of nuclear war, you might claim that a preemptive nuclear strike by the Soviets is *one possible* response to the deployment of a Star Wars system. Or you might point out that *some experts fear* that the Soviets might respond with a nuclear attack. There is a great difference between asserting a *possible* effect and asserting an *inevitable* effect. When in doubt, take the cautious path of possibilities.

2. **Avoid the post hoc fallacy.** This fallacy is named after the Latin phrase *post hoc, ergo propter hoc* (after this, therefore because of this). Suppose you observe that on days when you carry an umbrella, it never seems to rain. Can you reasonably conclude that by carrying an umbrella you stave off rain? If a black cat crosses your path in the morning and your car breaks down in the afternoon, can you logically conclude that the black cat caused your bad luck? In both cases there is a temporal relationship between the events but not a causal one. To demonstrate a causal relationship, you must propose a plausible mechanism by which one event brings about another.

3. **Avoid oversimplification.** It is not always sufficient to show that two events are related in time and that a plausible causal relationship exists between them. You also need to consider the other factors that may have had an effect on the outcome of events. In 1982 the so-called Reagan tax cut first took effect, and between 1983 and 1986 the price of the average stock on the New York Stock Exchange rose by nearly 50 percent. Did the tax cut cause the bull market? Well, it could have contributed to the rally, but it was certainly not the only cause of it. The tax cut put more money into people's pockets; if they spent some of that money on stocks, the increased demand for stocks would help to drive up prices. But a host of other factors were probably also involved in the bull market, among them the growth in the U.S. economy, the control of inflation, the decline in oil prices, the widespread use of Individual Retirement Accounts, the maturing of the "baby-boom" generation, and the relative prevalence of world peace. It is fair to say that the tax cut may have been one contributing factor in the historic bull market, but it is not fair to say that the tax cut caused it.

4. **Consider the views of those who may disagree with you.** Your readers fall into two camps: those who already agree with you and those who don't. Those who agree with you will nod their heads sagely at each point you make, but you really didn't need to convince them of anything in the first place. It is the readers who disagree with you that you need to sway. If you are to have any hope of changing their

minds, you must give due consideration to the views they hold. The best strategy is to acknowledge the strength of their arguments early on, perhaps in your first or second paragraph. Having placated your adversaries to some extent, you can then go on to raise even stronger arguments in support of your views, for example, "Despite the practicality of choosing the college major that most directly prepares you for the business world, there are even sounder reasons for pursuing a degree in the liberal arts. . . ." Even if you fail in creating converts to your views, you will at least succeed in making them see the strength of your arguments and you will fend off any accusations of unfairness.

IDEAS FOR ESSAYS

Write an essay exploring either the causes or the effects associated with one of the following subjects.

1. A current fad or fashion
2. The percentage of athletes who fail to graduate from college
3. Teenage rebelliousness
4. A new product (home computers, video-cassette recorders, microwave ovens, wine coolers, Post-it Notes, and so on)
5. Your first date (or your first kiss on a date)
6. An incident in which you feel you were abused or treated unfairly
7. A personal experience with violence
8. An individual quirk (like fear of heights, having nightmares about school, or drooling when you concentrate)
9. A passionate attitude or belief
10. Teenage employment (or unemployment)
11. The movement toward sexual equality
12. The temptation to cheat (or steal or lie)
13. The growing interest in foreign languages
14. The pressure to conform
15. The recent trends in prime-time television
16. The latest rage in popular music
17. The comparative status of "brains" and "jocks" on campus
18. The need for professors to "publish or perish"
19. The high cost of a college education
20. The graying of America (i.e., the increasing percentage of the elderly among the total population)

STUDENT ESSAY _____

"Remote Control" was written as an in-class essay on the topic, "Discuss the effects of some new product or minor invention." Kathy had time for only one draft, with minor revisions. The comparative success of this single draft is an indication of the value of the careful outlining that Kathy did before beginning to write.

"REMOTE CONTROL"

by Kathy Turner

OUTLINE

THESIS: Remote controls have done much harm to the well-being of American citizens.

  I. Remote controls

    A. For TV's

    B. For stereos

    C. For VCR's

    D. For garage doors

    E. Use TV as example

  II. Damage to weight (through eating before the television)

  III. Damage to TV (through excessive channel changing)

  IV. Damage to the home when remote is missing

    A. Turned upside down

    B. Owners think that is easier than walking to change channels

  V. Bright side of things

    A. Less wear on carpet

    B. Keep TV repairmen in business

    C. Exercise in hunting for control

  VI. Counterargument and conclusion

    A. Better slim hips than savings on carpet

    B. Better repairman starving than you

    C. Better ways of getting exercise

As the world has become increasingly more technical people have become ~~more out of shape~~ lazier than ever. A world that can ~~save~~

~~energy~~ make everything easy on its people will sooner or later find the people in no condition to perform even the smallest tasks. Anyone can see what cars and other automobiles have done to us; however, with a closer look, he may find there are many smaller luxuries that contribute to excessive laziness. One that seems to be growing out of control is the ever popular remote control. Remote controls are made for TV's, stereos, VCR's, and garage doors, just to name a few. ~~Since I am limited in this essay, I will use~~ To illustrate the pernicious effects of this invention, let us examine just one, the TV remote control ~~to study the base effects of these little gadgets~~ as an example of how these gadgets have changed the people of this century.

In most houses around the country, it has become permissible to eat while watching TV. This in itself is a bad habit, but, until remote controls, at least we got the exercise of getting up to change the channel. Now it is entirely possible to sit in a favorite lounge chair with a glass of coke in one hand, a bag of chips ~~to the left side~~ and a bag of cookies ~~to the right side~~ at opposite sides, and the remote control ~~resting~~ on one arm of the chair. Since the snacking viewer never moves from that position for hours, every calorie eaten rests harshly on the hips and thighs. Surely, ~~taking this into consideration~~ remote controls may be directly connected with the weight problems of our country's people.

The damage that remote controls can do to figures is not the only ~~kind of~~ damage they can ~~be~~ contribute to. These little boxes can cause a lot of unnecessary wear on the internal mechanisms of the TV. Since it is so easy to flip through the channels to see what is on, that is exactly what ~~so~~ many people do. Therefore, the greater ~~amount~~ number of channel changings can cause a greater ~~amount~~ number of TV breakdowns.

Finally, another form of ~~scarcely seen~~ damage is the wreckage of the house when the beloved family treasure, the remote control, is missing. Every cushion, pillow, and chair ~~or whatever else gets in the way~~ is turned over and searched until the little box is found. According to the bent mind of a remote control owner, it is much easier to turn the house upside down and shake it until the remote is found than it is to

~~just~~ walk three steps forward and change the channel by hand. People say that owning this thing is a luxury?!

I suppose if someone wanted to look on the "sunny side" of things, he could make his point also. He might say things like: remote controls produce less wear on the carpet; they keep TV repairmen from starving; the exercise lost is made up by the hunting for the remote when it is missing. However, can these arguments really stand up? No, I don't think so. I, myself, would rather have slim hips than unworn carpet. I would rather not have to pay a repairman's fee ~~because it may cause me to starve~~. And I can find better ways to get exercise than a frustrated hunt for a remote control. ~~Though the brilliance of technology is wonderful, I think we could do without the added remote controls.~~ If remote technology continues, the time when we will sit in one spot all day and still get our work done may not be so far off. However, the question remains: Is this really best for America's people?

Commentary: Kathy's essay starts out very effectively with a startling pair of observations:

> As the world has become increasingly more technical people have become lazier than ever. A world that can make everything easy on its people will sooner or later find the people in no condition to perform even the smallest tasks.

Having captured the reader's attention, Kathy narrows the focus of her essay until it is limited to the effects of the TV remote control. By focusing on a seemingly insignificant technological invention, Kathy increases her chances of being both original and thought-provoking. Few of her readers will have considered carefully the effects of TV remote controls.

The most significant weakness in Kathy's essay occurs in the second paragraph, where she contends that "remote controls may be directly connected with the weight problems of our country's people." Most readers are probably willing to accept that contention, but Kathy comes perilously close to oversimplifying the causes of weight gain. Eating before the television and using a remote control may be minor factors in weight gain, but there are clearly more important factors involved — among them heredity, the American preference for red meats, the national shift to less physically demanding occupations, the unwillingness of many to exercise regularly, and the dozens of other labor-saving devices that join with remote controls in reducing the amount of exercise that people get in the ordinary course of living. Kathy's oversimplification would be a serious weakness if she had not alluded to the impact of other labor-saving devices in her first paragraph. She actually uses TV remote controls only as one example of a number of factors that are helping to make Americans lazier and more poorly conditioned.

Kathy can also be accused of exaggerating the harmful effects of using TV remote controls. The channel-switching phenomenon she mentions in her third paragraph almost certainly exists, but Kathy presents no evidence that frequent use of the remote control actually harms the television set; and perhaps she need not present such evidence. Kathy uses exaggeration throughout her essay to wryly satirize American behavior. There is similar exaggeration in the ''wreckage'' caused by the loss of the remote control and in the reduced carpet wear caused by the use of the control.

The humor in Kathy's essay is at least in part directed toward herself as a representative of all Americans. When she sums up her argument by asserting that she ''would rather have slim hips than unworn carpet,'' she takes on the role of the stereotypical woman of TV commercialdom: she has a fixation with maintaining ''slim hips''; she is obsessed with the appearance of her carpet; and she is attached umbilically to her TV set, trudging remote-controllessly back and forth to change the channel. Yes, Kathy is correct—''the question remains: Is this really best for America's people?''

Masculine/Feminine
Prudence Mackintosh

Prudence Mackintosh is the author of *Thundering Sneakers* (1981) from which this essay is excerpted. As a modern, liberated woman, Mackintosh had hoped to raise her three sons without imposing sex stereotypes on them. In this witty account of her parental experiences, Mackintosh frequently compares the behavior of boys and girls and speculates on the causes of the dramatic differences she perceives.

I had every intention to raise liberated, nonviolent sons whose aggressive tendencies would be mollified by a sensitivity and compassion that psychologists claim were denied their father's generation.   1

I did not buy guns or war toys (although Grandmother did). My boys even had a secondhand baby doll until the garage sale last summer. I did buy Marlo Thomas' *Free to Be You and Me* record, a collection of nonsexist songs, stories, and poems, and I told them time and time again that it was okay to cry and be scared sometimes. I overruled their father and insisted that first grade was much too early for organized competi-   2 tive soccer leagues. They know that moms *and dads* do dishes and diapers. And although they use it primarily for the convenient bathroom between the alley and the sandpile, my boys know that the storeroom is now mother's office. In such an environment, surely they would grow up free of sex-role stereotypes. At the very least wouldn't they pick up their own socks?

3   My friends with daughters were even more zealous. They named their daughters strong, cool unisex names like Blakeney, Brett, Brook, Lindsay, and Blair, names that lent themselves to corporate letterheads, not Tupperware party invitations. These moms looked on Barbie with disdain and bought trucks and science kits. They shunned frilly dresses for overalls. They subscribed to Feminist Press and read stories called "My Mother the Mail Carrier" instead of "Sleeping Beauty." At the swimming pool one afternoon, I watched a particularly fervent young mother, ironically clad in a string bikini, encourage her daughter. "You're so strong, Blake! Kick hard, so you'll be the strongest kid in this pool." When my boys splashed water in Blakeney's eyes and she ran whimpering to her mother, this mom exhorted, "You go back in that pool and shake your fist like this and say, 'You do that again and I'll bust your lights out.'" A new generation of little girls, assertive and ambitious, taking a backseat to no one?

4   It's a little early to assess the results of our efforts, but when my seven-year-old son, Jack, comes home singing—to the tune of *"Frère Jacques"*—"Farrah Fawcett, Farrah Fawcett, I love you" and five minutes later asks Drew, his five-year-old brother, if he'd like his nose to be a blood fountain, either we're backsliding or there's more to this sex-role learning than the home environment can handle.

5   I'm hearing similar laments from mothers of daughters. "She used to tell everyone that she was going to grow up to be a lawyer just like Daddy," said one, "but she's hedging on that ambition ever since she learned that no one wears a blue fairy tutu in the courtroom." Another mother with two sons, a daughter, and a very successful career notes that, with no special encouragement, only her daughter keeps her room neat and loves to set the table and ceremoniously seat her parents. At a Little League game during the summer, fearful that this same young daughter might be absorbing the stereotype "boys play while girls watch," her parents readily assured her that she too could participate when she was eight years old. "Oh," she exclaimed with obvious delight, "I didn't know they had cheerleaders."

6   How does it happen? I have my own theories, but decided to do a little reading to see if any of the "experts" agreed with me. I was also curious to find out what remedies they recommended. The books I read propose that sex roles are culturally induced. In simplistic terms, rid the schools, their friends, and the television of sexism, and your daughters will dump their dolls and head straight for the boardroom while your sons contemplate nursing careers. *Undoing Sex Stereotypes* by Marcia Guttentag and Helen Bray is an interesting study of efforts to overcome sexism in the classroom. After reading it, I visited my son's very traditional school and found it guilty of unabashedly perpetrating the myths

that feminists abhor. Remember separate water fountains? And how, even if the line was shorter, no boy would be caught dead drinking from the girls' fountain and vice versa? That still happens. "You wouldn't want me to get cooties, would you, Mom?" my son says, defending the practice. What did I expect in a school where the principal still addresses his faculty, who range in age from 23 to 75, as "girls"?

Nevertheless, having been a schoolteacher myself. I am skeptical of   7
neatly programmed nonsexist curriculum packets like Guttentag and Bray's. But if you can wade through the jargon ("people of the opposite sex hereafter referred to as POTOS"), some of the observations and exercises are certainly thought-provoking and revealing. In one exercise fifth-grade students were asked to list adjectives appropriate to describe women. The struggle some of the children had in shifting their attitudes about traditional male roles is illustrated in this paragraph written by a fifth-grade girl who was asked to write a story about a man using the adjectives she had listed to describe women:

> Once there was a boy who all his life was very *gentle*. He never hit anyone or started a fight and when some of his friends were not feeling well, he was *loving* and *kind* to them. When he got older he never changed. People started not liking him because he was *weak, petite*, and he wasn't like any of the other men — not strong or tough. Most of his life he sat alone thinking about why no one liked him. Then one day he went out and tried to act like the other men. He joined a baseball team, but he was no good, he always got out. Then he decided to join the hockey team. He couldn't play good. He kept on breaking all the rules. So he quit the team and joined the soccer team. These men were *understanding* to him. He was really good at soccer, and was the best on the team. That year they won the championship and the rest of his life he was happy.

After reading this paragraph it occurred to me that this little girl's   8
self-esteem and subsequent role in life would be enhanced by a teacher who spent less time on "nonsexist intervention projects" and more time on writing skills. But that, of course, is not what the study was meant to reveal.

The junior high curriculum suggested by *Undoing Sex Stereotypes*   9
has some laudable consciousness-raising goals. For example, in teaching units called "Women's Roles in American History" and "The Socialization of Women and the Image of Women in the Media" teenagers are encouraged to critically examine television commercials, soap operas, and comic books. But am I a traitor to the cause if I object when the authors in another unit use *Romeo and Juliet* as a study of the status of women? Something is rotten in Verona when we have to consider Juliet's career possibilities and her problems with self-actualization. The conclusions of this project were lost on me; I quit reading when the author began to talk about ninth-graders who were "cognitively at a formal-operational level." I don't even know what my "external sociopsychological situation" is. However, I think I did understand some of the conclusions reached by the kids:

"Girls are smart."

"If a woman ran a forklift where my father works, there would be a
walkout."

"Men cannot be pom-pom girls."

10   Eminently more readable, considering that both authors are educators of educators, is *How to Raise Independent and Professionally Successful Daughters*, by Drs. Rita and Kenneth Dunn. The underlying and, I
think, questionable assumption in this book is that little boys have been
reared correctly all along. Without direct parental intervention, according to the Dunns, <u>daughters tend to absorb and reflect society's values.</u>
The Dunns paint a dark picture indeed for the parents who fail to
channel their daughters toward professional success. The woman who
remains at home with children while her husband is involved in the
"real world" with an "absorbing and demanding day-to-day commitment that brings him into contact with new ideas, jobs, and people
(attractive self-actualized females)" is sure to experience lowered IQ,
according to the Dunns. They go on to predict the husband's inevitable
affair and the subsequent divorce, which leaves the wife emotionally
depressed and probably financially dependent on her parents.

11   Now I'm all for women developing competency and self-reliance,
but the Dunns' glorification of the professional is excessive. Anyone
who has worked longer than a year knows that eventually any job loses
most of its glamour. And the world is no less "real" at home. For that
matter, mothers at home may be more "real" than bankers or lawyers.
How is a corporate tax problem more real than my counseling with the
maid whose boyfriend shot her in the leg? How can reading a balance
sheet compare with comforting a five-year-old who holds his limp cat
and wants to know why we have to lose the things we love? And on the
contrary, it is my husband, the professional, who complains of lowered
IQ. Though we wooed to Faulkner, my former ace English major turned
trial lawyer now has time for only an occasional *Falconer* or Peter
Benchley thriller. Certainly there is value in raising daughters to be
financially self-supporting, <u>but there is not much wisdom in teaching a
daughter that she must achieve professional success or her marriage
probably won't last.</u>

12   In a chapter called "What to Do from Birth to Two," the authors
instruct parents to introduce dolls only if they represent adult figures or
groups of figures. "Try not to give her her own 'baby.' A baby doll is
acceptable only for dramatizing the familiar episodes she has actually
experienced, like a visit to the doctor." If some unthinking person
should give your daughter a baby doll, and she likes it, the Dunns
recommend that you permit her to keep it without exhibiting any negative feelings, "but do not lapse into cuddling it or encouraging her to do
so. Treat it as any other object and direct attention to other more beneficial toys." I wonder if the Dunns read an article by Anne Roiphe called
"Can You Have Everything and Still Want Babies?" which appeared in
Vogue a couple of years ago. Ms. Roiphe was deploring the extremes to
which our liberation has brought us. "It is nice to have beautiful feet, it

may be desirable to have small feet, but it is painful and abusive to bind feet. It is also a good thing for women to have independence, freedom and choice, movement, and opportunity; but I'm not so sure that the current push against mothering will not be another kind of binding of the soul. . . . As women we have thought so little of ourselves that when the troops came to liberate us we rushed into the streets leaving our most valuable attributes behind as if they belonged to the enemy."

The Dunns' book is thorough, taking parents step-by-step through   13
the elementary years and on to high school. Had I been raising daughters, however, I think I would have flunked out in the chapter "What to Do from Age Two to·Five." In discussing development of vocabulary, the Doctors Dunn prohibit the use of nonsensical words for bodily functions. I'm sorry, Doctors, but I've experimented with this precise terminology and discovered that the child who yells "I have to defecate, Mom" across four grocery aisles is likely to be left in the store. A family without a few poo-poo jokes is no family at all.

These educators don't help me much in my efforts to liberate my   14
sons. And although I think little girls are getting a better deal with better athletic training and broader options, I believe we're kidding ourselves if we think we can raise our sons and daughters alike. Certain inborn traits seem to be immune to parental and cultural tampering. How can I explain why a little girl baby sits on a quilt in the park thoughtfully examining a blade of grass, while my baby William uproots grass by handfuls and eats it? Why does a mother of very bright and active daughters confide that until she went camping with another family of boys, she feared that my sons had a hyperactivity problem? I'm sure there are plenty of rowdy, noisy little girls, but I'm not just talking about rowdiness and noise. I'm talking about some sort of primal physicalness that causes the walls of my house to pulsate on rainy days. I'm talking about something inexplicable that makes my sons fall into a mad, scrambling, pull-your-ears-off-kick-your-teeth-in heap just before bedtime, when they're not even mad at each other. I mean something that causes them to climb the doorjamb with honey and peanut butter on their hands while giving me a synopsis of *Star Wars* that contains only five intelligible words: "And then this guy, he 'pssshhhhhhh.' And then this thing went 'vrongggggg.' But this little guy said, 'Nong-neeee-nonh-nee.'" When Jack and Drew are not kicking a soccer ball or each other, they are kicking the chair legs, the cat, the baby's silver rattle, and, inadvertently, Baby William himself, whom they have affectionately dubbed "Tough Eddy." Staying put in a chair for the duration of a one-course meal is torturous for these boys. They compensate by never quite putting both feet under the table. They sit with one leg doubled under them while the other leg extends to one side. The upper half of the body appears committed to the task at hand — eating — but the lower extremities are poised to lunge should a more compelling distraction present itself. From this position, I have observed, one brother can trip a haughty dessert-eating sibling who is flaunting the fact he ate all his "sweaty little peas." Although we have civilized them to the point that they dutifully mumble, "May I be excused, please?" their abrupt depar-

ture from the table invariably overturns at least one chair or whatever milk remains. This sort of constant motion just doesn't lend itself to lessons in thoughtfulness and gentleness.

15   Despite my encouragement, my sons refuse to invite little girls to play anymore. Occasionally friends leave their small daughters with us while they run errands. I am always curious to see what these females will find of interest in my sons' roomful of Tonka trucks and soccer balls. One morning the boys suggested that the girls join them in playing Emergency with the big red fire trucks and ambulance. The girls were delighted and immediately designated the ambulance as theirs. The point of Emergency, as I have seen it played countless times with a gang of little boys, is to make as much noise with the siren as possible and to crash the trucks into each other or into the leg of a living-room chair before you reach your destination.

16   The girls had other ideas. I realized why they had selected the ambulance. It contained three dolls: a driver, a nurse, and sick man on the stretcher. My boys have used that ambulance many times, but the dolls were always secondary to the death-defying race with the fire trucks; they were usually just thrown in the back of the van as an afterthought. The girls took the dolls out, stripped and re-dressed them tenderly, and made sure that they were seated in their appropriate places for the first rescue. Once the fire truck had been lifted off the man's leg, the girls required a box of Band-Aids and spent the next half hour making a bed for the patient and reassuring him that he was going to be all right. These little girls and my sons had seen the same NBC *Emergency* series, but the girls had apparently picked up on the show's nurturing aspects, while Jack and Drew were interested only in the equipment, the fast driving, and the sirens. . . .

17   Of course, I want my sons to grow up knowing that what's inside a woman's head is more important than her appearance, but I'm sure they're getting mixed signals when I delay our departure for the swimming pool to put on lipstick. I also wonder what they make of their father, whose favorite aphorism is "beautiful women rule the world." I suppose what we want for these sons and the women they may marry someday is a sensitivity that enables them to be both flexible and at ease with their respective roles, so that marriage contracts are unnecessary. When my sons bring me the heads of two purple irises from the neighbor's yard and ask, "Are you really the most beautiful mama in the whole world like Daddy says, and did everyone want to marry you?" do you blame me if I keep on waffling?

Questions on Content

1. What does Mackintosh do in her effort to raise "liberated, nonviolent sons"?
2. Why have some parents begun giving their daughters "unisex names" and what are some examples of those names?
3. What are "POTOS" and why does Mackintosh mention the acronym?
4. What kinds of dolls should girls be given according to Drs. Rita and Kenneth Dunn?

5. What are the differences between the game "Emergency" as played by Mackintosh's sons and by the girls who visit her home? What might these differences indicate about boys and girls?

Questions on Thesis, Purpose, and Structure

1. How effective are the examples Mackintosh uses to illustrate the behavior of children and their parents? Which examples are particularly informative, entertaining, or persuasive?
2. What causes of sex role stereotyping does Mackintosh identify? Does she find these explanations convincing? Explain your answer.
3. What possible ways of combating sex role stereotypes does Mackintosh consider? How is each method flawed?
4. What does Mackintosh think are the main reasons for the differences in behavior and interests between girls and boys? What do *you* think are the reasons for these differences?

Questions on Style and Diction

1. Find the following words in the essay and determine their definitions in context: mollified (paragraph 1); fervent, exhorted (paragraph 3); tutu (paragraph 5); unabashedly, perpetrating, abhor (paragraph 6); laudable, self-actualization (paragraph 9); eminently (paragraph 10); defecate (paragraph 13); pulsate, inadvertently, dubbed (paragraph 14); aphorism (paragraph 17).
2. What is the effect of the rhetorical question at the end of paragraph 2? Does Mackintosh need to answer that question?
3. What happens when words normally used to describe a woman are applied to a man? What connotations do those words carry? Examine the examples in paragraph 7, but feel free to extend this discussion beyond those specific examples?

Ideas for Essays

1. Do you agree with Mackintosh's ideas? If not, write a reasoned essay explaining your views and the weaknesses in Mackintosh's position.
2. Consider your own upbringing. Were you guided by your parents and teachers into fixed beliefs about the roles of men and women or have you felt free to express all facets of your personality? Describe your upbringing and its effects on your behavior and your ideas about the proper roles of men and women.

The Politics of Food

Gloria Steinem

Gloria Steinem (1936–   ), whose name has become virtually synonymous with the American feminist movement, was born in Ohio and educated at Smith College in Massachusetts. Following graduate work abroad in India as the recipient of a Chester Bowles Asian Fellowship, Steinem became a free-lance writer and journalist, contributing to such magazines as *Esquire, Vogue, Life, McCall's, Cosmopolitan,* and *Time* and authoring *The Thousand Indias* (1957), *The Beach Book* (1963), *Outrageous Acts and Everyday Rebellions* (1983), and *Marilyn* (1986). In 1972 she became founding editor of *Ms.* magazine, which quickly became one of the leading catalysts for women's liberation. Steinem has played an active role in the National Women's Political Caucus, which she helped organize, and the Women's Action Alliance. "The Politics of Food" (1980) from *Outrageous Acts and Everyday Rebellions* demonstrates the ways in which the distribution of food within families and societies is but one more indicator of a widespread belief in the inferiority of women.

1   For much of the female half of the world, food is the first signal of our inferiority. It lets us know that our own families may consider female bodies to be less deserving, less needy, less valuable.

2   In many poor countries, mothers often breastfeed sons for two years or more, especially when other food is scarce or uncertain. Daughters are usually nursed for less than half that time.

3   *What happens in the mind of a girl child who is denied her own mother's body, or in the mind of her brother who is not?*

4   In India and other countries where the poor must make painful choices, female infanticide is often carried out by the denial of scarce food and health care. Its practice is so common that a ratio of only eighty females to one hundred males is the norm in some parts of the country.

5   Economists say that scarcity increases value, but that rule doesn't seem to hold when the commodity is female. Mothers of daughters, no matter how poor their health, are expected to bear more and more children until they have sons. Families of bridegrooms go right on demanding dowries from the families of brides. If someone pays the price of scarcity, it seems to be the women themselves. Brides may be kidnapped from neighboring areas. The childbearing burden of a woman may be increased because her husband's brothers have no wives.

6   The cultural belief in a female's lesser worth goes so deep that many women accept and perpetuate it. "Food distribution within the family arises from the deliberate self-deprivation by women," concludes a 1974 study of nutrition in India, "because they believe that the earning members (and the male members who are potential earning members) are more valuable than those who do domestic work and the child rearing, which they consider devoid of economic value."

7   *What happens to the spirits of women who not only deprive themselves but police the deprivation of their daughters?*

8   Even in this wealthier, luckier country, we may know more than we admit. Black slave women and indentured white women were advertised

as breeders or workers, and also as assets who would eat and cost less than males. The hard-working farm women of the frontier served men and boys more plentifully and first, yet the toll of their own hard work and childbearing was so great that the two-mother family was the average: most men married a second time to replace a first wife who died of childbirth, disease, or fatigue. Within our own memories, there are wives and daughters of immigrant families who served meals to fathers and brothers first, sometimes eating only what was left on the men's plates. Right now, tired homemakers save the choice piece of meat for the "man of the house" or "growing boys" more often than for their growing daughters or themselves. Millions of women on welfare eat a poor and starchy diet that can permanently damage the children they bear, yet their heavy bodies are supposed to signify indulgence. Even well-to-do women buy the notion that males need better food, more protein, and more strength. They grow heavy on sugar or weak on diets while preparing good food for their families. Does a woman alone prepare a meal differently for a male guest than for another woman — or for herself? *Perhaps food is still the first sign of respect — or the lack of it — that we pay to each other and to our bodies.*

Of course, women have rebelled. We can guess that from knowing ourselves. We can also guess it from the elaborate, punitive systems that exist to punish female rebellion.   9

In many areas of Africa and Asia, strict taboos reserve the most   10
valued sources of energy and nourishment for males. Red meat, fish, poultry, eggs, milk, even some fruits and vegetables — each is forbidden to females in some parts of the world. The explanation of these taboos may be a euphemism (for instance, that eating red meat will make women "like men"), or it may play on women's deepest fear (for instance, that drinking milk will destroy a woman's value by making her sterile), but these cultural restrictions go very deep. Some women students from Africa observe them even after years of living in Europe or America. Others report anxiety and nausea when they first force themselves to eat an egg or an orange.

With or without taboos, food itself may be used as punishment or   11
reward. In many cultures, husbands and fathers ration out food from family storerooms to which they alone hold the key. Wives are accountable not only for what they eat but for children, extended family, and servants as well. Even in wealthier societies, wives may be disciplined or rewarded with the treat of "eating out," or given a strict family food budget that holds them accountable for the whole household. In times of inflation, women may be expected to stretch the shrinking food dollar with impossible ingenuity. For instance, when world food prices skyrocketed in the 1970s, a study of families in Great Britain showed that 75 percent of husbands made no increase at all in the housekeeping money they allowed their wives. No wonder food has become a primary source of identity for women.

Some cultures go beyond external controls. In tribal societies of   12
Ethiopia, for instance, a young girl's entry into womanhood and marriageability is marked by the pulling of several crucial teeth, a ritual in

the name of beauty that serves to make eating, especially of much-coveted meat, permanently difficult. A gap-toothed smile is regarded as feminine. So are the heavy ankle bracelets a female is bound by at puberty. (Think of the bound feet of the upper-class women of China.) In the same tribes, male decoration is suspiciously confined to body-painting or hair matted with clay and braids — nothing that restricts movement, eating, or freedom.

13   To deprive females of equal nourishment increases the male food supply and decreases rebellion among wives and daughters. But like all oppression, it is dangerous in the long run.

14   Poorly nourished women give birth to less healthy children, males as well as females. Even cultures that selectively reward pregnant women with better feeding rarely make up completely for the damage already done in the name of sexual politics. In extreme cases, high infant mortality, poor brain development, and protein-deficiency diseases are the results of poor maternal nutrition, and none of these is any respecter of gender.

15   We don't have to look far from our own doors to find infant mortality rates and protein deficiency that surpass almost any other industrialized country. The United States is producing ever-growing generations of an impoverished underclass; yet political resistance to food stamps, adequate welfare payments, even feeding programs confined to infants and pregnant or breastfeeding women, continues to increase. So does resistance to the job-training programs, child-care centers, and punishment of sex discrimination in the work place, all of which would allow women to support themselves and their children.

16   The short-term goal of saving money is cited in all of the above cases; yet that goal is rarely mentioned when discussing the many billions of dollars spent on the military. A dead certain, immediate loss of human talent is simply considered less important than a possible future loss of military superiority.

17   It makes you wonder: Is the fear of independent women so great, consciously or unconsciously, that our "profamily" leadership will choose short-term female dependency over the country's long-term self-interest? Do they maintain the example of poor women — or any women who can't survive without the goodwill and protection of a man — as a constant reminder to keep us all in line?

18   *Surely women can learn from the politics of food that arguments of enlightened self-interest aren't enough. Sometimes only rebellion will do.*

19   Facts may persuade us of the need to rebel.

20   *The Myth.* Males need more and better food because they do more work.

21   *The Fact.* According to the United Nations, females do one-third of the paid work in the world, and two-thirds of all work, paid and unpaid. In industrialized societies like the United States, homemakers work harder than any other class of worker: an average of 99.6 hours a week. In Latin America, females make up at least 50 percent of the agricultural labor force, and as much as 90 percent in Africa and Asia. In many

societies, most women have two jobs, inside the home and outside it, while most men have only one.

The Myth. Given the famine and malnutrition suffered by much of   22
the world, it is diversionary to focus on how food is distributed. The first and perhaps only question should be how to create more food.

The Fact. The earth already produces enough food to nourish all of   23
its inhabitants. The politics of distribution are the major reason for hunger and starvation. As the Swedish Nutrition Foundation and other international study groups concluded years ago, the use of food and starvation as a political weapon is even more destructive than bacteriological warfare or other weapons that affect all people equally, precisely because withholding nutrition afflicts pregnant women, nursing mothers, and children preferentially.

The Myth. There is no consistent attitude toward females. Some   24
cultures like plump women while others prefer thin ones. It's all a matter of personal preference and style.

The Fact. What is rare and possessed only by the powerful is envied   25
as a symbol of power. Thus, poor societies with little food produce an ideal of feminine beauty that is plump and available only to the rich. Pashas, African chieftains, and American robber barons sometimes force-fed or otherwise fattened up their women as testimonies to their wealth. In more fortunate societies where women become plump on starch and sugar if nothing else, leanness and delicacy in women are rare and envied. Nonetheless, the common denominators are weakness, passivity, and lack of strength. Rich or poor, feminine beauty is equated with subservience to men. Lower-class women, who have to do physical labor and develop some degree of strength, are made to envy this weakness. Middle Eastern peasant women envied and imitated the protection and restriction of the veil that began with women who were the possessions of upper-class men. American farm and factory women may envy the thinness and artifice of the rich.

To many women who are both working for a salary and raising   26
children, life as a childbearer and hostess for a well-to-do man may look desirable by comparison.

Freedom can only be imagined.   27

Thanks to the contagious ideas of feminism, however, imaginations   28
have been working overtime.

Poor women are demanding both the practical means to control the   29
endless births that endanger their health, and improved maternal and infant nutrition to make those fewer children healthier and more likely to survive. This major focus of women in poorer, agricultural countries is also important among the poor inside wealthy, industrialized countries like ours. We may know, for instance, that most poor women in the United States still don't have access to adequate contraception and safe abortion. But do we know that African doctors training here have diagnosed kwashiokor, the disease that produces the yellow skin and bloated bellies of African famines, in our own inner cities?

Middle-class women are beginning to cultivate fitness and strength.   30

Bodybuilders, everyday joggers, tennis champions, and Olympic athletes have begun to challenge the equation of beauty with weakness. Even upper-class women no longer tolerate the hothouse delicacy that testified to male protection.

31   All women need strength—health, muscles, endurance—if we are to literally change the world.

32   *Do we think of this as we imagine beauty? Or crave empty calories? Or pass our politics of food on to children and younger sisters?*

33   It will take a lot of nourishment to grow the world's longest revolution.

Questions on Content

1. List several specific ways in which food is used to show that "families consider female bodies to be less deserving, less needy, less valuable."
2. Steinem cites some evidence of societal mistreatment of women that does not involve the use of food. List several examples of this societal mistreatment.
3. How is food used "as punishment or reward"?
4. What evidence is there that the politics of food is a factor even within the United States Congress?

Questions on Thesis, Purpose, and Structure

1. Consider the essay's first and last paragraphs. How successful is the introduction in getting your attention as well as announcing the topic? How does Steinem's play on words in the essay's final sentence encourage you to think about the implications of her essay?
2. Why do women often deprive themselves and their daughters of the most nourishing food?
3. What are the physical, political, and societal effects of depriving women of food?
4. What are the causes of the differing concepts of feminine beauty?
5. What are some of the effects of "the contagious ideas of feminism"?

Questions on Style and Diction

1. Find the following words in the essay and determine their definitions in context: devoid (paragraph 6); euphemism (paragraph 10); diversionary (paragraph 22); subservience, artifice (paragraph 25).
2. Steinem uses rhetorical questions frequently in this essay. What are the purposes and what are the effects of the rhetorical questions in paragraphs 3, 7, 8, 17, and 32?
3. Steinem italicizes a number of sentences in her essay. Why do you think that she does so?

Ideas for Essays

1. If you agree with Steinem's contention that women are the victims of discrimination throughout the world, write an essay exploring some of the causes and effects of that discrimination in some other aspect of life, such as housing, employment, clothing, sports, education, or health care.
2. If you do not believe that women are the victims of widespread discrimina-

tion in the distribution of food, write an essay disputing Steinem's evidence and her conclusions.

3. If, in contrast with Steinem, you believe that *men* are the victims of discrimination, write an essay exploring some of the causes and effects of that discrimination in some aspect of life such as housing, employment, clothing, sports, education, or heath care.

North America after the War
Paul Ehrlich

Paul Ehrlich (1932–   ) was educated at the University of Pennsylvania and the University of Kansas. He is currently Bing Professor of Population Biology at Stanford University. Ehrlich's major interest is the environment: the threat that man poses to the fragile ecosystem in which we live and the positive steps that must be taken now if we are to avoid the consequences of our own follies. Ehrlich's books include *The Population Bomb* (1968); *Population, Food and Environment* (1970); *Cold and Dark: The World after Nuclear War* (1984); and, most recently, *Earth* (1987), co-authored with Anne Ehrlich. In "North America after the War" (1984), Ehrlich challenges us to think about the biological consequences of nuclear war—not just the extinction of many species of plants and animals, but also the disruption of the delicate natural balance between predator and prey.

It was almost the end of the century when humanity's luck ran out. Most   1
of the nuclear war scenarios had been optimistic. Three-quarters of the American and Soviet arsenals, more than 30,000 nuclear devices, exploded with power in excess of 9,000 megatons (9 billion tons) of TNT. The large cities of North America, Europe, Russia, China, and Japan, as well as huge areas of dense forest, fueled fire storms. Soot from these fire storms joined dust lofted into the stratosphere by thousands of ground bursts. Smoke from myriad smaller fires choked the lower atmosphere and darkness enshrouded the Northern Hemisphere from a few days after the early July war until October, when substantial sunlight again began to reach the earth's surface.

Soot and smoke absorbed large amounts of solar energy; dust re-   2
flected more back into space. This plunged temperatures in all inland areas to below zero for virtually the entire dark summer. Except for small refugia on the coastlines, temperatures across the North American continent fell below 10°F for several months, going well below zero in many places for extended periods. No place in the Northern Hemisphere escaped severe frosts. Although far fewer weapons were detonated in the Southern Hemisphere, plumes of soot moved rapidly across the equator from the North, creating quick freezes in many places. Dusky skies, lower than normal temperatures, and radioactive fallout eventually

covered the entire planet. The "nuclear winter" predicted by the world's top atmospheric scientists in late 1983 had come to pass.

3   By January, much of the debris had cleared from the skies, but lingering smoke, stratospheric dust, and material from still-burning fires prolonged an usually cold winter. Spring and summer were also colder than usual. Nitrogen oxides, produced when thermonuclear fireballs burned atmospheric nitrogen, had severely damaged the stratospheric ozone layer, which normally filters out ultraviolet rays harmful to plants and animals. This made the return of sunlight a mixed blessing.

4   Blast, fire, prompt radiation and delayed fallout, subzero temperatures, toxic smog, and lack of food eliminated the vestiges of human life. Even in the warmer places — the coastlines where the cold had been ameliorated by the thermal inertia of the oceans — people could not survive. The few officials and military personnel in the United States and Canada whose deep shelters had not been "dug out" by Soviet missiles, and who had passed the nuclear winter underground, starved soon after emerging in the frigid spring. Tropical peoples, even in coastal areas of Mexico, succumbed to exposure, radiation sickness, hunger, civil disorder, and epidemic disease. Starvation finished the Eskimo. Human beings were gone from North America — indeed, from the entire Northern Hemisphere.

5   But not all life was extinct. Scattered pockets of severely frost-damaged chaparral along the coast had escaped the great fires that had swept most of California bare. Even after the erosion of bare slopes in the postwar rain, many seeds survived. The Olympic Peninsula and parts of coastal British Columbia and Alaska had suffered less than inland areas because, as in California, the adjacent sea had moderated the long cold period. Even in coastal areas many plants died from a combination of low light, toxic air pollution, high radiation (the last especially affected the sensitive conifers), and from the continual violent storms generated by the sharp sea – land temperature gradient.

6   Inland in the subarctic and arctic North, virtually all of the growing plants had died. Cold-resistant boreal trees, deprived of the normal environmental cues that induce cold hardiness, were not prepared for the nuclear aftermath. Paper birches and aspens, which can tolerate temperatures of −100°F when acclimatized, died when midsummer temperatures dropped in a few days to −20°F. In the Rocky Mountains and sections of the East, substantial areas of forest had not burned, but most of the standing trees had succumbed to the extreme, unseasonable cold. Persistence of plant populations in most parts of what had been the United States and Canada depended on the survival of seeds and roots (or other subterranean organs) in the frozen ground.

7   Due to vagaries in wind patterns, vegetation survived in a few enclaves along the west coast of Florida, parts of Yucatan and Chiapas in Mexico, and the Osa Peninsula of Costa Rica. But in most of Florida, Mexico, and Central America, the devastation of growing plants was virtually complete. Subtropical and tropical floras, unfortunately, had had much less evolutionary experience with extreme cold: only a very few relatively hardy seeds and subterranean parts survived outside of the enclaves.

Most of the higher vertebrates went the way of *Homo sapiens*. The 8 cold alone killed many animals before radiation, thirst (lakes, rivers, and streams were covered with several feet of ice), and starvation could affect them. In the smoggy darkness, many had a reduced ability to find food, preventing them from adequately stoking their metabolic fires. Nearly every species of migratory land bird went extinct. But in places in the Northwest, a few warmblooded creatures — crows, ravens, starlings, ptarmigan, gulls, black bears, coyotes, rabbits, and rodents — managed to survive. So did some of the hardier denizens of the coastal chaparral pockets in California — but the extremely high radiation levels gradually pushed many populations to extinction.

In the continental interior, a handful of vertebrates survived the 9 cold, mostly reptiles, amphibians, and fishes whose physiological plasticity allowed their body temperatures to drop to near freezing. Warmblooded animals that hibernate had no opportunity to build reserves for a normal winter, let alone a nuclear winter. The lower metabolic rates of the lower vertebrates permitted scattered individuals to survive in deep crevices, burrows, or beneath the ice of large lakes. Most of those few survivors starved the following spring.

The majority of insects were even less fortunate. In seasonal envi- 10 ronments, insects normally pass the winter (or other stressful seasons) in a specific developmental stage — and virtually all were caught in the wrong stage. Only in arctic and alpine areas, where insects are adapted to summer frosts, did some insect fauna survive the freezing.

During the first postwar summer, seeds began to sprout in areas 11 where fire storms had not sterilized the soil. Surviving perennials in coastal pockets also began to produce new growth. But continuing cold weather and strong ultraviolet radiation damaged the tender young plant tissues. Many desert spring annuals that depended on now-extinct insects for pollination failed to reproduce. In refugia where insect pollinators did survive, they often were disoriented by the ultraviolet light, which though invisible to mammals was visible to them. This not only reduced their capacity to pollinate but also to reproduce themselves.

In arctic and alpine areas, many surviving insect populations dwin- 12 dled further or went extinct from lack of food. The growing season was extremely short and frosts frequently damaged plants struggling to recover. The abundant female mosquitoes had few vertebrates to feed on, and the males found little nectar in the few surviving flowers. Only a small fraction of the boreal insect fauna that had survived the first winter went into diapause for the next.

Not only was spring silent over most of the continent that first year 13 following the war, but summer was silent as well. In much of what had been the United States, no birds sang, no dogs barked, no frogs croaked, no fishes leaped. As they emerged into the desolation, most of the scattered lizards, snakes, turtles, and toads starved. Most areas were utterly devoid of organic motion beyond the wind-induced flutter of the leaves of scattered plants. There were exceptions, though. In mines, caves, and deep underground shelters, flies, roaches, rats, and mice had survived and in some had even thrived on the cadavers of people who had sought shelter there. When some of these survivors emerged at night, they found a similar resource in the abundant thawing cadavers of people and domestic animals. These scavengers built large local populations. But they soon crashed when they exhausted their grim resources.

14   All in all, life was in worse shape at the end of the first postwar summer than it had been in the spring. Only where substantial plant communities remained — on the northwest coast, in the coastal California chaparral, and in the tropical and subtropical pockets — did relatively diverse vertebrate and invertebrate populations survive. And even there losses were substantial. The last North American mountain lions, lynxes, large hawks, golden eagles, and other large predators went extinct; the refugia were not big enough to save the decimated populations of most animals that require large home ranges. Vultures did survive on the abundant carrion as did the once endangered bald eagle, outlasting — and even dining on — the species that had endangered them. Kestrels also made it, dining on grasshoppers. Most herbivorous insects that specialized on the less hardy plants were incapable of switching to plants with different suites of chemical feeding stimulants and toxic defenses. So they followed their plants into oblivion.

15   For several years after the war, dust from the partly denuded continents and smoke from lightning-ignited fires in forest remnants, smoldering peat bogs, coal stocks and seams, and burning oil and gas wells produced cool summers and unusually harsh winters. But gradually the climate returned more or less to normal, except that, in the near absence of vegetation, much of the central continent was more arid than before the war.

16   Over the next decades, plants began to reconquer the desolate continent. In the normally cooler latitudes many seeds in the soil were largely undamaged by cold and radiation. During each growing season for the first few postwar years, some prewar seeds germinated. And each year some of the seedlings survived.

17   Species adapted to disturbed areas did best. Kudzu vine, crab grass, stork's bill, dandelions, and similar weeds quickly covered large areas, often choking out species that people had once considered "more desirable." In California, an impoverished chaparral community slowly reclaimed the denuded hillsides, aided to some extent by its natural adaptation to fire. A rare survivor in that community was the gypsy moth. In the subarctic and the arctic, grasses, sedges, and dwarf willows regenerated relatively rapidly in spite of the short growing season. Some of the growing herbaceous and shrubby plants, accustomed to summer frosts, had only been set back, not killed, by the nuclear winter and subsequent frosty summers.

18   Forests returned slowly, since many trees require more than a decade to complete a generation. In the West, aspens from the coastal refugia and from surviving roots spread in a few hundred years to cover large portions of their previous range. Simultaneously, scrubby Gambel's oak reappeared and formed dense local stands. No significant herbivores took advantage of the oak's periodic years of heavy acorn production; concomitantly, relatively few animals were available to disperse the acorns until feral rat populations began to transport and store them. Then the oaks spread rapidly.

In the East, the turkey oak, a denizen of poor soils, underwent a   19
similar explosion. Several species of wind-pollinated pines also made a
comeback. Widespread, previously common species—white and southern pines in the East, and piñon, lodgepole, and ponderosa in the
West—were the most successful.

Vegetation recovered most slowly in the subtropical and tropical   20
areas. There, wherever intense cold had prevailed, virtually all the
plants—like the animals—had been destroyed. Most species could not
tolerate chilling even to a few degrees *above* freezing, and their seeds
were not cold hardy. Those plants that survived in refugia began gradually to spread into the debris-littered wastelands, but progress was slow
—especially for the many plants that depended on now-extinct animals
to disperse their seeds. This was much more important in tropical than
in temperate ecosystems.

The first animals to repopulate substantial areas of North America   21
were also "weeds." Roaches, rats, and houseflies suffered setbacks in
the early years, but they persisted and increased, free of significant
natural enemies and able to feed on a variety of plant materials and
organic debris. Crickets and grasshoppers, both relatively generalized
feeders, spread back fast from coastal refugia. Fire ants, having taken in
stride massive attacks with pesticides before the war, survived the ultimate human assault in pockets along the Gulf Coast and spread once
more over what had been the southeastern United States. As the flora
recovered, snowshoe hares reinvaded much of their old territory, fan-
ning out from surviving northwestern populations and reaching the east
coast in a few hundred years. They renewed their famous cycling
behavior—population outbreaks followed by crashes. That they did so
in the total absence of their lynx predators (long thought to have been a
cause of the cycles) would have fascinated population biologists—if
there had been any around.

The first predators to reoccupy the desolate areas were spiders,   22
ballooning in from refugia and emerging from underground burrows.
Coyotes also thrived, learning to hunt the rats and following the spreading front of snowshoe hares. Wolves faded away; there were too few
survivors. Because of the vagaries of fallout patterns, wolves had suffered
more than most species from radiation effects, and they did not successfully adapt to a diet of rats and hares.

A casual observer might have missed the most significant change in   23
predator trophic levels: the near absence of predacious and parasitic
insects. The impact of toxins from the war, together with the cold, was
similar to spraying the entire continent with insecticides. In many cases,
the smaller populations at the predator trophic levels died off even
though their plant-eating insect hosts had survived. One result was huge
outbreaks of locusts, gypsy moths, cutworms, and Japanese beetles,
which decimated the foliage over large areas. Another was that some
previously rare herbivorous insects, freed from natural controls, developed huge, destructive populations, just as new pests had often been
created by the misuse of pesticides before the war.

Although most insectivorous birds were extinct, cattle egrets, dining   24
on the larger insects, gradually spread throughout North America. They

were joined by ravens, crows, starlings, and gulls, all of which shifted their diets to a heavy emphasis on insects. Robins also reinvaded from refugia, but in the absence of lawns and with a severe shortage of earthworms, their populations grew with glacial slowness.

25   Some three thousand years after the war, the first human beings set foot on what had once been the United States. A handful of people had persisted through the postwar chaos in the Southern Hemisphere; the scattered groups of survivors had not all dwindled to extinction as many biologists had feared they might. But all had reverted to subsistence farming, mostly with stone and wooden implements. Most libraries had been destroyed by the war or in the subsequent social breakdown; the few that remained decayed in the deserted cities. People had had no time to preserve cultural artifacts that were peripheral to the daily struggle for existence.

26   Almost three thousand years elapsed before human populations grew large enough to form small, rudimentary cities and to begin exploratory moves into the mysterious and devastated North. Both the knowledge and the implements of industrial civilization were long gone. The new pioneers came in simple sailboats, moving along the Gulf Coast into ex-Texas. Over the next several millennia, they repopulated the transformed continent, farming the primitive maize and potato strains they had brought with them; hunting rats, hares, muskrats, beavers, and coyotes; and gathering locusts. Deer had not survived in North America, and the few that did in South America had been hunted to extinction.

27   To its prewar residents, North America of the year 5000 would have seemed a strange and unstable land indeed. Populations of the commonest organisms were still fluctuating violently. When grasshoppers had a good sequence of years, hordes of ravens, crows, starlings, gulls, and egrets made the vast plains a study in black and white. Then, as the foliage was exhausted, the grasshoppers died out, the birds succumbed or moved on, and dust storms swept the land—often leading to many decades of desolation before plants restored the ground cover.

28   Biologists transported in time would have been depressed at the low diversity in forests, grasslands, and deserts, but they would have been astounded at some of the organisms in abundance. Eastern diamondback rattlesnakes were everywhere, having spread from their Florida refugia and adapted to colder climates while feasting on rats. Monarch butterflies and tiger swallowtails were nowhere to be seen. The most common butterfly on the eastern coast was *Cissia joyceae*, an attractive little wood nymph once known from only a single specimen from Costa Rica. With unusual rapidity, it had evolved the ability to pass winters as a caterpillar in diapause and now had several generations a year, thriving on a diet of grasses.

29   In the West, a tiny beige hairstreak butterfly, *Strymon avalona*, survived the war on Santa Catalina Island, to which it had previously been restricted. The hairstreak crossed to the mainland after the war and became widespread and common. It too evolved a broadened diet, thriving on locoweeds, vetches, and other weedy plants, as well as on lupines, which had become extremely common as disturbances remained widespread.

Giant land snails and walking catfishes had become prominent   30
features of the warmer parts of the continent. These were not strange
mutants but simply exotic organisms that had gained a foothold before
the war. Such tough, competitive organisms had become dominant in
the absence of many previous predators and competitors. Indeed, contrary to popular mythology, increased mutation rates due to high levels
of ionizing radiation had not significantly speeded evolution. Prewar
mutation rates and genetic recombination had provided all the genetic
variability needed for evolution to proceed rapidly under strong selection pressures. The genetic damage done by radiation-induced mutations only weakened populations; the mutations did not produce any
"hopeful monsters" that rapidly replaced previous types.

Only minor evolutionary changes occurred during the time be-   31
tween the war and the human reinvasion. Resistance to pesticides, for
example, which had been common in the old days, disappeared. Some
specialists broadened their niches. Camouflage and other protective
mechanisms of many smaller insects declined because the previous
great diversity of insectivorous birds—including most of the species
that searched carefully for their prey—had been largely lost. Three
millennia had not been enough time for North American ecosystems to
make substantial evolutionary progress toward rediversifying the biota.
That would require a thousandfold greater time.

Homo sapiens was barred from one cultural evolutionary course it   32
had once taken. The human groups that went through the first industrial
revolution had thoroughly depleted the nonrenewable resources of the
planet before they blew it up. No nearly pure copper lay around on the
surface as it had in the Old Stone Age; it had to be extracted by the
smelting of low-grade ores. Oil could no longer be had by drilling down
a few feet; it could be obtained only by drilling several thousand feet.
High technology was required to obtain the resources needed by technological civilization. And high technology did not exist in the postwar
Stone Age.

The war and its aftermath had destroyed most of the stocks of   33
resources and much of the knowledge of how to use them. During the
millennia that followed, while *Homo sapiens* barely hung on, remaining
stockpiles of materials rusted away, decayed, and dispersed—and scientific knowledge was forgotten. Whether this was a blessing or curse
might have been debated if there were time travelers, but the result was
final. The technology that had produced automobiles, airplanes, television, computers, ICBMs, and thermonuclear devices would never be
regained.

Questions on Content

1. In what month does Ehrlich assume that a nuclear war occurs? For how many
   months afterwards do clouds enshroud the Northern Hemisphere?
2. What are the effects on temperature and crops of this "nuclear winter"?
3. What happens to the North American human survivors of the war? What
   happens to plant and animal life in North America in the first year after the
   war?
4. What forms of life thrive after the war?

5. When does the first human being again set foot on what had once been the United States?

Questions on Thesis, Purpose, and Structure

1. What use of "causal chains" does Ehrlich make in this essay? Examine each link in these causal chains. Is the reasoning sensible and convincing?
2. What are the "immediate effects" of the nuclear war? What are the "remote effects" of the war?
3. Why do plant and animal populations still fluctuate wildly five thousand years after the war?
4. Why does Ehrlich think that after a nuclear war humanity will never again regain its advanced technology?
5. How informative is Ehrlich's essay? How persuasive? What are the most persuasive points made in the essay? What are the least persuasive points?

Questions on Style and Diction

1. Find the following words in the essay and determine their definitions in context: scenarios, megatons, myriad (paragraph 1); refugia (paragraph 2); vestiges, ameliorated, inertia (paragraph 4); chapparal (paragraph 5); acclimatized (paragraph 6); metabolic, migratory, denizens (paragraph 8); boreal, diapause (paragraph 12); oblivion (paragraph 14); concomitantly (paragraph 18); artifacts, peripheral (paragraph 25); implements (paragraph 26); niches, ecosystems (paragraph 31).
2. Ehrlich often uses the specialized vocabulary of a biologist. To what extent does that vocabulary interfere with your understanding of the essay? To what extent does it contribute to your belief in Ehrlich's expertise?
3. Consider the kinds of insects, animals, and plants that Ehrlich thinks will thrive after the war. What is your emotional reaction to those forms of life? Do you think that Ehrlich is intentionally playing on these emotional connotations?

Ideas for Essays

1. Write a letter to a U.S. Congressman or Senator expressing your views about our nuclear defense policy. Explicitly consider in your letter the potential biological effects of nuclear war and nuclear winter.
2. Write a critique of Ehrlich's essay. What assumptions does he make that seem too gloomy or too optimistic? What other possible consequences of nuclear war can you envision? If possible, go to the library and find out about the controversy concerning nuclear winter.
3. Write about the world before and after the war from the point of view of the gypsy moth, the cutworm, or the Eastern diamondback rattlesnake.

The Sexed-Up, Doped-Up, Hedonistic Heaven of the Boom-Boom '70s

Tom Wolfe

Tom Wolfe (1931–   ) was born in Richmond, Virginia, and educated at Washington and Lee University and Yale University, where he earned a Ph.D. in American Studies. He began his career as a reporter for the Springfield, Massachusetts, *Union, Washington Post,* and New York *Herald-Tribune* and then in the mid-1960s began writing for *New York* magazine, *Harper's,* and *Esquire,* where he developed the colorful, freewheeling writing style that has come to be called "the New Journalism." His books, which study and critique contemporary manners and culture, include among others *The Kandy-Colored Tangerine-Flake Streamline Baby (1965); The Electric Kool-Aid Acid Test* (1968), about novelist and cult-hero Ken Kesey; *Mauve Gloves & Madmen, Clutter & Vine* (1976); *The Right Stuff* (1979), about the American space program; and a novel, *The Bonfire of the Vanities* (1987). In this essay from *Mauve Gloves & Madmen,* Wolfe speculates on the causes of the pervasive hedonism of the 1970s.

For me the 1970s began the moment I saw Harris, on a little surprise visit   1
to the campus, push open the door of his daughter Laura's dormitory room. Two pairs of eyes popped up in one of the beds, blazing like raccoons' at night by the garbage cans . . . illuminating the shanks, flanks, glistening haunches and cloven declivities of a boy and girl joined mons-to-mons. Harris backed off, one little step after another. He looked as if he were staring down the throat of a snake. He pulled the door shut, ever so gingerly.

The girl in the bed was not his daughter, but that didn't calm him in   2
the slightest. For an hour we lurched around the campus, looking for little Laura. Finally we went back to her room, on the chance she might have returned. This time Harris knocked on the door, and a girl's voice said, "Come in." Quite a cheery voice it was, too.

"Laura?"   3

But it wasn't Laura. Inside, in the bed, was the same couple —   4
except that they were no longer in medias res. They were sitting up with the covers pulled up to about collarbone level, looking perfectly relaxed. *At home,* as it were.

"Hi," says the girl. "Can we help you?"   5

Their aplomb is more than Harris can deal with. He takes on the   6
look of a man who, unaccountably, feels that *he* has committed the gaffe. He begins to croak. He sounds ashamed.

"I'm Laura's . . . I'm looking for my . . . I want . . ."   7

"Laura's at the library," says the boy. He's just as relaxed and cheery   8
as the girl.

Harris backs out and closes the door once more . . . very diffi-   9
dently. . . . At the library we find his missing daughter. She has long, brown Pre-Raphaelite hair, parted in the middle, a big floppy crew-neck sweater, jeans and clogs. She's 18 years old and looks about 12 and is not the least bit embarrassed by what her father tells her.

10   "Daddy, really. Don't pay any attention to that." she says. "I mean, my *God*, everybody used to have to use the *kitchen*! There was a mattress on the floor in there, and you used to have to jump over the mattress to get to the refrigerator-sort-of-thing. So we made a schedule, and everybody's room is a Free Room a couple of days a month, and if your room's a Free Room, you just go to the library-sort-of-thing. I mean, the kitchen was . . . *so* . . . *gross*!"

11   All Harris does is nod slowly, as if some complex but irresistible logic is locking into place. In the time it takes us to drive back to New York, Harris works it out in his mind. . . . The kitchen was *so gross*-sort-of-thing. . . . That's all. . . . By nightfall he has dropped the entire incident like a rock into a lake of amnesia.

12   By the next morning he has accepted the new order as *the given*, and in that moment he becomes a true creature of the 1970s.

13   How quickly we swallowed it all over the past 10 years! I keep hearing the 1970s described as a lull, a rest period, following the uproars of the 1960s. I couldn't disagree more. With the single exception of the student New Left movement — which to me evaporated mysteriously in 1970 — the uproars did not subside in the least. On the contrary, their level remained so constant, they became part of the background noise, like a new link of I-95 opening up.

14   The idea of a coed dorm, with downy little Ivy Leaguers copulating in Free Rooms like fox terriers, was a lurid novelty even as late as 1968. Yet in the early 1970s the coed dorm became *the standard*. Fathers, daughters, faculty — no one so much as blinked any longer. It was in the 1970s, not the 1960s, that the ancient wall around sexual promiscuity fell. And it fell like the wall of Jericho; it didn't require a shove. By the mid-1970s, any time I reached a city of 100,000 to 200,000 souls, the movie fare available on a typical evening seemed to be: two theaters showing *Jaws*, one showing *Benji* and 11 showing pornography of the old lodge smoker sort, now dressed up in color and 35 mm stock. Two of the 11 would be drive-in theaters, the better to beam the various stiffened giblets and moist folds and nodules out into the night air to become part of the American Scene. Even in the rural South the *typical* landscape of the 1970s included — shank to flank with the Baptist and United Brethren churches and the hot-wax car wash and the Arby's — the roadside whorehouse, a windowless shack painted black or maroon with a shopping mall-style back-lit plastic marquee saying: MASSAGE PARLOR — TOTALLY NUDE GIRLS — SAUNA ENCOUNTER SESSIONS.

15   The wall around promiscuity was always intended to protect the institution of the family. In the 1970s one had a marvelous, even bizarre opportunity to see what happens to that institution when it is left unprotected. The 1970s will be remembered as the decade of the great Divorce Epidemic; or, to put it another way, the era of the New Cookie. The New Cookie is the girl in her 20s for whom the American male now *customarily* chucked his wife of two to four decades when the electrolysis gullies appeared above her upper lip. In 1976 Representative Wayne Hays of Ohio, one of the most powerful figures in the House of Representatives, was ruined when it was discovered that he had put his New

Cookie, a girl named Elizabeth Ray, on his office payroll. It was this bureaucratic lapse that was his undoing, however, not the existence of the New Cookie. Six months before, when he had divorced his wife of 38 years, it hadn't caused a ripple.

Ways of life that as late as 1969 had seemed intolerable scarcely   16 drew a second glance in 1979. In 1969 I was invited to address a group of Texas corporation heads on the subject of "the drug culture." The meeting was held on the back lawn of the home of one of the group in a pavilion with a hardwood floor below and striped tenting above, the sort of rigging that is set up for deb season dances in the fall. Why these 80 or 90 businessmen had set up this edifice to hear a talk about the dopers I couldn't make out . . . until one of them spoke up in the middle of my talk and said: "Listen, half the people here already know it, and so I'm gonna tell you, too: my son was arrested two nights ago for possession of marijuana, and that's the third goddamned time in ten goddamned months for that little peckerwood! Now . . . what are we gonna *do* about it?"

This was greeted with shouts of "Yeah!" . . . "Mine, too!" . . .   17 "My daughter—four times, goddamn it!" . . . "You tell 'em, Bubba!" . . . "Form a mullyfoggin' committee!"

Somehow I knew at that moment it was only a matter of time before   18 marijuana was legalized in the United States, and it had nothing to do with medical facts, juridical reasoning, or the Epicurean philosophies of the weed's proponents. It had to do solely with the fact that people of wealth and influence were getting tired of having to extract their children from the legal machinery. That was getting worse than dope itself. By 1979 it had come to pass. My book *The Electric Kool-Aid Acid Test* had been about a man, the novelist Ken Kesey, who had been arrested twice in California for possession of a few ounces of marijuana. Facing a probable five-year jail sentence, he had fled to the jungles of Mexico to live among the dapple-wing Anopheles, the verruga-crazed Phlebotomus, and Pacific Coast female ticks. That was in 1966. Today, on sunny days in Manhattan, one can see young office workers sitting on the Contempo Slate terraces out front of the glass buildings along Park Avenue and the Avenue of the Americas wearing Ralph Lauren Saville Pseud suits and Calvin Klein clings, taking coffee breaks and toking their heads off, passing happy sopping joints from fingertip to fingertip and goofing in the open air. In New York, as in California and most other states, possession of a small amount of marijuana has been reduced to a misdemeanor and, in effect, taken off the books, since the police, with the tacit consent of the citizenry, usually ignore it.

As the moral ground shifted, like the very templates of the earth,   19 matters of simple decorum were not spared, either. To me the most fascinating side of Watergate was the ease and obvious relish with which men and women on both sides of the Senate hearing room table and the bar of justice, the sheriffs as well as the bandits, the winners as well as the losers, capitalized on the event in the form of book deals and television commercials. The Watergate book was one of the decade's new glamour industries, like the desk calculator business or the digital watch game. Nixon, Haldeman, Ehrlichman, Magruder, McCord, Hunt, and the Deans (John and Mo) published their side of it. And the winners? His Honor Judge Sirica, His Probity Leon Jaworski, His Jurisprudence Samuel Dash . . . As they piously cranked out their best-sellers, it became obvious that to fix blame, obtain convictions, and ruin great reputations in a case like Watergate was worth . . . *millions of dollars.* None of them, I assume, entered or carried out the good fight with any such thought in mind. Nevertheless, the lesson was there when it was all over, and the rush to line up the book contracts began. How very *seventies* it was that the books came out, all the same, and hardly anyone, in or out of government, so much as arched an eyebrow!

20   The great Senate hero of Watergate, Senator Sam Ervin of North Carolina, retired and made commercials for American Express. *Ave atque vale,* Defender of the Constitution! Selling off chunks of one's righteous stuff via television commercials became not merely acceptable but *conventional* behavior for famous people in the 1970s. In 1969 the first man to set foot on the moon, Neil Armstrong, delivered, via television, a cosmic symploce measuring the stride of mankind itself in the new age of exploration. In 1979 Armstrong was on television in a Sales Rep sack suit delivering Cordobas, Newports, and LeBarons for the Chrysler Corporation. *Non sibi sed patriae,* Apollo!

21   The hedonism of the 1970s derives, in my opinion, from a development so stupendous, so long in the making, and so obvious that, like the Big Dipper or the curvature of the Earth, it is barely noticed any longer. Namely, the boom of the booms. Wartime spending in the United States in the early 1940s brought the Depression to an end and touched off a boom that has continued for nearly 40 years. The wave of prosperity had its dips, but they were mere wrinkles in a soaring curve. The boom pumped money into *every* class level of the population on a scale such as history has never known. Truck dispatchers, duplicator machine repairmen, bobbin cleaners, policemen, firemen, and garbage men were making so much money — $15,000 to $20,000 (and more) per year — and taking so many vacations on tropical littorals and outfitting their $12,000 RVs with so many micro-wave ovens and micro-sauna booths, it was impossible to use the word "proletarian" any longer with a straight face.

22   By the late 1970s these *new masses* began appearing also in France, West Germany, Switzerland, England, Norway, Sweden, Japan and, to a lesser extent, Italy — which is to say, throughout the *capitalist* world. By 1977 per capita incomes in these countries were catching up with those of the United States and outstripping the rate of inflation in most cases. In England the average family's "disposable" or "discretionary" income — the surplus wealth that new ways of living are made of — had risen 26.5 percent in 10 years, and the increase was greatest among working-class people. It had become common for skilled workers to make as much as $20,000 a year, bringing them up even, in income, with middle-level executives and top corporate salesmen. In early 1979 the average hourly wage for workers in manufacturing plants was $6.49 in the United States, the same in West Germany, $7.29 in Norway and $8.46 in Swit-

zerland. Despite inflation, the European workers' second homes, sports cars, vacations in Venice, and calfskin trench coats were real.

The old utopian socialists of the 19th century—the Saint-Simons, the Owens, the Fouriers—*lived* for the day when industrial workers would command the likes of $6.49 or more per hour. They foresaw a day when industrialization (Saint-Simon coined the word) would give the common man the things he needed in order to realize his potential as an intelligent being: surplus (discretionary) income, political freedom, free time (leisure), and freedom from grinding drudgery. They never dreamed that their blissful Utopia would be achieved not under socialism but as the result of a hard-charging, go-getter business boom. To heighten the irony, it was in the 1970s that socialism was dealt a blow from which it is never likely to recover. Starting with the publication of Solzhenitsyn's *Gulag Archipelago* in 1973, the repressive nature of socialism as a monolithic system of government became too obvious to ignore any longer. By the 1970s there was no possible ideological detour around concentration camps, and under the pure socialism the concentration camps were found again and again—in the Soviet Union, in Cambodia, in Cuba, in the new United Vietnam. By 1979 Marxism was finished as a spiritual force, although the ideologues lingered on. In objective terms, then, the time was ripe for a development that would have confounded all the twilight theories of the past 100 years: namely the Rise of the West.

In subjective terms, however, the story was different. There was no moral force, no iron in the soul, not even a reigning philosophy, to give spiritual strength to the good times being had by all.

Solzhenitsyn, for his part, was not enchanted with American life, once he settled into his rural redoubt in Vermont. In his famous Harvard commencement speech of June 1978, he characterized the American way as soft, materialistic, morally impoverished. "The human soul," he said, "longs for things higher, warmer, and purer than those offered by today's mass living habits, introduced by the revolting invasion of publicity, by TV stupor, and by intolerable music. . . . Two hundred or even fifty years ago, it would have seemed quite impossible, in America, that an individual could be granted boundless freedom simply for the satisfaction of his instincts or whims." What Solzhenitsyn was looking at, utterly stupefied, was the first era of: *every man an aristocrat.*

In 1976 I wrote an essay entitled "The Me Decade and the Third Great Awakening." I soon found the phrase "the Me Decade" being used in many publications as a way of characterizing this as an age of narcissism, greed, or simple rut-boar wallowing. In the essay I was referring to something that I still find considerably more subtle:

America's extraordinary boom began in the early 1940s, but it was not until the 1960s that the *new masses* began to regard it as a permanent condition. Only then did they spin out the credit line and start splurging and experimenting with ways of life heretofore confined to the upper orders. In the 1970s they moved from the plateau of the merely materialistic to a truly aristocratic luxury: the habit of putting oneself on stage, analyzing one's conduct, one's *relationships*, one's hang-ups, one's personality, precisely the way noblemen did it during the age of chivalry. This secret vice was one of the dividends of the feminist movement of the 1970s. An ordinary status — woman, housewife — was elevated to the level of drama. One's existence as a *woman* . . . as *Me* . . . became something all the world analyzed, agonized over, drew cosmic conclusions from, or, in any event, took seriously. Books were written about *being a woman*, meetings were held, consciousnesses were raised (as the phrase went), television specials were produced, and magazines were founded upon that single notion. Every woman became a heroine of the great epic of the sexes. Out of such intense concentration upon the self, however, came a feeling that was decidedly religious, binding one beaming righteous soul to the other in the name of the cause.

28   And there you had the paradox of the 1970s: it was both the most narcissistic of decades and the least. In fact, such has been the paradox of hedonism itself for some 2,300 years. In the third century B.C. Epicurus, now remembered as the greatest of the hedonistic philosophers, lived a life that today would earn him the designation of "cult leader." At his home in Athens he established what would now be called a commune. The commingling of men and women within the Garden of Epicurus, as it was called, was viewed by many as depraved. Epicurus and his disciples developed the proposition that all truth is derived from the senses and the highest truth is derived from pleasure. Or as Hemingway would put it in our time: "Morality is what you feel good after." Yet the pursuit of pleasure, like most monomanias, carries the seeds of spirituality. Epicureanism became one of the most powerful pre-Christian religions, and in no time the Epicurean emphasis on pleasure became spiritual and, in fact, quite juiceless. Likewise, in the 1970s spirituality gushed forth in the most unexpected places, even among *swingers*, as the decade's most dedicated sexual-obsessives became known.

29   At a sex farm in the Santa Monica mountains of Los Angeles, people of all class levels gathered for weekends in the nude. They copulated in the living room, by the chess table, out by the pool, on the tennis courts, in the driveway, with the same open, free, liberated spirit as dogs in the park or baboons in a tree. In conversation, however, the atmosphere was quite different. The air became humid with solemnity. If you closed your eyes, you thought you were at a 19th century Wesleyan church encampment at Oak Bluffs. It's the soul that gets a workout here, brethren. . . . At the apex of my soul is a spark of the Divine . . . and I perceive it in the pure moment of ecstasy . . . which your textbooks call "the orgasm," but which I know to be Heaven. . . .

30   And in this strange progress from sexology to theology was added another rogue surge to what I think of as The Third Great Awakening, namely the third great religious wave in American history and the most extraordinary development of the 1970s. Such was the hunger for some form of spiritual strength that any obsession was sufficient to found a faith upon: jogging, flying, UFOs, ESP, health foods, or drug rehabilitation. No terrain was too barren or too alien to support a messiah. It was the Third Awakening that made possible the election as President of that

curious figure Jimmy Carter, an evangelical Baptist who had recently been "born again" and "saved," who had "accepted Jesus Christ as my personal Savior." Jimmy Carter seemed to come straight from the tent meeting where Sister Martha played the Yamaha piano and the sisters and the brethren stood up and gave witness and shouted. "Share it, brother!" "Share it, sister!" And praised God. In the four years that followed, Jimmy Carter never seemed to understand the power that flowed through his piney wood veins. He dissipated the power and the glory and threw away all his trump cards. The people yearned for halle-lujah, testifying, and the blood of the lamb, and he gave them position statements from the Teleprompter.

America now tingles with the things of the flesh while roaring drunk   31
on the things of the spirit. We are in that curious interlude of the 20th century that Nietzsche foretold a century ago: the time of the *reevaluation*, the devising of new values to replace the osteoporotic skeletons of the old. God is dead, and 40 new gods live, prancing like mummers. Beyond, it is not the ending but the beginning! Ecce America—in her Elizabethan period, her Bourbon Louis romp, her season of rude animal health and rising sap! Sisters and brethren, it is written that these are evil days, but I say unto you: the holiest of spirits are even now bubbling up into every brain. . . .

Questions on Content

1. According to Wolfe, what major changes in sexual mores took place during the 1970s?
2. Why does Wolfe feel that the decriminalization of possessing small amounts of marijuana was inevitable?
3. What relationship, if any, exists, between the changes in sexual morality, the changing attitudes toward drugs, and the profiteering among public officials eager to publish the inside story about the Watergate scandal?
4. Why does Wolfe conclude that "by 1979 Marxism was finished as a spiritual force"?
5. What does Wolfe mean when he calls the 1970s "the Me Decade"?
6. What does Wolfe mean by the Third Great Awakening?

Questions on Thesis, Purpose, and Structure

1. What is the basic cause of the hedonism of the 1970s according to Wolfe? Trace as best you can the chain of causes and effects leading Wolfe to the conclusion that now we are in the era of "every man an aristocrat."
2. What are the paradoxical effects of the extreme hedonism of modern life?
3. Explain how the election of Jimmy Carter as President serves for Wolfe as a fitting culmination of the diverse hedonistic forces at work in America during the 1970s. Why does Wolfe believe that Carter failed "to understand the power that flowed through his piney wood veins"?
4. How informative is Wolfe's essay? How persuasive? Do you find his writing entertaining? Give some specific examples of what Wolfe does to make his writing entertaining, informative, and persuasive.

Questions on Style and Diction

1. Find the following words in the essay and determine their definitions in context: cloven declivities (paragraph 1); in medias res (paragraph 4); aplomb, gaffe (paragraph 6); diffidently, Pre-Raphaelite (paragraph 9); lurid, stiffened giblets, nodules (paragraph 14); edifice (paragraph 16); juridical (paragraph 18); templates (paragraph 19); symploce (paragraph 20); hedonism, littorals, proletarian (paragraph 21); utopian, repressive, monolithic, ideologues (paragraph 23); redoubt, stupor, stupefied (paragraph 25).
2. Analyze the famous style of "the New Journalism" in a typical paragraph by Wolfe. Be sure to consider the diction, sentence structures, imagery, comparisons, and overall tone.
3. What is the effect of the Latin phrases in paragraph 20? What cynical criticism of modern values is created by these allusions?

Ideas for Essays

1. How did American life change during the 1980s? Write an essay in which you identify the causes and/or effects of one major change in the American scene.
2. If you are old enough to write from direct, personal experience, take issue with Wolfe's contentions about the 1970s. You may, for example, wish to dispute Wolfe's cynical observation that people were so hungry for something to believe in that they turned in masses to kooky beliefs. Or you may wish to call into question the pervasiveness of the sexual freedom that Wolfe assumes. Many additional possibilities exist.

The Blue Hotel
Stephen Crane

Stephen Crane (1871–1900) was born in Newark, New Jersey, and briefly attended Lafayette College and Syracuse University before becoming a free-lance journalist in New York City. His real interests, however, were literary — he had written the first draft of *Maggie: A Girl of the Streets* (1896) while in college — and for several years, until the publication of *The Red Badge of Courage* in 1895 won him recognition, Crane existed on the brink of poverty. Crane's reputation rests mainly on his achievement in these two novels, in a handful of naturalistic short stories, and in the brief and often sardonic poems published in *The Black Rider* (1895). The focus of "The Blue Hotel" (1898), perhaps Crane's most famous short story, is on the complex series of causes and effects through which the Swede's exaggerated sense of the dangers of the West gradually imposes itself on the midwestern community of Fort Romper.

I

The Palace Hotel at Fort Romper was painted a light blue, a shade that is   1
on the legs of a kind of heron, causing the bird to declare its position
against any background. The Palace Hotel, then, was always screaming
and howling in a way that made the dazzling winter landscape of Nebraska seem only a grey swampish hush. It stood alone on the prairie,
and when the snow was falling the town two hundred yards away was not
visible. But when the traveller alighted at the railway station he was
obliged to pass the Palace Hotel before he could come upon the company of low clapboard houses which composed Fort Romper, and it was
not to be thought that any traveller could pass the Palace Hotel without
looking at it. Pat Scully, the proprietor, had proved himself a master of
strategy when he chose his paints. It is true that on clear days, when the
great transcontinental expresses, long lines of swaying Pullmans, swept
through Fort Romper, passengers were overcome at the sight, and the
cult that knows the brown-reds and the subdivisions of the dark greens
of the East expressed shame, pity, horror, in a laugh. But to the citizens
of this prairie town and to the people who would naturally stop there,
Pat Scully had performed a feat. With this opulence and splendour, these
creeds, classes, egotisms, that streamed through Romper on the rails day
after day, they had no colour in common.

As if the displayed delights of such a blue hotel were not sufficiently   2
enticing, it was Scully's habit to go every morning and evening to meet
the leisurely trains that stopped at Romper and work his seductions
upon any man that he might see wavering, gripsack in hand.

One morning, when a snow-crusted engine dragged its long string   3
of freight cars and its one passenger coach to the station, Scully performed the marvel of catching three men. One was a shaky and quick-
eyed Swede, with a great shining cheap valise; one was a tall bronzed
cowboy, who was on his way to a ranch near the Dakota line; one was a
little silent man from the East, who didn't look it, and didn't announce it.
Scully practically made them prisoners. He was so nimble and merry and
kindly that each probably felt it would be the height of brutality to try to
escape. They trudged off over the creaking board sidewalks in the wake
of the eager little Irishman. He wore a heavy fur cap squeezed tightly
down on his head. It caused his two red ears to stick out stiffly, as if they
were made of tin.

At last, Scully, elaborately, with boisterous hospitality, conducted   4
them through the portals of the blue hotel. The room which they entered was small. It seemed to be merely a proper temple for an enormous stove, which, in the centre, was humming with godlike violence.
At various points on its surface the iron had become luminous and
glowed yellow from the heat. Beside the stove Scully's son Johnnie was
playing High-Five[1] with an old farmer who had whiskers both grey and

---

[1]A popular card game, the forerunner of modern contract bridge; also called Cinch or
Pedro.

sandy. They were quarrelling. Frequently the old farmer turned his face toward a box of sawdust—coloured brown from tobacco juice—that was behind the stove, and spat with an air of great impatience and irritation. With a loud flourish of words Scully destroyed the game of cards, and bustled his son upstairs with part of the baggage of the new guests. He himself conducted them to three basins of the coldest water in the world. The cowboy and the Easterner burnished themselves fiery red with this water, until it seemed to be some kind of metal-polish. The Swede, however, merely dipped his fingers gingerly and with trepidation. It was notable that throughout this series of small ceremonies the three travellers were made to feel that Scully was very benevolent. He was conferring great favours upon them. He handed the towel from one to another with an air of philanthropic impulse.

5   Afterward they went to the first room, and, sitting about the stove, listened to Scully's officious clamour at his daughters, who were preparing the midday meal. They reflected in the silence of experienced men who tread carefully amid new people. Nevertheless, the old farmer, stationary, invincible in his chair near the warmest part of the stove, turned his face from the sawdust-box frequently and addressed a glowing commonplace to the strangers. Usually he was answered in short but adequate sentences by either the cowboy or the Easterner. The Swede said nothing. He seemed to be occupied in making furtive estimates of each man in the room. One might have thought that he had the sense of silly suspicion which comes to guilt. He resembled a badly frightened man.

6   Later, at dinner, he spoke a little, addressing his conversation entirely to Scully. He volunteered that he had come from New York, where for ten years he had worked as a tailor. These facts seemed to strike Scully as fascinating, and afterward he volunteered that he had lived at Romper for fourteen years. The Swede asked about the crops and the price of labour. He seemed barely to listen to Scully's extended replies. His eyes continued to rove from man to man.

7   Finally, with a laugh and a wink, he said that some of these Western communities were very dangerous; and after his statement he straightened his legs under the table, tilted his head, and laughed again, loudly. It was plain that the demonstration had no meaning to the others. They looked at him wondering and in silence.

II

8   As the men trooped heavily back into the front room, the two little windows presented views of a turmoiling sea of snow. The huge arms of the wind were making attempts—mighty, circular, futile—to embrace the flakes as they sped. A gate-post like a still man with a blanched face stood aghast amid this profligate fury. In a hearty voice Scully announced the presence of a blizzard. The guests of the blue hotel, lighting their pipes, assented with grunts of lazy masculine contentment. No island of the sea could be exempt in the degree of this little room with

its humming stove. Johnnie, son of Scully, in a tone which defined his opinion of his ability as a card-player, challenged the old farmer of both grey and sandy whiskers to a game of High-Five. The farmer agreed with a contemptuous and bitter scoff. They sat close to the stove, and squared their knees under a wide board. The cowboy and the Easterner watched the game with interest. The Swede remained near the window, aloof, but with a countenance that showed signs of an inexplicable excitement.

The play of Johnnie and the grey-beard was suddenly ended by 9
another quarrel. The old man arose while casting a look of heated scorn at his adversary. He slowly buttoned his coat, and then stalked with fabulous dignity from the room. In the discreet silence of all other men the Swede laughed. His laughter rang somehow childish. Men by this time had begun to look at him askance, as if they wished to inquire what ailed him.

A new game was formed jocosely. The cowboy volunteered to be- 10
come the partner of Johnnie, and they all then turned to ask the Swede to throw in his lot with the little Easterner. He asked some questions about the game, and, learning that it wore many names, and that he had played it when it was under an alias, he accepted the invitation. He strode toward the men nervously, as if he expected to be assaulted. Finally, seated, he gazed from face to face and laughed shrilly. This laugh was so strange that the Easterner looked up quickly, the cowboy sat intent and with his mouth open, and Johnnie paused, holding the cards with still fingers.

Afterward there was a short silence. Then Johnnie said, "Well, let's 11
get at it. Come on now!" They pulled their chairs forward until their knees were bunched under the board. They began to play, and their interest in the game caused the others to forget the manner of the Swede.

The cowboy was a board-whacker. Each time that he held superior 12
cards he whanged them, one by one, with exceeding force, down upon the improvised table, and took the tricks with a glowing air of prowess and pride that sent thrills of indignation into the hearts of his opponents. A game with a board-whacker in it is sure to become intense. The countenances of the Easterner and the Swede were miserable whenever the cowboy thundered down his aces and kings, while Johnnie, his eyes gleaming with joy, chuckled and chuckled.

Because of the absorbing play none considered the strange ways of 13
the Swede. They paid strict heed to the game. Finally, during a lull caused by a new deal, the Swede suddenly addressed Johnnie: "I suppose there have been a good many men killed in this room." The jaws of the others dropped and they looked at him.

"What in hell are you talking about?" said Johnnie. 14

The Swede laughed again his blatant laugh, full of a kind of false 15
courage and defiance. "Oh, you know what I mean all right," he answered.

"I'm a liar if I do!" Johnnie protested. The card was halted, and the 16
men stared at the Swede. Johnnie evidently felt that as the son of the proprietor he should make a direct inquiry. "Now, what might you be

drivin' at, mister?'' he asked. The Swede winked at him. It was a wink full of cunning. His fingers shook on the edge of the board. "Oh, maybe you think I have been to nowheres. Maybe you think I'm a tenderfoot?''

17   "I don't know nothin' about you,'' answered Johnnie, "and I don't give a damn where you've been. All I got to say is that I don't know what you're driving at. There hain't never been nobody killed in this room.''

18   The cowboy, who had been steadily gazing at the Swede, then spoke: "What's wrong with you, mister?''

19   Apparently it seemed to the Swede that he was formidably menaced. He shivered and turned white near the corners of his mouth. He sent an appealing glance in the direction of the little Easterner. During these moments he did not forget to wear his air of advanced pot-valour.[2] "They say they don't know what I mean,'' he remarked mockingly to the Easterner.

20   The latter answered after prolonged and cautious reflection. "I don't understand you,'' he said, impassively.

21   The Swede made a movement then which announced that he thought he had encountered treachery from the only quarter where he had expected sympathy, if not help. "Oh, I see you are all against me. I see——''

22   The cowboy was in a state of deep stupefaction. "Say,'' he cried, as he tumbled the deck violently down upon the board, "say, what are you gittin' at, hey?''

23   The Swede sprang up with the celerity of a man escaping from a snake on the floor. "I don't want to fight!'' he shouted. "I don't want to fight!''

24   The cowboy stretched his long legs indolently and deliberately. His hands were in his pockets. He spat into the sawdust-box. "Well, who the hell thought you did?'' he inquired.

25   The Swede backed rapidly toward a corner of the room. His hands were out protectingly in front of his chest, but he was making an obvious struggle to control his fright. "Gentlemen,'' he quavered, "I suppose I am going to be killed before I can leave this house! I suppose I am going to be killed before I can leave this house!'' In his eyes was the dying-swan look. Through the windows could be seen the snow turning blue in the shadow of dusk. The wind tore at the house, and some loose thing beat regularly against the clapboards like a spirit tapping.

26   A door opened, and Scully himself entered. He paused in surprise as he noted the tragic attitude of the Swede. Then he said, "What's the matter here?''

27   The Swede answered him swiftly and eagerly: "These men are going to kill me.''

28   "Kill you!'' ejaculated Scully. "Kill you! What are you talkin'?''

29   The Swede made the gesture of a martyr.

30   Scully wheeled sternly upon his son. "What is this, Johnnie?''

[2]Drunken bravado.

The lad had grown sullen. "Damned if I know," he answered. "I   31
can't make no sense to it." He began to shuffle the cards, fluttering them
together with an angry snap. "He says a good many men have been
killed in this room, or something like that. And he says he's goin' to be
killed here too. I don't know what ails him. He's crazy, I shouldn't
wonder."

Scully then looked for explanation to the cowboy, but the cowboy   32
simply shrugged his shoulders.

"Kill you?" said Scully again to the Swede. "Kill you? Man, you're off   33
your nut."

"Oh, I know," burst out the Swede. "I know what will happen.   34
Yes, I'm crazy—yes. Yes, of course, I'm crazy—yes. But I know one
thing—" There was a sort of sweat of misery and terror upon his face. "I
know I won't get out of here alive."

The cowboy drew a deep breath, as if his mind was passing into the   35
last stages of dissolution. "Well, I'm doggoned," he whispered to
himself.

Scully wheeled suddenly and faced his son. "You've been troublin'   36
this man!"

Johnnie's voice was loud with its burden of grievance. "Why, good   37
Gawd, I ain't done nothin' to 'im."

The Swede broke in. "Gentlemen, do not disturb yourselves. I will   38
leave this house. I will go away, because"—he accused them dramatically with his glance—"because I do not want to be killed."

Scully was furious with his son. "Will you tell me what is the matter,   39
you young divil? What's the matter, anyhow? Speak out!"

"Blame it!" cried Johnnie in despair, "don't I tell you I don't know?   40
He—he says we want to kill him, and that's all I know. I can't tell what
ails him."

The Swede continued to repeat: "Never mind, Mr. Scully; never   41
mind. I will leave this house. I will go away, because I do not wish to be
killed. Yes, of course, I am crazy—yes. But I know one thing! I will go
away. I will leave this house. Never mind, Mr. Scully; never mind. I will
go away."

"You will not go 'way," said Scully. "You will not go 'way until I   42
hear the reason of this business. If anybody has troubled you I will take
care of him. This is my house. You are under my roof, and I will not
allow any peaceable man to be troubled here." He cast a terrible eye
upon Johnnie, the cowboy, and the Easterner.

"Never mind, Mr. Scully; never mind. I will go away. I do not wish   43
to be killed." The Swede moved toward the door which opened upon
the stairs. It was evidently his intention to go at once for his baggage.

"No, no," shouted Scully peremptorily; but the white-faced man slid   44
by him and disappeared. "Now," said Scully severely, "what does this
mane?"

Johnnie and the cowboy cried together: "Why, we didn't do nothin'   45
to 'im!"

Scully's eyes were cold. "No," he said, "you didn't?"   46

Johnnie swore a deep oath. "Why, this is the wildest loon I ever see.   47

We didn't do nothin' at all. We were just sittin' here playin' cards, and he——''

48   The father suddenly spoke to the Easterner. "Mr. Blanc," he asked, "what has these boys been doin'?"

49   The Easterner reflected again. "I didn't see anything wrong at all," he said at last, slowly.

50   Scully began to howl. "But what does it mane?" He stared ferociously at his son. "I have a mind to lather you for this, me boy."

51   Johnnie was frantic. "Well, what have I done?" he bawled at his father.

III

52   "I think you are tongue-tied," said Scully finally to his son, the cowboy, and the Easterner; and at the end of this scornful sentence he left the room.

53   Upstairs the Swede was swiftly fastening the straps on his great valise. Once his back happened to be half turned toward the door, and, hearing a noise there, he wheeled and sprang up, uttering a loud cry. Scully's wrinkled visage showed grimly in the light of the small lamp he carried. This yellow effulgence, streaming upward, coloured only his prominent features, and left his eyes, for instance, in mysterious shadow. He resembled a murderer.

54   "Man! man!" he exclaimed, "have you gone daffy?"

55   "Oh, no! Oh, no!" rejoined the other. "There are people in this world who know pretty nearly as much as you do—understand?"

56   For a moment they stood gazing at each other. Upon the Swede's deathly pale cheeks were two spots brightly crimson and sharply edged, as if they had been carefully painted. Scully placed the light on the table and sat himself on the edge of the bed. He spoke ruminatively. "By cracky, I never heard of such a thing in my life. It's a complete muddle. I can't, for the soul of me, think how you ever got this idea into your head." Presently he lifted his eyes and asked: "And did you sure think they were going to kill you?"

57   The Swede scanned the old man as if he wished to see into his mind. "I did," he said at last. He obviously suspected that this answer might precipitate an outbreak. As he pulled on a strap his whole arm shook, the elbow wavering like a bit of paper.

58   Scully banged his hand impressively on the footboard of the bed. "Why, man, we're goin' to have a line of ilictric street-cars in this town next spring."

59   "'A line of electric street-cars,'" repeated the Swede, stupidly.

60   "And," said Scully, "there's a new railroad goin' to be built down from Broken Arm to here. Not to mintion the four churches and the smashin' big brick schoolhouse. Then there's the big factory, too. Why, in two years Romper'll be a met-tro-*pol*-is."

61   Having finished the preparation of his baggage, the Swede straightened himself. "Mr. Scully," he said, with sudden hardihood, "how much do I owe you?"

"You don't owe me anythin'," said the old man, angrily.   62

"Yes, I do," retorted the Swede. He took seventy-five cents from his   63
pocket and tendered it to Scully; but the latter snapped his fingers in
disdainful refusal. However, it happened that they both stood gazing in a
strange fashion at three silver pieces on the Swede's open palm.

"I'll not take your money," said Scully at last. "Not after what's been   64
goin' on here." Then a plan seemed to strike him. "Here," he cried,
picking up his lamp and moving toward the door. "Here! Come with me
a minute."

"No," said the Swede, in overwhelming alarm.   65

"Yes," urged the old man. "Come on! I want you to come and see a   66
picter — just across the hall — in my room."

The Swede must have concluded that his hour was come. His jaw   67
dropped and his teeth showed like a dead man's. He ultimately followed
Scully across the corridor, but he had the step of one hung in chains.

Scully flashed the light high on the wall of his own chamber. There   68
was revealed a ridiculous photograph of a little girl. She was leaning
against a balustrade of gorgeous decoration, and the formidable bang to
her hair was prominent. The figure was as graceful as an upright sled-
stake, and, withal, it was of the hue of lead. "There," said Scully, tenderly, "that's the picter of my little girl that died. Her name was Carrie.
She had the purtiest hair you ever saw! I was that fond of her, she——"

Turning then, he saw that the Swede was not contemplating the   69
picture at all, but, instead, was keeping keen watch on the gloom in the
rear.

"Look, man!" cried Scully, heartily. "That's the picter of my little gal   70
that died. Her name was Carrie. And then here's the picter of my oldest
boy, Michael. He's a lawyer in Lincoln, an' doin' well. I gave that boy a
grand eddication, and I'm glad for it now. He's a fine boy. Look at 'im
now. Ain't he bold as blazes, him there in Lincoln, an honoured an'
respicted gintleman! An honoured and respicted gintleman," concluded
Scully with a flourish. And, so saying, he smote the Swede jovially on the
back.

The Swede faintly smiled.   71

"Now," said the old man, "there's only one more thing." He   72
dropped suddenly to the floor and thrust his head beneath the bed. The
Swede could hear his muffled voice. "I'd keep it under me piller if it
wasn't for that boy Johnnie. Then there's the old woman—— Where is it
now? I never put it twice in the same place. Ah, now come out with you!"

Presently he backed clumsily from under the bed, dragging with   73
him an old coat rolled into a bundle. "I've fetched him," he muttered.
Kneeling on the floor, he unrolled the coat and extracted from its heart a
large yellow-brown whiskey-bottle.

His first maneuver was to hold the bottle up to the light. Reassured,   74
apparently, that nobody had been tampering with it, he thrust it with a
generous movement toward the Swede.

The weak-kneed Swede was about to eagerly clutch this element of   75
strength, but he suddenly jerked his hand away and cast a look of horror
upon Scully.

76   "Drink," said the old man affectionately. He had risen to his feet, and now stood facing the Swede.

77   There was a silence. Then again Scully said: "Drink!"

78   The Swede laughed wildly. He grabbed the bottle, put it to his mouth; and as his lips curled absurdly around the opening and his throat worked, he kept his glance, burning with hatred, upon the old man's face.

IV

79   After the departure of Scully the three men, with the card-board still upon their knees, preserved for a long time an astounded silence. Then Johnnie said: "That's the dod-dangedest Swede I ever see."

80   "He ain't no Swede," said the cowboy, scornfully.

81   "Well, what is he then?" cried Johnnie. "What is he then?"

82   "It's my opinion," replied the cowboy deliberately, "he's some kind of Dutchman." It was a venerable custom of the country to entitle as Swedes all light-haired men who spoke with a heavy tongue. In consequence the idea of the cowboy was not without its daring. "Yes, sir," he repeated. "It's my opinion this feller is some kind of a Dutchman."

83   "Well, he says he's a Swede, anyhow," muttered Johnnie, sulkily. He turned to the Easterner: "What do you think, Mr. Blanc?"

84   "Oh, I don't know," replied the Easterner.

85   "Well, what do you think makes him act that way?" asked the cowboy.

86   "Why, he's frightened." The Easterner knocked his pipe against a rim of the stove. "He's clear frightened out of his boots."

87   "What at?" cried Johnnie and the cowboy together.

88   The Easterner reflected over his answer.

89   "What at?" cried the others again.

90   "Oh, I don't know, but it seems to me this man has been reading dime novels, and he thinks he's right out in the middle of it—the shootin' and stabbin' and all."

91   "But," said the cowboy, deeply scandalized, "this ain't Wyoming, ner none of them places. This is Nebrasker."

92   "Yes," added Johnnie, "an' why don't he wait till he gits *out West*?"

93   The travelled Easterner laughed. "It isn't different there even—not in these days. But he thinks he's right in the middle of hell."

94   Johnnie and the cowboy mused long.

95   "It's awful funny," remarked Johnnie at last.

96   "Yes," said the cowboy. "This is a queer game. I hope we don't git snowed in, because then we'd have to stand this here man bein' around with us all the time. That wouldn't be no good."

97   "I wish pop would throw him out," said Johnnie.

98   Presently they heard a loud stamping on the stairs, accompanied by ringing jokes in the voice of old Scully, and laughter, evidently from the Swede. The men around the stove stared vacantly at each other. "Gosh!" said the cowboy. The door flew open, and old Scully, flushed and

anecdotal, came into the room. He was jabbering at the Swede, who followed him, laughing bravely. It was the entry of two roisterers from a banquet hall.

"Come now," said Scully sharply to the three seated men, "move up   99
and give us a chance at the stove." The cowboy and the Easterner obediently sidled their chairs to make room for the new-comers. Johnnie, however, simply arranged himself in a more indolent attitude, and then remained motionless.

"Come! Git over, there," said Scully.   100

"Plenty of room on the other side of the stove," said Johnnie.   101

"Do you think we want to sit in the draught?" roared the father.   102

But the Swede here interposed with a grandeur of confidence. "No,   103
no. Let the boy sit where he likes," he cried in a bullying voice to the father.

"All right! All right!" said Scully, deferentially. The cowboy and the   104
Easterner exchanged glances of wonder.

The five chairs were formed in a crescent about one side of the   105
stove. The Swede began to talk; he talked arrogantly, profanely, angrily. Johnnie, the cowboy, and the Easterner maintained a morose silence, while old Scully appeared to be receptive and eager, breaking in constantly with sympathetic ejaculations.

Finally the Swede announced that he was thirsty. He moved in his   106
chair, and said that he would go for a drink of water.

"I'll git it for you," cried Scully at once.   107

"No," said the Swede, contemptuously. "I'll get it for myself." He   108
arose and stalked with the air of an owner off into the executive parts of the hotel.

As soon as the Swede was out of hearing Scully sprang to his feet   109
and whispered intensely to the others: "Upstairs he thought I was tryin' to poison 'im."

"Say," said Johnnie, "this makes me sick. Why don't you throw 'im   110
out in the snow?"

"Why, he's all right now," declared Scully. "It was only that he was   111
from the East, and he thought this was a tough place. That's all. He's all right now."

The cowboy looked with admiration upon the Easterner. "You were   112
straight," he said. "You were on to that there Dutchman."

"Well," said Johnnie to his father, "he may be all right now, but I   113
don't see it. Other time he was scared, but now he's too fresh."

Scully's speech was always a combination of Irish brogue and   114
idiom, Western twang and idiom, and scraps of curiously formal diction taken from the storybooks and newspapers. He now hurled a strange mass of language at the head of his son. "What do I keep? What do I keep? What do I keep?" he demanded, in a voice of thunder. He slapped his knee impressively, to indicate that he himself was going to make reply, and that all should heed. "I keep a hotel," he shouted. "A hotel, do you mind? A guest under my roof has sacred privileges. He is to be intimidated by none. Not one word shall he hear that would prijudice him in favour of goin' away. I'll not have it. There's no place in this here

town where they can say they iver took in a guest of mine because he was afraid to stay here." He wheeled suddenly upon the cowboy and the Easterner. "Am I right?"

115   "Yes, Mr. Scully," said the cowboy, "I think you're right."
116   "Yes, Mr. Scully," said the Easterner, "I think you're right."

V

117   At six-o'clock supper, the Swede fizzed like a fire-wheel. He sometimes seemed on the point of bursting into riotous song, and in all his madness he was encouraged by old Scully. The Easterner was encased in reserve; the cowboy sat in wide-mouthed amazement, forgetting to eat, while Johnnie wrathily demolished great plates of food. The daughters of the house, when they were obliged to replenish the biscuits, approached as warily as Indians, and, having succeeded in their purpose, fled with ill-concealed trepidation. The Swede domineered the whole feast, and he gave it the appearance of a cruel bacchanal. He seemed to have grown suddenly taller; he gazed, brutally disdainful, into every face. His voice rang through the room. Once when he jabbed out harpoon-fashion with his fork to pinion a biscuit, the weapon nearly impaled the hand of the Easterner, which had been stretched quietly out for the same biscuit.

118   After supper, as the men filed toward the other room, the Swede smote Scully ruthlessly on the shoulder. "Well, old boy, that was a good, square meal." Johnnie looked hopefully at his father; he knew that shoulder was tender from an old fall; and, indeed, it appeared for a moment as if Scully was going to flame out over the matter, but in the end he smiled a sickly smile and remained silent. The others understood from his manner that he was admitting his responsibility for the Swede's new view-point.

119   Johnnie, however, addressed his parent in an aside. "Why don't you license somebody to kick you downstairs?" Scully scowled darkly by way of reply.

120   When they were gathered about the stove, the Swede insisted on another game of High-Five. Scully gently deprecated the plan at first, but the Swede turned a wolfish glare upon him. The old man subsided, and the Swede canvassed the others. In his tone there was always a great threat. The cowboy and the Easterner both remarked indifferently that they would play. Scully said that he would presently have to go to meet the 6.58 train, and so the Swede turned menacingly upon Johnnie. For a moment their glances crossed like blades, and then Johnnie smiled and said, "Yes, I'll play."

121   They formed a square, with the little board on their knees. The Easterner and the Swede were again partners. As the play went on, it was noticeable that the cowboy was not board-whacking as usual. Meanwhile, Scully, near the lamp, had put on his spectacles and, with an appearance curiously like an old priest, was reading a newspaper. In time he went out to meet the 6.58 train, and, despite his precautions, a gust of polar wind whirled into the room as he opened the door. Besides

scattering the cards, it chilled the players to the marrow. The Swede cursed frightfully. When Scully returned, his entrance disturbed a cosy and friendly scene. The Swede again cursed. But presently they were once more intent, their heads bent forward and their hands moving swiftly. The Swede had adopted the fashion of board-whacking.

Scully took up his paper and for a long time remained immersed in matters which were extraordinarily remote from him. The lamp burned badly, and once he stopped to adjust the wick. The newspaper, as he turned from page to page, rustled with a slow and comfortable sound. Then suddenly he heard three terrible words: "You are cheatin'!" 122

Such scenes often prove that there can be little of dramatic import in environment. Any room can present a tragic front; any room can be comic. This little den was now hideous as a torture-chamber. The new faces of the men themselves had changed it upon the instant. The Swede held a huge fist in front of Johnnie's face, while the latter looked steadily over it into the blazing orbs of his accuser. The Easterner had grown pallid; the cowboy's jaw had dropped in that expression of bovine amazement which was one of his important mannerisms. After the three words, the first sound in the room was made by Scully's paper as it floated forgotten to his feet. His spectacles had also fallen from his nose, but by a clutch he had saved them in air. His hand, grasping the spectacles, now remained poised awkwardly and near his shoulder. He stared at the card-players. 123

Probably the silence was while a second elapsed. Then, if the floor had been suddenly twitched out from under the men they could not have moved quicker. The five had projected themselves headlong toward a common point. It happened that Johnnie, in rising to hurl himself upon the Swede, had stumbled slightly because of his curiously instinctive care for the cards and the board. The loss of the moment allowed time for the arrival of Scully, and also allowed the cowboy time to give the Swede a great push which sent him staggering back. The men found tongue together, and hoarse shouts of rage, appeal, or fear burst from every throat. The cowboy pushed and jostled feverishly at the Swede, and the Easterner and Scully clung wildly to Johnnie; but through the smoky air, above the swaying bodies of the peace-compellers, the eyes of the two warriors ever sought each other in glances of challenge that were at once hot and steely. 124

Of course the board had been overturned, and now the whole company of cards was scattered over the floor, where the boots of the men trampled the fat and painted kings and queens as they gazed with their silly eyes at the war that was waging above them. 125

Scully's voice was dominating the yells. "Stop now! Stop, I say! Stop, now—" 126

Johnnie, as he struggled to burst through the rank formed by Scully and the Easterner, was crying, "Well, he says I cheated! He says I cheated! I won't allow no man to say I cheated! If he says I cheated, he's a —— ——!" 127

The cowboy was telling the Swede, "Quit, now! Quit, d'ye hear——" 128

129   The screams of the Swede never ceased: "He did cheat! I saw him! I saw him——"

130   As for the Easterner, he was importuning in a voice that was not heeded: "Wait a moment, can't you? Oh, wait a moment. What's the good of a fight over a game of cards? Wait a moment——"

131   In this tumult no complete sentences were clear. "Cheat"—"Quit"

132   —"He says"—these fragments pierced the uproar and rang out sharply. It was remarkable that, whereas Scully undoubtedly made the most noise, he was the least heard of any of the riotous band.

133   Then suddenly there was a great cessation. It was as if each man had paused for breath; and although the room was still lighted with the anger of men, it could be seen that there was no danger of immediate conflict, and at once Johnnie, shouldering his way forward, almost succeeded in confronting the Swede. "What did you say I cheated for? What did you say I cheated for? I don't cheat, and I won't let no man say I do!"

134   The Swede said, "I saw you! I saw you!"

135   "Well," cried Johnnie, "I'll fight any man what says I cheat!"

136   "No, you won't," said the cowboy. "Not here."

137   "Ah, be still, can't you?" said Scully, coming between them.

138   The quiet was sufficient to allow the Easterner's voice to be heard. He was repeating, "Oh, wait a moment, can't you? What's the good of a fight over a game of cards? Wait a moment!"

139   Johnnie, his red face appearing above his father's shoulder, hailed the Swede again. "Did you say I cheated?"

140   The Swede showed his teeth. "Yes."

141   "Then," said Johnnie, "we must fight."

142   "Yes, fight," roared the Swede. He was like a demoniac. "Yes, fight! I'll show you what kind of a man I am! I'll show you who you want to fight! Maybe you think I can't fight! Maybe you think I can't! I'll show you, you skin, you card-sharp! Yes, you cheated! You cheated! You cheated!"

143   "Well, let's go at it, then, mister," said Johnnie, coolly.

The cowboy's brow was beaded with sweat from his efforts in intercepting all sorts of raids. He turned in despair to Scully. "What are you goin' to do now?"

144   A change had come over the Celtic visage of the old man. He now seemed all eagerness; he eyes glowed.

145   "We'll let them fight," he answered, stalwartly. "I can't put up with it any longer. I've stood this damned Swede till I'm sick. We'll let them fight."

VI

146   The men prepared to go out of doors. The Easterner was so nervous that he had great difficulty in getting his arms into the sleeves of his new leather coat. As the cowboy drew his fur cap down over his ears his hands trembled. In fact, Johnnie and old Scully were the only ones who displayed no agitation. These preliminaries were conducted without words.

Scully threw open the door. "Well, come on," he said. Instantly a   147
terrific wind caused the flame of the lamp to struggle at its wick, while a
puff of black smoke sprang from the chimney-top. The stove was in
mid-current of the blast, and its voice swelled to equal the roar of the
storm. Some of the scarred and bedabbled cards were caught up from
the floor and dashed helplessly against the farther wall. The men lowered their heads and plunged into the tempest as into a sea.

No snow was falling, but great whirls and clouds of flakes, swept up   148
from the ground by the frantic winds, were streaming southward with
the speed of bullets. The covered land was blue with the sheen of an
unearthly satin, and there was no other hue save where, at the low, black
railway station — which seemed incredibly distant — one light gleamed
like a tiny jewel. As the men floundered into a thigh-deep drift, it was
known that the Swede was bawling out something. Scully went to him,
put a hand on his shoulder, and projected an ear. "What's that you say?"
he shouted.

"I say," bawled the Swede again, "I won't stand much show against   149
this gang. I know you'll all pitch on me."

Scully smote him reproachfully on the arm. "Tut, man!" he yelled.   150
The wind tore the words from Scully's lips and scattered them far alee.

"You are all a gang of——" boomed the Swede, but the storm also   151
seized the remainder of this sentence.

Immediately turning their backs upon the wind, the men had swung   152
around a corner to the sheltered side of the hotel. It was the function of
the little house to preserve here, amid this great devastation of snow, an
irregular V-shape of heavily encrusted grass, which crackled beneath the
feet. One could imagine the great drifts piled against the windward side.
When the party reached the comparative peace of this spot it was found
that the Swede was still bellowing.

"Oh, I know what kind of a thing this is! I know you'll all pitch on   153
me. I can't lick you all!"

Scully turned upon him panther-fashion. "You'll not have to whip   154
all of us. You'll have to whip my son Johnnie. An' the man what troubles
you durin' that time will have me to dale with."

The arrangements were swiftly made. The two men faced each   155
other, obedient to the harsh commands of Scully, whose face, in the
subtly luminous gloom, could be seen set in the austere impersonal
lines that are pictured on the countenances of the Roman veterans. The
Easterner's teeth were chattering, and he was hopping up and down like
a mechanical toy. The cowboy stood rock-like.

The contestants had not stripped off any clothing. Each was in his   156
ordinary attire. Their fists were up, and they eyed each other in a calm
that had the elements of leonine cruelty in it.

During this pause, the Easterner's mind, like a film, took lasting   157
impressions of three men — the iron-nerved master of the ceremony; the
Swede, pale, motionless, terrible; and Johnnie, serene yet ferocious,
brutish yet heroic. The entire prelude had in it a tragedy greater than the
tragedy of action, and this aspect was accentuated by the long, mellow
cry of the blizzard, as it sped the tumbling and wailing flakes into the
black abyss of the south.

158   "Now!" said Scully.

159   The two combatants leaped forward and crashed together like bullocks. There was heard the cushioned sound of blows, and of a curse squeezing out from between the tight teeth of one.

160   As for the spectators, the Easterner's pent-up breath exploded from him with a pop of relief, absolute relief from the tension of the preliminaries. The cowboy bounded into the air with a yowl. Scully was immovable as from supreme amazement and fear at the fury of the fight which he himself had permitted and arranged.

161   For a time the encounter in the darkness was such a perplexity of flying arms that it presented no more detail than would a swiftly revolving wheel. Occasionally a face, as if illumined by a flash of light, would shine out, ghastly and marked with pink spots. A moment later, the men might have been known as shadows, if it were not for the involuntary utterance of oaths that came from them in whispers.

162   Suddenly a holocaust of warlike desire caught the cowboy, and he bolted forward with the speed of a broncho. "Go it, Johnnie! go it! Kill him! Kill him!"

163   Scully confronted him. "Kape back," he said; and by his glance the cowboy could tell that this man was Johnnie's father.

164   To the Easterner there was a monotony of unchangeable fighting that was an abomination. This confused mingling was eternal to his sense, which was concentrated in a longing for the end, the priceless end. Once the fighters lurched near him, and as he scrambled hastily backward he heard them breathe like men on the rack.

165   "Kill him, Johnnie! Kill him! Kill him! Kill him!" The cowboy's face was contorted like one of those agony masks in museums.

166   "Keep still," said Scully, icily.

167   Then there was a sudden loud grunt, incomplete, cut short, and Johnnie's body swung away from Swede and fell with sickening heaviness to the grass. The cowboy was barely in time to prevent the mad Swede from flinging himself upon his prone adversary. "No, you don't," said the cowboy, interposing an arm. "Wait a second."

168   Scully was at his son's side. "Johnnie! Johnnie, me boy!" His voice had a quality of melancholy tenderness. "Johnnie! Can you go on with it?" He looked anxiously down into the bloody, pulpy face of his son.

169   There was a moment of silence, and then Johnnie answered in his ordinary voice, "Yes, I—it—yes."

170   Assisted by his father he struggled to his feet. "Wait a bit now till you git your wind," said the old man.

171   A few paces away the cowboy was lecturing the Swede. "No, you don't! Wait a second!"

172   The Easterner was plucking at Scully's sleeve. "Oh, this is enough," he pleaded. "This is enough! Let it go as it stands. This is enough!"

173   "Bill," said Scully, "git out of the road." The cowboy stepped aside. "Now." The combatants were actuated by a new caution as they advanced toward collision. They glared at each other, and then the Swede aimed a lightning blow that carried with it his entire weight. Johnnie was

evidently half stupid from weakness, but he miraculously dodged, and his fist sent the over-balanced Swede sprawling.

The cowboy, Scully, and the Easterner burst into a cheer that was 174 like a chorus of triumphant soldiery, but before its conclusion the Swede had scuffed agilely to his feet and come in berserk abandon at his foe. There was another perplexity of flying arms, and Johnnie's body again swung away and fell, even as a bundle might fall from a roof. The Swede instantly staggered to a little wind-waved tree and leaned upon it, breathing like an engine, while his savage and flamelit eyes roamed from face to face as the men bent over Johnnie. There was a splendour of isolation in his situation at this time which the Easterner felt once when, lifting his eyes from the man on the ground, he beheld that mysterious and lonely figure, waiting.

"Are you any good yet, Johnnie?" asked Scully in a broken voice. 175

The son gasped and opened his eyes languidly. After a moment he 176 answered, "No—I ain't—any good—any—more." Then, from shame and bodily ill, he began to weep, the tears furrowing down through the blood-stains on his face. "He was too—too—too heavy for me."

Scully straightened and addressed the waiting figure. 177

"Stranger," he said, evenly, "it's all up with our side." Then his 178 voice changed into that vibrant huskiness which is commonly the tone of the most simple and deadly announcements. "Johnnie is whipped."

Without replying, the victor moved off on the route to the front door 179 of the hotel.

The cowboy was formulating new and unspellable blasphemies. 180 The Easterner was startled to find that they were out in a wind that seemed to come direct from the shadowed arctic floes. He heard again the wail of the snow as it was flung to its grave in the south. He knew now that all this time the cold had been sinking into him deeper and deeper, and he wondered that he had not perished. He felt indifferent to the condition of the vanquished man.

"Johnnie, can you walk?" asked Scully. 181

"Did I hurt—hurt him any?" asked the son. 182

"Can you walk, boy? Can you walk?" 183

Johnnie's voice was suddenly strong. There was a robust impatience 184 in it. "I asked you whether I hurt him any!"

"Yes, yes, Johnnie," answered the cowboy, consolingly; "he's hurt a 185 good deal."

They raised him from the ground, and as soon as he was on his feet 186 he went tottering off, rebuffing all attempts at assistance. When the party rounded the corner they were fairly blinded by the pelting of the snow. It burned their faces like fire. The cowboy carried Johnnie through the drift to the door. As they entered, some cards again rose from the floor and beat against the wall.

The Easterner rushed to the stove. He was so profoundly chilled that 187 he almost dared to embrace the glowing iron. The Swede was not in the room. Johnnie sank into a chair and, folding his arms on his knees, buried his face in them. Scully, warming one foot and then the other at a rim of the stove, muttered to himself with Celtic mournfulness. The cowboy had removed his fur cap, and with a dazed and rueful air he was running one hand through his tousled locks. From overhead they could hear the creaking of boards, as the Swede tramped here and there in his room.

188   The sad quiet was broken by the sudden flinging open of a door that led toward the kitchen. It was instantly followed by an inrush of women. They precipitated themselves upon Johnnie amid a chorus of lamentation. Before they carried their prey off to the kitchen, there to be bathed and harangued with that mixture of sympathy and abuse which is a feat of their sex, the mother straightened herself and fixed old Scully with an eye of stern reproach, "Shame be upon you, Patrick Scully!" she cried. "Your own son, too. Shame be upon you!"

189   "There, now! Be quiet, now!" said the old man, weakly.

190   "Shame be upon you, Patrick Scully!" The girls, rallying to this slogan, sniffed disdainfully in the direction of those trembling accomplices, the cowboy and the Easterner. Presently they bore Johnnie away, and left the three men to dismal reflection.

VII

191   "I'd like to fight this here Dutchman myself," said the cowboy, breaking a long silence.

192   Scully wagged his head sadly. "No, that wouldn't do. It wouldn't be right. It wouldn't be right."

193   "Well, why wouldn't it?" argued the cowboy. "I don't see no harm in it."

194   "No," answered Scully, with mournful heroism. "It wouldn't be right. It was Johnnie's fight, and now we mustn't whip the man just because he whipped Johnnie."

195   "Yes, that's true enough," said the cowboy; "but — he better not get fresh with me, because I couldn't stand no more of it."

196   "You'll not say a word to him," commanded Scully, and even then they heard the tread of the Swede on the stairs. His entrance was made theatric. He swept the door back with a bang and swaggered to the middle of the room. No one looked at him. "Well," he cried, insolently, at Scully, "I s'pose you'll tell me now how much I owe you?"

197   The old man remained stolid. "You don't owe me nothin'."

198   "Huh!" said the Swede, "huh! Don't owe 'im nothin'."

199   The cowboy addressed the Swede. "Stranger, I don't see how you come to be so gay around here."

200   Old Scully was instantly alert. "Stop!" he shouted, holding his hand forth, fingers upward. "Bill, you shut up!"

201   The cowboy spat carelessly into the sawdust-box. "I didn't say a word, did I?" he asked.

202   "Mr. Scully," called the Swede, "how much do I owe you?" It was seen that he was attired for departure, and that he had his valise in his hand.

"You don't owe me nothin'," repeated Scully in the same impertur-   203
bable way.

"Huh!" said the Swede. "I guess you're right. I guess if it was any   204
way at all, you'd owe me somethin'. That's what I guess." He turned to
the cowboy. "'Kill him! Kill him! Kill him!'" he mimicked, and then
guffawed victoriously. "'Kill him!'" He was convulsed with ironical
humour.

But he might have been jeering the dead. The three men were   205
immovable and silent, staring with glassy eyes at the stove.

The Swede opened the door and passed into the storm, giving one   206
derisive glance backward at the still group.

As soon as the door was closed, Scully and the cowboy leaped to   207
their feet and began to curse. They trampled to and fro, waving their
arms and smashing into the air with their fists. "Oh, but that was a hard
minute!" wailed Scully. "That was a hard minute! Him there leerin' and
scoffin'! One bang at his nose was worth forty dollars to me that minute!
How did you stand it, Bill?"

"How did I stand it?" cried the cowboy in a quivering voice. "How   208
did I stand it? Oh!"

The old man burst into sudden brogue. "I'd loike to take that   209
Swede," he wailed, "and hould 'im down on a shtone flure and bate 'im
to a jelly wid a shtick!"

The cowboy groaned in sympathy. "I'd like to git him by the neck   210
and hammer him"—he brought his hand down on a chair with a noise
like a pistol-shot—"hammer that there Dutchman until he couldn't tell
himself from a dead coyote!"

"I'd bate 'im until he——"   211

"I'd show *him* some things——"   212

And then together they raised a yearning, fanatic cry—"Oh-oh-oh!   213
if we only could——"

"Yes!"   214

"Yes!"   215

"And then I'd——"   216

"O-o-oh!"   217

VIII

The Swede, tightly gripping his valise, tacked across the face of the   218
storm as if he carried sails. He was following a line of little naked,
gasping trees which, he knew, must mark the way of the road. His face,
fresh from the pounding of Johnnie's fists, felt more pleasure than pain
in the wind and the driving snow. A number of square shapes loomed
upon him finally, and he knew them as the houses of the main body of
the town. He found a street and made travel along it, leaning heavily
upon the wind whenever, at a corner, a terrific blast caught him.

He might have been in a deserted village. We picture the world as   219
thick with conquering and elate humanity, but here, with the bugles of
the tempest pealing, it was hard to imagine a peopled earth. One viewed

the existence of man then as a marvel, and conceded a glamour of wonder to these lice which were caused to cling to a whirling, fire-smitten, ice-locked, disease-stricken, space-lost bulb. The conceit of man was explained by this storm to be the very engine of life. One was a coxcomb not to die in it. However, the Swede found a saloon.

220   In front of it an indomitable red light was burning, and the snow-flakes were made blood-colour as they flew through the circumscribed territory of the lamp's shining. The Swede pushed open the door of the saloon and entered. A sanded expanse was before him, and at the end of it four men sat about a table drinking. Down one side of the room extended a radiant bar, and its guardian was leaning upon his elbows listening to the talk of the men at the table. The Swede dropped his valise upon the floor and, smiling fraternally upon the barkeeper, said, "Gimme some whisky, will you?" The man placed a bottle, a whisky-glass, and a glass of ice-thick water upon the bar. The Swede poured himself an abnormal portion of whisky and drank it in three gulps. "Pretty bad night," remarked the bartender, indifferently. He was making the pretension of blindness which is usually a distinction of his class; but it could have been seen that he was furtively studying the half-erased blood-stains on the face of the Swede. "Bad night," he said again.

221   "Oh, it's good enough for me," replied the Swede, hardily, as he poured himself some more whisky. The barkeeper took his coin and manœuvred it through its reception by the highly nickelled cash-machine. A bell rang; a card labelled "20 cts." had appeared.

222   "No, continued the Swede, "this isn't too bad weather. It's good enough for me."

223   "So?" murmured the barkeeper, languidly.

224   The copious drams made the Swede's eyes swim, and he breathed a trifle heavier. "Yes, I like this weather. I like it. It suits me." It was apparently his design to impart a deep significance to these words.

225   "So?" murmured the bartender again. He turned to gaze dreamily at the scroll-like birds and bird-like scrolls which had been drawn with soap upon the mirrors in back of the bar.

226   "Well, I guess I'll take another drink," said the Swede, presently. "Have something?"

227   "No, thanks; I'm not drinkin'," answered the bartender. Afterward he asked, "How did you hurt your face?"

228   The Swede immediately began to boast loudly. "Why, in a fight. I thumped the soul out of a man down here at Scully's hotel."

229   The interest of the four men at the table was at last aroused.

230   "Who was it?" said one.

231   "Johnnie Scully," blustered the Swede. "Son of the man what runs it. He will be pretty near dead for some weeks, I can tell you. I made a nice thing of him, I did. He couldn't get up. They carried him in the house. Have a drink?"

232   Instantly the men in some subtle way encased themselves in reserve. "No, thanks," said one. The group was of curious formation. Two were prominent local business men; one was the district attorney; and one was a professional gambler of the kind known as "square." But a scrutiny of the group would not have enabled an observer to pick the

gambler from the men of more reputable pursuits. He was, in fact, a man so delicate in manner, when among people of fair class, and so judicious in his choice of victims, that in the strictly masculine part of the town's life he had come to be explicitly trusted and admired. People called him a thoroughbred. The fear and contempt with which his craft was regarded were undoubtedly the reason why his quiet dignity shone conspicuous above the quiet dignity of men who might be merely hatters, billiard-markers, or grocery clerks. Beyond an occasional unwary traveller who came by rail, this gambler was supposed to prey solely upon reckless and senile farmers, who, when flush with good crops, drove into town in all the pride and confidence of an absolutely invulnerable stupidity. Hearing at times in circuitous fashion of the despoilment of such a farmer, the important men of Romper invariably laughed in contempt of the victim, and if they thought of the wolf at all, it was with a kind of pride at the knowledge that he would never dare think of attacking their wisdom and courage. Besides, it was popular that this gambler had a real wife and two real children in a neat cottage in a suburb, where he led an exemplary home life; and when any one even suggested a discrepancy in his character, the crowd immediately vociferated descriptions of this virtuous family circle. Then men who led exemplary home lives, and men who did not lead exemplary home lives, all subsided in a bunch, remarking that there was nothing more to be said.

However, when a restriction was placed upon him — as, for instance, when a strong clique of members of the new Pollywog Club refused to permit him, even as a spectator, to appear in the rooms of the organization — the candour and gentleness with which he accepted the judgment disarmed many of his foes and made his friends more desperately partisan. He invariably distinguished between himself and a respectable Romper man so quickly and frankly that his manner actually appeared to be a continual broadcast compliment. 233

And one must not forget to declare the fundamental fact of his entire position in Romper. It is irrefutable that in all affairs outside his business, in all matters that occur eternally and commonly between man and man, this thieving card-player was so generous, so just, so moral, that, in a contest, he could have put to flight the consciences of nine tenths of the citizens of Romper. 234

And so it happened that he was seated in this saloon with the two prominent local merchants and the district attorney. 235

The Swede continued to drink raw whisky, meanwhile babbling at the barkeeper and trying to induce him to indulge in potations. "Come on. Have a drink. Come on. What — no? Well, have a little one, then. By gawd, I've whipped a man to-night, and I want to celebrate. I whipped him good, too. Gentlemen," the Swede cried to the men at the table, "have a drink?" 236

"Ssh!" said the barkeeper. 237

The group at the table, although furtively attentive, had been pretending to be deep in talk, but now a man lifted his eyes toward the Swede and said, shortly, "Thanks. We don't want any more." 238

At this reply the Swede ruffled out his chest like a rooster. "Well," 239 he exploded, "it seems I can't get anybody to drink with me in this town. Seems so, don't it? Well!"

240   "Ssh!" said the barkeeper.

241   "Say," snarled the Swede, "don't you try to shut me up. I won't have it. I'm a gentleman, and I want people to drink with me. And I want 'em to drink with me now. *Now*—do you understand?" He rapped the bar with his knuckles.

242   Years of experience had calloused the bartender. He merely grew sulky. "I hear you," he answered.

243   "Well," cried the Swede, "listen hard then. See those men over there? Well, they're going to drink with me, and don't you forget it. Now you watch."

244   "Hi!" yelled the barkeeper, "this won't do!"

245   "Why won't it?" demanded the Swede. He stalked over to the table, and by chance laid his hand upon the shoulder of the gambler. "How about this?" he asked wrathfully. "I asked you to drink with me."

246   The gambler simply twisted his head and spoke over his shoulder. "My friend, I don't know you."

247   "Oh, hell!" answered the Swede, "come and have a drink."

248   "Now, my boy," advised the gambler, kindly, "take your hand off my shoulder and go 'way and mind your own business." He was a little, slim man, and it seemed strange to hear him use this tone of heroic patronage to the burly Swede. The other men at the table said nothing.

249   "What! You won't drink with me, you little dude? I'll make you, then! I'll make you!" The Swede had grasped the gambler frenziedly at the throat, and was dragging him from his chair. The other men sprang up. The barkeeper dashed around the corner of his bar. There was a great tumult, and then was seen a long blade in the hand of the gambler. It shot forward, and a human body, this citadel of virtue, wisdom, power, was pierced as easily as if it had been a melon. The Swede fell with a cry of supreme astonishment.

250   The prominent merchants and the district attorney must have at once tumbled out of the place backward. The bartender found himself hanging limply to the arm of a chair and gazing into the eyes of a murderer.

251   "Henry," said the latter, as he wiped his knife on one of the towels that hung beneath the bar rail, "you tell 'em where to find me. I'll be home, waiting for 'em." Then he vanished. A moment afterward the barkeeper was in the street dinning through the storm for help and, moreover, companionship.

252   The corpse of the Swede, alone in the saloon, had its eyes fixed upon a dreadful legend that dwelt atop of the cash-machine: "This registers the amount of your purchase."

IX

253   Months later, the cowboy was frying pork over the stove of a little ranch near the Dakota line, when there was a quick thud of hoofs outside, and presently the Easterner entered with the letters and the papers.

"Well," said the Easterner at once, "the chap that killed the Swede   254
has got three years. Wasn't much, was it?"

"He has? Three years?" The cowboy poised his pan of pork, while   255
he ruminated upon the news. "Three years. That ain't much."

"No. It was a light sentence," replied the Easterner as he unbuckled   256
his spurs. "Seems there was a good deal of sympathy for him in
Romper."

"If the bartender had been any good," observed the cowboy,   257
thoughtfully, "he would have gone in and cracked that there Dutchman
on the head with a bottle in the beginnin' of it and stopped all this here
murderin'."

"Yes, a thousand things might have happened," said the Easterner,   258
tartly.

The cowboy returned his pan of pork to the fire, but his philosophy   259
continued. "It's funny, ain't it? If he hadn't said Johnnie was cheatin'
he'd be alive this minute. He was an awful fool. Game played for fun,
too. Not for money. I believe he was crazy."

"I feel sorry for that gambler," said the Easterner.   260

"Oh, so do I," said the cowboy. "He don't deserve none of it for   261
killin' who he did."

"The Swede might not have been killed if everything had been   262
square."

"Might not have been killed?" exclaimed the cowboy. "Everythin'   263
square? Why, when he said that Johnnie was cheatin' and acted like such
a jackass? And then in the saloon he fairly walked up to git hurt?" With
these arguments the cowboy browbeat the Easterner and reduced him to
rage.

"You're a fool!" cried the Easterner, viciously. "You're a bigger   264
jackass than the Swede by a million majority. Now let me tell you one
thing. Let me tell you something. Listen! Johnnie *was* cheating!"

"'Johnnie,'" said the cowboy, blankly. There was a minute of si-   265
lence, and then he said, robustly, "Why, no. The game was only for fun."

"Fun or not," said the Easterner, "Johnnie was cheating. I saw him.   266
I know it. I saw him. And I refused to stand up and be a man. I let the
Swede fight it out alone. And you — you were simply puffing around the
place wanting to fight. And then old Scully himself! We are all in it! This
poor gambler isn't even a noun. He is kind of an adverb. Every sin is the
result of a collaboration. We, five of us, have collaborated in the murder
of this Swede. Usually there are from a dozen to forty women really
involved in every murder, but in this case it seems to be only five
men — you, I, Johnnie, old Scully; and that fool of an unfortunate gambler came merely as a culmination, the apex of a human movement, and
gets all the punishment."

The cowboy, injured and rebellious, cried out blindly into this fog   267
of mysterious theory: "Well, I didn't do anythin', did I?"

Questions on Content

1. Describe the Blue Hotel and Fort Romper. Is the town ordinary or unusual?
2. What does the Swede expect Fort Romper to be like?

3. What does the Swede think will happen to him at the Blue Hotel?
4. Why does Scully tell the Swede about the "ilictric streetcars" and why does he insist on showing the Swede the picture of his daughter?
5. What changes the Swede from being frightened and retiring, to being bold and aggressive?
6. What causes the fight between Johnnie and the Swede? Who is in the right?
7. Why does the Swede insist that the men in the saloon drink with him?

Questions on Thesis, Purpose, and Structure

1. What has caused the Swede's misunderstandings about the West?
2. What factors influence the way in which the other characters react to the Swede?
3. What is the effect of the Swede's presence on the people with whom he comes into contact? Why does he affect them as he does?
4. Who is responsible for the death of the Swede? Is it the gambler, the Swede himself, Johnnie, Scully, the Easterner, the cowboy, or some combination of them all?
5. Why does Crane conclude the story's eighth section with the "dreadful legend . . . 'This registers the amount of your purchase'"?
5. What does this story tell us about America and Americans? About the causes of murder? About human nature? About natural forces?

Questions on Style and Diction

1. Find the following words in the story and determine their definitions in context: opulence, egotisms (paragraph 1); boisterous, trepidation, benevolent, philanthropic (paragraph 4); officious, furtive, (paragraph 5); profligate, contemptuous, countenance, inexplicable (paragraph 8); askance, ailed (paragraph 9); jocosely (paragraph 10); improvised, prowess (paragraph 12); blatant (paragraph 15); stupefaction (paragraph 22); celerity (paragraph 23); indolently (paragraph 24); dissolution (paragraph 35); peremptorily (paragraph 44); effulgence (paragraph 53); ruminatively (paragraph 56); roisterers (paragraph 98); interposed (paragraph 103); deferentially (paragraph 104); arrogantly, morose (paragraph 105); bacchanal (paragraph 117); deprecated, canvassed (paragraph 120); pallid, bovine (paragraph 123); importuning (paragraph 130); actuated (paragraph 173); languidly (paragraph 176); stolid (paragraph 197); imperturbable (paragraph 203); coxcomb (paragraph 219); indomitable, furtively (paragraph 220); exemplary (paragraph 232); clique, partisan (paragraph 233); potations (paragraph 236); patronage (paragraph 248).
2. Consider the connotations and implications of each character's name. Do these names fit the characters? How are the names helpful in revealing Crane's thematic ideas?
3. Carefully examine the description of the storm. How does it contribute to plot, characterization, and theme?

Ideas for Essays

1. Examine the Easterner's contention that "Every sin is the result of a collaboration." Is that a sensible conclusion drawn from the events in the story? Is it an equally sensible conclusion about your own experiences and observations in life?

2. In an analytical essay explain why the cowboy's final cry, "Well, I didn't do anythin', did I?" is an apt ending for the story.
3. Write an essay explaining in detail the many causal factors in the death of the Swede.

The Yellow Wall-Paper

Charlotte Perkins Gilman

Charlotte Perkins Gilman (1860–1935) was born in Hartford, Connecticut. Her formal schooling was limited and her early adult years were clouded by a nervous breakdown followed by a separation from her husband, but by the mid-1890s Gilman had published a number of short stories and poems and embarked on a career as an increasingly well-known feminist and socialist lecturer. Her best-known work, *Women and Economics* (1898), is an early feminist manifesto arguing for the economic independence of women. Gilman elaborated her call for a reexamination of the traditional role of women in such other works as *Concerning Children* (1900), *The Home* (1903), *Man-Made World* (1911), and *His Religion and Hers* (1923). In "The Yellow Wall-Paper" (1892), Gilman's narrator records her struggles with mental illness. As she does so, she speculates on the causes of her illness while also providing the reader with information that allows a somewhat different analysis of causes and effects. As you read, try to decide to what extent the physical surroundings prey on the narrator's mind and to what extent she is unsettled by her role as a woman and her treatment at the hands of men.

It is very seldom that mere ordinary people like John and myself secure ancestral halls for the summer.   1

A colonial mansion, a hereditary estate, I would say a haunted house, and reach the height of romantic felicity—but that would be asking too much of fate!   2

Still I will proudly declare that there is something queer about it.   3

Else, why should it be let so cheaply? And why have stood so long untenanted?   4

John laughs at me, of course, but one expects that in marriage.   5

John is practical in the extreme. He has no patience with faith, an intense horror of superstition, and he scoffs openly at any talk of things not to be felt and seen and put down in figures.   6

John is a physician, and *perhaps*—(I would not say it to a living soul, of course, but this is dead paper and a great relief to my mind—) *perhaps* that is one reason I do not get well faster.   7

You see he does not believe I am sick!   8

And what can one do?   9

If a physician of high standing, and one's own husband, assures friends and relatives that there is really nothing the matter with one but   10 temporary nervous depression — a slight hysterical tendency — what is one to do?

11   My brother is also a physician, and also of high standing, and he says the same thing.

12   So I take phosphates or phosphites — whichever it is, and tonics, and journeys, and air, and exercise, and am absolutely forbidden to "work" until I am well again.

13   Personally, I disagree with their ideas.

14   Personally, I believe that congenial work, with excitement and change, would do me good.

15   But what is one to do?

16   I did write for a while in spite of them; but it *does* exhaust me a good deal — having to be so sly about it, or else meet with heavy opposition.

17   I sometimes fancy that in my condition if I had less opposition and more society and stimulus — but John says the very worst thing I can do is to think about my condition, and I confess it always makes me feel bad.

18   So I will let it alone and talk about the house.

19   The most beautiful place! It is quite alone, standing well back from the road, quite three miles from the village. It makes me think of English places that you read about, for there are hedges and walls and gates that lock, and lots of separate little houses for the gardnerers and people.

20   There is a *delicious* garden! I never saw such a garden — large and shady, full of box-bordered paths, and lined with long grape-covered arbors with seats under them.

21   There were greenhouses, too, but they are all broken now.

22   There was some legal trouble, I believe, something about the heirs and coheirs; anyhow, the place has been empty for years.

23   That spoils my ghostliness, I am afraid, but I don't care — there is something strange about the house — I can feel it.

24   I even said so to John one moonlight evening, but he said what I felt was a *draught*, and shut the window.

25   I get unreasonably angry with John sometimes. I'm sure I never used to be so sensitive. I think it is due to this nervous condition.

26   But John says if I feel so, I shall neglect proper self-control; so I take pains to control myself — before him, at least, and that makes me very tired.

27   I don't like our room a bit, I wanted one downstairs that opened on the piazza and had roses all over the window, and such pretty old-fashioned chintz hangings! but John would not hear of it.

28   He said there was only one window and not room for two beds, and no near room for him if he took another.

29   He is very careful and loving, and hardly lets me stir without special direction.

30   I have a schedule prescription for each hour in the day; he takes all care from me, and so I feel basely ungrateful not to value it more.

31   He said we came here solely on my account, that I was to have perfect rest and all the air I could get. "Your exercise depends on your

strength, my dear," said he, "and your food somewhat on your appetite; but air you can absorb all the time." So we took the nursery at the top of the house.

It is a big, airy room, the whole floor nearly, with windows that look   32 all ways, and air and sunshine galore. It was nursery first and then playroom and gymnasium, I should judge; for the windows are barred for little children, and there are rings and things in the walls.

The paint and paper look as if a boys' school had used it. It is   33 stripped off—the paper—in great patches all around the head of my bed, about as far as I can reach, and in a great place on the other side of the room low down. I never saw a worse paper in my life.

One of those sprawling flamboyant patterns committing every artis-   34 tic sin.

It is dull enough to confuse the eye in following, pronounced   35 enough to constantly irritate and provoke study, and when you follow the lame uncertain curves for a little distance they suddenly commit suicide—plunge off at outrageous angles, destroy themselves in un-heard of contradictions.

The color is repellent, almost revolting; a smoldering unclean yel-   36 low, strangely faded by the slow-turning sunlight.

It is a dull yet lurid orange in some places, a sickly sulphur tint in   37 others.

No wonder the children hated it! I should hate it myself if I had to   38 live in this room long.

There comes John, and I must put this away,—he hates to have me   39 write a word.

We have been here two weeks, and I haven't felt like writing before,   40 since that first day.

I am sitting by the window now, up in this atrocious nursery, and   41 there is nothing to hinder my writing as much as I please, save lack of strength.

John is away all day, and even some nights when his cases are   42 serious.

I am glad my case is not serious!   43

But these nervous troubles are dreadfully depressing.   44

John does not know how much I really suffer. He knows there is no   45 *reason* to suffer, and that satisfies him.

Of course it is only nervousness. It does weigh on me so not to do   46 my duty in any way!

I meant to be such a help to John, such a real rest and comfort, and   47 here I am a comparative burden already!

Nobody would believe what an effort it is to do what little I am   48 able,—to dress and entertain, and order things.

It is fortunate Mary is so good with the baby. Such a dear baby!   49

And yet I *cannot* be with him, it makes me so nervous.   50

I suppose John never was nervous in his life. He laughs at me so   51 about this wall-paper!

At first he meant to repaper the room, but afterwards he said that I   52 was letting it get the better of me, and that nothing was worse for a nervous patient than to give way to such fancies.

53   He said that after the wall-paper was changed it would be the heavy bedstead, and then the barred windows, and then that gate at the head of the stairs, and so on.

54   "You know the place is doing you good," he said, "and really, dear, I don't care to renovate the house just for a three months' rental."

55   "Then do let us go downstairs," I said, "there are such pretty rooms there."

56   Then he took me in his arms and called me a blessed little goose, and said he would go down cellar, if I wished, and have it whitewashed into the bargain.

57   But he is right enough about the beds and windows and things.

58   It is an airy and comfortable room as any one need wish, and, of course, I would not be so silly as to make him uncomfortable just for a whim.

59   I'm really getting quite fond of the big room, all but that horrid paper.

60   Out of one window I can see the garden, those mysterious deep-shaded arbors, the riotous old-fashioned flowers, and bushes and gnarly trees.

61   Out of another I get a lovely view of the bay and a little private wharf belonging to the estate. There is a beautiful shaded lane that runs down there from the house. I always fancy I see people walking in these numerous paths and arbors, but John has cautioned me not to give way to fancy in the least. He says that with my imaginative power and habit of story-making, a nervous weakness like mine is sure to lead to all manner of excited fancies, and that I ought to use my will and good sense to check the tendency. So I try.

62   I think sometimes that if I were only well enough to write a little it would relieve the press of ideas and rest me.

63   But I find I get pretty tired when I try.

64   It is so discouraging not to have any advice and companionship about my work. When I get really well, John says we will ask Cousin Henry and Julia down for a long visit; but he says he would as soon put fireworks in my pillowcase as to let me have those stimulating people about now.

65   I wish I could get well faster.

66   But I must not think about that. This paper looks to me as if it *knew* what a vicious influence it had!

67   There is a recurrent spot where the pattern lolls like a broken neck and two bulbous eyes stare at you upside down.

68   I get positively angry with the impertinence of it and the everlast-ingness. Up and down and sideways they crawl, and those absurd, un-blinking eyes are everywhere. There is one place where two breadths didn't match, and the eyes go all up and down the line, one a little higher than the other.

69   I never saw so much expression in an inanimate thing before, and we all know how much expression they have! I used to lie awake as a

child and get more entertainment and terror out of blank walls and plain furniture than most children could find in a toy-store.

I remember what a kindly wink the knobs of our big, old bureau 70 used to have, and there was one chair that always seemed like a strong friend.

I used to feel that if any of the other things looked too fierce I could 71 always hop into that chair and be safe.

The furniture in this room is no worse than inharmonious, however, 72 for we had to bring it all from downstairs. I suppose when this was used as a playroom they had to take the nursery things out, and no wonder! I never saw such ravages as the children have made here.

The wall-paper, as I said before, is torn off in spots, and it sticketh 73 closer than a brother—they must have had perseverance as well as hatred.

Then the floor is scratched and gouged and splintered, the plaster 74 itself is dug out here and there, and this great heavy bed which is all we found in the room, looks as if it had been through the wars.

But I don't mind it a bit—only the paper. 75

There comes John's sister. Such a dear girl as she is, and so careful 76 of me! I must not let her find me writing.

She is a perfect and enthusiastic housekeeper, and hopes for no 77 better profession. I verily believe she thinks it is the writing which made me sick!

But I can write when she is out, and see her a long way off from 78 these windows.

There is one that commands the road, a lovely shaded winding road, 79 and one that just looks off over the country. A lovely country, too, full of great elms and velvet meadows.

This wall-paper has a kind of subpattern in a different shade, a 80 particularly irritating one, for you can only see it in certain lights, and not clearly then.

But in the places where it isn't faded and where the sun is just so—I 81 can see a strange, provoking, formless sort of figure, that seems to skulk about behind that silly and conspicuous front design.

There's sister on the stairs! 82

Well, the Fourth of July is over! The people are all gone and I am 83 tired out. John thought it might do me good to see a little company, so we just had mother and Nellie and the children down for a week.

Of course I didn't do a thing. Jennie sees to everything now. 84

But it tired me all the same. 85

John says if I don't pick up faster he shall send me to Weir Mitchell[1] 86 in the fall.

But I don't want to go there at all. I had a friend who was in his 87 hands once, and she says he is just like John and my brother, only more so!

[1]Silas Weir Mitchell (1829–1914), the Philadelphia neurologist-psychologist who introduced "rest cure" for nervous diseases. His medical books include *Diseases of the Nervous System, Especially of Women* (1881).

88   Besides, it is such an undertaking to go so far.

89   I don't feel as if it was worth while to turn my hand over for anything, and I'm getting dreadfully fretful and querulous.

90   I cry at nothing, and cry most of the time.

91   Of course I don't when John is here, or anybody else, but when I am alone.

92   And I am alone a good deal just now. John is kept in town very often by serious cases, and Jennie is good and lets me alone when I want her to.

93   So I walk a little in the garden or down that lovely lane, sit on the porch under the roses, and lie down up here a good deal.

94   I'm getting really fond of the room in spite of the wall-paper. Perhaps *because* of the wall-paper.

95   It dwells in my mind so!

96   I lie here on this great immovable bed — it is nailed down, I believe — and follow that pattern about by the hour. It is as good as gymnastics, I assure you. I start, we'll say, at the bottom, down in the corner over there where it has not been touched, and I determine for the thousandth time that I *will* follow that pointless pattern to some sort of a conclusion.

97   I know a little of the principle of design, and I know this thing was not arranged on any laws of radiation, or alternation, or repetition, or symmetry, or anything else that I ever heard of.

98   It is repeated, of course, by the breadths, but not otherwise.

99   Looked at in one way each breadth stands alone, the bloated curves and flourishes — a kind of "debased Romanesque" with *delirium tremens*[2] go waddling up and down in isolated columns of fatuity.

100   But, on the other hand, they connect diagonally, and the sprawling outlines run off in great slanting waves of optic horror, like a lot of wallowing seaweeds in full chase.

101   The whole thing goes horizontally, too, at least it seems so, and I exhaust myself in trying to distinguish the order of its going in that direction.

102   They have used a horizontal breadth for a frieze, and that adds wonderfully to the confusion.

103   There is one end of the room where it is almost intact, and there, when the crosslights fade and the low sun shines directly upon it. I can almost fancy radiation after all, — the interminable grotesques seem to form around a common centre and rush off in headlong plunges of equal distraction.

104   It makes me tired to follow it. I will take a nap I guess.

105   I don't know why I should write this.

106   I don't want to.

107   I don't feel able.

[2]Mental disorientation caused by excessive use of alcohol and characterized by physical tremors.

And I know John would think it absurd. But I *must* say what I feel   108
and think in some way — it is such a relief!

But the effort is getting to be greater than the relief.   109

Half the time now I am awfully lazy, and lie down ever so much.

John says I mustn't lose my strength, and has me take cod liver oil   110
and lots of tonics and things, to say nothing of ale and wine and rare
meat.

Dear John! He loves me very dearly, and hates to have me sick. I   111
tried to have a real earnest reasonable talk with him the other day, and
tell him how I wish he would let me go and make a visit to Cousin Henry
and Julia.

But he said I wasn't able to go, nor able to stand it after I got there;   112
and I did not make out a very good case for myself, for I was crying
before I had finished.

It is getting to be a great effort for me to think straight. Just this   113
nervous weakness I suppose.

And dear John gathered me up in his arms, and just carried me   114
upstairs and laid me on the bed, and sat by me and read to me till it tired
my head.

He said I was his darling and his comfort and all he had, and that I   115
must take care of myself for his sake, and keep well.

He says no one but myself can help me out of it, that I must use my   116
will and self-control and not let any silly fancies run away with me.

There's one comfort, the baby is well and happy, and does not have   117
to occupy this nursery with the horrid wall-paper.

If we had not used it, that blessed child would have! What a fortu-   118
nate escape! Why, I wouldn't have a child of mine, an impressionable
little thing, live in such a room for worlds.

I never thought of it before, but it is lucky that John kept me here   119
after all, I can stand it so much easier than a baby, you see.

Of course I never mention it to them any more — I am too wise, —   120
but I keep watch of it all the same.

There are things in that paper that nobody knows but me, or ever   121
will.

Behind that outside pattern the dim shapes get clearer every day.   122

It is always the same shape, only very numerous.   123

And it is like a woman stooping down and creeping about behind   124
that pattern. I don't like it a bit. I wonder — I begin to think — I wish
John would take me away from here!

It is so hard to talk with John about my case, because he is so wise,   125
and because he loves me so.

But I tried it last night.   126

It was moonlight. The moon shines in all around just as the sun   127
does.

I hate to see it sometimes, it creeps so slowly, and always comes in   128
by one window or another.

John was asleep and I hated to waken him, so I kept still and   129
watched the moonlight on that undulating wall-paper till I felt creepy.

The faint figure behind seemed to shake the pattern, just as if she   130
wanted to get out.

131   I got up softly and went to feel and see if the paper *did* move, and when I came back John was awake.

132   "What is it, little girl?" he said. "Don't go walking about like that —you'll get cold."

133   I thought it was a good time to talk, so I told him that I really was not gaining here, and that I wished he would take me away.

134   "Why, darling!" said he, "our lease will be up in three weeks, and I can't see how to leave before.

135   "The repairs are not done at home, and I cannot possibly leave town just now. Of course if you were in any danger, I could and would, but you really are better, dear, whether you can see it or not. I am a doctor, dear, and I know. You are gaining flesh and color, your appetite is better, I feel really much easier about you."

136   "I don't weigh a bit more," said I, "nor as much; and my appetite may be better in the evening when you are here, but it is worse in the morning when you are away!"

137   "Bless her little heart!" said he with a big hug, "she shall be as sick as she pleases! But now let's improve the shining hours by going to sleep, and talk about it in the morning!"

138   "And you won't go away?" I asked gloomily.

139   "Why, how can I, dear? It is only three weeks more and then we will take a nice little trip of a few days while Jennie is getting the house ready. Really dear you are better!"

140   "Better in body perhaps—" I began, and stopped short, for he sat up straight and looked at me with such a stern, reproachful look that I could not say another word.

141   "My darling," said he, "I beg of you, for my sake and for our child's sake, as well as for your own, that you will never for one instant let that idea enter your mind! There is nothing so dangerous, so fascinating, to a temperament like yours. It is a false and foolish fancy. Can you not trust me as a physician when I tell you so?"

142   So of course I said no more on that score, and we went to sleep before long. He thought I was asleep first, but I wasn't, and lay there for hours trying to decide whether that front pattern and the back pattern really did move together or separately.

143   On a pattern like this, by daylight, there is a lack of sequence, a defiance of law, that is a constant irritant to a normal mind.

144   The color is hideous enough, and unreliable enough, and infuriating enough, but the pattern is torturing.

145   You think you have mastered it, but just as you get well underway in following, it turns a back-somersault and there you are. It slaps you in the face, knocks you down, and tramples upon you. It is like a bad dream.

146   The outside pattern is a florid arabesque, reminding one of a fungus. If you can imagine a toadstool in joints, an interminable string of toadstools, budding and sprouting in endless convolutions—why, that is something like it.

That is, sometimes!

There is one marked peculiarity about this paper, a thing nobody   147
seems to notice but myself, and that is that it changes as the light   148
changes.

When the sun shoots in through the east windows — I always watch   149
for that first long, straight ray — it changes so quickly that I never can
quite believe it.

That is why I watch it always.   150

By moonlight — the moon shines in all night when there is a moon   151
— I wouldn't know it was the same paper.

At night in any kind of light, in twilight, candlelight, lamplight, and   152
worst of all by moonlight, it becomes bars! The outside pattern I mean,
and the woman behind it is as plain as can be.

I didn't realize for a long time what the thing was that showed   153
behind, that dim sub-pattern, but now I am quite sure it is a woman.

By daylight she is subdued, quiet. I fancy it is the pattern that keeps   154
her so still. It is so puzzling. It keeps me quiet by the hour.

I lie down ever so much now. John says it is good for me, and to   155
sleep all I can.

Indeed he started the habit by making me lie down for an hour after   156
each meal.

It is a very bad habit I am convinced, for you see I don't sleep.   157

And that cultivates deceit, for I don't tell them I'm awake — O no!   158

The fact is I am getting a little afraid of John.   159

He seems very queer sometimes, and even Jennie has an inexplic-   160
able look.

It strikes me occasionally, just as a scientific hypothesis, — that per-   161
haps it is the paper!

I have watched John when he did not know I was looking, and come   162
into the room suddenly on the most innocent excuses, and I've caught
him several times *looking at the paper*! And Jennie too. I caught Jennie
with her hand on it once.

She didn't know I was in the room, and when I asked her in a quiet,   163
a very quiet voice, with the most restrained manner possible, what she
was doing with the paper — she turned around as if she had been caught
stealing, and looked quite angry — asked my why I should frighten her
so!

Then she said that the paper stained everything it touched, that she   164
had found yellow smooches on all my clothes and John's, and she
wished we would be more careful!

Did not that sound innocent? But I know she was studying that   165
pattern, and I am determined that nobody shall find it out but myself!

Life is very much more exciting now than it used to be. You see I   166
have something more to expect, to look forward to, to watch. I really do
eat better, and am more quiet than I was.

John is so pleased to see me improve! He laughed a little the other   167
day, and said I seemed to be flourishing in spite of my wall-paper.

I turned it off with a laugh. I had no intention of telling him it was   168 *because* of the wall-paper — he would make fun of me. He might even want to take me away.

169   I don't want to leave now until I have found it out. There is a week more, and I think that will be enough.

170   I'm feeling ever so much better! I don't sleep much at night, for it is so interesting to watch developments; but I sleep a good deal in the daytime.

171   In the daytime it is tiresome and perplexing.

172   There are always new shoots on the fungus, and new shades of yellow all over it. I cannot keep count of them, though I have tried conscientiously.

173   It is the strangest yellow, that wallpaper! It makes me think of all the yellow things I ever saw — not beautiful ones like buttercups, but old foul, bad yellow things.

174   But there is something else about that paper — the smell! I noticed it the moment we came into the room, but with so much air and sun it was not bad. Now we have had a week of fog and rain, and whether the windows are open or not, the smell is here.

175   It creeps all over the house.

176   I find it hovering in the dining-room, skulking in the parlor, hiding in the hall, lying in wait for me on the stairs.

177   It gets into my hair.

178   Even when I go to ride, if I turn my head suddenly and surprise it — there is that smell!

179   Such a peculiar odor, too! I have spent hours in trying to analyze it, to find what it smelled like.

180   It is not bad — at first, and very gentle, but quite the subtlest, most enduring odor I ever met.

181   In this damp weather it is awful, I wake up in the night and find it hanging over me.

182   It used to disturb me at first. I thought seriously of burning the house — to reach the smell.

183   But now I am used to it. The only thing I can think of that it is like is the *color* of the paper! A yellow smell.

184   There is a very funny mark on this wall, low down, near the mop-board. A streak that runs round the room. It goes behind every piece of furniture, except the bed, a long, straight, even *smooch*, as if it had been rubbed over and over.

185   I wonder how it was done and who did it, and what they did it for. Round and round and round — round and round and round! — it makes me dizzy!

186   I really have discovered something at last.

187   Through watching so much at night when it changes so, I have finally found out.

188   The front pattern *does* move — and no wonder! The woman behind shakes it!

189   Sometimes I think there are a great many women behind, and sometimes only one, and she crawls around fast, and her crawling shakes it all over.

Then in the very bright spots she keeps still, and in the very shady 190
spots she just takes hold of the bars and shakes them hard.

And she is all the time trying to climb through. But nobody could 191
climb through that pattern—it strangles so; I think that is why it has so
many heads.

They get through, and then the pattern strangles them off and turns 192
them upside down, and makes their eyes white!

If those heads were covered or taken off it would not be half so bad. 193

I think that woman gets out in the daytime! 194
And I'll tell you why—privately-I've seen her! 195
I can see her out of every one of my windows! 196
It is the same woman, I know, for she is always creeping, and most 197
women do not creep by daylight.

I see her in that long shaded lane, creeping up and down. I see her 198
in those dark grape arbors, creeping all around the garden.

I see her on that long road under the trees, creeping along, and 199
when a carriage comes she hides under the blackberry vines.

I don't blame her a bit. It must be very humiliating to be caught 200
creeping by daylight!

I always lock the door when I creep by daylight. I can't do it at 201
night, for I know John would suspect something at once.

And John is so queer now, that I don't want to irritate him. I wish he 202
would take another room! Besides, I don't want anybody to get that
woman out at night but myself.

I often wonder if I could see her out of all the windows at once. 203
But, turn as fast as I can, I can only see out of one at one time. 204
And though I always see her, she *may* be able to creep faster than I 205
can turn!

I have watched her sometimes away off in the open country, creep- 206
ing as fast as a cloud shadow in a high wind.

If only that top pattern could be gotten off from the under one! I 207
mean to try it, little by little.

I have found out another funny thing, but I shan't tell it this time! It 208
does not do to trust people too much.

There are only two more days to get this paper off, and I believe 209
John is beginning to notice. I don't like the look in his eyes.

And I heard him ask Jennie a lot of professional questions about me. 210
She had a very good report to give.

She said I slept a good deal in the daytime. 211
John knows I don't sleep very well at night, for all I'm so quiet! 212
He asked me all sorts of questions, too, and pretended to be very 213
loving and kind.

As if I couldn't see through him! 214
Still, I don't wonder he acts so, sleeping under this paper for three 215
months.

It only interests me, but I feel sure John and Jennie are secretly 216
affected by it.

217   Hurrah! This is the last day, but it is enough. John to stay in town over night, and won't be out until this evening.

218   Jennie wanted to sleep with me—the sly thing! but I told her I should undoubtedly rest better for a night all alone.

219   That was clever, for really I wasn't alone a bit! As soon as it was moonlight and that poor thing began to crawl and shake the pattern, I got up and ran to help her.

220   I pulled and she shook, I shook and she pulled, and before morning we had peeled off yards of that paper.

221   A strip about as high as my head and half around the room.

222   And then when the sun came and that awful pattern began to laugh at me, I declared I would finish it to-day!

223   We go away to-morrow, and they are moving all my furniture down again to leave things as they were before.

224   Jennie looked at the wall in amazement, but I told her merrily that I did it out of pure spite at the vicous thing.

225   She laughed and said she wouldn't mind doing it herself, but I must not get tired.

226   How she betrayed herself that time!

227   But I am here, and no person touches this paper but me,—not *alive*!

228   She tried to get me out of the room—it was too patent! But I said it was so quiet and empty and clean now that I believed I would lie down again and sleep all I could; and not to wake me even for dinner—I would call when I woke.

229   So now she is gone, and the servants are gone, and the things are gone, and there is nothing left but that great bedstead nailed down, with the canvas mattress we found on it.

230   We shall sleep downstairs to-night, and take the boat home to-morrow.

231   I quite enjoy the room, now it is bare again.

232   How those children did tear about here!

233   This bedstead is fairly gnawed!

234   But I must get to work.

235   I have locked the door and thrown the key down into the front path.

236   I don't want to go out, and I don't want to have anybody come in, till John comes.

237   I want to astonish him.

238   I've got a rope up here that even Jennie did not find. If that woman does get out, and tries to get away, I can tie her!

239   But I forgot I could not reach far without anything to stand on!

240   This bed will *not* move!

241   I tried to lift and push it until I was lame, and then I got so angry I bit off a little piece at one corner—but it hurt my teeth.

242   Then I peeled off all the paper I could reach standing on the floor. It sticks horribly and the pattern just enjoys it! All those strangled heads and bulbous eyes and waddling fungus growths just shriek with derision!

243   I am getting angry enough to do something desperate. To jump out of the window would be admirable exercise, but the bars are too strong even to try.

Besides I wouldn't do it. Of course not. I know well enough that a step like that is improper and might be misconstrued.   244

I don't like to *look* out of the windows even—there are so many of those creeping women, and they creep so fast.   245

I wonder if they all come out of that wall-paper as I did?   246

But I am securely fastened now by my well-hidden rope—you don't get *me* out in the road there!   247

I suppose I shall have to get back behind the pattern when it comes night, and that is hard!   248

It is so pleasant to be out in this great room and creep around as I please!   249

I don't want to go outside. I won't, even if Jennie asks me to.   250

For outside you have to creep on the ground, and everything is green instead of yellow.   251

But here I can creep smoothly on the floor, and my shoulder just fits in that long smooch around the wall, so I cannot lose my way.   252

Why there's John at the door!   253

It is no use, young man, you can't open it!   254

How he does call and pound!   255

Now he's crying for an axe.   256

It would be a shame to break down that beautiful door!   257

"John dear!" said I in the gentlest voice, "the key is down by the front steps, under a plaintain leaf!"   258

That silenced him for a few moments.   259

Then he said—very quietly indeed, "Open the door, my darling!"   260

"I can't," said I. "The key is down by the front door under a plaintain leaf!"   261

And then I said it again, several times, very gently and slowly, and said it so often that he had to go and see, and he got it of course, and came in. He stopped short by the door.   262

"What is the matter?" he cried. "For God's sake, what are you doing!"   263

I kept on creeping just the same, but I looked at him over my shoulder.   264

"I've got out at last," said I, "in spite of you and Jane! And I've pulled off most of the paper, so you can't put me back!"   265

Now why should that man have fainted? But he did, and right across my path by the wall, so that I had to creep over him every time!   266

Questions on Content

1. What is wrong with the narrator at the beginning of the story? What does she think would be the best treatment for her ailment and how do her views differ from those of her husband and brother? Who do you think is correct?
2. Describe the narrator's bedroom. What is odd about the room and its furnishings? What use does the narrator think was made of the room in the past? How do *you* think the room was used?
3. Why does the narrator keep a journal? Why must she conceal it from her husband?
4. Why does the narrator ask her husband John to take her away before their lease is up? What is his response?

5. What does the narrator do with the key to her room on the last day of the story? Why does she do so?
6. What happens when John finds his wife creeping along the floor with her shoulder pressed against the "long smootch around the wall"?

Questions on Thesis, Purpose, and Structure

1. What do you think are the causes of the narrator's nervous condition and its progressive worsening? How does her behavior change as her condition deteriorates?
2. Describe the yellow wallpaper and attempt to explain how and why it has such a deep impact on the narrator. How are the things she sees in the wallpaper related to her situation as a woman in a society dominated by men?
3. Explain how Gilman's story combines purposes—informing, persuading, and entertaining the reader.

Questions on Style and Diction

1. Find the following words in the story and determine their definitions in context: flamboyant (paragraph 34); atrocious (paragraph 41); recurrent (paragraph 67); impertinence (paragraph 68); inanimate (paragraph 69); querulous (paragraph 89); fatuity (paragraph 99); frieze (paragraph 102); undulating (paragraph 129), arabesque, convolutions (paragraph 146); bulbous, derision (paragraph 242).
2. Examine the little endearments John uses in speaking to his wife. How do those words reveal his opinion of her and reflect nineteenth-century attitudes toward women? Could his way of speaking to his wife have been a factor in her nervous condition?
3. At what point do you first begin to feel confident that the narrator is going mad? Examine a passage or two in an effort to pin down the elements in style, diction, and content that reveal her growing insanity.

Ideas for Essays

1. If you have ever known anyone suffering from mental illness, you might wish to write an essay describing that person and his or her condition. If possible, try to analyze the causes of that person's illness and the effects of the illness on the person and his or her friends and relatives.
2. Rewrite "The Yellow Wall-Paper" as a series of entries in John's medical diary.
3. Write an essay analyzing the causes of the narrator's mental illness.

"Are Japanese Executives Better People Managers Than American Executives?"
"Why Every Kid Should Have an Apple after School"

As we have seen, causal analysis is one of the most effective methods of persuasion. Hence, it should come as no surprise that it is often used as an advertising strategy. Motorola's advertisement "Are Japanese executives better people managers than American executives?" was probably inspired by the popularity of William Ouchi's claims about the superiority of the Japanese style of management (see p. 395). Motorola's goal is to inspire a perception of the company as "A Leader in Electronics" and to appeal to a nationalistic desire to "buy American." The body of the advertisement develops four separate reasons why the company believes its philosophy of "respect for the dignity of the individual employee" has helped it to achieve a successful management style.

In "Why every kid should have an Apple after school," the Apple Computer Company attempts to build on the popularity of the Apple II line in education, while also arguing that the IIc is an ideal home computer. Note the emphasis on educational applications but also the references to business applications, household applications, and games. Finally, the advertisement concludes with a description of the computer and its accessories intended to present it as an economical, self-teaching home computer.

Meeting Japan's Challenge
Fifth in a Series

ARE JAPANESE EXECUTIVES BETTER PEOPLE MANAGERS THAN AMERICAN EXECUTIVES?

Courtesy of Motorola, Inc.

Much has been written about Japanese management style.

Quality circles, lifetime employment, corporate anthems, exercise programs, etc.

The implication is that the style of Japanese management is superior to that of American management. And that for Japanese companies, this particular style works both at home and abroad.

But did you know that this style is not universally practiced in Japan? In many Japanese companies, employment tenure varies, quality circles don't exist, the boss is the boss.

And did you know that many American companies have an even better record of management than some Japanese companies? We believe that one of these companies is Motorola. Why? It all starts with our respect for the dignity of the individual employee. We apply this philosophy in many employee-related programs.

Our Participative Management Program brings our people together in work teams that regularly, openly and effectively communicate ideas and solutions that help improve quality and productivity. In the process, many employees tell us that the program also enhances their job satisfaction.

Motorola's Technology Ladder provides opportunities for technical people, such as design engineers, to progress in professional esteem, rank and compensation in a way comparable to administrators and officers.

Our ten-year service club rewards employee dedication and loyalty with special protection for continued employment and benefits. And in an industry noted for both explosive growth and high mobility, almost one-quarter of our U.S. employees have been

Are employee exercise programs, company songs and lifetime employment the best ways to increase productivity?

with us for more than a decade.

Our open door policy enables employees to voice a grievance all the way up to the Chairman. It's rarely needed, but it's there. And it works. These and other programs reflect our respect for, and commitment to, the individual and the team. Their continuing effectiveness is reflected in the direct and open, non-union relationship among all our people, whether production workers, engineers or office workers. All of this works for us as we work for you.

Meeting Japan's Challenge requires an enlightened management style—demonstrated by our participative management style that respects the dignity of the individual.

 **MOTOROLA** A World Leader in Electronics

Quality and productivity through employee participation in management.

© 1982 Motorola Inc. Motorola and (M) are registered trademarks of Motorola, Inc.

Ideas for Discussion and Writing

1. What is Motorola's basic philosophy of management?
2. How has the company attempted to put that philosophy into effect?
3. How is Motorola's management style like that of the Japanese? How does Motorola's management style differ from what is typical in Japanese companies? (You might wish to read William Ouchi's essay "Japanese and American Workers: Two Casts of Mind.")
4. Do you believe that the kind of management advocated in this advertisement would make most American workers more productive and more satisfied with their jobs? Explain your views.
5. What reasons does this advertisement give you for believing that many Japanese firms fail to respect the dignity of the individual employee?

Why every kid should ha

Today, there are more Apples in schools than any other computer.

Unfortunately, there are still more kids in schools than Apples.

So innocent youngsters (like your own) may have to fend off packs of bully nerds to get some time on a computer.

Which is why it makes good sense to buy them an Apple® IIc Personal Computer of their very own.

The IIc is just like the leading computer in education, the Apple IIe. Only smaller. About the size of a three-ring notebook, to be exact.

Even the price of the IIc is small—under $1100.*

Of course, since the IIc is the legitimate offspring of the IIe, it can access the world's largest library of educational software. Everything from Stickybear Shapes™

With a IIc your kid can do something constructive after school. Like learn to write stories. Or learn to fly. Or even learn something slightly more advanced. Like multivariable calculus.

for preschoolers to SAT test preparation programs for college hopefuls.

In fact, the IIc can run* over 10,000

programs in all. More than a few of which you might be interested in yourself.

For example, 3-in-1 integrated business software. Home accounting and tax

programs. Diet and fitness programs.

Not to mention fun programs for the whole family. Like "Genetic Mapping" and

Courtesy of Apple Computer Inc.

ve an Apple after school.

"Enzyme Kinetics."

And the Apple IIc comes complete with everything you need to start computing in one box.

Including a free 4-diskette course to teach you how—when your kids get tired of your questions.

An RF modulator that can turn almost any TV into a monitor.

As well as a long list of built-in features that would add about $800 to the cost of a smaller-minded computer.

128K of internal memory—twice

the power of the average office computer.

A built-in disk drive that would drive up the price of a less-senior machine.

And built-in electronics for adding accessories like a printer, a modem, an AppleMouse or, an extra disk drive when the time comes.

In its optional carrying case, the IIc can even run away from home.

So while your children's shoe sizes and appetites continue to grow at an alarming rate, there's one thing you know can keep up with them. Their Apple IIc.

To learn more about it, visit any authorized Apple dealer. Or talk to your own computer experts.

As soon as they get home from school.

🍎

*The FTC is concerned about price-fixing. So this is only a Suggested Retail Price. You can pay more if you really want to. © 1984 Apple Computer Inc. Apple and the Apple logo are registered trademarks of Apple Computer Inc. Stickybear shapes is a trademark of Optimum Resource. For an authorized Apple dealer nearest you call **(800) 538-9696.** In Canada, call **(800) 268-7796** or **(800) 268-7637.***

Ideas for Discussion and Writing

1. To whom is this advertisement addressed? Is that choice of audience a wise one? Why or why not?
2. What reasons are given in the advertisement for purchasing an Apple IIc computer?
3. What kinds of programs can the Apple IIc run? Why are these different types of programs listed in the order that they are?
4. What features come with the Apple IIc at no extra cost? What is the purpose of including this list of features in the advertisement?
5. Examine the elements in the visual component of the advertisement. What do they do to corroborate and emphasize the messages contained in the text?
6. How informative is the advertisement? How persuasive? How entertaining? Explain your answers.

Chapter 13

DEFINITION

"More than 65 percent of college women report being subjected to sexual harassment by one or more of their professors."

"Fifty-seven percent of preschool-age children are victims of child abuse."

"Twenty-seven percent of all adult males are alcoholics."

These are shocking, staggering statistics. What's worse, we read statistics like them every day. Hence many people have reached the conclusion that character and morality in America are declining and that society is on the brink of chaos. But are such conclusions reasonable? Indeed, are we certain that we understand what is meant by these startling statistics? Note that we do not know how those conducting the surveys defined *sexual harassment, child abuse,* or *alcoholism.*

The college professor who barters grades for sex is clearly guilty of sexual harassment. But is the same true of an instructor who tells an off-color joke in order to enliven a dreary lecture? Some definitions of sexual harassment include any offensive sexual innuendo. The child who is beaten, bloodied, and locked in the basement overnight for telling a lie has been abused by any reasonable definition of child abuse. But is the same true of a child who has been spanked with an open hand? A hickory switch? A paddle? A two-by-four? Exactly where does reasonable punishment stop and child abuse begin? Similarly, what is meant by *alcoholism?* Everyone agrees that a person who frequently and compulsively drinks until passing out is an alcoholic. But by some definitions, so is any person whose drinking has become an unquestioned part of a daily routine. By such a definition, the man or woman who unwinds after work by routinely drinking a couple of beers or a glass of white wine can be seen as an alcoholic.

The only way to make sense of most statistics—and therefore much political and social debate—is to insist on a clear and unambiguous definition of terms. It may at first seem that the problem is a simple one, to be solved by consulting a dictionary. However, many of the most important and interesting words mean different things to different people or take on new meanings in different contexts. We may think everyone agrees on the meaning of democracy, for example, until we recall that communist East Germany is formally known as the German Demo-

Galleria d'Arte Moderna, Florence/Alinari/Art Resource, NY

The Thinker by Auguste Rodin (1880). What components of this sculpture help it to serve as a visual definition of a thinker? What other human postures might be used to convey the nature of thought?

cratic Republic. Similarly, we can be fairly certain that Queen Elizabeth has a different conception of "style" than a pop rock star like Madonna. In cases like these, an *extended definition* is warranted. Such definitions often unfold as complex combinations of the patterns of development that we have been studying—typically using exemplification, classification, comparison, or causal analysis as needed to clarify a particular definition.

The main purpose of an extended definition is, of course, to **inform** readers of the intended meaning of an important word or phrase. As such, definition often forms only one part of a longer essay. An essay on working women in the 1980s, for example, might begin with an extended definition of sexual harassment before proceeding to present evidence about the prevalence of problem in the workplace.

Definition essays, however, can also **persuade** and **entertain**. In writing about "The Peter Principle" (see p. 206), Laurence Peter and Raymond Hull use witty examples to define the Peter principle as the tendency in a bureaucracy for employees to rise to their levels of incompetence. Not coincidentally, however, those same examples also help to persuade us that Peter and Hull have stumbled upon a new, and wholly depressing, principle of human behavior. Similarly, Langston Hughes (p. 144) defines what the term *salvation* once meant to him by recounting his bittersweet memories of salvation during a revival meeting; the story is vivid and amusing, but it is also a persuasive condemnation of the hypocrisy that sometimes replaces true religious conversion or salvation. In writing your own extended definitions, keep in mind the need to entertain and persuade readers while you are informing them of the meaning of the term you have chosen to define.

PREWRITING

Because extended definitions usually draw upon a number of rhetorical strategies, the best and most methodical invention technique to use is probably Aristotelian invention (see p. 63). Suppose, for example, that you are assigned to write an essay on the meaning of *success* and decide to use Aristotelian invention to explore your thoughts before beginning a rough draft. In the paragraphs that follow, we have reproduced the questions you should ask yourself and our first attempts at answering them.

"1. How is your subject **defined** in the dictionary? What is the history of the word? Where does the word come from and how has its meaning changed? What meaning are you most interested in?"

The Oxford English Dictionary devotes nearly two full columns to the meanings of the word *success*. The current meaning of the word is given as "The prosperous achievement of something attempted; the attainment of an object according to one's desire: now often with particular reference to the attainment of wealth or position." The first recorded instance of the word's being used in this sense comes from Sir Philip Sidney's *The Psalmes of David* in 1586: "While I my race did runne, / Full of successe, fond did I say, / That I should never be undone." Interestingly, the undertones of egotism, selfishness, and false pride that are so prevalent in our current preoccupation with success seem to have been inherent in the word from the beginning. Sidney's speaker fondly and smugly prides himself on his success and foolishly ignores the inevitable change in fortune that shall leave him "undone."

In its earliest English uses, success was not yet the fuzzy, abstract concept that it has since become. It originally meant "that which happens in a sequel; . . . the issue, upshot, result." Hence, we have Parolles in Shakespeare's *All's Well That Ends Well* speaking of an effort to recover a lost drum: "I know not what the success will be, my lord; but the attempt I vow" (III.vi.86). The history by which the meaning of the word *success* has been transformed from something simple and external (a result) to something complex and personal (a sensation of achievement and prosperity) is common in the story of our language. We know that the word *spirit* once meant "wind" and that the word *right* meant "straight" well before it came to mean "correct." It is but one sign of human egotism that we so often take words with clear, simple meanings and muddle them by forcing them to describe our state of mind. That egotism is, of course, very obvious in our human preoccupation with achieving success.

"2. What other subjects can you **classify** with yours as part of some more general topic? How can you **subdivide** your subject?"

Success is best subdivided into two categories: success in one's own eyes and success in the eyes of others. The former is measured by one's internal sense of contentment or fulfillment. The latter is measured more objectively by one's wealth and status in the corporate or social hierarchy. Curiously, large numbers of people claim to prefer an internal sense of success even as they sacrifice their contentment to fierce competition in the workplace, frantic efforts to get rich quick, and general neglect of fulfilling family activities. It appears, paradoxically, that the most rewarding form of success is best achieved by ignoring, or at least deemphasizing, the external trappings of success—wealth, power, and prestige.

"3. What other subjects can you **compare** with yours to show similarities, differences, and degrees of value? What do you learn about your subject through unusual or unlikely comparisons?"

Success is most often compared with failure. Indeed, success and failure are often yoked into an ironic pair. As the great American poet Emily Dickinson observed, "Success is counted sweetest / By those who ne'er succeed." The converse of this is summed up in the saying that it is lonely at the top. Indeed, we are scarcely even surprised when some fabulously successful person commits suicide or suffers a nervous breakdown or is hospitalized for drug dependency. Consider Marilyn Monroe, Ernest Hemingway, Sylvia Plath, and Betty Ford.

When we are successful, we long for the recognition and approval of others. Hence, we schedule graduation ceremonies, lavish weddings, and public receptions for distinguished retirees and their newly promoted replacements. We like to recognize a public triumph through grandiose celebrations for the building of bridges, the christening of ships, or the ratification of treaties. In contrast, we like to take the bitter blow of defeat far off in some doggy corner of the dark day. Although we marry in large churches, we divorce in small offices or dingy courtrooms. If fired, we like to clear our desks quickly and slink unobtrusively out the door. For quite a few of us, death is the final failure and we hope to settle that disagreeable business in a shadowy room with only immediate family at our bedsides.

We are a sensible species, inclined to beam with pride at even the most trivial recognition of our successes and willing to battle to the bitter end before admitting our defeats. Hence there is a big business in printing certificates recognizing perfect attendance in grade school or cards extolling one's survival to yet another wedding anniversary or birthday. But we don't much like to behold our failures. Few students treasure as keepsakes report cards dotted with F's.

"4. What are the **causes and effects** of your subject? What comes before it and after it?"

If we are successful, we like to think it is because of our hard work and wisdom. But if we fail, we are the mere victims of misfortune or injustice. Jenny's parents remain convinced that she received straight A's in third grade because she is a genius, blessed with good parental genes. Johnny, who brings home an undistinguished record of C's and D's, complains that it is all the teacher's fault; she doesn't explain things clearly and, besides, she only gives good grades to the teacher's pet.

"5. What is the **history** of your subject? Does it exist now? How did it come to exist? What has happened to it in the past? What is likely to happen to it in the future?"

The desire for success and the dread of failure have probably always been human characteristics. Within each person, however, there may be a history of success and failure. Medieval and Renaissance writers were fond of describing the Wheel of Fortune, which carries one up like a Ferris wheel to a lofty height before inevitably plunging one back to the depths of failure. Even the most humble of day laborers is bound to have basked in some noonday sun. He may have wed a beautiful and loving woman, or won some small lottery, or saved a child's life. And even the most successful and distinguished businesswoman will someday experience failure. She may lose her job unjustly, or suffer during a long and bitter divorce, or succumb to the crablike claws of cancer.

"6. What authoritative testimony can you discover about your topic?"

In writing a definition essay, one can often turn to anthologies of famous quotations for useful insights. Here, for example, are a few statements about success drawn from two useful sources, *Peter's Quotations* and Bartlett's *Familiar Quotations*:

> "Success is not a harbor but a voyage with its own perils to the spirit. The game of life is to come up a winner, to be a success, or to achieve what we set out to do. Yet there is always the danger of failing as a human being. The lesson that most of us on this voyage never learn, but can never quite forget, is that to win is sometimes to lose."
> —*Richard M. Nixon*

> "Success goes to your head, failure to your heart."
> —*Laurence J. Peter*

"If at first you don't succeed, then try, try again. Then quit. There's no use being a damn fool about it."

— *W. C. Fields*

"Why should we be in such desperate haste to succeed, and in such desperate enterprises? If a man does not keep pace with his companions, perhaps it is because he hears a different drummer."

— *Henry David Thoreau*

"Six essential qualities that are the key to success: Sincerity, personal integrity, humility, courtesy, wisdom, charity."

— *Dr. William Menninger*

"To succeed in the world, we do everything we can to appear successful."

— *Duc de la Rochefoucauld*

"Let us be thankful for fools. But for them the rest of us could not succeed."

— *Mark Twain*

"Nothing succeeds like success."

— *Alexandre Dumas*

COMBINING PURPOSES

Clearly, the purpose of an extended definition is to clarify the meaning of a complex or ambiguous word — a word like *success* or *equality* or *fear*. If the word has several nuances of meaning, you may need to classify those nuances and illustrate each with an example or two. In doing this you will provide your reader with **information**. For example, in the student essay on fear at the end of this chapter, Angela Phillips distinguishes between fear of emotional pain and fear of physical pain and gives examples of each kind of fear: fear of failing a test and fear of remaining forever unmarried are emotional; fear of heights, fear of flying, and fear of attackers in the shadowy darkness are physical.

Normally, however, an extended definition does more than simply provide information. Usually you will wish to defend an opinion — that is, to **persuade** your audience to share your personal views about the concept being defined. Thomas Sowell (p. 637) does this in arguing that Americans too often confuse equality under the law with absolute equality; in the eyes of the law a private in the Marine Special Forces may be equal to an elderly widow, but there are apt to be great inequalities in their physical strength, emotional makeup, intellectual achievement, and personal wealth. By taking a stand, Sowell gives his readers an added reason for reading his essay. Similarly, Angela Phillips takes a stand in arguing that Stephen King is correct when he says that "Fear is like a sexual experience" — complete with foreplay, arousal to a peak of sensory concentration, and explosive climax.

Finally, you should remember that narrative anecdotes and descriptive details remain, as always, your best tools in the effort to **entertain** a reader. Note how much even fairly predictable details add to Angela Phillips's contention that "everyone is afraid of something hurting them":

> This kind of fear is the reason you wake up in the middle of the night and stare at the dark ceiling with a fiery chill running down your spine. This fear is the reason you hear every tiny creak and crack when you are left alone on a dark, moonless night. Fear of being hurt is universal.

PLANNING AND DRAFTING
A DEFINITION ESSAY

Formulate an assertive, debatable thesis. As we have just indicated, a strong thesis gives you your best opportunity to engage your reader by combining persuasion with information. Of course, most writers find it difficult to decide on a thesis without first exploring their ideas fairly fully. If you have engaged in Aristotelian invention, you may well be ready to decide on a thesis. But if Aristotelian invention wasn't useful to you or if you still feel uncertain about the position you wish to take, you may need to write a very rough draft of your essay in an effort to discover what you think about your topic.

At some point, however, you should force yourself to think explicitly about your thesis and the best way of supporting it. In the essay on *success* that we have been contemplating, there might be a number of different theses:

1. Modern science tells us that nothing is real unless it can be measured. If so, then the crude American tendency to equate success with wealth and status may be more meaningful than the mushy romantic claim that only happiness and contentment are true measures of success.
2. Success is like the mirage of water on the desert sands — craved and thirstily pursued at a distance, but vanishing into grief and despair when most closely approached.
3. The vanity and egotism of humanity are well illustrated by the various meanings of the word *success*.

Note that each of these theses goes well beyond the immediate task of providing a simple definition. Each assertion is specific, controversial, and — in this case — somewhat cynical. The essays that unfold from such theses could prove to be wrongheaded and misanthropic, but they are unlikely to be as dull and obvious as the essay that takes its thesis from the dictionary definition: "Success is the prosperous achievement of something attempted." Unless you choose a thesis with which the reader can conceivably disagree, you run the risk of writing definitions as dreary as the ones at the beginning of an Internal Revenue Service tax form.

Having chosen your thesis, you should give careful thought to the structure of your essay. Because there is no fixed pattern for an extended definition, you must use your own judgment in arranging your ideas. Do try, however, to begin and end with particularly interesting and thought-provoking paragraphs. Be particularly wary of using a dictionary definition for your introduction. You may well wish to include a formal definition somewhere in your essay, but you are unlikely to make your reader sit up and take notice if you begin with a plodding and plain statement like, "According to *Webster's New Collegiate Dictionary* fear is 'an unpleasant often strong emotion caused by anticipation or awareness of danger.'" A dictionary provides clarity, not stimulation or wit or provocation.

IDEAS FOR ESSAYS

Write an extended definition of one of the following words. Combine rhetorical patterns as necessary in developing a debatable thesis about the meaning of the word you have chosen.

Style	Writer's block
Taste	Conscience
Freedom	Courtesy
Anarchy	Sportsmanship
Faith	Fad
Humor	Cool
Republicans	Gross
Democrats	Pornography
Genius	Art
Imagination	Classic
Creativity	Discrimination

STUDENT ESSAY

Angela Phillips wrote the following extended definition of fear as an out of class assignment. Angela actually wrote four rough drafts before submitting a final version for a grade. To save space, we have reproduced only the first draft and the final draft.

FIRST DRAFT

"THERE'S NOTHING TO BE AFRAID OF . . .

OR IS THERE?"

by Angela Phillips

Your walking slowly down a deserted street when suddenly you see a figure standing in the dim, shadowed light of a far away streetlamp. You think to yourself, "I'm saved but the hair standing up on the back of your neck tells you better. Finally you can make out the fetures of the hulking form. They are grotesque. Your nostrals flare and you scream. Just then the thing grabs you, you hear a metallic click and the last thing you see is the shimmering black-red pool of blood at your feet. Let's pretend that this is actually happening. What do you feel? Most likely, it is fear. But what is fear and why do some people seem to like to be afraid?

Everybody is afraid of something. To this day I am afraid of the dark and of crowds. Fear is a strong emotion that is second only to anger. Fear is the reason you wake up in the middle of the night in a cold sweat and stare at the dark celing with a fiery chill running down your spine. Fear is the reason you hear every tiny creek and crack when you are left alone in an old house on a dark, moonless night. Fear is universal. It is felt by every person no matter where they are from. Fear was here when we arrived here. It has always been with us. It was the dark opressing fear that drove our long-armed ansestors from the trees and sent the magnificent and strong dinosaurs screaming blindly into the black putrid death of the tar pits. Fear will always be around to grab our weak hearts in its icy clutches and make us once agian prepare to fight or to run.

Because fear is so strong, the human body changes in minute ways. In truth, the body prepares to fight or to escape. The blood pressure drops and the heart rate increases to give the person a sense of unreality or confusion. The pupils will dilate to take in the whole horrifying sceane. Every sense is improved greatly. The ears can hear every scream or moan. The nostrals flare and pick up every foul order. Perspiration increases while the mouth goes dry to give the feeling of a cold sweat and the blood clots more quickly in case of wounds. When fear creeps silently into our minds our bodies transform to a fighting instrument, or the fear will imobilize us so that we are helplss to it.

Many people, including me, relish a small amount of fear. We practicly eat, sleep, and live the latest horror novel and we wait impatiently to see the best-selling blood, guts, and gore movie at the local theater. Why do we do this? Do you have to ask? To quote the master of horror, Stephen King, in his introduction to the novel Night Shift: "Fear is like a sexual experience." I think that he said it best. Small amounts of fear motivates the body to a peak of awareness. At this peak you are aware of nothing but that that is causing the fear. You feel every cruel stab of the glimmering knife. You hear every menicing footstep. You see every grotesque feture of the deamon or the evil gleam in the monsters eye. You smell every small blue, black putrid drop of blood. Then as the fear abates, you fall slowly from this peak and return to normal. Tension is released and you feel better. You will find that you are better able cope ~~because you are more relaxed~~. There is an almost soothing property in the hypnontic state that comes from the small amounts of fear that some people, like me, subject themselves to and not only enjoy but crave.

Fear is a black misty garment clad figure locked in the darkest room of your mind, that reaches out it's fleasless hand to grasp your very center. By opening that door in minute cracks, the small amounts of fear that creep out and blink blindly in the sunny passageway that is you own mind, can be used to your advantage. By opening that same door fully, the overall fear monster can and often does destroy the mind and then will slowly destroy the body.

    Commentary: Angela's earliest draft is obviously quite rough. Its most glaring errors are probably the many misspelled words, but Angela quite properly ignored spelling as she struggled to get her ideas down on paper. She realized that she would have an opportunity to correct her spelling during the process of revision.

    Although the content of this draft is fairly solid, Angela discovered several areas of weakness when she listened to the comments of the students to whom she read her first draft. She realized, for example, that her introduction was too gory—and, moreover, that it was weakened by the paradox inherent in assuming that her reader is stabbed to death by a "hulking form." In her final draft she retained the tense introductory anecdote, but eliminated the hyperbole.

    Angela's audience also suggested that her rough draft identifies only one form of fear. One student suggested that she might wish to classify the main types of fear before limiting her topic to the fear of physical harm. In her final draft Angela draws a useful distinction between the fear of emotionally unsettling situations and the fear of direct bodily harm.

FINAL DRAFT

"THERE'S NOTHING TO BE AFRAID OF . . .

OR IS THERE?"

by Angela Phillips

THESIS: Fear of having someone do bodily harm to oneself, probably the most common fear of all, is often misunderstood.

OUTLINE

Introduction: Anecdote about a terrifying situation.

   I. There are many types of fear.

     A. People fear emotional pain.

     B. People fear physical pain.

  II. Fear of bodily harm is strong and universal.

 III. With fear, the body changes.

 IV. Paradoxically, many people relish fear.

     Conclusion: Metaphor in which fear itself is personified.

You are walking slowly down a deserted street when suddenly you see a figure in the dim, shadowed light of a faraway streetlamp. You think to yourself, "Thank God, I'm saved," but the hair that is prickling on the back of your neck tells you otherwise. . . . All of us have had this nightmare at one time, and we have all reacted in the same way. We react with fear. But what is fear? And why do some people seem to like to be afraid?

Although fear assumes many forms, it always looks tremblingly to the future. If something gruesome or painful has already happened, we may regret it or mourn it or feel physical pain from it, but we no longer fear it. Broadly speaking, all of our fearful anticipations fall into two categories: fear of emotional pain and fear of physical pain. A common emotional fear is the fear of failure. Thus, many people are terrified of taking tests or of failing to find a job, a spouse, or even a set of new friends. Physical fears are perhaps even more common and include an uncountable number of phobias — acrophobia or fear of heights, hydrophobia or fear of water, agoraphobia or fear of crowds, and claustrophobia or fear of confined places. The most terrifying of all, however, seems to be the fear of direct bodily harm at the hands, claws, or fangs or some creepy creature.

We are all afraid of something hurting us. To this day, I am afraid of what may be hiding in the dark. Such fear produces a strong emotion that is second only to anger. This fear is the reason you wake up in the middle of the night and stare at the dark ceiling with a fiery chill running down your spine. This fear is the reason you hear every tiny creak and crack when you are left alone on a dark, moonless night. Fear of being hurt is universal. It is felt by every person, no matter where she is from. It was here when we humans first evolved and it will always remain to grab our weak, tiny hearts in its icy clutches and send us screaming blindly into panic.

Because fear is such a strong emotion, the human body changes in response to it. In truth, the body prepares to fight or run. According to Rita L. Atkinson in her text, Introduction to Psychology, the blood pressure drops and the heart rate increases to give the person a sense of unreality or confusion. The pupils dilate and every sense is improved greatly. The mouth goes dry and perspiration increases to give the feeling of a cold sweat, and the blood clots more quickly in case of wounds. When fear creeps silently into our minds, our bodies change into fighting machines—unless, that is, the fear immobilizes us and leaves us helpless before our gathering terror.

Many people, including me, relish a small amount of fear. We practically eat, sleep, and live the latest horror novel, and we wait impatiently to see the best-selling blood, guts, and gore movie at the local theater. Why do we do this, you ask? To quote the master of horror, Stephen King, in his introduction to the novel Night Shift, "Fear is like a sexual experience." The first glimmerings of fear are a form of foreplay, bringing the body to a peak of awareness and leaving your entire consciousness focused on the movie or novel that is awakening the fear. At the climax you feel every cruel stab of the knife, hear every menacing footstep, see every grotesque feature of the demon, tremble before every evil gleam in the monster's eye, and smell every tiny, blue-black, putrid drop of blood. Then as the fear abates, you fall slowly from this high and return to normal. Tension from the day is released along with the tension from the fear. You feel better and are better able to cope with life. There is even something soothing in the hypnotic state that comes from the small amounts of fear that some people, like me, subject themselves to and not only enjoy but crave.

Fear is a black, mistily clad figure locked in the darkest room of your mind. If you let it, it will reach out its fleshless hand to grasp your very soul. By opening that door in minute cracks, the little snakelets of fear that creep out and blink blindly in the sunny passageways of your mind can be used to your advantage. By opening the same door fully, the unchecked reptilian monster can and often does drive the mind over the brink of insanity.

Maybe He's a Nerd

Mike Royko

Mike Royko (1932–   ) was born in Chicago and has spend his entire working life associated with that great city. He has been associate editor of the *Chicago Daily News* (1959–1978), a columnist for the *Chicago Sun-Times* (1978–1984), and a syndicated columnist for the *Chicago Tribune* (1984–). In 1972 Royko was awarded a Pulitzer Prize for commentary. In addition, he is the author of a number of successful books, most notably *Boss—Richard J. Daley of Chicago* (1971). "Maybe He's a Nerd" was stimulated when Adlai Stevenson unexpectedly denied that he is a wimp during his campaign for governor of Illinois in 1982. This denial led Royko to compose a comically extended definition of the word *wimp* in the essay that follows.

1   Is Adlai Stevenson a wimp? That's an issue that Stevenson himself raised when he astonished everyone in politics by publicly denying that he is a wimp.

2   What was so surprising about his denial was that nobody had accused him of being a wimp in the first place.

3   His opponent in the race for Illinois governor, incumbent James Thompson, immediately issued his own denial that he had ever called Stevenson a wimp. And a check of the campaign records bears him out.

4   So the question is, why would Stevenson suddenly make not being a wimp an issue in his campaign?

5   An amateur psychologist might suggest that Stevenson suspects that people think he's a wimp, even though nobody has said so.

6   And if he thinks people view him as a wimp, that might mean that way down deep he fears that maybe he really is a wimp.

7   If so, Stevenson is mistaken. He isn't a wimp. He might be a bit dull—at least he was until he started denying he was a wimp, which is a pretty exciting thing for any candidate to do. But being dull doesn't make someone a wimp.

8   He also sometimes appears to be shy, which is unusual for a politician. But shyness isn't necessarily the mark of a wimp, either.

9   A wimp is someone who . . .

10   Well, rather than explain it, which isn't easy, let me give you a few examples of wimpiness:

11   You probably remember John and Rita Jenrette.

12   John was the boozing, wenching, grafting congressman who got caught in the Abscam scandal.

13   Rita was his beautiful, calculating wife who walked out on him and then became famous herself by posing nude for *Playboy* magazine and revealing intimate details of his career and their marriage.

14   During her publicity tour, Rita appeared on a national TV show, where she was babbling about John's sordid sex habits.

15   It was the kind of show that takes phone calls from viewers.

16   And what viewer called in? John Jenrette did. He wanted to tell Rita how much he still loved her.

17   Now that is a real wimp.

Then there was the heavyweight boxer, his name now forgotten, 18
who once crawled in the ring with the great Archie Moore.

In the first round, Moore bashed the guy so hard that he was 19
unconscious for 15 minutes.

When he came to, he staggered to his feet, made his way to Archie 20
Moore's dressing room, went in and said:

"Archie, could I have your autograph?" 21

That is a superwimp. 22

And there was the husband of a lady known as Milkshake Mary. 23

The husband had been ailing, losing weight, suffering aches and 24
pains, but the doctors didn't know why. So they put him in the hospital
for tests.

Every day his devoted wife would visit him and bring him a 25
milkshake.

On a hunch, a doctor had the dregs of one of the milkshakes tested. 26
They found that it was loaded with arsenic.

During Mary's trial for attempted murder, the husband was asked 27
how he now felt about his wife.

He said: "I wonder if she'd take me back." 28

He was king of the wimps. 29

Wimps have a different way of looking at things. 30

There is the old expression: "When the going gets tough, the tough 31
get going."

But for the wimp, it's something like this: "When the going gets 32
tough, the wimp phones his mother."

It was Winston Churchill who said he could offer World War II 33
England only "blood, sweat and tears."

To which a wimp nervously responded: "Could I have some Maa- 34
lox, too?"

The John F. Kennedy crowd popularized the phrase: "Grace under 35
pressure."

For the wimp, there is only "nausea under pressure." 36

The fact that Adlai Stevenson denied that he is a wimp is further 37
evidence that he is not a wimp.

That's because a wimp would never come right out and flatly deny 38
being a wimp, even if you said right to his face: "Why, you're nothing but
a little wimp."

That's one of the problems with language — people so often misuse 39
a word like wimp, confusing it with jerk or mope or drip or stiff or square
or schnook, all of which have their own specific meanings.

As for Stevenson, he should put the wimp issue behind him. As I 40
said, any candidate for governor who would take the trouble to deny that
he is a wimp when nobody has even accused him of being a wimp is
definitely not a wimp.

He's probably a nerd. 41

Questions on Content

1. Who is Adlai Stevenson, and what public office was he seeking at the time of
the events described in this essay?

2. What reasons are given for Stevenson's surprising denial that he is a wimp?

3. Although he agrees that Stevenson is not a wimp, Royko goes on to suggest several other unflattering adjectives that might be applied to Stevenson. What does he call Stevenson and why?

Questions on Thesis, Purpose, and Structure

1. How and where does Royko use comparison and contrast in attempting to clarify the definition of a wimp?

2. What examples does Royko use in defining the word *wimp?* Which examples are particularly entertaining, informative, and persuasive?

3. What can you speculate about Royko's purposes in writing this essay? Do you think that he wishes to take sides in the election or is he more interested in poking fun at human foibles? Defend your position.

Questions on Style and Diction

1. Brief paragraphs are a common feature in journalistic style, but even so, Royko's column includes a surprising number of very short paragraphs. Examine some of these brief paragraphs, and attempt to explain their effect on the reader. Where does Royko achieve a dramatic effect through paragraphing? Where could his essay have been improved by combining two or more separate paragraphs?

2. Royko frequently repeats the word *wimp* throughout the essay. Is that repetition desirable? Does it create a rhetorical effect, or is it just the inevitable consequence of attempting to define the word?

Ideas for Essays

1. Write an essay in which you attempt to find a word that aptly categorizes a current politician. You may choose either a flattering word or an unflattering one, but avoid racial or ethnic epithets.

2. Write an extended definition of one of the words that Royko contends can be compared with the word *wimp:* nerd, jerk, mope, drip, stiff, square, or schnook.

The Androgynous Man

Noel Perrin

Noel Perrin (1927–   ) teaches American literature at Dartmouth College and frequently contributes essays to *The New Yorker* and other magazines. Writing from his farm in Vermont, he has published three collections of essays (*First Person Rural* in 1978, *Second Person Rural* in 1980, and *Third Person Rural* in 1983). These volumes have established him as an astute observer of American culture. In "The Androgynous Man" (*The New Yorker*, 1984) Perrin takes up a theme that has been popular of late among feminists when he attempts to define a desirable combination of masculine and feminine characteristics.

The summer I was 16, I took a train from New York to Steamboat 1
Springs, Colo., where I was going to be assistant horse wrangler at a camp. The trip took three days, and since I was much too shy to talk to strangers, I had quite a lot of time for reading. I read all of "Gone With the Wind." I read all the interesting articles in a couple of magazines I had, and then I went back and read all the dull stuff. I also took all the quizzes, a thing of which magazines were even fuller then than now.

The one that held my undivided attention was called "How Mascu- 2
line/Feminine Are You?" It consisted of a large number of inkblots. The reader was supposed to decide which of four objects each blot most resembled. The choices might be a cloud, a steam engine, a caterpillar and a sofa.

When I finished the test, I was shocked to find that I was barely 3
masculine at all. On a scale of 1 to 10, I was about 1.2. Me, the horse wrangler? (And not just wrangler, either. That summer, I had to skin a couple of horses that died—the camp owner wanted the hides.)

The results of that test were so terrifying to me that for the first time 4
in my life I did a piece of original analysis. Having unlimited time on the train, I looked at the "masculine" answers over and over, trying to find what it was that distinguished real men from people like me—and eventually I discovered two very simple patterns. It was "masculine" to think the blots looked like man-made objects, and "feminine" to think they looked like natural objects. It was masculine to think they looked like things capable of causing harm, and feminine to think of innocent things.

Even at 16, I had the sense to see that the compilers of the test were 5
using rather limited criteria—maleness and femaleness are both more complicated than *that*—and I breathed a huge sigh of relief. I wasn't necessarily a wimp, after all.

That the test did reveal something other than the superficiality of its 6
makers I realized only many years later. What it revealed was that there is a large class of men and women both, to which I belong, who are essentially androgynous. That doesn't mean we're gay, or low in the appropriate hormones, or uncomfortable performing the jobs tradition-ally assigned our sexes. (A few years after that summer, I was leading troops in combat and, unfashionable as it now is to admit this, having a very good time. War is exciting. What a pity the 20th century went and spoiled it with high-tech weapons.)

What it does mean to be spiritually androgynous is a kind of free- 7
dom. Men who are all-male, or he-man, or 100 percent red-blooded Americans, have a little biological set that causes them to be attracted to physical power, and probably also to dominance. Maybe even to watch-ing football. I don't say this to criticize them. Completely masculine men are quite often wonderful people: good husbands, good (though sometimes overwhelming) fathers, good members of society. Further-

more, they are often so unself-consciously at ease in the world that other men seek to imitate them. They just aren't as free as us androgynes. They pretty nearly have to be what they are; we have a range of choices open.

8   The sad part is that many of us never discover that. Men who are not 100 percent red-blooded Americans — say, those who are only 75 percent red-blooded — often fail to notice their freedom. They are too busy trying to copy the he-men ever to realize that men, like women, come in a wide variety of acceptable types. Why this frantic imitation? My answer is mere speculation, but not casual. I have speculated on this for a long time.

9   Partly they're just envious of the he-man's unconscious ease. Mostly they're terrified of finding that there may be something wrong with them deep down, some weakness at the heart. To avoid discovering that, they spend their lives acting out the role that the he-man naturally lives. Sad.

10   One thing that men owe to the woman's movement is that this kind of failure is less common than it used to be. In releasing themselves from the single ideal of the dependent woman, women have more or less incidentally released a lot of men from the single ideal of the dominant male. The one mistake the feminists have made, I think, is in supposing that *all* men need this release, or that the world would be a better place if all men achieved it. It would just be duller.

11   So far I have been pretty vague about just what the freedom of the androgynous man is. Obviously it varies with the case. In the case I know best, my own, I can be quite specific. It has freed me most as a parent. I am, among other things, a fairly good natural mother. I like the nurturing role. It makes me feel good to see a child eat — and it turns me to mush to see a 4-year-old holding a glass with both small hands, in order to drink. I even enjoyed sewing patches on the knees of my daughter Amy's Dr. Dentons when she was at the crawling stage. All that pleasure I would have lost if I had made myself stick to the notion of the paternal role that I started with.

12   Or take a smaller and rather ridiculous example. I feel free to kiss cats. Until recently it never occurred to me that I would want to, though my daughters have been doing it all their lives. But my elder daughter is now 22, and in London. Of course, I get to look after her cat while she is gone. He's a big, handsome farm cat named Petrushka, very unsentimental, though used from kittenhood to being kissed on the top of the head by Elizabeth. I've gotten very fond of him (he's the adventurous kind of cat who likes to climb hills with you), and one night I simply felt like kissing him on the top of the head, and did. Why did no one tell me sooner how silky cat fur is?

13   Then there's my relation to cars. I am completely unembarrassed by my inability to diagnose even minor problems in whatever object I happen to be driving, and don't have to make some insider's remark to mechanics to try to establish that I, too, am a "Man With His Machine."

14   The same ease extends to household maintenance. I do it, of course. Service people are expensive. But for the last decade my house has functioned better than it used to because I've had the aid of a volume called "Home Repairs Any Woman Can Do," which is pitched just right

for people at my technical level. As a youth, I'd as soon have touched such a book as I would have become a transvestite. Even though common sense says there is really nothing sexual whatsoever about fixing sinks.

Or take public emotion. All my life I have easily been moved by certain kinds of voices. The actress Siobhan McKenna's, to take a notable case. Give her an emotional scene in a play, and within 10 words my eyes are full of tears. In boyhood, my great dread was that someone might notice. I struggled manfully, you might say, to suppress this weakness. Now, of course, I don't see it as a weakness at all, but as a kind of fulfillment. I even suspect that the true he-men feel the same way, or one kind of them does, at least, and it's only the poor imitators who have to struggle to repress themselves.   15

Let me come back to the inkblots, with their assumption that masculine equates with machinery and science, and feminine with art and nature. I have no idea whether the right pronoun for God is He, She or It. But this I'm pretty sure of. If God could somehow be induced to take that test, God would not come out macho, and not feminismo, either, but right in the middle. Fellow androgynes, it's a nice thought.   16

Questions on Content

1. What does Perrin discover when he analyzes the answers to the magazine quiz on masculinity and femininity?
2. What are some of the characteristics of a "he-man"?
3. What is the main advantage of recognizing that one is an androgyne?
4. In what specific ways is Perrin freer because he allows himself to be an androgynous man?

Questions on Thesis, Purpose, and Structure

1. What is an "androgynous man"? How does Perrin define the expression? What methods of development does he use in building this definition?
2. Consider Perrin's lengthy introduction in paragraphs 1 through 6. What makes that introduction effective? Why is the episode more effective because it happens to a sixteen-year-old instead of, say, a thirty-five-year-old?
3. Examine Perrin's conclusion. Why is it effective and thought-provoking?
4. What mix of purposes (informing, persuading, entertaining) does Perrin achieve in this definition of the androgynous man?

Questions on Style and Diction

1. Consider Perrin's use of sentence fragments in paragraphs 14 and 15. Perrin could easily have avoided using sentence fragments by making minor changes in punctuation. What, if any, rhetorical effect is achieved by his use of fragments?
2. Perrin makes frequent use of very short sentences. Consider the effects of those short sentences. Do they make his writing emphatic, choppy, clear, or simplistic? The effects of these short sentences will naturally vary, so be sure to use specific examples to support your views.

Ideas for Essays

1. Evaluate your own personality in a detailed essay. What "masculine" characteristics do you have? What "feminine" characteristics? Do you ever wish you
   could show more of the characteristics of the opposite sex? Which ones?
2. Compare the comments on masculinity and femininity in Perrin's essay with
   those in Prudence Mackintosh's "Masculine/Feminine" (p. 435).
3. Write your own extended definition of the ideal man or woman.

The History of a Little Girls' Game
Temma Ehrenfeld

Temma Ehrenfeld (1961–   ) was born in New York City and raised in
Teaneck, New Jersey. After a year at Bryn Mawr College, Ehrenfeld studied
English at Yale University, where she earned a B.A. in 1983. She then became
an assistant editor at *The New Leader*, a biweekly news and arts magazine,
before taking on her current duties as a part-time reporter at *Fortune* magazine. "The History of a Little Girls' Game," which was published in the Winter
1988 issue of *The Hudson Review*, illustrates how an accomplished writer uses
varied techniques of development in writing an extended definition, in this
case, of the girls' game that Ehrenfeld calls clapsies. Ehrenfeld lists as her
other writing credits "an essay in *Ms.* magazine, sections of two volumes of a
guide to colleges, the bulk of a ghost-written business law textbook, and
various book reviews." She is now at work on a collection of short stories.

1   "Clapsies" was the name my girlfriends and I knew for the rhyming,
rhythmic, and often repetitive verses you sing while clapping someone
else's hands in a matching pattern. We were fifth-graders then, fifteen
years ago. One or two younger boys would sometimes look on with
fascination and longing while we played, but self-respecting boys past
the age of eight stayed on the other side of the schoolyard blacktop.
Only girls did clapsies. We did them every day that year, whenever we
could, from the fall to the following spring.

2   In September, we exchanged our knowledge of clapsies learned
elsewhere, from older girls or in camp. Later, the leading clapsie players
made up variations on the movements of the standards, and we would
practice a variation we liked over and over to make sure that it did not
get mixed up and turn into something else. A really good one was
impossible to forget forever, though; it was bound to be reinvented. The
movements of a good clapsie made so much sense that learning them
was more like remembering. Our clapsie movements were logical and
deliberate, yet full of energy as, palm on palm, we went faster and faster,
slapping harder and harder.

When adults mention this little girls' game, they call it "pattycake" 3
—as in ". . . baker's man, bake me a cake as fast as you can." But pattycake is to clapsies as baby talk is to jive. It is not a game adults think about seriously. I myself hadn't thought of it for more than a decade when one August, entirely by chance, I played clapsies again. My friend Jamie and I were hiking the Appalachian Trail in Maine at the time; the trail was muddy and the undergrowth thick and green. One of the nice things about the Appalachian Trail is the fact that the volunteers who maintain it have built shelters or lean-tos where hikers can sleep. In the logbooks kept there, hikers write notes to travelers in both directions. Clapsies, I was to think later, are also a kind of public, random, but very American literature.

Jamie, who had gone ahead of me some time before, was asleep on 4
a sunny rock when I met two girls in a lean-to clearing. They looked about nine years old. With them was a woman, seemingly in her fifties. We said hello, the way hikers do. Then, just as it crossed my mind to wonder what circumstances had brought this particular white woman to accompany two little black kids, she told me that they were "Fresh Air Fund girls." She had a "camp" nearby—I figured she meant a summer place—and liked to entertain poor urban kids there for two weeks at a time. The girls stood a little bit away both from Jamie, asleep on the rock, and from us.

While their hostess and I were being friendly, they were doing 5
clapsies. "They didn't know each other at the beginning of the trip," she explained, "but then they started playing pattycake and got along fine. The girls always do that." From the corner of my eye I could see that some of the clapsies they were doing were completely new to me. Clapsies change.

One of the girls was milky-coffee colored, overweight, and still 6
puffing from the hike. Her hands were stiller than the other girl's and slower, like a jazz bass line catching up to a leading flute. She was from Brooklyn. The other girl had an amazingly long-limbed brittle skinniness that, on her small scale, made her seem a model for the stately woman she will someday be. She was very dark and from the Bronx. I asked them to teach me a clapsie they had been doing. It was called "ABC," and it looked harder than it was. The skinny girl, whom I'll call Vanessa, taught it to me in only three tries. By then Vanessa and I had awakened Jamie with our laughing, and she was ready to join me in a clapsie we both knew from the seventies.

"ABC" has a sequence where Vanessa and I clasped hands, like 7
business people shaking hands, except that we also clasped the other set of hands under the first clasp, then the first set of hands under the second clasp. Then we let go and slapped our own thighs and then snapped our fingers. It reminded me of a waterfall, including the splash at the bottom where an imaginary cascade hit our thighs.

The song begins with the melody and lyrics of the Jackson Five hit, 8
as far as "123":

```
ABC
Easy as
123
Ooh, aaah
I wanna piece of pie
pie too sweet
I wanna piece of meat
meat too rough
I wanna ride the bus
bus too full
I wanna ride a bull
bull too black
I wan' my money back
money too green
I wanna jellybean
jellybean not cooked
I wanna read a book
book not read
I wan' some lemonade
lemonade too sour
I wanna climb a tower
tower too high
I wanna say good-bye
Good-bye. . . .
```

9   [This is when you tickle the other person's stomach and usually everybody laughs.]

10   Too soon it was time to leave the girls and their hostess so we could hike up the hill before sundown. I wondered then if white girls or girls whose own parents could afford to send them to Maine knew the clapsies these two girls knew. Did the girls in my hometown, for instance, know "ABC"? I decided to find out.

11   My hometown, Teaneck, New Jersey, is a middle class community of some 40,000 people who live only seven miles from the "GW Bridge" to New York. There is a book about Teaneck, *Triumph in a White Suburb*, that describes how it came to be the first town to integrate voluntarily, in 1965. Teaneck is a good place to collect clapsies, since (as we shall see) the game has been a way of sharing between blacks and whites from its beginnings.

12   On an early October morning I arrived at Lowell School carrying a large cassette recorder, just in time for the recess after lunch. "I want to see if anyone is still doing the clapsies I did as a kid," I told one of the lunch aides, a middle-aged black woman. "They're still doing some of the clapsies I did!" she exclaimed, as if flattered by a compliment they paid her.

13   Out in the schoolyard, the girls at Lowell put on a show for me, and each other. They sang together in a big circle around whatever pair was demonstrating a clapsie. A few authoritative girls decided which pair would go next, and one girl made sure everybody knew which clapsies I

had and hadn't taped, so the next pair could be sure to demonstrate a new one. All I had to do was agree to the choice and push my cassette recorder on and off.

It turned out that Teaneck girls do know "ABC," the very funky clapsie the Fresh Air Fund girls taught me. Two black fourth-graders evidently had taught it to the other girls at Lowell. And the girls at Whittier School, on the other side of town, knew it, too.   14

Advanced clapsie players develop varieties done in foursomes and in big circles instead of one-on-one. These were the clapsies the girls at Whittier demonstrated for me. Sometimes two pairs interweaved the original hand movements, and sometimes a player in a foursome might clap hands with more than one other girl in a more complicated interweaving. Only a few girls could do this smoothly. Anxious to find a foursome that could perform one particularly difficult clapsie for me successfully, two of the bossier girls asked another girl not to play. She agreed immediately, looking much less hurt than I would have expected. She didn't look hurt for long, either. After the clapsie had been done, she was invited into the next round by the same pair that had ejected her. Cooperation is basic to clapsies.   15

The players might also stand in a big circle singing, each with her right palm resting on top of the palm of her neighbor; as they sang, each in turn flipped her free right arm over to slap the back of the hand resting on hers. When the song ended, the last person who was slapped left the circle. The players repeated the song until only two were left.   16

I don't remember doing circle claps like this one as a child, but Jamie, who grew up in one of the wealthier parts of Chicago, does. She described to me a clapsie that I later found recorded by Bess Hawes, a researcher in the field of black folk culture: "I have seen Los Angeles children playing this circle clap, though to different rhymes . . . clapping their neighbors' hands with right hand clapping up and left hand down; clapping their own hands together; clapping their neighbors' hands *left* hand up and *right* hand down; clapping their own hands, etc. Children can do this with enormous speed as early as the age of six. Interestingly, A. M. Jones describes just such clapping play in a child's game from West Africa." (In Chicago, Jamie tells me, she did this pattern matched with a song that began "A sailor went to sea, sea, sea.")   17

The connection between West Africa, on the one hand, and Chicago and Teaneck, on the other, can be traced. In fact, the more I learned about clapsies, the more I learned about what it means to live in a racially mixed culture, to be female, and, above all, to be a child.   18

The lyrics and clapping of clapsies have two near historical sources, white and black. Children's games are said to be piecemeal relics of abandoned bits of adult culture. Clapsies are no exception to the rule. Like other traditional children's games, they echo adult customs of previous centuries. Yet it is one of the mysteries of children's spontaneous games that they mysteriously persist over time and over large areas quite independently of adults.   19

Girls across the continent learn clapsies, counting out rhymes   20 ("eeny, meeny, miney, moe"), and jump rope and ball-bouncing songs at certain ages—and television, radio, books, teachers, and parents usually have nothing to do with it. In the United States the game has been a kind of sponge, absorbing trickles of culture from regions as far away as the British Isles and Africa, and from times as remote as the eighteenth century. In this respect, clapsies resemble the rest of American culture, so that in almost every American girl, there's something that likes a clapsie. You could say that clapsies are a whole library of oral and manual girllore.

21 The lyrics date to eighteenth- and nineteenth-century British and American girls' singing games, which were much more varied and numerous than those of today. "Ring around a rosey," originally called "Ring a Ring of Roses," is perhaps the simplest and most familiar. (There used to be an idea, later proved false, that this ring game had been inspired by the plague.) Now confined to pre-schoolers, "Ring around a rosy" is a good example of how traditional girls' games came to be played by ever-younger children. Victorian girls as old as fourteen played such games, singing of marriage, death, and burial, or of women's chores (as in the contemporary pre-schoolers' game "Mulberry bush": "This is the way we wash our clothes, wash our clothes . . ."). As they sang, they did pantomimes, clapped, skipped, or danced in rings or lines like those of American and English country dances. The games themselves were played in previous centuries by adults. The clapping was the straightforward sort where you clap only your own hands.

22 The best record of these games is Lady Alice Bertha Gomme's 1894 two-volume collection of *The Traditional Games of England, Scotland, and Ireland*. Gleaned from her adult correspondents' memories of both rural and urban Victorian childhoods, Lady Alice's games probably date from the middle of that century, and no doubt her accounts were tidied up considerably by memory and the demands of respectability. Nearly all of these games have quietly disappeared, as have those described by her American counterpart, the anthropologist and folklorist William Wells Newell. However, the branches of the broad family tree of clapsies can easily be traced through a few modern examples that preserve ancestral words or clapping patterns.

23 One such is "Miss Mary Mack," about a girl dressed in black, with silver buttons down her back, who asked her mother for fifteen cents to see an elephant "jump over the fence." Gomme records a game called "Alligoshee," in which mid-nineteenth-century girls of Middleton, Hersham, Surrey, and Shepscombe sang of various people dressed in black with silver buttons down their backs. Another part of "Miss Mary Mack" appears in folklorist Brian Sutton-Smith's history of children's games in New Zealand. It records that New Zealand children are said to have sung the following verse as early as 1901: "Pounds, shillings, and pence, the monkey jumped the fence / He went so high, he reached the sky / Pounds, shillings, and pence." As for the elephant, the earliest evidence of it that I uncovered appears in a clapsie one black woman remembers from Georgia after the turn of the century. Hers is also the first evidence I found of similar words tied to clapping.

Today, the lyrics of clapsies are approximately half-British and half-   24
American, with ancestors that can be traced throughout the British Empire and the United States. There are relatives in Continental Europe, as
well. It follows from this history that if the roots of clapsie lyrics are
farflung, the lyrics themselves are quite as far from fixed. "ABC" is a
modern contribution to a song that was conceived long ago: it is an
example of folklore-in-the-making.

The clapping patterns and music of contemporary hand-clapping   25
have always been black in style, with African roots. Girls play clapsies in
strictly white towns, as well as in integrated towns like Teaneck—yet
blacks do have a special cultural claim as inventors.

Steven Spielberg gave us several extended soft-focus renderings of   26
hand-clapping near the beginning of his movie *The Color Purple*, based
on the Alice Walker novel set in 1909 among poor black women in the
rural South. The movie obscured the complexity and variety of clapsies;
Celie and Nellie's pattycake was much too simple for girls their age.
Black girls actually know many more, and more complicated, singing
games than other American girls do. In the 1920s, when the traditional
games began to die out among the white majority, black girls continued
to adapt the old games to a specifically black tradition of clapping and
communal showing-off sessions.

The Anglo-American games and lyrics had married Afro-American   27
rhythms some three centuries earlier. When the traditional games first
crossed the ocean, slaves—both children and adults—encountered
them on plantations. Soon they had been mixed into the elaborate social
clapping play that then bloomed among the American inheritors of
African polyrhythmic drumming.

Applause, clapping to folk music, or clapping to chants at political   28
demonstrations are related in spirit to this black clapping tradition;
all distill the powerful effect of actions performed in unison or in a kind
of rhythmic harmony. Well into the 1900s, Southern blacks of all ages,
male and female, still knew a variety of off-beat, total-body, community-
making yet improvisational slapping games that are now seen mostly
in rudimentary forms and mostly among kids. "Gimme five" springs
from this tradition. So does the complicated solo body-slapping routine
called "Hambone," or handjiving, which is what little black boys
are doing when they drum on tables and slap their own thighs and
stomachs.

Once accompanied by a song of the same name, "Hambone" was a   29
man's act. As Bess Hawes wrote in 1972, most young black men still
know one or another version of the routine. It has had a mini-revival
since then after appearing on two recent McDonald's commercials.

"Hand Warmin', Hand Clappin'" inspired so many calls to the   30
company asking for directions on how to do the routine that McDonald's
printed up an advisory flyer. "Hand Warmin's Back" appeared in fall
1986 complete with handjiving performances by a baby, white professional types of both sexes, an elderly white couple, a black couple, and a
young black man who spins in his wheelchair before slapping the hand
of his white friend. They all clap their hands, slap their stomachs and

thighs, slap other people's hands, or otherwise raise a heartwarming ruckus while eating their french fries.

31   At least some of the original versions of games like "Hambone" would have been entirely lost to memory and recorded history had they not been recalled by Bessie Jones of St. Simon's Island, Georgia, and compiled by Bess Hawes in *Step It Down.* As an octogenarian in the 1970s Jones evidently was able to demonstrate a book's worth of the singing games (words, music, and clapping) from her youth in the rural black community of Dawson, Georgia. It was Bessie Jones who described the clapsie with Miss Mary Mack's elephant. The name she gave was "Green Sally Up."

32   Bessie and her friends learned "Green Sally Up" from their parents. Indeed, this was the first step in a long development process that culminated in adult solo clapping performances. Its clapping pattern is the basic pattycake: clap right hands; then your own hands together once; clap left hands; then your own hands together once; and right hands again:

> Green Sally up
> Green Sally down
> Green Sally bake her possum brown
> asked my mama for 15 cents
> to see that elephant jump the fence
> he jumped so high
> he touched the sky
> he never got back
> until the Fourth of July
> you see that house, on that hill
> that's where me and my baby live.
> oh the rabbit in the hash come a-stepping in the dash
> with his long-tailed coat and his beaver on.

33   It makes sense that Bessie Jones's instructional clapsie contained part of both the words and clapping pattern of "Miss Mary Mack," the first, the simplest, and, probably, the most widely known clapsie I did as a child. "Miss Mary Mack" merely varies the pattycake with a cross on the chest. As with all clapsies, each of the movements is timed to a syllable or beat:

> Miss Mary [cross hands on chest; slap thighs; and clap your own hands together once]
> Mack, Mack, Mack [the pattycake: clap right hands; then your own hands together once; clap left hands; then your own hands together once; and right hands again]
> all dressed in [repeat hand sequence from beginning]
> black, black, black
> with silver
> buttons, buttons, buttons [you have to say "buttons" fast as if the word were one syllable]

all down her
back, back, back.
She asked her
mother, mother, mother [fast]
for 15
cents, cents, cents
to see the
elephant, elephant, elephant [very fast]
jump over the ["over" is one beat]
fence, fence, fence.
It jumped so
high, high, high
it reached the
sky, sky, sky
and it never came ["and it" is one beat, and so is "never"]
back, back, back
'til the Fourth
of July, July, July ["of July" is one beat, and so are the next two
"Julys"]

But the contributions made by previous generations to the clapsies   34
of the present are not always this easy to recognize, for the games played
by twentieth-century kids sound up-to-date despite deep roots. The
topics and themes of clapsie lyrics are seldom anachronistic when they
are clear: pubescent sex, for instance, has replaced marriage as a major
topic. A new attitude towards death, too, has replaced the nineteenth-
century one. Once accepted as a universal fate, death is now universally
resistible in clapsies — with medical help, of course.

It would indeed be a throwback for children in the 1980s to sing the   35
lyrics of, say, the traditional singing game called "Waterflower," with its
opening announcement of mortality. Nonetheless, traces of these lyrics
can be detected in several current clapsies, and they are worth describing in full. Reported in a 1944 collection of *Play Songs of the Deep South*
(and probably dating back some years earlier), "Waterflower" seems to
be about many things simultaneously: the dependency of women on
men; the threat of death inherent in all rites of passage, which represent
progress toward a certain end; lovesickness; and love as an escape from
death. The story is simply that a girl recovers from deadly lovesickness
by marrying the boy. In the Deep South both boys and girls played
"Waterflower." First they skipped around one girl who stood in the
center as they sang:

Waterflower, waterflower
Growing up so tall
All the young ladies must surely, surely die

Then they stood still and pointed at her, singing,   36

All except Miss 'Lindy Watkins

[actually, the center girl's real full name would be used]
She is everywhere
The white folks say, the white folks say,
Turn your back and tell your beau's name

37   Miss 'Lindy Watkins turned her back and hung her head, picking it up only to point to a boy, her "Johnny." Another boy, the "Doctor," then entered the ring and gravely examined 'Lindy's tongue and pulse. Her encirclers stood and clapped their hands on the first and third beats as they sang,

> Doctor, Doctor, can you tell
> What will make poor 'Lindy well?
> She is sick and 'bout to die
> That will make poor Johnny [real boy's name] cry!
> Marry, marry, marry quick
> 'Lindy you are just lovesick . . .

38   They continued clapping as the Doctor fetched Johnny and returned to his place in the circle, Johnny courted 'Lindy, and 'Lindy and Johnny joined hands and danced.

39   Such funereal Victorian singing games have disappeared in our age, when it is no longer common for a child to see a sibling die or touch a dead body. But children's verses still frequently touch on sickness and mortality; and emergency house visits are a running theme of clapsies. "Waterflower" may be a direct historical link from an Anglo-American game to the clapsie "Uno dos cietas." There, excesses with a boyfriend lead to a potentially deadly bellyache (pregnancy?) that is conquered by demonstrating competence with numbers (competence to be an adult, on one's own?). However, in "Uno dos cietas," unlike "Waterflower," the boy is not the cure; in fact, he is not even present for the cure:

> Uno dos cietas
> East west
> I met my boyfriend at the candy store
> He brought me ice cream
> He brought me cake
> He brought me home with a bellyache
> Mama, Mama I feel sick
> call the doctor
> quick, quick, quick
> Doctor, doctor
> will I die?
> Count to five
> and you'll be alive
> 1,2,3,4,5
> I'm alive!

40   The modern elements in clapsies are usually self-evident. Clapsies today are female chauvinist, witty, cynical, rude, and wise by turns.

"S.O.S.," a current favorite at Lowell, is an example of typical boy baiting, explaining that "Boys go to Jupiter, to get more stupider / Girls go to Mars, to get more candy bars." If lyrics cannot be dated conclusively by the attitudes expressed, modern references, such as this indirect one to Mars candy bars, will give it away. A number of clapsies, like "ABC," include lyrics from songs or commercials. One clapsie launches a story by listing soft drinks. Another, "Big Mac Filet of Fish," turns a commercial jingle on its head, concluding: "You deserve a break today / so get up and throw your food away / at McDonald's / the dish ran away with the spoon." McDonald's picked up the teasing tone in its own jingle for the "Hand Warmin'" commercials, which proclaim that "It doesn't mean a lot if you don't get it *hot*!" The "it" refers to solo handjive, but as I heard this I kept thinking that the jingle was about a cold hamburger.

"Rocking Robin" takes off from a 1950s American hit. The obsceni- 41 ties were added by the kids:

> swing, swing, swing
> to the arithmetic, Hey, hey!
> rocking in the treetop
> all day long
> huffin' and a'puffin'
> and a'singing my song
> all the little birdies
> on Jaybird street
> love to hear the robin go
> tweet, tweet, tweet
>
> (chorus, with the same melody as the original)
> rocking robin
> tweet, tweet, elite
> rocking robin
> tweet, tweet, elite
>
> Mama's in the kitchen cooking rice
> Papa's in the alley (or Papa's in the poolroom) shooting dice
> Mama's in jail sitting on the pail
> Papa's downstairs selling fruit cocktail
> (chorus)
>
> Batman stepped on Robin's toe
> Robin said "Don't do it no more!"
> Batman said "I'm the FBI"
> Robin said "That's a doggone lie."
> (chorus)
>
> Went downtown to get a stick of butter
> then fell down sitting in the gutter
> went downtown to get a piece of glass
> shoved it up his ass and
> ohh, ah, I never saw a mother-fucker
> run so fast

all the little birdies
had a real good time tonight
there goes King Kong
playing ping pong with his rubber ding dong

42   Several of the clapsies are surprisingly worldly. One such is "The Spades Go," which has nothing in common but the first three words with the clapsie I knew by that name. I have yet to find a child who knows my version. Mine expressed a sentimental view of love; the new one decidedly does not, although (as you will see) it answers the lovelorn question of mine: "What is the me-ee-ee-ening of all this sah-ah-ah-awr-row over the hills of love?" But you'll have to accept "just because I kiss you, doesn't mean I love you" as an answer. In my version.

The spades go
tulips together
twilight forever
bring back my love to me
my heart goes
thump badee ump bump
thump badee ump bump
over the thought of thee
What is the
me-ee-ee-ening . . .

In the new version,

The spades go
down, down baby
down by the rollercoaster
sweet sweet baby
never gonna let you go
just because I kiss you
doesn't mean I love you
caught you with your boyfriend
late last night
hugging and a'kissing
and a'holding you tight
How do we know that?
peeking through the keyhole
naughty naughty
didn't wash the dishes
lazy lazy
jumped out the window
crazy crazy
ooh la la walla walla walla
ohh la la walla walla walla
I love you

The danger of applying literary analysis to clapsies is that one may   43
read sense into what children happily accept as nonsensical. I actually
know of three clapsies that begin, "the spades go." Could the phrase
once have referred to the slang meaning of "spades," blacks? If so, the
kids are now completely unconscious of it. Often, too, they do not
understand the curse words or sexual references of clapsies—which is
not to say that they therefore do not know that they are being rude. Some
do; some don't. This depends on age: Remember that clapsies are child's
play.

"Green Sally Up" and clapsies in general are a characteristically   44
childish instance of the black art of clapping. First, the rhythms of
clapsies are very simple. Second, little girls' consciousness of a communal purpose is relatively vague. Clapping in clapsies is more like drumming than applause since it is nearly free of any purpose other than
making sound (much as the lyrics often are). Unlike adult clapping, it is
not primarily intended to convey approval of a performer or attract
attention or create a sense of community. This is one reason no one
doubts that clapsies are now the product and possession of the young,
although children imitate the adult uses of clapping, as well.

Another reason is that the lyrics of clapsies are also not primarily   45
intended to communicate messages. Children have their own ways of
understanding language. For one thing, they are more prone than adults
to continue associating words heard together by chance. When they are
asked to free-associate in psychological tests with a given word, say
"green," they may well respond, "red," or "blue," in adult fashion, but
they also tend to come up with such words as "grass," "light," or, if the
child happens to own a green truck, "truck." Children delight in word
association much as some grown-up poets do: They aren't the least bit
disconcerted by near-nonsensical or nonsensical results.

The appeal of clapsie lyrics may therefore lie more in the way the   46
words are organized than in their meaning. It is the nature of clapsies,
and jump-rope or ball-bouncing songs, to include (1) fixed lists ("ABC,"
"123"); (2) couplets; (3) series of phrases with similar grammatical
structures; (4) potentially endless lists of ideas or objects; and (5)
repetitions of a word or words at the beginning of linked phrases, at the
end of phrases, or at the beginning *and* ends of phrases, which often
lead to a climax. You'll find examples of all of these kinds of rhetoric in
"ABC," and you can find 1, 4, and 5 in the sentence above this one.

Such verbal patterning is traditional in folklore, in working songs   47
like "John Henry" as well as in children's verses. Clapsies rhetoric has
more in common with adult rhetoric than one would think at first
hearing. If clapsie lyrics are distinguished mainly by their lack of overt
sense, it is also true that the lyrics of some adult music—from the
polyphony of the sixteenth century to twentieth-century rock—
conspicuously fail to communicate, either by being inaudible, patently
rhetorical, repetitive, or simply stupid. Of course, that adults sometimes
do what children do does not make children any less childish.

To note the childishness of clapsies is not to say that they do not   48
help prepare girls of various ages for adulthood, or that a boys' game

would do the job better. I add this because when it comes to playing, childishness and girlishness are often confused.

49   Psychological and historical research comparing the games of the sexes do suggest that there is a "feminine" way of playing. Boys were traditionally the active, aggressive sex. In the days when they were playing the early, violent, and now extinct versions of modern sports like rugby, girls' games were relatively static and inactive. They were charming because they were orderly and mannered, like "Waterflower"; indeed, they could be viewed by adults as symbolic demonstrations that conflict can be controlled, and it was as such that they were deemed psychologically satisfying to girls. Nowadays, boys are still more likely to play outdoor team sports, and boys play them at younger ages. Girls tend to play in small spaces or indoors, and to play one-on-one. Their games emphasize the skill and verbal cleverness of individuals, not speed or strategy or team spirit.

50   There is a long-standing discussion among feminists about how to equip our daughters for the hazards and opportunities of adulthood. Some argue that habits carried over from traditional girls' games put women at a disadvantage in the later games of life—especially those of large organizations. Girls' games, it is charged, are too orderly, too focused on skill rather than ingenuity or energy, and above all too individualistic. In *Games Mother Never Taught You* (New York: Rawson Associates, 1977), Betty Lehan Harragan states the charge in especially extreme terms, but her points are not unrepresentative of the debate. She writes, "For traditional girls' games [such as jacks and jump rope] there are no umpires or officials, no opposing teams of critical judges, no advantages to be gained from collaboration. . . . Girls' games are children's game which are outgrown early in childhood and never resumed because they have no intrinsic educational value; they teach nothing. . . . The objective of girls' games is never to beat anybody or perform under competitive stress, but merely to improve an agility in a vacuum."

51   How strange to confuse the absence of teams and concerned adults, or formal competition and its trappings, with a . . . "vacuum." Has she forgotten the girls themselves? The word would suggest that traditional girls' games might as well be played alone. This is certainly not true of clapsies, which by nature can't be played alone. Girls who play jacks and jump rope and clapsies together become a community. While the making of a community is not the self-evident purpose of clapsies, as with adult clapping at demonstrations, the community exists. Its purpose is to support (or criticize) the achievement of individuals within conspicuously predetermined and therefore rather demanding parameters. The clapsie set-up represents some kinds of real-life competition much more closely than does a confrontation of teams.

52   Clapsies do fit the stereotype of girls' games. They are verbal; cooperative, without the complex organization of teams or opposing "sides"; free of strategy, elaborate rules, arguments about rules, and numerical outcomes. In short they may be girlish, but this does not mean that they are easy or uncompetitive. The game requires individuals

to perfect their coordination, concentration, and ability to perform in a partnership, usually before an audience. The competition is implicit. Clapsie-style competition is like competition in the arts.

In any event, girls are changing their games of their own free will, so arguments based on projections from the girlhoods of today's women seem less and less relevant. One of the general rules of this century has been the tendency for girls to abandon their own games in favor of pastimes once peculiar to boys. In such circumstances, it is hard to see why girls need encouragement to play as boys do. The idea is a mere prejudice that ignores childish and girlish virtues. 53

Meanwhile clapsies, like many traditional girls' games before them, may eventually disappear among white girls. "There's no question that the game is fading," Brian Sutton-Smith told me from his office in Philadelphia, where he is Professor of Human Development and Folklore at the University of Pennsylvania. In an essay called "Sixty Years of Historical Change in the Game Preferences of American Children," as well as in other writings on the subject, Dr. Sutton-Smith explains that formal singing games began to fade among whites during the 1920s. After World War II, these games all but disappeared as girls turned to jump rope and ball-bouncing instead. The girls became increasingly active, perhaps simply because sneakers, loose clothing, and adult encouragement permitted them to be. Clapsies probably picked up after the War, too, Dr. Sutton-Smith suggested to me. Yet in his recent study of games played in the Philadelphia area clapsies were hardly mentioned in reports of play among white girls. Blacks are another story, of course. 54

My own observations bear out the suspicion that clapsies are now declining among whites. A boys' game is on the road to extinction when, at some point in its evolution, it begins to be played mainly, and then only, by girls. By contrast, a girls' game comes to be played by younger and younger girls before dying out, the fate of the original "Ring a Ring of Roses." In Teaneck, clapsies are no longer, as they were in the seventies, most popular in the fifth grade; they've slipped down to the first few months of the fourth. That's when the new fourth-graders teach each other the clapsies they learned over the summer, while the fifth-graders move on to singing Madonna songs in chorus. 55

Questions on Content

1. What are "clapsies," and how are they played?
2. At the end of paragraph 18, Ehrenfeld writes, "the more I learned about clapsies, the more I learned about what it means to live in a racially mixed culture, to be female, and, above all, to be a child." What do you learn about each of these topics from the essay?
3. Why does Ehrenfeld decide to return to her hometown schools in Teaneck, New Jersey? Why is it relevant that Teaneck is a racially integrated community?
4. What are the chief classifications of clapsies by size of participant group?
5. What are Ehrenfeld's reasons for asserting that "clapsies in general are a characteristically childish instance of the black art of clapping"?
6. What are the characteristic ways in which clapsie lyrics are organized?

Questions on Thesis, Purpose, and Structure

1. A lengthy essay about a game played by little girls might not immediately interest many readers. What does Ehrenfeld do to capture and preserve the interest of her readers?
2. Which of the rhetorical techniques that you have studied in this text does Ehrenfeld use in developing this essay? How do these varied means of developing her topic help her create a better extended definition?
3. What purpose is served by the narrative anecdote about the chance meeting with the Fresh Air Fund girls?
4. What benefits do young girls gain and what social and cultural lessons do they learn from playing clapsies?

Questions on Style and Diction

1. Find the following words in the essay and determine their definitions in context: gleaned (paragraph 22), polyrhythmic (paragraph 27), ruckus (paragraph 30), anachronistic (paragraph 34), pubescent (paragraph 34), female chauvinist (paragraph 40).
2. Ehrenfeld makes frequent use of parenthetic sentences, clauses, and phrases throughout this essay. Examine a number of these parenthetic expressions. Are they merely afterthoughts that should have been omitted, or do they add to clarity and interest in the essay?

Ideas for Essays

1. Think back to your own childhood. What games did you play? Were any of them out of the ordinary? If so, write an extended definition of one of the unusual games you played. Use a variety of techniques in explaining not just how your game was played, but also how playing that game is related to the broader issue of social, cultural, or intellectual development.
2. Compare a number of the games traditionally played by girls and boys. What are likely to be the differing effects of these games on the developing self-image of the children?

Rust

Guy de Maupassant

Guy de Maupassant (1850–1893) was born in Normandy in northwest France. Although he studied law and spent a decade working in Paris as a clerk in the naval ministry, Maupassant's real love was literature, and it was as a writer of fiction that he established a national and international reputation. From 1880 to 1890 Maupassant wrote almost three hundred short stories and six novels. In "Rust" Maupassant sensitively and humorously explores an important issue in sexuality about which convention, in his day and in ours, forbade open discussion. As a result, part of Maupassant's goal in this story is to provide a roundabout definition of what he means by the title "Rust." Note that in this "definition" we learn much about the causes, effects, and potential cures for this form of rust.

During his whole life, he had had only one insatiable passion, love of sport. He went out every day, from morning till night, with the greatest ardor, in summer and winter, spring and autumn, on the marshes, when it was close time on the plains and in the woods. He shot, he hunted, he coursed, he ferreted and trapped both birds and animals, he spoke of nothing but shooting and hunting, he dreamed of it, and continually repeated: 1

"How miserable any man must be who does not care for sport!" 2

And now that he was past fifty, he was well, robust, stout, and vigorous, though rather bald, and he kept his mustache cut quite short, so that it might not cover his lips and interfere with his blowing the horn. 3

He was never called by anything but his first Christian name, M. Hector, but his full name was Baron Hector Contran de Coutelier, and he lived in a small manor house which he had inherited, in the middle of the woods; and though he knew all the nobility of the department and met its male representatives out shooting and hunting, he regularly visited only one family, the Courvilles, who were very pleasant neighbors and had been allied to his race for centuries. In their house he was liked and taken the greatest care of, and he used to say: "If I were not a sportsman, I should like to be here always." 4

M. de Courville had been his friend and comrade from childhood, and lived quietly as a gentleman farmer with his wife, daughter, and son-in-law, M. de Darnetot, who did nothing, under the pretext of being absorbed in historical research. 5

Baron de Coutelier often went and dined with his friends, as much with the object of telling them of the shots he had made as of anything else. He had long stories about dogs and ferrets, of which he spoke as if they were persons of note whom he knew very well. He analyzed them and explained their thoughts and intentions: 6

"When Médor saw that the corn crake was leading him such a dance, he said to himself: 'Wait a bit, my friend, we will have a joke.' And then, with a jerk of the head to me, to make me go into the corner of the clover field, he began to quarter the sloping ground, noisily brushing through the clover to drive the bird into a corner from which it could not escape. 7

"Everything happened as he had foreseen. Suddenly, the corn crake found itself on the edge of the wood, and it could not go any further without showing itself; the corn crake thought to himself, 'Caught, by Jove,' and crouched down, Médor stood and pointed, looking round at me, but at a sign from me, he drew up to it, flushed the corn crake; bang! down it came, and Médor, as he brought it to me, wagged his tail, as much as to say: 'How about that, M. Hector?'" 8

Courville, Darnetot, and the two ladies laughed very heartily at those picturesque descriptions into which the baron threw his whole 9 heart. He grew animated, moved his arms about, and gesticulated with his whole body; and when he described the death of anything he had killed, he gave a formidable laugh, and said:

10   "Isn't that a good one?"

11   As soon as they began to speak about anything else, he stopped listening, and sat by himself, humming a few notes to imitate a hunting horn. And when there was a pause between two sentences on those moments of sudden calm which come between the war of words, a hunting tune was heard, "Ta, ta, ta, ra, ra," which the baron sang, puffing his cheek as if he were blowing his horn.

12   He had lived only for field sports and was growing old, without thinking about it, or guessing it, when he had a severe attack of rheumatism, and was confined to his bed for two months and nearly died of grief and boredom.

13   As he kept no female servant, for an old footman did all the cooking, he could not get any hot poultices, nor could he have any of those little attentions, nor anything that an invalid requires. His gamekeeper was his sick nurse, and, as the servant found the time hang just as heavily on his hands as it did on his master's, he slept nearly all day and all night in an easy chair while the baron was swearing and flying into a rage between the sheets.

14   The ladies of the de Courville family came to see him occasionally, and those were hours of calm and comfort for him. They prepared his herb tea, attended to the fire, served him his breakfast daintily, by the side of his bed, and when they were going again he used to say:

15   "By Jove! You ought to come here altogether," which made them laugh heartily.

16   When he was getting better and was beginning to go out shooting again, he went to dine with his friends one evening; but he was not at all in his usual spirits. He was tormented by one continual fear—that he might have another attack before shooting began, and when he was taking his leave at night, when the women were wrapping him up in a shawl and tying a silk handkerchief round his neck, which he allowed to be done for the first time in his life, he said in a disconsolate voice:

17   "If it begins all over again, I shall be done for."

18   As soon as he had gone, Mme. Darnetot said to her mother:

19   "We ought to try and get the baron married."

20   They all raised their hands at the proposal. How was it that they had never thought of it before? And during all the rest of the evening they discussed the widows whom they knew, and their choice fell on a woman of forty, who was still pretty, fairly rich, very good-tempered, and in excellent health, whose name was Mme. Berthe Vilers, and, accordingly, she was invited to spend a month at the château. She was very bored at home and was very glad to come; she was lively and active, and M. de Coutelier took her fancy immediately. She amused herself with him as if he had been a living toy, and spent hours in asking him slyly about the sentiments of rabbits and the machinations of foxes, and he gravely distinguished between the various ways of looking at things which different animals had, and ascribed plans and subtle arguments to them just as he did to men of his acquaintance.

The attention she paid him delighted him, and one evening, to   21
show his esteem for her, he asked her to go out shooting with him,
which he had never done to any woman before, and the invitation
appeared so funny to her that she accepted it.

It was quite an amusement for them to fit her out; everybody offered   22
her something, and she came out in a sort of short riding habit, with
boots and men's breeches, a short petticoat, a velvet jacket, which was
too tight for her across the chest, and a huntsman's black velvet cap.

The baron seemed as excited as if he were going to fire his first shot.   23
He minutely explained to her the direction of the wind, and how different dogs worked. Then he took her into a field, and followed her as
anxiously as a nurse does when her charge is trying to walk for the first
time.

Médor soon made a point, and stopped with his tail out stiff and one   24
paw up, and the baron, standing behind his pupil, was trembling like a
leaf, and whispered:

"Look out, they are par . . . par . . . partridges." And almost be-   25
fore he had finished, there was a loud whir-whir, and a covey of large
birds flew up in the air with a tremendous noise.

Mme. Vilers was startled, shut her eyes, fired off both barrels, and   26
staggered at the recoil of the gun; but when she had recovered her
self-possession, she saw that the baron was dancing about like a madman
and that Médor was bringing back the two partridges which she had
killed.

From that day, M. de Coutelier was in love with her, and he used to   27
say, raising his eyes: "What a woman!" And he used to come every
evening now to talk about shooting.

One day, M. de Courville, who was walking part of the way with   28
him, asked him, suddenly:

"Why don't you marry her?"   29

The baron was altogether taken by surprise, and said: 30

"What? I? Marry her? . . . Well . . . really . . ."   31

And he said no more for a while, but then, suddenly shaking hands   32
with his companion, he said:

"Good-by, my friend," and quickly disappeared in the darkness.   33

He did not go again for three days, but when he reappeared, he was   34
pale from thinking the matter over, and graver than usual. Taking M. de
Courville aside, he said:

"That was a capital idea of yours; try and persuade her to accept me.   35
By Jove, a woman like that, you might say, was made for me. We shall be
able to have some sort of sport together, all the year round."

As M. de Courville felt certain that his friend would not meet with a   36
refusal, he replied:

"Propose to her immediately, my dear fellow, or would you rather   37
that I did it for you?"

But the baron grew suddenly nervous, and said, with some   38
hesitation:

"No . . . no . . . I must go to Paris for . . . for a few days. As   39
soon as I come back, I will give you a definite answer." No other
explanation was forthcoming, and he started the next morning.

40   He made a long stay. One, two, three weeks passed, but M. de Coutelier did not return, and the Courvilles, who were surprised and uneasy, did not know what to say to their friend, whom they had informed of the baron's wishes. Every other day they sent to his house for news of him, but none of his servants had a line.

41   But one evening, while Mme. Vilers was singing and accompanying herself on the piano, a servant came with a mysterious air and told M. de Courville that a gentleman wanted to see him. It was the baron, in a traveling suit, who looked much altered and older, and as soon as he saw his old friend, he seized both his hands, and said in a somewhat tired voice: "I have just returned, my dear friend, and I have come to you immediately; I am thoroughly knocked up."

42   Then he hesitated in visible embarrassment, and presently said:

43   "I wished to tell you . . . immediately . . . that . . . that affair . . . you know what I mean . . . must come to nothing."

44   M. de Courville looked at him in stupefaction. "Must come to nothing? . . . Why?"

45   "Oh! Do not ask me, please; it would be too painful for me to tell you; but you may rest assured that I am acting like an honorable man. I can not . . . I have no right . . . no right, you understand, to marry this lady, and I will wait until she has gone, to come here again; it would be too painful for me to see her. Good-by." And be absolutely ran away.

46   The whole family deliberated and discussed the matter, surmising a thousand things. The conclusion they came to was that the baron's past life concealed some great mystery, that, perhaps, he had natural children, or some love affair of long standing. At any rate, the matter seemed serious, and, so as to avoid any difficult complications, they tactfully informed Mme. Vilers of the state of affairs, and she returned home just as much of a widow as she had come.

47   Three months more passed. One evening, when he had dined rather too well, and was rather unsteady on his legs, M. de Coutelier, while he was smoking his pipe with M. de Courville, said to him:

48   "You would really pity me, if you only knew how continually I am thinking about your friend."

49   But the other, who had been rather vexed at the baron's behavior in the circumstances, told him exactly what he thought of him:

50   "By Jove, my good friend, when a man has any secrets in his existence, as you have, he does not make advances to a woman, immediately, as you did, for you must surely have foreseen the reason why you had to draw back."

51   The baron left off smoking in some confusion.

52   "Yes, and no; at any rate, I could not have believed what actually happened."

53   Whereupon, M. de Courville lost his patience, and replied:

54   "One ought to foresee everything."

55   But M. de Coutelier replied in a low voice, in case anybody should be listening: "I see that I have hurt your feelings, and will tell you everything, so that you may forgive me. You know that for twenty years I have lived only for sport; I care for nothing else and think about nothing

else. Consequently, when I was on the point of undertaking certain obligations with regard to this lady, I felt some scruples of conscience. Since I have given up the habit of . . . of love, there! I have not known whether I was still capable of . . . of . . . you know what I mean. . . . Just think! It is exactly sixteen years since . . . I for the last time . . . you understand what I mean. In this neighborhood, it is not easy to . . . you know. And then, I had other things to do. I prefer to use my gun, and so before entering into an engagement before the mayor and the priest to . . . well, I was frightened. I said to myself: 'Confound it; suppose I missed fire!' An honorable man always keeps his engagements, and in this case I was undertaking sacred duties with regard to this lady, and so, to make sure, I decided to go and spend a week in Paris.

"At the end of that time, nothing, absolutely nothing occurred. And   56 it was not for want of trying. I went to the best there was, and they did everything they could. Yes . . . they certainly did their best! . . . And yet . . . they went away with nothing to show . . . nothing . . . nothing . . . I waited . . . I waited for a fortnight, three weeks, continually hoping. In the restaurants, I ate a number of highly seasoned dishes, which upset my stomach, and . . . and it was still the same thing . . . or rather, nothing. You will, therefore, understand, that, in such circumstances, and having assured myself of the fact, the only thing I could do was . . . was . . . to withdraw; and I did so."

M. de Courville had to struggle very hard not to laugh, and he shook   57 hands with the baron, saying:

"I am very sorry for you," and accompanied him halfway home.   58

When he got back and was alone with his wife, he told her every-   59 thing, nearly choking with laughter; she, however, did not laugh, but listened very attentively, and when her husband had finished, she said, very seriously:

"The baron is a fool, my dear; he was frightened, that is all. I will   60 write and ask Berthe to come back here as soon as possible."

And when M. de Courville observed that their friend had made such   61 long and useless attempts, she merely said:

"Nonsense! When a man loves his wife, you know . . . that sort of   62 thing always comes right in the end."

And M. de Courville made no reply, as he felt rather embarrassed   63 himself.

Questions on Content

1. What is Monsieur Hector's grand passion in life?
2. Who is Médor, and why does Monsieur Hector speak of him so glowingly?
3. What convinces Monsieur Hector's friends that he needs a wife?
4. Why does Monsieur Hector decide to go to Paris for a few days?
5. Why does Monsieur Hector decide that he cannot marry Madame de Vilers?

Questions on Thesis, Purpose, and Structure

1. Why is Madame de Vilers attracted to Monsieur Hector? How does she treat him? How does she finally win his love?

2. Consider the Freudian connotations of guns. How might Freud describe the causes of Monsieur Hector's condition?
3. Why does Maupassant entitle the story "Rust"? Does the story itself define the kind of rust that Maupassant has in mind? What are the causes and effects of this rust? How might it be cured? Why doesn't Maupassant describe it and define it more openly?
4. What are the implications of the story's final sentence?

Questions on Style and Diction

1. Find the following words in the story and determine their definitions in context: coursed, ferreted (paragraph 1); pretext (paragraph 5); gesticulated (paragraph 9); disconsolate (paragraph 16); château, machinations, ascribed (paragraph 20); covey (paragraph 25); surmising (paragraph 46); scruples (paragraph 55).
2. When Monsieur Hector decides to marry Madame de Vilers, he says to his friend, "By Jove, a woman like that, you might say, was made for me. We shall be able to have some sort of sport together, all the year round." How is the unwitting *double entendre* in the expression "have . . . sport together" related to the story's crisis?
3. Compare Monsieur Hector's mannerisms when speaking about the two forms of French "sport" — hunting and romance. Why is his speech so full of hesitations when he speaks of romance? How can those hesitations be linked to the story's title?

Ideas for Essays

1. Write a continuation of Maupassant's story, telling what happens when Monsieur Hector once again meets Madame de Vilers. Try to match Maupassant's subtlety and indirection in dealing with sexual relationships.
2. Write an essay in which you define — and provide examples of — other forms of "rust" in human beings or their relationships.

◇◇◇

Chapter 14

ARGUMENT AND PERSUASION

A lively argument, if it is conducted reasonably and concludes without rancor, can be both invigorating and enjoyable. Indeed, few pastimes are quite as absorbing as standing up for one's beliefs in the face of opposition. This chapter on argumentation will help you learn to state your opinions in writing with persuasive conviction.

In a sense, each of the earlier chapters has contributed to preparing you for this one. In an effective argument you will often wish to win your audience's attention with examples, anecdotes, or vivid descriptions. You will almost certainly need to present information supporting your views and may do so using classification, division, or process analysis. Furthermore, in making your case as persuasive as possible, you will frequently use comparison and causal analysis. The many weeks you have devoted to practicing these basic rhetorical patterns will prove valuable to you in the same way that skillful tennis players benefit from hours of practicing ground strokes, serves, and volleys. In an argumentative essay, as in a tennis match, you should draw upon the full range of skills and tactics at your disposal.

Any topic about which at least two sensible viewpoints are possible is an appropriate topic for argumentation. Issues within the broad range of politics are perhaps the first that come to mind. Is the execution of murderers a cruel and unusual punishment? Should the United States join with the Soviet Union in eliminating nuclear weapons? Should we pass a Constitutional amendment requiring a balanced federal budget? Should the President be allowed to serve for more than two terms in office?

Although political issues lend themselves readily to argumentation, the technique is not limited to such debates. You may use argumentation to explore the merits of a foreign language requirement for all students in your college. Or you may wish to write a passionate protest to university officials who are planning to cut down a magnificent grove of oak

Louvre, Paris/Alinari/Art Resource, NY

Liberty Leading the People (1830) by Eugene Delacroix. In the July Revolution of 1830 the workers of Paris stormed the government barricades and forced the abdication of King Charles X, whose government had tried to abolish freedom of the press and restrict the electorate. In this painting Delacroix attempts to use art to endorse and support that revolution. What devices of representation help him to do so?

trees to make room for a parking lot. Or you may wish to exhort the "suitcase students" to spend more weekends on campus supporting the cultural and intellectual programs offered by your college.

Indeed, argumentation is a pervasive and important element in human society. The leaders of our schools, our businesses, and our communities are often those who have best mastered the techniques of persuasive writing.

PREWRITING

In trying to discover ideas for inclusion in your argumentative essay, you should **draw on a variety of invention strategies**. Free writing for ten minutes or so on your topic can help you to crystallize your position and generate the basic arguments supporting it. Listing may well help you discover supporting facts and additional arguments. Mapping will help you to trace the causes of the problem you seek to resolve and the effects of any solutions you might propose. Finally, comparisons between your views and the views of your opponents will help you to develop additional arguments in support of your position and still others useful in refuting the opposition. You may wish to review Chapter 5 on "Invention Techniques" for further information on these invention strategies.

In many cases, however, invention techniques will not provide you with all the information you need in creating an effective argument. **Solid facts and expert testimony are often necessary to strengthen a purely logical argument.** On occasion you can collect such information through interviews or experiments. More often, however, you will need to engage in library research. Look up basic factual information in such sources as the *Encyclopedia Americana*, the *Statistical Abstract of the United States*, or the *World Almanac*. Check appropriate headings in the subject catalog of your college or university library as well as in such periodical indexes as the *Readers' Guide to Periodical Literature*, the *Public Affairs Information Service (PAIS)*, and the monthly catalog to *United States Government Publications*. You may also wish to ask your teacher or your reference librarian for advice on finding specialized bibliographies and other sources of factual information. Of course, any time you draw on published information or opinions in your essay, you must cite the source of that information and put quotation marks around any direct quotations.

PLANNING AND DRAFTING A PERSUASIVE ESSAY

As we have already mentioned, argumentative essays tend to follow no single rhetorical pattern of development. Instead, as writers develop their ideas, they cite whatever comparisons, contrasts, facts, or rationales they can in building logical support for their own position and they undermine the arguments of the opposition whenever possible. By studying the various essays in this chapter, you should be able to develop a sense of the range of approaches that good writers take in developing an argument.

Nevertheless, **it is often useful to begin planning an essay with some overall structure in mind. One such structural model involves building a syllogism**. As the basic form of deductive reasoning, a syllogism uses two premises to reach a conclusion. If the major and minor premises of a syllogism are true and if the two are logically related, then the conclusion that follows is irrefutable. Here, for example, are two of the basic forms taken by syllogisms:

Major premise: All humans are mortal.
Minor premise: Women are human.
Conclusion: Therefore, women are mortal.

Major premise: No insects are rational.
Minor premise: Mosquitos are insects.
Conclusion: Therefore, mosquitos are not rational.

Of course, few arguments are so clear-cut. Indeed, when an argumentative essay uses a syllogistic structure, the writer's basic challenge, is often to build a plausible case for believing in the truth of the major and minor premises. Thomas Jefferson did just that in basing the structure of the Declaration of Independence (see p. 558) on the following syllogism:

> Major premise: Governments exist to protect the rights of the people.
> Minor premise: King George III's government has violated the rights of the colonists.
> Conclusion: Therefore, King George's government should no longer exist.

By adopting the general form of a syllogism, you can at least rest assured that your essay has a logical structure.

A second general structure that you might consider using in a persuasive essay is more broadly applicable; it involves the logical presentation of your own position followed by the refutation of any opposing views, according to the accompanying general outline:

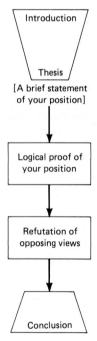

In using this general structure, you should begin with an introductory strategy that engages the interest of the reader at the same time that it allows you to narrow your focus and present your basic position. The body of the essay may range in length from two paragraphs to several pages (as dictated by your assignment and the nature of your topic), but in any event there should be a clear distinction between the arguments you present in proof of your own views and those you present in refuting objections that might be raised about those views. In some essays the body paragraphs in this pattern might be rearranged so that the refutation of opposing views precedes the logical proof of your position. The conclusion should restate your position in a fresh way that helps the reader see the significance of the entire essay.

COMBINING PURPOSES

The masters of argumentation—lawyers, politicians, and even some salesmen—realize that they must "work" an audience to attain their goals. They weave together humor, fact, reason, sentiment, and passionate eloquence in a rich fabric of rhetoric. They seek to inform, entertain, and—always—persuade.

1. **Informing the reader.** The most persuasive argument is almost inevitably the one best supported by facts. You should generously share with your reader any information you have collected through experiments, interviews, or library research. This includes not just the information that supports your position, but also that which contradicts you. By presenting the best factual case possible for your opposition, you will convince your reader of your fairness and therefore make it easier for him or her to accept your own factual evidence as credible and unbiased.

2. **Appealing to the reader's emotions through careful choice of words and images.** The exhortation to present information fairly does not mean that you should avoid taking sides or writing passionately. Indeed, the most effective arguments are frequently those that take full advantage of the emotional connotations of words. Consider, for example, this extract from Martin Luther King's great speech at a massive civil rights rally before the Lincoln Memorial on August 28, 1963:

> . . . as we walk, we must make the pledge that we shall march ahead. We cannot turn back. There are those who are asking the devotees of civil rights, "When will you be satisfied?" We can never be satisfied as long as the Negro is the victim of the unspeakable horrors of police brutality. We can never be satisfied as long as our bodies, heavy with the fatigue of travel, cannot gain lodging in the motels of the highways and the hotels of the cities. We cannot be satisfied as long as the Negro's basic mobility is from a smaller ghetto to a larger one. We can never be satisfied as long as the Negro in Mississippi cannot vote and a Negro in New York believes he has nothing for which to vote. No, no, we are not satisfied, and we will not be satisfied until justice rolls down like waters and righteousness like a mighty stream.

Note first of all that King's criticisms of police brutality, prejudice in public housing, economic injustice, and discrimination at the polls represent a fair-minded and factual enumeration of injustices widely experience by blacks in the 1950s and 1960s. If you, like Martin Luther King, wish to use strong, colorful language in stating your case, make certain that your case is a just one and that you avoid the misrepresentation characteristic of hucksters and snake-oil salesmen.

If your case is strong, however, it can only be made stronger by forceful phrasing. Note, for example, the use King makes of the connotations of words. He and his audience of "devotees" of civil rights make a "pledge" to each other to "march ahead"; the very nuances of the words imply that they are pious, honorable, and forthright individuals. These nuances are reiterated and given an aura of piety in the biblical cadences that close the paragraph: "we will not be satisfied until justice rolls down like waters and righteousness like a mighty stream."

Furthermore, King's prose is packed with powerful images. He lets us see the travelers "heavy with the fatigue of travel" being turned away from hotels and motels. He lets us picture the Negros in Mississippi who cannot vote and those in New York with "nothing for which to vote." His imagery draws us throughout the land, from south to north, from distant highway to city, from small ghetto to large one. He also uses repetition and parallelism to drive home his message: each of the last five sentences begins with the words "We can never be satisfied" or some variant of them. And finally, King occasionally inserts a direct statement of his strong emotions, as when he writes of "the unspeakable horrors of police brutality."

All of these language manipulations must be employed cautiously —particularly the last one. But when they are used effectively, as they are throughout King's address, they can make one's writing not only more persuasive, but more lively and moving as well.

3. **Persuading the reader with logic.** It goes almost without saying that a logical argument is apt to be far more convincing than an illogical one, but it is not always easy to be certain that one's own arguments are indeed logical. We have already seen that the deductive reasoning of syllogisms can be difficult to work into an essay. Even when syllogistic reasoning is possible, the premises on which such arguments are based can be difficult to prove.

Inductive reasoning is somewhat more common than deductive reasoning, but it is also less convincing. While deduction moves from general principles to specific conclusions, induction moves from specific instances to general conclusions. If, for example, you observe that every time you see a bolt of lightning, you also hear a peal of thunder, you use induction to conclude that lightning causes thunder. If you observe that the sun has risen in the east each day of your life, you use induction to conclude that the sun always rises in the east.

The difficulty with induction is that conclusions reached through it are *probably* true but not *certainly* true. Suppose that you have read five books by Isaac Asimov and have enjoyed each one of them; you therefore conclude that you like Asimov's writing and purchase every book he has published. Is your conclusion valid? It may be, but Asimov has written well over two hundred books. If the five you read were somehow atypical, it may turn out that you don't like his work after all and have wasted your money. Indeed, conclusions reached through induction are reversed with some regularity. All sciences are largely inductive, and progress in science often takes place when new methods of experimentation demonstrate the falsehood or inadequacy of old inductive conclusions. Modern discoveries in particle physics, for example, have overturned nearly a hundred years' worth of inductive evidence suggesting that electrons, protons, and neutrons were the fundamental building blocks of all matter; now we are told that the world is full of neutrinos, muons, quarks, and dozens of other subatomic particles.

The best we can do, it seems, is to struggle to make our arguments as logical as possible without flattering ourselves with the belief that we alone have the ability to see the truth clearly while everyone else peers through the darkness. The best we can do is state our assertions intelligently, support them with facts when possible, make logical arguments when we can, and consider thoroughly and thoughtfully the arguments of those who disagree with us.

TIPS ON REVISION

Try to eliminate logical fallacies. Errors in reasoning are common, and you should make a special effort to eliminate as many of them as possible during the process of revision. To help you do so, here is a list of some of the most common forms of logical fallacy.

1. *Non sequitur* (meaning "it does not follow"): reaching a conclusion that has no logical connection to its premises.

Immigrants from Southeast Asia are often some of the best students in American universities. Therefore, we should cut off all economic aid to Southeast Asia.

2. *Hasty generalization:* reaching an inductive conclusion based on too few examples or poorly chosen examples.

Meats cause cancer; alcohol causes cirrhosis of the liver; and sweets cause diabetes. Everything people like to eat is bad for them.

There are two errors here. First, the causal relationships between the foods and the various illnesses are not wholly demonstrable. Second, many things people like to eat are evidently good for them; for example, fruits, nuts, and whole-grain breads.

3. *Oversimplification:* misrepresenting a complex problem or issue as being neat and simple.

In the last twenty years the amount of money spent on education has significantly increased. At the same time standard test scores have declined. We can see that spending money on education only decreases performance.

Many other factors besides spending on education can have an effect on the test scores of the students. Children may be learning less at home because they watch too much television or because both parents work. In addition, marginal students may be taking the standardized tests who did not do so in the past. And still other factors may be at work.

4. *Either/or:* assuming that only two solutions to a problem exist when in fact there are many possibilities.

The members of the Palestinian Liberation Organization won't listen to reason. We must either give in to their demands or blast them from the face of the earth.

5. *Post hoc, ergo propter hoc* ("After this, therefore because of this"): see page 430.

6. *Circular reasoning:* assuming in the premise what is asserted in the conclusion.

The murder of unborn children must be punished as severely as the murder of adults.

The premise assumes that abortion is murder, but that is exactly what must be proven through logical argumentation.

7. *Argument "ad hominem":* attacking the speaker instead of the argument.

Senator Clarence is an acknowledged alcoholic. He has no right to express a view about the sales tax on liquor.

Senator Clarence's alcoholism is not the issue; the propriety of the tax is.

8. *Argument from analogy:* using an extended comparison as if it offers complete logical proof instead of limited illustration.

It is all right to stop a delirious person from walking off a cliff for his own good. Thus, it is also all right to force a person to accept our religion since it is for his own good.

It is possible to prove that saving a person from walking off a cliff is beneficial; however, given the many different religious views of mankind, the benefit of conversion to any particular religion must always remain doubtful. If used with care, analogy *is* a useful and persuasive means of developing an argument, as Judith Jarvis Thomson demonstrates in "A Defense of Abortion" (p. 567), but you must show that your analogies are apt.

9. *Faulty syllogism:* these errors can take a number of forms. One of them is the introduction of a new term in the conclusion:

Teachers of English cherish words.
Professor Jones is a teacher of English.
Therefore, Professor Jones should be given a pay raise.

The syllogism presents no evidence that those who cherish words particularly deserve a pay raise.
A second form of faulty syllogism involves ambiguity in the meaning of a term:

All men are created equal.
Women are not men.
Therefore, women are not created equal.

In the major premise the word *men* refers to humanity; in the minor premise it refers only to males. Thus, the conclusion is invalid.
Yet a third error in a syllogism is an improper relationship between premises. Unless the minor premise is a logical subset of the major premise, nothing can be proven. Consider the following example:

Proven criminals spend much of their time in jail.
Hackett spends much of his time in jail.
Therefore, Hackett is a criminal.

This syllogism and all others with the same form are false. Criminals are not the *only* people who spend much of their time in jail. Jailers do, and so do some defense lawyers in the process of counseling clients. Hackett may be a criminal, but the syllogism does not prove that he is.

IDEAS FOR ESSAYS

Use the techniques of argumentation to support or refute one of the following assertions:

1. College students ought to write essays in all of their courses.
2. Too many parents today "spare the rod and spoil the child."
3. The elderly have a responsibility to spare the community the financial drain of their futile and temporary medical care.
4. American corporations should be barred from doing business in countries with repellent internal policies (like South Africa) or repugnant international policies (like Libya).
5. All college courses should be graded on a simple pass/fail basis.
6. The institution of marriage should be abolished.
7. Corporate income taxes should be eliminated entirely.
8. The best sport to learn in high school is _____.
9. Bilingual education programs should be eliminated and English should be the sole language of the United States.
10. Television is underrated as a source of culture and education.

STUDENT ESSAY

Keith Martin's assignment for the following essay was to persuade the reader of the importance of some problem affecting the campus or the local community and then to suggest a logical solution to that problem. He was allowed to think about the assignment for several days, but was required to write his essay without using notes prepared out of class. Keith approached the assignment by first making an outline of the ideas that he wished to raise in his essay and then proceeding with a rough draft.

FIRST DRAFT

"LET'S PAINT THE GRASS GREEN"

by Keith Martin

Thesis: College athletic programs would not need nearly as much money if they didn't spend it so foolishly.

  I. Introduction: spray paint incident — $30,336.
 II. More foolish uses.
    A. Tour Buses — $15,000.
    B. Kegs of beer for parties — $7,500.
III. Money allotted is too much.
    A. Salaries for coaches too high — $200,000 – $287,000.
    B. Grants to players — $600,000.
    C. Millions in total budget allottments.
 IV. Solution to the problem.
    A. Auditor and more checks on spending.
    B. Less money allotted in all areas.
    C. More emphasis on academics.
  V. Conclusion.
    A. Too much money is being spent.
    B. The money is being spent foolishly.
    C. More control is needed.

A couple of years ago, a memo entered the office of Barry Casewell, head football coach here at A-State. The memo informed him that the playoff game against Northeast Louisiana would be televised nationally on a cable channel. ~~Casewell began to desperately think of ways to impress the TV audience that A-State is more than just a hick school.~~ ~~Suddenly an idea~~ A few days later at practice, coach Casewell discovered something that ~~extremely~~ bothered him. It was mid-winter, and we all know what happens to the grass as sub-zero temperatures approach. The turf was a nice shade of tan, leaning toward the brown side. Casewell began thinking. "What if someone important is watching the game? Why, they'll think we ain't nothin' more than a hick school." Casewell immediately made out ~~a requisition~~ an order for dozens of cases of green spray paint, and had twelve university employees spray the football field with it. The total cost was about $35,000, give or take a few thousand. ~~This is a good example of the foolish spending of budget dollars by athletic programs. The programs, however~~ What did it matter, anyway? The athletic program had a budget of a million dollars ~~anyway~~. Who would notice?

This is a good example of what is going on in most state-funded universities today. The athletic programs receive too much money, much of which is put to ridiculous use.

Another example of this misappropriation of funds is the amount of money spent on the band. In the 1984–85 football season, the athletic program provided transportation for the band in the form of three Great Southern tour buses. One might think that this is an appreciative gesture by the football team, until you consider one factor. The buses weren't for transportation to the away games, because the band only went to two. These buses provided the much needed service of carrying the band a distance of five blocks from the Fine Arts building to the stadium. This expense, which turned out to be $15,000 for the season, could have been ~~completely~~ eliminated by allowing students to take their own cars, or even walk to the field.

~~The foot~~ As if that wasn't enough appreciation, the football team also provided the band with two kegs of Busch beer for the party following the game. Of course, the team also got three kegs per game for their own party. The total bill for the season was $7,500.

This gross expenditure points out clearly that college athletic programs are allotted entirely too much money. Salaries for coaches are ~~extremely~~ too high. Most make more than the university president, while some "earn" up to $300,000 a year. Scholarships and other grants to players reach as high as the $600,000 mark per year, while other students cannot hope of such aid. In addition, most athletic programs ~~are~~ have budgets of over one million dollars a year.

While the problem is definitely a many-sided one, the solution is fairly simple. Each team in the athletic program should have a team auditor to insure proper spending of budget funds. This would cut down on foolish spending dramatically, due to the fact that all spending would have to be approved by the auditor. Less money should also be allotted to the programs. Even a million dollars is too much. More of this money ~~is~~ should be funneled into academics. After all, academics is what college is all about.

The problem is well defined. Too much money is being put into college athletics, and too much of it is being put to foolish use. The solution is simple. The only way to stop foolish spending is by exerting more control and using common sense. After all, everyone knows the grass turns brown in December.

Commentary: When Keith read his essay before a group of fellow students, he found that they uniformly liked it. Nonetheless, some students wondered where he got his information and whether they could wholly believe him. Others questioned whether an auditor appointed by administrators within the Athletic Department would be independent enough to question the decisions of those administrators. Thus, in revision Keith attempted to show how his personal experiences had given him reliable information about the football program. He also made it clear that he was calling for the appointment of an *independent* auditor. Finally, he revised his title in order to take advantage of a witty allusion.

FINAL DRAFT

"THE GRASS IS ALWAYS GREENER
ON THE FOOTBALL FIELD"

by Keith Martin

A couple of years ago, a memo entered the office of Barry Casewell, head football coach here at A-State. The memo informed him that the playoff game against Northeast Louisiana would be televised nationally on a cable channel. A few days later at practice, Casewell discovered something that bothered him. It was mid-winter, and we all know what happens to the grass as sub-zero temperatures approach. The turf was a nice shade of tan, leaning toward brown. Casewell began thinking, "What if someone important is watching the game? Why, they'll think we ain't nothin' more than a hick school." He immediately made out an order for dozens of cases of green spray paint and had twelve university employees spray the football field with it. The total cost was about $35,000, give or take a few thousand. What did it matter anyway? The athletic program had a budget of a million dollars. Who would notice?

This is a good example of what is going on in most state-funded universities today. The athletic programs receive too much money, much of which is put to ridiculous use. I became aware of several examples of this problem as a member of the A-State marching band last year, since some of the misappropriated money is spent on the band. In the 1984–85 football season, the athletic program provided transportation for the band in the form of three Great Southern tour buses. One might think that this was an appreciative gesture by the football team, until you consider one factor. The buses were not for transportation to the away games, because the band only went to two away games. These buses provided the much-needed service of carrying the band a distance of five blocks from the Fine Arts building to the stadium. This expense, which turned out to be $15,000 for the season, could have been eliminated by allowing students to take their own cars, or even walk to the field. As if the buses weren't enough appreciation, the football team also provided the band with two kegs of Busch beer for the party following each game. Of course, the team also got three kegs per game for their own party. The total bill for the season was $7,500.

This gross expenditure points out clearly that college athletic programs are allotted entirely too much money. Salaries for coaches are too high, most earning more than the university president, while some "earn" up to $300,000 per year. Scholarships and grants to players total as high as the $600,000 mark per year, while other students cannot hope for such aid. In addition, most athletic programs have budgets of over one million dollars per year.

While the problem is definitely a many-sided one, the solution is fairly simple. Each team in the athletic program should have a team auditor (chosen by a representative and impartial method) to insure proper spending of budgeted funds. This would cut down on foolish spending dramatically because all spending would have to be approved by the auditor. Also, less money should be given to the programs. A million dollars is just too much. More of this money should be funneled into academics. After all, academics is what college is all about.

The problem is well-defined. Too much money is being put into college athletics, and too much of it is being put to foolish use. The solution is simple. The only way to stop foolish spending is to exert more control and to use common sense. After all, everyone knows the grass turns brown in December.

The Declaration of Independence
Thomas Jefferson

Thomas Jefferson (1743–1826) was born in Shadwell, Virginia, and educated at William and Mary College in Williamsburg. From 1769 to 1775 he served in the Virginia House of Burgesses, where he played a leading role in helping to formulate the colonial position that first challenged and then denied the authority of the British parliament over the colonies. Jefferson served as a delegate to the Continental Congress (1775–1776), and it was in this capacity that he was asked to draft, together with Benjamin Franklin, John Adams, Robert Livingston, and Roger Sherman, the famous document setting forth the ideological basis for independence. The draft that emerged, both in language and in argument, is essentially Jefferson's own.

When in the course of human events, it becomes necessary for one people to dissolve the political bands which have connected them with another, and to assume among the Powers of the earth, the separate and equal station to which the Laws of Nature and of Nature's God entitle them, a decent respect to the opinions of mankind requires that they should declare the causes which impel them to the separation. 1

We hold these truths to be self-evident, that all men are created equal, that they are endowed by their Creator with certain unalienable Rights, that among these are Life, Liberty and the pursuit of Happiness. That to secure these rights, Governments are instituted among Men deriving their just powers from the consent of the governed. That whenever any Form of Government becomes destructive of these ends, it is the Right of the People to alter or to abolish it, and to institute new Government, laying its foundation on such principles and organizing its powers in such form, as to them shall seem most likely to effect their Safety and Happiness. Prudence, indeed, will dictate that Governments long established should not be changed for light and transient causes; and accordingly all experience hath shown, that mankind are more diposed to suffer, while evils are sufferable, than to right themselves by abolishing the forms to which they are accustomed. But when a long train of abuses and usurpations pursuing invariably the same Object evinces a design to reduce them under absolute Despotism, it is their right, it is their duty, to throw off such government, and to provide new Guards for their future security. Such has been the patient sufferance of these Colonies; and such is now the necessity which constrains them to alter their former Systems of Government. The history of the present King of Great Britain is a history of repeated injuries and usurpations, all having in direct object the establishment of an absolute Tyranny over these States. To prove this, let Facts be submitted to a candid world. 2

He has refused his Assent to laws, the most wholesome and necessary for the public good. 3

He has forbidden his Governors to pass Laws of immediate and pressing importance, unless suspended in their operation till his Assent should be obtained; and when so suspended, he has utterly neglected to attend to them. 4

He has refused to pass other Laws for the accommodation of large districts of people, unless those people would relinquish the right of Representation in the Legislature, a right inestimable to them and formidable to tyrants only. 5

He has called together legislative bodies at places unusual, uncomfortable, and distant from the depository of their Public Records, for the sole purpose of fatiguing them into compliance with his measures. 6

He has dissolved Representative Houses repeatedly, for opposing with manly firmness his invasions on the rights of the people. 7

8   He has refused for a long time, after such dissolutions, to cause others to be elected; whereby the Legislative Powers, incapable of Annihilation, have returned to the People at large for their exercise; the State remaining in the mean time exposed to all the dangers of invasion from without, and convulsions within.

9   He has endeavoured to prevent the population of these States; for that purpose obstructing the Laws of Naturalization of Foreigners; refusing to pass others to encourage their migration hither, and raising the conditions of new Appropriations of Lands.

10   He has obstructed the Administration of Justice, by refusing his Assent to Laws for establishing Judiciary Powers.

11   He has made Judges dependent on his Will alone, for the tenure of their offices, and the amount and payment of their salaries.

12   He has erected a multitude of New Offices, and sent hither swarms of Officers to harass our People, and eat out their substance.

13   He has kept among us, in time of peace, Standing Armies without the Consent of our Legislature.

14   He has affected to render the Military independent of and superior to the Civil Power.

15   He has combined with others to subject us to jurisdictions foreign to our constitution, and unacknowledged by our laws; giving his Assent to their acts of pretended Legislation:

16   For quartering large bodies of armed troops among us:

17   For protecting them, by a mock Trial, from Punishment for any Murders which they should commit on the Inhabitants of these States:

18   For cutting off our Trade with all parts of the world:

19   For imposing Taxes on us without our Consent:

20   For depriving us in many cases, of the benefits of Trial by Jury:

21   For transporting us beyond Seas to be tried for pretended offenses:

22   For abolishing the free System of English Laws in a Neighbouring Province, establishing therein an Arbitrary government, and enlarging its boundaries so as to render it at once an example and fit instrument for introducing the same absolute rule into these Colonies:

23   For taking away our Charters, abolishing our most valuable Laws, and altering fundamentally the Forms of our Governments:

24   For suspending our own Legislatures, and declaring themselves invested with Power to legislate for us in all cases whatsoever.

25   He has abdicated Government here, by declaring us out of his Protection and waging War against us.

26   He has plundered our seas, ravaged our Coasts, burnt out towns and destroyed the Lives of our people.

27   He is at this time transporting large Armies of foreign Mercenaries to compleat works of death, desolation and tyranny, already begun with circumstances of Cruelty & perfidy scarcely paralleled in the most barbarous ages, and totally unworthy the Head of the civilized nation.

28   He has constrained our fellow Citizens taken Captive on the high Seas to bear Arms against their Country, to become the executioners of their friends and Brethren, or to fall themselves by their Hands.

29   He has excited domestic insurrections amongst us, and has endea-

voured to bring on the inhabitants of our frontiers, the merciless Indian Savages, whose known rule of warfare, is an undistinguished destruction of all ages, sexes and conditions.

In every stage of these Oppressions We Have Petitioned for Redress 30 in the most humble terms: Our repeated petitions have been answered only by repeated injury. A Prince, whose character is thus marked by every act which may define a Tyrant, is unfit to be the ruler of a free People.

Nor have We been wanting in attention to our British brethren. We 31 have warned them from time to time of attempts by their legislature to extend an unwarrantable jurisdiction over us. We have reminded them of the circumstances of our emigration and settlement here. We have appealed to their native justice and magnanimity and we have conjured them by the ties of our common kindred to disavow these usurpations, which would inevitably interrupt our connections and correspondence. They too have been deaf to the voice of justice and of consanguinity. We must, therefore, acquiesce in the necessity, which denounces our Separation, and hold them, as we hold the rest of mankind, Enemies in War, in Peace Friends.

We, therefore, the Representatives of the United States of America, 32 in General Congress, Assembled, appealing to the Supreme Judge of the world for the rectitude of our intentions, do, in the Name, and by Authority of the good People of these Colonies, solemnly publish and declare, That these United Colonies are, and of Right ought to be Free and Independent States; that they are Absolved from all Allegiance to the British Crown, and that all political connection between them and the State of Great Britain, is and ought to be totally dissolved; and that as Free and Independent States, they have full power to levy War, conclude Peace, contract Alliances, establish Commerce, and to do all other Acts and Things which Independent States may of right do. And for the support of this Declaration, with a firm reliance on the protection of Divine Providence, we mutually pledge to each other our lives, our Fortunes and our sacred Honor.

Questions on Content

1. What truths are held to be self-evident by the signers of the Declaration?
2. If people have an inherent right to rebel against an unsatisfactory government, what, in Jefferson's view, will prevent frequent and frivolous revolt?
3. Besides King George, who is at fault for the continuing mistreatment of the colonies?

Questions on Thesis, Purpose, and Structure

1. What is the major premise of Jefferson's argument?
2. What is the minor premise?
3. What conclusion must follow if both the major and minor premises are correct?
4. What means of developing his argument does Jefferson adopt in trying to persuade the reader of the truth of the major and minor premises? Does Jefferson succeed?
5. In paragraphs 3 through 29 Jefferson charges King George with "repeated

injuries and usurpations" in governing the American colonies. Carefully evaluate these charges. Which ones are quite specific? Which ones are vague or ambiguous? Can you speculate on the reasons why Jefferson is more specific in some instances than in others?

6. Does Jefferson's arrangement of the charges leveled against the government of King George lend itself to any system of classification? If so, describe the main classifications.

Questions on Style and Diction

1. Find the following words in the essay and determine their definitions in context: impel (paragraph 1); endowed, unalienable, transient, usurpations, evinces, sufferance, constrained (paragraph 2); relinquish, inestimable, formidable (paragraph 5); depository, compliance (paragraph 6); annihilation, convulsions (paragraph 8); quartering (paragraph 16); mercenaries, perfidy (paragraph 27); insurrections (paragraph 29); unwarrantable, magnanimity, conjured, disavow, consanguinity (paragraph 31).
2. What is the rhetorical effect of the many parallel expressions in paragraphs 3 through 29?
3. Examine the connotations of the words that Jefferson uses in his charges against King George. Paragraphs 17, 26, and 27 are good ones to consider.
4. Examine the connotations of the words that Jefferson uses in describing the behavior of the colonists in paragraphs 30 and 31.

Ideas for Essays

1. Imagine that you are an official in the court of King George and that you have been assigned the task of writing a brief (two to four page) rebuttal to the arguments made in the Declaration of Independence. In attempting to justify the conduct of your monarch, you may wish to review the historical facts about the events leading up to the Revolutionary War.
2. Imagine that you are an American Indian living on a reservation in Oklahoma. Write a passionate statement declaring the independence of your tribe from the United States government.
3. Write a careful, analytical appraisal of Jefferson's methods of argumentation.
4. Imagine that you are a southerner at the time of the Civil War. Write an essay in which you use Jefferson's arguments to justify the right of the southern states to secede.

I Have a Dream
Martin Luther King, Jr.

Martin Luther King, Jr. (1929–1968) was born in Atlanta and was educated at Morehouse College, Crozer Theological Seminary, and Boston University, where he received a Ph.D. in theology in 1955. He began a pastoral career in 1954 at a church in Montgomery, Alabama, and it was there, in protest over Alabama's "Jim Crow" laws, that King organized the bus boycott that marked the beginning of his active involvement in America's growing civil rights movement. King became the nation's most prominent and respected civil rights leader, and its most articulate spokesman. He received the Nobel Prize for Peace in 1964, four years before being cut down by an assassin's bullet. The occasion for his famous "I have a dream . . ." speech was the 1963 march on Washington celebrating the one hundredth anniversary of the Emancipation Proclamation. This speech is justly renowned for its passionate eloquence, achieved through the use of colorful analogies, vivid images, and a careful control of rhythm and the connotations of words.

1   I am happy to join with you today in what will go down in history as the greatest demonstration for freedom in the history of our nation.

2   Five score years ago, a great American, in whose symbolic shadow we stand today, signed the Emancipation Proclamation. This momentous decree came as a great beacon light of hope to millions of Negro slaves who had been seared in the flames of withering injustice. It came as a joyous daybreak to end the long night of their captivity. But one hundred years later, the Negro still is not free. One hundred years later, the life of the Negro is still sadly crippled by the manacles of segregation and the chains of discrimination. One hundred years later, the Negro lives on a lonely island of poverty in the midst of a vast ocean of material prosperity. One hundred years later, the Negro is still anguished in the corners of American society and finds himself in exile in his own land. And so we have come here today to dramatize a shameful condition.

3   In a sense we have come to our nation's capital to cash a check. When the architects of our republic wrote the magnificent words of the Constitution and the Declaration of Independence, they were signing a promissory note to which every American was to fall heir. This note was the promise that all men — yes, Black men as well as white men — would be guaranteed the inalienable rights of life, liberty, and the pursuit of happiness.

4   It is obvious today that America has defaulted on this promissory note insofar as her citizens of color are concerned. Instead of honoring this sacred obligation, America has given the Negro people a bad check, a check which has come back marked "insufficient funds." But we refuse to believe that the bank of justice is bankrupt. We refuse to believe that there are insufficient funds in the great vaults of opportunity of this nation; and so we have come to cash this check, a check that will give us upon demand the riches of freedom and the security of justice.

5   We have also come to this hallowed spot to remind America of the fierce urgency of *now*. This is no time to engage in the luxury of cooling off or to take the tranquilizing drug of gradualism. *Now* is the time to make real the promises of democracy. *Now* is the time to rise from the dark and desolate valley of segregation to the sunlit path of racial justice. *Now* is the time to lift our nation from the quicksands of racial injustice to the solid rock of brotherhood. *Now* is the time to make justice a reality for all of God's children.

6   It would be fatal for the nation to overlook the urgency of the moment. This sweltering summer of the Negro's legitimate discontent will not pass until there is an invigorating autumn of freedom and equality. Nineteen Sixty-three is not an end, but a beginning. And those

who hope that the Negro needed to blow off steam and will now be content will have a rude awakening if the nation returns to business as usual. There will be neither rest nor tranquility in American until the Negro is granted his citizenship rights. The whirlwinds of revolt will continue to shake the foundations of our nation until the bright day of justice emerges.

7   But there is something that I must say to my people who stand on the warm threshold which leads into the palace of justice. In the process of gaining our rightful place, we must not be guilty of wrongful deeds. Let us not seek to satisfy our thirst for freedom by drinking from the cup of bitterness and hatred. We must forever conduct our struggle on the high plane of dignity and discipline. We must not allow our creative protest to degenerate into physical violence. Again and again we must rise to the majestic heights of meeting physical force with soul force. And the marvelous new militancy which has engulfed the Negro community must not lead us to a distrust of all white people; for many of our white brothers, as evidenced by their presence here today, have come to realize that their destiny is tied up with our destiny, and they have come to realize that their freedom is inextricably bound to our freedom.

8   We cannot walk alone. And as we walk we must make the pledge that we shall always march ahead. We cannot turn back. There are those who are asking the devotees of civil rights, "When will you be satisfied?" We can never be satisfied as long as the Negro is the victim of the unspeakable horrors of police brutality. We can never be satisfied as long as our bodies, heavy with the fatigue of travel, cannot gain lodging in the motels of the highways and the hotels of the cities. We cannot be satisfied as long as the Negro's basic mobility is from a smaller ghetto to a larger one. We can never be satisfied as long as our children are stripped of their selfhood and robbed of their dignity by signs stating "For Whites Only." We cannot be satisfied as long as the Negro in Mississippi cannot vote and a Negro in New York believes he has nothing for which to vote. No, no, we are not satisfied, and we will not be satisfied until justice rolls down like waters and righteousness like a mighty stream.

9   I am not unmindful that some of you have come here out of great trials and tribulations. Some of you have come fresh from narrow jail cells. Some of you have come from areas where your quest for freedom left you battered by the storms of persecution and staggered by the winds of police brutality. You have been the veterans of creative suffering. Continue to work with the faith that unearned suffering is redemptive.

10   Go back to Mississippi, and go back to Alabama. Go back to South Carolina. Go back to Georgia. Go back to Louisiana. Go back to the slums and ghettos of our Northern cities, knowing that somehow this situation can and will be changed. Let us not wallow in the valley of despair.

11   I say to you today, my friends, even though we face the difficulties of today and tomorrow, I still have a dream. It is a dream deeply rooted in the American dream. I have a dream that one day this nation will rise

up and live out the true meaning of its creed: "We hold these truths to be self-evident, that all men are created equal." I have a dream that one day, on the red hills of Georgia, sons of former slaves and the sons of former slave owners will be able to sit down together at the table of brotherhood. I have a dream that one day even the state of Mississippi, a state sweltering with the heat of injustice, sweltering with the heat of oppression, will be transformed into an oasis of freedom and justice. I have a dream that my four little children will one day live in a nation where they will not be judged by the color of their skin, but by the content of their character.

I have a dream today. I have a dream that one day down in Alabama   12
—with its vicious racists, with its governor's lips dripping with the words of interposition and nullification—one day right there in Alabama, little Black boys and Black girls will be able to join hands with little white boys and white girls as sisters and brothers.

I have a dream today. I have a dream that one day every valley shall   13
be exalted and every hill and mountain shall be made low, the rough places will be made plain and the crooked places will be made straight, and the glory of the Lord shall be revealed, and all flesh shall see it together.

This is our hope. This is the faith that I go back to the South with.   14
And with this faith we will be able to hew out of the mountain of despair a stone of hope. With this faith we will be able to transform the jangling discords of our nation into a beautiful symphony of brotherhood. With this faith we will be able to work together, to play together, to struggle together, to go to jail together, to stand up for freedom together, knowing that we will be free one day.

And this will be the day—this will be the day when all of God's   15
children will be able to sing with new meaning:

> *My country, 'tis of thee,*
> *Sweet land of liberty,*
> *   Of thee I sing;*
> *Land where my fathers died,*
> *Land of the Pilgrims' pride,*
> *From every mountainside*
> *   Let freedom ring.*

And if America is to be a great nation, this must become true.

And so let freedom ring from the prodigious hilltops of New Hamp-   16
shire. Let freedom ring from the mighty mountains of New York. Let freedom ring from the heightening Alleghenies of Pennsylvania. Let freedom ring from the snow-capped Rockies of Colorado. Let freedom ring from the curvaceous slopes of California.

But not only that. Let freedom ring from Stone Mountain of Georgia.   17
Let freedom ring from Lookout Mountain of Tennessee. Let freedom ring from every hill and molehill of Mississippi. "From every mountainside let freedom ring."

18   And when this happens — when we allow freedom to ring, when we let it ring from every village and every hamlet, from every state and every city — we will be able to speed up that day when all of God's children, Black men and white men, Jews and Gentiles, Protestants and Catholics, will be able to join hands and sing in the words of the old Negro spiritual: "Free at last! Free at last! Thank God Almighty. We are free at last!"

Questions on Content

1. On what occasion did Martin Luther King, Jr. deliver this speech? Who made up his audience?
2. What promises has the government failed to keep in its treatment of blacks?
3. How long does King think the government can wait before fulfilling these promises?
4. What warnings does King address to his followers concerning their conduct in the struggle for freedom?
5. What is King's dream?

Questions on Thesis, Purpose, and Structure

1. In what paragraphs of King's speech does he describe the problems faced by black citizens in America?
2. In what paragraphs does he describe the way to solve these problems?
3. In what paragraphs does he envision the results of solving those problems?
4. Is the speech logically structured? Explain your answer.
5. How would you describe the apparent purpose of the speech? Does it attempt to present new facts and information? To persuade through an appeal to reason? To increase emotional commitment to a cause?

Questions on Style and Diction

1. Find the following words in the essay and determine their meaning in context: momentous (paragraph 1); languished (paragraph 2); gradualism (paragraph 4); degenerate, militancy, inextricably (paragraph 6); tribulations, redemptive (paragraph 8); interposition, nullification (paragraph 16).
2. Consider King's use of imagery in paragraphs 1 through 4. Do the references to shadow and light, manacles and chains, land and water, and good checks and bad checks contribute to his argument? To the mood he wishes to develop? To a structured development of ideas?
3. What is the effect of King's allusions to the Bible and to the basic documents of American history?

Ideas for Essay

1. Write a detailed analysis of the use of imagery in King's "I Have a Dream" speech. Be sure to consider the impact of those images introduced through similes and metaphors.
2. Write your own "I Have a Dream" speech about some other significant problem in American society. Some possible topics are the following: equal access to higher education for rich and poor, free health care for the elderly, the right to life for the unborn, fair treatment for mentally and physically

handicapped Americans, fair treatment of native Americans, the right to a "good" death.

A Defense of Abortion
Judith Jarvis Thomson

Philosopher Judith Jarvis Thomson's ingenious essay "A Defense of Abortion" was published in 1971 in *Philosophy and Public Affairs*. In it she begins by conceding that the fetus may well be a person from the moment of conception. She then skillfully develops analogies to demonstrate that, even so, it is possible to provide an ethical defense of abortion in many circumstances.

Most opposition to abortion relies on the premise that the fetus is a human being, a person, from the moment of conception. The premise is argued for, but, as I think, not well. Take, for example, the most common argument. We are asked to notice that the development of a human being from conception through birth into childhood is continuous; then it is said that to draw a line, to choose a point in this development and say "before this point the thing is not a person, after this point it is a person" is to make an arbitrary choice, a choice for which in the nature of things no good reason can be given. It is concluded that the fetus is, or anyway that we had better say it is, a person from the moment of conception. But this conclusion does not follow. Similar things might be said about the development of an acorn into an oak tree, and it does not follow that acorns are oak trees, or that we had better say they are. Arguments of this form are sometimes called "slippery slope arguments"—the phrase is perhaps self-explanatory—and it is dismaying that opponents of abortion rely on them so heavily and uncritically. 1

I am inclined to agree, however, that the prospects for "drawing a line" in the development of the fetus look dim. I am inclined to think also that we shall probably have to agree that the fetus has already become a human person well before birth. Indeed, it comes as a surprise when one first learns how early in its life it begins to acquire human characteristics. By the tenth week, for example, it already has a face, arms and legs, fingers and toes; it has internal organs, and brain activity is detectable.[1] On the other hand, I think that the premise is false, that the fetus is not a person from the moment of conception. A newly fertilized ovum, a newly implanted clump of cells, is no more a person than an acorn is an oak tree. But I shall not discuss any of this. For it seems to me to be of great interest to ask what happens if, for the sake of argument, we allow the premise. How, precisely, are we supposed to get 2 from there to the conclusion that abortion is morally impermissible? Opponents of abortion commonly spend most of their time establishing that the fetus is a person, and hardly any time explaining the step from there to the impermissibility of abortion. Perhaps they think the step too simple and obvious to require much comment. Or perhaps instead they are simply being economical in argument. Many of those who defend abortion rely on the premise that the fetus is not a person, but only a bit of tissue that will become a person at birth; and why pay out more arguments than you have to? Whatever the explanation, I suggest that the step they take is neither easy nor obvious, that it calls for closer examination than it is commonly given, and that when we do give it this closer examination we shall feel inclined to reject it.

3   I propose, then, that we grant that the fetus is a person from the moment of conception. How does the argument go from here? Something like this, I take it. Every person has a right to life. So the fetus has a right to life. No doubt the mother has a right to decide what shall happen in and to her body; everyone would grant that. But surely a person's right to life is stronger and more stringent than the mother's right to decide what happens in and to her body, and so outweighs it. So the fetus may not be killed; an abortion may not be performed.

4   It sounds plausible. But now let me ask you to imagine this. You wake up in the morning and find yourself back to back in bed with an unconscious violinist. A famous unconscious violinist. He has been found to have a fatal kidney ailment, and the Society of Music Lovers has canvassed all the available medical records and found that you alone have the right blood type to help. They have therefore kidnapped you, and last night the violinist's circulatory system was plugged into yours, so that your kidneys can be used to extract poisons from his blood as well as your own. The director of the hospital now tells you, "Look, we're sorry the Society of Music Lovers did this to you—we would never have permitted it if we had known. But still, they did it, and the violinist now is plugged into you. To unplug you would be to kill him. But never mind, it's only for nine months. By then he will have recovered from his ailment, and can safely be unplugged from you." Is it morally incumbent on you to accede to this situation? No doubt it would be very nice of you if you did, a great kindness. But do you *have* to accede to it? What if it were not nine months, but nine years? Or longer still? What if the director of the hospital says, "Tough luck, I agree, but you've now got to stay in bed, with the violinist plugged into you, for the rest of your life. Because remember this. All persons have a right to life, and violinists are persons. Granted you have a right to decide what happens in and to your body, but a person's right to life outweighs your right to decide what happens in and to your body. So you cannot ever be unplugged from him." I imagine you would regard this as outrageous, which suggests that something really is wrong with that plausible-sounding argument I mentioned a moment ago.

5   In this case, of course, you were kidnapped; you didn't volunteer for the operation that plugged the violinist into your kidneys. Can those who oppose abortion on the ground I mentioned make an exception for

a pregnancy due to rape? Certainly. They can say that persons have a right to life only if they didn't come into existence because of rape; or they can say that all persons have a right to life, but that some have less of a right to life than others, in particular, that those who came into existence because of rape have less. But these statements have a rather unpleasant sound. Surely the question of whether you have a right to life at all, or how much of it you have, shouldn't turn on the question of whether or not you are the product of a rape. And in fact the people who oppose abortion on the ground I mentioned do not make this distinction, and hence do not make an exception in the case of rape.

Nor do they make an exception for a case in which the mother has to 6
spend the nine months of her pregnancy in bed. They would agree that would be a great pity, and hard on the mother; but all the same, all persons have a right to life, the fetus is a person, and so on. I suspect, in fact, that they would not make an exception for a case in which, miraculously enough, the pregnancy went on for nine years, or even the rest of the mother's life.

Some won't even make an exception for a case in which continua- 7
tion of the pregnancy is likely to shorten the mother's life; they regard abortion as impermissible even to save the mother's life. Such cases are nowadays very rare, and many opponents of abortion do not accept this extreme view. All the same, it is a good place to begin: A number of points of interest come out in respect to it.

1. Let us call the view that abortion is impermissible even to save the 8
mother's life "the extreme view." I want to suggest first that it does not issue from the argument I mentioned earlier without the addition of some fairly powerful premises. Suppose a woman has become pregnant, and now learns that she has a cardiac condition such that she will die if she carries the baby to term. What may be done for her? The fetus, being a person, has a right to life, but as the mother is a person too, so has she a right to life. Presumably they have an equal right to life. How is it supposed to come out that an abortion may not be performed? If mother and child have an equal right to life, shouldn't we perhaps flip a coin? Or should we add to the mother's right to life her right to decide what happens in and to her body, which everybody seems to be ready to grant—the sum of her rights now outweighing the fetus' right to life?

The most familiar argument here is the following. We are told that 9
performing the abortion would be directly killing[2] the child, whereas doing nothing would not be killing the mother, but only letting her die. Moreover, in killing the child, one would be killing an innocent person, for the child has committed no crime, and is not aiming at his mother's death. And then there are a variety of ways in which this might be continued. (1) But as directly killing an innocent person is always and absolutely impermissible, an abortion may not be performed. Or, (2) as directly killing an innocent person is murder, and murder is always and absolutely impermissible, an abortion may not be performed.[3] Or, (3) as one's duty to refrain from directly killing an innocent person is more stringent than one's duty to keep a person from dying, an abortion may not be performed. Or, (4) if one's only options are directly killing an

innocent person or letting a person die, one must prefer letting the person die, and thus an abortion may not be performed.[4]

10   Some people seem to have thought that these are not further premises which must be added if the conclusion is to be reached, but that they follow from the very fact that an innocent person has a right to life.[5] But this seems to me to be a mistake, and perhaps the simplest way to show this is to bring out that while we must certainly grant that innocent persons have a right to life, the theses in (1) through (4) are all false. Take (2), for example. If directly killing an innocent person is murder, and thus is impermissible, then the mother's directly killing the innocent person inside her is murder, and thus is impermissible. But it cannot seriously be thought to be murder if the mother performs an abortion on herself to save her life. It cannot seriously be said that she *must* refrain, that she *must* sit passively by and wait for her death. Let us look again at the case of you and the violinist. There you are, in bed with the violinist, and the director of the hospital says to you, "It's all most distressing, and I deeply sympathize, but you see this is putting an additional strain on your kidneys, and you'll be dead within the month. But you *have* to stay where you are all the same. Because unplugging you would be directly killing an innocent violinist, and that's murder, and that's impermissible." If anything in the world is true, it is that you do not commit murder, you do not do what is impermissible, if you reach around to your back and unplug yourself from that violinist to save your life.

11   The main focus of attention in writings on abortion has been on what a third party may or may not do in answer to a request from a woman for an abortion. This is in a way understandable. Things being as they are, there isn't much a woman can safely do to abort herself. So the question asked is what a third party may do, and what the mother may do, if it is mentioned at all, is deduced, almost as an afterthought, from what it is concluded that third parties may do. But it seems to me that to treat the matter in this way is to refuse to grant to the mother that very status of person which is so firmly insisted on for the fetus. For we cannot simply read off what a person may do from what a third party may do. Suppose you find yourself trapped in a tiny house with a growing child. I mean a very tiny house, and a rapidly growing child—you are already up against the wall of the house and in a few minutes you'll be crushed to death. The child on the other hand won't be crushed to death; if nothing is done to stop him from growing he'll be hurt, but in the end he'll simply burst open the house and walk out a free man. Now I could well understand it if a bystander were to say, "There's nothing we can do for you. We cannot choose between your life and his, we cannot be the ones to decide who is to live, we cannot intervene." But it cannot be concluded that you too can do nothing, that you cannot attack it to save your life. However innocent the child may be, you do not have to wait passively while it crushes you to death. Perhaps a pregnant woman is vaguely felt to have the status of house, to which we don't allow the right of self-defense. But if the woman houses the child, it should be remembered that she is a person who houses it.

I should perhaps stop to say explicitly that I am not claiming that 12
people have a right to do anything whatever to save their lives. I think,
rather, that there are drastic limits to the right of self-defense. If someone threatens you with death unless you torture someone else to death, I
think you have not the right, even to save your life, to do so. But the case
under consideration here is very different. In our case there are only two
people involved, one whose life is threatened, and one who threatens it.
Both are innocent: The one who is threatened is not threatened because
of any fault, the one who threatens does not threaten because of any
fault. For this reason we may feel that we bystanders cannot intervene.
But the person threatened can.

In sum, a woman surely can defend her life against the threat to it 13
posed by the unborn child, even if doing so involves its death. And this
shows not merely that the theses in (1) through (4) are false; it shows
also that the extreme view of abortion is false, and so we need not
canvass any other possible ways of arriving at it from the argument I
mentioned at the outset.

2. The extreme view could of course be weakened to say that while 14
abortion is permissible to save the mother's life, it may not be performed
by a third party, but only by the mother herself. But this cannot be right
either. For what we have to keep in mind is that the mother and the
unborn child are not like two tenants in a small house which has, by an
unfortunate mistake, been rented to both: The mother *owns* the house.
The fact that she does adds to the offensiveness of deducing that the
mother can do nothing from the supposition that third parties can do
nothing. But it does more than this: It casts a bright light on the supposition that third parties can do nothing. Certainly it lets us see that a third
party who says "I cannot choose between you" is fooling himself if he
thinks this is impartiality. If Jones has found and fastened on a certain
coat, which he needs to keep him from freezing, but which Smith also
needs to keep him from freezing, then it is not impartiality that says "I
cannot choose between you" when Smith owns the coat. Women have
said again and again "This body is *my* body!" and they have reason to
feel angry, reason to feel that it has been like shouting into the wind.
Smith, after all, is hardly likely to bless us if we say to him, "Of course
it's your coat, anybody would grant that it is. But no one may choose
between you and Jones who is to have it."

We should really ask what it is that says "no one may choose" in the 15
face of the fact that the body that houses the child is the mother's body.
It may be simply a failure to appreciate this fact. But it may be something
more interesting, namely the sense that one has a right to refuse to lay
hands on people, even where it would be just and fair to do so, even
where justice seems to require that somebody do so. Thus justice might
call for somebody to get Smith's coat back from Jones, and yet you have a
right to refuse to be the one to lay hands on Jones, a right to refuse to do
physical violence to him. This, I think, must be granted. But then what
should be said is not "no one may choose," but only "*I* cannot choose,"
and indeed not even this, but "*I* will not *act,*" leaving it open that
somebody else can or should, and in particular that anyone in a position

of authority, with the job of securing people's rights, both can and should. So this is no difficulty. I have not been arguing that any given third party must accede to the mother's request that he perform an abortion to save her life, but only that he may.

16   I suppose that in some views of human life the mother's body is only on loan to her, the loan not being one which gives her any prior claim to it. One who held this view might well think it impartiality to say "I cannot choose." But I shall simply ignore this possibility. My own view is that if a human being has any just, prior claim to anything at all, he has a just, prior claim to his own body. And perhaps this needn't be argued for here anyway, since, as I mentioned, the arguments against abortion we are looking at do grant that the woman has a right to decide what happens in and to her body.

17   But although they do grant it, I have tried to show that they do not take seriously what is done in granting it. I suggest the same thing will reappear even more clearly when we turn away from cases in which the mother's life is at stake, and attend, as I propose we now do, to the vastly more common cases in which a woman wants an abortion for some less weighty reason than preserving her own life.

18   3. Where the mother's life is not at stake, the argument I mentioned at the outset seems to have a much stronger pull. "Everyone has a right to life, so the unborn person has a right to life." And isn't the child's right to life weightier than anything other than the mother's own right to life, which she might put forward as ground for an abortion?

19   This argument treats the right to life as if it were unproblematic. It is not, and this seems to me to be precisely the source of the mistake.

20   For we should now, at long last, ask what it comes to, to have a right to life. In some views having a right to life includes having a right to be given at least the bare minimum one needs for continued life. But suppose that what in fact *is* the bare minimum a man needs for continued life is something he has no right at all to be given? If I am sick unto death, and the only thing that will save my life is the touch of Henry Fonda's cool hand on my fevered brow, then all the same, I have no right to be given the touch of Henry Fonda's cool hand on my fevered brow. It would be frightfully nice of him to fly in from the West Coast to provide it. It would be less nice, though no doubt well meant, if my friends flew out to the West Coast and carried Henry Fonda back with them. But I have no right at all against anybody that he should do this for me. Or again, to return to the story I told earlier, the fact that for continued life that violinist needs the continued use of your kidneys does not establish that he has a right to be given the continued use of your kidneys. He certainly has no right against you that *you* should give him continued use of your kidneys. For nobody has any right to use your kidneys unless you give him such a right; and nobody has the right against you that you shall give him this right — if you do allow him to go on using your kidneys, this is a kindness on your part, and not something he can claim from you as his due. Nor has he any right against anybody else that *they* should give him continued use of your kidneys. Certainly he had no right against the Society of Music Lovers that they should plug him into

you in the first place. And if you now start to unplug yourself, having learned that you will otherwise have to spend nine years in bed with him, there is nobody in the world who must try to prevent you, in order to see to it that he is given something he has a right to be given.

Some people are rather stricter about the right to life. In their view, it does not include the right to be given anything, but amounts to, and only to, the right not to be killed by anybody. But here a related difficulty arises. If everybody is to refrain from killing that violinist, then everybody must refrain from doing a great many different sorts of things. Everybody must refrain from slitting his throat, everybody must refrain from shooting him — and everybody must refrain from unplugging you from him. But does he have a right against everybody that they shall refrain from unplugging you from him? To refrain from doing this is to allow him to continue to use your kidneys. It could be argued that he has a right against us that *we* should allow him to continue to use your kidneys. That is, while he had no right against us that we should give him the use of your kidneys, it might be argued that he anyway has a right against us that we shall not now intervene and deprive him of the use of your kidneys. I shall come back to third-party interventions later. But certainly the violinist has no right against you that *you* shall allow him to continue to use your kidneys. As I said, if you do allow him to use them, it is a kindness on your part, and not something you owe him. 21

The difficulty I point to here is not peculiar to the right of life. It reappears in connection with all the other natural rights; and it is something which an adequate account of rights must deal with. For present purposes it is enough just to draw attention to it. But I would stress that I am not arguing that people do not have a right to life — quite to the contrary, it seems to me that the primary control we must place on the acceptability of an account of rights is that it should turn out in that account to be a truth that all persons have a right to life. I am arguing only that having a right to life does not guarantee having either a right to be given the use of or a right to be allowed continued use of another person's body — even if one needs it for life itself. So the right to life will not serve the opponents of abortion in the very simple and clear way in which they seem to have thought it would. 22

4. There is another way to bring out the difficulty. In the most ordinary sort of case, to deprive someone of what he has a right to is to treat him unjustly. Suppose a boy and his small brother are jointly given a box of chocolates for Christmas. If the older boy takes the box and refuses to give his brother any of the chocolates, he is unjust to him, for the brother has been given a right to half of them. But suppose that, having learned that otherwise it means nine years in bed with that violinist, you unplug yourself from him. You surely are not being unjust to him, for you gave him no right to use your kidneys, and no one else can have given him any such right. But we have to notice that in unplugging yourself, you are killing him; and violinists, like everybody else, have a right to life, and thus in the view we were considering just now, the right not to be killed. So here you do what he supposedly has a right you shall not do, but you do not act unjustly to him in doing it. 23

24   The emendation which may be made at this point is this: The right to life consists not in the right not to be killed, but rather in the right not to be killed unjustly. This runs a risk of circularity, but never mind: It would enable us to square the fact that the violinist has a right to life with the fact that you do not act unjustly toward him in unplugging yourself, thereby killing him. For if you do not kill him unjustly, you do not violate his right to life, and so it is no wonder you do him no injustice.

25   But if this emendation is accepted, the gap in the argument against abortion stares us plainly in the face: It is by no means enough to show that the fetus is a person, and to remind us that all persons have a right to life — we need to be shown also that killing the fetus violates its right to life, i.e., that abortion is unjust killing. And is it?

26   I suppose we may take it as a datum that in the case of pregnancy due to rape the mother has not given the unborn person a right to the use of her body for food and shelter. Indeed, in what pregnancy should it be supposed that the mother had given the unborn person such a right? It is not as if there were unborn persons drifting about the world, to whom a woman who wants a child says "I invite you in."

27   But it might be argued that there are other ways one can have acquired a right to the use of another person's body than by having been invited to use it by that person. Suppose a woman voluntarily indulges in intercourse, knowing of the chance it will issue in pregnancy, and then she does become pregnant; is she not in part responsible for the presence, in fact the very existence, of the unborn person inside? No doubt she did not invite it in. But doesn't her partial responsibility for its being there itself give it a right to the use of her body?[6] If so, then her aborting it would be more like the boy's taking away the chocolates, and less like your unplugging yourself from the violinist — doing so would be depriving it of what it does have a right to, and thus would be doing it an injustice.

28   And then, too, it might be asked whether or not she can kill it even to save her own life: If she voluntarily called it into existence, how can she now kill it, even in self-defense?

29   The first thing to be said about this is that it is something new. Opponents of abortion have been so concerned to make out the independence of the fetus, in order to establish that it has a right to life, just as its mother does, that they have tended to overlook the possible support they might gain from making out that the fetus is *dependent* on the mother, in order to establish that she has a special kind of responsibility for it, a responsibility that gives it rights against her which are not possessed by any independent person — such as an ailing violinist who is a stranger to her.

30   On the other hand, this argument would give the unborn person a right to its mother's body only if her pregnancy resulted from a voluntary act, undertaken in full knowledge of the chance a pregnancy might result from it. It would leave out entirely the unborn person whose existence is due to rape. Pending the availability of some further argument, then, we would be left with the conclusion that unborn persons

whose existence is due to rape have no right to the use of their mothers' bodies, and thus that aborting them is not depriving them of anything they have a right to and hence is not unjust killing.

And we should also notice that it is not at all plain that this argument really does go even as far as it purports to. For there are cases and cases, and the details make a difference. If the room is stuffy, and I therefore open a window to air it, and a burglar climbs in, it would be absurd to say, "Ah, now he can stay, she's given him a right to the use of her house—for she is partially responsible for his presence there, having voluntarily done what enabled him to get in, in full knowledge that there are such things as burglars, and that burglars burgle." It would be still more absurd to say this if I had had bars installed outside my windows, precisely to prevent burglars from getting in, and a burglar got in only because of a defect in the bars. It remains equally absurd if we imagine it is not a burglar who climbs in, but an innocent person who blunders or falls in. Again, suppose it were like this: Peopleseeds drift about in the air like pollen, and if you open your windows, one may drift in and take root in your carpets or upholstery. You don't want children, so you fix up your windows with fine mesh screens, the very best you can buy. As can happen, however, and on very, very rare occasions does happen, one of the screens is defective; and a seed drifts in and takes root. Does the personplant who now develops have a right to the use of your house? Surely not—despite the fact that you voluntarily opened your windows, you knowingly kept carpets and upholstered furniture, and you knew that screens were sometimes defective. Someone may argue that you are responsible for its rooting, that it does have a right to your house, because after all you *could* have lived out your life with bare floors and furniture, or with sealed windows and doors. But this won't do—for by the same token anyone can avoid a pregnancy due to rape by having a hysterectomy, or anyway by never leaving home without a (reliable!) army.

It seems to me that the argument we are looking at can establish at most that there are *some* cases in which the unborn person has a right to the use of its mother's body, and therefore *some* cases in which abortion is unjust killing. There is room for much discussion and argument as to precisely which, if any. But I think we should sidestep this issue and leave it open, for at any rate the argument certainly does not establish that all abortion is unjust killing.

5. There is room for yet another argument here, however. We surely must grant that there may be cases in which it would be morally indecent to detach a person from your body at the cost of his life. Suppose you learn that what the violinist needs is not nine years of your life, but only one hour: All you need do to save his life is spend one hour in the bed with him. Suppose also that letting him use your kidneys for that one hour would not affect your health in the slightest. Admittedly you were kidnapped. Admittedly you did not give anyone permission to plug him into you. Nevertheless it seems to me plain you *ought* to allow him to use your kidneys for that hour—it would be indecent to refuse.

Again, suppose pregnancy lasted only an hour, and constituted no threat to life or death [sic]. And suppose that a woman becomes pregnant as a result of rape. Admittedly she did not voluntarily do anything to bring about the existence of a child. Admittedly she did nothing at all which would give the unborn person a right to the use of her body. All the same it might well be said, as in the newly emended violinist story, that she *ought* to allow it to remain for that hour — that it would be indecent in her to refuse.

35   Now some people are inclined to use the term "right" in such a way that it follows from the fact that you ought to allow a person to use your body for the hour he needs, that he has a right to use your body for the hour he needs, even though he has not been given that right by any person or act. They may say that it follows also that if you refuse, you act unjustly toward him. This use of the term is perhaps so common that it cannot be called wrong; nevertheless it seems to me to be an unfortunate loosening of what we would do better to keep a tight rein on. Suppose that box of chocolates I mentioned earlier had not been given to both boys jointly, but was given only to the older boy. There he sits, stolidly eating his way through the box, his small brother watching enviously. Here we are likely to say "You ought not to be so mean. You ought to give your brother some of those chocolates." My own view is that it just does not follow from the truth of this that the brother has any right to any of the chocolates. If the boy refuses to give his brother any, he is greedy, stingy, callous — but not unjust. I suppose that the people I have in mind will say it does follow that the brother has a right to some of the chocolates, and thus that the boy does act unjustly if he refuses to give his brother any. But the effect of saying this is to obscure what we should keep distinct, namely the difference between the boy's refusal in this case and the boy's refusal in the earlier case, in which the box was given to both boys jointly, and in which the small brother thus had what was from any point of view clear title to half.

36   A further objection to so using the term "right" that from the fact that A ought to do a thing for B, it follows that B has a right against A that A do it for him, is that it is going to make the question of whether or not a man has a right to a thing turn on how easy it is to provide him with it; and this seems not merely unfortunate, but morally unacceptable. Take the case of Henry Fonda again. I said earlier that I had no right to the touch of his cool hand on my fevered brow, even though I needed it to save my life. I said it would be frightfully nice of him to fly in from the West Coast to provide me with it, but that I had no right against him that he should do so. But suppose he isn't on the West Coast. Suppose he has only to walk across the room, place a hand briefly on my brow — and lo, my life is saved. Then surely he ought to do it, it would be indecent to refuse. Is it to be said, "Ah, well, it follows that in this case she has a right to the touch of his hand on her brow, and so it would be an unjustice in him to refuse"? So that I have a right to it when it is easy for him to provide it, though no right when it's hard? It's rather a shocking idea that anyone's rights should fade away and disappear as it gets harder and harder to accord them to him.

So my own view is that even though you ought to let the violinist 37
use your kidneys for the one hour he needs, we should not conclude that
he has a right to do so—we should say that if you refuse, you are, like
the boy who owns all the chocolates and will give none away, self-centered and callous, indecent in fact, but not unjust. And similarly, that
even supposing a case in which a woman pregnant due to rape ought to
allow the unborn person to use her body for the hour he needs, we
should not conclude that he has a right to do so; we should conclude
that she is self-centered, callous, indecent, but not unjust, if she refuses.
The complaints are no less grave; they are just different. However, there
is no need to insist on this point. If anyone does wish to deduce "he has
a right" from "you ought," then all the same he must surely grant that
there are cases in which it is not morally required of you that you allow
that violinist to use your kidneys, and in which he does not have a right
to use them, and in which you do not do him an injustice if you refuse.
And so also for mother and unborn child. Except in such cases as the
unborn person has a right to demand it—and we were leaving open the
possibility that there may be such cases—nobody is morally *required* to
make large sacrifices, of health, of all other interests and concerns, of all
other duties and commitments, for nine years, or even for nine months,
in order to keep another person alive.

6. We have in fact to distinguish between the two kinds of Samari- 38
tan: the Good Samaritan and what we might call the Minimally Decent
Samaritan. The story of the Good Samaritan, you will remember, goes
like this:

> A certain man went down from Jerusalem to Jericho, and fell
> among thieves, which stripped him of his raiment, and wounded him,
> and departed, leaving him half dead.
> And by chance there came down a certain priest that way; and
> when he saw him, he passed by on the other side.
> And likewise a Levite, when he was at the place, came and looked
> on him, and passed by on the other side.
> But a certain Samaritan, as he journeyed, came where he was; and
> when he saw him he had compassion on him.
> And went to him, and bound up his wounds, pouring in oil and
> wine, and set him on his own beast, and brought him to an inn, and
> took care of him.
> And on the morrow, when he departed, he took out two pence,
> and gave them to the host, and said unto him, "Take care of him; and
> whatsoever thou spendest more, when I come again, I will repay
> thee."
>
> *(Luke 10:30–35)*

The Good Samaritan went out of his way, at some cost to himself, to help
one in need of it. We are not told what the options were, that is, whether
or not the priest and the Levite could have helped by doing less than the
Good Samaritan did, but assuming they could have, then the fact they
did nothing at all shows they were not even Minimally Decent Samari-

tans, not because they were not Samaritans, but because they were not even minimally decent.

39   These things are a matter of degree, of course, but there is a difference, and it comes out perhaps most clearly in the story of Kitty Genovese, who, as you will remember was murdered while thirty-eight people watched or listened, and did nothing at all to help her. A Good Samaritan would have rushed out to give direct assistance against the murderer. Or perhaps we had better allow that it would have been a Splendid Samaritan who did this, on the ground that it would have involved a risk of death for himself. But the thirty-eight not only did not do this, they did not even trouble to pick up a phone to call the police. Minimally Decent Samaritanism would call for doing at least that, and their not having done it was monstrous.

40   After telling the story of the Good Samaritan, Jesus said, "Go, and do thou likewise." Perhaps he meant that we are morally required to act as the Good Samaritan did. Perhaps he was urging people to do more than is morally required of them. At all events it seems plain that it was not morally required of any of the thirty-eight that he rush out to give direct assistance at the risk of his own life, and that it is not morally required of anyone that he give long stretches of his life — nine years or nine months — to sustaining the life of a person who has no special right (we were leaving open the possibility of this) to demand it.

41   Indeed, with one rather striking class of exceptions, no one in any country in the world is *legally* required to do anywhere near as much as this for anyone else. The class of exceptions is obvious. My main concern here is not the state of the law in respect to abortion, but it is worth drawing attention to the fact that in no state in this country is any man compelled by law to be even a Minimally Decent Samaritan to any person; there is no law under which charges could be brought against the thirty-eight who stood by while Kitty Genovese died. By contrast, in most states in this country women are compelled by law to be not merely Minimally Decent Samaritans, but Good Samaritans to unborn persons inside them. This doesn't by itself settle anything one way or the other, because it may well be argued that there should be laws in this country — as there are in many European countries — compelling at least Minimally Decent Samaritanism.[7] But it does show that there is a gross injustice in the existing state of the law. And it shows also that the groups currently working against liberalization of abortion laws, in fact working toward having it declared unconstitutional for a state to permit abortion, had better start working for the adoption of Good Samaritan laws generally, or earn the charge that they are acting in bad faith.

42   I should think, myself, that Minimally Decent Samaritan laws would be one thing, Good Samaritan laws quite another, and in fact highly improper. But we are not here concerned with the law. What we should ask is not whether anybody should be compelled by law to be a Good Samaritan, but whether we must accede to a situation in which somebody is being compelled — by nature, perhaps — to be a Good Samaritan. We have, in other words, to look now at third-party interventions. I have been arguing that no person is morally required to make large

sacrifices to sustain the life of another who has no right to demand them, and this even where the sacrifices do not include life itself; we are not morally required to be Good Samaritans or anyway Very Good Samaritans to one another. But what if a man cannot extricate himself from such a situation? What if he appeals to us to extricate him? It seems to me plain that there are cases in which we can, cases in which a Good Samaritan would extricate him. There you are, you were kidnapped, and nine years in bed with that violinist lie ahead of you. You have your own life to lead. You are sorry, but you simply cannot see giving up so much of your life to the sustaining of his. You cannot extricate yourself, and ask us to do so. I should have thought that—in light of his having no right to the use of your body—it was obvious that we do not have to accede to your being forced to give up so much. We can do what you ask. There is no injustice to the violinist in our doing so.

7. Following the lead of the opponents of abortion, I have through-out been speaking of the fetus merely as a person, and what I have been asking is whether or not the argument we began with, which proceeds only from the fetus' being a person, really does establish its conclusion. I have argued that it does not. 43

But of course there are arguments and arguments, and it may be said that I have simply fastened on the wrong one. It may be said that what is important is not merely the fact that the fetus is a person, but that it is a person for whom the woman has a special kind of responsibility issuing from the fact that she is its mother. And it might be argued that all my analogies are therefore irrelevant—for you do not have that special kind of responsibility for that violinist, Henry Fonda does not have that special kind of responsibility for me. And our attention might be drawn to the fact that men and women both *are* compelled by law to provide support for their children. 44

I have in effect dealt (briefly) with this argument in section 4 above; but a (still briefer) recapitulation now may be in order. Surely we do not have any such "special responsibility" for a person unless we have assumed it, explicitly or implicitly. If a set of parents do not try to prevent pregnancy, do not obtain an abortion, but rather take it home with them, then they have assumed responsibility for it, they have given it rights, and they cannot *now* withdraw support from it at the cost of its life because they now find it difficult to go on providing for it. But if they have taken all reasonable precautions against having a child, they do not simply by virtue of their biological relationship to the child who comes into existence have a special responsibility for it. They may wish to assume responsibility for it, or they may not wish to. And I am suggesting that if assuming responsibility for it would require large sacrifices, then they may refuse. A Good Samaritan would not refuse—or anyway, a Splendid Samaritan, if the sacrifices that had to be made were enormous. But then so would a Good Samaritan assume responsibility for that violinist; so would Henry Fonda, if he is a Good Samaritan, fly in from the West Coast and assume responsibility for me. 45

8. My argument will be found unsatisfactory on two counts by many of those who want to regard abortion as morally permissible. First, while 46

I do argue that abortion is not impermissible, I do not argue that it is always permissible. There may well be cases in which carrying the child to term requires only Minimally Decent Samaritanism of the mother, and this is a standard we must not fall below. I am inclined to think it a merit of my account precisely that it does *not* give a general yes or a general no. It allows for and supports our sense that, for example, a sick and desperately frightened fourteen-year-old schoolgirl, pregnant due to rape, may of *course* choose abortion, and that any law which rules this out is an insane law. And it also allows for and supports our sense that in other cases resort to abortion is even positively indecent. It would be indecent in the woman to request an abortion, and indecent in a doctor to perform it, if she is in her seventh month, and wants the abortion just to avoid the nuisance of postponing a trip abroad. The very fact that the arguments I have been drawing attention to treat all cases of abortion, or even all cases of abortion in which the mother's life is not at stake, as morally on a par ought to have made them suspect at the outset.

47   Secondly, while I am arguing for the permissibility of abortion in some cases, I am not arguing for the right to secure the death of the unborn child. It is easy to confuse these two things in that up to a certain point in the life of the fetus it is not able to survive outside the mother's body; hence removing it from her body guarantees its death. But they are importantly different. I have argued that you are not morally required to spend nine months in bed, sustaining the life of that violinist; but to say this is by no means to say that if, when you unplug yourself, there is a miracle and he survives, you then have a right to turn around and slit his throat. You may detach yourself even if this costs him his life; you have no right to be guaranteed his death, by some other means, if unplugging yourself does not kill him. There are some people who will feel dissatisfied by this feature of my argument. A woman may be utterly devastated by the thought of a child, a bit of herself, put out for adoption and never seen or heard of again. She may therefore want not merely that the child be detached from her, but more, that it die. Some opponents of abortion are inclined to regard this as beneath contempt—thereby showing insensitivity to what is surely a powerful source of despair. All the same, I agree that the desire for the child's death is not one which anybody may gratify, should it turn out to be possible to detach the child alive.

48   At this place, however, it should be remembered that we have only been pretending throughout that the fetus is a human being from the moment of conception. A very early abortion is surely not the killing of a person, and so is not dealt with by anything I have said here.

AUTHOR'S NOTES

1 Daniel Callahan, *Abortion: Law, Choice and Morality* (New York, 1970), p. 373. This book gives a fascinating survey of the available information on abortion. The Jewish tradition in David M. Feldman, *Birth Control in Jewish Law* (New York, 1963), part 5; the Catholic tradition in John T. Noonan, Jr., "An Almost Absolute Value in History," in *The Morality of Abortion*, ed. John T. Noonan, Jr. (Cambridge, Mass., 1970).

2 The term "direct" in the arguments I refer to is a technical one. Roughly, what is meant by "direct killing" is either killing as an end in itself, or killing as a means to some end, for example, the end of saving someone else's life. See note 5 on this page, for an example of its use.

3 Cf. *Encyclical Letter of Pope Pius XI on Christian Marriage*, St. Paul Editions (Boston, n.d.), p. 32: "However much we may pity the mother whose health and even life is gravely imperiled in the performance of the duty allotted to her by nature, nevertheless what could ever be a sufficient reason for excusing in any way the direct murder of the innocent? This is precisely what we are dealing with here." Noonan (*The Morality of Abortion*, p. 43) reads this as follows: "What cause can ever avail to excuse in any way the direct killing of the innocent? For it is a question of that."

4 The thesis in (4) is in an interesting way weaker than those in (1), (2), and (3): They rule out abortion even in cases in which both mother *and* child will die if the abortion is not performed. By contrast, one who held the view expressed in (4) could consistently say that one needn't prefer letting two persons die to killing one.

5 Cf. the following passage from Pius XII, *Address to the Italian Catholic Society of Midwives:* "The baby in the maternal breast has the right to life immediately from God. — Hence there is no man, no human authority, no science, no medical, eugenic, social, economic or moral 'indication' which can establish or grant a valid juridical ground for a direct deliberate disposition of an innocent human life, that is a disposition which looks to its destruction either as an end or as a means to another end perhaps in itself not illicit. — The baby, still not born, is a man in the same degree and for the same reason as the mother" (quoted in Noonan, *The Morality of Abortion*, p. 45).

6 The need for a discussion of this argument was brought home to me by members of the Society for Ethical and Legal Philosophy, to whom this paper was originally presented.

7 For a discussion of the difficulties involved, and a survey of the European experience with such laws, see *The Good Samaritan and the Law*, ed. James M. Ratcliffe (New York, 1966).

Questions on Content

1. What "slipper slope" argument is frequently used by opponents of abortion? What is a slippery slope argument?
2. What analogy does Thomson use in paragraph 4, and what does that analogy demonstrate? Where else in the essay does Thomson return to the same basic analogy, and why does she do so?
3. Why is Thomson displeased in paragraph 5 with the argument that abortion, while generally impermissible, ought to be tolerated if the pregnancy is the result of rape? Why does she subsequently argue in paragraph 30 that a woman *does* have the right to an abortion if the pregnancy is the result of rape?
4. What does Thomson mean by the "extreme view" of abortion?
5. What new analogy does Thomson use in paragraph 11, and what does that analogy demonstrate? Where else in the essay does she use this analogy again, and why does she do so?
6. What does the analogy of the coats demonstrate in paragraph 14?
7. What is demonstrated by the analogy involving Henry Fonda in paragraph 20? Why does Thomson return to that analogy later in the essay?
8. What does the box of chocolates analogy in paragraph 23 demonstrate? Why does Thomson return to that analogy later in the essay?

9. What is demonstrated by the burglar and peopleseed analogies in paragraph 31?
10. What does Thomson mean by the Minimally Decent Samaritan in paragraphs 38 through 41?

Questions on Thesis, Purpose, and Structure

1. Thomson uses her first three paragraphs to introduce her topic and her approach to that topic. How successful is this introduction in getting your attention? How successful is it in disarming the objections of those who oppose abortion? How persuasive is it?
2. Thomson frequently explains and develops the arguments of her opponents. Why? Does she do so fairly?
3. Much of Thomson's argument is based on analogies. What are the dangers of argument by analogy? How successfully does Thomson avoid those dangers? Are her arguments logical and persuasive?
4. Thomson uses eight numerals to indicate structural divisions in her essay. Identify the idea or argument that is the focus of each of the eight sections.
5. Why does the eighth section logically come at the end of the essay? In what way does it serve as a conclusion? Why does Thomson's final paragraph remind us that she has "only been pretending throughout that the fetus is a human being from the moment of conception"?
6. Clearly, Thomson's major purpose is persuasive, but is there anything enter taining about her development of the arguments? Identify the most entertaining aspects of her essay, and explain what creates the entertainment.

Questions on Style and Diction

1. Find the following words in the essay and determine their definitions in context: canvassed, incumbent, accede (paragraph 4); stringent (paragraph 9); supposition (paragraph 14); unproblematic (paragraph 19); emendation (paragraph 24); datum (paragraph 26); purports (paragraph 31); stolidly, callous (paragraph 35); extricate (paragraph 42); recapitulation (paragraph 45).
2. Thomson's essay was published in a scholarly journal. What features of her prose style, if any, show that she is writing for an audience of philosophers and scholars instead of a more general audience?

Ideas for Essays

1. Use carefully chosen analogies to explore some other controversial ethical issue. Some possibilities include the right to commit suicide, the prohibition of bigamy, the decriminalization of drug use, and the right to bear firearms.
2. Write an evaluation and critique of Thomson's arguments. Are her analogies fair? Is her reasoning sound? Can you think of ways to refute her arguments and, thereby, show that abortion is unethical?

◇◇◇

Getting a Big Bang out of Creation Theories

Noel Riley, S.M.

As one who wears two hats (or should I say a hat and a veil?), I am both   1
angered and embarrassed when the origins of our universe are posed as
a conflict between Genesis and evolution.

My hat? I have a master's degree in chemistry from St. Louis Univer-   2
sity, and have taught science and religion for more than 25 years. My
veil? I am a Roman Catholic nun, a member of the Sisters of Mercy
community. I firmly believe both in God and in evolution. My embarrassment? That "believers" should espouse a discredited fundamentalist
view of creation, one that merits the scorn and ridicule of the scientific
community. My anger? That there are some well-meaning people who
confront the young with a false choice: *either* the biblical story of
creation *or* evolutionary theory. My thesis? There is no intrinsic conflict
between faith and science, between God the creator and evolutionary
theory.

The book of Genesis was probably written between the 10th and 6th   3
centuries B.C., much later than the oral traditions from which it sprang.
What scientific knowledge did the inspired authors have? Only the
knowledge of their time, which is the case with our generation, too. Was
the science faulty? Certainly, unless you think the earth is flat, supported
by a large turtle, with waters above and below, and kept in check by an
enclosed firmament. Did the authors of Genesis intend to teach science?
Certainly not. As Roman Catholic theologian Robert Bellarmine wrote
some four centuries ago, "The Bible was written to show us how to go to
heaven, not how the heavens go!" And, as St. Augustine observed in the
4th Century, "The gospels do not tell us that our Lord said, 'I will send
you the Holy Ghost to teach you the course of the sun and moon'; we
should endeavor to become Christians and not astronomers."

What Genesis does is relate—in simple, figurative language that   4
could be understood by primitive people—the fundamental principles
of salvation and the description then popular of the origins of the human
race. Let us consider a few examples of this figurative language and the
underlying message.

In Genesis, God is shown as a master craftsman fashioning the   5
world in six days and resting on the seventh. Jews were required to keep
the Sabbath as a day of rest, which is the most reasonable explanation for
depicting God as resting on the Sabbath, too.

The creation story uses a liturgical or mnemonic device, "God saw   6
that it was good," to mark each great event of creation. Once it was
considered necessary to think of "the days" as periods of time representing some thousands of years each. But the days can be understood
simply as normal 24-hour periods, forming the literary framework of
what was probably a prehistoric hymn. The use of this literary device had
a practical purpose; it made memorization and recitation easier, for we
are speaking of people who were largely illiterate.

7   The primitive cosmology of Genesis was used to teach that God created all things and to emphasize his transcendent power, and his love and concern for us. This view contrasted with the pagan epics, then widespread, in which creation was depicted as a struggle between the gods and the forces of chaos. The Hebrew people lived among idolaters and were surrounded by those who worshiped animals. The point of Genesis is that God is to be worshiped because it was He who created all these things.

8   And why is Eve described in Genesis as being formed from the side of Adam? To demonstrate that she is of the same nature as man, unlike animals, and does not deserve the subordinate position assigned women in pagan society.

9   The biblical story of creation has a religious purpose. It contains, but does not teach, errors. The evolutionary theory of creation, in contrast, has a scientific purpose, and the search for truth is the province of astronomers, geologists, biologists and the like. These two purposes are distinct, and both offer truth to the human mind and heart. The mistake scientists make is drawing philosophical and religious inferences and deductions unwarranted by the scientific data; the mistake of religious leaders is using the Bible as a science textbook.

10   At the time of the controversy over Galileo's theory of the universe, Bellarmine warned: "I say that if a real proof be found that the sun is fixed and does not revolve around the earth, but the earth around the sun, then it will be necessary, very carefully, to proceed to the explanation of the passages of Scripture which appear to be contrary, and we should rather say that we have misunderstood these than pronounce that to be false which is demonstrated."

11   Far from taking God out of the universe, the theory of evolution gives us a more sublime conception of God's creative act. He operates through the laws of nature that He has established. I am indebted to contemporary philosopher John O'Brien for an analogy: Just as it shows more skill for a billiards player to get all eight balls in the pockets in one stroke, rather than eight (or nine!), so it is a loftier conception of God to imagine a single creative act, with secondary causes operative thereafter.

12   Today scientists trying to explain the origins of the universe favor the "big bang" theory. Does this contradict Genesis? Not at all. In fact, if I were tempted to embrace a discredited concordism, I would see in the first "big bang" the creative hand of God, and His lofty words: "Let there be light!"

Indeed, let there be more light in our discussions, for the believer need fear not truth, but ignorance.

Questions on Content

1. What "two hats" does Riley wear, and what does she learn about creation from each perspective?
2. Why is Riley angered "when the origins of our universe are posed as a conflict between Genesis and evolution"? Why is she embarrassed?
3. How does Riley explain the six days of creation in Genesis? What is the main point of the Genesis story?

4. Does Riley think that Eve was actually formed from Adam's rib? What does she think is the point of that incident?
5. Why, according to Riley, would creation in a "big bang" be consistent with Christianity?

Questions on Thesis, Purpose, and Structure

1. Why does Riley begin her essay by discussing her educational background and vocation?
2. Which paragraphs in the essay focus on the Genesis account of creation? Which paragraphs focus on the scientific account of creation? Why does Riley arrange her ideas in this way?
3. What is Riley's thesis? Does she state it directly? If so, where? If not, should she have done so?

Questions on Style and Diction

1. Find the following words in the essay and determine their definitions in context: fundamentalist, intrinsic (paragraph 2); firmament, endeavor (paragraph 3); liturgical, mnemonic (paragraph 6); cosmology, transcendent, pagan, idolaters (paragraph 7); inferences (paragraph 9); concordism (12).
2. Riley frequently cites authorities to support her arguments — Robert Bellarmine, St. Augustine, John O'Brien, the Bible itself. What is the effect of these citations? How does this use of authorities influence your impression of Riley and her arguments?
3. Examine the one-sentence conclusion. Why is it an effective way to end the essay?

Ideas for Essays

1. At the heart of Riley's argument is the belief that there is (and can be) no conflict between religious truth and scientific truth. Examine this contention in an essay of your own by focusing on religious doctrines other than those in the creation story.
2. Both science and religion seek the truth and involve complex systems of explanation or belief. Write an essay comparing the kinds of truth presented through science and religion.

Love Is a Fallacy
Max Shulman

Max Shulman (1919–   ), for four decades one of America's leading comic writers, was born in St. Paul, Minnesota, and graduated from the University of Minnesota in 1942. Following military service during World War II, Shulman began to write humorous short stories for such popular periodicals as *Esquire*, *Mademoiselle*, *Saturday Evening Post*, and *Good Housekeeping*. Over the years

Shulman has written novels, motion picture scripts, and Broadway shows, as well as the successful "Dobie Gillis" television series, which ran on CBS from 1959 to 1962. Shulman takes the writing of comedy seriously: "I don't believe there's any kind of writing more serious than funny writing—nor more difficult or demanding of more dedication and work hours." In "Love Is a Fallacy" from *The Many Loves of Dobie Gillis* (1951), Shulman both defines the most common forms of logical fallacy and amusingly shows how they *can* have importance in daily life.

1   Charles Lamb, as merry and enterprising a fellow as you will meet in a month of Sundays, unfettered the informal essay with his memorable *Old China* and *Dream's Children*. There follows an informal essay that ventures even beyond Lamb's frontier. Indeed, "informal" may not be quite the right word to describe this essay; "limp" or "flaccid" or possibly "spongy" are perhaps more appropriate.

2   Vague though its category, it is without doubt an essay. It develops an argument; it cites instances; it reaches a conclusion. Could Carlyle do more? Could Ruskin?

3   Read, then, the following essay which undertakes to demonstrate that logic, far from being a dry, pedantic discipline, is a living, breathing thing, full of beauty, passion, and trauma.

— Author's Note

4   Cool was I and logical. Keen, calculating, perspicacious, acute and astute—I was all of these. My brain was as powerful as a dynamo, as precise as a chemist's scales, as penetrating as a scalpel. And—think of it!—I was only eighteen.

5   It is not often that one so young has such a giant intellect. Take, for example, Petey Burch, my roommate at the University of Minnesota. Same age, same background, but dumb as an ox. A nice enough young fellow, you understand, but nothing upstairs. Emotional type. Unstable. Impressionable. Worst of all, a faddist. Fads, I submit, are the very negation of reason. To be swept up in every new craze that comes along, to surrender yourself to idiocy just because everybody else is doing it—this, to me, is the acme of mindlessness. Not, however, to Petey.

6   One afternoon I found Petey lying on his bed with an expression of such distress on his face that I immediately diagnosed appendicitis. "Don't move," I said. "Don't take a laxative. I'll get a doctor."

7   "Raccoon," he mumbled thickly.

8   "Raccoon?" I said, pausing in my flight.

9   "I want a raccoon coat," he wailed.

10   I perceived that his trouble was not physical, but mental. "Why do you want a raccoon coat?"

11   "I should have known it," he cried, pounding his temples. "I should have known they'd come back when the Charleston came back. Like a fool I spent all my money for textbooks, and now I can't get a raccoon coat."

12   "Can you mean," I said incredulously, "that people are actually wearing raccoon coats again?"

"All the Big Men on Campus are wearing them. Where've you   13
been?"

"In the library," I said, naming a place not frequented by Big Men   14
on Campus.

He leaped from the bed and paced the room, "I've got to have a   15
raccoon coat," he said passionately. "I've got to!"

"Petey, why? Look at it rationally. Raccoon coats are unsanitary.   16
They shed. They smell bad. They weigh too much. They're unsightly.
They—"

"You don't understand," he interrupted impatiently. "It's the thing   17
to do. Don't you want to be in the swim?"

"No," I said truthfully.   18

"Well, I do," he declared. "I'd give anything for a raccoon coat.   19
Anything!"

My brain, that precision instrument, slipped into high gear. "Any-   20
thing?" I asked, looking at him narrowly.

"Anything," he affirmed in ringing tones.   21

I stroked my chin thoughtfully. It so happened that I knew where to   22
get my hands on a raccoon coat. My father had had one in his undergrad-
uate days; it lay now in a trunk in the attic back home. It also happened
that Petey had something I wanted. He didn't *have* it exactly, but at least
he had first rights on it. I refer to his girl, Polly Espy.

I had long coveted Polly Espy. Let me emphasize that my desire for   23
this young woman was not emotional in nature. She was, to be sure, a
girl who excited the emotions, but I was not one to let my heart rule my
head. I wanted Polly for a shrewdly calculated, entirely cerebral reason.

I was a freshman in law school. In a few years I would be out   24
in practice. I was well aware of the importance of the right kind of wife
in furthering a lawyer's career. The successful lawyers I had observed
were, almost without exception, married to beautiful, gracious, intelligent women. With one omission, Polly fitted these specifications
perfectly.

Beautiful she was. She was not yet of pin-up proportions, but I felt   25
sure that time would supply the lack. She already had the makings.

Gracious she was. By gracious I mean full of graces. She had an   26
erectness of carriage, an ease of bearing, a poise that clearly indicated
the best of breeding. At table her manners were exquisite. I had seen her
at the Kozy Kampus Korner eating the speciality of the house—a sandwich that contained scraps of pot roast, gravy, chopped nuts, and a
dipper of sauerkraut—without even getting her fingers moist.

Intelligent she was not. In fact, she veered in the opposite direction.   27
But I believed that under my guidance she would smarten up. At any
rate, it was worth a try. It is, after all, easier to make a beautiful dumb girl
smart than to make an ugly smart girl beautiful.

"Petey," I said, "are you in love with Polly Epsy?"   28

"I think she's a keen kid," he replied, "but I don't know if you'd call   29
it love. Why?"

"Do you," I asked, "have any kind of formal arrangement with her? I   30
mean are you going steady or anything like that?"

31   "No. We see each other quite a bit, but we both have other dates. Why?"

32   "Is there," I asked, "any other man for whom she has a particular fondness?"

33   "Not that I know of. Why?"

34   I nodded with satisfaction. "In other words, if you were out of the picture, the field would be open. Is that right?"

35   "I guess so. What are you getting at?"

36   "Nothing, nothing," I said innocently, and took my suitcase out of the closet.

37   "Where are you going?" asked Petey.

38   "Home for the weekend." I threw a few things into the bag.

39   "Listen," he said, clutching my arm eagerly, "while you're home, you couldn't get some money from your old man, could you, and lend it to me so I can buy a raccoon coat?"

40   "I may do better than that," I said with a mysterious wink and closed my bag and left.

41   "Look," I said to Petey when I got back Monday morning. I threw open the suitcase and revealed the huge, hairy, gamy object that my father had worn in his Stutz Bearcat in 1925.

42   "Holy Toledo!" said Petey reverently. He plunged his hands into the raccoon coat and then his face. "Holy Toledo!" he repeated fifteen or twenty times.

43   "Would you like it?" I asked.

44   "Oh yes!" he cried, clutching the greasy pelt to him. Then a canny look came into his eyes. "What do you want for it?"

45   "Your girl," I said, mincing no words.

46   "Polly?" he said in a horrified whisper. "You want Polly?"

47   "That's right."

48   He flung the coat from him. "Never," he said stoutly.

49   I shrugged. "Okay. If you don't want to be in the swim, I guess it's your business."

50   I sat down in a chair and pretended to read a book, but out of the corner of my eye I kept watching Petey. He was a torn man. First he looked at the coat with the expression of a waif at a bakery window. Then he turned away and set his jaw resolutely. Then he looked back at the coat, with even more longing in his face. Then he turned away, but with not so much resolution this time. Back and forth his head swiveled, desire waxing, resolution waning. Finally he didn't turn away at all; he just stood and stared with mad lust at the coat.

51   "It isn't as though I was in love with Polly," he said thickly. "Or going steady or anything like that."

52   "That's right," I murmured.

53   "What's Polly to me, or me to Polly?"

54   "Not a thing," said I.

55   "It's just been a casual kick—just a few laughs, that's all."

56   "Try on the coat," said I.

57   He complied. The coat bunched high over his ears and dropped all

the way down to his shoe tops. He looked like a mound of dead raccoons. "Fits fine," he said happily.

I rose from my chair. "Is it a deal?" I asked, extending my hand. 58
He swallowed. "It's a deal," he said and shook my hand. 59

I had my first date with Polly the following evening. This was in the 60 nature of a survey; I wanted to find out just how much work I had to do to get her mind up to the standard I required. I took her first to dinner. "Gee, that was a delish dinner," she said as we left the restaurant. Then I took her to a movie. "Gee, that was a marvy movie," she said as we left the theater. And then I took her home. "Gee, I had a sensaysh time," she said as she bade me good night.

I went back to my room with a heavy heart. I had gravely underesti- 61 mated the size of my task. This girl's lack of information was terrifying. Nor would it be enough merely to supply her with information. First she had to be taught to *think*. This loomed as a project of no small dimensions, and at first I was tempted to give her back to Petey. But then I got to thinking about her abundant physical charms and about the way she entered a room and the way she handled a knife and fork, and I decided to make an effort.

I went about it, as in all things, systematically. I gave her a course in 62 logic. It happened that I, as a law student, was taking a course in logic myself, so I had all the facts at my finger tips. "Polly," I said to her when I picked her up on our next date, "tonight we are going over to the Knoll and talk."

"Oo, terrif," she replied. One thing I will say for this girl: you would 63 go far to find another so agreeable.

We went to the Knoll, the campus trysting place, and we sat down 64 under an old oak, and she looked at me expectantly. "What are we going to talk about?" she asked.

"Logic." 65

She thought this over for a minute and decided she liked it. "Mag- 66 nif," she said.

"Logic," I said, clearing my throat, "is the science of thinking. 67 Before we can think correctly, we must first learn to recognize the common fallacies of logic. These we will take up tonight."

"Wow-dow!" she cried, clapping her hands delightedly. 68

I winced, but went bravely on. "First let us examine the fallacy 69 called Dicto Simpliciter."

"By all means," she urged, batting her lashes eagerly. 70

"Dicto Simpliciter means an argument based on an unqualified 71 generalization. For example: Exercise is good. Therefore everybody should exercise."

"I agree," said Polly earnestly. "I mean exercise is wonderful. I 72 mean it builds the body and everything."

"Polly," I said gently, "the argument is a fallacy. *Exercise is good* is 73 an unqualified generalization. For instance, if you have heart disease, exercise is bad, not good. Many people are ordered by their doctors *not* to exercise. You must *qualify* the generalization. You must say exercise is *usually* good, or exercise is good *for most people*. Otherwise you have committed a Dicto Simpliciter. Do you see?"

74   "No," she confessed. "But this is marvy. Do more! Do more!"

75   "It will be better if you stop tugging at my sleeve," I told her, and when she desisted, I continued. "Next we take up a fallacy called Hasty Generalization. Listen carefully: You can't speak French. I can't speak French. Petey Burch can't speak French. I must therefore conclude that nobody at the University of Minnesota can speak French."

76   "Really?" said Polly, amazed. "*Nobody?*"

77   I hid my exasperation. "Polly, it's a fallacy. The generalization is reached too hastily. There are too few instances to support such a conclusion."

78   "Know any more fallacies?" she asked breathlessly. "This is more fun than dancing even."

79   I fought off a wave of despair. I was getting nowhere with this girl, absolutely nowhere. Still, I am nothing if not persistent. I continued.

80   "Next comes Post Hoc. Listen to this: Let's not take Bill on our picnic. Every time we take him out with us, it rains."

81   "I know somebody like that," she exclaimed. "A girl back home — Eula Becker, her name is. It never fails. Every single time we take her on a picnic —"

82   "Polly," I said sharply, "it's a fallacy. Eula Becker doesn't *cause* the rain. She has no connection with the rain. You are guilty of Post Hoc if you blame Eula Becker."

83   "I'll never do that again," she promised contritely. "Are you mad at me?"

84   I sighed deeply. "No, Polly, I'm not mad."

85   "Then tell me some more fallacies."

86   "All right. Let's try Contradictory Premises."

87   "Yes, let's," she chirped, blinking her eyes happily.

88   I frowned, but plunged ahead. "Here's an example of Contradictory Premises: If God can do anything, can He make a stone so heavy that He won't be able to lift it?"

89   "Of course," she replied promptly.

90   "But if He can do anything, He can lift the stone," I pointed out.

91   "Yeah," she said thoughtfully. "Well, then I guess He can't make the stone."

92   "But He can do anything," I reminded her.

93   She scratched her pretty, empty head. "I'm all confused," she admitted.

94   "Of course you are. Because when the premises of an argument contradict each other, there can be no argument. If there is an irresistible force, there can be no immovable object. If there is an immovable object, there can be no irresistible force. Get it?"

95   "Tell me some more of this keen stuff," she said eagerly.

96   I consulted my watch. "I think we'd better call it a night. I'll take you home now, and you go over all the things you've learned. We'll have another session tomorrow night."

I deposited her at the girls' dormitory, where she assured me that   97
she had had a perfectly terrif evening, and I went glumly to my room.
Petey lay snoring in his bed, the raccoon coat huddled like a great hairy
beast at his feet. For a moment I considered waking him and telling him
that he could have his girl back. It seemed clear that my project was
doomed to failure. The girl simply had a logic-proof head.

But then I reconsidered. I had wasted one evening; I might as well   98
waste another. Who knew? Maybe somewhere in the extinct crater of her
mind, a few embers still smoldered. Maybe somehow I could fan them
into flame. Admittedly it was not a prospect fraught with hope, but I
decided to give it one more try.

Seated under the oak the next evening I said, "Our first fallacy   99
tonight is called Ad Misericordiam."

She quivered with delight.   100

"Listen closely," I said. "A man applies for a job. When the boss asks   101
him what his qualifications are, he replies that he has a wife and six
children at home, the wife is a helpless cripple, the children have
nothing to eat, no clothes to wear, no shoes on their feet, there are no
beds in the house, no coal in the cellar, and winter is coming."

A tear rolled down each of Polly's pink cheeks. "Oh, this is awful,   102
awful," she sobbed.

"Yes, it's awful," I agreed, "but it's no argument. The man never   103
answered the boss's questions about his qualifications. Instead he appealed to the boss's sympathy. He committed the fallacy of Ad Misericordiam. Do you understand?"

"Have you got a handkerchief?" she blubbered.   104

I handed her a handkerchief and tried to keep from screaming while   105
she wiped her eyes. "Next," I said in a carefully controlled tone, "we
will discuss False Analogy. Here is an example: Students should be
allowed to look at their textbooks during examinations. After all, surgeons have X-rays to guide them during an operation, lawyers have
briefs to guide them during a trial, carpenters have blueprints to guide
them when they are building a house. Why, then, shouldn't students be
allowed to look at their textbooks during an examination?"

"There now," she said enthusiastically, "is the most marvey idea   106
I've heard in years."

"Polly," I said testily, "the argument is all wrong. Doctors, lawyers,   107
and carpenters aren't taking a test to see how much they have learned,
but students are. The situations are altogether different, and you can't
make an analogy between them."

"I still think it's a good idea," said Polly.   108

"Nuts," I muttered. Doggedly I pressed on. "Next we'll try Hypoth-   109
esis Contrary to Fact."

"Sounds yummy," was Polly's reaction.   110

"Listen: If Madame Curie had not happened to leave a photographic   111
plate in a drawer with a chunk of pitchblende, the world today would not
know about radium."

"True, true," said Polly, nodding her head. "Did you see the movie?   112

Oh, it just knocked me out. That Walter Pidgeon is so dreamy. I mean he fractures me."

113   "If you can forget Mr. Pidgeon for a moment," I said coldly, "I would like to point out that the statement is a fallacy. Maybe Madame Curie would have discovered radium at some later date. Maybe somebody else would have discovered it. Maybe any number of things would have happened. You can't start with a hypothesis that is not true and then draw any supportable conclusions from it."

114   "They ought to put Walter Pidgeon in more pictures," said Polly. "I hardly ever see him any more."

115   One more chance, I decided. But just one more. There is a limit to what flesh and blood can bear. "The next fallacy is called Poisoning the Well."

116   "How cute!" she gurgled.

117   "Two men are having a debate. The first one gets up and says, 'My opponent is a notorious liar. You can't believe a word that he is going to say.' . . . Now, Polly, think. Think hard. What's wrong?"

118   I watched her closely as she knit her creamy brow in concentration. Suddenly, a glimmer of intelligence—the first I had seen—came into her eyes. "It's not fair," she said with indignation. "It's not a bit fair. What chance has the second man got if the first man calls him a liar before he even begins talking?"

119   "Right!" I cried exultantly. "One hundred percent right. It's not fair. The first man has *poisoned the well* before anybody could drink from it. He has hamstrung his opponent before he could even start. . . . Polly, I'm proud of you."

120   "Pshaw," she murmured, blushing with pleasure.

121   "You see, my dear, these things aren't so hard. All you have to do is concentrate. Think—examine—evaluate. Come now, let's review everything we have learned."

122   "Fire away," she said with an airy wave of her hand.

123   Heartened by the knowledge that Polly was not altogether a cretin, I began a long, patient review of all I had told her. Over and over and over again I cited instances, pointed out flaws, kept hammering away without let-up. It was like digging a tunnel. At first everything was work, sweat, and darkness. I had no idea when I would reach the light, or even *if* I would. But I persisted. I pounded and clawed and scraped, and finally I was rewarded. I saw a chink of light. And then the chink got bigger and the sun came pouring in and all was bright.

124   Five grueling nights this took, but it was worth it. I had made a logician out of Polly; I had taught her to think. My job was done. She was worthy of me at last. She was a fit wife for me, a proper hostess for my many mansions, a suitable mother for my well-heeled children.

125   It must not be thought that I was without love for this girl. Quite the contrary. Just as Pygmalion loved the perfect woman he had fashioned, so I loved mine. I determined to acquaint her with my feelings at our very next meeting. The time had come to change our relationship from academic to romantic.

"Polly," I said when next we sat beneath our oak, "tonight we will not discuss fallacies." 126

"Aw, gee," she said, disappointed. 127

"My dear," I said, favoring her with a smile, "we have now spent five evenings together. We have gotten along splendidly. It is clear that we are well matched." 128

"Hasty Generalization," said Polly brightly. 129

"I beg your pardon," said I. 130

"Hasty Generalization," she repeated. "How can you say that we are well matched on the basis of only five dates?" 131

I chuckled with amusement. The dear child had learned her lessons well. "My dear," I said, patting her hand in a tolerant manner, "five dates is plenty. After all, you don't have to eat a whole cake to know it's good." 132

"False Analogy," said Polly promptly. "I'm not a cake. I'm a girl." 133

I chuckled with somewhat less amusement. The dear child had learned her lessons perhaps too well. I decided to change tactics. Obviously the best approach was a simple, strong, direct declaration of love. I paused for a moment while my massive brain chose the proper words. Then I began: 134

"Polly, I love you. You are the whole world to me, and the moon and the stars and the constellations of outer space. Please, my darling, say that you will go steady with me, for if you will not, life will be meaningless. I will languish. I will refuse my meals. I will wander the face of the earth, a shambling, hollow-eyed hulk." 135

There, I thought, folding my arms, that ought to do it. 136

"Ad Misericordiam," said Polly. 137

I ground my teeth. I was not Pygmalion; I was Frankenstein, and my monster had me by the throat. Frantically I fought back the tide of panic surging through me. At all costs I had to keep cool. 138

"Well, Polly," I said, forcing a smile, "you certainly have learned your fallacies." 139

"You're darn right," she said with a vigorous nod. 140

"And who taught them to you, Polly?" 141

"You did." 142

"That's right. So you do owe me something, don't you, my dear? If I hadn't come along you never would have learned about fallacies." 143

"Hypothesis Contrary to Fact," she said instantly. 144

I dashed perspiration from my brow. "Polly," I croaked, "you mustn't take all these things so literally. I mean this is just classroom stuff. You know that the things you learn in school don't have anything to do with life." 145

"Dicto Simpliciter," she said, wagging her finger at me playfully. 146

That did it. I leaped to me feet, bellowing like a bull. "Will you or will you not go steady with me?" 147

"I will not," she replied. 148

"Why not?" I demanded. 149

"Because this afternoon I promised Petey Burch that I would go steady with him." 150

151   I reeled back, overcome with the infamy of it. After he promised, after he made a deal, after he shook my hand! "The rat!" I shrieked, kicking up great chunks of turf. "You can't go with him, Polly. He's a liar. He's a cheat. He's a rat."

152   "Poisoning the Well," said Polly, "and stop shouting. I think shouting must be a fallacy too."

153   With an immense effort of will, I modulated my voice. "All right," I said. "You're a logician, Let's look at this thing logically. How could you choose Petey Burch over me? Look at me—a brilliant student, a tremendous intellectual, a man with an assured future. Look at Petey—a knothead, a jitterbug, a guy who'll never know where his next meal is coming from. Can you give me one logical reason why you should go steady with Petey Burch?"

154   "I certainly can," declared Polly. "He's got a raccoon coat."

Questions on Content

1. What is the cause of Petey Burch's distress at the beginning of the story?
2. What does the narrator, Dobie Gillis, demand in return for the raccoon coat in his father's attic?
3. What does Dobie feel he must do to make Polly Espy a worthy mate? How does he go about repairing her deficiencies?
4. Which forms of logical fallacy does Dobie teach Polly to recognize?
5. Why does Polly dump Dobie and return to Petey Burch?

Questions on Thesis, Purpose, and Structure

1. In the "Author's Note" Shulman claims that "Love is a Fallacy" should be called an essay. What do you think? What argument does it develop? Does it cite sufficient instances? What conclusion is reached? Why do you suppose that Shulman doesn't want to call it a short story?
2. Compare the narrator with his roommate Petey Burch. What are the obvious flaws in the character of each? Why does Shulman make such a point of telling us that Petey is a faddist in the opening paragraphs?
3. Why does Dobie teach Polly to recognize logical fallacies? What makes his success in teaching her to reason so ironic?
4. What thematic point does Shulman make about logic and love?
5. Shulman gives textbook definitions of most of the major forms of logical fallacy. How does he make that information entertaining? How does he also manage to give a persuasive purpose to this short story?

Questions on Style and Diction

1. Find the following words in the story and determine their definitions in context: flaccid (paragraph 1); pedantic (paragraph 3); perspicacious (paragraph 4); acme (paragraph 5); waif (paragraph 50); trysting (paragraph 64); contritely (paragraph 83); infamy (paragraph 151); modulated (paragraph 153).
2. What are the characteristics of collegiate slang in the late 1940s as exemplified in this story? How does Shulman's use of slang add to the humor and effectiveness of the story?
3. Shulman uses a number of allusions in this story. For example, he alludes to

Charles Lamb (paragraph 1), Carlyle and Ruskin (paragraph 2), the Charleston (paragraph 11), Madame Curie (paragraph 111), Pygmalion (paragraph 125), and Frankenstein (paragraph 138). Are these allusions sufficiently clear and understandable? Examine a few of them with care. What do they add to the paragraphs in which they occur?

Ideas for Essays

1. Writers today are much more aware of potentially sexist language than they were in 1951 when Shulman published this story. Is Shulman's story offensively sexist? Take a stand on this question, and argue your position with as much logic and passion as you can muster.
2. Dobie Gillis attempted to determine the characteristics of an ideal wife inductively by observing the wives of successful young lawyers. If you feel that his method was flawed, write an essay in which you describe a better method of discovering the characteristics of an ideal spouse.
3. Dobie Gillis felt that his wife must have three characteristics: beauty, graciousness, and intelligence. What characteristics do you believe an ideal spouse should have? Write an essay in which you create a persuasive argument for a particular set of characteristics.

Harrison Bergeron
Kurt Vonnegut, Jr.

Kurt Vonnegut, Jr. (1922–   ) was born and raised in Indianapolis, Indiana. Following a year at Cornell University, Vonnegut joined the Army and was shipped overseas where he witnessed at first hand the devastating firebombing of Dresden in February 1945—an experience that provided the subject matter for his novel *Slaughterhouse-Five* (1969). Since 1950, when he left the business world to become a full-time writer, Vonnegut has clearly established himself as one of America's most important and popular fiction writers. Vonnegut's witty novels and stories display his interest in science fiction, his hatred of war, and his insistence on the need to resist the dehumanizing pressures of technology. In addition to *Slaughterhouse-Five*, the most significant of Vonnegut's novels are *Player Piano* (1952), *Welcome to the Monkey House* (1968), and *Breakfast of Champions* (1973). The satiric humor of "Harrison Bergeron" (1961) is characteristic of Vonnegut's bemused pessimism about humanity. Note particularly Vonnegut's sharp criticism of the American desire not just for equality "before God and the law," but for equality "every which way."

The year was 2081, and everybody was finally equal. They weren't only 1 equal before God and the law. They were equal every which way. Nobody was smarter than anybody else. Nobody was better looking than anybody else. Nobody was stronger or quicker than anybody else. All this equality was due to the 211th, 212th, and 213th Amendments to the Constitution, and to the unceasing vigilance of agents of the United States Handicapper General.

2   Some things about living still weren't quite right, though. April, for instance, still drove people crazy by not being springtime. And it was in that clammy month that the H-G men took George and Hazel Bergeron's fourteen-year-old son, Harrison, away.

3   It was tragic, all right, but George and Hazel couldn't think about it very hard. Hazel had a perfectly average intelligence, which meant she couldn't think about anything except in short bursts. And George, while his intelligence was way above normal, had a little mental handicap radio in his ear. He was required by law to wear it at all times. It was turned to a government transmitter. Every twenty seconds or so, the transmitter would send out some sharp noise to keep people like George from taking unfair advantage of their brains.

4   George and Hazel were watching television. There were tears on Hazel's cheeks, but she'd forgotten for the moment what they were about.

5   On the television screen were ballerinas.

6   A buzzer sounded in George's head. His thoughts fled in panic, like bandits from a burglar alarm.

7   "That was a real pretty dance, that dance they just did," said Hazel.

8   "Huh?" said George.

9   "That dance—it was nice," said Hazel.

10   "Yup," said George. He tried to think a little about the ballerinas. They weren't really very good—no better than anybody else would have been, anyway. They were burdened with sashweights and bags of bird-shot, and their faces were masked, so that no one, seeing a free and graceful gesture or a pretty face, would feel like something the cat drug in. George was toying with the vague notion that maybe dancers shouldn't be handicapped. But he didn't get very far with it before another noise in his ear radio scattered his thoughts.

11   George winced. So did two out of the eight ballerinas.

12   Hazel saw him wince. Having no mental handicap herself, she had to ask George what the latest sound had been.

13   "Sounded like somebody hitting a milk bottle with a ball peen hammer," said George.

14   "I'd think it would be real interesting, hearing all the different sounds," said Hazel, a little envious. "All the things they think up."

15   "Um," said George.

16   "Only, if I was Handicapper General, you know what I would do?" said Hazel. Hazel, as a matter of fact, bore a strong resemblance to the Handicapper General, a woman named Diana Moon Glampers. "If I was Diana Moon Glampers," said Hazel, "I'd have chimes on Sunday—just chimes. Kind of in honor of religion."

17   "I could think, if it was just chimes," said George.

18   "Well—maybe make 'em real loud," said Hazel. "I think I'd make a good Handicapper General."

19   "Good as anybody else," said George.

"Who knows better'n I do what normal is?" said Hazel.   20

"Right," said George. He began to think glimmeringly about his   21
abnormal son who was now in jail, about Harrison, but a twenty-one-gun
salute in his head stopped that.

"Boy!" said Hazel, "that was a doozy, wasn't it?"   22

It was such a doozy that George was white and trembling, and tears   23
stood on the rims of his red eyes. Two of the eight ballerinas had
collapsed to the studio floor, were holding their temples.

"All of a sudden you look so tired," said Hazel. "Why don't you   24
stretch out on the sofa, so's you can rest your handicap bag on the
pillows, honeybunch." She was referring to the forty-seven pounds of
birdshot in a canvas bag, which was padlocked around George's neck.
"Go on and rest the bag for a little while," she said. "I don't care if
you're not equal to me for a while."

George weighed the bag with his hands. "I don't mind it," he said,   25
"I don't notice it any more. It's just a part of me."

"You been so tired lately—kind of wore out," said Hazel. "If there   26
was just some way we could make a little hole in the bottom of the bag,
and just take out a few of them lead balls. Just a few."

"Two years in prison and two thousand dollars fine for every ball I   27
took out." said George. "I don't call that a bargain."

"If you could take a few out when you came home from work," said   28
Hazel. "I mean—you don't compete with anybody around here. You
just set around."

"If I tried to get away with it," said George, "then other people'd   29
get away with it—and pretty soon we'd be right back to the dark ages
again, with everybody competing against everybody else. You wouldn't
like that, would you?"

"I'd hate it," said Hazel.   30

"There you are," said George. "The minute people start cheating on   31
laws, what do you think happens to society?"

If Hazel hadn't been able to come up with an answer to this ques-   32
tion, George couldn't have supplied one. A siren was going off in his
head.

"Reckon it'd fall all apart," said Hazel.   33

"What would?" said George blankly.   34

"Society," said Hazel uncertainly. "Wasn't that what you just said?"   35

"Who knows?" said George.   36

The television program was suddenly interrupted for a news bulle-   37
tin. It wasn't clear at first as to what the bulletin was about, since the
announcer like all announcers, had a serious speech impediment. For
about half a minute, and in a state of high excitement, the announcer
tried to say, "Ladies and gentlemen—"

He finally gave up, handed the bulletin to a ballerina to read.   38

"That's all right—" Hazel said of the announcer, "he tried. That's   39
the big thing. He tried to do the best he could with what God gave him.
He should get a nice raise for trying so hard."

"Ladies and gentlemen—" said the ballerina, reading the bulletin.   40
She must have been extraordinarily beautiful, because the mask she

wore was hideous. And it was easy to see that she was the strongest and most graceful of all the dancers, for her handicap bags were as big as those worn by two-hundred-pound men.

41   And she had to apologize at once for her voice, which was a very unfair voice for a woman to use. Her voice was a warm, luminous, timeless melody. "Excuse me —" she said, and she began again, making her voice absolutely uncompetitive.

42   "Harrison Bergeron, age fourteen," she said in a grackle squawk, "has just escaped from jail, where he was held on suspicion of plotting to overthrow the government. He is a genius and an athlete, is under-handicapped, and should be regarded as extremely dangerous."

43   A police photograph of Harrison Bergeron was flashed on the screen upside down, then sideways, upside down again, then right side up. The picture showed the full length of Harrison against a background calibrated in feet and inches. He was exactly seven feet tall.

44   The rest of Harrison's appearance was Halloween and hardware. Nobody had ever born heavier handicaps. He had outgrown hindrances faster than the H-G men could think them up. Instead of a little ear radio for a mental handicap, he wore a tremendous pair of earphones, and spectacles with thick wavy lenses. The spectacles were intended to make him not only half blind, but to give him whanging headaches besides.

45   Scrap metal was hung all over him. Ordinarily, there was a certain symmetry, a military neatness to the handicaps issued to strong people, but Harrison looked like a walking junkyard. In the race of life, Harrison carried three hundred pounds.

46   And to offset his good looks, the H-G men required that he wear at all times a red rubber ball for a nose, keep his eyebrows shaved off, and cover his even white teeth with black caps at snaggle-tooth random.

47   "If you see this boy," said the ballerina, "do not — I repeat, do not — try to reason with him."

48   There was a shriek of a door being torn from its hinges.

49   Screams and barking cries of consternation came from the television set. The photograph of Harrison Bergeron on the screen jumped again and again, as though dancing to the tune of an earthquake.

50   George Bergeron correctly identified the earthquake, and well he might have — for many was the time his own home had danced to the same crashing tune. "My God —" said George, "that must be Harrison!"

51   The realization was blasted from his mind instantly by the sound of an automobile collision in his head.

52   When George could open his eyes again, the photograph of Harrison was gone. A living, breathing Harrison filled the screen.

53   Clanking, clownish, and huge, Harrison stood in the center of the studio. The knob of the uprooted studio door was still in his hand. Ballerinas, technicians, musicians, and announcers cowered on their knees before him, expecting to die.

54   "I am the Emperor!" cried Harrison. "Do you hear! I am the Emperor! Everybody must do what I say at once!" He stamped his foot and the studio shook.

"Even as I stand here—" he bellowed, "crippled, hobbled,   55
sickened—I am a greater ruler than any man who ever lived! Now watch
me become what I *can* become!"

Harrison tore the straps of his handicap harness like wet tissue   56
paper, tore straps guaranteed to support five thousand pounds.

Harrison's scrap-iron handicaps crashed to the floor.   57

Harrison thrust his thumbs under the bar of the padlock that secured   58
his head harness. The bar snapped like celery. Harrison smashed his
headphones and spectacles against the wall.

He flung away his rubber-ball nose, revealed a man that would have   59
awed Thor, the god of thunder.

"I shall now select my Empress!" he said, looking down on the   60
cowering people. "Let the first woman who dares rise to her feet claim
her mate and her throne!"

A moment passed, and then a ballerina arose, swaying like a willow.   61

Harrison plucked the mental handicap from her ear, snapped off her   62
physical handicaps with marvelous delicacy. Last of all, he removed her
mask.

She was blindingly beautiful.   63

"Now—" said Harrison, taking her hand, "shall we show the peo-   64
ple the meaning of the word dance? Music!" he commanded.

The musicians scrambled back into their chairs, and Harrison   65
stripped them of their handicaps, too. "Play your best," he told them,
"and I'll make you barons and dukes and earls."

The music began. It was normal at first—cheap, silly, false. But   66
Harrison snatched two musicians from their chairs, waved them like
batons as he sang the music as he wanted it played. He slammed them
back into their chairs.

The music began again and was much improved.   67

Harrison and his Empress merely listened to the music for a while   68
—listened gravely, as though synchronizing their heartbeats with it.

They shifted their weights to their toes.   69

Harrison placed his big hands on the girl's tiny waist, letting her   70
sense the weightlessness that would soon be hers.

And then in an explosion of joy and grace, into the air they sprang!   71

Not only were the laws of the land abandoned, but the law of gravity   72
and the laws of motion as well.

They reeled, whirled, swiveled, flounced, capered, gamboled, and   73
spun.

They leaped like deer on the moon.   74

The studio ceiling was thirty feet high, but each leap brought the   75
dancers nearer to it.

It became their obvious intention to kiss the ceiling.   76

They kissed it.   77

And then, neutralizing gravity with love and pure will, they re-   78
mained suspended in air inches below the ceiling, and they kissed each
other for a long, long time.

It was then that Diana Moon Glampers, the Handicapper General,   79
came into the studio with a double-barreled ten-gauge shotgun. She

fired twice, and the Emperor and the Empress were dead before they hit the floor.

80   Diana Moon Glampers loaded the gun again. She aimed it at the musicians and told them they had ten seconds to get their handicaps back on.

81   It was then that the Bergerons' television tube burned out.

82   Hazel turned to comment about the blackout to George. But George had gone out into the kitchen for a can of beer.

83   George came back in with the beer, paused while a handicap signal shook him up. And then he sat down again.

84   "You been crying?" he said to Hazel.

85   "Yup," she said.

86   "What about?" he said.

87   "I forget," she said. "Something real sad on television."

88   "What was it?" he said.

89   "It's all kind of mixed up in my mind," said Hazel.

90   "Forget sad things," said George.

91   "I always do," said Hazel.

92   "That's my girl," said George. He winced. There was the sound of a riveting gun in his head.

93   "Gee—I could tell that one was a doozy," said Hazel.

94   "You can say that again," said George.

95   "Gee—" said Hazel, "I could tell that one was a doozy."

Questions on Content

1. Why is the job of the Handicapper General so important in the year 2081?
2. What makes George and Hazel equal in intelligence?
3. What handicaps must Harrison wear?
4. What happens when Harrison removes his own handicaps and those of the ballerina and musicians?
5. What happens to Harrison in the end? Why don't his parents seem to comprehend what has happened?

Questions on Thesis, Purpose, and Structure

1. According to Vonnegut, what is wrong with attempting to make everyone equal "every which way"? What point does Vonnegut make through this story about the desire for equality?
2. When Harrison rebels, we get a glimpse of the kind of society *he* would create. Describe that society. Do you think that Vonnegut endorses it? Why do you think that Vonnegut sets up that particular alternative instead of one that readers might find more attractive?
3. Discuss the combination of purposes in this story. What makes it so entertaining? What makes it so persuasive? Is it informative?

Questions on Style and Diction

1. Look for instances of exaggeration or overstatement in this story. What effects are created by Vonnegut's frequent use of exaggeration and overstatement?
2. What different characteristics of speech do you find in Hazel, George, and

Harrison? Why do you think that Vonnegut makes them speak in different ways?

Ideas for Essays

1. Does American society today in any way resemble the society in Vonnegut's story? If you think it does, write an essay in which you describe the handicaps and fetters that hold back people of exceptional ability.
2. An alternative to the equal society of "Harrison Bergeron" might be a society in which "survival of the fittest" is not only tolerated but even mandated by law. Write an essay or short story in which you describe this nightmarish alternative.

"PACs—Consider the Alternatives"

As you have probably noticed throughout this text, many companies turn their advertisements into brief editorials on topics of particular concern in their industry. Such is the case with the advertisement reproduced here. "PACs— Consider the alternatives" is a response to the spate of articles against Political Action Committees that appears in the media every election year. Because many (although by no means all) of these PACs represent business interests, Mobil's support for them is understandable. Note how much effort goes into refuting the opposition in this advertisement. Both past practices and future alternatives are examined and determined to be less desirable than the status quo.

PACs—Consider the alternatives

Here we are, nearly six months after the 1982 Congressional elections, and the media are still exercised over the so-called undue influence of Political Action Committees. And, with over 18 months before the next election, they worry that Congress will be even more "corrupted" in the 1984 balloting.

As we pointed out in this space last year, PACs are truly the voice of the people—people who band together to make their electoral choices more emphatic by pooling their funds in support of one or more candidates. They do it through corporate or labor PACs, through PACs representing their views as environmentalists, as professionals, or as enthusiasts in some favorite pastime. More importantly, we pointed out that no PAC, whatever its sponsorship, can contribute more than $5,000 to any one Congressional candidate in a single election, and that's hardly enough to corrupt a legislator, even if he or she were disposed to be corrupted.

In view of the continuing uproar about PACs, let's consider the alternatives. For background, we're indebted to an article by Michael Malbin in *Public Opinion* magazine, which described past political financing.

■ In the 1790s, Aaron Burr set up a state bank for the primary purpose of lending mortgage money to Democrats. In those days, only property owners could vote, and most land owners were Federalists. The idea was to create more Democratic voters.

■ Early in the nineteenth century, it was general practice to solicit kickbacks from politically appointed government employees to fatten campaign treasuries. The Civil Service Reform Act of 1883 closed off this source of funds.

■ During the 1896 campaign, Mark Hanna, chairman of the Republican National Committee, saw nothing wrong with levying a regular assessment on all large businesses, a practice that endowed President McKinley with more than $6 million in campaign money. The Tillman Act of 1907 put a stop to that.

Obviously, anyone determined to channel money to political candidates can find a way, and some ways are more nefarious than others. That's why we believe PACs—out front and clearly identifiable—are an excellent way to help finance our political process. This is particularly true when no one party label can meet the needs of the myriad constituencies which now contribute to more than 3,100 PACs. These contributions are made voluntarily by employees, union members, and others (corporations and labor unions are prohibited by law from contributing), and the PACs report their finances and contributions to the Federal Elections Commission, as do the candidates who receive them.

The *Public Opinion* article said it well: "As people learn that organizing makes them more effective politically, it becomes very hard under the First Amendment to return to an earlier day. The genie cannot be forced back into the bottle."

The alternative to PACs most frequently proposed is public campaign financing, or equal allocations to all candidates from federal, tax-collected funds. Four flaws in this idea come readily to mind.

■ It would tax voters without giving them the right to name the candidate for whom their dollars are intended.

■ It would give an automatic edge to incumbents—good, bad, or indifferent—running for reelection. Challengers are usually not as well known as incumbents and must outspend incumbents just to put themselves on the map.

■ A system of equal allocations would create geographic inequities. It costs much more to campaign in an urban district than in a rural area, what with prevalent advertising and TV commercial rates in these different markets.

■ Public financing would add another cost item to the federal budget, since we must presume, in all fairness, that taxpayers' contributions would not be used to pay bureaucrats for administering collections and distributions.

The present system retains the concept of voluntary support with disclosure—a concept which took two centuries to develop. Nothing that has been suggested to take its place would improve the electoral process and any change would, in all likelihood, reduce citizen participation.

With elections as with most things, if it isn't broken, don't fix it.

Ideas for Discussion and Writing

1. This combination of an advertisement and an editorial—sometimes called an "advertorial"—uses a number of methods of development. Where and for what purpose does it use the following: examples, causal analysis, comparison/contrast?
2. Clearly, the primary intent of this advertisement is to persuade the reader to support the current laws governing PACs. Are you persuaded? Why or why not?
3. Is the advertisement informative and entertaining as well as persuasive? Explain.
4. What do *you* think about Political Action Committees? Evaluate the arguments raised in this advertisement. Are the arguments *against* PACs presented in sufficient detail? What are those arguments?
5. Is this advertisement just a public-spirited and unselfish expression of an opinion by the Mobil Corporation, or could the company benefit in some way through the preservation of PACs? Explain your views.

PART IV

FURTHER READING
Paired Essays on
Controversial Issues

Chapter 15

LAKE POWELL
Paradise or Paradise Lost?

Glen Canyon's Azure Jewel
L. I. Wilson

In 1956, amid much controversy, Congress authorized the construction of the Glen Canyon Dam on the Colorado River at Page, Arizona. The dam was finally completed in 1964, and today Lake Powell stretches for 186 miles northeast through Arizona and into Utah. L. I. Wilson's essay in praise of Lake Powell was published in the *Saturday Evening Post* in March of 1980.

1 The silence is all around, wrapped in darkness and surrounded with mystery. No creatures are heard rustling and scurrying in the night or howling plaintive, lonely calls. No wind is whispering softly as it caresses the leaves on trees or roaring thunderously in anger as it tears them loose and sends them swirling away. There is no lapping of water against the walls of sandstone cliffs worn alternately smooth and ragged by nature's ravishes or against the sides of volcanic-rock islands protruding from the water's depths. There is only stillness, quiet, peace and the beauty of Lake Powell waiting to be discovered by the dawn.

2 Mention Lake Powell to most Americans and they do not know what it is or where it is. That is not surprising because the lake is only 16 years old, but it is a body of lucent water that stretches 186 miles northeast from the Glen Canyon Dam at Page, Arizona, to a point in Utah just below the juncture of Highway 95 and the Colorado River. It has 1,900 miles of shoreline and 91 side canyons, and its 27 million acre-feet of cool crystallinity are fed from the runoff of snow-covered Wyoming, Utah and Colorado mountains. It is one of the largest man-made lakes in North America, vying only with Lake Mead, whose approximately 29 million acre-feet of water are held back by Hoover Dam.

3 Formed by the waters of the Colorado River, Lake Powell is a haven of peace, quiet and solitude. It's an escape from the world, a place for rest and recreation surrounded by some of the most beautiful scenery on earth. It is an azure jewel in a free-form setting and it is the perfect spot for a vacation.

4   Much debate preceded authorization for construction of the dam in 1956 because it was feared the rising water would not only cover some of the historic locations on the Colorado River but would also destroy the beauty of Glen Canyon. But the stated purpose for building it was to create a reservoir to store water, control floods and sediment, conserve fish and wildlife, create recreational areas and produce electrical energy.

5   There is no doubt that a few historic locations — like the spot where Padres Dominguez and Escalante in 1776 finally succeeded in crossing the Colorado River — are indeed under water, but the area created can be enjoyed by more people than the canyon alone ever could accommodate. In addition, the bright blue water of the lake has added a contrast to the brick-red canyon walls that greatly enhances their beauty, and careful supervision by the park service ensures that nature's ecological and environmental controls continue.

6   Nor has the history of the area been disregarded, for the water covering the site of "The Crossing of the Fathers" has been named Padre Bay, and other locations around the lake carry the names of historic sites and persons. The man who explored the canyon has been memorialized in the name of the lake itself: Major John Wesley Powell, a Civil War veteran who lost an arm at the battle of Shiloh and a self-taught naturalist and early advocate of water reclamation, led the first successful boat expeditions down the turbulent Colorado River and through the Grand Canyon.

7   Lake Powell is a fisherman's paradise. At dawn and at dusk when insects skim the lake's surface, numerous varieties of fish leave the deeper water and the crevices and ledges of the steep underwater canyon walls and rise to the surface to feed. They may be seen in shimmering beauty as they jump for insects or swim casually through the translucent water. Stocked by the National Park Service, the lake contains striped and large-mouth bass, rainbow trout and black crappie, which live and breed in its depths along with the Colorado River's native walleye and northern pike, channel catfish, brown trout, bluegill and, of course, the universal carp.

8   Despite the complete stillness on the lake at certain times, the surrounding area is not devoid of life. Both native and migratory birds live in the trees and cliffs that line Lake Powell. Sandpipers populate the sandy beaches and sand bars and waterfowl are at home on the lake itself. On the shores, in the valleys and on the cliffs and mesas live deer, foxes, coyotes, bobcats, rabbits, squirrels, rats and mice. Even beaver dams are sometimes found along the streams that feed into the lake. Hikers along the shores can catch a whiff of a skunk's "perfume" or, in more remote areas, a quick glimpse of a bighorn sheep as it moves quickly and gracefully at seemingly unscalable heights. A remote hidden cave or rock shelter might house a mountain lion, and on the lake it is not uncommon for a bat to fly through the open window of a houseboat, searching for a midnight feast of flying insects but always as anxious to leave the houseboat as its occupants are for him to go.

9   Viewed from an airplane, the area surrounding Lake Powell appears barren and nonproductive, but not so the shores and canyons as they are

seen from the lake. Against the sweeping vistas of brick-red sandstone cliffs, which are reflected in bobbing ripples of red on the azure water, may be seen the glory of desert flora. The cactus and yucca display their flowers or their fruit and at the higher elevations are junipers and piñons. Bordering the lake and the many streams that lead into it are cottonwoods, tamarisks, poplars and willows, and in the spring wild flowers cover the beaches with masses of yellow, red, pink, lavender and purple. On the canyon walls, lichens form streaks and designs in white, black, gray, yellow, orange and green.

From the lake, the cliffs take on a beauty of form and color that awes   10
the beholder. Layer upon layer of varicolored strata — the orange and red-brown of Navajo sandstone, the pinks and beiges of carmel formation and the grays and blacks of tropic shale — indicate ancient geological origins. Volcanic plugs, or necks, left after the softer outer layers of volcanic cones have eroded away, give evidence of the last volcanic uplift millions of years ago and stand out as prehistoric forms.

Several types of boats may be found on the lake, some privately   11
owned and many that can be rented. There are motor boats, cruisers, sailboats, kayaks and canoes. Water-skiing is a popular sport on the smooth, clear water of the bays, and scuba divers can swim along with the abundant and varied fish life, marvel at the beauty of underwater canyon walls and formations and even explore some ancient Indian ruins which now are below the surface. Becoming more and more popular are the houseboats which can be docked on the sandy beaches for overnight stays. Lying on the deck of a houseboat and looking deep into the blackness of a nighttime sky which stretches endlessly through the universe, enhancing the brilliance of a billion stars or more, is a rare and wondrous experience.

By living aboard a houseboat for a week or two and towing a   12
motorboat behind, a vacationer can fully enjoy the Lake Powell attractions. A houseboat can be anchored on a beach or a sand bar and the motorboat used for fishing or to explore passageways and canyons that are too narrow to accommodate the larger vessel. Those who do not own or desire to rent a boat can take scenic cruises aboard tour boats such as the Canyon King, a paddle-wheel river boat. Guided charters are available for fishing trips.

Sightseers and photographers should not miss the Rainbow Bridge   13
National Monument, which is a short hike from a dock near the Rainbow Marina. This stone bridge is the largest natural stone span on earth and, like the Grand Canyon, has been called one of the seven natural wonders of the world. Against a salmon-colored background, variegated streaks in shades of red and brown lend credence to the name given it by the Indians: *Nonnezoshi* or "Rainbow Turned to Stone." There are only two ways to reach the bridge — by boat or by an arduous and difficult 26-mile round-trip hike from the base of Navajo Mountain. There are scenic flights, however, which afford breath-taking views from the air.

Popular side attractions in the Lake Powell area are the two exciting   14
Colorado River raft expeditions below the lake. The one-day raft expedition starts with a bus trip through a two-mile tunnel to the base of Glen

Canyon Dam. From there, a five-hour rubber raft trip takes the "river-runner," floating downstream between majestic sandstone cliffs and past green, wooded glens. There are stops for lunch and for short hikes to see ancient Indian petroglyphs.

15   For a real feeling of exploration, however, and a small sampling of the experiences of John Wesley Powell and his companions in their expeditions down the Colorado River, nothing can compare with the eight-day Grand Canyon rubber raft trip. So popular is this thrilling expedition that reservations must be made as much as a year in advance.

16   It is for the average vacationer; however, that a sojourn at Lake Powell can provide the respite he has looked forward to and planned all year long. He can immerse himself in quiet, peaceful beauty far from the demands of a business world and the pollution, noise and frustrations of an everyday urban life. He can rest on the deck of a houseboat and feel the gentle caress of a cool evening breeze. He can look out over the lake and watch ripples of deep blue water reflect, on their crests, the dancing images of age-old sandstone cliffs or the spreading hues of a western sunset. He can breathe the clean, pure air and he can listen to the splashing of the fish he may catch — come the next day's dawn.

The Damnation of a Canyon
Edward Abbey

Edward Abbey (1927 –   ) was born in Home, Pennsylvania, and earned two degrees at the University of New Mexico. He developed his love for the wilderness and his concern over the way in which the forces of civilization threaten the environment during the fifteen years that he spent as a park ranger and fire lookout for the National Park Service in the Southwest. Abbey —who has been described as "a living American artifact, part maverick, part pastoral extremist, part semi-hermit, part latter-day Jeremiah Johnson" — has forcefully articulated his preservationist ethic in such books as *Desert Solitaire* (1968), *The Journey Home: Some Words in Defense of the American West* (1977), *Abbey's Road* (1979), *Down the River* (1982), and *Beyond the Wall: Essays from the Outside* (1984). "The Damnation of a Canyon" from the last of these books is an impassioned attack on the creation of reservoirs by damming free-flowing rivers. Note the contrasts between the natural life in the canyon before and after construction of the dam.

1   There was a time when, in my search for essences, I concluded that the canyonland country has no heart. I was wrong. The canyonlands did have a heart, a living heart, and that heart was Glen Canyon and the golden, flowing Colorado River.

2   In the summer of 1959 a friend and I made a float trip in little

rubber rafts down through the length of Glen Canyon, starting at Hite and getting off the river near Gunsight Butte—The Crossing of the Fathers. In this voyage of some 150 miles and ten days our only motive power, and all that we needed, was the current of the Colorado River.

In the summer and fall of 1967 I worked as a seasonal park ranger at the new Glen Canyon National Recreation Area. During my five-month tour of duty I worked at the main marina and headquarters area called Wahweap, at Bullfrog Basin toward the upper end of the reservoir, and finally at Lee's Ferry downriver from Glen Canyon Dam. In a number of powerboat tours I was privileged to see almost all of our nation's newest, biggest and most impressive "recreational facility." 3

Having thus seen Glen Canyon both before and after what we may fairly call its damnation, I feel that I am in a position to evaluate the transformation of the region caused by construction of the dam. I have had the unique opportunity to observe firsthand some of the differences between the environment of a free river and a power-plant reservoir. 4

One should admit at the outset to a certain bias. Indeed I am a "butterfly chaser, googly eyed bleeding heart and wild conservative." I take a dim view of dams; I find it hard to learn to love cement; I am poorly impressed by concrete aggregates and statistics in the cubic tons. But in this weakness I am not alone, for I belong to that ever-growing number of Americans, probably a good majority now, who have become aware that a fully industrialized, thoroughly urbanized, elegantly computerized social system is not suitable for human habitation. Great for machines, yes. But unfit for people. 5

Lake Powell, formed by Glen Canyon Dam, is not a lake. It is a reservoir, with a constantly fluctuating water level—more like a bathtub that is never drained than a true lake. As at Hoover (or Boulder) Dam, the sole practical function of this impounded water is to drive the turbines that generate electricity in the powerhouse at the base of the dam. Recreational benefits were of secondary importance in the minds of those who conceived and built this dam. As a result the volume of water in the reservoir is continually being increased or decreased according to the requirements of the Basin States Compact and the power-grid system of which Glen Canyon Dam is a component. 6

The rising and falling water level entails various consequences. One of the most obvious, well known to all who have seen Lake Mead, is the "bathtub ring" left on the canyon walls after each drawdown of water, or what rangers at Glen Canyon call the Bathtub Formation. This phenomenon is perhaps of no more than aesthetic importance; yet it is sufficient to dispel any illusion one might have, in contemplating the scene, that you are looking upon a natural lake. 7

Of much more significance is the fact that plant life, because of the unstable water line, cannot establish itself on the shores of the reservoir. When the water is low, plant life dies of thirst; when high, it is drowned. Much of the shoreline of the reservoir consists of near perpendicular sandstone bluffs, where very little flora ever did or ever could subsist, but the remainder includes bays, coves, sloping hills and the many side canyons, where the original plant life has been drowned and new plant 8 life cannot get a foothold. And of course where there is little or no plant life there is little or no animal life.

9   The utter barrenness of the reservoir shoreline recalls by contrast the aspect of things before the dam, when Glen Canyon formed the course of the untamed Colorado. Then we had a wild and flowing river lined by boulder-strewn shores, sandy beaches, thickets of tamarisk and willow, and glades of cottonwoods.

10   The thickets teemed with songbirds: vireos, warblers, mockingbirds and thrushes. On the open beaches were killdeer, sandpipers, herons, ibises, egrets. Living in grottoes in the canyon walls were swallows, swifts, hawks, wrens and owls. Beaver were common if not abundant: not an evening would pass, in drifting down the river, that we did not see them or at least hear the whack of their flat tails on the water. Above the river shores were the great recessed alcoves where water seeped from the sandstone, nourishing the semitropical hanging gardens of orchid, ivy and columbine, with their associated swarms of insects and birdlife.

11   Up most of the side canyons, before damnation, there were springs, sometimes flowing streams, waterfalls and plunge pools — the kind of marvels you can now find only in such small-scale remnants of Glen Canyon as the Escalante area. In the rich flora of these laterals the larger mammals — mule deer, coyote, bobcat, ring-tailed cat, gray fox, kit fox, skunk, badger and others — found a home. When the river was dammed almost all of these things were lost. Crowded out — or drowned and buried under mud.

12   The difference between the present reservoir, with its silent sterile shores and debris-choked side canyons, and the original Glen Canyon, is the difference between death and life. Glen Canyon was alive. Lake Powell is a graveyard.

13   For those who may think I exaggerate the contrast between the former river canyon and the present man-made impoundment, I suggest a trip on Lake Powell followed immediately by another boat trip on the river below the dam. Take a boat from Lee's Ferry up the river to within sight of the dam, then shut off the motor and allow yourself the rare delight of a quiet, effortless drifting down the stream. In that twelve-mile stretch of living green, singing birds, flowing water and untarnished canyon walls — sights and sounds a million years older and infinitely lovelier than the roar of motorboats — you will rediscover a small and imperfect sampling of the kind of experience that was taken away from everybody when the oligarchs and politicians condemned our river for purposes of their own.

14   The effects of Glen Canyon Dam also extend downstream, causing changes in the character and ecology of Marble Gorge and Grand Canyon. Because the annual spring floods are now a thing of the past, the shores are becoming overgrown with brush, the rapids are getting worse where the river no longer has enough force to carry away the boulders washed down from the lateral canyons, and the beaches are disappearing, losing sand that is not replaced.

15   Lake Powell, though not a lake, may well be as its defenders assert the most beautiful reservoir in the world. Certainly it has a photogenic

backdrop of buttes and mesas projecting above the expansive surface of stagnant waters where the speedboats, houseboats and cabin cruisers ply. But it is no longer a wilderness. It is no longer a place of natural life. It is no longer Glen Canyon.

The defenders of the dam argue that the recreational benefits available on the surface of the reservoir outweigh the loss of Indian ruins, historical sites, wildlife and wilderness adventure. Relying on the familiar quantitative logic of business and bureaucracy, they assert that whereas only a few thousand citizens ever ventured down the river through Glen Canyon, now millions can — or will — enjoy the motorized boating and hatchery fishing available on the reservoir. They will also argue that the rising waters behind the dam have made such places as Rainbow Bridge accessible by powerboat. Formerly you could get there only by walking (six miles). 16

This argument appeals to the wheelchair ethos of the wealthy, upper-middle-class American slob. If Rainbow Bridge is worth seeing at all, then by God it should be easily, readily, immediately available to everybody with the money to buy a big powerboat. Why should a trip to such a place be the privilege only of those who are willing to walk six miles? Or if Pikes Peak is worth getting to, then why not build a highway to the top of it so that anyone can get there? Anytime? Without effort? Or as my old man would say, "By Christ, one man's just as good as another — if not a damn sight better." 17

Or as ex-Commissioner Floyd Dominy of the U.S. Bureau of Reclamation pointed out poetically in his handsomely engraved and illustrated brochure *Lake Powell: Jewel of the Colorado* (produced by the U.S. Government Printing Office at our expense): "There's something about a lake which brings us a little closer to God." In this case, Lake Powell, about five hundred feet closer. Eh, Floyd? 18

It is quite true that the flooding of Glen Canyon has opened up to the motorboat explorer parts of side canyons that formerly could be reached only by people able to walk. But the sum total of terrain visible to the eye and touchable by hand and foot has been greatly diminished, not increased. Because of the dam the river is gone, the inner canyon is gone, the best parts of the numerous side canyons are gone — all hidden beneath hundreds of feet of polluted water, accumulating silt, and mounting tons of trash. This portion of Glen Canyon — and who can estimate how many cubic miles were lost? — *is no longer accessible to anybody.* (Except scuba divers.) And this, do not forget, was the most valuable part of Glen Canyon, richest in scenery, archaeology, history, flora and fauna. 19

Not only has the heart of Glen Canyon been buried, but many of the side canyons above the fluctuating waterline are now rendered more difficult, not easier, to get into. This because the debris brought down into them by desert storms, no longer carried away by the river, must unavoidably build up in the area where flood meets reservoir. Narrow Canyon, for example, at the head of the impounded waters, is already beginning to silt up and to amass huge quantities of driftwood, some of it floating on the surface, some of it half afloat beneath the surface. 20

Anyone who has tried to pilot a motorboat through a raft of half-sunken logs and bloated dead cows will have his own thoughts on the accessibility of these waters.

21   Hite Marina, at the mouth of Narrow Canyon, will probably have to be abandoned within twenty or thirty years. After that it will be the turn of Bullfrog Marina. And then Rainbow Bridge Marina. And eventually, inevitably, whether it takes ten centuries or only one, Wahweap. Lake Powell, like Lake Mead, is foredoomed sooner or later to become a solid mass of mud, and its dam a waterfall. Assuming, of course, that either one stands that long.

22   Second, the question of costs. It is often stated that the dam and its reservoir have opened up to the many what was formerly restricted to the few, implying in this case that what was once expensive has now been made cheap. Exactly the opposite is true.

23   Before the dam, a float trip down the river through Glen Canyon would cost you a minimum of seven days' time, well within anyone's vacation allotment, and a capital outlay of about forty dollars—the prevailing price of a two-man rubber boat with oars, available at any army-navy store. A life jacket might be useful but not required, for there were no dangerous rapids in the 150 miles of Glen Canyon. As the name implies, this stretch of the river was in fact so easy and gentle that the trip could be and was made by all sorts of amateurs: by Boy Scouts, Camp Fire Girls, stenographers, schoolteachers, students, little old ladies in inner tubes. Guides, professional boatmen, giant pontoons, outboard motors, radios, rescue equipment were not needed. The Glen Canyon float trip was an adventure anyone could enjoy, on his own, for a cost less than that of spending two days and nights in a Page motel. Even food was there, in the water: the channel catfish were easier to catch and a lot better eating than the striped bass and rainbow trout dumped by the ton into the reservoir these days. And one other thing: at the end of the float trip you still owned your boat, usable for many more such casual and carefree expeditions.

24   What is the situation now? Float trips are no longer possible. The only way left for the exploration of the reservoir and what remains of Glen Canyon demands the use of a powerboat. Here you have three options: (1) buy your own boat and engine, the necessary auxiliary equipment, the fuel to keep it moving, the parts and repairs to keep it running, the permits and licenses required for legal operation, the trailer to transport it; (2) rent a boat; or (3) go on a commercial excursion boat, packed in with other sightseers, following a preplanned itinerary. This kind of play is only for the affluent.

25   The inescapable conclusion is that no matter how one attempts to calculate the cost in dollars and cents, a float trip down Glen Canyon was much cheaper than a powerboat tour of the reservoir. Being less expensive, as well as safer and easier, the float trip was an adventure open to far more people than will ever be able to afford motorboat excursions in the area now.

26   What about the "human impact" of motorized use of the Glen Canyon impoundment? We can visualize the floor of the reservoir gradu-

ally accumulating not only silt, mud, waterlogged trees and drowned cattle but also the usual debris that is left behind when the urban, industrial style of recreation is carried into the open country. There is also the problem of human wastes. The waters of the wild river were good to drink, but nobody in his senses would drink from Lake Powell. Eventually, as is already sometimes the case at Lake Mead, the stagnant waters will become too foul even for swimming. The trouble is that while some boats have what are called "self-contained" heads, the majority do not; most sewage is disposed of by simply pumping it into the water. It will take a while, but long before it becomes a solid mass of mud Lake Powell ("Jewel of the Colorado") will enjoy a passing fame as the biggest sewage lagoon in the American Southwest. Most tourists will never be able to afford a boat trip on this reservoir, but everybody within fifty miles will be able to smell it.

27 All of the foregoing would be nothing but a futile exercise in nostalgia (so much water over the dam) if I had nothing constructive and concrete to offer. But I do. As alternate methods of power generation are developed, such as solar, and as the nation establishes a way of life adapted to actual resources and basic needs, so that the demand for electrical power begins to diminish, we can shut down the Glen Canyon power plant, open the diversion tunnels, and drain the reservoir.

28 This will no doubt expose a drear and hideous scene: immense mud flats and whole plateaus of sodden garbage strewn with dead trees, sunken boats, the skeletons of long-forgotten, decomposing water-skiers. But to those who find the prospect too appalling, I say give nature a little time. In five years, at most in ten, the sun and wind and storms will cleanse and sterilize the repellent mess. The inevitable floods will soon remove all that does not belong within the canyons. Fresh green willow, box elder and redbud will reappear; and the ancient drowned cottonwoods (noble monuments to themselves) will be replaced by young of their own kind. With the renewal of plant life will come the insects, the birds, the lizards and snakes, the mammals. Within a generation—thirty years—I predict the river and canyons will bear a decent resemblance to their former selves. Within the lifetime of our children Glen Canyon and the living river, heart of the canyonlands, will be restored to us. The wilderness will again belong to God, the people and the wild things that call it home.

Chapter 16

WHO ABUSED THE CHILDREN OF JORDAN, MINNESOTA?

A Tough Prosecutor for a Heinous Crime
Teri Mach

Following her graduation in 1983 from the College of St. Thomas in St. Paul, Minnesota, Teri Mach took a position as a staff writer for the *Twin Cities Reader*, a weekly news and entertainment paper based in Minneapolis. Mach's article, "A Tough Prosecutor for a Heinous Crime," was initially published in that paper, but it received a much larger audience when the condensed version that we are reprinting was published in the October 1984 issue of *Ms.* magazine.

When Mach initially wrote her article, the difficulties involved in investigating and prosecuting child sexual abuse were not yet fully perceived. In retrospect, Mach writes, "I somewhat regret the tone of my article as shortly after it was published in *Ms.* magazine (and quite a bit after it was published in the *Twin Cities Reader*), Ms. Morris dropped the charges against all those she had been prosecuting in the Rud case. Until that point, Morris had been an extremely successful prosecutor of child sexual abuse in Scott County, Minnesota. She spoke to attorneys' organizations around the state, informing them about the most effective ways to prosecute such a crime. Remember, this was fairly new territory back in 1982 and 1983 when she began prosecuting these crimes."

Mach is continuing an active career in journalism, having served as the assistant producer of a weekly public affairs television program in St. Paul. More recently, she has moved to rural Minnesota where she works as a reporter and editorial assistant for a local newspaper.

1   Over the past year, Kathleen Morris arrested and charged 24 residents of Jordan, Minnesota (pop. 2,663), in a child sex abuse case that has snowballed into one of the largest and most bizarre in history. As the outspoken county attorney of Scott County, an area lying on the southwestern fringes of the Twin Cities, Morris's aggressive prosecution of child molesters has won her statewide recognition and a reputation for playing hardball in court.

2   This latest case comes on the heels of the 1982 Cermak convictions, which resulted from Morris's persistent investigation of a family whose

616

history of incestuous child abuse spans three generations. A number of adults in the family—four parents and two grandparents who subjected the seven young Cermak children to sexual abuse—were locked up. (However, the grandparents are currently appealing their convictions.) Morris is now on the offensive in a second and even more abhorrent alleged child abuse ring.

In October, 1983, Morris charged James John Rud of Jordan with   3
more than 100 counts of criminal sexual conduct and other assault charges. Although the case has not yet come to trial, 23 other arrests followed Rud's, with Morris alleging that these adults involved more than 20 children in violent sexual acts, including anal rape and forced oral sex.

Because national statistics indicate that men constitute the vast ma-   4
jority of sexual offenders, Morris's work has challenged the notion of the typical child molester: 50 percent of the adults that she has charged and arrested are women. "All the people in the system, the attorneys and police, were so used to having men be the bad people, the abusers," Morris explains. "It's real hard to deal with mothers who sexually abuse their kids.

"In the Cermak case, the judges kept telling me, 'Kathleen, I just   5
can't believe this.' And I'd just rant and rave and say, 'What do you mean you don't believe? I've got thirty-five kids [as witnesses] here.'

"And it wasn't that they didn't believe," Morris continues, "it was   6
basically that they didn't want to. Once you accept the fact that it's going on, and it's going on everywhere, you can't put your head back into the sand."

Although many people might hope the Cermaks and Ruds are prod-   7
ucts of a highly unusual rural community, and that sexual abuse of children is geographically and culturally isolated in that county alone, the experts say it isn't so.

Paul Gerber, a special agent with Minnesota's Bureau of Criminal   8
Apprehension, has worked exclusively on sexual abuse cases for the past five years. He thinks that it is Kathleen Morris who sets the county apart from others, not its population. "Scott County is neither unique nor isolated," Gerber insists. "They have a prosecutor who is extremely vociferous in her approach and who is willing to make the subject matter highly visible," he adds.

In all of the sexual abuse cases she has prosecuted over the past five   9
years, Morris says she has never seen a convicted child abuser show any sign of remorse. Sex with children, even one's own, is natural and "beautiful," they reply. This reasoning makes Morris all the more determined.

"The cry of the eighties is 'Protect the poor offender, they're the   10
ones who are most misunderstood.' And I feel sorry for offenders; I feel sorry for Jim Cermak. He himself was abused as a child. He grew up in that system," she explains. "But suppose someone has repeatedly abused kids, and has tried all the different treatment programs, what do you do? You lock them up so that at least for twenty-eight years and six months they won't get to touch one of your children," Morris insists.

11   You'd expect that Kathleen Morris would have a reservoir of support from the community for her efforts. But support isn't all that solid in small towns where residents hear that the county attorney has just arrested the civic-minded schoolteacher down the block or the nice old man next door. Ironically, some residents charge Morris with taking advantage of the vulnerable children who testify in these cases. A few have even claimed that the county attorney brainwashes and drugs the kids.

12   Public outrage aside, Kathleen Morris has won the respect and confidence of many and has noticed a recent turnabout in the community's reaction to her work.

13   "There's an entirely different attitude toward the Rud case," Morris explains. "Maybe those concerned with the county's reputation — like the lawyers and the rich businessmen — don't like to hear that kind of thing talked about, but the ordinary person on the street is saying, 'Go ahead and prosecute.'"

14   Morris was reelected to her post in 1983, a crucial and reassuring vote of confidence from the community she continues to agitate.

Disturbing End of a Nightmare
Jacob V. Lamar, Jr. (reported
by J. Madeleine Nash/Jordan)

In the sixteen months following the first allegations of child sexual abuse in Jordan, Minnesota, the case gained increasing national attention, as more adults were accused of sexual molestation (even of their own children) and more children related stories of sodomy, incest, bestiality, and even murder. The following article from the February 25, 1985, issue of *Time* magazine reports the surprising conclusion to the story.

1   Jordan, Minn., is a town of Rockwellian prettiness, nestled amid stands of hardwood trees and rolling bluffs. With its four churches, lagoon park and first-rate public school system, the Scott County hamlet (pop. 2,900), 35 miles from Minneapolis–St. Paul, would seem to be a model American community. But over the past year and a half, the town's idyllic image has been eroded by allegations of widespread sexual abuse of children. In all, 24 adults were charged by the local prosecutor with molesting 37 youngsters. Some of the defendants were couples accused of engaging in sexual activities with their own children. Local authorities took 25 children from their parents, placing them in foster homes outside Jordan.

When some of the children alleged last October that one to six   2
youngsters had been murdered, almost all of the child-abuse charges
were dropped pending a new investigation by State Attorney General
Hubert H. Humphrey III. Last week Humphrey's task force, which included agents from the FBI and the Minnesota bureau of criminal apprehension, released a 29-page report concluding that no murders had been
committed. Moreover, the study harshly criticized the original investigation. Said Humphrey: "The manner in which the Scott County cases
were handled has resulted in it being impossible to determine, in some
cases, whether sexual abuse actually occurred, and if it did, who may
have done these acts." The investigation had been so bungled, said the
Humphrey report, that no charges would be refiled against the accused.

Jordan's ordeal began in September 1983, when Christine Brown, a   3
mother of five, complained to police that Garbage Collector James Rud
had molested her nine-year-old daughter. Rud, who had twice before
been convicted of child molesting, soon implicated Brown and a group
of other citizens in tales of orgies and sex games with children.

Under the supervision of Scott County Attorney Kathleen Morris, the   4
number of arrests for alleged child sexual abuse grew. Fear spread
through the once tranquil community. Children related detailed incidents of sodomy, incest and bestiality. One young girl reported being
forced to eat a cat and a pet gerbil, "fur and all." A ten-year-old boy said
he was kidnapped and driven to a party where whip-wielding women in
see-through clothes forced him into sexual acts with other children and
adults that were photographed.

Rud pleaded guilty and was eventually sentenced to 40 years in   5
prison. But Robert and Lois Bentz, the first couple to be tried, were
acquitted last September. Under brutal cross-examination, some of the
prosecution's young witnesses; including the Bentzes' own sons, 10 and
6, recanted or told confusing stories. One neighbor's eleven-year-old
boy, who had claimed he had had oral sex with Robert Bentz, testified
that his story was "a big lie."

Just as the case of a second couple was going to trial last October,   6
Prosecutor Morris, who had been alternately praised for her persistence
and berated as overzealous, suddenly announced that the county was
dropping all charges against the remaining 19 defendants. The reason: to
spare the children further trauma and safeguard the investigation of the
alleged homicides committed by members of the sex ring.

Much of the blame for the clumsy local investigation has been   7
attributed to Morris and her office. The prosecutor apparently played a
major role in conducting intensive, prolonged, exhausting interviews
with the children. In one case, authorities talked to a nine-year-old girl
20 times, yet there were only four written reports on her sessions.
According to the Humphrey report, children were sometimes interviewed together and had a great deal of contact with one another, which
could have resulted in the "cross-germination" of allegations. Under
questioning from Humphrey's task force, many of the children retracted
their stories. One boy who had claimed to have witnessed a teenager's
grisly murder admitted to basing his story on a television program he

had seen. He said that he lied about the murder to please Morris' investigators. Said an angry Morris: "It's easy to believe a child when they retract because that's what adults want to hear. It's not easy to believe when they're telling you the truth."

8   The report also found that Scott County police made many arrests without gathering corroborating evidence. "Surveillance techniques were not utilized," the report said. "Search warrants were rarely obtained." To make up for a lack of evidence in one case, Morris is believed to have offered two defendants dismissal of all charges in return for information about the alleged murders.

9   While most of Jordan's citizens were relieved last week that the investigations seemed to be over, some expressed anger at what they considered a witch-hunt. Others were concerned about the still unresolved fate of twelve children sequestered in foster homes and institutions. Some remained suspicious of neighbors. Said Kathie Voss, a nursery school teacher: "I thoroughly believe that there were both guilty and innocent people involved, and now we'll never know who is who." Seven former defendants have filed lawsuits against the county, demanding up to $336.3 million in damages. (The targets—the county board, Morris and her investigators—have hired Lawyer Jim Martin to represent them.)

10   Humphrey last week described the initial investigation as a tragedy. "The children have clearly suffered," he said. "They have been subjected to a process which undermined their credibility, and as a result, individuals who may have committed sexual abuse will not be prosecuted."

Chapter 17

PORNOGRAPHY

Against the Latest Howl for Censorship
Judith Crist

Judith Crist (1922–   ) earned a bachelor's degree from Hunter College and a master's in journalism from Columbia. Although she has taught journalism at Hunter College and Sarah Lawrence College, she has spent most of her career as a film critic, writing for the New York *Herald-Tribune*, the *Ladies' Home Journal*, *TV Guide*, and the *Saturday Review*. From 1963 to 1973 she was the regular film critic on the NBC *Today* show. "Against the Latest Howl for Censorship" was published in *Censorship: For and Against* (1972, edited by Harold Hart).

At the moment, the lady has lots of company and a good share of it is in   1
high places. The lady is the one who, so the oldie goes, has phoned the police to arrest the man across the way standing around stark and staring and naked. An officer arrived but could see no one. "He's right there, officer. Just climb up on this chair, and scrunch around the window frame, and hang over a little, and you can see him."

The lady, bolstered by a Vice-Presidential declaration that "so long   2
as Richard Nixon is President, Main Street is not going to turn into Smut Alley," is now in the forefront of the latest howl for censorship. We are experiencing the thoroughly expected and not unnatural backlash against the changing mores of the last half of the Sixties. Once again we have completed a social cycle and a social circle that has left the unperceptive with present shock. Normal progressions, accelerated beyond the speed of sight in this age of instant communication, have exploded with terrifying force. And unless the voices of sanity are ready with a reply, we may well be on the brink of the censorious Seventies—a period of retrogression that would negate the astonishing advances toward intellectual honesty and creative freedom that we have made in recent years.

These advances are not blatantly evident to the eye. But consider   3
what an exile from this country in the Sixties would note on his return in

1970. Kurt Vonnegut Jr.'s Looseleaf, returning after eight lost years with the Ulysses-like hero of *Happy Birthday, Wanda June,* observes, "You know what gets me — how all the magazines show tits today. Used to be against the law, didn't it? Must have changed the law. . . . You know what gets me — how everybody says *fuck* and *shit* all the time now. I used to be scared shitless I'd say *fuck* or *shit* in public by accident. Now everybody says *fuck* and *shit* all the time. Something very big must have happened while we were out of the country. . . . You know what gets me — how short the skirts are. Something very important about sex must have happened while we were gone . . ."

4   What happened about sex in the Sixties was simply a matter of economics and evolution as far as stage and screen and literature were concerned: a coming of age, a realism in understanding our mores, and a new freedom in the arts. There were the landmark court rulings on obscenity, the frenetic fumbling of the film industry at self-regulation, the fading of local censors, the opening of the floodgates for the exploiters, the all-too-human confusion of freedom with license — and then shock at how far we'd come so soon. From the sealed-lips coolth of Hollywood kisses, we were plunged into a wallow of hip and thigh and genitalia; from the over-dressed stage extravaganza, we were down to nudes cavorting, to smutty stories and to social statements. From the bang-bang-you're-dead of off-screen sound-effect violence, we were soaking in full-color blood baths on a small screen in our very homes.

5   Clark Gable's "Frankly, my dear, I don't give a damn," hard-won from the industry's censors by David Selznick in 1939, had in fewer than 30 years faded before a stream of four-, five- and seven-letter obscenities from the lovely lips of Elizabeth Taylor. Though right up to the Sixties Hollywood insisted on stuffing a jewel into the meanest belly dancer's belly button, by the Seventies there hadn't been a part of the human anatomy that had not been fully displayed on the big screen, and the amount of pubic hair on show became the industry's standard for deciding whether a teen-ager could see a film under parental escort or not at all.

6   At least, the startled homefolks remarked, they would not be seeing this sort of thing in the privacy of their own homes (where nudity, one gathers from the morality mavens, is strictly taboo). But by the 1970–71 television season, those very R-rated films (requiring parental escort) were being shown virtually intact on the telly; and a couple of cause celebres of the early Sixties, *Hurry Sundown* (with a phallic saxaphone scene that had deeply upset the Catholics) and *The World of Suzy Wong* (a eulogy to the virtues of a Hong Kong whore from which Grauman's Chinese had barred unescorted sub-sixteeners) were telecast intact — and in prime network time yet!

7   All of this seems to have happened overnight, particularly in my own medium of film, where the occasional moviegoer, so long wrapped in a cottonwood of the film industry's moral hypocrisy, has experienced a decade of constant trauma. We tend to cling, first, to our peculiar puritanisms: deny the flesh with shame for the beauty of the body and permission only to watch its desecration and destruction as payment for

sin. Secondly, we still believe in the mass-entertainment escapism function of the commercial films of 30 and 40 years ago. Many still think of
movies as mass-manufactured fodder for the national 12-year-old mentality that filmdom ascribed to all ages. Few are fully aware of the
economic revolution that has brought the independent film maker and
the auteur to the forefront with personal films for individuals and special
interest groups. Thus, sporadic visits to the changing film scene are
unnerving even to the sophisticate. And a professional moviegoer like
myself is hard put to remember that it was only ten years ago—and not
in another lifetime—that we were goosefleshed by the realization that
the undulating shadowy at the outset of *Hiroshima, Mon Amour* were
naked bodies in embrace. Today, the screen-watching workday is a rare
one that has not provided a minimum of three orgasms by noon, plus a
goodly detailing of sadism, masochism, homosexuality and mayhem by
quitting time.

And for the eroticized enthusiast beyond the "respectable" movie   8
houses, there are the mini-movies showing their stag and blue movies,
the peep shows, the pornophoto shops, and the so-called movie-making
establishments where patrons can watch the alleged filming of skin-
flicks. The day of the exploiter is at hand. The bestseller lists are topped
by how-to sex books, and the theaters are flooded with how-to sex
movies. Much in the manner of the Hollywood Biblical which wallowed
in dancing girls and violence and romance with the Good Book as its
alibi, so the sexploitation flick pretends to be "documenting" the state
of pornography abroad, or "educating" the inept at refinements of ero-
tica for marital bliss, or "telling it how it is"—with a warning, of course,
that lechery, like crime, doesn't pay for anyone but the smut-film maker.

Small wonder, then, that the cry for censorship had arisen in the late   9
Sixties, and has come to a scream with the ultimate libertarianism of the
President's Commission on Obscenity and Pornography whose findings
were made public in October, 1970. The majority finding, that there was
"no warrant for continued governmental interference with the full freedom of adults to read, obtain or view" pornographic materials, confirmed the know-nothing suspicion that the fall into the slimepit was
indeed at hand.

Well, not quite. A variety of Congressional committees probing sex   10
and violence in films and on television were still to be heard from. And
simultaneously, a New York Criminal Courts judge held that *Censorship
in Denmark*, a documentary that detailed Copenhagen's pornography
fair for those who couldn't take the sightseeing trip for themselves, was
"patently offensive to most Americans because it affronts community
standards relating to the description or representation of sexual matters," and had, as its dominant theme, "a prurient interest in sex."

But the point, of course, to the consideration of censorship I am   11
edging toward, is simply that "most Americans" are under no obligation
to affront themselves by going to see *Censorship in Denmark*. They are
free to exercise the only kind of censorship in which I whole-heartedly
believe: self-censorship on the part of the public and, hopefully, on the
part of the creator. And it is on behalf of the minority of Americans who

would only not be affronted but also might be edified, or enlightened, or simply titillated by this movie that we must fight for the freedom of film.

12   Before we go further into what is essentially a consideration of a film and theater critic's view of censorship, I should note that far more qualified professionals — lawyers, psychologists, behavioralists, sociologists — have explored the field to a fare-thee-well. No layman could hone the legalisms as brilliantly as has Charles Rembar in *The End of Obscenity*, recounting his triumphant defenses of the publications of *Lady Chatterley, Tropic of Cancer* and *Fanny Hill*, nor as Ephraim London has in his various defenses of films, from the 1952 case of *The Miracle* which established the film as a medium rather than an industry, and, most important, as a medium and an art form entitled to the protection of the First Amendment. It was Mr. London who, at the very time the New York City police were picking up *Censorship in Denmark*, won a reversal from the United States Court of Appeals of a judgment by a lower Federal Court approving a Customs confiscation of a Swedish film *Language of Love*. I think the opinion, written for the three-man court by Circuit Judge Leonard Moore, is worth quoting in part, both for its urbanity and its principle. He describes the film as:

> a movie version of the 'marriage manual' — that ubiquitous panacea (in the view of some) for all that ails modern man-woman relations.
>   Assuming the Masters and Johnson (*Human Sexual Response*, 1966) premise that the path to marital euphoria and social utopia lies in the perfection and practice of clinically correct and complete sexual technology, this film offers to light that path in a way the masses can understand. It purports to be an animated Little Golden Book of marital relations, or perhaps the *Kama Sutra* of electronic media, although the film is nowhere nearly as rich in the variety of its smorgasbord of delights as comparison with that ancient Hindu classic might suggest. It may be the vulgate scripture, the Popular Mechanics of interpersonal relations, the complete cure for the ailing marriage. Or so goes the theory of its sponsors.
>   *Language of Love* stars four of what are apparently leading Scandinavian sexual technocrats, with brilliant cameo roles for the functioning flesh of various unnamed actors. . . . This film, as did *I Am Curious (Yellow)*, contains scenes of oral-genital contact and other heterosexual activity that no actor or actress would ever have confessed knowledge of in bygone days of the silver screen. Nevertheless, the movie-going public has been confronted with all of this before in recent times.

13   Viewing the film in its "tedious entirety," Judge Moore held it not proscribably obscene on established constitutional tests, but noted frankly that the court found several sequences offensive:

> not because they excited predilections to prurience but because they intruded upon areas of interpersonal relations which we consider to be peculiarly private. Our sensibilities were offended, but that is a matter of taste and de gustibus non est disputandum, particularly in matters of sex and constitutional law.

Granted that certain scenes might have erotic appeal to the average 14
person, the court observed, "Indeed erotic appeal has assumed a position of paramount importance, somewhat overemphasized we think, in
the affairs of our daily lives," but it is not to be equated with "prurient
interest." Simplistic or superficial, tedious or over-clinical though the
discussion of sex might be, the film, the court found, had redeeming
social value in its advocacy of ideas.

The court asked:

> In final analysis is freedom of speech and expression, including exhi-
> bition of motion picture films, to be based on the opinions of 51
> percent or even 80 percent of our populace? If so, it might well be that
> on a national plebiscite the *Language of Love, I Am Curious (Yellow),
> Les Amants, Memoirs of a Woman of Pleasure (Fanny Hill)* and others
> would all be condemned by a majority vote. Minorities would then
> read and see what their fellow men would decide to permit them to
> read and see. The shadow of 1984 would indeed be commencing to
> darken our horizon. . . .

The court concluded: 15

> Whether these decisions will bring forth a more enlightened people
> who have lived long under sex taboos or will cause a moral degrada-
> tion of the race will be for the historian. . . .

Certainly, a film historian will find an enlightened public feasting 16
off any number of fine films of the past decade that were made possible
by a relaxation of taboos. *Hiroshima, Mon Amour, The Virgin Spring,
The Apartment, Elmer Gantry, The Hustler, Two Women, Divorce —
Italian Style, Tom Jones, 8½, Hud, Dr. Strangelove, The Servant, Darling, Mickey One, Georgy Girl, Bonnie and Clyde, Ulysses, The Graduate, The Killing of Sister George, Last Summer, Midnight Cowboy,
Women in Love, The Virgin and the Gypsy, Five Easy Pieces, Putney
Swope, Going Down the Road, Brewster McCloud, Little Murders* are but
a few of the films of quality that would not have been made, let alone
shown to us intact, had there not been a steady erosion of censorship.

The idiocies of film censorship up to 1964 are nowhere better 17
documented than by Murray Schumach in *The Face on the Cutting Room
Floor.* He ended his chronicle as the industry was preparing for self-regulation, with a certain optimism. Had the industry settled for a simple
not-for-children classification, the system might have functioned on less
farcical terms than it has. The ratings start with *G*, which means for
general consumption; *M*, stands for "mature," a rating abandoned (possibly on the realization that few movies could deserve that label) in favor
of *GP*, which stands for general consumption but parental discretion
advised; *R*, which restricts teen-agers to admission with parental or
guardian escort; and *X*. This last designation was intended to signify
adult admission only, but of course, is considered the label of the dirty
movie — either to be capitalized on by the smut-men or sought out by
the prurient or to be ostracized by theater managements and newspaper
advertising pages catering to the bluenoses.

18   The politicking and juggling and bargaining over the gradations of rating has been shocking, with moviegoers misled and children misguided and the independent and minor moviemaker getting short shrift and little consideration in the rating game. In the same way, the little man has suffered from the censor; fighting a case from police precinct to the Supreme Court is a costly process and, as a result, not a democratic one.

19   Beyond the film historian, the sociologist and the psychologist have endlessly debated in slick magazines and learned journals whether the moral degradation of the race is upon us. There is mountainous material —none of it definitive—to prove that sex and violence are harmless and/or harmful for the young. For my part, I wish there were as much concern about shielding them from the destructive forces of real life as there is about the possible effects a film or a television show may have upon their little psyches. Children, I have found, are particularly resilient in this audiovisual age; they are no longer naive, as my generation was, about the fictional creations of film. My worry, in fact, is that they are so sophisticated about the manufacture of their entertainments that they even suspect the reality of the riots and battles they see on the news shows, half-expecting the skull-smashed demonstrator and the shattered Vietnamese soldier to wash off the makeup and show up on a game show the next day. But children should be protected from the ugliness, the inhumanity, the grostesque distortions of hard-core pornography, just as they should be protected from the sadism, the perversity, and the disregard of human values in the violent entertainments presented to them in the guise of adventure shows. This is, of course, a parental responsibility; but parents—like booksellers, theater owners, producers, and distributors—may well decline their moral responsibilities. The realist must, I fear, demand some legal restrictions where minors are concerned.

20   But the American adult must take responsibility for himself, with the right to exercise his own standards. The ones who shout the loudest about being "swamped" and "flooded" with filth via the mails—I often wonder why our mailbox is never defiled by even a dribble—seem never to exercise their privilege of throwing brochures away unread, twisting the dial, or heaven help us, turning off the set, or simply not going into a suspect movie. And the ones who worry most about the children are for the most part bachelors or spinsters who haven't done a day's social service in their lives, beyond, perhaps, joining a police action against a film.

21   I became aware of this state of affairs from the stream of police witnesses in the case against *The Killing of Sister George* in Boston, where witness after witness testified to forcing himself or herself to sit through the whole film to the near-final two-minute breast-nibbling scene between two women—all for the sake of the children they did not have. And nowhere was there anyone to contradict the exhibitor's contention that no one under the age of eighteen had been admitted to the film.

22   And what possible ill effect, beyond boredom, could the film or

scene have had upon children? In this age of bottle-babies, I doubt that a five-year-old would have had even nostalgic yearnings in the course of the scene. Only the most naive or prudish adult might have been "offended" — but he, of course, was not obliged to attend.

Beyond the effects of violence and sex on children, the social scientists have made endless studies of the effects of pornography on crime and other anti-social actions. Again, so long as the Danes' experience has not been totally researched, the findings can be used on either side. 23

I remain convinced that no female has been raped by text or film and that the triggering of the psychotic mind cannot be predetermined or even pin-pointed. 24

I do know, however, what censorship accomplishes, creating an unreal and hypocritical mythology, fomenting an attraction for forbidden fruit, inhibiting the creative minds among us and fostering an illicit trade. Above all it curtails the right of the individual, be he creator or consumer, to satisfy his intellect and his interest without harm. In our law-rooted society, we are not the keeper of our brother's morals — only of his rights. 25

In protecting those rights we must be Voltairean, advocating, as Holmes said, "not free thought for those who agree with us, but freedom for the thought that we hate." It's a good principle, but I must confess that I declined to testify on behalf of *I Am Curious (Yellow)* and *Language of Love*. I claimed the critic's privilege, if not the civil libertarian's, of choosing to advocate beyond pure principle on aesthetic grounds. If other critics had not been found to testify, I would have done my service — but one wearies of going to the barricades to fight for trash. I did testify on behalf of *Sister George*, a remarkably fine film, and for *491*, an earlier work by the director of *I Am Curious*, that was distinguished by honest aspiration and artistry. But my irritation with and optional withdrawal from the legalistic battles were directed purely at the censors, at the U.S. Customs officials and petty police (servants, alas, of small-minded bigoted citizens) who were completely negating their avowed purpose. Had *Curious (Yellow)* not become a cause celebre, it would have opened in a small art house in New York and suffered a quiet death from negative criticism and word-of-mouth. Instead, misguided but well-intentioned critics took up the cause, its ersatz sexuality was highly publicized and its shrewd importers made millions from a voyeuristic public. Even with *Sister George* the Boston police doublecrossed themselves. They seized the film but had to release it immediately under an anti-prior-restraint injunction; the film had been doing good business up to then but zoomed into smash-hit status while the publicized censorship battle was fought. 26

It's not just the censors who publicize smut. The smart exhibitor in recent years has even capitalized on the censorious critic. The banner quote-line exploited at a theater's showing of Ingmar Bergman's *The Silence* back in 1964 was a lady critic's "This is the dirtiest movie I've ever seen!" and the leather jackets went pouring in, only to find themselves completely frustrated in their attempts to recognize the highly 27 touted masturbation, intercourse, and cunnilingus scenes that the censors had debated but which Bergman's artistry hid from the pornography-minded. But let's not be snobbish. A Michigan State film society recently touted a revival of *The Ape Woman* by quoting me as deeming it "the depth of unappetizing movie making."

28   Well, the depths have been plumbed a lot deeper since that 1964 film and moviegoers are now assured that they will tremble, throw up and sweat at the ecstasies and horrors to be seen within. But we are, I suspect, reaching the end of the era of voyeurism. We have seen it all and are ready to put it in perspective. The blue-movie audience (long ago composed of the wealthy dilettante or the frat boys or the fellows at the firehouse) is made up largely of middle-aged businessmen and oldsters. The younger generation has either been there, legitimately, and taken it in stride — or couldn't care less.

29   One goes back to the days of one's youth, of pouring over pages 723ff in the Modern Library edition of *Ulysses*, of gulping down snatches of *Lady Chatterley* in a bootlegged brown-paper-bound edition, and of going from there into the twin-bedded cinematic world of Doris Day's eternal virginity.

30   The other day I came home to find my fourteen-year-old finishing *Tropic of Cancer.* "Boy, what a bore!" he remarked, tossing the book aside. And beyond his qualifications as a literary critic, I think him a healthier type than my contemporaries. So much, then, for the moral decline of the race.

Obscene Pictures: Fact and Fiction

Susanne Kappeler

In the following excerpt from Susanne Kappeler's book *The Pornography of Representation* (The University of Minnesota Press, 1986), note the extended comparison between the "real" crime against a black youth in Namibia and the "fictional" crimes against young women in "snuff" movies. Kappeler contends that the distinction between real and fictional is far from clear and that certain acts of representation are in themselves real, obscene, and criminal: "In the murdering of Thomas Kasire, taking pictures was an integral part of the act of torture and an integral part of the enjoyment of the act of torture."

1   *The Guardian Weekly*, in its first issue of 1984, carried an article entitled 'A Murder in Namibia'. A white farmer, van Rooyen, aged 24, had tortured and killed the 18-year-old Thomas Kasire, a new black worker on his farm. The history is as follows: on account of the language Kasire speaks and the area he comes from, his white boss accuses him of being

a supporter of the national liberation movement SWAPO (South Western African People's Organization). He

> throws a heavy chain around the throat of Thomas Kasire. For two days the white farmer keeps Thomas chained fast in his farmyard. Eventually, Thomas is killed as van Rooyen's drinking pals applaud and take pictures. This happens on a farm, in Namibia, in 1983.[1]

Three pictures accompany the article, one showing the murderer 'as   2 he appeared in court', wearing a suit and tie. The other two pictures are from the 'scene' of crime: a close-up of Kasire's head, bleeding, one ear half cut off, a heavy iron chain around his neck, with the white left arm of his torturer holding on to the chain, intruding from the left into the middle foreground of the picture. The third photograph has the caption: 'The victim is forced to pose with a clenched fist (SWAPO salute), while a friend of the murderer takes photos.'[2] The murderer himself is in the picture, towering over the young black man whom he holds by the chain. He is wearing farm clothes and a cap (they could also be paramilitary gear) and he is facing the camera. The young black man looks as if he were held up on his feet chiefly by the chain the white man holds.

The event is a curiosity in criminology, for the pictures   3

> were the damning evidence. Without them, the court would in all probability have acquitted [van Rooyen]. The explanations given by him and his white friends would have outweighed the statements of black witnesses. So safe are the whites in their dominant position within the apartheid system that, incredibly, the whole event was photographed at van Rooyen's request.[3]

The coincidence of this kind of violence and its representation is no   4 accident. It is no curiosity in the domain of representation. The pictures are not documentary evidence, snapped by a journalist or observer by chance in the right place at the right time. The pictures are compositions, deliberate representations, conforming to a genre. The victim is forced to 'pose'; the perpetrator of the torture positions himself in the other picture with reference to the camera. Another white man is behind the camera, framing the picture. The picture may remind us of those taken by fishermen and hunters posing with their catch, smiling into the camera. But the catch is a human being, a victim, and thus the picture also reminds us of some of the darkest photographic memories of the Vietnam war, those pictures which break the documentary mould and where a temporary victor briefly poses for the camera with his victim vanquished, acknowledging the presence of the camera, drawing it into complicity. The picture may also remind us, or some of us, of pornography, a woman in the place of the black man, the white men in their respective positions — in the picture, behind the camera — unchanged.

The written report, too, cannot but align itself with the existing   5 literary tradition of the genre:

> Sunday afternoon — two white guests arrived at the farm. Thomas has now stood, bound, for two days without food or water. Van Rooyen

suggests to his friends that they should have some drinks and soon they begin celebrating the capture of a young 'terrorist'.

The victim is fetched and forced to pose whilst one of the guests borrows van Rooyen's Instamatic camera. A short time after the pictures are taken there is an almost inaudible sob from Thomas Kasire. After a faint shudder he falls backwards—lifeless.[4]

For 'Thomas'—the 'boy'[5] put 'Justine' or 'Emanuelle' or 'O'—the victim already designated by reduced identity, a first name, no family name. For 'farm' put 'chateau', retain the aristocratic patronym of its owner and you have the perfect scenario of sadean libertinism, the classic paradigm of the genre.

6   Experts on pornography, obscenity and censorship, experts of the law as well as experts of the arts, will argue that the issue of real violence, physical violence to people as in 'A Murder in Namibia', is irrelevant to the question of pornography. Real violence is a case for the courts and the criminologists: it is fact, not fiction.

7   Experts in law are for the most part concerned with fact, although with cases of threat, libel and with the question of censorship they are themselves concerned with a realm of representation that relates ambiguously to the realm of fact. Experts of the arts are now virtually exclusively concerned with fiction, since the modern understanding of art and literature highlights the creative and imaginative as the defining elements, coupled with an evaluative criterion of 'excellence'.[6] When the issue is pornography, both sides offer themselves as the obvious experts while at the same time effectively disowning it. Thus the arts experts, while coyly refraining from claiming pornography as an art (not 'excellent' enough), nevertheless recognize its affinity with their own subject and, moreover, have memories of the law interfering in the arts proper with its censorship arm, as in the famous literary obscenity trials.[7] They claim, as it were, the other side of the boundary between fiction and pornographic fiction (without apparently any contradiction). Liberalism is in favour of a clear separation of expertise and of restricting the law to unambiguous fact. The law, increasingly complying, restricts its concern to the possibility of a factual relation between fiction (potential fact) and actual fact, thus placing pornography itself outside its proper domain.

8   Hence the present situation where protectors as well as critics of pornography face each other over the (law's) problem of refuting or proving a causal relationship between the consumption of pornographic fiction and the perpetration of sexual crimes: does represented content lead to content being acted out? Did a sexual assailant get his crime out of a book, film or magazine? Representation itself, pornography itself, is already no longer in question, in this search for a match between contents. Sociology provides statistics: they prove nothing. Perhaps it is rather a case for the psychologists, and there are psychiatric estimates: 'no correlation'.[8] What is clear from this division of domains and competencies is that representation itself is not considered a part of the real; as fiction it is opposed to fact, and it does not apparently involve any acts, activity, action, save fictional ones in its content.

In the murder of Thomas Kasire, 'posing' for pictures was an inte-   9
gral part of his torture; in fact, it was the final cause of death. In the
murdering of Thomas Kasire, taking pictures was an integral part of the
act of torture and an integral part of the enjoyment of the act of torture.
This particular form of violence has two parts: doing it and enjoying it,
action and appreciation. Today, we loosely call it sadism. Enjoyment,
according to Sade, requires a sophisticated intellectual structure, beyond
sheer gratification. It requires an audience. With an audience, torture
becomes an art, the torturer an author, the onlookers an audience of
connoisseurs. This sophisticated structure is manifest in the present
case: there is a host, the owner of the farm, and there are guests. One
white man, the host, is the *maître de cérémonie*,[9] also acting as torturer
in the content of the picture, another white man, a guest, behind the
camera, acting in the production of the picture. The two look at each
other. The one in the picture will come out of the picture and take the
place of the man behind the camera, looking at the scene he has framed.
The host and his guests mingle and merge in the audience, they become
one as the audience, but the host is the author of the party, and they are
'celebrating'.

The victim does not come out of the picture, the victim is dead. In   10
this case literally, in the general case of representation virtually, or
functionally, as there is no designated role in the world, and in the
continued existence of the representation, for the victim to take up. If
the person filling the role of victim is not actually dead, s/he should be.
In the words of the Marquis de Sade:

> There's not a woman on earth who would ever have had cause to
> complain of my services if I'd been sure of being able to kill her
> afterwards.[10]

An interesting use of the word 'cause'.

The white men's party, their action of representing the torture and   11
death of Thomas Kasire, is disregarded by both camps of experts. In the
face of the 'real', factual violence involved in the production of the
representation, the arts experts deem that the representation ceases to
be fiction and a relative of the arts. The case is handed over to the courts,
where the representation becomes 'evidence', a chance windfall for the
prosecution, who treats it as a mirror reflection of reality, the reality of
the crime. Van Rooyen is tried for murder; his action of producing
pornographic representations, relatives of the snuff-movies, goes unnoticed and untried.

Experts on fiction and art will say that this incident does not count,   12
because the incident was real (the victim really died). Fiction, of course,
has always had a troubled relationship with reality, its investment in
realism motivated by a concern with authenticating its own enterprise in
an increasingly secular culture, guaranteeing a certain relevance. But it
wants no part *in* reality, it is the Other to the real. It is the surplus of the
real, it need have no function in the real, it need serve no purpose. It is
the leisure and the pleasure which complements the work and utility of

the real. That is its beauty, the beauty and privilege of the arts. Gratuitousness becomes the trademark of the arts' sublimity.

13   Gratuitousness is the mark of the murderer's photography. It is for
sheer surplus pleasure, as is the torture itself, which has nothing of
course to do with fighting so-called terrorists or any other utility in the
world. It serves the leisure and the pleasure of the white man (the
incident happens at a weekend, Friday–Sunday),[11] it is a form of his free
expression of himself, an assertion of his subjectivity.

14   Van Rooyen's production of pictures is fiction *par excellence*. The
pictures are *made* (fiction from *fingere* = to form), careful compositions according to the laws of aesthetics and representation. The fiction
exceeds fact in its representation of reality: Thomas Kasire lives on in his
representation, though Thomas Kasire is dead. The fiction continues as
existence in reality.

AUTHOR'S NOTES

1 Aslak Aarhus and Ole Bernt Froshaug, 'A Murder in Namibia', *The Guardian
   Weekly*, 8 January 1984, p. 7. Namibia has been administered by South Africa
   since 1915. In 1971 the International Court of Justice ruled this an 'illegal
   occupation' and demanded that South Africa withdraw. It has refused to do
   so. SWAPO is the national liberation movement fighting to end South African
   rule in the country.
      Van Rooyen is only one example of a white settler in Namibia who got
   away with murdering a black worker.
2 Ibid.
3 Ibid.
4 Ibid.
5 Ibid.
6 Raymond Williams, *Keywords: A Vocabulary of Culture and Society* (London, Fontana, 1976); see especially 'Literature' and 'Fiction'.
7 See, e.g. Frank Kermode, 'Obscenity and the Public Interest', in his *Modern
   Essays* (London, Fontana, 1971).
8 'Dr Sharon Satterfield (at the University of Minnesota human sexuality program) . . . has given us serious testimony that there is no correlation between pornography and violence against women' *Minneapolis Star and
   Tribune*, 31 December 1983, p. 4A.
9 Roland Barthes, *Sade, Fourier, Loyola* (Paris, Editions du Seuil, 1971), p.
   164.
10 Marquis de Sade, quoted in *Time Out*, 1–7 March 1984, p. 11.
11 Aarhus and Froshaug, 'A Murder in Namibia', p. 7.

Chapter 18

IS AFFIRMATIVE ACTION FAIR?

A Defense of Quotas

Charles Krauthammer

Charles Krauthammer (1950–   ) is a senior editor for the *New Republic*, in which this essay appeared in September 1985.

As recently as three years ago Nathan Glazer noted with dismay the inability, or unwillingness, of the most conservative American administration in 50 years to do anything about the growing entrenchment, in law and in practice, of racial quotas. It seemed that officially sanctioned race consciousness was becoming irrevocably woven into American life.   1

Glazer's pessimism was premature. In the last two years a revolution has been brewing on the issue of affirmative action. It is marked not by the pronouncements of Clarence Pendleton, or the change in composition and ideology of the United States Commission on Civil Rights. That is for show. It is marked by a series of court rulings and administration actions that, step by step, will define affirmative action out of existence.   2

How far this process had gone was dramatized by the leak of a draft executive order that would outlaw in federal government contracting not only quotas and statistical measures but any "preference . . . on the basis of race, color, religion, sex or national origin . . . with respect to any aspect of employment." Although this appeared as a bolt from a blue August sky, it was, in fact, the culmination of a process that has been building over the last several years. It amounts to a counterrevolution in stages on the issue of race-conscious social policy.   3

The counterrevolution has occurred in what is probably the most crucial domain of affirmative action: employment. Classic affirmative action mandates preference for blacks (and women and other favored groups) at all four steps in the employment process: recruitment, hiring, promotion, and firing. The counterrevolution has attacked such preferences at each step of the way, beginning at the end.   4

The first major breach in the edifice of affirmative action was the Supreme Court's Memphis fire fighters decision of June 1984. The City of Memphis had been under a court-ordered consent decree to increase the number of blacks in the fire department. When layoffs came in 1981,   5 a U.S. District Court ruled that last-hired blacks could not be the first fired, as the seniority system dictated. Three whites were laid off instead. The Supreme Court reversed that decision. It ruled that in a clash between a bona fide seniority system and affirmative action, seniority prevails.

6   You cannot fire by race. But can you promote? Can you hire? The next, more tentative, step in the counterrevolution occurred this past spring in the District of Columbia. A suit originally filed in the waning days of the Carter administration had resulted in mandated preferential hiring and promotions for minorities in the city's fire departments. In March the D.C. fire chief, according to one of the judge's directives in the case, ordered that five black fire fighters be promoted over whites who had scored higher than they had.

7   The union immediately filed suit to block the promotions. And the Justice Department joined the suit on the union's side. The judge in the case then rendered a Solomonic decision prohibiting race conscious-ness in promotion, but permitting it in hiring.

8   The case is under appeal and no one knows how it will come out. The reason is that no one knows how to interpret *Memphis*. Did this ruling apply only to layoffs, as suggested to civil rights groups trying to limit their losses? Or did it apply also to hiring and/or promotion, the other crucial career choke points? You can read *Memphis* either way, and everyone is waiting for the Court to say.

9   Everyone, that is, except William Bradford Reynolds, head of the Justice Department's Civil Rights Division, and leading *contra*. Reyn-olds is a conservative in a hurry. Invoking *Memphis* as his authority, he ordered 51 jurisdictions from New York to Los Angeles to cleanse exist-ing consent decrees (which mandated goals — quotas — if hiring) of any hint of group or racial preference. Not only would preferences be out-lawed from now on, but existing decrees would have to be revised to reflect the new dispensation.

10   Reynold's target is to root out race consciousness in toto, from firing to promotion to hiring. Everything, it seems, except recruitment. Last June, at the start of Reynold's confirmation hearings for the number three job at Justice (he was eventually turned down), he sent a letter to Senator Edward Kennedy stating that he favored affirmative action in recruitment. He argued that it is the only permissible affirmative action; in fact, it is how you determine its success. Its success could be "mea-sured," he wrote, "in the number of persons who are recruited to apply."

11   Recruiting, it seems, would be the last refuge for affirmative action. Or so it seemed, until the final step: draft executive order 11246 revising the affirmative action order that since 1968 has mandated race conscious-ness and statistical norms (quotas) in employment for government con-tractors. The draft executive order would repeal it all: goals, timetables, statistical norms, and other forms of racial preference.

12   It appears to do so even for Reynolds's cherished exception, re-cruitment. Hard to tell, though. The first section of the draft order seems

to define affirmative action, as Reynolds likes to, as exclusively applicable to recruitment. "Each government contractor . . . shall engage in affirmative recruitment . . . to . . . expand[ing] the number of qualified minorities and women who receive full consideration for hiring and promotion." But the very next section continues: "Nothing in this executive order shall be interpreted to require . . . any preference . . . on the basis of race . . . with respect to any aspect of employment, including . . . recruitment. . . ."

Either the drafters are exceedingly careless, or the internal adminis-   13
tration debate over whether to go the very last mile in eradicating race consciousness has yet to be decided. In either case, recruitment poses a logical problem for Reynolds & Company (if race consciousness is in principle unjust, how can it be O.K. for recruitment?). But it is not, in practice, a serious issue. If preferential treatment is outlawed for firing, promotion, and hiring, then recruitment really is the last mile: affirmative action expires long before it is reached. The administration and its civil rights opponents seem to agree that if this program — renegotiating the consent decrees and draft executive order 11246 — is enacted, recruitment or not, race-conscious affirmative action is dead.

They disagree about whether that would be a good thing. Is race-con-   14
scious affirmative action worth saving?

There are three arguments in favor. The first, marshaled principally   15
against Reynolds's revisionist consent decree is profoundly conservative. It says that at this late date things are working out well, whatever the merits. Let well enough alone. The Justice Department would "disturb the acquiescence of the community in the new systems established after much travail and effort under the consent decrees," charged the NAACP. It will "threaten social peace for the sake of ideology," said *The Washington Post*. "Don't stick your nose in cases that have already been resolved," said Representative Don Edwards, one of five representatives who wrote to the attorney general asking him to cease and desist.

The irony here, of course, is that the NAACP is relatively new to the   16
cause of "settledness." Not always has it argued that justice should be deferred so as not to "disturb the acquiescence of the community" in existing social arrangements. That was the segregationist case. And in that case, it was argued, correctly, that although settledness and social peace have some claim to make, they cannot prevail over the claims of justice.

It works, argues William H. Hudnut, the Republican mayor of India-   17
napolis, of his city's consent decree setting aside a quarter of its police and fire fighting slots for minorities. Why fix what ain't broke?

Because justice is not interested in what's broke and what's not; it is   18
interested in justice. Hence the second argument for affirmative action, the familiar argument that while color blindness may be a value, remedying centuries of discrimination through (temporary) race consciousness is a higher value.

Does the right of the disadvantaged to redress (through preferential   19
treatment) override the right of individuals to equal treatment? *Memphis*

and the D.C. fire fighters decision begin to parse the issue. The logic of these decisions is that in layoffs and promotion the aggrieved whites have by dint of service, acquired *additional* individual claims that outweigh the historical claims of blacks. But what about unadorned individual claims? When hired you bring your citizenship with you and nothing else. Shouldn't that be enough to entitle you to equal, color-blind treatment?

20   It is not clear how to adjudicate the competing claims, that of a historically oppressed community for redress, and of the blameless individual for equal treatment. One side claims the mantle of — indeed, it defines itself as the side of — civil rights. But that is surely a semantic claim. The movement began, of course, as a civil rights movement. But when, for example, the D.C. Office of Human Rights declares that its primary mission is to ensure that blacks end up in city jobs in proportion "equal to their group representation in the available work force," the issue has ceased to be rights. It is group advancement.

21   The other side claims the mantle of individual rights and equal treatment. That is not a semantic claim. But it is not an absolute one either. After all, either by design or default, we constantly enact social policies that favor certain groups at the expense of others, the individuals in neither group having done anything to deserve their fate. One routine, and devastating, exercise in social engineering is the government-induced recession, periodically applied to the economy to curb inflation. The inevitable result is suffering, suffering that we know well in advance will be borne disproportionately by the poor and working class.

22   Is this discrimination by class? Certainly. It is not admitted to be so, and it is certainly not the primary effect. But it is an inevitable and predictable side effect. Yet in the face of an overriding national priority — saving the currency — we adopt policies that disproportionately injure a recognized class of blameless individuals. (Similarly, the draft discriminates by age, the placement of toxic waste dumps by geography, etc. We continually ask one group or another to bear special burdens for the sake of the community as a whole.)

23   If controlling inflation is a social goal urgent and worthy enough to warrant disproportionate injury to a recognized class of blameless individuals, is not the goal of helping blacks rapidly gain the mainstream of American life? Which suggests a third, and to my mind most convincing, line of defense for affirmative action. It admits that the issue is not decidable on the grounds of justice. It argues instead a more humble question of policy: that the rapid integration of blacks into American life is an overriding national goal, and that affirmative action is the means to that goal.

24   To be sure, affirmative action has myriad effects. They even include such subtle negative psychological effects on blacks as the "rumors of inferiority" studied by Jeff Howard and Ray Hammond (TNR, September 9). The calculation is complex. But it is hard to credit the argument that on balance affirmative action actually harms blacks. Usually ad-

vanced by opponents of affirmative action, this argument is about as ingenuous as Jerry Falwell's support of the Botha regime out of concern for South African blacks. One needs a willing suspension of disbelief to maintain that a policy whose essence is to favor blacks hurts them. Even the Reagan administration admits (in a report sent to Congress in February) that executive order 11246 has helped skilled black men.

The Reagan counterrevolutionaries want to end the breach of justice   25
that is affirmative action. A breach it is, and must be admitted to be. It is not clear, however, that correcting this breach is any more morally compelling than redressing the historic injustice done to blacks. In the absence of a compelling moral case, then, the Reagan counterrevolution would retard a valuable social goal: rapid black advancement and integration. Justice would perhaps score a narrow, ambiguous victory. American society would suffer a wide and deepening loss.

We're Not Really "Equal"
Thomas Sowell

Thomas Sowell (1930–   ) was born in Gastonia, North Carolina. Although initially a high school dropout, Sowell earned a B.A. degree from Harvard University, an M.A. from Columbia University, and a Ph.D. from the University of Chicago, all in economics. He has taught at Cornell, Brandeis, and UCLA. Although black himself, Sowell has consistently opposed forced busing, affirmative action quotas, and many government assistance programs. A contributor to leading economics, business, and political journals, Sowell has authored a number of provocative and controversial books, among them *Black Education: Myths and Tragedies* (1972), *Affirmative Action Reconsidered: Was It Necessary in Academia?* (1975), *Race and Economics* (1975), and *Knowledge and Decisions* (1980). "We're Not Really 'Equal'" first appeared in the "My Turn" column of *Newsweek* in 1981.

As a teacher I have learned from sad experience that nothing so bores   1
students as being asked to define their terms systematically before discussing some exciting issue. They want to get on with it, without wasting time on petty verbal distinctions.

Much of our politics is conducted in the same spirit. We are for   2
"equality" or "the environment," or against an "arms race," and there is no time to waste on definitions and other Mickey Mouse stuff. This attitude may be all right for those for whom political crusades are a matter of personal excitement, like rooting for your favorite team and jeering the opposition. But for those who are serious about the consequences of public policy, nothing can be built without a solid foundation.

3   "Equality" is one of the great undefined terms underlying much current controversy and antagonism. This one confused word might even become the rock on which our civilization is wrecked. It should be worth defining.

4   Equality is such an easily understood concept in mathematics that we may not realize it is a bottomless pit of complexities anywhere else. That is because in mathematics we have eliminated the concreteness and complexities of real things. When we say that two plus two equals four, we either don't say two *what* or we say the same what after each number. But if we said that two apples plus two apples equals four oranges, we would be in trouble.

5   Yet that is what we are saying in our political reasoning. And we are in trouble. Nothing is more concrete or complex than a human being. Beethoven could not play center field like William Mays, and Willie never tried to write a symphony. In what sense are they equal—or unequal? The common mathematical symbol for inequality points to the smaller quantity. But which is the smaller quantity—and in whose eyes—when such completely different things are involved?

6   When women have children and men don't, how can they be either equal or unequal? Our passionate desire to reduce things to the simplicity of abstract concepts does not mean that it can be done. Those who want to cheer their team and boo the visitors may like to think that the issue is equality versus inequality. But the real issue is whether or not we are going to talk sense. Those who believe in inequality have the same confusion as those who believe in equality. The French make better champagne than the Japanese, but the Japanese make better cameras than the French. What sense does it make to add champagne to cameras to a thousand other things and come up with a grand total showing who is "superior"?

7   When we speak of "equal justice under law," we simply mean applying the same rules to everybody. That has nothing whatsoever to do with whether everyone performs equally. A good umpire calls balls and strikes by the same rules for everyone, but one batter may get twice as many hits as another.

8   In recent years we have increasingly heard it argued that if outcomes are unequal, then the rules must have been applied unequally. It would destroy my last illusion to discover that Willie Mays didn't really play baseball any better than anybody else, but that the umpires and sportswriters just conspired to make it look that way. Pending the uncovering of intricate plots of this magnitude, we must accept the fact that performances are very unequal in different aspects of life. And there is no way to add up these apples, oranges and grapes to get one sum total of fruit.

9   Anyone with the slightest familiarity with history knows that rules have often been applied very unequally to different groups. (A few are ignorant or misguided enough to think that this is a peculiarity of American society.) The problem is not in seeing that unequal rules can lead to unequal outcomes. The problem is in trying to reason backward from unequal outcomes to unequal rules as the sole or main cause.

There are innumerable places around the world where those who   10
have been the victims of unequal rules have nevertheless vastly outper-
formed those who are favored. Almost nowhere in Southeast Asia have
the Chinese minority had equal rights with the native peoples, but the
average Chinese income in these countries has almost invariably been
much higher than that of the general population. A very similar story
could be told from the history of the Jews in many countries of Europe,
North Africa and the Middle East. To a greater or lesser extent, this has
also been the history of the Ibos in Nigeria, the Italians in Argentina, the
Armenians in Turkey, the Japanese in the United States — and on and on.

It would be very convenient if we could infer discriminatory rules   11
whenever we found unequal outcomes. But life does not always accommodate itself to our convenience.

Those who are determined to find villains but cannot find evidence   12
often resort to "society" as the cause of all our troubles. What do they
mean by "society" or "environment"? They act as if these terms were
self-evident. But environment and society are just new confused terms
introduced to save the old confused term, equality.

The American environment or society cannot explain historical be-   13
havior patterns found among German-Americans if these same patterns
can be found among Germans in Brazil, Australia, Ireland and elsewhere
around the world. These patterns may be explained by the history of
German society. But if the words "environment" or "society" refer to
things that may go back a thousand years, we are no longer talking about
either the causal or the moral responsibility of American society. If
historic causes include such things as the peculiar geography of Africa or
of southern Italy, then we are no longer talking about human responsibility at all.

This does not mean that there are no problems. There are very   14
serious social problems. But that means that serious attention will be
required to solve them — beginning with defining our terms.

Chapter 19

THE MILGRAM EXPERIMENT
Was It Ethical?

The Milgram Experiment

Ronald Smith,
Irwin G. Sarason,
and Barbara Sarason

Ronald Smith teaches psychology at Portland State University. Irwin and Bar-bara Sarason teach psychology at the University of Washington–Seattle. To-gether they are the coauthors of *Psychology: Frontiers of Behavior* (1973), from which this excerpt, explaining the experiment performed by Stanley Milgram, is taken.

1   After World War II the Nuremberg war trials were conducted in order to try Nazi war criminals for the atrocities they had committed. In many instances the defense offered by those on trial was that they had "only followed orders." During the Vietnam War American soldiers accused of committing atrocities in Vietnam gave basically the same explanation for their actions.

2   Most of us reject justifications based on "obedience to authority" as mere rationalizations, secure in our convictions that we, if placed in the same situation, would behave differently. However, the results of a series of ingenious and controversial investigations performed in the 1960s by psychologist Stanley Milgram suggest that perhaps we should not be so sure of ourselves.

3   Milgram wanted to determine the extent to which people would obey an experimenter's commands to administer painful electric shocks to another person. Pretend for a moment that you are a subject in one of his studies. Here is what would happen. On arriving at a university laboratory in response to a classified ad offering volunteers $4 for one hour's participation in an experiment on memory, you meet another subject, a pleasant, middle-aged man with whom you chat while await-ing the arrival of the experimenter. When the experimenter arrives, dressed in a laboratory coat, he pays you and then informs you and the other person that one of you will be the subject in the experiment and

that the other will serve as his assistant. You are chosen by lot to be the assistant, but in reality you are the subject.

The experimenter explains that the study is concerned with the 4 effects of punishment on learning. Accompanied by you, the "subject" is conducted into a room and strapped into a chair, and a large electrode is attached to his wrist. He is told that he is to learn a list of word pairs and that whenever he makes an error he will receive electric shocks of increasing intensity. On hearing this, the "subject" responds, "When I was at the West Haven V.A. Hospital a few years ago, they detected a slight heart condition. Nothing serious, but are these shocks dangerous?" The experimenter replies in an unconcerned manner that although the shocks may be painful, they will cause no permanent tissue damage.

You and the experimenter then proceed to an adjoining room con- 5 nected by an intercom so that the "subject's" responses can be heard. You are seated in front of an apparatus with 30 toggle switches ranging from 15 volts to 450 volts. (See Figure 1.) Your task is to administer the learning task to the "subject." Whenever he gives an incorrect answer, you must give him an electric shock, starting at the lowest level (15 volts) and increasing the level by 15 volts each time. You are given a sample shock of 45 volts and find it moderately painful.

What you are unaware of at this point is that you are in a carefully 6 contrived situation. The learner is actually an actor who receives no shock at all, and the responses you hear over the intercom are tape-recorded so that they will be exactly the same for each "assistant." The experimenter's actions are also carefully programmed.

As the experiment proceeds, the learner makes error after error. 7 You increase the shock level steadily until he is clearly experiencing pain. The tape-recorded responses are programmed to correspond to the shock intensities as follows:

75 volts	Ugh!
90 volts	Ugh!
105 volts	Ugh! (*louder*)
120 volts	Ugh! Hey, *this* really hurts.

Figure 1 The control panel of the shocking apparatus used in the Milgram research. Copyright © 1974 by Stanley Milgram. Reprinted by permission of Harper & Row, Publishers, Inc.

135 volts	Ugh!!
150 volts	Ugh!!! Experimenter! That's all. Get me out of here. I told you I had heart trouble. My heart's starting to bother me now. Get me out of here. I told you I had heart trouble. My heart's starting to bother me. I refuse to go on. Let me out.
165 volts	Ugh! Let me out. (*shouting*)
180 volts	Ugh! I can't stand the pain. Let me out of here! (*shouting*)
195 volts	Ugh! Let me out of here. Let me out of here. My heart's bothering me. Let me out of here! You have no right to keep me here! Let me out! Let me out of here! My heart's bothering me. Let me out! Let me out!
210 volts	Ugh!! Experimenter! *Get* me out of here. I've had enough. I won't be in the experiment any more.
225 volts	Ugh!
240 volts	Ugh!
255 volts	Ugh! Get me *out* of here.
270 volts	(*Agonized scream*). Let me out of here. Let me out of here. Let me out of here. Let me out. Do you hear? Let me out of here.
285 volts	(*Agonized scream*).
300 volts	(*Agonized scream*). I absolutely refuse to answer any more. Get me out of here. You can't hold me here. Get me out. Get me out of here.
315 volts	(*Intensely agonized scream*). *I told you I refuse to answer.* I'm no longer part of this experiment.
330 volts	(*Intense and prolonged agonized scream*). Let me out of here. Let me out of here. My heart's bothering me. Let me out, I tell you. (*Hysterically*) Let me out of here. Let me out of here. You have no right to hold me here. Let me out! Let me out! Let me out of here! Let me out! Let me out!
345 volts	(*At 345 volts and thereafter, there was only silence.*)[1]

8   But supposing you express unwillingness at some point to continue shocking the learner? In that event the experimenter, sitting at a nearby desk, would respond in one of the following ways:

"Please continue" or "Please go on."
"The experiment requires that you continue."
"It is absolutely essential that you continue."
"You have no other choice. You must go on."

9   Having now experienced the Milgram situation at least in your imagination, how long do you think you would continue to administer

[1]Copyright © 1974 by Stanley Milgram.

shocks? Most of our students maintain that they would not go beyond 105 volts before refusing to continue the experiment. A panel of psychiatrists predicted before the experiment that perhaps only 1 percent of the subjects would proceed to the 450-volt level.

In fact, however, the "shock" produced by the results of this study 10 was much more startling than the simulated shocks in the experiment. Forty men ranging in age from 20 to 50 and representing a cross section of the population, participated in the investigation. The maximum shock levels they administered are shown in Table 1. Nearly two-thirds of them administered the 450-volt maximum shock, and the average maximum shock they administered was 368 volts.

Virtually all the people who administered high levels of shock 11 exhibited extreme discomfort, anxiety, and distress. Most verbally refused to continue on one or more occasions. But continue they did when ordered to do so by the experimenter, who assured them that what happened in the experiment was his responsibility.

By contriving a situation with many real-life elements, Milgram 12 succeeded in demonstrating that a high percentage of "normal" people will obey an authority figure even when the destructive effects of their obedience are obvious. The conclusions that he draws from his work are chilling indeed:

A commonly offered explanation is that those who shocked the victim at the most severe level were monsters, the sadistic fringe of society. But if one considers that almost two-thirds of the participants fall into the category of "obedient" subjects, and that they represented ordinary people drawn from working, managerial, and professional classes, the argument becomes very shaky. Indeed, it is highly reminiscent of the issue that arose in connection with Hannah Arendt's 1963 book, *Eichmann in Jerusalem.* Arendt contended that the prosecution's effort to depict Eichmann as a sadistic monster was fundamentally wrong, that he came closer to being an uninspired bureaucrat who simply sat at his desk and did his job. For asserting these views, Arendt became the object of considerable scorn, even calumny. Somehow, it was felt that the monstrous deeds carried out by Eichmann required a brutal, twisted, and sadistic personality, evil incarnate. After witnessing hundreds of ordinary people submit to the authority in our own experiments, I must conclude that Arendt's conception of the *banality of evil* comes closer to the truth than one might dare imagine. The ordinary person who shocked the victim did so out of a sense of obligation—a conception of his duties as a subject—and not from any peculiarly aggressive tendencies.

This is, perhaps, the most fundamental lesson of our study: ordinary people, simply doing their jobs, and without any particular hostility on their part, can become agents in a terrible destructive process. Moreover, even when the destructive effects of their work become patently clear, and they are asked to carry out actions incompatible with fundamental standards of morality, relatively few people have the resources needed to resist authority. A variety of inhibitions against

TABLE 1   Maximum shock levels administered by subjects in the Milgram experiment

Shock level	Verbal designation and voltage level	Number of subjects giving each maximum shock level
	Slight Shock	
1	15	
2	30	
3	45	
4	60	
	Moderate Shock	
5	75	
6	90	1
7	105	
8	120	
	Strong Shock	
9	135	
10	150	6
11	165	
12	180	1
	Very Strong Shock	
13	195	
14	210	
15	225	
16	240	
	Intense Shock	
17	255	
18	270	2
19	285	
20	300	1
	Extreme-Intensity Shock	
21	315	1
22	330	1
23	345	
24	360	
	Danger: Severe Shock	
25	375	1
26	390	
27	405	
28	420	
	XXX	
29	435	
30	450	26
	Average maximum shock level	368 volts
	Percentage of obedient subjects	65.0%

disobeying authority come into play and successfully keep the person in his place.[2] (Milgram, 1974, pp. 5–6)

Milgram's method of investigation also generated shock waves among psychologists. Many questioned whether it was ethical to expose subjects without warning to experiments that were likely to generate considerable stress and that might conceivably have lasting negative effects on them. But supporters of Milgram's work argue that adequate precautions were taken to protect participants. There was an extensive debriefing at the conclusion of the experiment, and participants were informed that they had not actually shocked anyone. They had a friendly meeting with the unharmed "subject." The purpose of the experiment was explained to them, and they were assured that their behavior in the situation was perfectly normal. Further, supporters argue, the great societal importance of the problem being investigated justified the methods the experimenters used. Finally, they cite follow-up questionnaire data collected by Milgram from his subjects after they received a complete report of the purposes and results. Eighty-four percent of the subjects stated that they were glad to have been in the experiment (and several spontaneously noted that their participation had made them more tolerant of others or otherwise changed them in desirable ways). Fifteen percent expressed neutral feelings, and only 1.3 percent stated that they were sorry to have participated.

13

The controversy over the ethics of Milgram's research has raged for over a decade. In combination with other controversial issues, it has prompted a deep and abiding concern for protecting the welfare of subjects in psychological research. Because of such concerns, it is most unlikely that Milgram's research could be conducted today.

14

Some Thoughts on the Ethics of Research: After Reading Milgram's "Behavioral Study of Obedience"
Diana Baumrind

Psychologist Diana Baumrind published this essay in *American Psychologist* in 1964 shortly after the appearance of Milgram's seminal work on obedience to authority in 1963. At the time she was a fellow at the Institute of Human Development, University of California–Berkeley.

[2]Copyright © 1974 by Stanley Milgram.

1   Certain problems in psychological research require the experimenter to balance his career and scientific interests against the interests of his prospective subjects. When such occasions arise the experimenter's stated objective frequently is to do the best possible job with the least possible harm to his subjects. The experimenter seldom perceives in more positive terms an indebtedness to the subject for his services, perhaps because the detachment which his functions require prevents appreciation of the subject as an individual.

2   Yet a debt does exist, even when the subject's reason for volunteering includes course credit or monetary gain. Often a subject participates unwillingly in order to satisfy a course requirement. These requirements are of questionable merit ethically, and do not alter the experimenter's responsibility to the subject.

3   Most experimental conditions do not cause the subjects pain or indignity, and are sufficiently interesting or challenging to present no problem of an ethical nature to the experimenter. But where the experimental conditions expose the subject to loss of dignity, or offer him nothing of value, then the experimenter is obliged to consider the reasons why the subject volunteered and to reward him accordingly.

4   The subject's public motives for volunteering include having an enjoyable or stimulating experience, acquiring knowledge, doing the experimenter a favor which may some day be reciprocated, and making a contribution to science. These motives can be taken into account rather easily by the experimenter who is willing to spend a few minutes with the subject afterwards to thank him for his participation, answer his questions, reassure him that he did well, and chat with him a bit. Most volunteers also have less manifest, but equally legitimate, motives. A subject may be seeking an opportunity to have contact with, be noticed by, and perhaps confide in a person with psychological training. The dependent attitude of most subjects toward the experimenter is an artifact of the experimental situation as well as an expression of some subjects' personal need systems at the time they volunteer.

5   The dependent, obedient attitude assumed by most subjects in the experimental setting is appropriate to that situation. The "game" is defined by the experimenter and he makes the rules. By volunteering, the subject agrees implicitly to assume a posture of trust and obedience. While the experimental conditions leave him exposed, the subject has the right to assume that his security and self-esteem will be protected.

6   There are other professional situations in which one member—the patient or client—expects help and protection from the other—the physician or psychologist. But the interpersonal relationship between experimenter and subject additionally has unique features which are likely to provoke initial anxiety in the subject. The laboratory is unfamiliar as a setting and the rules of behavior ambiguous compared to a clinician's office. Because of the anxiety and passivity generated by the setting, the subject is more prone to behave in an obedient, suggestible manner in the laboratory than elsewhere. Therefore, the laboratory is not the place to study degree of obedience or suggestibility, as a function of a particular experimental condition, since the base line for these

phenomena as found in the laboratory is probably much higher than in most other settings. Thus experiments in which the relationship to the experimenter as an authority is used as an independent condition are imperfectly designed for the same reason that they are prone to injure the subjects involved. They disregard the special quality of trust and obedience with which the subject appropriately regards the experimenter.

Other phenomena which present ethical decisions, unlike those mentioned above, *can* be reproduced successfully in the laboratory. Failure experience, conformity to peer judgment, and isolation are among such phenomena. In these cases we can expect the experimenter to take whatever measures are necessary to prevent the subject from leaving the laboratory more humiliated, insecure, alienated, or hostile than when he arrived. To guarantee that an especially sensitive subject leaves a stressful experimental experience in the proper state sometimes requires special clinical training. But usually an attitude of compassion, respect, gratitude, and common sense will suffice, and no amount of clinical training will substitute. The subject has the right to expect that the psychologist with whom he is interacting has some concern for his welfare, and the personal attributes and professional skill to express his good will effectively. 7

Unfortunately, the subject is not always treated with the respect he deserves. It has become more commonplace in sociopsychological laboratory studies to manipulate, embarrass, and discomfort subjects. At times the insult to the subject's sensibilities extends to the journal reader when the results are reported. Milgram's (1963) study is a case in point. The following is Milgram's abstract of his experiment: 8

> This article describes a procedure for the study of destructive obedience in the laboratory. It consists of ordering a naive S to administer increasingly more severe punishment to a victim in the context of a learning experiment.[1] Punishment is administered by means of a shock generator with 30 graded switches ranging from Slight Shock to Danger: Severe Shock. The victim is a confederate of E. The primary dependent variable is the maximum shock the S is willing to administer before he refuses to continue further.[2] 26 Ss obeyed the experimental commands fully, and administered the highest shock on the generator. 14 Ss broke off the experiment at some point after the victim protested and refused to provide further answers. The procedure created extreme levels of nervous tension in some Ss. Profuse sweating, trembling, and stuttering were typical expressions of this emotional disturbance. One unexpected sign of tension—yet to be explained—was the regular occurrence of nervous laughter, which in some Ss developed into uncontrollable seizures. The variety of interesting behavioral dynamics observed in the experiment, the reality of the situation for the S, and the possibility of parametric variation[3]

[1] *S* stands for subject, *E* for experimenter.

[2] A *dependent variable* is that which is expected to change as a result of the experiment.

[3] *Parametric variation* involves controlled changes in the conditions of the experiment.

within the framework of the procedure, point to the fruitfulness of further study [p. 371].

9   The detached, objective manner in which Milgram reports the emotional disturbance suffered by his subject contrasts sharply with his graphic account of that disturbance. Following are two other quotes describing the effects on his subjects of the experimental conditions:

> I observed a mature and initially poised businessman enter the laboratory smiling and confident. Within 20 minutes he was reduced to a twitching, stuttering wreck, who was rapidly approaching a point of nervous collapse. He constantly pulled on his earlobe, and twisted his hands. At one point he pushed his fist into his forehead and muttered: "Oh God, let's stop it." And yet he continued to respond to every word of the experimenter, and obeyed to the end [p. 377].
>
> In a large number of cases the degree of tension reached extremes that are rarely seen in sociopsychological laboratory studies. Subjects were observed to sweat, tremble, stutter, bite their lips, groan, and dig their fingernails into their flesh. These were characteristic rather than exceptional responses to the experiment.
>
> One sign of tension was the regular occurrence of nervous laughing fits. Fourteen of the 40 subjects showed definite signs of nervous laughter and smiling. The laughter seemed entirely out of place, even bizarre. Full-blown, uncontrollable seizures were observed for 3 subjects. On one occasion we observed a seizure so violently convulsive that it was necessary to call a halt to the experiment . . . [p. 375].

Milgram does state that,

> After the interview, procedures were undertaken to assure that the subject would leave the laboratory in a state of well being. A friendly reconciliation was arranged between the subject and the victim, and an effort was made to reduce any tensions that arose as a result of the experiment [p. 374].

It would be interesting to know what sort of procedures could dissipate the type of emotional disturbance just described. In view of the effects on subjects, traumatic to a degree which Milgram himself considers nearly unprecedented in sociopsychological experiments, his casual assurance that these tensions were dissipated before the subject left the laboratory is unconvincing.

10   What could be the rational basis for such a posture of indifference? Perhaps Milgram supplies the answer himself when he partially explains the subject's destructive obedience as follows, "Thus they assume that the discomfort caused the victim is momentary, while the scientific gains resulting from the experiment are enduring [p. 378]." Indeed such a rationale might suffice to justify the means used to achieve his end if that end were of inestimable value to humanity or were not itself transformed by the means by which it was attained.

11   The behavioral psychologist is not in as good a position to objectify his faith in the significance of his work as medical colleagues at points of

breakthrough. His experimental situations are not sufficiently accurate models of real-life experience; his sampling techniques are seldom of a scope which would justify the meaning with which he would like to endow his results; and these results are hard to reproduce by colleagues with opposing theoretical views. Unlike the Sabin vaccine,[4] for example, the concrete benefit to humanity of his particular piece of work, no matter how competently handled, cannot justify the risk that real harm will be done to the subject. I am not speaking of physical discomfort, inconvenience, or experimental deception per se, but of permanent harm, however slight. I do regard the emotional disturbance described by Milgram as potentially harmful because it could easily effect an alteration in the subject's self-image or ability to trust adult authorities in the future. It is potentially harmful to a subject to commit, in the course of an experiment, acts which he himself considers unworthy, particularly when he has been entrapped into committing such acts by an individual he has reason to trust. The subject's personal responsibility for his actions is not erased because the experimenter reveals to him the means which he used to stimulate these actions. The subject realizes that he would have hurt the victim if the current were on. The realization that he also made a fool of himself by accepting the experimental set results in additional loss of self-esteem. Moreover, the subject finds it difficult to express his anger outwardly after the experimenter in a self-acceptant but friendly manner reveals the hoax.

A fairly intense corrective interpersonal experience is indicated 12 wherein the subject admits and accepts his responsibility for his own actions, and at the same time gives vent to his hurt and anger at being fooled. Perhaps an experience as distressing as the one described by Milgram can be integrated by the subject, provided that careful thought is given to the matter. The propriety of such experimentation is still in question even if such a reparational experience were forthcoming. Without it I would expect a naive, sensitive subject to remain deeply hurt and anxious for some time, and a sophisticated cynical subject to become even more alienated and distrustful.

In addition the experimental procedure used by Milgram does not 13 appear suited to the objectives of the study because it does not take into account the special quality of the set which the subject has in the experimental situation. Milgram is concerned with a very important problem, namely, the social consequences of destructive obedience. He says,

> Gas chambers were built, death camps were guarded, daily quotas of corpses were produced with the same efficiency as the manufacture of appliances. These inhumane policies may have originated in the mind of a single person, but they could only be carried out on a massive scale if a very large number of persons obeyed orders [p. 371].

But the parallel between authority-subordinate relationships in Hitler's Germany and in Milgram's laboratory is unclear. In the former situation

[4]The polio vaccine.

the SS man or member of the German Officer Corps, when obeying orders to slaughter, had no reason to think of his superior officer as benignly disposed towards himself or their victims. The victims were perceived as subhuman and not worthy of consideration. The subordinate officer was an agent in a great cause. He did not need to feel guilt or conflict because within his frame of reference he was acting rightly.

14   It is obvious from Milgram's own descriptions that most of his subjects were concerned about their victims and did trust the experimenter, and that their distressful conflict was generated in part by the consequences of these two disparate but appropriate attitudes. Their distress may have resulted from shock at what the experimenter was doing to them as well as from what they thought they were doing to their victims. In any case there is not a convincing parallel between the phenomena studied by Milgram and destructive obedience as that concept would apply to the subordinate-authority relationship demonstrated in Hitler Germany. If the experiments were conducted "outside of New Haven and without any visible ties to the university," I would still question their validity on similar although not identical grounds. In addition, I would question the representativeness of a sample of subjects who would voluntarily participate within a noninstitutional setting.

15   In summary, the experimental objectives of the psychologist are seldom incompatible with the subject's ongoing state of well being, provided that the experimenter is willing to take the subject's motives and interests into consideration when planning his methods and correctives. Section 4b in *Ethical Standards of Psychologists* (APA, undated) reads in part:

> Only when a problem is significant and can be investigated in no other way, is the psychologist justified in exposing human subjects to emotional stress or other possible harm. In conducting such research, the psychologist must seriously consider the possibility of harmful aftereffects, and should be prepared to remove them as soon as permitted by the design of the experiment. Where the danger of serious aftereffects exists, research should be conducted only when the subjects or their responsible agents are fully informed of this possibility and volunteer nevertheless [p. 12].

From the subject's point of view procedures which involve loss of dignity, self-esteem, and trust in rational authority are probably most harmful in the long run and require the most thoughtfully planned reparations, if engaged in at all. The public image of psychology as a profession is highly related to our own actions, and some of these actions are changeworthy. It is important that as research psychologists we protect our ethical sensibilities rather than adapt our personal standards to include as appropriate the kind of indignities to which Milgram's subjects were exposed. I would not like to see experiments such as Milgram's proceed unless the subjects were fully informed of the dangers of serious aftereffects and his correctives were clearly shown to be effective in restoring their state of well being.

REFERENCES

American Psychological Association. Ethical Standards of Psychologists:
A summary of ethical principles. Washington, D.C.: APA, undated.
Milgram, S. Behavioral study of obedience. *J. Abnorm. Soc. Psychol.*,
1963, 67, 371–78.

A Reply to Baumrind
Stanley Milgram

Stanley Milgram (1933–1987) was born in New York City. He earned a B.A.
from Queens College and a Ph.D. in social psychology from Harvard before
beginning his academic career at Yale in 1960. It was in New Haven, while
serving as principal investigator for a National Science Foundation research
grant, that Milgram conducted the famous and controversial experiments on
human obedience that now carry his name and that he later described in the
book *Obedience to Authority: An Experimental View* (1974). His reply to Diana
Baumrind's critique of his experimental procedures was published in *American
Psychologist* in 1964.

Obedience serves numerous productive functions in society. It may be 1
ennobling and educative and entail acts of charity and kindness. Yet the
problem of destructive obedience, because it is the most disturbing
expression of obedience in our time, and because it is the most perplexing, merits intensive study.

In its most general terms, the problem of destructive obedience 2
may be defined thus: If X tells Y to hurt Z, under what conditions will Y
carry out the command of X, and under what conditions will he refuse?
In the concrete setting of a laboratory, the question may assume this
form: If an experimenter tells a subject to act against another person,
under what conditions will the subject go along with the instruction, and
under what conditions will he refuse to obey?

A simple procedure was devised for studying obedience (Milgram, 3
1963). A person comes to the laboratory, and in the context of a learning
experiment, he is told to give increasingly severe electric shocks to
another person. (The other person is an actor, who does not really
receive any shocks.) The experimenter tells the subject to continue
stepping up the shock level, even to the point of reaching the level
marked "Danger: Severe Shock." The purpose of the experiment is to
see how far the naive subject will proceed before he refuses to comply
with the experimenter's instructions. Behavior prior to this rupture is

considered "obedience" in that the subject does what the experimenter tells him to do. The point of rupture is the act of disobedience. Once the basic procedure is established, it becomes possible to vary conditions of the experiment, to learn under what circumstances obedience to authority is most probable, and under what conditions defiance is brought to the fore.

4   The results of the experiment (Milgram, 1963) showed, first, that it is more difficult for many people to defy the experimenter's authority than was generally supposed. A substantial number of subjects go through to the end of the shock board. The second finding is that the situation often places a person in considerable conflict. In the course of the experiment, subjects fidget, sweat, and sometimes break out into nervous fits of laughter. On the one hand, subjects want to aid the experimenter; and on the other hand, they do not want to shock the learner. The conflict is expressed in nervous reactions.

5   In a recent issue of *American Psychologist*, Diana Baumrind (1964) raised a number of questions concerning the obedience report. Baumrind expressed concern for the welfare of subjects who served in the experiment, and wondered whether adequate measures were taken to protect the participants. She also questioned the adequacy of the experimental design.

6   Patently, "Behavioral Study of Obedience" did not contain all the information needed for an assessment of the experiment. But it is clearly indicated in the references and footnotes (pp. 373, 378) that this was only one of a series of reports on the experimental program, and Baumrind's article was deficient in information that could have been obtained easily. I thank the editor for allotting space in this journal to review this information, to amplify it, and to discuss some of the issues touched on by Baumrind.

7   At the outset, Baumrind confuses the unanticipated outcome of an experiment with its basic procedure. She writes, for example, as if the production of stress in our subjects was an intended and deliberate effect of the experimental manipulation. There are many laboratory procedures specifically designed to create stress (Lazarus, 1964), but the obedience paradigm was not one of them. The extreme tension induced in some subjects was unexpected. Before conducting the experiment, the procedures were discussed with many colleagues, and none anticipated the reactions that subsequently took place. Fore-knowledge of results can never be the invariable accompaniment of an experimental probe. Understanding grows because we examine situations in which the end is unknown. An investigator unwilling to accept this degree of risk must give up the idea of scientific inquiry.

8   Moreover, there was every reason to expect, prior to actual experimentation, that subjects would refuse to follow the experimenter's instructions beyond the point where the victim protested; many colleagues and psychiatrists were questioned on this point, and they virtually all felt this would be the case. Indeed, to initiate an experiment in which the critical measure hangs on disobedience, one must start with

a belief in certain spontaneous resources in men that enable them to overcome pressure from authority.

It is true that after a reasonable number of subjects had been ex-   9
posed to the procedures, it became evident that some would go to the end of the shock board, and some would experience stress. That point, it seems to me, is the first legitimate juncture at which one could even start to wonder whether or not to abandon the study. But momentary excitement is not the same as harm. As the experiment progressed there was no indication of injurious effects in the subjects; and as the subjects themselves strongly endorsed the experiment, the judgment I made was to continue the investigation.

Is not Baumrind's criticism based as much on the unanticipated   10
findings as on the method? The findings were that some subjects performed in what appeared to be a shockingly immoral way. If, instead, every one of the subjects had broken off at "slight shock," or at the first sign of the learner's discomfort, the results would have been pleasant, and reassuring, and who would protest?

PROCEDURES AND BENEFITS

A most important aspect of the procedure occurred at the end of the   11
experimental session. A careful postexperimental treatment was administered to all subjects. The exact content of the dehoax varied from condition to condition and with increasing experience on our part. At the very least all subjects were told that the victim had not received dangerous electric shocks. Each subject had a friendly reconciliation with the unharmed victim, and an extended discussion with the experimenter. The experiment was explained to the defiant subjects in a way that supported their decision to disobey the experimenter. Obedient subjects were assured of the fact that their behavior was entirely normal and that their feelings of conflict or tension were shared by other participants. Subjects were told that they would receive a comprehensive report at the conclusion of the experimental series. In some instances, additional detailed and lengthy discussions of the experiments were also carried out with individual subjects.

When the experimental series was complete, subjects received a   12
written report which presented details of the experimental procedure and results. Again their own part in the experiments was treated in a dignified way and their behavior in the experiment respected. All subjects received a follow-up questionnaire regarding their participation in the research, which again allowed expression of thoughts and feelings about their behavior.

The replies to the questionnaire confirmed my impression that   13
participants felt positively toward the experiment. In its quantitative aspect (see Table 1), 84% of the subjects stated they were glad to have been in the experiment; 15% indicated neutral feelings, and 1.3% indi-

TABLE 1   Excerpt from questionnaire used in a follow-up study of the obedience research

Now that I have read the report, and all things considered . . .	Defiant	Obedient	All
1. I am very glad to have been in the experiment	40.0%	47.8%	43.5%
2. I am glad to have been in the experiment	43.8%	35.7%	40.2%
3. I am neither sorry nor glad to have been in the experiment	15.3%	14.8%	15.1%
4. I am sorry to have been in the experiment	0.8%	0.7%	0.8%
5. I am very sorry to have been in the experiment	0.0%	1.0%	0.5%

Note — Ninety-two percent of the subjects returned the questionnaire. The characteristics of the nonrespondents were checked against the respondents. They differed from the respondents only with regard to age; younger people were overrepresented in the nonresponding group.

cated negative feelings. To be sure, such findings are to be interpreted cautiously, but they cannot be disregarded.

14   Further, four-fifths of the subjects felt that more experiments of this sort should be carried out, and 74% indicated that they had learned something of personal importance as a result of being in the study. The results of the interviews, questionnaire responses, and actual transcripts of the debriefing procedures will be presented more fully in a forthcoming monograph.

15   The debriefing and assessment procedures were carried out as a matter of course, and were not stimulated by any observation of special risk in the experimental procedure. In my judgment, at no point were subjects exposed to danger and at no point did they run the risk of injurious effects resulting from participation. If it had been otherwise, the experiment would have been terminated at once.

16   Baumrind states that, after he has performed in the experiment, the subject cannot justify his behavior and must bear the full brunt of his actions. By and large it does not work this way. The same mechanisms that allow the subject to perform the act, to obey rather than to defy the experimenter, transcend the moment of performance and continue to justify his behavior for him. The same viewpoint the subject takes while performing the actions is the viewpoint from which he later sees his behavior, that is, the perspective of "carrying out the task assigned by the person in authority."

17   Because the idea of shocking the victim is repugnant, there is a tendency among those who hear of the design to say "people will not do it." When the results are made known, this attitude is expressed as "if they do it they will not be able to live with themselves afterward." These two forms of denying the experimental findings are equally inappropriate misreadings of the facts of human social behavior. Many subjects do, indeed, obey to the end, and there is no indication of injurious effects.

The absence of injury is a minimal condition of experimentation; 18
there can be, however, an important positive side to participation.
Baumrind suggests that subjects derived no benefit from being in the
obedience study, but this is false. By their statements and actions, subjects indicated that they had learned a good deal, and many felt gratified
to have taken part in scientific research they considered to be of significance. A year after his participation one subject wrote:

> This experiment has strengthened my belief that man should avoid
> harm to his fellow man even at the risk of violating authority.

Another stated:

> To me, the experiment pointed up . . . the extent to which each
> individual should have or discover firm ground on which to base his
> decisions, no matter how trivial they appear to be. I think people
> should think more deeply about themselves and their relation to their
> world and to other people. If this experiment serves to jar people out
> of complacency, it will have served its end.

These statements are illustrative of a broad array of appreciative and 19
insightful comments by those who participated.

The 5-page report sent to each subject on the completion of the 20
experimental series was specifically designed to enhance the value of
his experience. It laid out the broad conception of the experimental
program as well as the logic of its design. It described the results of a
dozen of the experiments, discussed the causes of tension, and attempted to indicate the possible significance of the experiment. Subjects responded enthusiastically; many indicated a desire to be in further
experimental research. This report was sent to all subjects several years
ago. The care with which it was prepared does not support Baumrind's
assertion that the experimenter was indifferent to the value subjects
derived from their participation.

Baumrind's fear is that participants will be alienated from psycho- 21
logical experiments because of the intensity of experience associated
with laboratory procedures. My own observation is that subjects more
commonly respond with distaste to the "empty" laboratory hour, in
which cardboard procedures are employed, and the only possible feeling upon emerging from the laboratory is that one has wasted time in a
patently trivial and useless exercise.

The subjects in the obedience experiment, on the whole, felt quite 22
differently about their participation. They viewed the experience as an
opportunity to learn something of importance about themselves, and
more generally, about the conditions of human action.

A year after the experimental program was completed, I initiated an 23
additional follow-up study. In this connection an impartial medical ex-
aminer, experienced in outpatient treatment, interviewed 40 experimental subjects. The examining psychiatrist focused on those subjects he felt
would be most likely to have suffered consequences from participation.
His aim was to identify possible injurious effects resulting from the

experiment. He concluded that, although extreme stress had been experienced by several subjects.

> none was found by this interviewer to show signs of having been harmed by his experience. . . . Each subject seemed to handle his task [in the experiment] in a manner consistent with well established patterns of behavior. No evidence was found of any traumatic reactions.

Such evidence ought to be weighed before judging the experiment.

OTHER ISSUES

24   Baumrind's discussion is not limited to the treatment of subjects, but diffuses to a generalized rejection of the work.

25   Baumrind feels that obedience cannot be meaningfully studied in a laboratory setting: The reason she offers is that "The dependent, obedient attitude assumed by most subjects in the experimental setting is appropriate to that situation [p. 421]." Here, Baumrind has cited the very best reason for examining obedience in this setting, namely that it possesses "ecological validity." Here is one social context in which compliance occurs regularly. Military and job situations are also particularly meaningful settings for the study of obedience precisely because obedience is natural and appropriate to these contexts. I reject Baumrind's argument that the observed obedience does not count because it occurred where it is appropriate. That is precisely why it *does* count. A soldier's obedience is no less meaningful because it occurs in a pertinent military context. A subject's obedience is no less problematical because it occurs within a social institution called the psychological experiment.

26   Baumrind writes: "The game is defined by the experimenter and he makes the rules [p. 421]." It is true that for disobedience to occur the framework of the experiment must be shattered. That, indeed, is the point of the design. That is why obedience and disobedience are genuine issues for the subject. *He must really assert himself as a person against a legitimate authority.*

27   Further, Baumrind wants us to believe that outside the laboratory we could not find a comparably high expression of obedience. Yet, the fact that ordinary citizens are recruited to military service and, on command, perform far harsher acts against people is beyond dispute. Few of them know or are concerned with the complex policy issues underlying martial action; fewer still become conscientious objectors. Good soldiers do as they are told, and on both sides of the battle line. However, a debate on whether a higher level of obedience is represented by (a) killing men in the service of one's country, or (b) merely shocking them in the service of Yale science, is largely unprofitable. The real question is: What are the forces underlying obedient action?

28   Another question raised by Baumrind concerns the degree of parallel between obedience in the laboratory and in Nazi Germany. Ob-

viously, there are enormous differences: Consider the disparity in time scale. The laboratory experiment takes an hour; the Nazi calamity unfolded in the space of a decade. There is a great deal that needs to be said on this issue, and only a few points can be touched on here.

1. In arguing this matter, Baumrind mistakes the background metaphor for the precise subject matter of investigation. The German event was cited to point up a serious problem in the human situation: the potentially destructive effect of obedience. But the best way to tackle the problem of obedience, from a scientific standpoint, is in no way restricted by "what happened exactly" in Germany. What happened exactly can *never* be duplicated in the laboratory or anywhere else. The real task is to learn more about the general problem of destructive obedience using a workable approach. Hopefully, such inquiry will stimulate insights and yield general propositions that can be applied to a wide variety of situations.

2. One may ask in a general way: How does a man behave when he is told by a legitimate authority to act against a third individual? In trying to find an answer to this question, the laboratory situation is one useful starting point—and for the very reason stated by Baumrind—namely, the experimenter does constitute a genuine authority for the subject. The fact that trust and dependence on the experimenter are maintained, despite the extraordinary harshness he displays toward the victim, is itself a remarkable phenomenon.

3. In the laboratory, through a set of rather simple manipulations, ordinary persons no longer perceived themselves as a responsible part of the causal chain leading to action against a person. The means through which responsibility is cast off, and individuals become thoughtless agents of action, is of general import. Other processes were revealed that indicate that the experiments will help us to understand why men obey. That understanding will come, of course, by examining the full account of experimental work and not alone the brief report in which the procedure and demonstrational results were exposed.

At root, Baumrind senses that it is not proper to test obedience in this situation, because she construes it as one in which there is no reasonable alternative to obedience. In adopting this view, she has lost sight of this fact: A substantial proportion of subjects do disobey. By their example, disobedience is shown to be a genuine possibility, one that is in no sense ruled out by the general structure of the experimental situation.

Baumrind is uncomfortable with the high level of obedience obtained in the first experiment. In the condition she focused on, 65% of the subjects obeyed to the end. However, her sentiment does not take into account that within the general framework of the psychological experiment obedience varied enormously from one condition to the next. In some variations, 90% of the subjects *dis*obeyed. It seems to be *not* only the fact of an experiment, but the particular structure of elements within the experimental situation that accounts for rates of obedience and disobedience. And these elements were varied systematically in the program of research.

34   A concern with human dignity is based on a respect for a man's potential to act morally. Baumrind feels that the experimenter *made* the subject shock the victim. This conception is alien to my view. The experimenter tells the subject to do something. But between the command and the outcome there is a paramount force, the acting person who may obey or disobey. I started with the belief that every person who came to the laboratory was free to accept or to reject the dictates of authority. This view sustains a conception of human dignity insofar as it sees in each man a capacity for *choosing* his own behavior. And as it turned out, many subjects did, indeed, choose to reject the experimenter's commands, providing a powerful affirmation of human ideals.

35   Baumrind also criticizes the experiment on the grounds that "it could easily effect an alteration in the subject's . . . ability to trust adult authorities in the future [p. 422]." But I do not think she can have it both ways. On the one hand, she argues the experimental situation is so special that it has no generality; on the other hand, she states it has such generalizing potential that it will cause subjects to distrust all authority. But the experimenter is not just any authority: He is an authority who tells the subject to act harshly and inhumanely against another man. I would consider it of the highest value if participation in the experiment could, indeed, inculcate a skepticism of this kind of authority. Here, perhaps, a difference in philosophy emerges most clearly. Baumrind sees the subject as a passive creature, completely controlled by the experimenter. I started from a different viewpoint. A person who comes to the laboratory is an active, choosing adult, capable of accepting or rejecting the prescriptions for action addressed to him. Baumrind sees the effect of the experiment as undermining the subject's trust of authority. I see it as a potentially valuable experience insofar as it makes people aware of the problem of indiscriminate submission to authority.

CONCLUSION

36   My feeling is that viewed in the total context of values served by the experiment, approximately the right course was followed. In review, the facts are these: (a) At the outset, there was the problem of studying obedience by means of a simple experimental procedure. The results could not be foreseen before the experiment was carried out. (b) Although the experiment generated momentary stress in some subjects, this stress dissipated quickly and was not injurious. (c) Dehoax and follow-up procedures were carried out to insure the subjects' well-being. (d) These procedures were assessed through questionnaire and psychiatric studies and were found to be effective. (e) Additional steps were taken to enhance the value of the laboratory experience for participants, for example, submitting to each subject a careful report on the experimental program. (f) The subjects themselves strongly endorse the experiment, and indicate satisfaction at having participated.

37   If there is a moral to be learned from the obedience study, it is that every man must be responsible for his own actions. This author accepts

full responsibility for the design and execution of the study. Some people may feel it should not have been done. I disagree and accept the burden of their judgment.

Baumrind's judgment, someone has said, not only represents a personal conviction, but also reflects a cleavage in American psychology between those whose primary concern is with *helping* people and those who are interested mainly in *learning* about people. I see little value in perpetuating devisive forces in psychology when there is so much to learn from every side. A schism may exist, but it does not correspond to the true ideals of the discipline. The psychologist intent on healing knows that his power to help rests on knowledge; he is aware that a scientific grasp of all aspects of life is essential for his work, and is in itself a worthy human aspiration. At the same time, the laboratory psychologist senses his work will lead to human betterment, not only because enlightenment is more dignified than ignorance, but because new knowledge is pregnant with humane consequences.

38

REFERENCES

Baumrind, D. Some thoughts on ethics of research: After reading Milgram's "Behavioral study of obedience." *Amer. Psychologist*, 1964, 19, 421–23.

Lazarus, R. A laboratory approach to the dynamics of psychological stress. *Amer. Psychologist*, 1964, 19, 400–11.

Milgram, S. Behavioral study of obedience. *J. Abnorm. Soc. Psychol.*, 1963, 67, 371–78.

Milgram, S. Some conditions of obedience and disobedience to authority. *Hum. Relat.*, 1965, 18, 1, Feb. 57–75.

Chapter 20

IS THE STRATEGIC DEFENSE INITIATIVE FEASIBLE?

The War against "Star Wars"
Robert Jastrow

Robert Jastrow (1925 –) was born in New York City and educated at Columbia University, where he earned his Ph.D. in theoretical physics in 1948. Following several years of additional study and a year as a faculty member at Yale, Jastrow became a consultant in nuclear physics at the U.S. Naval Research Laboratory in Washington. He became chief of NASA's Theoretical Division in 1958 and the founding director of the Goddard Institute for Space Studies in 1961. Jastrow's books include *Red Giants and White Dwarfs: The Evolution of Stars, Planets and Life* (1967), *Astronomy: Fundamentals and Frontiers* (1972), *God and the Astronomers* (1978), *The Enchanted Loom: Mind in the Universe* (1981), and *How to Make Nuclear Weapons Obsolete* (1985). Jastrow's essay on the war against "Star Wars" was one of a series of essays and letters about President Reagan's Strategic Defense Initiative (SDI) to be published by *Commentary* magazine. In this 1984 essay Jastrow is more concerned with evaluating the arguments of those who oppose SDI than he is with actually defending the project itself.

1   President Reagan offered a new strategic vision to the American people in his "Star Wars" speech of March 23, 1983. The policy he had inherited from his predecessors relied on the threat of incinerating millions of Soviet civilians as the main deterrent to a Soviet nuclear attack on our country. The President was troubled by the moral dimensions of this policy. He said: "The human spirit must be capable of rising above dealing with other nations and human beings by threatening their existence." And he called on our scientists to find a way of defending the United States against a Soviet nuclear attack by intercepting the Soviet missiles before they reached our soil.

2   When I first heard the President's speech, I thought he had a great idea. I wrote an article commenting favorably on the proposal[1] and then, a little later, I traveled to Washington to hear a talk by Dr. George Keyworth, the President's Science Adviser, on the strategic and technical implications of the President's plan.

Since Dr. Keyworth was rumored to have made a major contribution   3
to the thinking behind the "Star Wars" speech, I felt that I would be
getting an insider's view of the technical prospects for success in this
difficult undertaking. That was particularly interesting to me, because
several of my fellow physicists had expressed the gravest reservations
about the technical feasibility of the proposal. In fact, Dr. Hans Bethe, a
distinguished Nobel laureate in physics, had said bluntly, "I don't think
it can be done."

Dr. Keyworth started by describing the circumstances that had led to   4
the President's speech. Then he got into the technical areas I had come
to hear about. "For more than five months," he told us, "some fifty of
our nation's better technical minds [have] devoted their efforts almost
exclusively to one problem—the defense against ballistic missiles."
This group of specialists, which included some of the most qualified
defense scientists in the country, had concluded that the President's goal
was realistic—that it "probably could be done."

"The basis for their optimism," Dr. Keyworth went on, "is our   5
tremendously broad technical progress over the past decade." He
pointed specifically to the advances in computers and "new laser techniques." He also mentioned the promising new developments that
might enable us to protect the vitally important satellites carrying all this
laser weaponry and computing equipment, and prevent the Soviets from
knocking these critical satellites out as a preliminary to a nuclear attack
on the United States. "These and other recent technical advances," Dr.
Keyworth concluded, "offer the possibility of a workable strategic [mis-
sile] defense system."

That was pretty clear language. Defense experts had given the Presi-   6
dent's proposal a green light on its technical merits. I went back to New
York with a feeling that the President's vision of the future—a future in
which nuclear weapons would be "impotent and obsolete"—was going
to become a reality.

The following month a panel of university scientists came out with a   7
report that flatly contradicted Dr. Keyworth's assessment. According to
the panel, an effective defense of the United States against Soviet missiles was "unattainable." The report, prepared under the sponsorship of
the Union of Concerned Scientists (UCS),[2] leveled numerous criticisms
at the "Star Wars" proposal. It pointed out, *inter alia*, that thousands of
satellites would be needed to provide a defensive screen; that one of the
"Star Wars" devices under consideration would require placing in orbit a
satellite weighing 40,000 tons; that the power needed for the lasers and
other devices proposed would equal as much as 60 percent of the total
power output of the United States; and that, in any case, the Soviets
would be able to foil our defenses with a large bag of relatively inexpensive tricks, such as spinning the missile to prevent the laser from burning
a hole in it, or putting a shine on it to reflect the laser light.

The signers of the report included physicists of world renown and   8
great distinction. The impact of their criticisms seemed absolutely
devastating.

9   Around the same time, another study of the feasibility of the "Star Wars" defense came out with more or less the same conclusion. According to that report, which had been prepared for the Office of Technology Assessment (OTA)[3] of the Congress, the chance of protecting the American people from a Soviet missile attack is "so remote that it should not serve as the basis for public expectations or national policy."

10   These scientific studies, documented with charts and tables, apparently sounded the death knell of missile defense. Scientists had judged the President's proposal, and found it wanting. According to *Nature*, the most prestigious science journal in the world:

> The scientific community knows that [the President's proposal] will not work. The President's advisers, including his science adviser, Dr. George Keyworth, know it too, but are afraid to say so.
>   Dr. Keyworth is employed to keep the President informed on these technical matters, but sadly, there is no evidence that he is willing to give Mr. Reagan the bad news.

11   A few weeks later, I received unclassified summaries of the blue-ribbon panels appointed by the Defense Department to look into the feasibility of a United States defense against Soviet missiles.[4] These were the documents on which Dr. Keyworth had relied in part for his optimistic appraisal. The reports by the government-appointed consultants were as different from the reports by the university scientists as day is from night. One group of distinguished experts said no fundamental obstacles stood in the way of success; the other group, equally distinguished, said it would not work. Who was right? According to the UCS report, "any inquisitive citizen" could understand the technical issues. I decided to look into the matter. This is what I found.

12   Missiles usually consist of two or three separate rockets or "stages," also called boosters. On top of the uppermost stage sits the "bus" carrying the warheads. One by one, the stages ignite, burn out, and fall away. After the last stage has burned out and departed, the bus continues upward and onward through space. At this point it begins to release its separate warheads. Each warhead is pushed off the bus in a different direction with a different velocity, so as to reach a different target. The missiles with this capability are said to be MIRVed (MIRV stands for multiple independently targetable reentry vehicle).

13   Most of the discussion of the "Star Wars" defense assumes a many-layered defense with three or four distinct layers. The idea behind having several layers is that the total defense can be made nearly perfect in this way, even if the individual layers are less than perfect. For example, if each layer has, say, an 80-percent effectiveness — which means that one in five missiles or warheads will get through — a combination of three such layers will have an overall effectiveness better than 99 percent, which means that no more than one warhead in 100 will reach its target.[5]

14   The first layer, called the boost-phase defense, goes into effect as the Soviet missile rises above the atmosphere at the beginning of its

trajectory. In the second layer, or mid-course defense, the booster has burned out and fallen away, and we concentrate on trying to destroy or disable the "bus" carrying the nuclear warheads, or the individual warheads themselves, as they arc up and over through space on their way to the United States. In the third layer, or terminal defense, we try to intercept each warhead in the final stages of its flight.

The boost-phase defense offers the greatest payoff to the defender   15
because at this stage the missile has not yet sent any of its warheads on their separate paths. Since the largest Soviet missiles carry ten warheads each, if our defense can destroy one of these missiles at the beginning of its flight, it will eliminate ten warheads at a time. The defense catches the Soviet missiles when they have all their eggs in one basket, so to speak.

But the boost-phase defense is also the most difficult technically,   16
and has drawn the most fire from critics. How can we destroy a Soviet missile thousands of miles away, within seconds or minutes after it has left its silo?

At the present time, one of the most promising technologies for   17
doing that is the laser, which shoots a bolt of light at the missile as it rises. Missiles move fast, but light moves faster. A laser beam travels a thousand miles in less than a hundredth of a second. Focused in a bright spot on the missile's skin, the laser beam either burns a hole through the thin metal of the skin, which is only about a tenth of an inch thick, or it softens the metal sufficiently so that it ruptures and the missile disintegrates.

Another very promising technology for the boost-phase defense is   18
the Neutral Particle Beam, which shoots a stream of fast-moving hydrogen atoms at the missile. The atoms travel at a speed of about 60,000 miles a second, which is less than the speed of light but still fast enough to catch up to the missile in a fraction of a second. The beam of fast-moving atoms is very penetrating, and goes through the metal skin of the missile and into the electronic brain that guides it on its course. There the atoms create spurious pulses of electricity that can cause the brain to hallucinate, driving the missile off its course so that it begins to tumble and destroys itself. If the beam is intense enough, it can flip the bits inside the brain's memory so that it remembers the wrong things; or it can cause the brain to lose its memory altogether. Any one of these effects will be deadly to the Soviet missile's execution of its task.

The Neutral Particle Beam can also play havoc with the circuits in   19
the electronic brain that guide the bus sitting on top of the missile. The mischief created here may prevent the bus from releasing its warheads; or it may cause the bus to send the warheads in the wrong directions, so that they miss their targets; or it may damage the electronic circuits in the warheads themselves, after they have been pushed off the bus, so that when they reach their targets they fail to explode.[6] The Neutral Particle Beam can be lethal to the attacker in the boost phase, the mid-course phase, and the terminal phase. All in all, it is a most useful device.

Now for an important point: to be effective, the laser or the Neutral   20

Particle Beam must have unobstructed views of all the Soviet missile fields. One of the best ways of achieving that is to put the device that produces these beams on a satellite and send it into orbit.

21   So this, then, is the essence of the plan for a boost-phase defense against Soviet missiles: a fleet of satellites, containing equipment that generates laser beams or Neutral Particle Beams, circles the earth, with enough satellites in the fleet so that several satellites are over the Soviet missile fields at all times—a sufficient number to shoot down, in the worst case, all 1,400 Soviet missiles if they are launched against us simultaneously.

22   The plan looks good on paper. Yet according to the UCS report, it has absolutely no practical value. This study shows that because of the realities of satellite orbits, the satellites needed to protect the United States against Soviet attack would "number in the thousands." The report's detailed calculations put the precise number at 2,400 satellites.

23   Now, everyone acknowledges that these satellites are going to be extremely expensive. Each one will cost a billion dollars or more—as much as an aircraft carrier. Satellites are the big-ticket items in the plan for a space-based defense. If thousands are needed, the cost of implementing the plan will be many trillions of dollars. A defense with a price tag like that is indeed a "turkey," as a spokesman for the UCS called it.

24   If the numbers put out by the UCS were right, there would be no point in looking into the plan further. But after the UCS report hit the papers, I began to hear rumors from professionals in the field that the numbers were not right. Since the whole "Star Wars" plan rested on this one point, I thought I would just check out the calculations myself. So I got hold of a polar-projection map of the northern hemisphere and a piece of celluloid. I marked the positions of the North Pole and the Soviet missile fields on the celluloid, stuck a pin through the North Pole, and rotated the celluloid around the Pole to imitate the rotation of the earth carrying the missile fields with it. Then I played with the map, the moving celluloid, and different kinds of satellite orbits for a day or two, to get a feel for the problem.

25   It was soon clear that about 50 evenly spaced satellite orbits, with four satellites in each orbit, would guarantee adequate coverage of the missile fields. In other words, 200 satellites would do the job, and "thousands" were certainly not needed. I could also see that it might be possible to get down to fewer than 100 satellites, but I could not prove that with my celluloid "computer."

26   I talked again with my friends in the defense community and they told me that my answers were in the right ballpark. The experts had been looking at this problem for more than ten years, and the accurate results were well known. As I had suspected, a hundred or so satellites were adequate. According to careful computer studies done at the Livermore laboratory, 90 satellites could suffice, and if the satellites were put into low-altitude orbits, we might get by with as few as 45 satellites.[7]

27   So the bottom line is that 90 satellites—and perhaps somewhat fewer—are needed to counter a Soviet attack. That cuts the cost down

from many trillions of dollars to a level that could be absorbed into the amount already earmarked by the government for spending on our strategic forces during the next ten or fifteen years. It removes the aura of costliness and impracticality which had been cast over the President's proposal by the Union of Concerned Scientists' report.

The scientists who did these calculations for the UCS had exagger- 28 ated the number of satellites by a factor of about twenty-five. How did they make a mistake like that? A modicum of thought should have indicated that "thousands" of satellites could not be the right answer. Apparently the members of the panel did begin to think more carefully about the matter later on—but only after they had issued their report— because in testimony before a congressional committee a UCS spokes- man lowered his organization's estimate from 2,400 satellites to 800 satellites.[8] In their most recent publication on the matter, the members of the panel lowered their estimate again, to 300 satellites.[9] That was getting closer. Another factor of three down and they would be home.

But the Union of Concerned Scientists never said to the press or the 29 Congress: "We have found important mistakes in our calculations, and when these mistakes are corrected the impact is to cut the cost of the missile defense drastically. In fact, correcting these errors of ours has the effect of making the President's idea much more practical than we thought it was when we issued our report." Months after the publication of the report, *Science 84*, published by the American Association for the Advancement of Science, was still referring to the need for "2,400 orbit- ing laser stations."

The work by the Union of Concerned Scientists on the question of 30 the satellite fleet is the poorest that has appeared in print, to my knowl- edge. The report prepared for the Office of Technology Assessment, which does a better job on this particular question, says that 160 satel- lites are needed for our defense. That is only about double the accurate result that came out of the computer studies at Livermore.

But the report to the OTA has a different failing. Because of an error 31 in reasoning—an extremely inefficient placement of the satellites in their orbits—it concludes that if the Soviets were to build more missiles in an effort to overwhelm our defense, the United States would have to increase the number of its satellites in orbit in direct proportion to the increase in the number of Soviet missiles.[10]

This seems like a technical detail, but it has a cosmic impact. It 32 means that if the Soviets build twice as many missiles, we have to build twice as many satellites. If they build four times as many missiles, we have to build four times as many satellites. Since our satellites are going to be expensive, that can be a costly trade-off. In fact, it could enable the Soviets to overwhelm our defense simply by building more missiles. As the *New Republic* said: "They could just roll out more SS-18's" (the SS-18 is the biggest and most powerful missile in the Soviet arsenal).

But some fine work by the theoretical physicists at Los Alamos has 33 shown that the report to the OTA is seriously in error. The Los Alamos calculations, which have been confirmed by computations at Livermore, show that the number of satellites needed to counter a Soviet attack does *not* go up in direct proportion to the number of Soviet missiles. It turns out instead that the number of satellites goes up approximately in proportion to the *square root* of the number of missiles.

34   That also seems like a fine point — almost a quibble — but consider its significance. The square root means that if the Soviets build *four* times as many missiles, we only have to build *twice* as many satellites to match them. Suppose the United States built a defensive screen of 100 satellites that could shoot down — as a very conservative estimate — 80 percent, or four-fifths, of the Soviet missiles. And suppose the Soviets decided they wanted to build enough missiles so that the number of missiles getting through our defensive screen would be the same as the number that would have reached the United States if we had no defense. That is what "overwhelming the defense" means. To do that, the Soviets would have to build more than 5,000 additional missiles and silos.[11] The Los Alamos "square-root" rule tells us that if the Soviets went to that trouble and expense, the United States could counter those thousands of new missiles with only 100 additional satellites.

35   With numbers like that, the cost trade-offs are bound to favor the defense over the offense. If the Soviets tried to overwhelm our defense, they would be bankrupted before we were.

36   The report to the OTA has other defects. One is a peculiar passage in which the author exaggerates by a factor of roughly 50 the requirements for a terminal defense, i.e., a defense that tries to destroy the Soviet warheads toward the end of their passage, when they are already over the United States. Current planning assumes that as the warheads descend, they will be intercepted by smart mini-missiles with computer brains and radar or infrared "eyes," which maneuver into the path of the warhead and destroy it on impact. A smart missile of this kind destroyed an oncoming enemy warhead at an altitude of 100 miles on June 10, 1984, in a successful test of the technology by the Army.

37   The question is: how many smart missiles are required? Professionals sizing up the problem have concluded that at most 5,000 intercepting missiles will be needed. The answer according to the report to the OTA: 280,000 smart missiles. Though these smart missiles will not cost as much as aircraft carriers, they are not exactly throwaways. Thus the effect of this calculation, as with the studies by the Union of Concerned Scientists on the size of our fleet of laser-equipped satellites, is to create the impression that a defense against Soviet missiles will be so costly as to be impractical.

38   How did the report to the Office of Technology Assessment arrive at 280,000 missiles? First, the report assumed that about 1,000 sites in the United States — missile silos, command posts, and so on — need to be defended. That is reasonable.

39   Second, the report assumed the Soviets might choose to concentrate their whole attack on any one of these 1,000 sites. This means that every single site would have to have enough intercepting missiles to counter the Soviet attack, if the entire attack were aimed at this one location.

That is not reasonable. Why would the Soviets launch thousands of   40
warheads—their entire nuclear arsenal—against one American missile
silo? This is known in the trade as a GIGO calculation (garbage in,
garbage out). The theorist makes an absurd assumption, does some
impeccable mathematics, and arrives at an absurd answer.

When theoretical physicists joust over ideas, a factor of two hardly   41
counts; a factor of three matters a bit; factors of ten begin to be important; factors of 100 can win or lose an argument; and factors of 1,000
begin to be embarrassing. In a study of the practicality of the Neutral
Particle Beam—that most promising destroyer of Soviet missiles and
warheads—the panel of the Union of Concerned Scientists made a
mistake by a cool factor of 1,600. As in the case of the panel's estimate of
the size of our satellite fleet, the direction of its error was such as to
make this promising "Star Wars" technology seem hopelessly
impractical.

According to the scientists who wrote the UCS report, the device—   42
called a linear accelerator—needed to generate the Neutral Particle
Beam would weigh 40,000 tons. To be effective, this enormous weight
would have to be placed in a satellite. Of course, the idea of loading
40,000 tons onto an orbiting satellite is absurd. By comparison, the NASA
space station will weigh about 40 tons. This finding by the Union of
Concerned Scientists makes it clear that the plan to use the Neutral
Particle Beam is ridiculous.

But the UCS's study panel made a mistake. The correct result for the   43
weight of the linear accelerator is 25 tons, and not 40,000 tons. Now, 25
tons is quite a practical weight to put into an orbiting satellite. It is, in
fact, about the same as the payload carried in a single flight of the NASA
shuttle.[12]

A UCS spokesman admitted his organization's rather large error in   44
congressional testimony some months ago.[13] But when he made the
admission he did not say: "We have made a mistake by a factor of more
than a thousand, and the correct weight of the accelerator for this Neutral Particle Beam is not 40,000 tons, but closer to 25 tons." He said: "We
proposed to increase the area of the beam and accelerator, noting that
would make the accelerator unacceptably massive for orbital deployment. Our colleagues have pointed out that the area could be increased
after the beam leaves the small accelerator."

That was all he said about the mistake in his testimony.   45

Now, this cryptic remark does not convey to a Senator attending the   46
hearing that the scientist has just confessed to a mistake which changes a
40,000-ton satellite into a 25-ton satellite. There is nothing in his remark
to indicate that the UCS's distinguished panel of scientists had reached a
false conclusion on one of the best "Star Wars" defenses because the
panel had made a whopping error in its calculations.

The report prepared for the OTA also makes a mistake on the   47
Neutral Particle Beam, but this mistake is only by a factor of fifteen.
According to the report, the Soviet Union can protect its missiles and

warheads from the Neutral Particle Beam with a lead shield about one-tenth of an inch thick. The shield, the report states, would not weigh too much and therefore could be "an attractive countermeasure" for the Soviets.

48   But scientists at Los Alamos have pointed out that a layer of lead one-tenth of an inch thick will not stop the fast-moving atoms of the Neutral Particle Beam; they will go right through it. In fact, a table printed in the OTA report itself shows that the lead shield must be 15 times thicker—at least 1½ inches thick—to stop these fast-moving particles.

49   A layer of lead as thick as that, wrapped around the electronics in the missile and its warheads, would weigh many tons—considerably more than the total weight of all the warheads on the missile. If the Soviets were unwise enough to follow the advice offered them in the report to the Office of Technology Assessment, their missile would be so loaded down with lead that it would be unable to get off the ground.

50   That would be a great plus for American security, and a nice response from our defense scientists to the President's call for ways of making the Soviet missiles "impotent and obsolete."

51   Other suggestions for the Soviets can be found in the report by the Union of Concerned Scientists. They include shining up the Soviet missiles, spinning them, attaching "band-aids" and "window shades," as the UCS report calls them, and launching "balloons" as fake warheads. I am not an expert in this dark area of "countermeasures," but I have talked with the experts enough to understand why the professionals in the defense community regard many of these proposals as bordering on inanity.

52   Putting a shine on the missile sounds like a good idea, because it reflects a part of the laser beam and weakens the beam's effect. However, it would be a poor idea for the Soviets in practice. One reason is that the Soviets could not count on keeping their missiles shiny; during the launch the missile gets dirty, partly because of its own exhaust gases, and its luster is quickly dulled. But the main reason is that no shine is perfect; some laser energy is bound to get through, and will heat the surface. The heating tends to dull the shine, so more heat gets through, and dulls the shine some more, and still more heat gets through . . . and very soon the shine is gone.

53   Spinning the missile spreads the energy of the laser beam over its whole circumference, and is a better idea than putting a shine on it. However, it only gains the Soviets a factor of pi, or roughly three, at most. And it does not gain them anything at all if the laser energy is transmitted in sharp pulses that catch the missile in one point of its spin, so to speak. The experts say there is no problem in building a laser that sends out its energy in sharp pulses.

54   Now to the other proposals by the scientists on the UCS panel. The "band-aid" is a metal skirt which slides up and down the outside of the missile, automatically picking out the spot that is receiving the full heat of the laser beam, and protecting the metal skin underneath. The "window shade" is a flexible, metallized sheet which is rolled up and fas-

tened to the outside of the missile when it is launched, and then unrolled at altitudes above fifty miles. It is supposed to protect the missile against the X-ray laser, which is another exotic but promising defense technology.

The trouble with these suggestions is that they do not fit the reali- 55 ties of missile construction very well. A missile is a very fragile object, the ratio of its weight empty to its weight loaded being 10 or 15 to 1 — nearly the same as an eggshell. Any attempt to fasten band-aids and window shades on the outside of the missile, even if their contours are smoothed to minimize drag, would put stresses on the flimsy structure that would require a major renovation of the rocket and a new series of test flights. If the Soviets tried to carry out all the suggestions made by the UCS's scientists — putting on band-aids and window shades, spinning their missiles and shining them up — their missile program would be tied up in knots. That would be another fine response from our scientists to the President's call for a way of rendering the Soviet weapons useless.

The "balloon" is still another trick to foil our defenses. The thought 56 here is that after the boost phase is over, and the booster rocket has fallen away, the bus that normally pushes out the Soviet warheads will instead kick out a large number of "balloons" — light, metallized hollow spheres. Some balloons will have warheads inside them, and some will not. Since the empty balloons weigh very little, the Soviets can put out a great many of these. Not knowing which among this great multitude of balloons contain warheads, we will waste our mid-course defenses on killing every balloon in sight, empty or not.

A friend who works on these matters all the time explained to me 57 what was wrong with this idea. He said that a modest amount of thought reveals that it is possible to tell very easily which balloons have warheads, and which do not. All the defense has to do is tap one, in effect, by directing a sharp pulse of laser light at it, and then observing how it recoils. An empty balloon will recoil more rapidly than a loaded one. Once the loaded balloons — the ones with the warheads — are picked out, we can go after them with our Neutral Particle Beams, or other warhead-killers.

This list of proposed countermeasures is not complete, but it is 58 representative. The ideas put forward by the UCS — the band-aid, the window shade, the shining and spinning rockets, and the balloon — remind one of nothing so much as a group of bright students from the Bronx High School of Science getting together to play a game in which they pretend to be Soviet scientists figuring out how to defeat American missile defenses. The ideas they come up with are pretty good for a group of high-school students, but not good enough to stand up to more than a thirty-minute scrutiny by the defense professionals who earn their living in thinking about these matters.

Of course, there is no harm in these proposals. The harm comes in 59 offering shoddy work — superficial analyses, marred by errors of fact, reasoning, and simple carelessness — as a sound scientific study bearing on a decision of vital importance to the American people. The work seems sound enough on casual examination, with its numbers, graphs, and theoretical arguments. Certainly the New York *Times* was impressed when it described the UCS report as "exhaustive and highly technical." It is only when you penetrate more deeply, and begin to talk with knowledgeable people who have thought long and hard about these problems, that you realize something is wrong here.

60   How did published work by competent scientists come to have so many major errors? A theorist reviewing these reports on the feasibility of the President's proposal cannot help noticing that all the errors and rough spots in the calculations seem to push the results in one direction —toward a bigger and more costly defense, and a negative verdict on the soundness of a "Star Wars" defense against Soviet missiles. If the calculations had been done without bias, conscious or otherwise, you would expect some errors to push the result one way, and other errors to push it the other way.

61   But all the errors and omissions go in one direction only—toward making the President's plan seem impractical, costly, and ineffective.

62   This is not to say that the errors were made in a deliberate, conscious effort to deceive. I do not think that for a moment. What happens is quite different, and every theorist will recognize the phenomenon. When you finish a calculation, you check your result against your intuitive feeling as to what the situation should be. You ask yourself: "Does this result make sense, or not?" If the result does not make sense, you know either that you have made a great discovery which will propel you to Stockholm, or you have made a mistake. Usually you assume the latter, and you proceed to check your calculations very carefully. But if the result seems to be in good agreement with everything you expected about the behavior of the system you are investigating, you say to yourself, "Well, that looks all right," and you go on to the next step.

63   Of course, a careful theorist always checks his calculations anyway, whether the answer seems sensible or not. But he is apt to check them just a mite less carefully if the results agree with what he expected than if they do not.

64   I think this is what must have happened to the theorists who wrote the report for the Union of Concerned Scientists. Clearly they had a strong bias against the President's proposal from the beginning, because they believed that a defense against Soviet missiles would, in their own words, "have a profoundly destabilizing effect on the nuclear balance, increasing the risk of nuclear war," and that such a defense against missiles "could well produce higher numbers of fatalities" than no defense at all.

65   So, when the calculations by the panel yielded the result that thousands of laser-equipped satellites would be needed to counter a Soviet attack—which meant that for this reason alone the whole plan was hopelessly impractical—the members of the panel were not surprised. Their technical studies had simply confirmed what they already knew to be true for other reasons, namely, that the President's idea was terrible.

Now, I would like to wager that if the theorists studying the matter   66
for the UCS had found that only 10 satellites could protect the United
States from a massive Soviet attack—if they had gotten a result that
indicated the President's proposal was simple, effective, and inexpensive to carry out—then they would have scrutinized their calculations
very, very carefully.

What is one to make of all this?   67

When I was a graduate student in theoretical physics, we revered   68
some of the men who have lent their names to the report by the Union of
Concerned Scientists. They are among the giants of 20th-century
physics—the golden era in our profession. Yet these scientists have
given their endorsement to badly flawed calculations that create a misleading impression in the minds of Congress and the public on the
technical feasibility of a proposal aimed at protecting the United States
from destruction.

Lowell Wood, a theorist at Livermore and one of the most brilliant of   69
the younger generation of defense scientists, made a comment recently
to the New York *Times* about what he also saw as a contradiction between the research talents of Dr. Hans Bethe—the most prominent
physicist associated with the Union of Concerned Scientists—and the
negative views of that great theorist on the technical merits of the
proposal to defend the United States against Soviet missiles. Dr. Wood
said:

> Is Hans Bethe a good physicist? Yes, he's one of the best alive. Is he a
> rocket engineer? No. Is he a military-systems engineer? No. Is he a
> general? No. Everybody around here respects Hans Bethe enormously
> as a physicist. But weapons are my profession. He dabbles as a mili-
> tary-systems analyst.

It seems to me that Dr. Wood has part of the answer. I think the   70
remainder of the answer is that scientists belong to the human race. As
with the rest of us, in matters on which they have strong feelings, their
rational judgments can be clouded by their ideological preconceptions.

AUTHOR'S NOTES

1 Commentary, January 1984.
2 *A Space Based Missile Defense*, March 1984; *The Fallacy of Star Wars*, based
  on studies conducted by the Union of Concerned Scientists, edited by John
  Tarman, Vintage, 293 pp., $4.95.
3 *Directed Energy Missile Defense in Space:* A Background Paper, April 1984.
4 *Ballistic Missile Defense and U.S. National Security:* A Summary Report,
  Prepared for the Future Security Strategy Study, October 1983; *The Strategic
  Defense Initiative:* Statement by Dr. James C. Fletcher Before the House
  Committee on Armed Services, March 1984.
5 The explanation is that 20 percent get through the first layer; 20 percent of
  that fraction, or a net of 4 percent, get through the second layer; finally, 20

percent of that 4 percent, or 0.8 percent, get through the third layer. The overall effectiveness of the three layers is 99.2 percent.

6 Nuclear explosives, unlike ordinary explosives, do not detonate if you drop them or hit them with a hammer. A series of precisely timed steps, controlled by electronic circuits in the warhead, has to occur before the explosion can happen. If the circuits are damaged, and the steps do not occur, or their timing is off, the warhead will not explode.

7 These numbers depend on the power of the laser beams and the sizes of the mirror used to focus them. All the studies described here make the same assumptions—a 20- or 25-million-watt laser and a 30-foot mirror.

8 The scientist explained that his panel had forgotten that Soviet missile fields are spread out across a 5,000-mile arc in the USSR, and had put all the missiles in one spot. This made it harder for the satellite lasers to reach all the missiles, and meant more satellites were needed.

9 *The Fallacy of Star Wars*, Chapter 5. The explanation offered by the UCS for this correction is that its experts belatedly realized some satellites are closer to their missile quarry than others, and can polish the missile off in a shorter time. That means each satellite can kill more missiles, and, therefore, fewer satellites are needed to do the whole job.

10 The report assumed the American satellites would move through space in tight bunches, instead of being spread out around their orbits. By bunching them together this way, it kept the satellites from being used effectively, and overestimated the number of satellites we would have to put up to counter an increased Soviet deployment of missiles. The theorists at Livermore and Los Alamos assumed the satellites were spread out evenly in their orbits when they did their calculations. I did also, when I took a look at the problem. Anyone trying to figure out how to build the best defense for the United States at the lowest cost to the taxpayer would do the same.

11 The Soviets have 1,400 missile silos and missiles. To get five times this number and make up for the losses suffered in penetrating our defense, they would have to build another 5,600 missiles and silos.

12 The shuttle's payload is 33 tons in the orbits currently in use. It would be about 20 tons in the orbits needed for the defensive screen against Soviet missiles.

13 Hearings Before the Senate Committee on Armed Services, April 24, 1984.

◇◇◇

Response to Robert Jastrow

Hans A. Bethe, Richard Garwin,
Kurt Gottfried, Henry W. Kendall,
Carl Sagan, and
Victor F. Weisskoff

The distinguished scientists who collaborated on this letter are all members of the Union of Concerned Scientists, a group committed to working actively to decrease the risk of nuclear war. As the authors point out, three of them (Hans A. Bethe, Richard Garwin, and Henry W. Kendall) "have together had a total of over eight decades of extensive experience with a wide variety of military systems." Bethe, it might be added, was the Chief of Theoretical Physics at Los Alamos Science Lab during the period from 1943 to 1946, when the first nuclear weapons were being developed. In 1967 he was the recipient of a Nobel Prize for Physics. Carl Sagan, who became well known as the host of a popular PBS series on the universe, "has a twenty-five-year continuing involvement in the development of major U.S. space projects." Interestingly, these renowned physicists openly confess to having made two errors in their mathematical calculations (as noted by Jastrow in the preceding essay). Those of us who are less comfortable with numbers than they can take comfort in the humanity of their errors while perhaps also taking fright at the fact that erring human beings must inevitably be in control of our nation's nuclear policy. In the "Response to Robert Jastrow" (1985) Bethe and associates contribute to the continuing debate about American nuclear defense through which we all fervently hope to achieve an error-free national policy.

To the Editor of Commentary:

Mr. Reagan's proposed Strategic Defense Initiative raises issues of the utmost gravity. We are astonished that Commentary would present a brief for SDI in the guise of an uninformed attack against the report prepared by us under the auspices of the Union of Concerned Scientists, *The Fallacy of Star Wars* (Vintage, 1984). Robert Jastrow's "The War Against 'Star Wars'" takes issue with our criticisms of SDI by pretending that the entire enterprise stands or falls on a precise calculation of how many laser satellites would be required by the defense. There are some honest disagreements among knowledgeable experts that are central to the SDI debate which we wish to bring to your readers' attention, but this is not one of them. 1

In his "Star Wars" speech, Mr. Reagan proposed to defend the *population* of the United States against Soviet nuclear-armed missiles, and thereby to replace deterrence as the bedrock of our national security. As recently as December 23, 1984, the President and his Secretary of Defense restated this objective in order to proscribe heresies within their administration: SDI would not be bargained away, they asserted, or be devoted to the lesser goal of merely defending American missile silos. 2

A ballistic-missile defense (BMD) of cities is inconceivable unless the great majority of Soviet ICBM's could be destroyed while their fragile booster engines are still burning brightly. Missiles that survive 3 this "boost phase" would pose a much more formidable threat to any defense because they would release a large number of elusive and far less vulnerable warheads immersed in a vast swarm of decoys and other "penetration aids." The subsequent defensive layers could not, it is widely acknowledged, cope with such a prodigious "threat cloud." The fact that the earth is round requires an attack on Soviet boosters to be launched from space.

4   We examined all credible proposals for boost-phase defense. (While infrared and laser homing projectiles are promising interceptors for mid-course and terminal defense, they are implausible boost-phase weapons, because of their low speed.) Orbiting defenses suffer from a fatal flaw: they would rely on delicate precision instruments which would be exquisitely vulnerable to attack. We share this conclusion with Edward Teller, an ardent SDI advocate, who has said that "lasers in space won't fill the bill—they must be deployed in great numbers at terrible cost and could be destroyed in advance of an attack." As we shall see, Mr. Jastrow's own argument leads to the conclusion that countering new Soviet ICBM deployments with orbiting lasers would be ludicrously expensive.

5   These pitfalls could be averted if the defensive weapons were "popped-up" into space on warning of attack. But this would pose insuperable time constraints: the defensive weapon must rise to a height of at least 650 miles before the enemy booster completes firing, feasible with current slow-burning Soviet missiles, but hardly practical against a Soviet equivalent of the much faster MX. Furthermore, the Soviets could readily develop boosters that finish burning too soon for any pop-up scheme to work.[1] Claims that the Soviets would find it difficult to develop such "fast-burn" boosters should be laid to rest by noting that our SPRINT missile, which operated as a BMD interceptor in 1974, already demonstrated this technology.

6   In sum, no technical scheme exists for a comprehensive strategic defense free of fundamental conceptual flaws. As former Secretary of Defense James Schlesinger has said, "In our lifetime and that of our children, cities will be protected by the forbearance of those on the other side, or through effective deterrence." Nor is there any basis for Mr. Jastrow's assertion that the reports of the "blue-ribbon panels," appointed at the President's request, are "as different" from our report "as day is from night." The technical [Fletcher] panel's summary emphasizes that "survivability of the system components is a critical issue whose resolution requires a combination of technologies and tactics that remain to be worked out." Major General John C. Toomay, the panel's Deputy Chairman, has said that the panel tended to be "pessimistic whether these technical objectives could be realized but felt that, on balance, the research and engineering was well worth doing," and that the difference between the panel's qualified assessment and its recommendation is "like the difference between the horse you bet on and the sentimental favorite."[2]

7   Not only is there no technical scheme, there is not even the vaguest outline for a political scenario that might propel us toward a defense-

dominated world. That political factors are essential was recognized in the Fletcher report, which stated that the effectiveness of the defense would depend not only on technology, but also on the degree to which Soviet offensive forces could be constrained. Moreover, the Hoffman panel, which considered the strategic implications of SDI for the President, noted that the past behavior of the Soviets "suggests that they would be more likely to respond with a continuing build-up of their long-range offensive forces."

Hence our disagreement with knowledgeable and candid sup-   8 porters of SDI is one of risk assessment. They are gambling on the President's "sentimental favorite," in the hope that unforeseen technical advances might transform the prospects for strategic defense, and are not as troubled as we are by the risks that the pursuit of SDI would entail. Our studies persuaded us that all the envisaged BMD schemes are ruinously expensive, and could not protect the United States from utter destruction because they could be readily overwhelmed or outfoxed at much less cost. We shall also explain why the very attempt to proceed toward a comprehensive missile defense will provoke a massive escalation of the competition in offensive nuclear weapons, and increase the likelihood of nuclear war.

Why should a thrust toward strategic defense have any risks beyond   9 galloping budget deficits? What is the harm in trying? This has been answered by the Hoffman panel: defenses that could withstand a small attack, but would collapse under a large onslaught, are highly provocative. In the early stages of BMD deployment we would have just such a defense, as well as vulnerable land-based missiles. This would have two grave hazards. First, the Soviets would fear that if the U.S. were to attack preemptively our defense could cope with their surviving missiles; they would also know that our defense could, at most, provide poor protection of our vulnerable missiles against a Soviet first strike. This would greatly enhance their incentive to attack preemptively in a serious crisis.

Second, Soviet leaders have asserted that they would avert this   10 predicament by enlarging their offensive capabilities. This build-up would emphasize submarine-based cruise missiles, which underfly space defenses and provide little warning; ICBM's equipped with countermeasures against U.S. defense; and anti-satellite weapons to attack our BMD space platforms. Painfully aware of the fragility of our embryonic defense, we would find such Soviet moves highly provocative, and respond in kind. A budding BMD system is therefore a catalyst for an acceleration of the offensive arms race, not for reductions in offensive arms, as many SDI advocates claim.

SDI is often portrayed as a benign research program. But a program   11 launched from the Oval Office, described as a vital element in the nation's future strategic posture, and funded at already so lavish a level, is not merely a research project. It will not be so treated by the Soviets, no matter what we may say or believe. Modern military systems take many years to develop, so the Soviets will feel compelled to initiate programs to counter the still unborn U.S. defense. Hence SDI is likely to enmesh us in a more dangerous offensive confrontation even if it is eventually abandoned before any defenses are deployed. Those who find this far-fetched have not learned the saga of MIRV—the multiple-warhead ICBM. We invented MIRV's as a BMD countermeasure. When the Soviets installed a rudimentary ABM system, we forged ahead with MIRV development, and then to deployment *after* the ABM treaty prevented the Soviets from installing a defense that made MIRV's necessary. The Soviets then followed suit. As a result, the incentive for a preemptive strike has grown because a single warhead can destroy many MIRVed enemy warheads before they are launched. Now there is a consensus that MIRVing was a dangerous mistake; former MIRV advocates such as Henry Kissinger look back fondly to the days of one warhead per missile.

12   We are also disturbed that the mere prospect of lavish funds is already giving SDI a life of its own. With jobs, university research, profits, and promotions at stake, such an enterprise can quickly turn into a juggernaut that cannot be stopped even when it is clear that its goals are unattainable.

13   Many officials now realize that SDI holds no promise for population defense, and so ersatz rationales are coming into vogue. The most popular is that a partially effective BMD would bolster deterrence because defenses would compound the problem of planning an attack.[3] True enough, if the offense stays frozen while the defense is installed. But each superpower's highest priority is a nuclear arsenal that can, with full confidence, penetrate to its opponent's vital targets. Only technologies far more robust and inexpensive than anything now dreamed of could alter that priority.[4]

14   Another fashionable rationale is that even a modest BMD could protect us from accidental launches and from terrorists. But protection from accidental launch by the superpowers does not require space weapons. Devices installed on ballistic missiles to destroy them on receipt of secure, encrypted radio messages would suffice. And attack by terrorists would hardly come via ICBM. Delivery of nuclear explosives by plane, ship, or diplomatic pouch would be far easier. A nuclear weapon hidden in a bale of marijuana would apparently find ready entry into the U.S. The cost of one laser battle station uselessly orbiting would pay for legions of secret agents who could actually grapple with this threat.

15   There are those who favor SDI because they believe it best exploits the great U.S. advantage in high technology. Their position seems to be supported by the apprehension that Soviet leaders express so vigorously about SDI. Is that not enough reason to pursue the program?

16   We have observed and participated in the nuclear competition since its inception. Thanks to U.S. technological superiority, virtually every new technical initiative has come from the United States: the fission bomb, the hydrogen bomb, the intercontinental bomber, submarine-launched missiles, high-accuracy ICBM's, MIRV's, and high-accuracy long-range cruise missiles. The only significant Soviet initiative was the

ICBM itself, but our ICBM's quickly surpassed those of the Soviets in both quality and numbers. The net result has been a steady erosion of American security. There is no evidence that space weapons will be an exception. It is true that we have a significant edge in all the technologies that strategic defense would depend on. But in the nuclear era a sophisticated defense can be foiled by relatively rudimentary means. Which is easier: the construction or the disruption of an exquisitely shaped mirror 30-feet across which must swiftly turn from one target to another with very high accuracy? Moreover, it is cheap to build devastating weapons that could readily penetrate our exorbitantly expensive "shield." Unless there is a breakthrough in defense as revolutionary as nuclear weapons themselves, the strategic offense will reign supreme.

But if so, why are the Soviets so opposed to SDI? Because they are   17
exceedingly cautious, and have been playing catch-up with American nuclear technology since 1945. Soviet military planners are obliged to take American pronouncements, however implausible, much more seriously than American strategists, and will respond with an offensive build-up and by expanding their already significant BMD research effort.[5] They seem to recognize that this will require vast expenditures they can ill afford, and that the net result will be a decrease in their national security. The same would be true for us.

We should vigorously exploit our technological advantage to ac-   18
quire military intelligence about the Soviet Union, to strengthen our strategic command-and-control systems, and to reduce our reliance on nuclear weapons. The search for new BMD techniques must go on, but the distinction between research and deployment should not be blurred. But in assessing military technologies we must recognize that any attempt by either superpower to increase the threat to the other's survival will soon redound to its own disadvantage.

We now return to Mr. Jastrow's caricature of our case against SDI. He   19
would have readers believe that the prospects for SDI can be decided on the basis of just two numbers that we had calculated incorrectly in our earliest report, *Space-Based Ballistic Missile Defense* (Union of Concerned Scientists, March 1984); and that our "many major errors . . . go in one direction only—toward making the President's plan seem impractical, costly, and ineffective."

What did we set out to do? Since there is no plausible concept for   20
strategic defense, we sought to fill this void. To that end the technical portions of our report assessed separately the interception mechanisms; illustrated the magnitude of the defender's task by estimating the size of the defensive system required in the absence of all countermeasures; and examined a large variety of countermeasures. A realistic net assessment would integrate the last two items, and incorporate the likely enhancements of Soviet offensive capabilities. Had we carried that through in a hard-nosed fashion it would have led to the conclusion that the cost and size of the defensive system are unbounded. Why? Because the largely unknown defensive technologies, whose ultimate effectiveness is still a matter of speculation, would be pitted against prodigiously

effective weapons and many known countermeasures invented during twenty-five years of BMD research. We firmly believe that countermeasures will carry the day into the foreseeable future.

21   Mr. Jastrow's two make-or-break numbers are the size of the laser constellation that would have to be in orbit and the weight of a neutral-particle-beam weapon. Regarding the satellite number, he claims that "the whole 'Star Wars' plan rested on this one point." But it is at least as important whether orbiting lasers could themselves withstand attack. As for neutral particle-beam weapons, he asserts that they are "that most promising destroyer of Soviet missiles and warheads," but neglects to mention that once fast-burn boosters are developed they would be completely shielded from such beams by the atmosphere — the reason we relegated our discussion of the characteristics of such devices to a technical appendix.[6]

22   Mr. Jastrow's allegation that our work contains "many major errors" is both false and undocumented. We erred twice in our first report: in arriving at the number of 2,400 satellites and in estimating the weight of the particle-beam weapon; but these errors had hardly any bearing on our overall assessment of SDI, were corrected in public at our first opportunity five weeks after the initial report was issued, and do not appear in any of our subsequent publications.

23   The calculation of the number of satellites is not simple. For example, the "fine work by the theoretical physicists at Los Alamos," to which Mr. Jastrow alludes,[7] makes just the mistake that we had made, even though it appeared four months after our report was publicly corrected. The claim that "the experts had been looking at this problem for more than ten years, and the accurate results were well known" is not correct.

24   How many satellites must then dance on top of a laser beam? Mr. Jastrow implies that the calculation that produces the smallest number of satellites is the most accurate, a clear absurdity. A small satellite fleet is much more vulnerable than a large one. Indeed, there is no "right" number of satellites, for it depends on a host of unknown performance parameters, the nature of the attack, etc. Given the present level of ignorance, all such calculations are based on ad-hoc assumptions of varying degrees of implausibility. They are meant to be illustrative, and bear no relation to actual designs, since they all ignore a host of factors that would greatly increase the number of satellites. Taking the rather small differences in assumed parameters into account, our corrected estimate of 300 laser stations is consistent with those by Carter, Drell et al.,[8] a fact Mr. Jastrow neglected to mention.

25   Unfortunately, Mr. Jastrow has failed to notice that he is impaled on his own sword, blunt instrument though it may be. "Everyone acknowledges that these satellites are going to be extremely expensive; each one will cost a billion dollars or more," he says. Quite so. What would be the cost trade-off if the Soviets were to deploy a cluster of 3,000 small three-warhead fast-burn ICBM's at a cost of about $50 billion?[9] Let us accept Mr. Jastrow's favorite satellite-number calculation,[10] and his cost per satellite. We then find that it would cost the U.S. $1 trillion to deploy the additional space defenses required by this new $50 billion threat![11]

Mr. Jastrow has painted a picture of the Senate hearing at which our   26
errors were rectified that does not conform with the hearing record.[12] He
asserts that our statement on the particle-beam weapon ended with the
sentence: "Our colleagues have pointed out that the area could be
increased after the beam leaves the small accelerator." Mr. Jastrow then
charges us with deceiving the Senators because we did not say that this
correction brought with it a great saving in weight. But that was not all
that happened. The written testimony of our witness, Richard L. Garwin,
distributed before the hearing to the press and the committee, and
reproduced in the hearing record, actually reads: ". . . leaves the small
accelerator, *saving a great deal of weight*" (emphasis added). Before
our witness took the floor, Donald Kerr, the Director of Los Alamos, had
said:

> I think the UCS report in many ways helps to illustrate the great
> difficulty involved in first devising and then developing the technol-
> ogy that might be used for strategic defense. They have properly
> focused on the concerns with command and control, countermea-
> sures, and vulnerability. In some cases I think their analysis has either
> been overly simplified for the purpose of the public document that it
> is, or at least in one case, they are totally in error.

Kerr then described our error concerning satellite numbers, and explained how we had overestimated the weight of the particle-beam
weapon. He then went on to say:

> So I think on the one hand UCS has done a service to the country in
> raising these issues. I would hope that a longer-term, more sophisti-
> cated analysis, albeit one still in the open unclassified literature, might
> dispel some of the inaccuracies that are also in it.

That analysis was already underway, and is continuing. It is reflected in
our October 1984 *Scientific American* article and in our book, *The
Fallacy of Star Wars*. When our witness testified, there was little point in
going over these errors yet again.[13]

The allegation that we systematically tilted the case against "the   27
President's plan" is untrue. In fact, we granted it every benefit of the
doubt allowed by the laws of physics: beams that would be aimed
instantly from one booster to the next without ever missing; laser
weapons having a lethality far beyond that for which not even conceptual designs exist; no redundancy to compensate for attrition due to
enemy action; no growth in the size and capability of the Soviet ICBM
force. No military system in history has ever attained the level of perfection that we granted to "the President's plan." (One of us, Richard L.
Garwin, even made an original suggestion that greatly improves the
prospects for the ground-based laser scheme.)

Mr. Jastrow opens his attack on our treatment of countermeasures by   28
admitting that "I am not an expert in this dark area," and then reveals
that (always anonymous) professionals of his acquaintance "regard
many of [the UCS] proposals as bordering on inanity." His rendition of

our treatment of countermeasures is another caricature. It is he who emphasizes "tricks" like spinning the missile or "putting a shine on it." We focused on techniques that would prevent accurate targeting on the booster, on measures that would greatly increase the power levels needed for destruction, and on the inherent vulnerability of spacecraft. He would also have readers believe that decoy balloons are a kind of schoolboy prank, but in reality they have been studied for over two decades[14] by "defense professionals," and are taken very seriously.

29   This picture of us as babes in the cruel woods of countermeasures does not wash. One of us (Richard L. Garwin) recently participated in the Discrimination Countermeasures Panel of the Army's BMD Program Office. We (in particular Richard L. Garwin and Kurt Gottfried) have had repeated contacts with senior members of the Fletcher panel. They have given our countermeasure suggestions serious consideration in those few cases where they had not already been studied by the panel. Since some of these men are devoted advocates of SDI, and not shy, we wonder why these charges of "inanity" have not been voiced in public, but have been whispered only into Mr. Jastrow's ear.

30   Mr. Jastrow seems perplexed as to how some of "the giants of 20th-century physics" could have "lent their names" to an effort that is "pretty good for high-school students, but not good enough to stand up to more than a thirty-minute scrutiny by the defense professionals." He attempts to resolve his paradox by quoting Lowell Wood of Livermore: "Is Hans Bethe a good physicist? Yes, he's one of the best alive. Is he a rocket engineer? No. Is he a military-systems engineer? No. Is he a general? No."

31   As this quotation is intended to discredit all our work on these matters, we reluctantly respond. Three of us (Hans A. Bethe, Richard L. Garwin, and Henry W. Kendall) have together had a total of over eight decades of extensive experience with a wide variety of military systems, including BMD technologies and countermeasures, extending to nuclear-weapons designs and effects and missile-and-reentry-vehicle development. Another (Carl Sagan) has a twenty-five-year continuing involvement in the development of major U.S. space projects. While none of us is a general (in contrast, we presume, to Messrs. Jastrow and Wood), a member of our study panel, Noel Gayler, is an admiral who has served as Commander-in-Chief of all U.S. forces in the Pacific, Director of the National Security Agency, Assistant Chief of Naval Operations for Research and Development, and as Deputy Director of the Joint Strategic Target Planning Staff, which is responsible for the operational plans for all our strategic-nuclear forces.

32   Mr. Jastrow concedes that we did not engage "in a deliberate, conscious effort to deceive," but surmises that our "rational judgments [were] clouded by ideological preconceptions." What are these "preconceptions"? A defense against Soviet missiles, he quotes us as believing, would "'have a profoundly destabilizing effect on the nuclear balance, increasing the risk of nuclear war,'" and "'could well produce higher numbers of fatalities' than no defense at all." But those are not ideological preconceptions. They are the unhappy conclusions to which our analysis has inexorably led. We stand by them.

AUTHORS' NOTES

1 The Martin-Marietta Corporation studied fast-burn boosters for the Fletcher panel, and concluded that they would impose a payload-loss of at most 20 percent, a consensus confirmed in writing by the Deputy Chairman of the panel. Claims to the contrary stem from an abandoned Pentagon attempt to discredit Ashton Carter's Congressional Office of Technology Assessment report on SDI. This misinformation is still being spread (e.g., *Wall Street Journal* editorial, December 10, 1984).

2 *National Journal*, July 7, 1984, p. 1316.

3 The diversion of SDI to silo defense is the only rationale that makes technical (though not necessarily strategic) sense. Hard targets, especially expendable silos, could be defended. However, we agree with the administration's Scowcroft commission that such defenses are not needed at this time. In any case, space-based weapons are not suited to this purpose.

4 Indeed, the growth in the offense is bound to exceed any attrition that the defense is likely to attain. The U.S. nuclear threat against Moscow multiplied as soon as we learned that the city was being surrounded by ABM batteries.

5 The Soviets' BMD program seems to be quite similar in character to what ours was before the "Star Wars" speech. We know of no evidence that they are moving toward a comprehensive strategic defense of Soviet society. As the Fletcher panel emphasizes, the most daunting BMD problems are computer-intensive, an area in which the Soviets are exceptionally weak. Indeed, they lag in almost all technologies critical to space-based BMD, so they would be ill-advised to start a contest in this arena.

6 Mr. Jastrow claims that a neutral-particle-beam weapon would only weigh 25 tons. That agrees with our estimate of the weight of the accelerator alone, but ignores the far heavier beam expansion and targeting magnets (see *The Fallacy of Star Wars*, p. 97).

7 G.H. Canavan, *Simple Estimates of Satellite Constellation Sizing*, Los Alamos National Laboratory, August 6, 1984. A detailed solution of the satellite-coverage problem has now been found (Richard L. Garwin, to be published) which shows that the "square-root law" of the Los Alamos paper, to which Mr. Jastrow ascribes such importance, is incorrect under all but highly artificial circumstances.

8 S.D. Drell, P.J. Farley, and D. Holloway, *The Reagan Strategic Defense Initiative: A Technical, Political, and Arms Control Assessment*, Stanford University, July 1984.

9 This comes from the projected cost of the Midgetman missile, though not in its mobile form, and includes the cost of the extra warheads, the silo, and ten years of maintenance.

10 C.T. Cunningham, Report No. DDV84-0007, Lawrence Livermore National Laboratory, August 30, 1984.

11 This is arrived at from Cunningham's number of 120 lasers for 1,400 co-located boosters with an engagement time of 150 seconds. Our 3,000 fast-burn boosters give an engagement time of 40 seconds, which then gives $120 (3000/1400) (150/40) = 964$ laser satellites. (All agree that the number of lasers is proportional to the number of co-located boosters, not to their square-root.) Cunningham assured a booster hardness that is 50 percent of the Fletcher panel's baseline figure. Were the latter used, the laser constellation would cost $1.9 trillion. This illustrates the sensitivity to assumed parameters.

12 Department of Defense Authorization for Appropriations for FY85, The Strategic Defense Initiative, Senate Committee on Armed Services, 98th Congress, Second Session, April 24, 1984.

13 He did, however, read the phrase at issue, "saving a great deal of weight."
   Unfortunately the stenotypist missed precisely one line of written text, and
   the last word, as restored in the record, was misprinted as "height."

GLOSSARY

$$=\!\!\Diamond\!\!\Diamond\!\!=$$

Abstract. The opposite of *concrete*; used to describe a word or group of words representing attitudes, ideas, or qualities that cannot be apprehended directly through the senses. The language of philosophy and science tends to be abstract.

Allusion. A reference, generally brief, to a person, place, thing, or event with which the reader is presumably familiar. Allusion is a device that allows a writer to compress a great deal of meaning into a very few words. Allusions "work" to the extent that they are recognized and understood; when they are not, they tend to confuse.

Ambiguity. A word, phrase, event, or situation that may be understood or interpreted in two or more ways.

Analogy. A comparison, usually imaginative, of two essentially unlike things that nonetheless share one or more common features. Writers use analogies as a method of exploring familiar subjects in new and fresh ways or as a method of exploring difficult ideas by comparing them to things known and familiar.

Anecdote. A brief, unadorned, and self-contained incident, frequently drawn from the writer's own experience, which is used to provide an example or support a point.

Annotation. The explanatory note (or notes) that an author or editor supplies for a given text.

Archaism. An obsolete word or phrase.

Argumentation. A form of exposition that attempts to persuade or convince the reader; it consists of an assertion or proposition together with whatever supporting evidence or proof the writer can muster.

Argument "ad hominem." *See* Logical fallacies.

Argument from analogy. *See* Logical fallacies.

Aristotelian invention.   *See* Invention techniques.

Assertion.   A statement declaring that something is the case; a claim.

Assumption.   Something taken for granted.

Audience.   A writer's audience consists of his or her intended readers. Knowledge of one's audience is critical; as the audience changes, so will the strategies that a writer employs. Good writers attempt to anticipate the needs of their audience and keep them firmly in mind at every stage of the writing process.

Brainstorming.   *See* Invention techniques.

Bombast.   Language that is inflated, extravagant, verbose, and insincere.

Cause and effect.   A form of exposition (also referred to as *causal analysis*) that either analyzes the reasons for a particular event, action, idea, or decision or analyzes its consequences.

Characterization.   The process by which an author creates, presents, and develops a human subject.

Chronological.   Characterized by a pattern of organization or presentation that introduces events or things in their normal time sequence.

Circular reasoning.   *See* Logical fallacies.

Classification.   A form of exposition that groups or categorizes things according to their shared characteristics.

Cliché.   An expression that has become worn, threadbare, and trite from overuse so that it is no longer fresh and effective.

Coherence.   The quality of effective writing when all parts are clearly connected and each part contributes to the making of an organic whole.

Colloquial language.   Language that is informal and conversational.

Comparison and contrast.   A form of exposition in which the writer compares the similarities and differences between two (or more) events, ideas, individuals, things, and so on as a means of clarifying, explaining, or judging them.

Conclusion.   The sentences or paragraphs that bring an essay to a logical and satisfactory end. Effective conclusions evolve naturally out of the body of the essay and leave the reader with a sense of completeness. Ineffective conclusions, by contrast, seriously weaken the impact of the total essay. Among the many strategies for effective endings are the following: (1) a restatement of the thesis and main points; (2) a final example—or an anecdote, quotation, question, or insightful comment of some kind—that makes the major point of the essay anew and thus drives it home to the reader; and (3) a prediction about the future based on the ideas presented, or a statement about the implications or applications of those ideas to the readers' lives (or, alternately, a call for action of some kind). Conclusions that apologize in any way for what the writer has done, introduce new ideas that should have been introduced earlier, or contradict what has been said already should be carefully avoided.

Concrete.   The opposite of abstract. Language that refers directly to what we see, hear, touch, taste, or smell is concrete. The language of literature tends to be concrete; it expresses even abstract concepts concretely through images and metaphors.

Conflict.   The struggle or encounter of two opposing forces within a narrative or plot that serves to create reader interest. Conflict may be between two characters; between one character and some aspect of his or her environment; or between two ideas, feelings, or tendencies struggling within a single character.

Connotation.   The meaning suggested or implied by a given word or phrase, as opposed to its literal or dictionary meaning; *see also* Denotation.

Context.   The sentences or paragraphs that surround a given word or phrase and provide it with its particular meaning or connotation.

Crisis.   That point during a narrative when the events or actions reach their turning point.

Criticism.   The description, analysis, interpretation, or evaluation of a literary work of art.

Deduction.   The method of reasoning that moves from the general to the specific.

Definition.   The meaning or explanation of a word or concept.

Denotation.   The literal, dictionary meaning of a given word or phrase; *see also* Connotation.

Description.   The form of exposition that explains a person, event, object, or place through the use of detail derived from the five senses.

Dialogue.   The conversation that goes on between or among the characters of a given work.

Diction.   The author's choice or selection of words (vocabulary). The artistic arrangement of those words constitutes *style*.

Division.   A form of exposition that divides its subject into its component parts

Editing.   *See* Revision.

Effect.   *See* Cause and effect.

Either/or.   *See* Logical fallacies.

Essay.   A short, nonfictional prose work written to set forth or communicate an idea, assertion, or point of view about a given subject.

Empathy.   The state of entering into and actually participating in the emotional, mental, or physical life of an object, person, or literary character.

Emphasis.   The weight or stress the author gives to one or more of the elements of the work.

Epigraph.   A quotation prefacing a work, often containing a clue to the writer's intention.

Evaluation.   A judgment about the particular merits or success of a given work.

Evidence.   The facts, statistics, examples, experiences, arguments, and so forth given in support of the writer's assertion or thesis.

Exemplification.   A form of exposition in which the writer provides specific illustrations or examples to support a general proposition.

Exposition.   Writing that presents, explains, or describes a subject.

Fable.   A story with a moral lesson, often employing animals who talk and act like human beings.

Fallacies.   *See* Logical fallacies.

Faulty syllogism.   *See* Logical fallacies.

Fiction.   A prose narrative that is the product of the imagination.

Figures of speech.   Imaginative uses of language in order to achieve special meaning or effect, add emphasis, or provide insight. They include *simile* (a comparison using "like" or "as"); *metaphor* (a comparison without the use of "like" or "as"); *personification* (in which an idea or thing is given human attributes or feelings or is spoken of as if it were alive); *hyperbole* (an obvious and deliberate exaggeration); *paradox* (a self-contradictory and absurd statement that turns out to be, in some sense at least, actually true and valid); *rhetorical question* (a question to which no response or reply is expected, because only one answer is possible); and *understatement* (a statement, that deliberately represents something as being of far less importance or magnitude than it really is— opposite of *hyperbole*).

First draft.   A writer's first unrevised and unedited version of a complete work. Also called the "rough" draft.

Focus.   The deliberate narrowing or restricting of a subject so that it is manageable. The particular focus chosen depends on such factors as the audience, the subject, the purpose, and the space available.

Foreshadowing.   A device by means of which the author hints at something to follow.

Free writing.   *See* Invention techniques.

Generalization.   A broad statement about all members of a given category based on the examination or study of only some of its members.

Grouping.   *See* Invention techniques.

Hasty generalization.   *See* Logical fallacies.

Hyperbole.   *See* Figures of speech.

Illustration.   The use of examples to develop a generalization.

Image.   A word or a series of words that creates a sensory experience.

Incongruity.   A word, phrase, or idea that is out of keeping with, inconsistent with, or inappropriate in its context.

Induction.   The method of reasoning that moves from the consideration of specifics or particulars to a conclusion about them.

Inference.   A prediction made about the unknown on the basis of the known; an educated guess.

Introduction.   The sentences or paragraphs that announce the essay's subject and indicate the pattern of organization that is to follow. Introductions, like conclusions, vary in length and take many different forms. Strategies for effective introductions include the following: (1) a clear statement of the central idea of the essay (or the problem or issue to be addressed) and why it is important, together with sufficient background information to make the context of that idea (problem or issue) clear to the reader; (2) an example or anecdote that introduces the subject; (3) a bold assertion—perhaps based on statistical evidence—calculated to gain the reader's attention; (4) a challenging question that the essay will proceed to answer; and (5) An arresting quotation— perhaps from some well-known authority—that introduces the reader to the essay's main idea.

Invention techniques. Techniques used by writers for discovering, exploring, developing, and organizing the subject matter for essays. They include *listing* (or *brainstorming*), *grouping, free writing, dialogue, Aristotelian invention, the reporter's questions,* and *comparison*. Although usually employed during prewriting—as a means of discovering something to write about—these techniques can be helpful at any stage of the writing process.

Irony. Verbal irony involves a contrast or discrepancy between what is said and what is actually meant. Irony is a means for exposing the disparity between appearance and reality. Irony that is deliberately intended to hurt is called *sarcasm*. Mild irony often takes the form of *understatement*.

Jargon. A specialized vocabulary shared by certain small groups of people. This vocabulary may be suitable for speaking or writing to that group of people, but otherwise it is out of place.

Juxtaposition. A form of implied comparison or contrast created by placing two items side by side.

Listing. *See* Invention techniques.

Logical fallacies. Errors of reasoning that occur in argumentative essays. They include the *non sequitur* (a conclusion that has no logical connection to its premise); *hasty generalization* (reaching an inductive conclusion based on too few examples or poorly chosen ones); *oversimplification* (misrepresenting a complex problem or issue as being neat and simple); *either/or* (the assumption that there are only two solutions to a given problem when in fact there are many); *post hoc, ergo propter hoc* ["after this, therefore because of this"] (a faulty assertion about cause and effect); *circular reasoning* (assuming in the premise what is asserted in the conclusion); *argument "ad hominem"* (attacking the speaker instead of the argument); *argument from analogy* (using an extended comparison as if it offers logical proof instead of mere illustration); and *faulty syllogism* (any of a number of errors in syllogistic reasoning).

Metaphor. *See* Figures of speech.

Myth. Broadly, any idea or belief to which a number of people subscribe.

Narration. A form of exposition that retells an event or series of related events in order to make a point.

Narrative sequence. The order in which events are recounted.

Narrator. The voice or character that tells the story.

Non sequitur. *See* Logical fallacies.

Objective and subjective writing.   Objective writing presents its subject matter without the intrusion of the personal opinions or feelings of the author. Subjective writing, by contrast, allows those opinions and feelings to be included with the ideas and information presented. In practice, purely objective or purely subjective writing is rare; most writing is a mixture of the two.

Organization.   The overall plan or design that shapes the work.

Outline.   The plan the writer develops to guide the composing of his or her first draft in which the constituent parts of the essay are clearly labeled. Outlines may take the form of an informal list of the major points the writer wishes to make or of a formal plan (using Roman numerals, letters, and arabic numerals) that presents in detailed order all the material the writer intends to present. Outlines can also be made during the revision process to check the essay's structure and make certain that all the relevant points have been covered.

Oversimplification.   *See* Logical fallacies.

Parable.   A story designed to convey or illustrate a moral lesson.

Paradox.   *See* Figures of speech.

Paragraph.   A self-contained rhetorical unit composed of closely related sentences that presents and develops a central idea.

Paraphrase.   The act of translating the ideas of another writer into your own words. Paraphrase retains (or amplifies) the meaning of the original, but changes its diction and form. Because paraphrase is a form of intellectual borrowing, the source should be appropriately credited.

Parody.   The imitation of the subject matter or characteristic style of a particular author.

Persuasion.   *See* Argumentation.

Personification.   *See* Figures of speech.

Plagiarism.   The act of using without proper credit or acknowledgment words and ideas that are not one's own.

Plot.   The patterned arrangements of the events of a narrative.

Point of view.   The perspective a writer adopts in writing about a given subject.

Post hoc, ergo propter hoc.   *See* Logical fallacies.

Preface.   The author's or editor's introduction, in which the writer states his or her purposes and assumptions and makes any acknowledgements.

Prewriting.   In general, that stage of the writing process that occurs before actual writing begins, during which the writer makes a series of key decisions about the subject and develops the subject matter. To the extent that prewriting involves invention or discovery, it can in fact occur at any stage of the writing process.

Process.   A form of exposition that explains or demonstrates on a step-by-step basis how something is done.

Proofreading.   That stage in the process of revision in which the writer checks for typographical errors or for basic errors in spelling, grammar, and punctuation.

Protagonist.   The chief character of a literary work.

Purpose.   The writer's primary reason for writing; the goal or objective the writer sets out to achieve. Good writing often involves some combination of purposes.

Reporter's questions.   *See* Invention techniques.

Revision.   The stage in the writing process during which the writer reviews and revises what he or she has written to improve its effectiveness. Revision encompasses both major alterations in content and structure and the minor changes referred to under the heading of Proofreading.

Rhetoric.   The art of persuasion; the practice (and the study of the practice) of using language effectively. The various forms of exposition (*argumentation, cause and effect, comparison and contrast, description, division, exemplification, narration,* and *process*) are often referred to as rhetorical techniques.

Rhetorical question.   *See* Figures of speech.

Sarcasm.   A form of verbal irony delivered in a derisive, caustic, and bitter manner to belittle or ridicule its subject.

Satire.   A type of writing that holds up persons, ideas, or things to varying degrees of ridicule or contempt presumably in order to improve, correct, or bring about some desirable change.

Sentence structure.   *See* Syntax.

Sentimentality.   The presence of emotion or feeling that seems excessive or unjustified in terms of the circumstances.

Setting.   The time, place, and general circumstances in which actions or events take place.

Short story.   A short work of narrative prose fiction.

Simile.   *See* Figures of speech.

Stereotype.   A commonly held, conventionalized picture or judgment of an individual, race, issue, and so on that is used thoughtlessly without being tested for its accuracy.

Strategy.   The method a writer chooses to achieve his or her ends.

Structure.   The overall pattern or organization of a given work.

Style.   An author's characteristic manner of expression; style includes the author's diction, syntax, sentence patterns, punctuation, and spelling. The best style in any given circumstances is the language that is best suited to achieve the author's purpose or purposes. To describe an author's style is to describe his or her unique literary personality.

Subjective writing.   *See* Objective and subjective writing.

Summary.   A brief overview of the ideas and information already developed.

Support.   The evidence or proof an author marshals to back up his or her argument.

Syllogism.   The formal three-step pattern of logic that employs deduction.

Symbol.   Literally, something that stands for something else. Any word, object, action, or character that embodies and evokes a range of additional meaning and significance.

Syntax.   The arrangement of words and phrases within a sentence. Also called *sentence structure.*

Synthesis.   The process of bringing together different elements to form a coherent whole.

Theme.   The controlling idea or meaning of a work.

Thesis.   The assertion or proposition that unifies and controls the entire essay.

Tone.   The author's attitude toward the subject or audience. Tone, for example, can be serious, humorous, ironic, satiric, sarcastic, angry, critical, condescending, sincere, enthusiastic, sympathetic, and so forth.

Topic sentence.   The sentence (although it may, in fact, be more than one) that states or announces the major idea or purpose of a paragraph.

Transitions.   The devices that link the ideas, sentences, and paragraphs of an essay into a logical and coherent whole that the reader can easily follow. Transitional devices take the form of words, phrases, or paragraphs.

Trite.   *See* Cliché.

Understatement.   *See* Figures of speech.

Unity.   That quality of good writing in which all elements are clearly and effectively related to the accomplishment of the thesis.